2

Brian Clough:
Nobody Ever Says Thank You

Previous titles by the same author

Behind the Curtain: Travels in Eastern European Football
Sunderland: A Club Transformed
Inverting the Pyramid: A History of Football Tactics
The Anatomy of England: A History in Ten Matches

Brian Clough:
Nobody Ever Says Thank You

THE BIOGRAPHY

JONATHAN WILSON

This edition first published in Great Britain in 2011 by
Orion Books
an imprint of the Orion Publishing Group Ltd
Orion House, 5 Upper St Martin's Lane,
London WC2H 9EA
An Hachette UK Company

1 3 5 7 9 10 8 6 4 2

A CIP catalogue record for this book is available
from the British Library.

ISBN: 978 1 4091 2317 0

Typeset by Input Data Services Ltd, Bridgwater, Somerset

Printed and bound by CPI Group (UK) Ltd, Croydon, CR0 4YY

The Orion Publishing Group's policy is to use papers
that are natural, renewable and recyclable and made from
wood grown in sustainable forests. The logging and
manufacturing processes are expected to conform to the
environmental regulations of the country of origin.

Every effort has been made to fulfil requirements with regard to
reproducing copyright material. The author and publisher
will be glad to rectify any omissions at the earliest opportunity.

Contents

Acknowledgements

A couple of months before my dad died, I told him that I'd agreed a deal to write a biography of Brian Clough. His memory had gone by then, but when I asked if he remembered Clough, he looked at me like I was an idiot. 'Of course I do,' he snapped, and mentioned a hat-trick Clough had scored for Sunderland against Grimsby in 1962. He had no idea what he'd had for lunch.

Like most of his generation of Wearsiders, my dad mythologised Clough. Growing up as a Sunderland fan, I could never quite understand why he was so popular, how a player who had played only a season and a half for us could have had such an impact. I now realise that the brevity is the point. Nobody had time to get frustrated with him; there was no long tailing off into retirement or sense of betrayal as he joined another club.

More than that, Clough offered an excuse, a ready counterfactual. If he hadn't wrecked his knee on Boxing Day, Sunderland would surely have been promoted in 1962–63 and would have attacked the First Division with momentum and a sense of self-belief. Given the readiness of the board to invest, there might have been a return to the glory days of the thirties. Even after the injury, there were intriguing possibilities. What if the board hadn't sacked the manager George Hardwick and Clough, who was coaching the youth team? Could Clough have risen as a manager at Roker Park? Perhaps then it would have been Sunderland lifting the European Cup rather than Nottingham Forest. But Clough was ousted, leaving a bitterness that conditioned his attitude to football's hierarchy that lasted for the rest of his career.

It is that context that this book tries to restore. There have been several memoirs about Clough published in the past decade or so, many of them excellent, but this is the first full biography of Clough from birth to death. It is based on conversations with almost 200 interviewees, for whose time

I thank them. Many asked not to be named or quoted; I hope I've respected their privacy. I'm very grateful to Richard Williams, Iain Macintosh and Richard Jolly for their help in tracking down and interviewing so many people who had a connection to Clough.

The memory being as fallible as it is, and Clough being a rather better anecdotalist than he was historian, this book has also involved hours and hours in the British Library at St Pancras and British Newspaper Library at Colindale checking dates and facts. My thanks to the staff at both establishments.

For their help in correcting and improving the manuscript, I thank Kat Petersen, Chris Hawkes, John English and, particularly, Ian Preece, my editor at Orion. Thanks also to my agent, David Luxton, for his constant support.

A huge number of people have helped in other ways, whether by offering an opinion or anecdote, loaning books and tapes, or suggesting lines of enquiry. I'm especially grateful to: Araceli Alemán, Dave Allan, Philippe Auclair, Gary Bowyer, Jeff Brown, Paul Fraser, Nick Harris, Matt Hockin, Will Jago, Mark Metcalf, Jimmy Nelson, Dominic Sandbrook, Robin Simpson, Doug Weatherall and Scott Wilson. Brighton and Hove Albion, Hartlepool United and Middlesbrough football clubs were all extremely helpful. And thanks also to all those who responded to appeals for information in the *Northern Echo* and the *Middlesbrough Evening Gazette*.

Captain Ahab stood erect, looking straight out beyond the ship's ever-pitching prow. There was an infinity of firmest fortitude, a determinate, unsurrenderable wilfulness, in the fixed and fearless, forward dedication of that glance. Not a word he spoke; nor did his officers say aught to him; though by all their minutest gestures and expressions, they plainly showed the uneasy, if not painful, consciousness of being under a troubled master-eye. And not only that, but moody stricken Ahab stood before them with a crucifixion in his face; in all the nameless regal overbearing dignity of some mighty woe.

Herman Melville, *Moby-Dick*

I

1935–1962

The young have aspirations that never come to pass;
the old have reminiscences of what never happened.

Saki, *Reginald at the Carlton*

His Mother's Boy

W alk out of Albert Park by the south-east corner, cross the road with the grass bank of the Clairville Stadium to the left and the brown-grey mass of the Cleveland Fire Station to the right, and you come to Valley Road. Cross over and walk down the left side, and at the end of the first block of four you come to number 11. It was there, on 21 March 1935, that Brian Howard Clough was born.

These days the street feels like any other on a pre-war estate: modest, unpretentious, perhaps a little shabby in places as age takes its toll, but pleasant enough; far, certainly, from the impoverished back-to-backs in which footballers of his era stereotypically grew up. This was one of the 1.5 million houses built with state or council subsidy to fulfil Lloyd George's promise of 'homes fit for heroes' back from the First World War, part of a so-called garden-city development, bounded by a park and lighter and airier than the terraces of the town centre. This was council housing, aimed at the working class, but the area was desirable enough that the original residents included teachers, insurance agents and company directors. For the Cloughs, with their comparatively large garden, where they grew roses as well as the vegetables that were a significant part of their diet, the area must have carried a sense of aspiration.

Much of Middlesbrough, after all, was a grim place, even by the standards of industrial cities between the wars. In his *English Journey*, published a year before Clough's birth, J.B. Priestley described it as 'a dismal town, even with football and beer', which he isolated as the town's two key leisure pursuits. Middlesbrough had grown faster than any other town in the country in the nineteenth century, the combination of iron ore in the Cleveland Hills and the coal from the Durham pits leaving it ideally placed to answer the world's increasing demand for iron and then for steel. The difficulties it faced were the same as those faced by any town with a rapidly expanding population; because Middlesbrough's population grew faster than anywhere else, so too did its problems. After the Wall Street crash of

1929, Middlesbrough was hit as hard as anywhere, many of the shipyards and the steelworks standing idle as demand plummeted. As a consequence, the thirties were a time of hardship and unemployment. The heavy industry may have been ugly, but its redundant trappings were even worse.

Locals were well aware of their town's status. 'Not long ago,' Priestley wrote, 'I wrote an article in which I attacked a certain industrial town, which I did not name, for its miserable appearance and lack of civilised gaiety. The actual town I was describing was not Middlesbrough, was not even in the same part of the country. But at once an official of that town angrily protested in the local paper against my writing in such a fashion about Middlesbrough. I did not tell him that I had not had Middlesbrough in mind at all. If the cap fits, I thought, let them all wear it.'

The new garden estates were an attempt to rectify that, and the sense of space remains striking: the streets are broad and beyond the garden at the back there is a stretch of grassland even before you reach the oval that used to be the sports ground of the Acklam steelworks. So rural was the feel, in fact, that it was common in Clough's day to hear owls hoot at night, while a beck runs behind the even-numbered houses, through a clutch of shrubs and into Albert Park. It was the slates on that side of the street that the young Brian used anxiously to watch on damp days; only when they were dry would his mother allow him out to play, and until he suffered his knee injury aged twenty-seven – and beyond – playing was all Clough wanted to do.

And it was in the park, given to the people of Middlesbrough in 1868 by the steel magnate Henry Bolckow, that Clough would walk with Peter Taylor discussing the game; and, today, it is there that a statue of him now stands, striding purposefully towards the town centre in kit and boots, with another pair of boots, laces tied together, slung around his neck. On his way he would pass the war memorial, and see on the marble slabs of remembrance the names of two of his relatives, John Jas Clough and William Clough, both of whom were killed in the First World War.

Clough's father, Joe, very nearly went the same way. He was precisely one of those soldiers home from the war for whom the garden estates had been designed; he had fought with the King's Own Yorkshire Light Infantry and walked with a limp after being shot in the ankle. A scar on his nose, where he had been clipped by another bullet, showed how close he had come to death, but rather than dwelling on the fortune of his escape, the family preferred to tease him with the story that he had been shot as he ran away from the enemy, and had suffered the facial wound when he had turned back over his shoulder to make sure the Germans weren't closing in. Perhaps that was an example of the rough, mocking humour in which Clough would later specialise – something Harry Pearson, in *The Far Corner*, suggests is characteristic of the area; perhaps for a generation to whom death was such a constant presence, mortality was an issue best avoided.

Joe worked as a sugar-boiler at Garnett's sweet factory, a quarter of a mile from Ayresome Park, leaving home at 7.30 in the morning and returning at 6 for his bath. He later rose to become manager, but at home it was Clough's mother, Sally, who was in charge. She demanded the family were on time for dinner, refused to allow Joe to smoke in the house and ensured the household chores were done with rigorous punctuality. Despite frequent migraines, she maintained order, Clough recalled in his first autobiography, with 'a thin belt' she kept 'across the back of a wooden chair'. She insisted that Sundays be observed, leading her brood to the Anglican church, and refusing to allow them to play football; instead, the 'other room', out of bounds for the rest of the week, would be opened and she would play the piano while the rest of the family sang along.

Hers was a typically northern Anglicanism, in which cleanliness wasn't so much next to godliness as integral to it, and entwined with a furious work ethic. 'Cleanliness was a main theme of my mam's,' said Clough's brother Joe. 'We didn't have any money, but that didn't prevent her from keeping everything spotless.' She scrubbed the front step incessantly, proudly maintained the net curtains and regarded it as a great virtue that she'd had the same stair-carpet for thirty years. She insisted that the sheets be on the line by 8.30am on washing day – scorning a neighbour who never got them out before 10 – and ensured all her children had three sets of clothes: one for school, one for Sunday best, and an old set to be worn at all other times, which for Clough tended to mean playing football or cricket in the park. The outside window-sills, meanwhile, were to be painted once a year.

Clough seems to have been quite happy mucking in and running errands – he even put his balance as a striker down to the practice he had had at carrying a sack of potatoes in either hand – but the sills were a job he tried to avoid: 'It was more than your life was worth if you got paint on the glass,' he said in his second autobiography. He clearly adored his mother, while acknowledging that 'she had a short temper'. In her brusqueness and sense of order, perhaps, lay the germ of Clough's managerial style. 'There was discipline in our house,' he said, 'because, with eight of us, there had to be.'

It wasn't just Sally who imposed it. Joe remembered his father having 'big bony hands ... they would leave a mark'. Sally's only prohibition on the punishment he could administer was that it shouldn't be 'on the head'.

Joe and Sally's first child, Betty, died of septicaemia when she was four, before Brian was born. He thus became the fifth in a line of eight who survived, younger than Joe, Doreen, Des and Bill, and older than Gerald, Deanna and Barry. The brothers slept three to a bed – more if the cousins came to visit – all in the same room. It was, as Clough put it, 'a hard-working, often hard-up house' but, while they certainly weren't well-off, the Cloughs were comfortable and well-fed and, once the war was over, managed to scrape together enough for a fortnight's holiday in Blackpool every year. They regarded the resort as some kind of earthly paradise, even if money was so tight that candyfloss could only be bought every third day or so and one stick had to be shared among the whole family.

Clough later idealised his childhood, almost fetishising it in the form of his mother's mangle which he had restored and kept in his dining-room in Quarndon alongside his scroll certifying he was a Freeman of the City of Nottingham. In his first autobiography, Clough spoke lovingly of 'the smell of liver and onions and the thought of dumplings, always crispy and then her [his mother's] own rice pudding with nutmeg on the top to follow', which for him equated to what he called in his second autobiography 'the feeling of being wanted and safe'.

His family also gave Clough his love of football, which soon became an obsession in an area that lived for the game. So intrinsic was the sport to the fabric of the town that ICI, the major employer on Teesside, changed shift patterns to fit around Middlesbrough's home matches. Joe was a regular on the terraces at Ayresome Park. He idolised Wilf Mannion, who, Clough said, 'played football the way Fred Astaire danced'. When Clough later found himself sharing a dressing-room with the great inside-forward he 'couldn't help but stare at him'. 'I felt,' he said, 'as if I was watching somebody who lived on the moon.' Mannion, his fellow England international George Hardwick and other players often visited the sweet factory, where Joe would hand out bags of rejects. Sally also loved the game, and would lean out of the back bedroom window to shout encouragement during matches played at the Acklam steelworks sports ground, which lay a few dozen yards away, beyond the gardens and a triangle of rough grass. Barbara Clough, Brian's wife, remembered sitting next to Sal at Ayresome Park early on in their relationship, not knowing who she was. 'She was kicking every ball and heading every ball, and I thought, "Oooh gosh, she's keen." At one point she apologised. "Sorry, pet, did I kick you?" because her foot used to go out.' That perhaps suggests Clough's later fears that his mother didn't respect his football career were unfounded.

Clough would also have watched matches played on the steelworks ground, but the first games he saw in which he had an emotional involvement were the 'bob-a-man' games on the cinder pitches on the common in which his eldest brother, Joe, used to play. Men, often wearing work boots with trousers tucked into socks, would pay a shilling each to join in, with the winning side taking the pot. The games were fiercely contested, and would often draw crowds of several hundred. One of those who learned his football in such games was Don Revie, Clough's eternal rival. Eight years older than Clough, he grew up just a fifteen-minute walk from Valley Road in Bell Street near Ayresome Park.

Visiting his father at the factory, Clough would hang around to watch the Middlesbrough players arriving at Ayresome Park for training. Harold Shepherdson, who, having recently retired as a player, was then Middlesbrough's assistant trainer and would later be part of Alf Ramsey's backroom staff when England won the World Cup, remembered seeing the young Clough and hearing him say that one day he would play for Boro. He had heard dozens of dreamers looking to avoid the pit, ICI or the steelworks say much the same, but he later insisted that there was something in the tone of voice, the certainty with which the words were spoken, that made him pay attention. Perhaps he romanticised or exaggerated the anecdote, although there is something about Clough that makes it believable, but what is not in doubt is that a few years later he heard the same voice asserting with the same conviction that he would score forty goals the following season. Clough achieved that as well.

Clough himself had first caught the eye at an almost incredibly young age. 'We would go to Stewart's Park on a Sunday and people would stop and watch him kick a ball and head a ball from being two,' his sister Doreen recalled in a podcast produced for Middlesbrough council. 'He always liked to kick a ball,' Joe said. 'We had a fairish back garden and half of it was cultivated and half of it was lawn. We weren't allowed a big ball. We just played with a tennis ball, something like that.'

After the garden, Clough graduated to kickabouts on Clairville Common. 'For our Christmas box, we all got a pair of boots and a ball between us,' Joe recalled. 'It would be a £5 ticket from Carey's because that's how people bought stuff – on the drip – in those days. We'd be out there every night; that was the routine – if it was dry. We weren't allowed out if it was wet or in the dark. There were two cinder pitches, and the top was just rough common. We managed to get a little bit flattened out – just enough for one goal. That was OK because as kids you'd be chased from the cinder pitch if the older lads came to play.'

It soon became apparent he was better than his peers and he would hustle to join in with the older children. That was a risk, for they reacted to being embarrassed by somebody younger with crunching challenges but, as he later told it, Clough revelled in the physicality, and attributed the toughness he showed as a professional to his early experiences as a slight child being bullied by bigger and older opponents. Although several other players must have suffered something similar, it is tempting to wonder whether this too contributed to Clough's managerial style: his mother kept him in line by use of a belt and a sharp word; other players kept him in line with their own form of physical discipline.

There was no football team in the junior section at Marton Grove School, only a games lesson every Tuesday. Pupils would line up in twos, and then embark on 'the long march' for half a mile through the town to 'another local school, a snobby one', as Clough put it, that had a sports field. Every night, though, Clough would rush home, change into his old clothes and, provided the slates were dry, be straight out to play either football or cricket according to the season. Cricket remained a passion for Clough, and he would often be seen for an hour or two at Test matches at Trent Bridge. For a time, Len Hutton was a bigger hero to him than any footballer, and opening the batting for England was a greater dream than playing at centre-forward for them.

In those days, Clough wrote, 'I was no genius on the field or off it. I was just a raggy-arsed lad, one of the gang, one of the Bowery boys who got up to everything that fell short of breaking the law.' For Clough, the notion of what breaking the law entailed was always flexible. He was somebody who seems instinctively to have pushed against any and every authority, with the possible exception of his mother. He played truant. He stole apples and pears 'from the posh areas of the neighbourhood' to eat, and stamps from Woolworths for no reason other than that he could. When the children's railway was running in the park, he and his friends would wait for lunch-time or the evening when the ticket-collector took his break and, if he'd forgotten to 'empty his container . . . we'd grab enough tickets to do us for a couple of days'.

Much of what he got up to was no more than standard schoolboy mischief, but it is perhaps significant that, even years later, he saw his catalogue of minor thefts as essentially innocent. He became a keen bird's-nester, and his approach to that seems to have followed similar principles. 'I was never a cruel child,' he said, 'and we were told that to take one egg caused no distress to the mother.' He was, in other words, taking something that wasn't his in the hope it wouldn't be missed; when applied to the fruit he stole from 'posh areas' the theory could even be construed as a crude form of vigilante socialism.

Poaching, perhaps, is the most romantic of the poor man's crimes against the rich, and Clough was involved in that as well, after being taken onto the moors and shown how to hunt grouse by a friend called Brian Harrison, who sold washing-machines for a living. 'They are the most stupid birds imaginable,' Clough wrote unapologetically in his second autobiography. 'We would take an airgun and shoot the first one to show itself, only for three or four more to look up to see where the noise had come from.'

It was a similar story with the flowers in Albert Park, even after he'd been taken on by Middlesbrough. From his regular walks there with Peter Taylor later in life, Clough came to know the gardeners who maintained it. Every year, the council would plant the beds with wallflowers, and the day before they did so, the gardeners would tip Clough off. The next day, he'd turn up with a wheelbarrow, and take home a few specimens to liven up the garden on Valley Road. It wouldn't be until he arrived in Nottingham that Clough was portrayed as Robin Hood, posing by his statue in the town centre, but from an early age he was robbing the rich to give to the poor; his generosity later in life to those worse off than himself would be well-documented, but at this stage, he was very much part of the poor.

Thanks to his mother, Clough said, he and his brothers 'all grew up with that essential quality . . . the awareness of what is right and what is wrong'. In some ways, with his insistence on respect for referees and playing football in a particular way, he did seem to have a clear set of moral values; and yet in others – most notably his huckster's eye for the main chance – those values seem rather more blurred. To call him a hypocrite would be trite, but it would be fair to say that his ethical system was complex and that for him what was right and what was legal were not necessarily the same thing.

Physically, Clough developed rapidly, thanks to a combination of regular games and running while 'doing the messages' for his mother (which Doreen suggested he would only do 'for money'). At 10am, he would wait for a man who rode past on his bike on his way to work every day, and would chase after him, keeping up as far as possible, effectively using him as a pacemaker. He would even run when going to collect pease-pudding and faggots in a dish, something that also required great balance if he weren't to spill any on the way back.

At school, though, Clough's development was rather more pedestrian. 'Academically, I was thick,' he wrote in his first autobiography, although given the sharpness that was so evident later in life, that seems to have been through a lack of application rather than a lack of intelligence. 'I was a disgrace,' he admitted, 'such was my lack of interest in anything other than games.' As with so much else, Clough dealt with the issue with bluster – and given he subsequently became head boy at Marton Grove, it evidently didn't hold him back – but that failure does seem to have troubled him. 'Bit of a let-down to the family I was,' he said in a BBC interview. 'Everybody else made it to the grammar school.'

In both autobiographies, he recounts the tale of the day he got the results of his eleven-plus. 'I was standing at our little wooden gate having just heard that I'd failed' when Bill 'breezed in from his posh grammar school' and shouted to his mates, 'See our Bri's failed his exam then . . .' To Clough's mortification, 'half of Middlesbrough heard him', while Bill 'just wheeled his bike through the gate and past me as though I wasn't there'.

It is perfectly natural, of course, that Clough should dwell on what must have been an embarrassing moment, perhaps the first time he had really known failure, but what is striking is what follows: 'I'm glad I made something of myself in the end.' The implication seems to be that by becoming one of the best centre-forwards of his generation and then one of the greatest managers of all time, Clough was redressing his failure in the eleven-plus. 'I don't have any O-levels, I don't have any A-levels, and when my children chastise me and give me stick about my lack of this,' he said in a television interview fully fifty years after that failure, 'I put my European Cup medals on the table, my Championship medals. I've got a tableful – they're my O-levels and A-levels.'

From what both said at various times, it seems that Brian and Bill – who was the nearest brother to him in age – remained close for many years despite being, as Bill put it, 'chalk and cheese', and yet that incident at the gate rankled. There is something slightly uncomfortable about a man who humiliated others so effectively and yet who was clearly so sensitive about what was, after all, merely a child's statement of fact. Given the – good-natured? – mockery of Bill in which Clough dresses the anecdote, it doesn't seem too great a leap to suggest it betrays an intellectual insecurity.

Bill, Clough said, was the only one of the brothers who didn't play football – which isn't true, given it was Bill who found Brian a place in the Great Broughton team, where he himself had been playing for a season, although it may be that he was less gifted and less dedicated than the others. He was 'the studious one' who was always 'immaculate'. Clough portrays him as an obsessive who would spend three hours every Sunday cleaning his bike and later in life insisted that the cord on the iron was wound clockwise. 'He was the only one to get a divorce – he was that clever,' Clough wrote. Is teasing a man over a broken marriage in a book that sold tens of thousands of copies – however gently – really less hurtful than an offhand comment to a few mates about his eleven-plus? There are times when Clough, for all his stated love of northern bluntness, seems to have been remarkably thin-skinned.

'Bill,' Clough went on, 'finished up in Germany with the army and

11

learned Russian, which must have been very useful in Middlesbrough where few could actually speak English.' His anti-intellectualism is readily apparent, and it crops up frequently in his dismissal of Walter Winterbottom and other coaches who possessed a more theoretical approach, but he also seems to have been fascinated by book-learning. Duncan Hamilton wrote of having to buy two copies of any book he was taking on away trips because Clough, after some gentle teasing, would always want to borrow one, and even of having to dredge up the name of James Joyce from a vague description because Clough wanted to compare Martin O'Neill to another Irishman whom nobody could understand.

What also comes across in Clough's description of Bill, is how much he (Brian) needed his mother's approval. Bill said they had a 'special kind of rapport', but Clough insisted that Bill 'was Mam's favourite son. I never was. Perhaps it was because he won the teapot in a "lovely baby" competition and I didn't. Still ... I had a reasonable consolation prize by winning the European Cup – twice.' It's notable, too, that at least half of his delight at being named head boy was the 'pleasure, pride and satisfaction' it gave his mother, who seems to have been rather more impressed by that local achievement than she was by what he achieved in football.

Clough himself revelled in the responsibility. 'I actually enjoyed standing at the top of the stairs and warning the late arrivals,' he said – an irony, given his later attitude to punctuality. 'As a prefect, Cloughie was a little bit of a bully to young kids,' the school goalkeeper Keith Harkin recalled in an interview with Roger Hermiston. 'I think it went to his head a bit. He laid the law down to young kids – stop running, take your hands out of your pockets and so on – but he would be the first to be running or to have his bloody hands in his pockets.' According to his brother Joe, the headmaster, Mr Turnbull, considered him 'the best prefect we've ever had'.

Clough may have portrayed himself as an anti-establishment iconoclast – may even have been so – but he expected respect for authority where it was due. Usually, particularly later in life, that meant with him at the top of the hierarchy, but he never seems to have challenged Alan Brown, his dictatorial manager at Sunderland, and certainly never his mother. 'My mam was the biggest influence of all, the way she ran her orderly house, overcrowded as it was,' he wrote in his second autobiography. 'The routine and the pecking order established, it was an environment where we all knew our place and the expectations of us.'

To suggest that Clough was driven by an urge for his mother's approval even after her death is probably overly simplistic, but there is one other very good reason for him to associate silverware with her memory. In 1972, Derby had completed their fixtures before their challengers for the title, and Clough was on a family holiday to the Scilly Isles when he learned that Leeds had lost at Wolves and Liverpool had failed to beat Arsenal and that his side were thus champions. He bought champagne for the whole dining-room of the hotel where they were staying in, and it is easy to imagine Clough's parents' pride at their boy's achievement. Later on that trip, though, Sally fell ill. She never fully recovered, and died in March the following year. That night, Clough's thirty-eighth birthday, Derby over-turned a one-goal first-leg deficit against the Czechoslovak champions Spartak Trnava at the Baseball Ground to reach the European Cup semi-final. Naturally, the European Cup that year became a way of honouring her memory and, equally naturally, when Derby then lost in controversial circumstances to Juventus, winning the European Cup took on the nature of a quest.

Failing his eleven-plus clearly hurt, but Clough's self-assurance soon took over, as Tony Rowell, who taught him English, maths, geography, history and religious instruction as well as games, recalled in an interview with Tony Francis. 'He was bright and alert and seemed to have an opinion on everything,' he said. When subjects were thrown open for discussion, 'he would argue with teachers, which was rare in a thirteen-year-old boy.'

Clough also showed early signs of the sense of loyalty that would be such a trait later in life. Rowell was adept at throwing chalk at boys who weren't paying attention. On one occasion, sensing Clough's mind had drifted, he sought a missile to jolt him back to attention. Reaching around his desk, though, he found only a gym slipper. He hurled that, but Clough ducked, and the slipper crashed through a glass window behind him. Unfortunately for Rowell, the school's headmaster was walking by at the time, and burst into the room in a fury. When Rowell admitted he had thrown the slipper, the headmaster gave Rowell 'the biggest rollicking I've ever had'. As soon as he'd gone, Clough stood up and apologised, and admitted that what had happened had been unfair. Significantly, he didn't appear perturbed that discipline should be maintained by slippers thrown with such force that they could break a window.

By the time Rowell began to coach him, Clough had developed into 'a sturdily built boy' who was 'nimble with it'. Even as a third-former, he was assertive on the pitch, often arguing with the captain. 'Clough was usually right in what he said,' Rowell told Francis, 'but at times I had to tell him to shut up and get on with it.'

Clough started out as a centre-half, but was soon moved to centre-forward. At school level he could be devastating. His goals helped Marton Grove to the final of the Dorman Cup in 1949, but the game that stuck in Harkin's memory was one he played against Clough, for Tollsby against Grove Hill. Tollsby led 3–0 at half-time, but the fourteen-year-old Clough scored five in the second half to turn the game.

Clough left school at fifteen and, following his mother's advice, joined ICI, initially as a messenger. His leadership qualities were evidently clear immediately, for he was put in charge of the other fifteen-year-old apprentices on his first day. 'It must have seemed automatic,' one said, 'because he had such a forceful nature.'

After a while, Clough tried out as a turner and fitter. 'I didn't know I was going to be a footballer,' he said. 'In those days, everything was airy-fairy. They wanted to put you into a trade.' The work bored and confused him, and when he was taken down an anhydrite mine, he was terrified. Not surprisingly, he failed the apprenticeship – 'I couldn't put on a screw to save my life' – but he was given another chance, working as a junior clerk at Casebourne's cement works, an offshoot of ICI. 'It was a good time,' he said, 'except I had to ride seven miles to work. I'd have a drop of milk in a sauce-bottle, and every time you came off your bike going round a roundabout, which inevitably you did in the winter in Middlesbrough in those days, the first thing that went was your milk bottle, so you had to find another sauce-bottle for the next day.'

Work began at 7.12 each morning – start times were staggered at three-minute intervals to prevent queues at the clocking-in machine – but he was allowed five minutes' grace for lateness over a week. Pushing authority to the limit as ever, he would make sure he turned up punctually every day and then clocked off five minutes early on a Friday. At the same time, his brother Joe had him help out on the wagon he drove at the plasterer's yard, building up his biceps and chest by carrying bags of plaster.

Work, though, was just the prelude to a Saturday, when Clough got to do what he was best at: playing football and, specifically, scoring goals. After starting at ICI, he had a spell of just over a year in which he didn't play much football, but he then joined Marton Grove Youth Club. They were not, it's fair to say, a great side, and on one occasion lost 20–0 to South Park Rovers. Clough saw so little of the ball that day that he dropped back into midfield.

At the same time, Bill Clough was playing for Great Broughton, a village about fifteen miles from Middlesbrough in the Cleveland hills, and he persuaded them to recruit his sixteen-year-old brother. In the 1952–53 season, there were four Cloughs – Joe, Des, Bill and Brian – in the side, as well as Doreen's husband Sid. After Brian, Des was probably the best player among the brothers, going on to play at centre-half for Bishop Auckland and to captain Whitby Town. He didn't give up the game until 1986, by which time he was well into his fifties.

The pitch was simply a farmer's field, indistinctly marked, and had to be cleared of sheep and their dung before matches. The league itself largely catered for farmers, and was noted for the ferocity of the rivalry when neighbouring villages played each other. This was far from a gentle baptism for Clough. On one occasion, in a match against Dunsdale, Great Broughton's keenest rivals, Des Clough suffered a cut above the eye, was rushed to the hospital in Guisborough, had it stitched up and returned to finish the match. Little wonder Clough later had no time for malingerers.

The team was managed by Nancy Goldsborough, who ran the local post office, and made a point of washing the team's dark green shirts herself; players wore whatever shorts and socks they could get their hands on. Like Clough's mother, she imposed a stern discipline and, in consideration of her female sensitivities, it was frowned upon to swear in her presence. That – if anything can – may help to explain Clough's odd campaign against swearing at the City Ground in the mid-eighties (despite the fact he himself, of course, swore liberally).

Team-mates remember Clough insisting on wearing the number nine shirt, moving little, and scoring a lot. On one occasion, against Skinningrove in the Cup, he helped clear three inches of snow from the pitch, persuaded the referee it was playable, and then scored ten goals in a 16–0 victory. Hat-trick followed hat-trick and even though Great Broughton, with its remote location, wasn't the best place to be spotted by a professional scout, word soon got around that Clough was a player of some potential. So much promise, in fact, that as well as Great Broughton and Marton Grove, Clough also turned out for Marske Rovers, Acklam steelworks and, in the interdepartmental tournament at ICI, Casebourne's, often playing as many as six games a week. 'I was so tired,' he said, 'that I was almost falling asleep at work, much to the annoyance of my boss, who advised that I should give a little less time to football and more to the job for which I was being paid.'

Having been tipped off by a friend, Ray Grant, who was headmaster of Hugh Bell secondary school and who ran Middlesbrough's junior side, sent the former England forward George Camsell to watch Clough in a game for Great Broughton against Stokesley in the Jefferson Cup. Given he once hit sixty-three goals in a season for Middlesbrough, Camsell might have been expected to recognise a goalscorer when he saw one, but he reported back that Clough wouldn't make it.

Grant, though, decided to take a look for himself, and called Clough up to play for Middlesbrough Juniors against Huddersfield. Clough had had a quiet game, but in the second half, Albert Mendham, the left-winger, attempted to switch the play with a cross-field pass just behind Clough. Instinctively, Clough half-turned, stretched out a leg, flicked the ball over his shoulder, ran on, and crashed a shot into the top corner. Grant told Middlesbrough to ignore Camsell's report.

When Clough joined Middlesbrough as an amateur in November 1951 it was the fulfilment of a dream. 'We didn't really know anything else,' he said. 'Newcastle and Sunderland were on Mars as far as we were concerned. Middlesbrough were the odd one out in that they didn't win anything: Newcastle did their bit in the Cup and Sunderland were the moneybags club, but we were as good as them.'

He soon began playing regularly for the Juniors, but he didn't want to miss out on his games with his brothers for Great Broughton. Happily, Middlesbrough's youth side played in the mornings and Great Broughton in the afternoon so, having played one game, Clough would meet his brothers at the Linthorpe Hotel, where one of the farmers would pick them up in his potato truck. They'd then travel to Great Broughton where most of the family would tuck into a pie and a pint in the Black Horse as their pre-match meal. Clough, in those days, preferred a lemonade. Two teams, though, weren't enough to sate Clough's desire to play, and he began turning out for South Bank, a top local amateur side, and Billingham Synthonia, who paid him £1 a match for five games in April and May 1953. He didn't declare it, and insisted in his autobiography that that was the only time he'd ever cheated the Revenue. Clough's debut for Synthonia came away at Evenwood. 'With the looks of an adolescent,' the local paper reported, 'Clough combines the skill, vigour and guile of a veteran campaigner.'

Clough soon found the life of a footballer wasn't quite what he'd expected it to be. 'I used to run to training through Albert Park,' he said, 'and I used to say that I did more training running there than I did when I got there, because we were always cleaning boots and you got a clip round the ear if you looked the wrong way. It was a class system in football in those days. Lindy [Delapenha, the right-winger] would walk in and just throw his boots. Then it would be "pass me a towel ... do this ... do that." I never thought anything of it.'

As soon as he turned seventeen, Clough signed professional forms with Middlesbrough, bringing to an end his heavy schedule of games for amateur and semi-pro teams. According to Joe and Doreen, it was his mother rather than Clough who registered him – suggesting perhaps that he was unsure whether he wanted to be a footballer and perhaps hinting at the indecisiveness that occasionally gripped him later in life. Joe even said that he suspected Clough signed up principally for the £1-a-week retainer he was due while he performed his National Service. 'He was always careful with money,' he said.

A week or two after signing for Middlesbrough, Clough joined the RAF and did his square-bashing at Padgate near Manchester, before being transferred, after a brief time in Dumfries, to Watchet in Somerset. It was there that he got the close-cropped hairstyle he wore throughout his playing days. In Scotland, Clough had managed to secure a number of forty-eight-hour passes so that he could return to Middlesbrough to play – although, to his frustration, he was often deployed as an inside-left rather than in the centre.

After being sent to Somerset, he had expected to be redeployed to Catterick in North Yorkshire, which would have allowed him to carry on playing for Middlesbrough, but that plan was blocked by his warrant officer, 'a bloke called Stevenson', who recognised his talent and wanted him playing for the regiment. With only two weeks' annual leave and the length of the journey making it hardly worth negotiating a forty-eight-hour pass-out, Clough was restricted to an occasional game for Middlesbrough's reserves or thirds, even if the £7 it brought was very welcome. Stevenson's attitude may have frustrated Clough, but at least he recognised he could play; the RAF's national selectors, by contrast, never called him up, something that left him 'miffed' and probably helped reinforce his scorn for those in positions of authority.

National Service also introduced him, for the first time, to girls, who by his own account had barely figured in his life in Middlesbrough between work and football (although, according to Joe and Doreen, not for the lack of options: 'he was good-looking in a quiet sort of a way,' Joe said). His first 'physical contact', as he put it in his first autobiography, although it seems to have been very innocent, came after a match in Wales as the team attended a social put on by the home side. As his team-mates got up to dance, Clough was left alone at the table until a 'dark-haired, pretty girl' from the Rhondda came over, 'grabbed my hand and asked me to dance. It seemed more like a command than a request.' Clough slithered inexpertly over the dance-floor with her, but when the social was over 'she disappeared into the night'. Nonetheless, she made enough of an impression that for a few months whenever Clough was in the area, he'd take her a box of chocolates. For Clough, National Service consisted mainly of marching, running, playing football and sneaking off to listen to the cricket on the radio.

That was frustrating enough, for all Clough wanted to do was to get back to the north-east to play football. When he did finally get back there, though, aged twenty, released from the RAF and desperate to unleash his goalscoring ability in a professional environment, life became even more frustrating, as he found himself only Middlesbrough's fifth-choice centre-forward.

Local Hero

Clough chafed at the delay to his progress. 'I sensed injustice,' he wrote in his first autobiography. 'I was confined to the reserves, while Doug Cooper had the No 9 shirt in the first team. I knew I was streets ahead of him, that he was too big, too fat, and that I could have stuck the ball through his legs five times before he blinked.' This was one of Clough's odd hobby-horses. It must have been irritating that Cooper, eighteen months younger than Clough, was able to perform his National Service at Catterick and so didn't face the same obstacles he had, but there was never a time when Cooper was an obvious first-choice ahead of Clough. Cooper seems rather, in Clough's mind, to have become the embodiment of his frustrations at that time, and in the emphasis on his physique there is perhaps also a back-projection of the player who was regularly selected ahead of him for England: Derek Kevan.

It wasn't just Clough's football that was held up by the manager Bob Dennison's refusal to pick him: every aspect of his life served to remind him that his progress had stalled. Clough played a lot of tennis in Albert Park with a girl called Wendy whose family 'lived in one of the posher parts of town' on Devonshire Road. On a visit to her home, Clough was told by her father that he wasn't 'the right one' for his daughter, something Clough took as a class-based snub. Once he'd started scoring regularly for Middles-brough, her father had second thoughts, and wrote to him to say he was welcome at their house at any time. Clough, though, could be as loyal to a grudge as he was to a friend. 'I wouldn't have gone round there to see her or him for anything,' he said.

It was an earlier, less-overt jibe that nagged him, though. He would have married his first 'serious girlfriend', Mary, an 'absolutely beautiful brunette', had she not insisted on a Catholic service – 'she missed out poor girl' – but once, when he got uppity, she had reminded him he was 'only a reserve-team centre-forward'.

It was a truth that needled away in him, and was fostered by Peter Taylor, a goalkeeper who arrived from Coventry City for £3,500 in 1955 and who was convinced immediately of Clough's talents. Taylor had never fulfilled the promise he had shown as a player in Nottingham schools football – 'Perfect with his angles,' said the winger Billy Day.

'Crosses were his weakness. He wasn't agile enough, but he was the best in the country at throwing a ball out' – and, even at twenty-six, he was beginning to consider what he might do when his playing career was over. Heavily influenced by his former manager at Coventry, Harry Storer, he saw coaching as his future, and let those around him know it, much to the irritation of team-mates and coaching staff who wondered why a goalkeeper who was rarely first choice had so much to say about how the game should be played.

'Peter Taylor was a really shrewd guy,' said the defender Mick McNeil. 'A bugger, he was. A nice guy. I got on well with him and Cloughie, although Cloughie was very outspoken. I remember Peter Taylor came to me one day and he said, "Hey, Mick," – he was blowing on his fag – and he said, "You know, how many games have you played now?"

'I said, "I think I've played about twelve, something like that."

'He said, "Yes, and you've played damned well, haven't you?"

'I said, "Well, yes, I'm really pleased. You think Bob's pleased?"

'He said, "Yes, I've just been talking to him. What weight are you?"

'I said, "Twelve stone."

'He said, "I told him so! You're just the right weight."

'And he took a last draw on his cigarette and tossed it to the floor. "Put your foot on that."

'The whole rigmarole, the story, he gets you thinking that he's about to say something really interesting, and then . . . "Put your foot on that." He was a sod for that.'

Taylor first saw Clough playing in the traditional pre-season Probables v Possibles trial match and was so taken by 'the way this crew-cut unknown shielded the ball and how cleanly he struck it' that he immediately sought out Dennison, the manager, to tell him how good a prospect he considered him. Having done that, he sought out Clough. The first words he said to him, if Clough's first autobiography is to be believed, were, 'I don't know what's going on at this club. You're better than anybody here.'

It was exactly what Clough wanted to hear – perhaps what he needed to hear, for he said it was the first time anybody had confirmed what he felt in his own mind – and it persuaded him immediately of Taylor's ability to assess a player. 'That was him throughout the rest of his life – instant judgement, taking little or no time, as long as it was based on what he considered to be solid evidence,' he said.

There were two things about Clough's game that really impressed Taylor: his ability to generate power in shots with hardly any backlift, and his calm in front of goal. Taylor always said it was a goal Clough scored in a reserve game against Stoke that persuaded him of his talent, as he ran on to a loose ball, held off a defender and, under pressure, fired his shot low past the goalkeeper. Taylor asked him afterwards what had gone through his mind as he'd entered the box. A puzzled Clough replied that nothing had, and that, Taylor told him, was the key.

'His shooting was so powerful because he was an excellent trainer, building up his legs and thighs,' said the Middlesbrough forward Alan Peacock. 'He may have been physically slight, but he made a point of developing the key muscles, and was technically excellent.' Alan Durban, who played with and against Clough in training at Derby, remembered being struck by his heading ability. 'He would use a golfer's stance to get strength in a certain part of his body without needing to jump,' he told Pat Murphy. 'Too many centre-forwards jump and in so doing, they lose power in the header. But Cloughie would stand there, really give it some oomph and his headers would rocket in from twelve yards.'

So taken was Taylor by Clough, so frustrated by Dennison's refusal to select him, that in September 1955 he took Clough to see Hartlepools United play Derby County, who were by then managed by Harry Storer. After the game, Taylor introduced the two and, in a conversation conducted in the centre-circle so they could be assured of not being overhead, Taylor tried to persuade Storer to sign Clough. Derby, though, had no funds available for transfers and so nothing came of it, which was probably just as well, given that Taylor's actions were blatantly against FA regulations.

Taylor and Clough rapidly became close friends. 'I was a stranger in a dull town,' Taylor wrote in *With Clough by Taylor*. 'Middlesbrough of the mid-fifties was a place where you could see hundreds of men shuffling on the pavements of the main street on Sunday mornings, gazing expectantly at the town hall clock. At the first stroke of noon, they tensed like runners on a starting line. By the twelfth stroke, they had vanished into the opening doors of pubs. What drab pubs too.'

Clough was a welcome distraction for Taylor and together they coached

21

schoolboys in Redcar – a useful supplement to their wages – and travelled all round the north-east to watch midweek football, in Sunderland, Gateshead, South Shields, Newcastle and Darlington. Initially neither he nor Clough had a car, so they would either try to persuade Delapenha to drive them or take the bus, trying to sit at the front upstairs so they could put their feet up on the ledge under the window. 'I just wanted to be involved in football every moment of the day,' Taylor said. 'I loved the atmosphere, loved assessing players.'

In those days, Taylor had strong left-wing beliefs, and he introduced Clough to politics, taking him to see the Shadow Chancellor Harold Wilson speak at a working-men's club. Clough, who still lived with his parents and so perhaps was glad of the freedom, regularly visited Taylor's house opposite Price's clothing factory on Saltwells Crescent. In the mornings, they would meet in Albert Park on the way to training. 'Peter Taylor and Cloughie used to walk together talking about football,' remembered Billy Day, 'and me and Eddie [Holliday] would walk about ten yards behind talking about the dogs the day before or the racing in the afternoon.'

Most evenings they would sit, smoking and talking football, while Taylor's wife, Lill, made them dinner; Clough's only reference to her in his auto-biographies is to note that she made 'smashing chips', pancakes and door-steps of bread with golden syrup.

Neither had many other friends – Peacock, in fact, suggested they deliberately excluded others to the extent of locking the door of their compartment on train journeys so they could play dominoes and talk football together without interruption – and so Taylor naturally became a regular visitor at the Clough home as well. When Lill went into labour with their second child, Phillip, it was Barry Clough's bike he borrowed to collect the gas and the air-box from the midwife. Clough and his sister Deanna became godparents although, given Taylor's suspicion of religion, that probably says more about Clough's belief in the traditions of the church and his willingness to browbeat others into doing things his way than anything else. In the summer, Clough would follow Taylor to the family home in Nottingham, less it seems for a holiday than to be with his great friend; he spent most of his time helping out selling dried peas in the grocery shop run by Taylor's brother Don.

It has become a cliché to describe their relationship as being like a marriage, but then Taylor spoke of them as 'an incompatible couple fatally attracted to each other by a single passion' and there was certainly something akin to courtship about the way Clough described their life at Middlesbrough. After training, they would walk home for lunch through Albert Park, 'talking football the whole of the way'.

With the rest of his Middlesbrough team-mates, it was less of a discussion. Others, perhaps, had the cockiness knocked out of them by National Service, but not Clough. Even as a junior, Clough would spend the taxi journey back from games analysing what had happened and telling other players, even those older than himself, what they should have done. The coach Jimmy Gordon was so concerned by his attitude that he suggested to Harold Shepherdson, by then Boro's trainer, that Clough had to be reined in, but neither he nor Dennison ever found a way of tempering his aggressive self-confidence.

Mick McNeil, four years Clough's junior, remembered clearly the first time he met him, when he was fourteen years old. 'We [he and Bob Appleby, a young goalkeeper] used to go along in the evenings after work and train under the stand, in the sweat box, the "soot box" we called it because it was full of dust. One evening Cloughie was there, playing table-tennis with some first-team player. We were just young lads doing our training. We were doing step-ups. The box had a wooden base and it moved when you tried to do these things as quickly as you could. So the floor was bouncing. I heard this voice: "Hey, Buster!" The first words Cloughie ever spoke to me. "Hey, Buster – do you mind? We're trying to play table-tennis." Bobby and I said, under our breaths, "And we're trying to train." But we sat on the seat and watched him finish his game, then we carried on.'

The swagger is even apparent in early family photographs, in which Clough, no matter his position in the frame, always seems the dominant figure, with his chest-out pose, his easy grin and the glint of superiority in his eye. Failing his eleven-plus either did nothing to dampen his self-belief or, more likely, it prompted him to express it so overtly that nobody could ever suspect how keenly he had felt the failure. 'He wasn't frightened of anyone,' Joe said. 'He'd tell anyone what he thought. He was always "right".' The only person he wouldn't challenge, Joe and Doreen recalled, was their mother.

*

Middlesbrough's start to the 1955–56 season was indifferent. A 1–1 draw against Fulham on 3 September meant they had taken five points from five games, but, Cliff Mitchell wrote in the *Middlesbrough Evening Gazette*, it might have been a lot better had they taken their chances. 'The forwards looked good,' he wrote, 'until they got within sight of the Fulham goal.'

There was an obvious solution, and he was making his presence felt. Clough scored two and hit the woodwork twice as the reserves won the North Riding Senior Cup with a 4–2 victory over Scarborough. Two days later, he banged in four in a 4–2 win over Stockton, taking his tally for the season to thirteen from eight games. After a 1–1 draw at Bury on 10 September, Mitchell advocated change.

Clough finally won selection against Barnsley the following Saturday, as Mitchell was able to reveal on the Thursday. 'BRIAN CLOUGH GETS HIS BIG CHANCE,' the headline in the *Gazette* read. 'Two-footed, and a good header, Clough's zest and dash have proved too much for the defences opposing him in the North Eastern League,' Mitchell wrote, reflecting on his record of fifteen goals in nine games that season. There was, fans of the time recall, a great sense of expectation. 'We'd all heard about the goals he'd been scoring for the reserves,' said Leslie Wilson, a regular in the 'bob end' with his father. 'We'd been struggling a bit so everybody was calling for him to be in the side, and there was a lot of excitement about it.'

Clough walked into the home dressing-room at Ayresome Park, and saw the shirts arranged in numerical order. He went to sit by the number nine shirt, which hung next to the radiator. A few minutes later Jimmy James, a local comedian, came in with Ely, the stooge from his stage act, and sat down next to Clough, telling jokes and puffing away on a cigarette, blowing the smoke alternately from one side of his mouth then the other. He was a regular at home games and, although Clough was initially unsettled by his presence in the dressing-room, he later became close enough to agree to James's suggestion that he and Lindy Delapenha appear on stage at the Palladium and put on a show of head tennis.

Although he tried to hide it, Clough was nervous, and his mental state wasn't eased when Dennison told him he'd been picked, and the rest was 'up to him'. Perhaps Dennison thought it important to encourage a player to take responsibility, to try to ensure he involved himself in the game and didn't hide behind more senior players, but the incident rattled Clough sufficiently that he made it his policy as a manager to tell a debutant that he'd been picked because he was good enough, and to try to ensure he was as relaxed as possible. 'When footballers go out on the field they have to be relaxed, not frightened. Sometimes that frame of mind is difficult to achieve, but they simply have to relax,' he wrote in his first autobiography. 'I don't know anyone who can do anything to the best of his ability if he is taut with apprehension.' That became such a central tenet of his thinking that Gary Megson was sold five months and one game after signing for Forest because he would get so nervous before matches he'd vomit, something Clough felt was unsettling the rest of the team.

Tense Clough may have been, but his debut was encouraging. 'He didn't score,' Leslie Wilson went on, 'and the game finished 1–1, but I remember the final minutes, with everybody urging him on to get the winner on his debut. We had a load of corners, and he headed a couple just over, but that was as close as he got.'

The following Monday, the *Gazette* was cautiously impressed. 'Judgement reserved: Clough's pleasing game,' ran the headline above Mitchell's report, in which he urged against snap judgements. 'To those who grumbled over the weekend that Brian was "raw", was well held by his opposing centre-half and failed to score, I would advise patience and understanding. To start with, he came into a Middlesbrough side that was up to all its old tricks of inaccurate passing, bunching, hesitancy and lack of plan. The support he received, in these circumstances, was rather less than moderate. He has probably had more effective backing in the reserves. Clough has a lot to learn. He is "green" and is finding difficulty in bridging the gap between the North Eastern League and the Second Division. He did enough in the 1–1 draw on Saturday to suggest that he will bridge that gap. His was a debut of promise. I think he'll be among the goals for Boro's first team in the near future.'

It took some time, though. Clough played the following week in a 1–1 draw at Anfield, the trip exposing further unexpected anxieties as he encountered situations he had never previously experienced. He described his panic in a hotel dining-room when a waiter arrived to ask players what they wanted as a starter. Never having had one before, he had no idea what to say, so when Lindy Delapenha ordered a prawn cocktail, he blurted out that he'd have the same. It made little difference to his performance.

'Clough's headed flicks, his persistence and promise must have earned him continued favour,' Mitchell wrote.

It did, but a 2–0 defeat at Bristol City had Mitchell reporting that Dennison had 'some blinding headaches' over the forward line which 'with two exceptions . . . had been uniformly and consistently poor since the start of the season'. Clough, he said, 'was a trier all the way, but gave his least impressive display. It could be argued that he lacked support, but he failed to produce any threat to the opposing goal. And he did have more than one good chance. I still feel he can make the grade.'

At that stage there was still a sense of anxiety about Clough when he was forced out of his comfort zone. On long away trips, for instance, the team would take the train from Middlesbrough to Darlington to connect with mainline services heading south. Clough, in those early days, would find his compartment immediately and settle himself down for the journey, whereas Taylor would take any extra tickets the club had bought and wander up and down the platform selling them, splitting the proceeds with Dennison. His streetwiseness was something Clough clearly admired, and in time came to ape.

His first goal for the club came the following Saturday, as a Boro side including the young winger Billy Day for the first time, came from 2–0 down to beat Leicester City 4–3. Clough then got the winner in a 2–1 victory over Lincoln City. After a 3–1 home defeat to Stoke City in which, in Mitchell's words, 'Clough was blotted out by [Ken] Thomson, Stoke's fine centre-half', though, he was dropped as the prolific Charlie Wayman returned for an away game at Hull. Peter Taylor made his Middlesbrough debut in that game, called up after Rolando Ugolini, Boro's Scottish-Italian goalkeeper, had suffered a gashed head in a car crash. Clough responded by banging in four in eleven minutes as the reserves beat Gateshead reserves 6–2, but he never got another run in the first team that season, and it seemed that Day was emerging as the bigger star.

Alan Peacock, another young local forward, made his debut that November and Ken McPherson, who had begun the season as first reserve for Wayman, was sold to Coventry the following month having been rendered redundant by the crop of emerging talent. Wayman, presumably reasoning that he too would soon have outlived his usefulness despite having averaged roughly two goals every three games throughout his career, soon applied for a player-manager's position at Workington of the Third Division (North) and, having failed to land that, was then linked with a similar role at York.

Clough returned after a seven-game absence but had 'a poor match' in a 5–0 defeat at Notts County before being used to give Wayman a break in the third of the four Christmas matches, a 1–0 reverse at West Ham. It was another six weeks before he was given another chance, at home to Bristol City. 'Clough,' Mitchell wrote, 'despite missing some chances, helped to make the first goal and scored the second' in a 2–1 win.

He suffered a knee injury in that game and, after ten days in plaster, his season was effectively over. It had ended in frustration, but most players would probably have considered three goals in nine games as a reasonable enough start to life in the first team. Clough, though, was not most players. On 26 April, he put in a transfer request, although only after he'd sold the story that he was about to do so to the local paper for £50.

'I think that a change of club would be of benefit to me,' Clough told the *Gazette*. 'It may seem surprising for a young player like myself, who hasn't been in the game five minutes, to ask for a move, and there is something I would like to say right away. I have no quarrel with any of my team-mates at Ayresome Park. I have always got along well with the lads. The trouble is that I feel I am no further forward now than I was when I first played for the senior team near the beginning of the season. I want to improve all the time and I think that any big improvement will come quicker if I move away from Ayresome Park. I would be struggling to get another club and so I would like Middlesbrough to cancel my contract, then I could go for trials with other clubs and maybe make the grade eventually.'

It was an odd statement to make, for there had been no suggestion – or at least nothing that had reached the *Gazette* – that Clough had fallen out with anybody. Perhaps his abrasive self-assertiveness had already started to antagonise his team-mates. Clough had pushed ICI's timekeeping to the limit, and he did the same at Middlesbrough, making a point of turning up for training after most of his team-mates so he could make a grand entrance in his gabardine coat when they were half-changed and throw his cap at the peg; the general consensus is that he hit the target five times out of six. Shepherdson spoke of his 'amazing aura of self-confidence', recalling how from the very beginning he was 'dedicated ... desperate for success', seemingly capable of talking about nothing other than football.

Clough's frustration at his failure to become a clear first-team regular can only have been heightened by the fact that Boro weren't doing particularly well without him. They finished that 1955–56 season fourteenth, twelve points off promotion, but there were signs that Dennison was beginning to see the potential of his young local forwards, as he placed Wayman, then thirty-four, on a sliding scale salary – £15 per match if he played in the first team and £12 if he played in the reserves. Wayman, recognising that probably meant his time as an automatic starter was coming to an end, admitted he felt 'bitter and resentful'.

Perhaps that encouraged Clough, or perhaps he decided that if he wasn't getting a game he had nothing to lose, but having failed to secure a move he asked for a raise. Dennison initially demurred, but Clough, in a flash of the smart-alec logic that would become one of his most famous characteristics, asked whether the reason players were paid less in the summer than the winter was that they didn't play. Dennison confirmed it was, at which Clough pointed out that in the summer he was just as good a player as Len Shackleton and therefore should be paid the same as anybody else. Dennison upped his basic weekly wage from £9 to £11, which was probably an indication that Clough was becoming more central to his thinking for the 1956–57 season.

Sure enough – or perhaps because Cooper was unable to secure leave from the base at Catterick – Clough was given his chance in the final practice game before the 1956–57 season, and was named in the Reds, the Probables, to face the Whites, the Possibles. Heavy rain, though, forced the game to be abandoned and Cooper was recalled to face Stoke City for the opening game of the season.

Clough fumed, his mood worsened by a piece in that Saturday's *Evening Gazette*. Under the headline, 'Football, the Problem Child of British Sport', it lamented that 'promising young players are not coming into the game in such numbers because of better wages and conditions available in more secure professions. A lot of those who do make football their livelihood are unsatisfactory pupils; they will not train the hard way.' Clough had never had any thought but to go into football, had trained hard and had scored hatfuls of goals, and yet still he kept being denied his chance.

Boro began the season with a 1–1 draw against Stoke, Bill Harris levelling with four minutes remaining. Mitchell was not impressed. 'Here we go again,' read the headline, 'the mixture as before.' Cooper who presumably, like Clough, was cursing his lack of opportunities and his bad luck when they presented themselves, twisted his knee, and so Clough returned to face Bury at Gigg Lane that Tuesday. This time, the chance was seized.

Clough 'led "giant" Norman Nielsen a merry dance,' Mitchell reported. He scored twice – both equalisers – and was denied a hat-trick by a brilliant save before hitting the post. Boro lost 3–2, but at least, Mitchell's tone suggested, Clough represented something fresh, something different, something that might shake Boro from their cycle of underachievement. Clough scored two more the following Saturday in a 3–1 win at Barnsley. 'At twenty-one, and with only a handful of League appearances behind him, Brian Clough has quite a lot to learn,' Mitchell wrote. 'Fortunately for Middlesbrough, and happily for himself, he is learning fast and, in the process, is helping himself to a healthy tally of goals. For four goals from his two games this season is a fine return and it is a fact that he is unlucky not to have twice as many to his credit. Some of his best efforts, headers and shots, have been brilliantly saved or have gone just wide; on the four occasions on which he did score, he was "Johnny on the spot", succeeding from close range each time. A bustling, strong opportunist, Clough has started the season in heartening style and gives promise of adding needed finish to the often clever approach work of his colleagues in the forward line.'

He rattled in an 'unstoppable left-foot drive' in a 2–2 home draw against Bury, and then got the goal in a 1–1 draw at Leicester in which he was 'always harassing and bustling the defence ... several times beating experienced centre-half Jack Froggatt in the air and on the ground'.

Two more goals in a 3–2 defeat at Grimsby took his tally to eight in five, but the overall performance had Mitchell complaining that Boro were 'one of the most exasperating teams in the country'. He got the second as Boro beat Bristol City and Mitchell, never quick to leap to judgement, was becoming increasingly convinced that Clough might just be as special as he seemed. 'Brian Clough is going from strength to strength,' he wrote. 'He played a vital part in Middlesbrough's 3–2 victory ... and the Ayresome Park crowd of almost 20,000 was quick to show its recognition of the fact. What a fine goal he scored; and you must have noticed how the accuracy of his passing has increased and how much more mature is his play. Clough, in a short time, has made big strides. With further experience, and the continued support of his colleagues, he could develop into a top-class centre-forward. Meanwhile, nine goals in six games is good enough!'

His value was seen again the following Wednesday, as Boro played Grimsby at home. A Bob Crosbie free-kick had cancelled out Delapenha's penalty and Boro again looked like dropping a point in a game they should have won. 'But this season,' Mitchell wrote, 'Middlesbrough have a twenty-one-year-old match-winner called Brian Clough. And in the seventy-fourth-minute this local lad hit a typically opportunistic goal.' For once, Mitchell was speaking not of exasperation but of a 'real bid' for promotion.

Ten goals in seven games was enough to draw the attention of the national press. 'I first spoke to him in 56–57, my first full season as a football writer on the *Daily Herald*,' said Doug Weatherall, who after moving to the *Mail* became one of the most respected voices in north-eastern journalism. 'I cut my teeth as he was cutting his teeth. So I was the first person to interview him in a biggish way. I remember the first time I saw him play, at Ayresome against Grimsby. I was moved by him straightaway and I wrote that he was the most exciting player I'd seen in a penalty area for years.'

He turned out to be one of the most exciting interviewees as well. 'I'll never forget that first interview. I asked routine questions but I didn't get routine answers,' Weatherall said. 'He was a genius – it was clear even then. He was the only player who ever said this: I asked him who'd helped him and he said he'd tell me who hadn't. It wasn't so-and-so and it wasn't so-and-so. Then he told me who had – the youth team coach Jimmy Gordon and the reserve team coach Mickey Fenton.'

Middlesbrough's next game was away at Notts County, who hadn't won since Easter. The outcome was inevitable; as Mitchell said, he 'should have known better' than to get his hopes up. Boro lost 2–1 and Mitchell highlighted Clough as one of only three players to have given 'adequate performances'. There followed goals in draws against Liverpool and Leyton Orient, then in wins over Port Vale and Rotherham, and when he scored the first two in a 4–1 victory over Bristol City, Mitchell was again speaking of promotion, while praising the understanding Clough and the inside-forward Derek McLean had struck up in the reserves.

Boro drew at Swansea, then beat Fulham 3–1, Clough getting the second, at the beginning of November. A week later, in a 4–0 victory away to Nottingham Forest, Clough struck his first senior hat-trick. 'It's wonderful, absolutely wonderful,' he told the *Evening Gazette*. 'Lindy Delapenha gave me the first goal, Ronnie Burbeck the second, and Arthur Fitzsimons the last. And don't forget the work Derek McLean put in – what a fighter he is – and how the lads in defence held out when Forest were on top. I couldn't have done a thing without the lads. It's grand to play in the side these days because everybody is fighting and helping you all they can.'

His team-mates may not have recognised the modest figure being presented, but at the time, few cared. Clough's goals had transformed the season from the 'here we go again' of its opening into something far more exciting. A crowd of over 32,000 turned out to see Boro beat West Ham 3–1: 'Four times Clough was right out of luck not to score,' Mitchell wrote. 'The young leader failed for only the third time this season to be in the list of marksmen – and there were no complaints!' Even when he didn't score, Clough was the news.

With petrol rationing imposed because of the Suez Crisis likely to curtail future away trips, several hundred Middlesbrough fans made the journey to Blackburn on 25 November and, of course, it was then, with optimism at its height, that Middlesbrough crumbled, losing 1–0. Clough was back on target a week later in a 3–0 win over Lincoln, but the glorious form of the autumn had deserted him, as Mitchell hinted following a 2–1 defeat at Sheffield United. 'Some sympathy there must be for a team which outplays its opponents to the extent of having five forwards, two wing-halves and, at times, a full-back blazing into the attack – yet which loses . . .' he wrote. 'It was almost solely in the marksmanship that they fell down.'

It would become a recurring theme: it was clear that when Clough played well, Middlesbrough played well. What was less certain was whether his centrality to their hopes was a tribute to his ability, or an indication of his insistence on being at the centre of everything. Just as Clough's form dipped, the England manager Walter Winterbottom came to take a look at him in Middlesbrough's away game at Stoke. Two other recurring themes presented themselves as Boro lost 3–1 to a Neville Coleman hat-trick: that Thomson should mark Clough out of the game, and that Clough should not play well with Winterbottom watching.

Any lingering thought that promotion might be possible was as good as extinguished three days before Christmas as Boro lost their fourth game in five, going down 2–1 at home to Barnsley. The Cup offered brief hope as a 1–1 draw against First Division Charlton was followed with a 3–2 win in the replay at the Valley. Clough, for once, played well with Winterbottom in attendance, and levelled the match at 2–2 as he seized on Joe Scott's pass, held off John Hewie and scored with a left-foot strike. Ayresome was packed for the fourth-round tie against Aston Villa, and Clough gave Boro a 2–1 lead just before half-time. Fatigue overcame them, though, and Villa came back to win 3–2; Boro's season, effectively, was over by the end of January.

Clough's, however, was not. Winterbottom had seen enough in those two matches in which he'd watched him to follow the hype and select Clough for the B international against Scotland in Birmingham on 6 February. 'I found it a bit fast,' Clough said. 'Some of the lads were bit above me in class, but I enjoyed every minute.' It was modesty his performance didn't warrant. 'I don't think I've ever seen him distribute the ball better than in the first half,' said Dennison, who attended the game at St Andrews, 'and he had a hand in every goal.'

The first came in the opening minute as Clough swept a ball to the left for Brian Pilkington to cut in and score. Twelve minutes later, as Cliff Mitchell's report relayed it, Alfred 'Stokes cut in along the goal-line before hitting the ball, hard and low, into the middle. Boro's young leader was there to smash it home.' And after twenty-one minutes, Clough slipped in Peter Thompson for the third. It was Clough's pass to the right-winger Harry Hooper – then at Wolves but later a team-mate at Sunderland – that led to the penalty from which Hooper made it four in the second half.

Basil Easterbrook, the great authority on football and cricket for the Kemsley Group of newspapers, was convinced of Clough's quality, describing him as 'a man in a number 9 shirt showing the boldness, assurance, decisiveness and all-round ability so long lacking in the middle of England forward lines. Clough is a natural in the direct lineal descent of such pre-war Middlesbrough leaders as George Camsell and Mickey Fenton. Barring injury his future must be bright and that means England's is too.'

Later that month, Clough made his debut for the England Under-23 side in a 1–1 draw against Scotland at Ibrox. Johnny Haynes created three fine chances for him, and John Dyson another, but he took none and played so poorly that he was mocked by the train driver at Darlington as he changed on his way back to Middlesbrough. After the praise that had greeted his first appearance in an England shirt, doubts had begun to emerge.

Clough was watched once more by an England selector, heading the opener as Boro won 2–1 at Fulham in March, the second in an unbeaten run of nine games with which they finished the campaign, the young local forward-line offering hope for the following season. Clough himself finished on forty goals, and was told by England to secure himself a passport as he was under consideration for the national squad and the Under-23 tour to eastern Europe.

His final chance to impress the selectors came in a game for Young England against Old England at Highbury. On a pitch that was 'largely barren of grass and iron-hard', Clough had a difficult game as Old England won 2–1. 'He was often beaten for possession by Billy Wright,' Mitchell wrote. 'In spite of poor service from his colleagues in a rather disjointed forward line, he did put in a couple of good shots and a fine header, any one of which might well have registered.' He did enough, though, to be selected for the Under-23 tour.

England went first to Sofia, where Clough got their goal in a 2–1 defeat to Bulgaria with what the *Middlesbrough Evening Gazette* described as 'a flying header.' It was an unsatisfying, niggly game though, in which Stan Anderson, who would be Clough's captain at Sunderland, became the first player to be sent off playing for an England team after punching a Bulgarian he said had spat at him.

The accommodation, Jimmy Armfield recalled in *150BC*, was Spartan, two camp-beds in each room with a rudimentary wash-basin at one end. Armfield was in the next room to Clough and popped in to find him 'creating merry hell' about a large beetle he'd found on the rug. 'That was when I first became aware that he had an inner confidence about himself that set him apart,' Armfield said. 'The rest of us were basically quite quiet young men, a bit hesitant to take on authority. Things were different in those days, but Cloughie would speak his mind.'

Clough's room-mate on that trip was the Blackburn winger Bryan Douglas. 'He had strong opinions about Middlesbrough and the management,' he remembered. 'He used to put the fear up people. If you were a bit weak-willed he could be a bit nasty off the field.' Clough was among

33

a group of players who passed the spare time between games playing cards – mainly solo. 'He was just as aggressive playing cards as football,' Douglas said. 'If you played the wrong card he'd hit the roof.'

When England beat Romania 1–0 in Bucharest a week later, Clough was omitted as West Brom's Derek Kevan – nicknamed 'The Tank' for his robust style – moved from inside-forward to centre-forward, his number ten shirt going to Haynes who, like Ronnie Clayton, Duncan Edwards and David Pegg, had missed the first game of the tour, playing for the senior side against the Republic of Ireland. According to Armfield, Clough was 'astounded' and, he later claimed, let Winterbottom know how he felt, although given only five players were retained – and only four in the same position – it probably shouldn't have been regarded as too much of a slight. Three days after that, Winterbottom made just once change for a game against Czechoslovakia in Bratislava. England won 2–0, and despite a general feeling the tour had been a success, Clough came home dis-appointed.

The forthrightness Clough had shown in facing down Winterbottom and his readiness to dissect the games of others caused hostility among some players, particularly as it was allied to a personality so single-minded as to seem selfish. There was an abrasiveness, a willingness to leap on the weaknesses of others. The winger Edwin Holliday, for instance, despite his reputation for being, in Peacock's words, 'bloody wild', used to become so nervous before games that he'd repeatedly visit the toilet. Once, as Clough watched him walk back across the dressing-room to his seat, Clough asked him in front of the whole dressing-room whether he'd remembered to wash his hands. Given his later obsession with relaxing players before games, it's hard to see such a jibe as anything other than a casual desire to assert his superiority.

Shepherdson, though, believed Clough's main problem was one of tone, and that he genuinely believed what he was doing was for the greater good. 'He wanted the others to do well also, and he was no back-stabber,' Boro's trainer told Pat Murphy. 'A few of the others resented his blunt speaking, but at least you knew where you stood with Brian.'

He had a level of competitiveness few of his team-mates could under-stand, something that often manifested itself away from football. That summer, Middlesbrough sent a team to play cricket against Redcar Cricket

Club. Clough, coming in at six, scored 4 and Peter Taylor top-scored with 31 as Middlesbrough, fielding twelve men, won by a wicket. The game was such a success it was reprised a year later, when Taylor scored 41, and Clough, having taken 2 for 21, scored 15 not out to guide the football club to a six-wicket victory. A year after that, in a benefit for the Redcar groundsman, Ted Johnson, Clough was unbeaten on 24 with Middlesbrough 117 for 7 chasing 170 to win when bad light stopped play.

'He wasn't a bad cricketer,' said Stan Wilson, who played for Redcar. 'There was him and Lindy Delapenha could play a bit, but the others were just there to sign autographs. But he hadn't come to sign autographs. He'd come to win. I remember him nagging these fellas; he might have been playing in the Cup final the way he was bollocking them. He couldn't understand not playing to win. But that was him: he was a winner.'

Others were less charitable. Gordon saw the problems early, after Clough had attacked Shepherdson and Mickey Fenton for staying inside by a radiator while the players trained outside in the cold and the wet. He also complained constantly about the tedium of training, which invariably consisted of ten laps of the pitch, followed by five half laps, followed by twelve sprints, with only very occasional training games to provide variety. Clough was not alone in his frustration, and eventually Delapenha took matters into his own hands, asking for volunteers to come back and play head-tennis in the afternoon. They strung a rope between the back of a stand and the factory wall behind and would have regular games of six-a-side for a shilling a man.

On away trips, Shepherdson would check the players' rooms on a Friday night to make sure they hadn't snuck off drinking. Often, if players were missing, he would find them in Clough's room, being given a team-talk they didn't necessarily appreciate. Clough could also be an irritant in training. In exercises he was lazy, following Taylor's advice – 'don't leave it on the track; save it for the next match' – but in practice matches he was as competitive as he was on a Saturday afternoon, constantly niggling, tugging shirts, even elbowing his marker, as the centre-half Brian Phillips clearly remembered. 'He used to back into me and pull my shirt, and I said, "Hey, Clow" – that's what I called him – "Hey, Clow, stop fucking around."

'He says, "Ah, fucking get on with it."

'I say, "Look, cut it out!"

'Anyway, next thing the ball comes round, and as he turns round, that way' – he mimed Clough turning to his left – 'he can't turn the other way because he's got no left foot – as he turned round, I fucking hit him. He went down squealing, "You wait till I get up!"

'I said, "When you get up, I'll still be here." Because he couldn't burst a paper bag. Do you know what I mean? I could have blown him over. So that was the start of it.'

Phillips – 'a real party man' according to Mick McNeil; 'he was a Jack the Lad and God he could sink them (it didn't touch the sides)' – was Clough's most vocal critic, and there were times when Gordon had to abandon team-talks because they'd descended into slanging matches between the pair. Clough, Phillips believed, was interested only in himself and Dennison was too weak to stop him. 'We'd be flogging our guts out for a 0–0 draw and Cloughie would be strolling around at the other end quite unconcerned,' he said. 'He did bugger all when the pressure was on. Then we'd have to read in the *Gazette* what a great game he'd had.'

From a very early stage, Clough cultivated the local media. In an age in which most players were hesitant or lacked eloquence in their dealings with the press, Clough was something radically different. Almost from the moment he made the Middlesbrough first team, he was quoted far more often than any of his team-mates in the papers, and it's easy to see why: where others spoke in clichés, he was forthright, opinionated and funny. At times, particularly after a good performance, he would hold court to a circle of writers, but he was also adept at playing one journalist off against another. Doug Weatherall recalled the sinking feeling he sometimes had when pulling up outside Clough's house and seeing another journalist's car already there. It was that skill, that ability to manipulate people, of course, that allowed him so often to sell exclusives – as, for instance, when he had handed in that first transfer request. And as Clough and his opinions increasingly became a story, so those terrified of missing out on them began to realise the benefits of viewing his performances in a favourable light. 'He was well in with the reporters at that particular time,' said Peacock. 'John Corner, Joe Etherington, Cliff Mitchell at the *Middlesbrough Gazette*, Ray Roberts who worked for the *Northern Echo* ... I thought they were too Cloughie, if you know what I mean. It was all Brian. I think that went against some of the senior players, as well. They were too close to him,

I thought. Behind the scenes he had a go at certain players without actually naming them and that was a big thing at the club at the time.'

That was one irritation, but there was the issue of Clough's selfishness in front of goal. Clough would always be demanding the ball, and at times would almost barge a team-mate out of the way in his desperation to get a shot in. Dennison once told him that a player had complained that Clough shouted for the ball even if the player in possession had a better shooting opportunity, and asked him why. 'Because I'm better at it than he is,' Clough replied. He was similarly dismissive of Jimmy Gordon's suggestion that the team would be better off if he focused less on scoring and more on setting up chances for his team-mates.

'In seven years I don't think me or Eddie [Holliday] hit the side-netting with a shot,' Billy Day said. 'You'd cut it back to him and if you didn't, he'd say, "I've run forty yards to get up with you." He was a brilliant striker of a moving ball. His timing was perfect. It was a miracle if he shot over the bar. He used to have his knee always at the right angle to the ground. If I'd thrown a hand grenade over, he'd have volleyed it. That was his thinking. One of his abilities was that if it was 50–50 with a defender, he would still kick through it to score. Basically it was that bravery that got him injured, wasn't it? He couldn't stand a coward. He did his job. He used to say "I'm not wasting energy running out to the wings or chasing back. That's what you lot get paid for." He'd say, "My job's in the penalty area, scoring goals and that's what I get paid for." And you wouldn't argue because he was the one that got you the win bonus.'

His attitude may have bred frustration, but the evidence suggested Middlesbrough were better off when Clough was focused on scoring goals. Certainly Clough preferred it. 'When he scored he was like a man on drugs,' Peacock said. 'He just lived for that on the field.' And when he was getting his fix, he tended to be more generous to others. Delapenha fondly recalled having laid on a goal for Clough when he might have scored himself, and Clough rushing straight for him and holding his arm aloft like a heavyweight champion.

He began the next season, if not in a withdrawn role, then at least offering evidence that he had taken Gordon's advice to heart. Middlesbrough opened away to Stoke with the same side that had won the final game of the previous season 1–0 at Huddersfield. Clough, for once escaping Thomson, got the opener, but, Mitchell reported, 'Boro lost their poise and, with it, their confidence ... The rearguard was bulldozed into making a series of mistakes and City cracked home four in less than half an hour.'

It soon got worse as an unchanged team drew 2–2 at home to Rotherham. 'How,' Mitchell asked, 'can a side which presents goals to its opponents and at the same time spurns wonderful chances be rated as unlucky? It's not bad luck, it's bad play ... Scoring chances? Plenty of them. Every forward missed at least one and special mention has to be made of Fitzsimons who missed four.' By the following Saturday, the *Gazette*'s headline was noting how 'Disappointment turns to bitterness' as Boro were held to a 0–0 draw at home by Bristol City. 'Every member of the line was remiss in his shooting,' Mitchell wrote. 'There could be no suggestion of bad luck. Clough tried to make up for his own lack of power-shooting by spraying passes through the middle. He laid on some good chances too, though I suppose we've come to expect goals from Brian.'

They soon came and, once they did, the mood changed abruptly. Away to Rotherham, Mitchell reported, 'Clough, scourge of defences last season, cut his deep-lying tactics right out and, instead, lay well upfield, made direct tracks for goal, and shot whenever he got the chance. Result – he scored twice and was unfortunate not to have made it four ...' Boro won 4–1. 'If they can retain this dynamic form,' Mitchell continued, 'then surely they can be at least among the challengers when April comes round.'

Two days later, Boro won 2–0 at Cardiff: 'It all added up to a roasting for a Cardiff side that was, I know, relieved to get away with only a 2–0 defeat. And the player chiefly responsible was Brian Clough. As at Rotherham, he usually stayed upfield and was the spearhead of the attack. As at Rotherham, he scored twice and but for a combination of bad luck and good goalkeeping would undoubtedly have notched a hat-trick.' Mitchell noted how often Taylor found Clough with quick clearances, which is revealing for two reasons. For one, it suggests the closeness of the relationship between goalkeeper and striker, and it's easy to imagine it was something they'd discussed while walking through Albert Park or eating Lill's pancakes. But it also perhaps suggests Clough's growing influence over Mitchell, whose earlier reports, frankly, don't suggest somebody likely to have noted such a tactic unless he'd been prodded towards it. It's probably significant how often he refers in copy to 'Brian'; he very rarely referred to any other player by forename alone, and it's tempting even to wonder whether Clough might have planted the idea that he was better deployed as an out-and-out goalscorer. For all his legendary bluntness, there was a cunning about Clough, a willingness and an ability to play the political game.

The following Wednesday, Clough helped himself to four more – which made it eight goals in a week – as Middlesbrough beat Doncaster 5–0. 'Clough great – but it was no one-man act,' claimed the headline in the *Gazette*, but given he'd set up the one goal he hadn't scored, Mitchell didn't sound convinced. 'Chances come to every team in every match,' he wrote. 'Whether or not they are converted means the difference between success and failure. There are forwards who are brilliant at working the ball, but who fall down repeatedly when the final touch is required. That type of forward has often worn the red shirt of Middlesbrough FC in the post-war years. We welcome now a forward who can work the ball, move it to the advantage of his colleagues and who also possesses the priceless gift of marksmanship. Yes, Clough's the name. And if anyone can shoot Middlesbrough back into the First Division, it is this twenty-two-year-old Teessider with a load of dynamite in both feet and with the guts to give as much as it takes. Second Division rearguards stand on no ceremony – and it takes a good 'un to breach them regularly.'

Just as everything seemed to be going perfectly, misfortune struck. Middlesbrough fought back from 2–0 down for a worthy 2–2 draw at Liverpool, but the devil was in the aside that Fitzsimons had missed the game with flu. It tore through the squad, and Clough was one of a number of players who missed the 3–2 defeat at Doncaster and a 1–1 draw at home to Barnsley. The promotion charge was checked, but even worse, at least as far as Clough was concerned, it meant he missed the Under-23 international against Bulgaria at Stamford Bridge. The physically imposing Derek Kevan played, while Jimmy Greaves, a rapid slip of a seventeen year old who had played only six league games for Chelsea, came in at centre-forward. Greaves scored twice in a 6–2 win, and Clough had another rival for the national team.

With the flu bug lingering, Boro lost 4–0 at Leyton Orient, but as players returned they were exceptional in beating Charlton 2–0, Clough scoring the first. Charlton's manager Sam Lawrie described Boro as the best side his team had faced that season, and admitted he couldn't have complained if it had finished 5–0.

That Wednesday, Clough was picked for an FA Representative XI to play an RAF XI made up of players at league clubs. 'Clough's speed was allied with clever ball distribution,' Mitchell wrote, as the FA won 5–2, Clough scoring one and setting up two others. That, though, was not enough to earn him a recall to the England Under-23 side for the game against Romania the following Saturday. A furious Mitchell – perhaps influenced by Clough – noted that it was entirely logical that the selectors should stick with the side that had beaten Bulgaria, rather less so that when Kevan was elevated to the senior squad they should replace him with Newcastle's Bill Curry.

The good news for Middlesbrough was that it meant Clough could play for them in a 2–0 win over Fulham. Mitchell was still seething. 'Fulham centre-half Stapleton and goalkeeper Black were left gasping as Clough robbed the former, waltzed past the latter and cracked the ball home,' he wrote. 'It was a goal that would have delighted anyone. Even those officials responsible for the selection of England's Under-23 team.' Given Curry got one and Greaves two as the Under-23s won 3–2, the selectors probably weren't too concerned.

When Boro followed up that win with a 4–1 victory at Swansea, Clough scoring the fourth, they closed to within a point of the leaders, Blackburn. He then got the opener in a 3–2 win over Derby, and the blip caused by the outbreak of flu seemed to have been negotiated. There was a further positive for Clough too, as he was selected for an FA XI to face the Army on 30 October. He produced perhaps the greatest display of his career to date, hitting five in a 6–3 win; that one Under-23 performance in Glasgow aside, he had shone every time he'd played in a representative side and the *Express* started suggesting he could be a possible replacement for Tommy Taylor in the England team.

That high was rapidly followed by a low as Middlesbrough suffered one of their characteristic lapses. As Mitchell bemoaned a 'lack of fight', they lost 5–0 at Bristol Rovers. Two Clough goals in the opening twelve minutes restored some confidence as they beat Lincoln City 3–1, but the doubts returned a week later with a 2–0 defeat away to bottom-of-the-table Notts County. Inconsistency was Middlesbrough's hallmark throughout the late fifties, and it was hard to know whether they didn't play well if Clough didn't score or whether Clough didn't score if they didn't play well.

Still, they remained within touching distance, and when Clough hit four to take his season's tally to twenty in a 5–2 home win over Ipswich, promotion still seemed within their grasp. But Boro took a single point from the next three games then lost 3–1 to Stoke (where Thomson again kept Clough on a tight leash), before back-to-back 1–0 defeats to Huddersfield over Christmas derailed the promotion charge.

With nothing else to play for, Dennison began to experiment, implementing a dual striker plan with Clough partnered by Alan Peacock. A goalless draw away to Bristol City wasn't necessarily the most encouraging start, even if Clough did have what Mitchell insisted was a good goal ruled out, but then Dennison would probably have argued that at least it stopped the rot.

New Year 1958 brought new hope, if not for that season, then for the future. It wasn't just that Boro hammered Derby 5–0 in the third round of the FA Cup, or even that 'Clough and Peacock moved about the field to the obvious bewilderment of Derby's defence', vindicating Dennison's tactical switch, it was that the average age of the team was only twenty-three and that of the front five – Day, McLean, Clough, Peacock and Holliday – just twenty. Better still, all of them were local apart from Holliday, and even he came from no further away than Leeds. 'It gelled straightaway,' said Peacock, 'but the guy who made it tick – apart from the wingers, and we had Billy Day and Edwin Holliday who could catch pigeons or flies – but Bill Harris was the mainstay. He was a terrific player – great sense and great vision.'

Cardiff came to Middlesbrough on the back of four straight victories, including a 6–1 win over the league-leaders Liverpool, but they were despatched 4–1. Mitchell's optimism was born again. 'The fact that the gloomy outlook of a few weeks ago has been banished by quite a young defence and the youngest forward line in the football league, suggests that the future could hold something worthwhile for Middlesbrough. Such as promotion for instance. Not this season perhaps. That run of defeats over Christmas means there is tremendous leeway to make up. But there is something to build on and the Boro boys should be a real force in soccer before so very long.'

The twin centre-forward plan worked perfectly, as Cardiff kept a close eye on Clough and in so doing neglected Peacock, who scored a hat-trick. 'They were right, of course, to keep a tight rein on Clough, for this fine young forward has proved his menace so often,' Mitchell wrote. 'But, in any case, they could not subdue him entirely, and his whole-hearted persistent work in midfield and in the goalmouth did much to bring about the win.'

In his post-match quotes, at least, Clough was a team-man personified. 'What does it matter who gets the goals, as long as it's a Boro player?' he asked. 'I'm all for the plan, even if it means I do not score so many myself.' Peacock, though, maintained that Clough hated it if others took the headlines.

Then it was on to Anfield, where Middlesbrough had a remarkably good record, but where Liverpool, still top of the table, hadn't lost since Middlesbrough themselves had beaten them in February. The army's refusal to grant Billy Day leave meant Boro couldn't name an unchanged team for a fourth straight game, Ron Burbeck replacing him on the wing. 'Liverpool,' Mitchell wrote, 'were shocked by the speed, challenge and skill of their opponents and could not complain at the surrendering of a proud record' as they lost 2–0. 'Clough led the line with tenacity and intelligence' and scored the first on fifty minutes, Burbeck sealing the win three minutes from time.

There is a degree to which the job of a local sports reporter is to be a cheerleader for the local team, for generating interest in them is what sells copies, but Mitchell's excitement is palpable as he highlights four 'good and satisfying features' from the game: 'The sprightly display on a good and heavy pitch; the way players came to each other's help when it was needed; the continued success of the twin centre-forward plan; the swift, stern tackling of the defence.'

After every surge in form, though, comes an away game at Stoke, this time in the fourth round of the FA Cup. Clough gave Boro an early lead, but they couldn't get their passing game together on 'a gluey mudheap' and they lost 3–1. A 3–1 win over Barnsley had Mitchell purring again – 'Chiefly responsible was "the plan". Clough (2) and Peacock were the scorers and these two dynamic young forwards might well have shared half a dozen goals. Clough is maturing swiftly' – but Boro's momentum had gone.

Clough's momentum, though, was upwards, and with his team-mates he became increasingly self-assertive. His habit of settling in early for long train trips soon deserted him, and it was not uncommon to see Dennison and Shepherdson pacing the platform before the departure for an away game, worried that Clough wouldn't make it. But he would always be there in the nick of time, swaggering along with his bag in his hand and his boots slung around his neck. So often did he arrive at the very last second that his team-mates wondered if he hid at the end of the platform, waiting to make as dramatic an entry as possible. Yet the suspicion remains that the brazenness was at least in part a mask for profound insecurities.

With women, for instance, Clough was reticent. In his first autobiography he spoke of how after training he would talk football with Taylor 'until we were interrupted by the factory girls coming out of Price's for their break. Peter could never understand why I wasn't more interested, being single and not having much to do.' Lill Taylor remembered Clough being so alarmed by the way they would stop and stare at somebody who was rapidly becoming a local hero that if he saw the factory emptying from their front room, he would hide himself in the curtains until they had gone.

In neither autobiography does Clough offer much of an explanation for his apparent lack of interest. Perhaps it was, as Lill suggested, simply the shyness of somebody who was still a reluctant – and at the time still very minor – celebrity, but it is also tempting to see the influence of his dominant mother over Clough, whether consciously or unconsciously, who refused to allow a rival female figure to rise up in his affections. Or perhaps it was simply that Clough's world, as he progressed from school, to ICI, to national service, to football, was a profoundly male one, and it is natural the bonds he formed were homosocial, and that led to an innocence around women. In the first autobiography, for instance, he describes in sympathetic detail his anxious expectancy as he leaned against a garden wall talking to a girl, desperate to be allowed to hold her hand.

Clough and the other younger members of the team used to meet in Rea's cafe and ice-cream bar, a Middlesbrough institution owned by the family of the singer Chris Rea. 'It was Edwin [Holliday]'s favourite,' the forward Alan Peacock remembered. 'We'd start off at Rea's and walk down Linthorpe Road – all the girls used to walk up and down there. I was very naive. I think Cloughie was too. Edwin was a bit of a lad. Billy [Day]'s quiet. So was Derek [McLean]. And believe it or not Clough was very quiet then. If you looked at the five of us, there was only Edwin who was a bit of a wild boy.'

The cafe was run in Clough's time by Camillo Rea, whose father had established the business after leaving Italy to work on building sites in New York and Panama. 'Clough was a nice fellow,' he said. 'Quite gentle, really. People used to talk about him being rather egoistic, but to me he was a proper gentleman. He always respected you. I remember Taylor very well. He and Brian were good buddies. They were in and out of the shop all the while. Taylor was a much quieter man. He relied on Brian such a lot. If they were talking, Brian made all the conversation and Peter would be in the background. I think he felt inferior to Brian, somehow or other.'

Drink may have become a major part of his life later on, but back then Clough was almost tee-total. 'You couldn't have wished for a nicer lad,' said McLean. 'He'd give you his last penny. He never had a smoke or a drink – well, maybe a half, you know, when he went out.'

At Rea's, certainly, there was never a suggestion of booze. 'The players would come in at lunchtime, mainly for milkshakes,' said Camillo. 'But I got Brian on to Oxo. He came in one day and said, "They're talking about Oxo. All the fellows go crazy on Saturday."

'I said, "I've got it here."

'He said, "I'll have one."

'Then he said, "Our players should have this – get it down to the club for half-time." He always had Oxo after that.'

With the World Cup in Sweden coming up in the summer, the season became less about Middlesbrough than whether Clough would make it into the England squad. The Munich air crash that February had robbed England of Roger Byrne, Duncan Edwards, David Pegg and Tommy Taylor and, as a piece in the *Gazette* rather tactlessly put it, Clough was one of four possible replacements for Taylor at centre-forward.

Winterbottom watched Clough twice – in defeats at West Ham and Derby – and on the day Clough tore Notts County apart at home on 29 March, scoring twice, the England manager was at White Hart Lane to see Bobby Smith score five as Tottenham beat Aston Villa 6–2. Mitchell suggested then that the fight was between Clough, Smith and Jimmy Murray, who was on his way to becoming top-scorer for Wolves as Stan

Cullis's side won the title. There was one other candidate, though: Clough's eternal nemesis Derek Kevan, who three days earlier had scored a hat-trick as the English League beat the Scottish League 4–1 in Newcastle.

On 12 April, Clough scored twice as Middlesbrough lost 3–2 at home to Blackburn. 'There may be better centre-forwards in the country,' said Mitchell, 'but I haven't seen one. And several of my colleagues, who cover First Division matches too, tell me that they rate Clough the best of them all.' Sure enough, three days later. Clough was selected for the England Under-23 side to meet Wales on 23 April; it was his first call-up for a representative side since scoring five for an FA XI against the Army the previous October.

Clough got the equaliser in a match England lost 2–1, but the reviews were mixed. 'Middlesbrough's generously-touted centre-forward did himself no good at all,' said the *Mail*. 'He was pocketed by the match's strong man [Mel] Charles from the word go. There was hardly a peep out of Clough all evening.' The *News Chronicle*, meanwhile, saw promise: 'Clough, providing many neat flicks, was not happy in a forward line which lacked both a plan and a general. His great moment came when he finished off a movement by Greaves and [Alan] A'Court. Touches of this description must keep him in the reckoning.'

The *Express* went even further. 'I was sorry for Clough who had a perfect case for a moan,' wrote Desmond Hackett. 'He had scant support, and just had not a hope of producing the shooting power the crowd expected. But despite his difficulties, Clough's flicks and positional play did not go unnoticed and determination brought him an equalising goal when he shrugged off three defenders and drove low into the net.'

He did enough, at least, to earn selection for an England Under-23 side – to be supplemented by four overage players – to face England at Stamford Bridge on 2 May, the day before the FA Cup final. Clough scored with a neat sidefoot finish, but was only fleetingly involved as the senior England side won 4–2. Still, Mitchell was encouraged. 'Clough came through with as much credit as his lacklustre colleagues would permit,' he wrote – and again it's hard not to wonder what influence Clough had over those words. 'I think he has enhanced his chances of going to Sweden.'

Those chances were enhanced further as England, with Kevan wearing the number nine shirt, struggled to a 2–1 win over Portugal on 7 May. Clough's 'claims, strong enough to start with, hardened tremendously . . . .' Mitchell wrote, 'for this England was a team without a leader . . . [Kevan] . . . is not the answer and never has been. He has done his best, but that best has not been good enough for the national side.' That wasn't just local pride or words from those with whom Clough had fraternised; the report put out by the Press Association made much the same point: 'On last night's showing, and that of both the World Cup trial last Friday and the game against Scotland, Derek Kevan, the burly West Bromwich inside-left, is not the answer to the centre-forward gap left by the death of Tommy Taylor.' Two days later, Clough was named as part of a twenty-man England party to travel to Yugoslavia and the USSR before the World Cup. 'We all thought that meant we were going to the World Cup,' said Bryan Douglas, who was also named in the squad.

After a chat with Winterbottom on the flight to Belgrade, Clough believed he would start against Yugoslavia. It seems likely that was Winterbottom's intention – whatever faults players may have seen in him, nobody ever questioned his integrity – but the team was picked by the selectors, who had been impressed by Kevan's link-up with Bobby Charlton in a 4–0 away win over Scotland that April, in which he had scored twice and Charlton once, and in the 2–1 win over Portugal in May, in which Charlton had netted both goals.

Although Clough later expressed outrage about his non-selection – and perhaps it would have been better for the selectors to have looked at another option before the World Cup – the fact remains that after Tommy Taylor's death, Kevan was the man in possession. Winterbottom acknow-ledged that Kevan was 'as slow as a carthorse' while 'Clough could score from any distance and any angle', but he saw advantages in 'the tremendous energy' of the West Brom forward. And, while the gulf between the top two divisions was nowhere near as vast then as it would become, Kevan was a proven player in the top flight.

The match in Belgrade could hardly have gone worse. Kevan was played at centre-forward with Bobby Charlton to his left and Johnny Haynes to his right, but England rarely had the ball enough for that to matter, losing 5–0. 'We have given a real lecture to the masters of football,' claimed the report in the Yugoslav paper Borba; England, following years of tradition, blamed the heat. 'It was eighty, eighty-five degrees,' said Douglas. 'We got a real hiding.'

Winterbottom made four changes for the match in Moscow a week later, bringing in Bobby Robson for Charlton and naming three uncapped players – but Clough wasn't one of them. Kevan scored as England played much better and drew 1–1. Still, the columnist ELT reflected in the *Gazette*, as one of twenty to go on tour, it stood to reason that Clough would be in the twenty-two for the World Cup, even if Kevan kept his place in the starting XI. That, though, was to reckon without Clough's talent for self-destruction.

Never a great traveller to anywhere apart from Mallorca, Clough seems to have had a thoroughly miserable time of it in Moscow, gloomily detailing in his autobiography the queues he saw everywhere and the unsettling sight of soldiers marching outside Lenin's tomb. His room-mate, Bobby Charlton, experienced in trips behind the iron curtain, advised him to take plenty of chocolate to eat, advice for which he was grateful when his first meal in Moscow consisted of a bowl of clear soup at the bottom of which lay a raw egg 'looking at me like a single eye'. To repay the favour and to try to lift the boredom, Clough took Charlton bird-nesting in the hotel grounds. 'There is only one thing,' he said, 'worse than a bored footballer – a footballer who can't play.' He was bored, but Kevan, he clearly felt, fell into the latter category. Charlton, meanwhile, still struggling to come to terms with the Munich air crash, played against Yugoslavia but not against the USSR and effectively ruled himself out of the World Cup squad.

Climbing trees had taught Clough to appreciate them, and they became one of his odd obsessions. 'Who really looks at trees and sees their shapes and colours?' he once asked. 'They're magic.' What Clough liked, he accumulated: he persuaded Jan Einar Aas, the Norwegian who played briefly for Nottingham Forest, to smuggle a sapling out of Norway for his garden, and on one return flight from Amsterdam, each Forest player had a conifer on the floor between his feet as customs officers conveniently turned a blind eye. He even had the Forest squad spend one training session planting conifers by the side of the training pitch to help block the wind.

In training before the USSR game, England practised in the grounds of their hotel. 'We played the attack we thought would play against the defence we thought would play,' said Douglas. 'And Brian was in the team then.

When the eleven was read out the next day, though, he missed out. He was the only one. Who knows why? He was very volatile and, I'm only guessing, but he maybe had an argument with Billy Wright or Tom Finney. Walter Winterbottom was a schoolteacher, very old-school, and that wouldn't have gone down well.'

Certainly Clough clashed with Wright after the game. He wasn't the only player irritated by the closeness of the captain's relationship with Winterbottom, but he was probably the only one to let it show quite so blatantly. After Wright had spent several minutes talking about how good the Soviet centre-forward had been – trying, perhaps, to justify his own poor performance – Clough snapped, saying he hadn't thought much of him and felt he had pretty much given up after an hour. (Here, for once, Clough's judgement of a player was awry, for that centre-forward was Eduard Streltsov, widely acknowledged as the best Russian outfielder there has ever been.)

Wright ignored Clough, turning away and continuing his conversation, but Clough assumed that Winterbottom had overheard, or that Wright had told him, and that he looked dimly on an uncapped player criticising his captain. Whatever the reason, Clough and Jim Langley, who had played at left-back against Yugoslavia, were taken aside before the flight back from Moscow and told they would not be part of the World Cup squad. 'Perhaps Brian's confident manner ruffled a few feathers,' Peacock said. 'It can't have been because he played in the Second Division, because anybody could see he was a natural, whatever team he was in.'

'It rankles,' Clough said in an interview with Tyne-Tees Television in 2000. 'Winterbottom was definitely an amateur. His name suggests it and he was. He was well-spoken, very presentable, well-liked in the FA. He never caused a ripple in his life ... We were gluttons for talent – it was coming at us from all angles. If he couldn't get a side out of that ... there was five for every position. Sir Walter was in charge and where he really killed me was before the World Cup in Sweden. I'd gone through all the training and played in all the games and I'd got my suit from Simpsons in London – best suit I've ever had; it lasted years.

'Then the day he was going to announce his squad he said to me, "I've got a bit of a shock for you; you're not going." So I said, "Why not?" And he said, "Well, we've got two centre-forwards," and he took a lad called

Derek Kevan from West Brom.' The use of the 'a something called some-thing' construction was characteristic, conveying the impression, according to context, either that the person Clough was speaking to couldn't possibly be aware of the subject or, as in this case, that the subject wasn't worth knowing about.

'Brian was quite annoyed,' said Douglas. 'As I understand it, he had a few words with Walter Winterbottom on the way back to the extent of saying that if he wasn't going to play him then don't bother calling him up. And, of course, after that he didn't. Brian was a bit like that. He had an opinion on everything – football, politics, everything.'

Even by 2000, the anger hadn't gone away. 'Derek Kevan couldn't play at all compared to me,' Clough said. 'He never scored a blinking goal, but he was big and strong and caught people's eye. People hadn't woken up to the fact that other people could play football: Hughie Gallacher, for a start, who was before my time; he was like a ha'penny rabbit but he was one of the best and bravest centre-forwards that's ever played football.' There is significance, surely, in the comparison. Gallacher, five foot five inches and slightly built, had been a hero at Newcastle in the twenties, captaining them to the league title at twenty-three while drawing criticism for his outspokenness. He then led Derby to second in 1936; their highest position until Clough took them to the championship. Gallacher's goals came at a ratio only slight slower than Clough. 406 in 554 league games for Queen of the South, Aidrieonians, Newcastle, Derby, Notts County, Grimsby and Gateshead, plus twenty-three in twenty internationals for Scotland. When his career came to an end, he turned to journalism, but was banned from St James' Park for the caustic nature of his match reports. He turned to drink after the sudden death of his wife and, while facing prosecution for throwing an ashtray at his son in 1957, committed suicide by placing his head on the track in front of an express train at Low Fell.

Clough must have seen the parallels, perhaps even saw an example of what he might have become. Like Gallacher, he was a scrapper and, as a player at least, he felt that, like Gallacher, he hadn't had the recognition he deserved. 'They used to go for the big type, strong with a bit of pace,' he said. 'Blond hair always caught their imagination as well.' The accusation sounds ridiculous, but in *Why England Lose*, Simon Kuper and Stefan Szymanski give a scientific reason why it may be true: because of what they call the 'availability heuristic', blond players are more likely to be recommended by scouts: 'the more available a piece of information is to the memory,' they explain, 'the more likely it is to influence your decision, even when the information is irrelevant. Blonds stick in the memory.' Part of Clough's genius was that he understood that intuitively.

That said, Kevan's hair was actually mid-brown, and for all Clough's scorn, he had a reasonable World Cup. Although Keith Dewhurst of the Press Association was moved to note 'Kevan gave his usually blundering act' in the 0–0 draw against Brazil, he also scored in the first game against the USSR and against Austria. One of the reasons for his inclusion, though, his partnership with Bobby Charlton, was rendered invalid as Charlton, still traumatised by the Munich air-crash, was left at home. Kevan failed to strike up such an understanding with either Bobby Robson or Peter Broadbent, and England went out following a play-off with the Soviets having finished the group level with them in second place.

Clough spent the summer stewing. Part of him was furious he'd been dragged round eastern Europe without ever being given the chance to prove himself; part of him wondered whether there was anything he could have done to improve his chances or whether perhaps the time had come to move on from Middlesbrough. 'I scored so many goals,' he wrote, 'because I followed my mam's insistence that whatever I did I should do to the best of my ability, and that I should keep trying harder and harder to be better still, even if I thought I had nothing more to give.' What the cleanliness of the front doorstep was to his mother, so goals were to Clough.

He was constantly pushing for the next level, and for him that meant international football. He came to blame Middlesbrough's trainer Harold Shepherdson, who also worked as Winterbottom's trainer – and was next to Alf Ramsey on the bench when England won the World Cup – for not pushing his case more strongly and asked whether the Middlesbrough director Harry French, who sat on the board of selectors, could have done more to advance his cause.

Clough decided to leave, and again asked Dennison for a transfer. Conveniently, rumours began to appear linking Manchester United with a bid for Clough. Dennison responded by taking the captaincy from Bill Harris and offering it to Clough, which both played to his ego and ensured he received more money. 'Bill is not the type to shout at players on the field and I know he is happier when he is allowed to get on with his own job,' the manager said. 'That is one of the reasons why I have appointed Clough. He has almost three years' League experience behind him and I am sure that he has the aptitude for the job – so that age does not matter. Brian has that drive on the field that can win matches and as captain I'm certain he can inspire his colleagues. I feel a captain should be keen to do the job on the field.'

It was a controversial move however he justified it. Even Shepherdson, who was broadly sympathetic to Clough, was opposed. 'Clough was a bad influence on the team,' he said. 'He created jealousy. He and Taylor were loners who chose certain people to communicate with. I wasn't one of them.' Before long, Clough and Taylor were meeting Dennison in his office on a Friday afternoon to select the team for the following afternoon. 'I was aware of a certain amount of resentment towards me from some of the other players,' Clough said, 'partly because I always said what I thought, but mainly because I was bloody good at what I did and made no excuses for believing I was the best.'

'I think it was probably the worst thing that could have happened, that Clough and Taylor got together,' said the centre-half Brian Phillips. 'It was Taylor who'd got the brains. I said all the way along that Taylor pulled the strings. Even when Cloughie came out with stuff, Taylor had manufactured it. He made the bullets. But Taylor, in a way, hadn't got the bottle. He'd got the brains; Cloughie had the mouth.'

The England issue still rankled with Clough, and it's not hard to see his hand at work in a column by ELT published in the *Gazette* the week before the season began. 'All Teesside football followers are fervently hoping that he will show form in Middlesbrough's opening games which will force the selectors to remedy the blunder they were guilty of last June when they left him out of our World Cup party,' it read. 'Clough's form last season should have earned him an England cap, but he has only to continue scoring goals with the regularity he has done in the last two seasons and I feel sure his ability will be recognised. We look to the Middlesbrough director, Mr Harry French, to try to convince his co-selectors that Brian is the man to wear England's number nine shirt.'

Having rallied the press to his cause, Clough then did his own bit of self-promotion, starting the 1958–59 season by scoring five in a 9–0 win over newly promoted Brighton. 'It was the added responsibility of being captain held me back,' he said, which might have been nothing more than an obvious gag, were it not for the suspicion that Clough didn't do obvious gags: this was a dig at those who had criticised his accession.

The good start was maintained as Clough got the only goal in an away win at Sheffield United, firing in first time after McLean had challenged for a ball hooked over his head by Harris. They twice had the lead at Grimsby the following Saturday as well but, this being Middlesbrough, optimism couldn't be allowed to get out of hand, and they wilted on a hot afternoon, losing 3–2. 'Clough usually had no one to help him – and was opposed by a most resolute young centre-half in [Keith] Jobling,' Mitchell wrote. 'It was a hard game and Boro were not disgraced. But they were neither dynamic in attack nor watertight in defence.'

Boro had 'an erratic, disjointed air about them' as they drew 0–0 with Sheffield United, but they came from behind to beat Liverpool 2–1 with a Clough double. Mitchell had begun ghosting Clough's column in the Saturday Sports Edition of the *Gazette*, and the striker's influence is easy to discern. 'Clough was always threatening despite being monumentally marked . . .' Mitchell wrote, 'again there was moderate support at inside-forward.' Little wonder Peacock at times became irritated by the coverage.

It's become a commonplace to suggest that Peacock and Clough didn't get on, but he insisted that isn't true. 'I'm the type that's quite happy going along with anything,' Peacock said. 'I didn't go looking for headlines. I like to keep in the background. He was a lovely lad. That's how I remember him. Clean-living, good family man, thought the world of his wife, thought the world of his kids, and he was always . . . like when he met my wife for the first time, when we were just courting, he went straight up to her and said how nice it was to see her. He was nice to people like that. Sometimes he could be a little bit over the top, and that was when he annoyed people, when he went too far.'

When Clough scored two and laid on another for the eighteen-year-old debutant Alan Rodgerson in a 4–1 win at Rotherham, Boro had dropped only three points from their first six games and appeared genuine promotion candidates. On 13 September, though, Boro had to travel to Stoke and, even worse, Winterbottom came to watch Clough. Predictably, Thomson marked Clough out of the game, and Boro lost 3–1.

Mitchell, whether he was acting as Clough's mouthpiece or not, clearly wasn't the only one worried about Boro's inside-forwards. The following Tuesday, Middlesbrough and Sunderland reached agreement on terms for the transfer of Don Revie. He had been voted Footballer of the Year in 1956 while at Manchester City, when, aping the Hungarian Nándor Hidegkuti, he had operated as a deep-lying centre-forward, but his time at Roker Park hadn't gone well and he had fallen out with the manager, Alan Brown. Revie, though, wanted a move to a First Division club, and although Dennison spent the next three weeks trying to persuade him to join Boro, he refused. Given Clough's capacity to cling to grudges, it may be that the roots of his later antipathy to Revie lay in that aborted deal; in *Clough & Revie*, Roger Hermiston even suggested that one of Revie's reasons for rejecting the deal was that he couldn't imagine himself ever forging an effective partnership with somebody as tempestuous and individualistic as Clough. Clearly there were other and greater causes, but here Clough saw the chance to play alongside a respected former England international – something that could only have helped his own game – only for Revie to snub him and the team they had both grown up supporting. As it became apparent Revie wasn't going to move, Dennison turned his attentions to Albert Quixall of Sheffield Wednesday, but he joined Manchester United instead. Had either arrived, it would almost certainly have meant Derek McLean making way, and it might have ended Dennison's use of twin centre forwards.

On the pitch, the mood of discontent was spreading. Harris missed a penalty as Middlesbrough lost 2–1 at home to Rotherham, while Mitchell's report added fuel to the anti-Clough fire. 'It was only when Clough was in possession that a goal seemed likely,' he wrote. 'Boro's young captain scored a great goal and came close on two other occasions – but he needed better support than that which came his way.'

The morning of the next game, away to Charlton, Taylor approached Peacock as he ate his breakfast and told him there'd be a team meeting at eleven. When he got there, he found Clough and Taylor, plus the other members of the forward line. Clough told them that Winterbottom would be watching, and that he'd therefore be grateful if they could help make him look good. That could be construed as a slightly pitiful plea from somebody desperate for international recognition, but it was part of a wider pattern of self-obsession.

Clough, struggling with a calf injury, perhaps shouldn't even have played, but did so and was dreadful in a 1–0 defeat. 'Not for years have I seen a worse performance from a Boro forward line,' Mitchell wrote. 'It had scarcely a shot in its locker; it had neither plan, nor purpose, nor cohesion; it lacked any semblance of accuracy in the pass. And it fiddled.' Fiddling was something Mitchell, in common with most of the football writers of his age, couldn't abide.

Dennison seemingly agreed, dropping all four members of the forward line other than Clough. The result was a 0–0 draw at home to Bristol City. By the beginning of October, Middlesbrough's promotion hopes were already over.

For Clough, selection for an English League XI to face the Scottish League at Ibrox on 8 October must have been a welcome distraction, and he scored in a 1–1 draw. 'Everything about his goal,' Basil Easterbook wrote, 'stamped Clough as a leader above average – the way he collected the ball after [Willie] Toner had missed it, his acceleration as he set off down the clear path to Scotland's goal, his timing, force and placing of shot. Great – that was the only word to describe Clough's effort. How tragic, then, that for the remainder of the match he should be reduced to the occasional clever flick or pass. This was not the Middlesbrough man's fault in any way. Full responsibility for the Football League's failure to win this match rests with Quixall and Greaves, our bitterly disappointing inside-forwards.' Strange, Peacock may have noted, how inside-forwards so often disappointed when playing alongside Clough.

By the time two signings were finally made at the beginning of November, Boro had gone nine games without a win. The arrivals were hardly of the calibre of Revie and Quixall: the right-half Ray Yeoman was bought from Northampton and the left-half Brian Jordan from Rotherham. Even as Clough posed for welcome photographs in the *Gazette* it's not hard to imagine that behind his stiff grin he was wondering how Boro had started out bidding for international inside-forwards and ended up buying journeymen wing-halves.

Boro at last won again on 8 November, Clough and Peacock both scoring hat-tricks as Scunthorpe were beaten 6–1. The next home game brought a 5–0 win over Derby, but that game was sandwiched between defeats at Leyton Orient and Bristol Rovers. Dennison moved again to strengthen the side, signing the inside-forward Willie Fernie for £19,000 from Celtic. He, at least, had some pedigree, having won sixteen caps for Scotland and earned a reputation that led Mitchell to describe him as the 'ball-playing artist of the twinkling feet'.

Defeats at Ipswich and the leaders Sheffield Wednesday meant Boro had taken a single point from their previous nine away games and relegation had become a serious concern, but back-to-back wins – 6–4 at Brighton, in which Clough got a hat-trick, and 3–1 at home to Barnsley, in which he scored twice – eased the pressure. Nonetheless, when Mitchell noted after a 1–0 home defeat to Birmingham in January 1959 that 'this Boro side isn't yet good enough to hold its own in the First Division' it seemed bizarre he should even be contemplating promotion.

Willie Fernie, certainly, had rapidly become disillusioned. 'We used to get changed, and we had the numbers of our shirts – eight, nine, ten . . .' Peacock remembered. 'It finished with eight; then there was the door, and then nine and ten, so me and Cloughie were always together. Anyway, Willie came in, and Cloughie must have been in the toilet or somewhere, and Willie said, "How the hell do you play with this bloke? He can't play. I might as well have that bloody pillar there. At least if I hit it, it'll come back to me." Probably that went against Cloughie. He wasn't the best player, but if you were prepared to play as Middlesbrough played, and he's getting the goals, that's it.'

A 3–1 defeat at home to Charlton at the beginning of February had Mitchell suggesting the twin centre-forward plan had 'outlived its usefulness' and complaining that Clough and Peacock 'more than once got in each other's way': on-field difficulties, perhaps, reflected their off-field niggles.

By March, Middlesbrough had accumulated enough points to render relegation only a distant threat, but with promotion even more remote, the *Gazette* ran three in-depth features asking 'What's Wrong with the Boro?'

Mitchell went first. 'There is sufficient talent on the books of Middlesbrough FC now for a genuine promotion challenge to be embarked upon ...' he insisted. 'Some of the young hopefuls who were drafted in have not sustained their initial promise ... Too many established players have been persevered with in spite of consistently moderate displays; too few promising young men have been given the chance to settle down into the first team. Adequacy has been tolerated in some, not in others. And that doesn't make for the happiest of dressing-rooms.'

The lack of team spirit was obvious, and it was something upon which the veteran reporter To'T remarked the following day. Unlike Mitchell, he suggested Clough's leadership may be to blame. 'It was not a popular choice with the players then, nor is it now,' he wrote. 'Clough looks like proving one of the twenty or so Middlesbrough FC greats of the last forty years, but a man of authority and experience, in a more convenient part of the side than centre-forward, would have made his presence and his displeasure felt when a number of recent games at Ayresome Park were petering away to ignoble failure.' The more common complaint was surely that Clough had, at times, made his displeasure all too obvious, but the general point remains valid.

'There have been,' To'T continued, 'and will continue to be, occasions when Clough's dexterity as a goal-getter has given to the side sufficient stimulus for the maintenance of morale, but responsibility for team spirit should be broader based than on one man's marksmanship. The urgent need is of some personality capable of rousing and getting the best out of the side.'

The third analysis was written by George Hardwick, the former Middlesbrough and England forward who at the time was coach of PSV Eindhoven. Mitchell, perhaps recognising his position demanded good relations with Dennison, had refused to blame the manager, describing his task as 'Herculean', but Hardwick was scathing. 'I cannot understand how a team, having played three-quarters of a season together can still fail to understand each other's play,' he said. 'It boils down to a need for still more team coaching and team discussion – and perhaps the feeling between players could be better.'

He was sceptical too about Clough's captaincy, although rather more sympathetic than To'T. 'I am firmly convinced,' he wrote, 'this appointment has hindered Clough's development as a footballer and jeopardised his chance of an international career.'

With the season petering out and Clough apparently no nearer the England call-up he so craved, the first half of 1959 might have been forgettable for Clough had it not been for his wedding. He fell out with journalists, he fell out with directors and he fell out with players, but his marriage to Barbara remained strong; when he died in 2004, they had been together for over forty-five years.

Clough had been in Rea's café when he first saw her, a girl 'with a smile that seemed to light up the entire north-east'.

'It was some time before I plucked up the courage to introduce myself,' he wrote in his autobiography. He bought himself a strawberry milkshake, wandered over, and said, 'Hello, my name is Brian,' then bought her a coffee. She replied that her name was Barbara Glasgow. She lived on Gifford Street, about three-quarters of a mile from Valley Road.

'My dad was aware of him [Clough] because he didn't miss a match at Ayresome Park,' Barbara said. 'He just came up one evening, introduced himself and said would I like to go to the pictures. I sort of knew about him vaguely. My dad used to come home raving about this centre-forward who was scoring all these goals. I went home and said who I was going out with. And he said, "The young man I've been watching every week?"

'And I said yes, so he had a big beam on his face.

'And my mother said, "A footballer?"

'She had her reservations.'

Barbara had gone to Kirby Grammar School and, when she'd left, her parents had wanted her to go into teaching. Instead, she became a shorthand typist and worked at ICI; although he hadn't known it at the time, Clough and Barbara had briefly been work colleagues. Clough was devoted to her, sending a telegram from every away game he played in and relishing visits to her house to enjoy her mother's 'gorgeous coconut cakes'. Barbara taught Clough how to dance – a relief after his slithering ineptitude while playing for his RAF side in Wales – but he didn't get too many opportunities to practise. He was still living at home and that meant obeying his mother's strict 9.30pm curfew. If he were late, his mother wouldn't let him out the following night and would find unpleasant chores for him to do, such as picking the sprouts from the vegetable patch on a frosty morning. In his first autobiography, Clough claimed that he himself would insist on being home by 10pm 'for *Match of the Day* as much as anything', saying that meant catching the bus outside the Gaumont cinema at 9.50, which in turn often led to them missing the last few minutes of films. It's a nice detail, suggesting his early obsession with the game, but like so many Clough anecdotes, it doesn't stand up, given *Match of the Day* didn't start until 1964, long after he'd left Middlesbrough.

On Sundays, he and Barbara would walk in Albert Park with their own groups of friends and perhaps go rowing on the lake. In winter, Clough would usually wear a ribbed sweater a couple of sizes too big for him and a muffler, which embarrassed Barbara to such an extent that she'd turn aside rather than have to acknowledge him.

For all that, she agreed to marry him. At the time, the only Boro player with a car was Lindy Delapenha, who owned a battered maroon Ford Anglia. He would give players lifts home from training, but strictly in order of seniority (which he seems to have interpreted by age rather than rank), meaning Clough was usually left to walk or take the bus. Having heard of his engagement, though, Delapenha gave Clough and Barbara a lift to Stockton to visit a jeweller. As he got out of the car outside H Samuel, the door came off in Clough's hand, and he was left trying desperately to reattach it as Barbara went in to choose her ring.

They were married in St Barnabas Church on the morning of Saturday, 4 April 1959, choosing the date 'to make sure we got the maximum allowance from the tax-man'. They held the reception at the Linthorpe Hotel, where Clough had once waited for the potato truck to ferry him to Great Broughton. After rushing through the speeches so he could get off to play against Leyton Orient that afternoon, Clough handed his brother Des £25 and told him to buy everybody a drink. 'Let them buy their own,' he replied; Clough evidently wasn't the only member of his family who was cautious with money.

The lift Clough had arranged was late, leading him to try – without success – to commandeer a police car, but he made it to Ayresome Park in time for his name to be included on the team-sheet before it was submitted at 2pm. Inevitably, he scored in a 4–2 win. The next day, he and Barbara travelled to London, where they spent their honeymoon – all four days of it – in the familiar footballers' haunt of the Russell Hotel: Clough sleeping; Barbara sightseeing.

On the Wednesday they went on to Liverpool where, with Barbara watching from the directors' box, Clough scored twice in the final two minutes to secure an unlikely victory.

'He's not had a kick,' Bill Shankly is supposed to have growled at Boro's trainer Harold Shepherdson as they shook hands after the final whistle.

'He's had at least two to my knowledge, Bill,' Shepherdson replied.

Or at least that's how Clough tells the story and how it has entered legend. In fact, although Middlesbrough won 2–1, the order and timings of the goals were rather different. Holliday got the first eight minutes after half-time following a combination between Clough and Fernie and, ten minutes later, Clough scored his fortieth goal of the season after Fernie and Holliday returned the favour; Jimmy Melia pulled one back late on. This is a perennial problem with Clough: the anecdotes are often good to start with, but have been polished to greatness by manipulations over time – whether by Clough or those who have delighted in telling his tale; the legend has supplanted the facts.

Middlesbrough finished the 1958–59 season thirteenth, with Clough scoring forty-three goals in all competitions. It still wasn't enough, though, to earn him a call-up to the England side for the tour to the Americas. 'Throughout the country, heads were shaken in wonder when the names were announced ... of the men chosen to tour the Americas,' Mitchell wrote. 'In this part of the world the dominant feeling would appear to be anger, mixed with incredulity, that the ace marksman in the country has again been given the cold shoulder.'

Although England ended the tour with an 8–1 win over the USA, defeats to Brazil, Peru and Mexico meant it was generally regarded as a failure. In three of the games, Winterbottom had fielded Greaves, Bobby Charlton and Haynes; in the other, Peter Broadbent of Wolves replaced Greaves. The *Gazette* columnist ELT considered the whole strategy misplaced. 'The scheme of three interchanging inside-forwards,' he wrote, 'with no orthodox centre-forward seems to have been a dismal failure so far as producing goals is concerned.'

The new season didn't begin promisingly, a goalless draw with

Portsmouth being followed by a 2–0 defeat to Cardiff, but it was ignited in the third game, away at Derby, when Boro 'achieved brilliance in the last forty minutes' to win 7–1. 'The twin centre-forward plan worked with a vengeance,' Mitchell wrote. 'Clough, who had a good game, took burly centre-half [Les] Moore, and usually one or two other defenders, out to the wings and Peacock was there to crack home four glorious goals.' Remarkably, Clough didn't score.

A 1–1 draw at home to Cardiff followed, but Clough was still to get off the mark for the season. When the drought was broken, it went in a rush, as he scored four in fourteen minutes in Boro's 6–2 win over Plymouth. Hull were beaten 4–0 and for the fourth season in a row, Boro won at Anfield, where Winterbottom saw Clough 'play a strong, hard game and distribute the ball well'. It was enough to earn a call-up for the English League to play the Irish League, but before that Clough had scored a hat-trick in a 3–0 win over Charlton to take Boro to within a point of the top of the table.

The representative game in Belfast fell on Barbara's birthday. Clough promised her a goal; he delivered all five in a 5–0 win. 'Brian Clough, for so long an international outcast, MUST have won his cap,' the report in the *Mail* said. 'He shattered the Irish defence with five brilliantly taken goals. Here was his answer to those selectors who for so long have rated him no more than a successful goalgetter in the Second Division.' The *Mirror* was even more explicit: 'Get that England No 9 jersey ready for Brian Clough.'

A fortnight later came the long-awaited news, with an added bonus. 'Clough, Holliday in!' the front page of the *Gazette* exulted. Having waited so long for his England call-up, Clough ended up having to share the glory with a younger team-mate. 'This is one of the happiest days of my life and I only hope I can do well on Saturday,' he told Mitchell. 'I want to succeed for my own sake, of course, but also for those wonderful Boro supporters who have always cheered me on. I just hope I don't let anyone down.'

That last line sounds uncharacteristic, laced with none of the self-confident bombast that usually characterised his speech, and it betrayed a genuine anxiety that was probably intensified by the interest his call-up generated on Teesside. His father organised a bus for his workmates at ICI Wilton to travel down to watch the game, while around two hundred fans took advantage of a special excursion train that travelled overnight from Middlesbrough to Cardiff for the game against Wales.

'At the team hotel I felt nervous and vulnerable, twenty-four years old but a young twenty-four and hardly a man of the world,' he wrote in his first autobiography. The squad's first meal together was breakfast, and Clough could hardly have made a worse impression, his nervousness causing him to spill his plate of bacon and baked beans onto his lap. Fortunately Tom Finney stepped in, lending Clough a pair of trousers and taking his only pair of flannels to be cleaned.

Worse soon followed, as Clough realised he'd forgotten his boots, prompting a panicky phone call to Dennison, who sent them down to Cardiff with his wife. It was hardly worth the effort; Clough barely got a kick as Graham Moore cancelled out Greaves's opener in the final minute of a poor game. 'He was intelligent and thoughtful in his distribution, worked non-stop and was always on the look-out for an opening in the Welsh rearguard,' Mitchell wrote. 'He laid on a number of good chances for his colleagues – but he waited, and waited, and waited for a return pass that would put him in with a scoring chance.'

Few others were so generous but, having scored the winner in a patchy 3–2 win over Lincoln, Clough was retained for the match at Wembley against Sweden eleven days later. The selectors, obsessed by the idea of letting the side develop together as Hungary had at the beginning of the decade, had picked a young team and insisted on retaining it, leaving Winterbottom concerned as to how they would perform against a side as experienced as Sweden, who had reached the World Cup final a year before (although neither of their biggest stars of that tournament – Gunnar Gren and Nils Liedholm – made the trip to Wembley).

'I seem to recall Brian Clough having two real scoring chances,' wrote Mitchell. 'The first was created by his own opportunism, when he tore in as the Swedish goalkeeper was about to clear. The Boro captain shot against the upright and just couldn't force the ball over the line when it rebounded across the face of goal. The second came when Greaves centred and Clough headed against the crossbar . . . Why didn't Charlton and Greaves play just a little bit more to their centre-forward? I just don't know, unless it was that their essentially individualistic styles meant that each wanted to win the game on his own. Brian Clough did not fail. He didn't get the chance to fail – or succeed.' Again, that is a kind reading of the game.

'They took us apart,' Greaves admitted. Sweden won 3–2, but the gulf in quality seemed far greater than that. Clough set up the opener for John Connelly, but he was haunted by a chance he'd missed, running on to an underhit backpass, only to shoot against the bar. As the ball bounced down, he seemed likely to get to the rebound, but lost his footing and ended up sprawled on the ground, unable to turn it in with either head or boot and jabbing at it ineffectually with his knee.

Clough blamed Winterbottom, pointing out that the balance of the team was all wrong because he, Greaves and Charlton – a more orthodox forward in those days – were too similar and ended up chasing the same ball or making the same runs. 'It didn't work, it couldn't work,' Clough said, 'but it was his job to find a way of producing a combination that made best use of us.'

Dennison, who had taken the rest of the Middlesbrough squad to Wembley to watch, was used to Clough casting around for someone to blame, but he wondered whether the selectors' reluctance to turn to Clough again was down to more than just his attitude. 'He told Winterbottom he would have to drop either Greaves or Charlton,' Dennison said. 'No wonder he didn't get the chance. Those matches seemed to prove to me that he wasn't quite up to it.'

Greaves, having played with Clough twice, was rather more positive. 'He was everything you have to be as a striker,' he said. 'Fearless, physically and morally tough, and greedy.' He felt that it was the fact that Clough was scoring his goals in the Second Division that was raising doubts in the selectors' minds. Hardwick, meanwhile, suggested playing in the second flight was holding Clough back not merely in terms of recognition, but also in terms of the development of his game. 'I couldn't see him scoring so many goals in Division One because top-class centre-halves weren't likely to be beaten by his quick reflexes,' he said. 'They'd have smothered him before he got into position. Against Sweden I watched with great sadness. The local press put it down to the poor service he got from his wingers and half-backs, but every time they looked for him, he was heavily marked. He didn't escape – never got into space.'

Clough's critics among the Middlesbrough squad had made similar complaints, but it was perhaps only then that he really began to take them on board. The suspicion was always that his bluster hid a fragile self-belief, and Clough so hated not scoring that during the odd barren run Dennison would have him play against the youths in training, just to restore his confidence.

After that match against Sweden, he perhaps learned two things. From a managerial point of view, Clough saw that balance in a team was crucial. His teams almost always had a fine natural balance, which explains why they were able to play so coherently with so little formal tactical training, and also why so many players seemed to overperform under Clough: in his side they had a specific function that tended to match their skill set; elsewhere the fit wasn't so good and so they were asked to play beyond the boundaries of their talent without team-mates whose skills complemented theirs and covered for their deficiencies. And from a playing point of view he perhaps realised that goals alone were not enough; by the time he had reached Sunderland two years later, he seemed – relatively speaking – a more complete player, a passer and creator as well as a goal-scorer; he had shown those qualities at Middlesbrough, but only in patches. Then again, perhaps it was simply that at Sunderland he felt he had a better class of player around him and that giving them the ball seemed more worthwhile.

Clough's initial reaction, though, was one of gloom, as he reflected on the opportunity he had wasted, and the fact that other Middlesbrough players, many of whom he knew had been only too keen to see him fail, had watched him struggle. That Saturday, Middlesbrough were away at Leyton Orient, and Clough was subdued in a 5–0 defeat. 'There can be no excuses,' Mitchell wrote, 'and I can think of no extenuating circumstances.' Mick McNeil would later offer an explanation, claiming the game had been fixed.

Middlesbrough then took the train north to Edinburgh for a friendly against Hibernian, whose centre-forward, Joe Baker, was widely expected to replace Clough in the England side. As the other players chatted and played cards or dominoes, Clough and Taylor sat in a compartment by themselves, analysing the England match and what had gone wrong for Clough. To him, the attempt to learn from his mistakes may have seemed entirely natural, laudable even, but it intensified the sense that he was too aloof, too wrapped up in himself, to be an effective captain.

There were two major opponents to Clough's captaincy. Most vociferous was Brian Phillips, who felt he should lead the team. 'The only massive mistake that was made at Ayresome Park,' Phillips said, 'was making him captain, the centre-forward who was after catching goals and wanted all the rest of the fucking side to go and help him knock them in – but that would have made no difference. Arrogant I would say is the best word. He was arrogant to a lot of people, and the reason he fell out with people was that they wouldn't stand for it.'

Alongside Phillips stood Bill Harris, the former captain, a Wales international of undoubted ability with a reputation for shirking the more physical side of the game. Clough used to rant at him for not chasing back and putting in tackles, and on one occasion even called him a 'coward' during a match. On the journey north, they plotted a challenge to Clough's leadership, and were joined by a third conspirator, Willie Fernie. He had never got on with Clough, who felt he held on to the ball for too long, and was inclined to try to beat an extra man rather than playing the sort of quick pass on which Clough thrived. Clough called him 'My-ball Fernie' and, the Scot believed, was responsible for turning a section of the Middlesbrough crowd against him.

By the time they reached Edinburgh, the plot was sufficiently advanced to have tainted the atmosphere. Most players seem to have believed that Phillips was the ringleader, but he denied that, and when asked even produced a photograph of himself standing on a balcony in Edinburgh with Clough and Taylor, the three apparently getting along perfectly well. 'I was more or less conned into being involved with it,' Phillips insisted. 'Whatever anybody says, I didn't organise that.'

The full-back Derek Stonehouse hadn't played at Orient because of injury, and travelled separately from Middlesbrough to Edinburgh. When he got there, he said, he found players whispering in corners while Clough and Taylor were nowhere to be seen. Doug Weatherall, similarly, was instantly aware that something was amiss. 'My angle was Joe Baker against Brian Clough as contenders for the England team,' he said. 'I turned up on my own and when I got to the hotel the team was already there. I remember going in and I heard a player say, "Oh, he'll have somebody to talk to now," meaning one of Brian's friends had arrived.'

The match itself finished in a 6–6 draw, and Baker was widely considered to have outplayed Clough who, in the agency copy used in the *Gazette*, was accused of having played too deep – the lessons of the Sweden game, perhaps, too well-learned. Like Stonehouse, Peacock, who was still finishing his national service, travelled to the game alone. 'I travelled up there on the Army warrant, got off at Edinburgh and went to play in the game, take my uniform off and get changed to play. I remember getting a ball and knocking it past the keeper and just overrunning it a little bit. I was at an angle and I looked up and there was Clough, so I slid it across and he knocked it in. In those days you just used to shake hands – none of this dancing business. But half the lads came up to me and started bollocking me: "What do you think you're doing?"'

Clough, driven by the lack of service, similarly dropped deep in a 1–0 win over Huddersfield the following Saturday. 'Again it was the England goal-making Brian Clough we saw, rather than the Boro goal-scoring Brian Clough,' Mitchell wrote, 'and while his pass to Holliday led to the winning goal, I think a lot of us yearn for the pulse-quickening sight of this fine centre-forward in full cry for goal, and finishing off with a fierce, unstoppable drive.'

With the rebel movement gathering momentum, Middlesbrough beat Hibs 4–3 in a return friendly, with Clough this time outshining Baker. 'In approach, distribution, leadership and finishing,' Mitchell said, 'the Boro captain underlined his mastery'. A 1–0 defeat at Ipswich followed, and only then did the story break. Phillips, it transpired, had approached Taylor, by then essentially a second-team player but important because of his relationship to Clough, and told him that a round-robin petition was being raised to have Clough stripped of the captaincy. Taylor tried to talk him out of it, but the letter, bearing nine signatures (but not Peacock's, Holliday's or Day's), was presented to Dennison and the board, accusing Clough of 'sulking' after England's defeat to Sweden, and complaining of 'harsh words on the pitch'. 'It was his pure arrogance that turned the lads against him,' said McNeil. 'They just felt that he was on the management's side rather than the team's side.' Who actually got round to drafting the petition remains unclear, but it seems likely that it was instigated by Harris with ready support from Phillips, Fernie and the full-back Ray Bilcliff.

'With us walking to the ground with Brian and Peter, the team didn't ask me,' said Day. 'I thought it was good of them. It would have put us in difficulties. I didn't go to the meeting and I was never asked to sign the letter. I wouldn't have signed it, obviously. You couldn't betray ... It was the older players. Basically I think he upset one or two of them. If he didn't see them make a tackle ... what you call hiding on the pitch. That's all it was. To be fair, some of them were really good players and they just weren't tacklers. He loved tacklers.' Holliday dismissed the round-robin as 'blatant stupidity', particularly as he was under the impression that Clough had never really wanted the captaincy anyway.

Others that Clough would have considered his friends, though, did sign. 'I signed it,' McLean admitted. 'I regret it when I look back.'

'Everybody signed it,' said McNeil. 'Bob Appleby and me were young lads. Bob said to me, "What are you going to do?" I said I didn't want to sign it, but they said everybody had to sign, either yes or no. Obviously as young boys [he was nineteen at the time] you go with the majority. So yes, I signed it. But I couldn't see who else we could have had as captain – except Bill Harris, whom we respected as a player but who wasn't forceful on the field, or mouthy. You want somebody who's going to open their mouth. Looking at it now, clinically, I still think Cloughie was the best man for the job, although I don't believe centre-forward is the best position for a captain. I think you're better to have a centre-half, or somebody in midfield, who sees the whole thing.'

Middlesbrough's vice-chairman, Eric Thomas, reacted by calling the players and coaching staff to his office for a meeting with the chairman, W.S. Gibson, and Dennison. Various players – 'mostly the defenders,' McLean said, 'because he always used to go on about the defenders' – spoke up, in a precursor of the notorious meeting that would cost Clough his job at Leeds. 'They just said why they didn't want him as captain.' Even saying that, though, was itself a major step, and gives some indication of just how annoying several of his team-mates considered Clough.

Word leaked out and the national media decamped to Middlesbrough; even back then, Clough and controversy seemed inseparable. 'I'd covered a match at Carlisle on the Tuesday and I was in the station hotel there because I was covering a game at Workington on the Wednesday,' Weatherall remembered. 'I got a call from the *Herald*'s office; they'd got the first editions and there was a story being put around by a freelance from Teesside that the majority of players at Middlesbrough had signed a petition asking the management to take the captaincy from Clough. So my plan was to get back first thing the next morning and get down to Teesside to see Brian.

'As soon as I got to his house I knew I was too late. I recognised the car outside – it belonged to Len Shackleton, who worked for the *Express* at the time. Brian came to the door, but I could tell straightaway that he'd got something tied up with the *Express*. So I tried to get the story as best I could without knowing much. "It's broken my heart," he told me.'

The *Express* even had a loudspeaker van to advertise the fact that the news of a rebellion against Clough would be in their paper the following morning. Clough was devastated, his usual bullish façade cracked by his performances for England, and shattered by this.

On Wednesday, 18 November, Mitchell, perhaps trying to play down a story he'd missed, wrote off the whole affair (in a front-page piece; his editor presumably was rather more convinced of the significance of the affair than he was) as 'a storm in a tea-cup' and cited a conversation with Clough. 'Nobody is going to get me away from Ayresome Park with stories like this,' he had said. 'The spirit in the dressing-room is good. We are all fighting for one thing, promotion, and I want to play my part in that fight.'

'Some of the players,' Mitchell explained, 'had, apparently, taken exception to Brian Clough's attitude – a "lone wolf" who did not always train with them was one reported complaint. These players had their say at the meeting; Clough acknowledged that he might well have been in the wrong in one or two instances – and it all ended amicably enough. With Clough still captain. It was noticeable that there was nothing wrong with Middlesbrough's team spirit at Ipswich last Saturday, when the Teessiders, weakened by an injury to their centre-half, went down only 1–0 after a great fight. The impression given was that the airing of the players' grievances had done them good and that, having got it all "off their chests" they felt all the better for it.'

Gibson, meanwhile, insisted the meeting had been called not in direct response to the round-robin, but to improve relations between players and board. 'Players expressed their views and it was a harmonious meeting,' he said.

Even Clough at that stage seemed conciliatory. 'Some of the lads raised one or two good points,' he said. 'Everything was sorted out and it all ended very happily. It is a pity for the club that things like this should get the wrong sort of publicity, when actually it was a very good thing it happened, and it helped to make for good team spirit. As far as the captaincy is concerned, if the Middlesbrough manager should, at any time, feel that it would be to the club's benefit if I were to resign the captaincy I would not hesitate to do so. Meanwhile, the lads are content that I should carry on as captain and I shall do just that.'

A day later, though, the full extent of the furore Mitchell had tried to ignore was revealed as Clough handed in a transfer request. 'I don't want this thing hanging on and on,' he said. 'I want to be freed so I can join another club, preferably in the First Division. The only thing I am interested in is to settle down and get on with my game of football. I am absolutely adamant about this. I don't want to stay with Middlesbrough five minutes longer than necessary and the sooner something is fixed up the happier I will be. I have always fought for Middlesbrough and always done my best, but I am sick of it all now.' A storm in a tea-cup it may have been, but it had led to Middlesbrough's best striker since the war seeking to leave the club.

Dennison refused to place him on the list – and, perhaps significantly, offloaded Phillips at the end of the season and Bilcliff a year after that – at which Clough, without withdrawing the request, vowed that despite everything that had happened, he would give his all on Saturday, at home to Bristol Rovers. Most fans were supportive – one even ran onto the pitch to confront Bilcliff – but as Clough led the side out, there was some barracking, the first time he had suffered such abuse. Clough didn't react, but stared straight ahead. He began quietly, but twenty minutes in he received the ball in the inside-left channel, about ten yards inside the Rovers half. He turned and ran, carrying the ball on a diagonal as Rovers backed off and then, about thirty yards out, he struck a ferocious drive into the top corner. 'The place erupted,' said Leslie Wilson, who was in the 'bob end'. 'I can still see it clearly. I was standing next to my dad and it absolutely flew in, one of those memories you'll always keep. Whenever people mention Clough I think of that.'

It was a goal that seemed almost a visible manifestation of the unleashing of his frustration. 'You had to admire him for doing that while under such pressure,' said Hardwick. 'He resisted the temptation to walk around the ground with two fingers up to the crowd.' Clough added two more, one from a Fernie pass and one from a weak back-pass as Boro won 5–1. 'I have not seen a Boro side play better for a long time,' Mitchell wrote, presumably glad the whole affair was over and he could get back to the simple routine of ringing Dennison for team news on a Thursday morning.

A 3–1 defeat on a muddy pitch at Swansea checked any thought that a refocused squad might surge up the table, but Boro then hammered Charlton 4–1, Clough scoring two, winning a penalty and setting up the other when his shot was parried. He followed that up with a hat-trick at, remarkably, Stoke, his old nemesis Ken Thomson having been left out as he finalised a move to Teesside. Boro lost 6–3 at Portsmouth, but back-to-back Christmas wins over second-placed Rotherham, who had gone sixteen games unbeaten, lifted Middlesbrough to within three points of the promotion places.

The momentum disappeared in the new year. Although Boro beat Derby 3–0, Mitchell was troubled by 'a lack of snap and crispness'. He was right to be so. Boro went out of the FA Cup to Sheffield Wednesday, were guilty of 'an inordinate amount of fussing and fiddling' in drawing at Plymouth, drew with Liverpool, and then suffered 'a body blow' in going down 1–0 at Charlton as a 'dallying' Bilcliff was caught in possession by Billy Kiernan and Clough, in front of the watching Winterbottom, missed a sitter.

A 6–3 victory over Bristol City, in which Clough scored a hat-trick, restored some hope, but the season dwindled away in draws with Scunthorpe and Sunderland. A first home defeat of the season followed against Aston Villa, and when Boro went down 5–2 at Lincoln, Mitchell admitted Boro had 'no longer even an academic interest in the promotion race'.

They ended the 1959–60 season fifth, ten points behind Cardiff who were promoted in second, and the last month of the season was characterised by speculation about Clough's future, something, it is safe to assume, he was happy enough to encourage. Fiorentina expressed their interest, at which the club admitted, as a headline in the *Gazette* had it, that they 'might not say no to a big offer for Clough'. Clough himself said he would fancy joining 'a glamour club like Manchester United or Wolves'. After a 2–2 draw with Leyton Orient on the final day of the season, Clough, Mitchell reported, 'seemed . . . rather relieved when the whistle blew'. He'd scored another forty goals, and under his captaincy Middlesbrough had finished higher than in any season since they were relegated in 1954, but it had been another year of frustration: he had secured a place in neither a First Division side, nor in the national team.

Not only that, but the hurt of the round-robin issue lingered. 'If it hadn't been for my wife I might have quit football,' he said in an interview with the *Mail*. 'I don't want to endure another nine months like last season, with so many old spinsters bickering behind the scenes. Indeed, if we can't all row together I want no part of the Middlesbrough programme.'

Clough pestered Dennison about a transfer and he responded by offering various financial incentives, recognising, presumably, that Clough's ambition, to a large extent, was fuelled by his fear of ending up with nothing. His insecurity could occasionally be glimpsed in the columns he wrote for the *Middlesbrough Evening Gazette*. 'I have no trade outside football,' he wrote. 'If I could start again as a bright-eyed youngster living his every moment for football, I would take an apprenticeship.' Clough, of course, had tried an apprenticeship, but had failed. 'After all, everyone doesn't make the grade. What happens then? If a man has no trade, he has little future. That might have been me.' A few years later, it was.

Clough told Dennison he wanted to set up a small business to supplement his income as a footballer. Dennison approached Albert King, an ice-cream merchant from Redcar who later joined the Middlesbrough board, and asked him for help. He recognised the marketing potential of the Clough name, and suggested a £2,000 loan to buy a general store or newsagents. Clough, though, wasn't sure how Barbara would take to living above a shop and dithered for so long that King lost interest.

Dennison didn't give up. He knew a boot manufacturer near Northampton that had done well by having Tom Finney endorse their product. Ideas for a Clough design were knocked around, and Clough even visited the factory with Dennison to discuss a deal. Initially he seemed keen, but as they left, Clough commented that the 2.5 per cent he was being offered didn't seem like much. Dennison pointed out that he didn't have to do anything other than allow his name to be used, and that Finney, a far bigger name, had been on the same deal. A week later the contract was drawn up, but again Clough hesitated. Two weeks after that, the company gave the deal to Jimmy Greaves instead.

*

Clough was hesitant too about his Middlesbrough future. By mid-June the whole squad had re-signed their contracts, apart from Clough, Holliday and the inside-forward Ray Henderson. The other two eventually sorted out their deals, but Clough remained reluctant. By 8 July, the *Gazette's* front page was carrying the headline 'I will NOT re-sign – Clough'. A week later, Clough admitted he was eager for Dennison to return from holiday so he could either sort out his contract or arrange a transfer. 'I am so anxious to see Mr Dennison that I would sit on his doorstep until he arrived back if I thought it would stop some people chasing me around,' he said.

On 28 July, Mitchell went to a party Clough threw for Ray Barnard, who was leaving the club for Lincoln. Day, Thomson, Waldock, Stonehouse, Taylor and Holliday were all there – which presumably gives some indication of who Clough's friends in the squad were – and after a lengthy chat with Clough, Mitchell reported that he believed he would stay. It wasn't till 11 August, though, nine days before the season began, that Clough finally signed his contract. By then, Ken Thomson had taken over the captaincy, and Dennison was warning Clough that he couldn't expect simply to walk back into the side.

Having missed the bulk of the pre-season fitness work, he was left out for the opening fixture, away at Bristol Rovers, his place being taken by the eighteen-year-old Joe Livingstone, who at that stage hadn't even played for the reserves. 'I asked Clough if he felt up to it,' Dennison explained, 'and the player replied that he did not think he was yet fit enough, an opinion held all along by our trainer Harold Shepherdson.' He wasn't unduly missed, a Peacock double and another from Holliday securing a 3–2 win.

Against Derby that Wednesday, though, Boro were 'ragged, desperate' in losing 2–1, and so Clough was recalled for the first Saturday home game, against Liverpool. 'Clough has now had two weeks full training,' Dennison said. 'He has been at the ground every morning and afternoon and we now consider him to be fully fit.' After a 1–1 draw, Mitchell was less convinced. In the return at Derby, Clough was 'bottled up by County's confident young centre-half, [Ray] Young', and Boro lost 1–0: three points from four games and the season was in danger of being still-born.

But then Clough turned in 'a vastly improved display' in a 2–1 win at Rotherham, and scored twice in a 5–0 victory over Southampton that Mitchell reported was less convincing than the scoreline may have suggested. 'Clough maintained his improved form and looks like getting back to something like his best,' he wrote. 'That's good enough for any team in the country.'

Still, all was not well: Boro were fortunate to draw 1–1 with Scunthorpe, and defended abysmally in drawing 4–4 with Leeds. They lost at home to Scunthorpe and, with Esmond Million saving a penalty from Ernie Taylor, beat Sunderland 1–0. Two defensive lapses meant Boro drew against Brighton in what an increasingly irritated Mitchell described as an 'apology for a game of football'. They went out of the League Cup 4–3 to Cardiff and then threw away 2–0 and 3–1 leads in a 3–3 draw with Plymouth.

On 15 October, Boro beat Norwich 2–0, but the main football story in the *Gazette* the following Monday was far more serious. Under the headline, 'Soccer Bribery – FA and League act,' it cited an FA statement: 'The Consultative Committee, on behalf of the Council, has decided as a first step to refer the evidence which has reached them to the Director of Public Prosecutions to take such action as he might think fit. This procedure is without prejudice to any subsequent action that may be taken in respect of offences against the rules of the FA and the Football League.' The statement went on to reference rule 35b, which prohibits 'an official of an association or club, referee, linesman or player' from betting on any football match. It may have been couched in the fusty language of the committee room, but the implication was clear: the FA believed matches were being fixed.

Perhaps it was that story that set Clough thinking, or perhaps he already had his suspicions. 'I sensed a nasty smell,' Clough wrote in his second autobiography. 'There was something wrong, something obvious even to a blind man. . . . It was happening on a regular basis and I was totally pissed off.' He began to suspect that Middlesbrough's fallibility at the back went beyond simple ineptitude.

He wasn't the only one. 'I could never understand why we leaked goals in the Middlesbrough defence,' said Mick McNeil. 'I always thought we had a reasonable side, looking at other teams. Yet there seemed to be times when goals were scored and . . . I don't know. Back then there was a lot of things going on.'

'It was just common sense,' said Billy Day. 'They used their common sense. Basically it was a couple of the older players. They were in their twilight and there were certain grounds where they weren't going to get a kick, which is common sense, isn't it? Maybe they knew they were going to get put on the list at the end of the season.'

The following Saturday, Boro drew 6–6 at Charlton. 'I can't imagine a more thrilling tussle than this one,' wrote Mitchell. Clough scored a hat-trick, and Boro held the lead at 2–1, 4–3 and 6–4. '[Middlesbrough's goalkeeper Bob] Appleby made some fine saves and was, I'm told, hindered by a Charlton forward as he tried to collect the dropping centre by [Johnny] Summers that went over his hands into the net in the last minute,' Mitchell went on. 'And Charlton's fifth goal was surely an offside job. Thomson, too, put in a lot of whole-hearted work at centre-half but, as with all the defenders, found recovery difficult in the mud. Bilcliff and McNeil were apt to give the wingers opposing them too much scope, while both Harris and Yeoman were seen to better advantage in attack than in defence.'

Clough was furious and again he found support from McNeil. 'It was a farce,' he said. 'They were letting the goals in. It was a betting syndicate.' Presented with the team that played that day, he went through it one by one. 'Bobby Appleby was as straight as a die, the same as I am. Ray Yeoman wasn't a better either. So, Ken Thomson ...' and he gave one more name, not of a player who played that day, but of, given Clough's visceral loathing of match-fixing, the least likely of players.

'And Peter Taylor.' Taylor? 'Ken Thomson and Peter Taylor. They were the two. Taylor was a better. I remember at Leyton Orient [the 5–0 defeat in October 1959], running back and the winger hits the ball from the left, an easy catch for Peter, and just as it was there, I never ever understood how the ball came through. It hit me on the back of the neck and flew into the net. Peter said, "Oh, bad luck." It definitely went on. ... a hell of a lot. I think we should have had promotion on three occasions when I was there and I think it was betting against the side was the reason we didn't. Purely that.'

On the train back to the north-east from Charlton, Clough walked down the corridor to the compartment where many of his team-mates were sitting, and made his feelings known. 'If I can manage to score four next week,' he said, 'you never know, we might even win.' They responded by suggesting that if Clough actually moved away from his marker they might have an outlet ball from the back and so be able to control possession.

Clough, though, was sure the issue went beyond tactics. 'I'd kept an eye on our defenders and to my mind something had to be wrong,' he said. 'Not even incompetent or crap players could explain the way Middlesbrough were letting in goals. I watched two of our lot in particular, Brian Phillips and Ken Thomson . . . I couldn't believe those two were genuinely as bad as they appeared to be.'

The details of Clough's allegations remain unclear (and it should be said that in his account of the game he mistakenly claims to have salvaged a point from the game with a late equaliser; his memory of it was clearly imperfect). 'As a centre-forward, I was usually somewhere near the halfway line when the opposition were scoring against us, so I didn't always have the best of angles to see what was going on,' Clough wrote in his second autobiography, published in 2002.

'But I did know how and when Phillips or Thomson should have been heading the ball clear and I did know when they seemed to be missing it. I remember them doing it against Doncaster.' Given Doncaster were relegated in 1958, and didn't play Middlesbrough again until 1967, Clough may mean Middlesbrough's 3–2 defeat at Belle Vue on 18 September 1957 (although they also lost there, 2–1, the season before). Thomson, though, only joined from Stoke in 1960 and so wasn't involved in that game. Besides which, given Clough's intemperate nature, it seems improbable that he would have allowed a suspicion to fester for three years before doing anything about it. More likely, his memory forty years on simply confused Doncaster with another club. There are plenty of other candidates that season, given how many high-scoring draws and defeats Middlesbrough were involved in, but perhaps the most likely, given the stature of the club, its geographical location and colours, are Rotherham, against whom they drew 2–2 at home, or Lincoln City, where they lost 5–2.

Clough went to Dennison with his suspicions, but 'he wanted no bother, no trouble whatsoever, and avoided it wherever possible'. That was a regular criticism of the manager, with many fans troubled by the fact that most of the players knew him as 'Bob'; he did not, it was often claimed, command the respect he should have done. 'Any time he went anywhere,' Mick McNeil said, 'he had what I would call a nervous or an embarrassing cough. Whenever he came into the dressing-room, or going out training, before any time he'd talk to you.'

Clough seems to have regarded his reluctance to act on his allegations as, if not cowardice, then at least moral laziness, but the circumstances under which Dennison had taken over Middlesbrough in 1954 must be considered. The club, £60,000 in debt, had just been relegated, was mired in scandal and struggling to survive. One of Dennison's first tasks as manager had been to travel to Seaburn to identify the body of the club secretary who had committed suicide after it had been discovered that money had gone missing from the club safe and insurance cards had been left unstamped. The club then took one point from his first nine games in charge. That he not only kept them in the Second Division that season but went on to bring a level of stability was a remarkable achievement, and having established Boro as a solid top-half side with aspirations of promotion, the last thing he needed was further controversy. The ambitions of a hot-headed young forward to play in the First Division are understandable, but it is equally understandable if Dennison preferred a period of consolidation, even if that meant turning a blind eye to certain dubious practices.

There had already been one match-fixing scandal in April 1956, just before Clough became a regular in the side. In an away game at Port Vale, Rolando Ugolini had been beaten late on by a soft shot that bobbled over his body to cost Boro a 3–2 defeat. Most were inclined to regard it as misfortune, until he got on the team bus afterwards and, on discovering that Aston Villa and Rangers had both won, let out a shout of celebration, announcing he had a treble. When he then admitted the third team had been Port Vale, club staff had to intervene to prevent him being beaten up by his team-mates. Ugolini was sold to Wrexham the following year. Technically, what he had done was not illegal – and there's no evidence to say that the late goal was anything other than accidental. As fixed-odds betting became increasingly popular, it was an open secret that a number of players would hedge by backing against their own side: win, and they collected their bonus from the club; lose and they collected a bonus of a different kind from the bookmaker. While the reaction of the other Middlesbrough players suggests Ugolini's bet was unusual at the time – one player accused him of having cost his daughter a pair of shoes that would have been bought with the bonus for a draw – it did perhaps open their eyes to the possibilities of fixed-odds betting.

Undeterred, and perhaps driven by a slightly warped sense of natural justice – Clough may have flirted with illegality for much of his life, but in both autobiographies he proudly describes how he would, for instance, berate bus conductors if they drove past a stop claiming to be full when empty seats remained – Clough took his complaint higher, approaching a director, Harold Thomas. He was a solicitor in the town, in Clough's description, a Rumpole of the Bailey figure with his portly frame and horn-rimmed spectacles. He too was reluctant to take action: 'a nice man, I'm sure,' Clough said, 'but ... he didn't want trouble on the scale I was suggesting.'

Trouble was never something that deterred Clough, who approached Mitchell, looking to use his regular column in the *Evening Gazette* to accuse his team-mates of throwing games having backed against Middlesbrough on the fixed odds. Mitchell's editor blocked the article, presumably for fear of libel action, but he wrote it up anyway and read it out to other players, warning them that he knew what was going on.

Whether there actually were anything going on is impossible to say, although both Phillips and Thomson were later exposed in the *Sunday People*'s investigation into widespread match-fixing in the English game. Million, a reserve goalkeeper at Middlesbrough who briefly courted Clough's sister Deanna, despite Clough's best efforts to dissuade him, admitted that he had deliberately conceded two goals while playing for Bristol Rovers against Mansfield Town, claiming to have been offered a bribe of £300 by Phillips, who was by then at Mansfield. Both were subsequently jailed and banned from football. Thomson, meanwhile, was banned after throwing a game while playing for Hartlepools United, but Phillips always maintained there was no organised racket when Clough made the complaint – in fact, he has always denied any involvement in match-fixing.

'I never,' he said, 'and this is the truth, on my kids' honour, even though I went to prison, I never played in a game that I thought was thrown. Even though I ended up in jail, I never played in a game I thought was fixed. That's the truth. On my kids' lives. I came across it, and I'll tell you when, when I thought "these fuckers have thrown this". Not me – it was Boro against Port Vale.' The Ugolini game, in other words. For what happened at Mansfield, he blamed Jimmy Gaunt, a forward who put together a betting syndicate while recovering from a broken leg.

The full-back Ray Bilcliff, though, admitted that there was dressing-room talk of players backing against Middlesbrough in the late fifties, although it was never clear who they were.

The allegations seem, briefly, to have galvanised Boro and after 3–1 wins over Sheffield United and Swansea and a 1–1 draw at Stoke, they lay, almost despite themselves, two points off second. Nothing, though, was as damaging to Middlesbrough as hope, and they crashed to a 6–1 defeat at Luton in a game in which they conceded three penalties, only two of them converted. It was, the *Gazette*'s headline said, 'so bad it hurt'. 'They were given the run-around by a side which was then one point better off than the two bottom clubs; they were outplayed and outclassed; they were a bad second in challenge and determination; almost from the first whistle they played like a beaten team …' Mitchell wrote. 'McNeil had a bad time; Thomson played his worst game since joining the club; Harris and Yeoman were never on top of their jobs.'

After a draw at home to Lincoln was followed by a 2–1 win over Huddersfield, Clough heading the winner five minutes from time, Middlesbrough had lost only one of their last eleven. 'If you are a cynic,' Mitchell admitted, 'you could suggest that this is a sorry commentary on the strength of the rest of the teams; that if Boro, on their recent form, are still able to stay in the race, then there can't be anything to beat.' The crowds tended to agree, and after ten home matches they were 97,958 down on the previous season; patience, evidently, was wearing thin.

A 1–1 draw at Bristol Rovers showed 'how much depends on Clough's marksmanship' as he missed two chances and so Boro failed to turn a 'four-star display' into two points, but he got the breakthrough in a 2–0 win over Leyton Orient, and struck twice in the final eleven minutes to win a 'red-blooded thriller' 4–3 at Anfield.

Boro went out of the FA Cup to Manchester United and 'looked a long way below First Division class' as Clough scored a late equaliser in a 2–2 draw against Rotherham, but even after a defeat at Southampton, a Clough hat-trick in a win at Portsmouth left them third in the table having lost just two of their previous seventeen games.

They beat Leeds, Brighton and Plymouth, but lost at Sunderland, so that by the end of February they were fourth, six points behind Sheffield United, four behind Ipswich and two behind Liverpool but with two games in hand on the leaders. March, though, was the killer as Boro took just two points from four games. 'Clough,' Mitchell noted, 'has hit a nightmare spell with one goal in seven matches and with scarcely a vestige of the dash, enthusiasm and challenge we used to see from him.' In the midst of it all, almost unnoticed on Teesside, Don Revie was appointed manager of Leeds.

Against Stoke, 'Clough scored the only goal in the forty-sixth minute and was livelier than of late, but he still missed a couple of great chances that would have been snapped up by the Clough we remember,' but any lingering hopes Boro could still claw their way into the First Division disappeared with a 3–1 defeat at Ipswich. As they had the previous season, Boro finished fifth on forty-eight points, ten points off promotion. A haul of thirty-six goals made it Clough's poorest season since he'd become a first-team regular.

Clough's final game for Middlesbrough came on 29 April in a 4–1 defeat at Sheffield United; he had scored his final goal a week earlier in a 3–0 home win over Portsmouth. On 4 May, Taylor, having slipped to third choice behind Appleby and Million, was transfer-listed, and the following month Jimmy Gordon left to take up a coaching role at Blackburn. With Clough's key allies leaving – although at that stage he and Gordon were far from close and regularly rowed – he was always likely to follow, and if Middlesbrough had any resolve to keep him, it must have been eroded by financial results that showed gate receipts had fallen 28 per cent from the previous season – a particular concern as the maximum wage was abolished that summer.

As Clough 'steadfastly refused to sign' his contract for the 1961–62 season, Dennison transfer-listed him for £55,000. 'People were resigned to it,' said Leslie Wilson. 'There was a lot of disillusionment among fans because of the constant failure to win promotion.'

There was talk of Arsenal coming in for him, while the Sunderland manager Alan Brown had made his interest clear, but Clough was doubtful about joining another Second Division club, even one with Sunderland's history and obvious ambition. Clough himself favoured a move to Wolves, who had won the league in 1958 and 1959 and the FA Cup in 1960. In Stan Cullis, they had a tough, disciplinarian manager – a type to which

Clough seems to have been drawn – and their style of play, focused on quick long balls out from the back and crosses to direct wingers, seemed a perfect fit for Clough's attributes, even if the style of football was far more direct than that of the teams Clough managed would be.

Eager to sort out his future before he went on holiday – a Mediterranean cruise he admitted he only tolerated for Barbara's benefit – and unsure what to do, Clough went to Scarborough to see Taylor, who was holidaying with his family in the apartment he owned there. They discussed the situation on a pair of deck-chairs on the beach and then Taylor, who had tried to sell Clough to Harry Storer at Derby County six years earlier, decided – in contravention of all regulations – to play middleman again. Still in his beach shorts, he went to the nearest phone-box and rang Cullis at Molineux. Cullis, though, was away, and so Clough went on his cruise without having given Brown a definite answer. Taylor knew he would join, though, and bet £18 at 100–6 that Sunderland would be promoted; after Clough signed, those odds came in to 7–2.

Brown himself was on holiday with his family at Bude in Cornwall, but he was a man who never really switched off. Learning that Clough was due into Southampton at 5am on Monday, 10 July, he drove 140 miles through the night to meet him off the boat. Seeing Clough collecting his trunk, he paid a porter to attract Clough's attention. 'Barbara said, "There's a fella down there waving at you,"' Clough recalled. 'And I looked at him and said, "Well I don't know him," and it was Alan Brown.'

Brown reached over a five-foot fence, introduced himself and shook Clough's hand. He told him Sunderland had agreed a £45,000 fee with Middlesbrough and offered him £40 a week. 'I'm known as the one who speaks his mind,' Clough wrote in his second autobiography, 'but Browny was the master at it. I didn't know Alan Brown personally, but I knew of him. I was aware of his reputation as a strict and honest man. I took him at his word.'

Two days later, Clough met Brown in Sunderland and, according to the report in the *Sunderland Echo*, 'expressed himself delighted with the housing accommodation which was offered'. He signed his contract at midday on the Friday, allowing the *Echo* that night to announce 'the biggest soccer surprise of the close season'.

'They didn't like it in Middlesbrough,' Clough said. 'They called me a traitor. I'd never had it so intense in my own mind, but I remember one of my brothers saying, "not Sunderland. You can go anywhere but Sunderland." And I said, "Look, why not?" and he said, "They're our enemies." It was terms like that they used to use.'

Clough himself seems to have regarded his days at Middlesbrough with ambivalence, and certainly by the end he was, he acknowledged, 'sick of the place'. As he said in his second autobiography, though, they 'taught me a fundamental fact of life – defenders need to be as good at their jobs as any forward. They are not there to clatter the opposition, to kick people, to destroy. Their job is to protect their own goal with skill and intelligence.' In Charlie Hurley, still widely regarded by fans as their greatest ever player, Sunderland had a defender in just that mould: a tough, strong centre-half who played with immense restraint and understanding and could pass a ball. For that, and other reasons, Clough found Sunderland a far happier place than Middlesbrough, even if the frustrations he eventually endured there outstripped anything he'd experienced at Ayresome Park.

A Dream Destroyed

Clough was the third of three major signings made by Sunderland that year, following the right-half George Herd, who had been bought from Clyde for £40,000, and Harry Hooper, a Durham-born right-winger who joined from Birmingham City for £17,000.

In the years immediately after the War, Sunderland had never been afraid to spend, gates that regularly reached 50,000 allowing them to bring in the likes of Len Shackleton, Trevor Ford and Ivor Broadis and earning them the nickname The Bank of England club. As the fifties went on and silverware proved elusive, the spending became increasingly desperate and in 1957 a Football League commission, investigating an anonymous tip-off, found Sunderland guilty of making payments to players in excess of the maximum wage, and fined them £5,000. The manager, Bill Murray, resigned, and the chairman Bill Ditchburn and three directors were suspended. A year later, Sunderland suffered their first relegation.

For a side that believed itself one of England's elite, that had won six league titles – only Arsenal at that stage had won more – that was a staggering psychological blow. Looking to restore the club's reputation,

Sunderland turned to Alan Brown. He was, as Jimmy Nelson, Sunderland's reserve left-back at the time, put it, 'a fearsome character'; Charlie Hurley called him 'the strictest man in football'. Born in Corbridge in Northumberland, Brown soon demonstrated an ascetic streak he would carry into management. Aged sixteen, he ran seventeen miles along the Tyne into Newcastle, rested for a few minutes and then ran back, all part of his efforts to improve his fitness. As a centre-half for Huddersfield, Burnley and Notts County, he developed a reputation for toughness and honesty.

At Burnley, his first job in management, Brown established a strong youth set-up, and oversaw the development of a training complex on the edge of town, helping with much of the physical work himself, and insisting his players also did their share. That nobody should be treated differently remained a central tenet, and he would regularly have the first team act as ball-boys for the youths or order his stars to brew tea for everybody else, a habit Clough copied exactly. After three years at Burnley, Brown saw it as his duty to return to the north-east to rescue the club he had supported as a boy in its hour of need. There he had the players concrete the car-park at the new training-ground at Washington.

'You lived in fear of him but there was no need to be because he was a really genuine, nice guy,' said Nelson. 'He kept a very strict ship. In that winter of 1962–63 when we had all the snow and all those games were called off, he would have us training in the space under the Roker End where there were huge concrete pillars so that if you didn't keep your head up you'd brain yourself. Or we'd go down to Seaburn beach and we'd be training in skins in January – I don't think bibs had been invented then. He'd have us training till the water lapped in over our ankles. We had individual baths then – slipper baths we called them – and you'd end up two of you sharing one of them because nobody wanted to wait. We'd all race back to the ground and get straight in just to thaw out.'

Clough was well aware of Sunderland's history. The side of the early to mid-fifties might not have won anything, and might have been riven by cliques, but it was still a team packed with stars and capable of producing, when the mood took it, exhilarating football. 'I was taking over from the greats,' he said in 2000. 'Trevor Ford had just gone when I got there and the moneybags team had broken up.'

Sunderland may since have become used to mediocrity, to hovering between the top two divisions for most of the past fifty years, but when Clough joined, even after three seasons in the Second Division, there was a sense that this was an outrageous exile, an inexplicable fall from grace that would inevitably soon be rectified, and that meant money would be spent in pursuit of promotion. To an extent, Brown was to blame for the relegation. When he had arrived, he'd found a dressing-room packed with players bought at great expense and all pulling in different directions. 'He got rid of all the older people and the so-called stars,' said Jimmy Montgomery, who was making his way through the youth ranks at the time. 'He brought all the younger people in, who he knew would work for him and graft for him and do specific jobs for him.' Initially, the shock was too much, and Sunderland were relegated, but the underlying philosophy was sound. Brown is remembered with great affection on Wearside for the quality of football his young team played, even if it was in the Second Division and, as Montgomery, who finished his career playing under Clough at Nottingham Forest, pointed out, Brown's methods clearly struck a chord. 'Brian was exactly the same,' he said, not only in terms of the emphasis on the team over the individual, but even down to 'the little mannerisms'.

The night Clough signed, Sunderland's chairman Syd Collings explained his thinking. 'I would rather see Sunderland in the First Division with an overdraft than in the Second Division with money in the bank . . .' he said. 'In the view of the signing today you must be wondering how near we are to the workhouse. We are at the first door and we have to get out again. I am not worried about the overdraft because I am confident that with the team we can put on the field we will get our money back next season. It is better to spend and look for success than to wait and hope.'

His ambition had certainly struck a chord; even before the Clough signing, season ticket sales had reached record levels – £26,503 as opposed to £12,100 at the same stage the previous year. Clough's arrival unleashed a new wave of enthusiasm. 'Autograph hunters thronged the entrance to the Roker Park ground . . .' said the report in the *Echo* as the players reported for pre-season training on 24 July. 'They were eager to catch a glimpse of Sunderland's new £45,000 signing from Middlesbrough, sharp-shooting centre-forward Brian Clough. Inside the ground Brian strolled over the lush green carpet of the playing area and talked over tactics with his new colleagues, skipper Stan Anderson, burly Charlie Hurley and last season's Scottish newcomer, inside-forward George Herd.'

Clough was a particular fan of Hurley. 'He was regarded in the north-east as the best ball-playing centre-half there was,' Clough said. 'He could do it, he could beat a man. He had beautiful balance and he didn't kick that much for a centre-half, which was incredible because, in my day, if you didn't kick as a centre-half you couldn't play.'

The respect went both ways. Clough's arrival seemed like the final part of the jigsaw. 'When we signed him I thought we'd hit the jackpot,' said Hurley. 'We had all the build-up, but just missed out – we needed the goals a good goalscorer would score.

'When I played against Cloughie, I would say "leave Cloughie to me" and I'd track him. You might not see me an awful lot, but you wouldn't see him either. I'd stick right by him for ninety minutes. I remember once after coming off after a game at Boro and he turned to me and said, "You know the best thing that's happened to me today is full-time, so I can turn round and not see you right behind me." And that was a great compliment, because he was the best goalscorer I ever played against. He was the best in the Second Division by a mile, but I include my games in the First Division and at international level in that. He was the player I took most satisfaction from stopping scoring: you'd come off the pitch and think, "Cloughie didn't score. I've done my job."'

Still wearing his red Middlesbrough training gear, Clough was perhaps carried away by the exuberance and goodwill he experienced at that first training session. Catching sight of an acquaintance walking past the training ground at Whitburn, Clough wandered over to chat to him, at which Brown gave him an almighty public dressing-down. After that, Brown said, Clough was always 'the model of respect', and it is a sign both of their mutual admiration and Clough's importance to the club that when the team photograph was taken the following day, manager and centre-forward sat next to each other in the middle of the middle row.

Unlike Gordon and Shepherdson at Middlesbrough, Brown was always involved in training, relishing the worst of conditions. 'He seemed to take a perverse pleasure from it,' Jimmy Nelson said. Brown was not just a hard taskmaster, though; he had a fine tactical mind and was regarded as one of Britain's most innovative coaches. He developed shadow play – essentially practice without the ball to work on positioning – long before Arrigo Sacchi was deemed a revolutionary for introducing it at AC Milan, and implemented other ideas that didn't catch on quite so well. At one training session during his second stint as Sunderland manager, for instance, he had his defenders practising heading with golf-balls, insisting it wouldn't hurt if their technique was right.

'He was different to Bob Dennison,' Clough said. 'Bob was a very soft-spoken man, a quiet man, I suppose in his own way an imposing man. He was six foot, dark hair and everything, but he didn't used to say a lot. When I got to Sunderland it was the exact opposite. Browny was there with his shorts on – he had the body of a twenty year old; muscles all over. If he got into you after a match, short and sweet, and you never answered back. He was a stickler for discipline, a right bugger. That was the side I got from Alan Brown. He detested shabby clothing and he insisted his players always had a regular trim . . . Alan Brown was not simply my manager, he was my mentor.'

Pre-season brought two convincing wins on a tour of Denmark, and there was more than the usual optimism about the start of the new campaign. It lasted less than a fortnight. Clough made his debut on the opening day away to Walsall, who had been promoted in each of the previous two seasons. Walsall went ahead from a disputed twelfth-minute penalty, but Herd levelled, and then teed up Clough for a debut goal. As Herd pulled a thigh muscle and was reduced to limping on the wing, though, Walsall came back to win 4–3. 'Clough,' the *Sunderland Echo*'s correspondent Argus noted, 'in the right spot to grab the goal made by Herd, made it a scoring League debut for Sunderland, but there was little chance of him distinguishing himself in such a game. He was fiercely marked, poorly supported and most of the time quite subdued.'

Had it not been for the injury to Herd, Argus suggested, Sunderland probably would have won, but he saw cause for concern in their apparent lack of sharpness. 'Their own football played with the same dedication and drive as Walsall's could put them right out in front at the top of the Second Division,' he noted. 'Without it, they may not even be in the hunt.'

Similar bad luck with injury undermined Sunderland's second match, away to Liverpool the following Wednesday. With the score at 0–0 after thirty-five minutes, their centre-half Charlie Hurley suffered a cut eye.

Patched-up, he returned at centre-forward for the second half, but Sunderland lost 3–0. They came from behind to beat Stoke 2–1 with two Ambrose Fogarty goals in their first home game, but Clough was so peripheral he wasn't even mentioned in the *Echo's* match report. The following Wednesday, at home to Liverpool, Clough at least scored, ramming in a low drive from twenty yards just before half-time, but that was to reduce Liverpool's lead to 2–1, and Sunderland went on to concede two more. Liverpool would go on to walk away with the Second Division championship, but that was little consolation at the time. After all the investment, financial and emotional, Sunderland had suffered three defeats in their first four games, their new centre-forward had done little other than score twice in losing causes, and the First Division looked an awfully long way away.

'When Clough first arrived he had a chip on his shoulder,' remembered Sunderland's captain, Stan Anderson. 'He'd been scoring all these goals but Middlesbrough weren't going anywhere, just hanging around mid-table, so he was frustrated. He brought that with him, but it only lasted a couple of weeks. I could understand it. He would say, "Just give me the ball and I'll stick it in the net for you." That might have sounded like a bit of a boast, but it was true; he very rarely missed. He wasn't the quickest, but he had the knack of being in the right position, which is what football's all about. He got into some strange positions, but the ball used to come to him. There were times when he'd go to the back post and there'd be three or four defenders in front of him, but they'd all miss the cross and he'd score.'

Sunderland clung on to win 3–2 at Bristol Rovers having been 2–0 up inside thirteen minutes, but it was an essentially unconvincing performance, and the season – and Clough – didn't really get going until the 3–1 home win over Leeds United – with their player-manager Don Revie at right-half – on 11 September. Clough scored two and could have had far more in what Argus in the *Echo* described as 'the finest exhibition of centre-forward play seen at Roker Park for years'. Clough, he went on, 'was in tune with everyone around him, making good service look extra good and doing his share of the foraging too. Over the ninety minutes he was so often in the finishing position that it became almost a personal duel between him and a brave, inspired goalkeeper in Alan Humphreys.'

Significantly for those at Middlesbrough who had criticised Clough's selfishness, his single-minded focus on the goal and nothing but the goal,

Argus also praised his 'brilliant reverse passes to both wings'. At that stage, Clough was still a popular figure in the Sunderland dressing-room, admired for his competitive spirit. 'We always wanted to be on Cloughie's side in five-a-sides,' said Jimmy Nelson, 'not just because he scored goals but because he wanted to win so much, all the time. He was strong; whenever he got a chance you expected him to finish. Even when he got the injury he was going in to finish. But he was much more than a poacher. I don't think he ever worked back, but that wasn't his game, and not many did then.'

Clough, though, injured his knee in a League Cup tie at Bolton and without him and Anderson, Sunderland went down 3–1 at Norwich. Clough returned at Bury the following Tuesday, and pounced on a Bob Stokoe error to score, but by then Sunderland were already 2–0 down; they went on to lose 3–2, and the *Echo*'s headline lamented their 'lack of fight'. It was a theme that recurred throughout the season; Sunderland defeats were invariably put down to them being outfought: 'strolling players became sitting ducks for Bury's businesslike tactics,' Argus moaned. Eight games into the season, Sunderland had just six points.

Herd returned and scored two in a 4–0 win over Scunthorpe, Clough turned in a Hooper cross to see off Bolton in a League Cup replay, and the winger set up all three of Clough's goals against Bury as he scored his first Sunderland hat-trick in a 3–0 win. Come the Saturday, though, and there was further frustration as Sunderland drew 1–1 at Brighton. They were the only team to have taken a point off Liverpool, but Sunderland dominated and, according to Argus, should have recorded a 'handsome win'. For the first time, he dared a little – mild – criticism of Clough: 'So far on top and yet only one goal to show for it? It sounds as though the forwards were at fault for not finishing the job, but there was, in fact, very little fault to be found anywhere along the line. Just one instance, perhaps, where a make-sure effort by Brian Clough ran him into trouble when a first-time shot could have been the answer.'

Clough's response was his second hat-trick in successive home games as Sunderland beat Walsall 5–2 in the League Cup, the match in which, thanks to a broken cheekbone Peter Wakeham had suffered at Brighton, Jimmy Montgomery made his debut in goal for Sunderland, four days before his eighteenth birthday. The injury, Clough suggested, was the best

The young centre-forward contemplates a bright future at Middlesbrough (PA).

Preparing for another windswept day of training in the mud (Getty Images).

Clough and Barbara, and her 'smile that seemed to light up the entire north-east' on their wedding day at St Barnabas church. Later that day he scored against Leyton Orient (PA).

Clough looking remarkably like his son in an FA Cup third-round replay
away to Charlton (PA).

Clough holds off Charlton's Gordon Jago to attempt a left-foot strike in a
Division Two match at the Valley (PA).

His two caps: Clough goes close in 1–1 draw against Wales at Ninian Park, and is thwarted by Sweden's goalkeeper Bengt Nyholm in a 3–2 defeat at Wembley (both PA).

A smiling Clough looks
forward to Sunderland's
away match at Chelsea;
Clough studies the
programme in the Roker
Park dressing-room
(PA and Getty Images).

Alan Brown, Clough and a young Jim Montgomery (lower right) in the
Sunderland team photo for 1961 (Colorsport).

Clough in action for Sunderland, up against Preston's George Ross.
Sunderland won 1–0 at Deepdale, October 1961 (Colorsport).

The attempted comeback: Clough plays his first game for 20 months in a draw against West Bromwich Albion (Getty Images).

thing that could have happened. 'The crowd didn't like Peter Wakeham at all,' he said. 'He used to get some right stick. That was the last thing he needed because he was nervous enough.' Perhaps because of the influence of Taylor, and perhaps having seen the points dropped by Wakeham's errors, Clough recognised the value of a top-class goalkeeper in an era in which many of his contemporaries were sceptical, something he showed most definitively in spending £270,000 to sign Peter Shilton for Nottingham Forest.

The goals against Walsall prompted Argus rapidly to backtrack from his earlier criticism, and again suggested that Clough had learned from his experiences with England, and had become a more complete player. 'He has built his reputation on goal-scoring ability and the three which he claimed last night made it clear that he is worthy of all the praise which has been heaped upon him on that account,' he wrote. 'His use of the ball however – and particularly the devastating passes with which he manages to bring his wingers into the game – underlined a less-publicised quality which carries tremendous value.'

A Charlie Hurley header earned a draw at Derby, before Clough inspired a 2–1 victory against Leyton Orient. 'Clough shines in fighting role,' said the sub-head in the *Echo*, below a headline announcing that 'Off-form Sunderland were lucky to win'. Clough had gathered a long-ball from the left-back Len Ashurst to cancel out an early Orient goal with the assistance of a goalkeeping error, then added the winner with a right-foot shot through a crowded goalmouth. 'The lion's share of the honours in attack must obviously go to Brian Clough,' said Argus. 'Not only for those match-winning goals, but because he made a fight of it all the way through and his challenging play in the later stages helped to take a great deal of weight off the defence.'

It may not have been convincing, but the victory provided a sense of momentum which Sunderland maintained with a 1–0 win at Preston, in a game in which Clough was again praised for his selflessness in creating space for others. 'His whole aim was to score goals,' said Hurley, 'but he created a lot of space for others just because the marking on him would be so severe. He was an out-and-out lazy striker, not a grafter at all. He'd do sod all for eighty-nine minutes, then score a goal and come in and say, "I scored. If you'd kept a clean sheet we'd have won."'

He was rewarded with another hat-trick at home to Plymouth, meaning he had rattled in eleven in four consecutive home games, taking his tally to seventeen in seventeen games in all competitions for the season. Argus hailed 'Clough, the ace goal-grabber, who gives a new value to half chances and leads his line with that eye-for-everyone touch which helps him to make dramatic changes in the point of attack; Hooper, with uncanny control and devastating burst of speed; and Herd, the wee genius who has brought automation to soccer by coming up with split-second answers to the trickiest of problems ... it must have been sheer delight for bang-in-form Stan Anderson to feed the ball into this soccer brains trust and see his service put to such excellent use.' For all that, though, he seemed no nearer a return to the England side, in part because of Greaves's form, but presumably also because Winterbottom saw him as being more trouble than he was worth.

Sunderland suddenly were third, a point behind Southampton with a game in hand, with Liverpool six points clear of them and already looking certain to be promoted. Sunderland's unbeaten run of nine league games came to an end as they were outmuscled in a 2–0 defeat at Southampton. When that was followed with a 2–2 draw at home to Luton, the warning signs were beginning to crystallise, but faded again as Clough scored two equalisers in a 2–2 draw in the derby against Newcastle, a game that, in Weatherall's mind, highlighted just what made him so special. 'Afterwards,' he said, 'a Newcastle fan said to me that everybody was saying Clough was this, that and the other, but his two goals were tap-ins. So I said, "If it's that easy why isn't everybody doing it?" He was brilliant at getting the first touch on hard, low crosses. He was the best centre-forward I ever saw play for Middlesbrough or Sunderland. He was the finest I'd seen in the north-east until Alan Shearer. You could smell the goals. He did score from outside the box, but he was great in the six-yard box. People say anybody can score from there, but centre-forwards have to get the first touch, and that's what he was great at.'

That was down in part, of course, to natural ability, but it was also something Clough worked on tirelessly. 'He wasn't that quick – just normal pace you expect from a forward, wasn't great in the air, but his timing of his runs and of striking the ball was brilliant,' said Hurley. 'He'd practise fifteen, twenty minutes, maybe half an hour, after training every day, getting players to put in balls for him and hitting them first time – high balls, low balls, everything. He wouldn't take the ball down, because that can give a centre-half time to get in a tackle, would always strike it first time. He never placed a shot in his life – if you did, he said, you weren't hitting it as hard as you could, but if you hit it hard first time, maybe it flew in the top-corner, maybe the keeper saved it and somebody else stuck it in.'

When Clough followed up those two goals at Newcastle with his fourth hat-trick of the season, in a 7–2 victory over Swansea, it seemed the season was back on track, especially when Walsall were beaten 3–0 on 16 December, despite Anderson breaking a cheekbone in the fourth minute. That injury, though, meant Sunderland went into the Christmas programme without him, Herd and Hurley. They lost at Stoke and Charlton, and were probably fortunate the return against Charlton on 30 December became the first match to be postponed at Roker Park for thirty-six years as floodwater froze over the pitch.

The momentum of the autumn stalled, but Southampton were beaten after a replay in the third round of the FA Cup, the attendance of 58,527 for the second game – a record for a floodlit match at Roker – suggesting there was still a widespread belief that this was a team that could bring success. Clough played despite a heavy cold, but suffered a bruised foot that ruled him out of the league match against Bristol Rovers the following Saturday. With Hurley playing with stitches in a head wound and Hooper slowed by a thigh injury, there were reasons for concern, particularly when Rovers took an early lead. The twenty-year-old Northern Irish forward Jimmy O'Neill enjoyed a goalscoring debut as Clough's replacement, and Sunderland went on to win 6–1. The worries about the depth of the squad were justified, though, and that was the last good news for some time.

Sunderland, 'the team that forgot to fight until it was too late', as Argus dubbed them in his match report, lost 1–0 at Leeds and, in the FA Cup, were held to a goalless draw at home by Port Vale, who were then in Division Three. 'They will have to do better than this for the wages some players are getting,' said a letter-writer to the *Echo*, 'because the fans are getting fed up with the excuses they've had to put up with all this season.'

The intended target, presumably, was Clough, who had gone seven games without a goal. Brown's patience was evidently beginning to fray, and he dropped Clough and the left-winger Jack Overfield for the visit of

Norwich on 3 February. Only 18,000 turned out to see O'Neill, Clough's replacement, end thirty-eight minutes of anxiety with the opener in a 2–0 win.

It was, though, a brief respite. Clough was restored to the team for the League Cup fifth-round tie against Norwich that Wednesday, but although he scored with a waist-high volley, Sunderland lost 4–1. 'Beyond his well-taken goal,' Argus noted, 'Clough shows no sign he is playing himself out of his lean spell.'

It got worse. Sunderland lost 3–1 at Scunthorpe and drew 0–0 at home to Brighton. 'Three times from no more than eight yards Clough failed to accept chances that would have made the game safe,' Argus reported. 'Shocking misses all of them, but Clough is the sort of player who does not need to be told or reminded he has made a hash of things. He criticises himself more severely than anyone else does . . . he is having a bad time of it . . . yet it was to him alone that supporters looked for even the hope of a goal.'

Not Brown, though, and he dropped Clough, Anderson, Hooper and Wakeham for the home game against Derby, handing Montgomery his home debut in goal. Goals from Hurley and Herd gave Sunderland a 2–1 win, but the suspicion was that it was too little too late. If they were to have 'the slightest chance of getting back into the promotion race', Argus noted, they had to get a result away to promotion-chasing Leyton Orient the following Saturday.

Clough was furious at being omitted, but knew better than to question his manager. 'Alan Brown was a very domineering manager – you had to do what he wanted even if you didn't agree with it,' said Anderson. 'Brian appreciated Alan Brown later in life – I don't think he appreciated it at the start, but that's how he finished up: very domineering. You know the famous quote about if there was a disagreement Brian would sit down with the player, they'd talk about it for twenty minutes and then they'd decide he was right? Well, that was Alan Brown. There were no clashes between Brian and Alan Brown because you couldn't clash with Alan Brown.'

They drew 1–1, but Argus saw reasons for hope. 'Sunderland needed both points from their visit to Leyton Orient . . .' he wrote. 'For most of the game they looked like getting them.' There were signs of 'spirit' in 'their brightest display away from home for some time'. As Preston's progress in the FA Cup gave Sunderland a weekend off, results left them eighth, eleven points behind the leaders Liverpool and five behind Leyton Orient in second, with a game in hand. A record of twelve home wins and only two away left little doubt where their problems lay.

O'Neill, still in for Clough, scored in a 4–1 home win over Charlton and then got two in a 3–2 defeat against Plymouth, where Sunderland lost yet another player, the young centre-half Dickie Rooks, to a fractured cheekbone. After a 0–0 draw at home to Preston, Clough was at last recalled for the game against Huddersfield on 24 March, as was Hooper. He hadn't hit a league goal since mid-December, but after outmuscling John Codding-ton to latch on to a Len Ashurst ball to give Sunderland an eighth-minute lead, he went on to complete his fifth hat-trick of the season in a 3–0 win. Both he and Hooper, Argus said, had 'recaptured the dash and power which was slipping from their game'. Clough thought he'd made a point to Brown, and suggested he should never have been dropped. 'The rest did you good,' Brown replied.

Suddenly the surge was on. Clough got the only goal away at Middles-brough, who had effectively been reduced to nine men by injury before half-time, and climbed to fourth, ten points behind Liverpool and four behind Leyton Orient in second. Willie McPheat laid on goals for Clough and Herd as Southampton were beaten 3–0. Sunderland then went to Luton, where they had never previously won.

With Hurley injured, Clough took over the captaincy and, according to Ashurst, before kick-off called a group of senior players over to one touch-line. Clough told them that a Luton player had offered to sell the game, and asked what they thought. The players rejected the offer, but Sunderland won 2–1 anyway, with Montgomery saving a late penalty. Sunderland remained fourth, two points behind Leyton Orient with four games to play, and belief was building, particularly when Orient could only draw 0–0 with Luton.

Heavy rain fell on the morning of the Tyne–Wear derby, Saturday, 21 April, but that didn't stop the crowds. The *Echo* spoke of the 'siege of the town' and featured several interviews with fans who had travelled for hours without getting even as far as Roker. At the ground, the gates were locked forty minutes before kick-off with over 50,000 inside and thousands more in the streets outside. It was, every report agreed, a tremendous game.

91

Clough played in Herd to give Sunderland a nineteenth-minute lead, and then McPheat tapped in the second after Dave Hollins had saved from Hooper. Clough 'rarely broke clear' from the attentions of Bill Thompson and Newcastle had their chances, but Herd made the game safe with a drive from the edge of the box. Even better, Leyton Orient drew 0–0 at Norwich. Going into the final week of the season, Sunderland trailed Leyton Orient by two points with a marginally inferior goal average, but had three games to play to Orient's two. Three wins by reasonable margins would be enough.

On the Monday, Leyton Orient won 3–1 at Luton, while Sunderland hammered Rotherham 4–0, Clough pulling down a Herd cross at shoulder height and lashing in the last of them. That meant a 2–0 win at Rotherham on the Tuesday would lift Sunderland above Leyton Orient on goal average. Midway through the second half it was still goalless, but then Clough turned in a McPheat cross and Hurley headed a second within three minutes. Clough added his second to make it 3–0 from a Cec Irwin free-kick with seven minutes to go. After seven straight wins, Sunderland, playing away at Swansea, needed only to match the result Orient achieved at home to Bob Stokoe's Bury to return to Division One.

Overnight trains were laid on to Wales as thousands of Sunderland fans travelled south in expectation of the club's first promotion. Again, an opponent offered to throw the game; Hurley rejected the offer without consultation. It looked as though Sunderland would get the win they needed when Clough seized the loose ball after Ashurst had been fouled and, taking full advantage of the referee's decision to allow play to continue, wriggled through two challenges to open the scoring. But twenty minutes into the second half, a Swansea corner found Brayley Reynolds. He hooked the ball over his shoulder and Ashurst, Montgomery and Irwin on the line were unable to prevent it sneaking in. Leyton Orient won 2–0, and Sunderland's great charge had been in vain. Clough had scored thirty-four goals in all competitions and had come closer than ever before to promotion, but again, he had failed.

Gates were up 269,872 on the previous season to 949,766 – an average of 32,986 for league games – while Sunderland made a profit of £16,713, despite increased wages after the abolition of the maximum wage. For all the eventual disappointment, Clough had made Sunderland exciting to watch, and that perhaps explains why fans of the era remember him with such fondness despite the relatively short time he spent there. For those eighteen months, he was the spearhead who gave potency to an adept but occasionally clawless side. By 10 July, when Sunderland held their AGM for 1962, Collings was able to report season ticket sales were already in excess of £38,000 – up £4,000 on the total figure for the previous season.

Clough himself, after a minor car-crash in which the driver of another car was left concussed after apparently driving into his path, spent his summer playing tennis at Ashbrooke, where Harry Hooper was also a member. He also became friendly with Lance Gibbs, the West Indies Test cricketer, who played for Whitburn in the Durham Senior League.

Failure to win promotion had only persuaded Sunderland that more needed to be spent. The emergence of Montgomery meant that Wakeham, who had never been popular, could be sold to Charlton, while Sunderland were linked with moves for Aberdeen's outside-left George Mulhall and Johnny Crossan, a Northern Irish inside-left then playing for Standard Liege after receiving a lifetime ban from British football for irregularities in his move from Derry City to Coleraine and subsequent payments he received while theoretically an amateur.

England performed reasonably in the World Cup, reaching the quarter-final, where they lost to the eventual champions Brazil. In three of their four matches, England played Gerry Hitchens at centre-forward, flanked by Jimmy Greaves and Johnny Haynes, but in the goalless draw with Bulgaria, it was Clough's former Middlesbrough team-mate Alan Peacock who led the line. Clough himself seemingly hadn't even been considered (and if playing in the Second Division had been a reason why he hadn't been selected in 1958, how galling that it should not have been a barrier to Peacock's call-up four years later), which can only have intensified his irritation at his lack of opportunity. The best news of the summer for him, in fact, was probably Winterbottom's decision to quit the FA to take a post at the Central Council for Physical Recreation.

Sunderland began the 1962–63 season at home to Middlesbrough, and it was indicative of the spirit of optimism that 48,106 turned out to see Clough score twice in a 3–1 win. They scraped a 1–0 victory in windy conditions against Charlton – Wakeham flapping at a cross to gift McPheat the goal – but the injury problems that had plagued them the previous season returned as McPheat broke his leg in a 1–0 defeat at Leeds. 'I have seen nothing so far to convince me that referees are putting into effect their high-sounding ideas for cleaning up the game . . .' Argus noted. 'What a tragedy that a fine young player like McPheat should be put out of the game for months by an undetected foul of the variety of which referees as a body seem curiously blind.'

Away form was again Sunderland's major problem, defeats at Chelsea and Rotherham meaning the home wins over Swansea and Rotherham were needed just to stay in touch. Mulhall joined from Aberdeen and made his debut in a 3–1 home win over Luton and then scored as Sunderland at last registered their first away win of the season, beating Southampton 4–2; Clough got the other three. 'Freescoring forwards can usually be listed as goalpoachers,' Argus noted, 'but Clough has progressed beyond that stage to become an important link in a hard-working system.' He scored another two in a 7–1 League Cup win over Oldham, and two more in a 3–0 home win over Derby.

Even with Mulhall, the pattern of home wins and points dropped away continued. When they were good, they were exceptional, as was the case in the 6–2 win over Grimsby that marked Johnny Crossan's debut, a game in which Clough scored another hat-trick. And when they were off-colour, they were still good enough that, by December 1962, they were comfortable in second behind Chelsea. A 3–2 League Cup quarter-final victory over Blackburn Rovers, not merely a First Division side but one that had won eight and drawn two of their previous ten games, offered proof of just what they were capable of. Clough contributed 'a beauty' to cancel out an early Rovers goal, running on to a long ball, holding off two challenges and skipping by another before driving in left-footed, and then scored a late third as Sunderland, as the Guardian's report said, 'took command'. Here, it seemed, was evidence not merely that Sunderland could cope at a higher level, but that they might thrive there.

In the league, Cardiff, fellow promotion hopefuls, were beaten 2–1 at home, and then Sunderland went to Huddersfield, another side jockeying near the top of the table. Only the excellence of Montgomery kept Huddersfield out in the first half, but the game changed with two goals in the first three minutes of the second. Both came from sharp passing moves, and both were scored by Clough. At that stage Sunderland – and Clough in particular – seemed to be flying, playing fast, dynamic football that was laying on chance after chance for the most prolific forward in the division. 'He brought something different to the club,' said Montgomery. 'You need to have a little bit of arrogance about you if you're going to be successful. The ones who're shy and retiring, they soon go out of the game. The players knew that as long as he was banging the goals in, we were earning money. We were getting our bonuses. Because the wages weren't the best in the world, but the bonuses were very, very good. You could get a bonus of £60 a point – when you weren't getting anything like £60 in wages. You could treble your wages with a 1–0 win, so Brian's contribution was vital.'

'It was the happiest time of my life in terms of football,' Clough told Pat Murphy. 'Sunderland folk are beautiful, much warmer and more genuine than those in Middlesbrough and we had a wonderful relationship going. I was young, happily married . . . I was cracking in the goals. Lovely days.' Misfortune, though, was lurking, unseen and unexpected. It was hardly, though, unimagined: Sunderland were perhaps especially unfortunate, but looking back through old match reports, the staggering thing to modern eyes is how often teams were reduced to ten men by injury, and how common broken bones – especially cheekbones – were.

With hindsight, Clough's last games are barely credible, reading almost like a carefully arranged valedictory tour. He played his last away game and scored his last goal before the injury, appropriately enough, at Ayresome Park, as Sunderland overcame the early loss of McNab to injury to draw 3–3. Clough's strike, Sunderland's second, came from a long forward pass from Ashurst, exactly the sort of move that, a fortnight later, led to the injury that ended his career. It took his tally to 250 goals in 269 league games; no player has reached the mark in fewer matches.

Then came Leeds, managed by the man who would become Clough's managerial arch-rival, Don Revie. Their defensive approach was criticised by Argus, who praised Clough's 'hard-working display'. He beat Jack Charlton in the air to head back across goal for Mulhall to score the first, and Hurley added the second in a 2–1 win. Immediately after Revie's Leeds came Bob Stokoe's Bury, completing the triangle of loathing that would connect the three men, born within fifty miles of each other, for the rest of their careers.

Each came to despise the other two: the teams Clough and Revie managed became great rivals, embodying wholly differing conceptions of football; Stokoe accused Revie of having tried to bribe him to throw a match, and had his revenge by upsetting Leeds in the 1973 FA Cup final with, of all sides, Sunderland; and Clough hated Stokoe for an ill-judged comment as he tried to pick himself up after suffering the injury that effectively ended his playing career. As he blacked out on the icy mud in the corner of the penalty area at the Fulwell End, leaving behind the first period of his life and emerging with desperate, painful uncertainty into the second, he heard Stokoe shouting, 'He's only coddin' ref.' They were words Clough would never forget. 'I had a joke with my sons,' he said, 'that if they got naughty I'd send them upstairs to their room to throw darts at Bob Stokoe's picture,' Clough said.

If only he had only been coddin', but the referee, Kevin Howley, himself from Middlesbrough, knew Clough too well. 'He doesn't cod, not this lad,' he replied. He was grimly correct.

It had been a ferocious winter and there were so many postponements that the FA Cup final had to be pushed back by three weeks. Boxing Day was raw and cold, 'the kind of day when seagulls flew backwards to stop their eyes watering,' as Clough put it in his autobiography, but having inspected the pitch ninety minutes before kick-off, Howley decided it was playable. At Ayresome Park, thirty-two miles to the south, Middlesbrough's game against Norwich was called off, and several have since suggested that Sunderland's match should also have been postponed. Nobody suggested that at the time, though, and Clough even congratulated Howley, a respected referee who had taken charge of the 1960 FA Cup final, on his decision, joking about the softies down the road. As when he'd helped clear the snow from Great Broughton's pitch before scoring ten against Skinningrove, the desire to play outweighed all else.

Half an hour before kick-off, an ugly yellow-grey cloud that had been lurking off the coast and that had caused Howley his only hesitation, drifted over the ground, bringing a torrential hailstorm that further worsened conditions. Sunderland had gone thirty-one home games without defeat, but they struggled for rhythm on the difficult surface and Charlie Hurley had missed a penalty when, after twenty-seven minutes, they suffered what Argus described as 'their greatest blow in years'. 'If I hadn't missed that penalty,' Hurley said, the regret clear in his voice even half a century later, 'the game would have panned out differently. But fate's fate.'

Ashurst marginally overhit a through-ball, and Clough gave chase. 'I was never to be distracted in circumstances like that,' he said. 'Suddenly it was as if someone had just turned out the light. The Bury goalkeeper, Chris Harker, had gone down for the ball, and his shoulder crunched into my right knee.' On video, the incident looks innocuous enough, goalkeeper and forward colliding as they went for the ball, the sort of thing that happens dozens of times every weekend. Only when Clough tried and failed to get up, flopping like a dazed rag-doll, did it become apparent that something was seriously amiss. 'The ball came forward and Brian was chasing,' Harker said. 'I came out and dived across him, which goalkeepers do to block the ball, and Brian came over the top of me.'

He hit the ground hard, and photographs show blood smeared across his forehead. 'I was slightly off balance, with my head down ...' Clough said. 'I didn't see him. My head hit the ground, and for a second or two I didn't know a thing. Only blackness. I'd done my knee but I couldn't feel that. The ground was icy and I'd gone over the goalkeeper and hit my head and I was in a daze and I came round and I was crawling, not able to get up because of my knee and I heard Bob saying, "Get up you lazy bastard, there's nowt the matter with you."' There, in that moment, Clough's life changed; he came round a different person, one who could no longer play football at the highest level.

Unable to stand, Clough was carried from the field and then lifted onto a couch in the dressing-room, the white sheet with which it was covered soon being stained with blood. Johnny Watters, Sunderland's physio, said Clough should go to hospital and made to take off his boots, but Brown stopped him. Clough suggested Brown still thought he could be patched up and go out and play, but Brown later said he had known instantly that Clough's career was probably over, and had been trying to hide that fact from him through his initial recovery.

Sunderland went on to lose 1–0, 'only a minor tragedy' Argus noted, beside the fact that 'Clough could be out for rest of season'. It would, of course, be even worse than that, and what made it all the more cruel was that Clough had been playing so well – twenty-four league appearances that season had brought twenty-four goals, to go with four in four in the

League Cup – that he'd seemed, as Argus said, 'set fair for an all-time club and league goal-scoring record in the brightest season of an already brilliant career'. That career was effectively over: the great goalscorer had been cut down in his prime.

II

1962–1972

Nor shall this peace sleep with her; but as when
The bird of wonder dies, the maiden phoenix
Her ashes new-create another heir
As great in admiration as herself

(William Shakespeare, *Henry VIII*, Vv40)

Iron in the Soul

The stricken Clough was taken from Roker Park to Sunderland General Hospital, where Watters's worst fears were realised. Both the medial and cruciate ligaments were completely torn and, realistically, that meant the end of Clough's career. He had an operation on his knee on 29 December and, for the next three months, he was in plaster from groin to ankle. That, though, wasn't the end of the bad news. As Clough lay on his hospital bed wondering whether he would ever play again, Barbara stopped visiting. When she returned after an absence of five days, it was to tell him she'd suffered a miscarriage. Clough hadn't even known she'd been pregnant. The happiest time of his life was over, and in a matter of days he went from being a carefree young talent whose biggest worry was whether the new England manager would be as blind to his talents as the old one, to a man who had known real pain, physical and emotional, and who, with his career in jeopardy, was starkly aware of his responsibilities.

It wasn't just Barbara who stopped visiting. 'Alan Brown didn't allow players to go and see him till four days after the injury,' said Stan Anderson. 'That's what he did. I remember when I broke my cheekbone he wouldn't let my wife come and see me, said "Oh, his face is all swollen, you wouldn't want to see him."' Quite why he did that is unclear; a worry that seeing an injured team-mate might make players fear for their own safety at least has a certain logic; hiding an injury from a spouse just seems bizarre. It's often assumed that Clough's aversion to injured players, his occasionally pathological refusal to engage with them, was a result of his own injury. In fact, it may in part have been another case of him implementing one of Brown's strategies.

It was Brown who gave Clough a lift home from hospital, something he did in typically unsentimental style. He helped Clough out of the car, gave him a piggy-back to the door, went back, got the crutches from the boot and handed them to Clough. 'See you tomorrow,' he said, returned to his car and drove away. That at least gave Clough a sense that he was wanted at the club; he later admitted how, as he'd lain in his hospital bed, unable to move, his mind had dwelt on how little he had to offer. All his life had been focused on scoring goals, and that was what had taken him to the brink of greatness. Without his goals, though, without football, he was just a failed turner-and-fitter. Self-pity, a devil that haunted Clough in his darkest moments, was never far away, despite the hundreds of letters of support he received from Sunderland fans, confirming the extraordinary bond he'd formed with them in eighteen months. 'I took to Sunderland,' he said, 'and they took to me.'

Without Clough, Sunderland faltered. They lost to Aston Villa in the League Cup semi-final and, although they made it to the fifth round of the FA Cup, it wasn't until mid-March that they won another league game. That was largely due to a series of postponements brought about by a harsh winter – the run without a win lasted only four games – but the momentum of December was gone, and promotion was lost in a run of eight matches between 30 March and 30 April in which Sunderland won just once. Five of them were drawn, and at least four of those matches Sunderland dominated; with a fit and firing Clough, a forward to turn control into goals, it seems reasonable to believe a couple of those may have been won. Even if only one of them had been, it would have been enough not only to take the second from Chelsea, who beat Sunderland at Roker Park on the final day of the season, but to take top spot in the division from Stoke. As it was, Sunderland finished third, denied promotion on goal average. Clough had never been closer to promotion, yet that summer he had probably never felt further away from being a First Division footballer.

The doctors cut two holes in the plaster, allowing Watters to work the muscle with electricity, but it was after the plaster came off at the end of March that the hard work began: eighteen months of brutal, unremitting effort to try to get back to playing. 'The surgeon set my knee in plaster to try to get the medial ligament strong,' Clough explained, 'which he did – a magnificent job. But coming out of plaster after three months, it took me three months to get my leg straight. And if you can't get your leg straight you can't work the quadriceps. It took me ages and ages and ages.'

Brown had Clough report for training at 9am each day to run up and down the steps of the Roker End, the only alteration in routine coming when he allowed him to run down to the beach at Roker and slog along the sand and up the Cat and Dog Stairs at the south end of the promenade. The bend in the cliff, where a ravine cuts inland through Roker Park (the park) towards Roker Park (the football ground), took its name, gruesomely, from the fact that a century or two earlier it had been there that the corpses of cats and dogs drowned in the river would wash up; here, the metaphor was all too obvious and all too appropriate. Only after two months, when the season was over and the other players went on holiday, did Brown finally let Clough have a day off. 'I was too hard on him,' Brown later acknowledged. 'He must have thought I was a beast.' Clough's only relaxation in those days was, during the summer, to head south to Acklam Park or Scarborough to watch Yorkshire play cricket; it was then that he first met Geoff Boycott, a friendship that endured for the rest of his life.

The biggest problem for Clough – and those around him – though, was less the physical side of the training than his mental torment. 'The so-called rehabilitation period was hard because I was so difficult to live with,' he said. Clough would scream at the coaches supervising his running, telling them to join him on the steps. Often Brown did, but resentment set in, and when Sunderland finally won promotion in 1964, Clough congratulated the manager but refused to shake his hand.

They later made up and remained close long after both had left Sunderland. Clough always referred to him as 'Mr Brown' and, years later, after Brown had moved into a retirement home in Devon, sent him regular letters. When Brown and his wife went to California to visit their daughter, Clough even sent them a cheque 'to have your first sandwich together on us'. When Clough's son Nigel first began to emerge in the Nottingham Forest first team, Clough sent Brown a newspaper clipping about him. With it was a note in which he said that he wished Nigel could have worked with Brown, because it was Brown who had taught him discipline.

'When a footballer's getting over a bad injury, he's mentally ill as well,' Brown said. 'It showed in Clough's behaviour. He was under dreadful strain – frightened to death about what would become of him after football.' Clough the manager had a clear aversion to injuries and injured players, almost as though he couldn't bear the sight of a plaster cast for the memories it brought back. He banned Trevor Francis, who had damaged his Achilles, from attending the 1980 European Cup final for instance and, in 1986, having diverted the Nottingham Forest team coach to the hospital where the former Forest defender Paul Hart was recovering after breaking his leg in his first game after moving to Birmingham, he stayed on the coach while his players went in to visit. Duncan Hamilton, author of *Provided You Don't Kiss Me*, raised the issue with Clough once as they drank together; Clough changed the subject while giving Hamilton the impression that he acknow-ledged he had a phobia.

Clough's fears for his future led him to supplement his income without the regular win bonuses to boost his salary. He did some media work, but he also turned to less conventional means. 'There wasn't exactly a rota or a roster, but we took turns to visit,' said Jimmy Nelson. 'I remember going with Cec Irwin and Billy Richardson to his house near the Barnes. We went in and the whole front room was full of shoes. The bay window was stacked up with boxes like it was a shoe shop, all properly arranged in order of size. You went, "How's your knee?" and he said, "Come and have a look at the shoes ... " He had everything in there, brogues, smart shoes, the lot ...'

Nobody seems to know quite where they came from, but Nelson had his suspicions. 'He and Ambrose Fogarty were great friends,' he said. 'Ambrose was a right little leprechaun. It wouldn't surprise me if the shoes came off the back of an Irish ship. Cec might have bought a pair, but I certainly didn't.' You wonder what his mother, whom Clough insisted so often had taught him right from wrong, thought of it.

The surgeon didn't want Clough even to attempt a comeback, but he insisted that he had at least to try. On 21 December 1963, though, Argus announced Clough's retirement in his column in the *Football Echo*. 'The outside chance – it was never more – that Brian Clough might be able to recover from the worst type of knee injury which can befall a player was abandoned on medical advice last week,' he wrote. 'The brave battle which Clough had waged for nearly a year kept everyone hoping that this would be the exception to the rule. But it was a forlorn hope and the verdict which everyone feared was, perhaps, inevitable ... There is no coming back from the cruciate ligament injury.' And yet, within a few weeks, Clough had second thoughts, raising the possibility that the club had tried to push through his retirement so they could collect the insurance money. Argus's column the previous week, perhaps not coincidentally, had reflected on how the attack lacked a 'leader' and wondered whether Sunderland needed to sign a Clough-type player to replace Nic Sharkey.

The next six months evidently offered some promise and, by the start of the 1964–65 season, Clough was back training with the squad. Among the *Echo's* traditional start-of-term photographs showing players stretching, jogging and playing leapfrog, there was Clough lying on his back, the familiar grin on his face as George Herd performed a handstand on his stomach. The training ground on Moor Lane, past the pond in Whitburn on the road to Cleadon, can be a desolate place, muddy and windswept, the hills behind stretching up to the water tower and the ruined mill as though in one of Andrew Wyeth's gloomier landscapes. That morning, though, the sun was out, the grass freshly cut, and there was a palpable sense of hope. It was illusory.

On 15 August, Clough made his return as a second-half substitute for Nic Sharkey in a 3–2 friendly defeat to Huddersfield, his every touch cheered by the Roker Park crowd. 'There is now no doubt that Clough can play football again,' Argus reported. 'The big question is whether he can play it at the top class. Only he can provide the answer and it is more important that he should provide it to his own satisfaction than that he should convince anyone else.'

A week later, Clough started for the reserves away at Grimsby and scored with a low twenty-yard free-kick in a 2–2 draw. Unusually, the *Echo* carried a match report of a second-team fixture, an indication of the level of expectation that surrounded Clough even as the first team began its first season back in the top flight for six years. 'There was little fault in his positional play and his ability to reach high balls gave Sunderland the edge in second-half corners,' wrote Vedra, the *Echo's* underused reserve-team correspondent. 'For one fifteen-minute period he was everything a centre-forward should be and only brilliant goalkeeping and a large helping of good luck [presumably for the keeper] stopped him from scoring at least a hat-trick.'

Clough was even more impressive a week later as he played for the reserves at home against Halifax, scoring a hat-trick and setting up two in a 7–1 win. The first team, meanwhile, had been badly shaken by Alan Brown's decision at the end of July to quit the club for Sheffield Wednesday. Even worse, an injury to Jim Montgomery left the fifteen-year-old Derek

Forster as the only fit goalkeeper on the books. The result was one point from three games, and the clamour for Clough's inclusion became impossible to ignore – even if the bigger problem were the ten goals conceded rather than the five goals scored.

Sure enough, the following Wednesday, Clough returned to face West Brom, who had already beaten Sunderland 4–1 that season. Sunderland were improved, and Clough hit the post and went close to a late winner in a 2–2 draw. 'There were the reminders,' Argus wrote, 'that Clough still carries much of his former dash and fire. And though over the ninety minutes the overall impression was that he found it increasingly difficult to get into the game after a tremendous first-half effort, there was the evidence that he can still see the half chance taking shape and be in a position to have a go.

'As a starting point for him, it was encouraging enough and, though, as a perfectionist, he was far from satisfied with himself, he is entitled to know that he shaped a good deal better than might have been expected.'

Clough retained his place for the Saturday game against Leeds, in which Sunderland, trailing 2–0, were jeered off at half-time. Clough nutmegged Jack Charlton then headed in a Roger Usher cross to spark a comeback. Johnny Crossan scored twice as Sunderland went 3–2 up, but then conceded a late equaliser. There was a caution, though, to Argus's verdict. 'Because they snatched the vital goals, both Clough and Crossan could be well-pleased with their afternoon's work,' he wrote, 'yet over the ninety minutes they contributed less in constructive play than their colleagues in attack.'

That same day Barbara's mother, who had been staying with them, died. There'd be no more coconut cake and, Clough began to realise, there'd soon be no more football.

Argus had even more doubts after a 2–2 draw against Aston Villa a week later. 'The men who took all the power out of the attack were Crossan and Clough, neither of whom made any real impression upon the Villa defence . . .' he wrote. 'It was uphill all the way for Clough, who was so comfortably held by [John] Sleeuwenhoek that this was the position from which Villa had least to fear. It is in such games as this that Clough, lacking his old pace and power, is shown up to his greatest disadvantage. He obviously carries the sympathy of the crowd, but Sunderland officials must surely be convinced that Clough's cause might have been better served if they had given him a longer build-up in the reserves.'

His team-mates had been desperate for him to return. 'I loved him on the pitch,' said Hurley. 'You don't have to love him off the pitch – if you've got a player who scores goals you've got respect for him. I said to all the lads, "Whatever happens, however he plays, if there are any signs of anything we've got to tell him he's on the way back." We needed him, but there was nothing.'

Clough was left out for the 3–1 defeat at Arsenal the following week and never returned to the first team. His next appearance in the *Echo*, in fact, was campaigning for Labour in the Sunderland South constituency at the general election. By Christmas it had become apparent he would never play again. His pace was gone, and nothing, he began to realise, would bring it back. 'I'd encountered an injustice or two already, but nothing compared with this ...' Clough said. 'I suddenly knew the meaning of the word desolation ... Life had seemed so good and so promising. Suddenly, I had nothing but worries. I was finished, an ex-footballer who knew how to do nothing other than play football.'

He'd failed his eleven-plus. He'd failed his apprenticeship. He may have had great self confidence but, in his professional life at least, it was validated only by his football. It was football that gave him an income, that from which he drew his sense of self-worth, and in the fraction of a second it took for his knee to hit Harker's shoulder, it was over, for all his efforts to make a comeback. Alan Peacock said that 'when he scored he was like a man on drugs – he just lived for that on the field'. That terrible accident ensured he would never get his fix again.

'Brian was a very sick and sad young man,' said George Hardwick, who eventually succeeded Alan Brown as manager (Revie, intriguingly, turned down an approach). 'He hated every member of the club from the first team down to the A-team because they could do something he couldn't – go out on a Saturday and play football. Boy, was he bitter. He'd meet his team-mates in the tunnel at half-time and give them the biggest rollickings. He even told the trainer and coach they hadn't a clue.'

Jim Montgomery remembered one incident in particular. 'I used to smoke in those days, me and Brian Usher and Jimmy Davison, we were sitting in what they called the counting house, where they used to count the money on a Saturday, and the laundry was just there, and we were standing there having a cigarette after training and Brian walked in and gave us a bollocking, the biggest bollocking of our lives, really. For smoking. I think he smoked himself at times, but to see younger lads smoking . . .' And here the great conundrum of Clough emerges: he could be absurdly harsh and openly hypocritical – and it wasn't as though the three were youth-team players; all were first-team players at the time – and yet somehow his words had a positive effect. 'It was taken on board,' Montgomery said. 'I did stop soon after that. It made an impression.'

Cigarettes weren't Clough's only vice. It was around then that he first turned to alcohol for solace. 'I went berserk for a time,' he said. 'I drank heavily. I wasn't very manly.' Barbara gave birth to Simon, Clough's eldest boy, that year, and on the day he was born Clough got so drunk on champagne with Lance Gibbs at Wetherall's club in the centre of Sunderland that the sister at the hospital was reluctant to allow him in to see his son. 'Some welcome to fatherhood,' as he put it in his autobiography. Clough's devotion to his family is not in doubt – even if, as Tony Francis's biography suggests, tensions emerged in the eighties when his children began to leave the family home – but Simon's birth, by increasing Clough's responsibilities, can only have increased the pressure upon him: losing his income as a footballer would have been bad enough anyway, but now he had a son to provide for as well.

Clough lashed out at those around him, apparently blaming Len Ashurst for having played the pass that led to his collision – or at least that is what Ashurst says; Clough himself, when pressed on the issue by Jeff Brown in an interview in 2000, expressed surprise, saying he thought it had been Jim McNab who played the ball. What is certainly true is that Ashurst walked out of a Round Table lunch after being criticised in a speech by Clough and refused to play in his testimonial. In his autobiography, Ashurst claimed that other players agreed to take the same stand only to be won around by an offer of cash.

'He was never the same person after he got injured,' Ashurst said. 'Not that I thought much of him before. You could just about deal with his abrasiveness because he did score a lot of goals for us. But he manufactured his image after all those wasted months, trying to get back playing he adopted that drawl and started courting controversy, getting the press in his pocket.'

Charlie Hurley, as gentlemanly as ever, said he felt sorry for him, recognising that Clough was 'broken-hearted' and that his anger was a means of releasing his frustration, but he soured the atmosphere around the team. By December 1964, Sunderland were bottom of the table having picked up just nine points, and seemed likely to suffer an immediate return to the Second Division. By then, Clough was even railing against directors, something that would ultimately cost him his job.

Hardwick, sick of Clough moping around 'like a North Sea fret', as he put it, decided to offer him a job working with the youth set-up. 'One day I was walking along the passage,' Clough said, 'and he shouted, "Hey, Cloughie!" get here! If you think you're going to wander around for twelve months doing nowt and just collect your wages on a Friday, you've another thing coming."'

For Clough, this seemed at first like insult added to injury. 'Now to start with,' he said, 'he hurt me with that because one of the worst things for a footballer is being injured and the second worst is having to train on your own, and I was having to train on my own. I knew every step down to Seaburn beach and every house and every grain of sand. It was murder. But he said, get with the A-team, the third team, and that was my first job in management. I got a year's experience because the guy who was in charge, who was called Bill Scott, was in his late sixties and he'd shot it. He was there just, as they used to do in those days, to give somebody a job.'

Giving Clough a coaching role was something Brown always insisted he had intended to do. Such is Brown's reputation for integrity he probably did, and certainly his logic for not telling Clough of his plan fits with his bracing personality. The worst thing for Clough in the long term, he felt, would be to look back and wonder if he could have given more to resume his playing career. That was why he drilled him mercilessly, that was why he refused to offer him the comfort of a job in coaching. Footballers, he knew, needed only the slightest excuse to ease off, and so he wanted Clough to think playing was his only way of safeguarding a secure future.

After those three games, it became obvious that Clough's days as a player were over. He had given everything, but the damage to his knee was too great. His future lay in coaching. At times Clough spoke of the advantage he had of having an early start in management, but the suspicion remains that Brown, cruel as he may have seemed, was right: Clough had to be persuaded that not only was there no hope of him getting back to playing, but that there could never have been. 'Nothing I did in the rest of my career,' Clough said, 'compares with being young, fit and scoring goals by the barrowload. Management is only a substitute for playing football.'

Nonetheless, it soon became apparent that Clough was good at it. 'I was always interested in management,' he said, 'because I used to talk a lot about football and you'd be amazed how many footballers didn't talk about football. Far too many just switched off at 12.30, went home and couldn't fill their time in because academically we weren't Einsteins and so we didn't know what to do. So some ended up in the snooker-hall and some got into horse-racing. I wasn't into that, because I never had any money, but I used to play a bit of snooker because we had a table at Middlesbrough. It was normal carry-on for me to go into management because I had no qualifications off the field, but I couldn't just take my boots off and go into training because I wasn't that well known.'

This was what all those conversations with Taylor, those hours spent wandering round Albert Park, eating Lill's chips and criss-crossing the north-east by bus had prepared him for. There's a gulf, of course, between theory and practice, but Clough bridged it almost instinctively. 'I found, instantly, I could teach,' he said, and he also relished working with a group of players prepared to listen to his theories and act upon them. 'Brian was a revelation,' Hardwick said. 'His mind was occupied and he was achieving something. He *has* to achieve. He loved working with the kids, and they loved working with him. Instead of condemning, he was encouraging.'

Clough went on an FA coaching course in Durham, run by Charles Hughes, the notorious long-ball theorist who would later become technical director of the FA. Unsurprisingly, Clough, who even then had purist tendencies, was not impressed, and so began one of his longest-running battles. He derided Hughes's approach as 'primitive' and later said he'd never worked with anyone who had less idea about football than Hughes.

One of the exercises Hughes set up involved a prospective coach running down the wing and crossing for a forward to head in. Most of the people on the course had not played football to any level, and so Clough became frustrated by a series of scuffed and mishit crosses. When one did eventually come across at the right height, he casually glanced a side-header into the bottom corner. To his disbelief, Hughes stopped the session to tell him that he should always head with his forehead because that's where the bone is strongest and so it was from there that the most power could be generated. That finesse had anything to do with football was a notion with which Hughes never seemed comfortable.

Clough set out to prove Hughes wrong whenever he could, and left the course insisting that the other students had learnt more from him than from the man who was actually employed to teach them. More confident than ever, Clough decided to disregard convention and implement his own ideas with Sunderland's youth side. He scrapped the tedious lapping of the pitch, and instead introduced more five- and six-a-side games.

The players responded and a side featuring Colin Todd, Colin Suggett and John O'Hare reached the FA Youth Cup semi-final, at which Hardwick gave Clough the title of youth-team manager. 'He took to the job with relish,' O'Hare said. 'It seemed to me like he really enjoyed his job, and he was certainly enjoyable to be with. He was quite different, really, in his approach to how we trained, with a lot of ball work, shooting, all that sort of stuff, instead of the laps or half-laps of the field that we'd been used to.'

Todd admitted that, at that stage, he found Clough an intimidating figure. 'But as a kid you just get on with what you're doing,' he said. 'Whatever he said, we'd do, knowing that he had that much knowledge anyway. We were frightened, because of how the man was, but we were only sixteen or seventeen. We used to have a laugh, he wasn't all serious. As a youngster, I knew from the dressing-room at Sunderland that he was a very outspoken player. I wouldn't say [the injury] made him bitter, but it made [him] feel that he'd lost something. He had had everything going for him. But he had to look forward and the next best thing was to be involved in a coaching capacity. Throughout his career in management, his philosophy was to control and pass that ball. With him being a striker, the one bit that he always wanted was to make sure the strikers get quality. He once said, "I would hate to deal with some of the balls people are trying to play to our strikers so make sure they're good quality." He always believed that the strikers had the hardest job on the pitch.'

Hardwick's plan – although he never let Clough know for fear of expanding his ego to bursting point – was eventually to install Clough as his assistant, but he never got the chance. After promoting Clough, Hardwick was called in to see Laurie Evans, one of the directors, who demanded to know why Clough had been appointed. Hardwick explained the progress the youth side had made under Clough, at which Evans told him he didn't care: the board just wanted Clough out of the club. It's astonishing how much of Clough's career, even at that stage, was played out in wood-panelled rooms. Quite why they wanted rid of him so badly is less clear: perhaps it was simply that his bad temper and outspokenness had created a bad atmosphere, perhaps the board had been irritated by Clough's criticism of them, or perhaps, as Clough later claimed, it had more to do with the £40,000 insurance pay-out they received when Clough's career was formally terminated. Clough himself picked up only £1,500, plus around £10,000 in proceeds from a testimonial arranged by Hardwick. That 31,000 turned out for it suggests just how popular Clough remained among fans.

Hardwick refused to get rid of Clough, and that, he believed, was his downfall. Sunderland rallied after Christmas, winning eight of their last nine home games to avoid relegation comfortably, but Hardwick was sacked nonetheless. When he asked for an explanation, he was told he'd been too friendly with the press and too hard on the players, neither of which he considered particularly convincing reasons. He drew his own conclusions. 'I was fired because I stood by Brian and refused to climb down,' he said. 'Any fool could see that. That's how much they despised him.' Hardwick was left, as he put it, 'sickened', so disgusted that he effectively retired from professional football. Clough, though, was too young to walk away; he had almost three decades of battles left to fight. It was because of Sunderland's callousness rather than the injury itself, Taylor said, that the 'iron entered deeper into his soul'.

The Only Reasonable Means of Governance

Those months in the summer of 1965 were the worst for Clough. He was thirty and, for the first time in his adult life, he was out of work. In truth, he had few prospects: a prolific goalscorer he may have been, but why would any club take a chance on a thirty year old with a little over a year's coaching experience at youth level, especially one with such a reputation for chippiness? And to add to the pressure, Barbara was pregnant again; Nigel would be born the following March.

Clough desperately needed a break, and it came in the form of Hartlepools United, who were in an even worse shape than he was. A 2–0 defeat at Colchester on 16 October left Pools second bottom of the Fourth Division with eight points from twelve games. It wasn't an unfamiliar position – they had finished in the bottom two five times in a row between 1960 and 1964 – but after the hope offered by a fifteenth-place finish the previous season, Geoff Twentyman, who had been in the job only 150 days, was sacked, leaving the club to look for their eighth manager in the eight years since the death of Fred Westgarth. The same day, Ernest Ord resigned as chairman because of ill health; a day earlier, his twenty-seven-year-old son David, who was also a director, had been hospitalised with severe burns to his right hand and both legs after a blowback on the coke central heating system in his home. To add to the sense of chaos, Hartlepools's trainer, Peter Gordon, then quit the club to move to Southend, where he joined up with Twentyman's predecessor, Alvan Williams.

Two days after he'd resigned, Ord was persuaded to continue and revealed he had three names in mind to replace Twentyman: the former Pools player Len Richley, George Hardwick, and Clough, on whose behalf the former Sunderland great Len Shackleton, by then a writer on the *Sunday People* and an influential figure in north-eastern football, was lobbying hard, perhaps recognising in Clough's sparky abrasiveness a kindred spirit.

That wasn't enough to convince the players, and four of them – the right-back Stan Storton, the wing-halves Barry Ashworth and Eric Harrison and the goalkeeper Ken Simpkins – asked to be put on the transfer list. A day later, Pools lost 2–1 to Barnsley and had their captain, Clough's former Sunderland team-mate Ambrose Fogarty, sent off – their third sending-off of the season.

Alvan Williams was approached about a return – he was, after all, the only manager in recent memory to have spared Pools the embarrassment of applying for re-election at the end of the season – but he rejected the offer and so Ord turned to Hardwick. He too turned him down, but recommended Clough. With both Shackleton and Hardwick backing him, Ord decided Clough was his man. Talks were scheduled for the following Monday, but had to be cancelled as the chairman was confined to bed. By

113

the time they did meet, on the Wednesday, things had got even worse as the reserve-team manager Bill Heselton quit, blaming 'the frustration brought on by trying to find eleven men for the reserves. Last week it was midnight on Friday before I had a full side fixed for the trip to Bradford City. And it was only with the help of Mr Bobby Waller, secretary of Seaton Holy Trinity, who allowed me to play two of his lads, that I eventually made up the team. The directors selected the first team last week, and now they have my deepest sympathy when choosing the reserves.'

Hartlepools were falling apart, literally and metaphorically. 'It wasn't a tip,' Clough said. 'To call Hartlepools a tip would make a tip ashamed to be called a tip.' When Ord approached him on the night of his testimonial, despite seemingly taking an instant dislike to him, Clough seized the opportunity. As he put it in *Walking on Water*, he 'needed a job, needed the money and needed a future'. The playing part of his career was over, and the managerial chapter had begun.

Clough accepted the job that night, and even spoke about it at the dinner that followed his testimonial. 'Hartlepools won't be at the bottom of the Fourth Division for very much longer,' he said. 'They have the players to climb up. If you want to see some good stuff from Saturday onwards, get yourself down to a little place called Hartlepools. It won't be a little place for very long.'

What is remarkable is how much that sounds like the older Clough; in fact, with those words, Clough already sounds less like himself than like somebody impersonating him. There is the swagger, the braggadocio, the insistence that now that he's in charge success is inevitable. And there too is the familiar trope – 'a little place called Hartlepools' – emphasising the remoteness and the lack of stature of the club by suggesting his audience may not have heard of it, as though it were some village in an obscure corner of Africa rather than a major port twenty-odd miles down the coast.

Twentyman's departure had made front-page news in the *Hartlepool Mail*; Clough's appointment did not, but then that was a day on which Ian Smith met with Harold Wilson to discuss the mounting crisis in Rhodesia and Ian Brady and Myra Hindley appeared in court to face the first charges over the Moors murders. On the back page, Sentinel, the newspaper's football reporter, greeted Clough's appointment with no great enthusiasm, not particularly because he doubted Clough, but because he despaired of the team. It would, he wrote, be 'a formidable task' to drag Pools out of the bottom four.

Asked about his aims, Clough found the Clough-tone immediately: awkward, mocking, bullish, asserting his own superiority over the questioner, but giving him copy good enough that he'd have no hesitation in coming back for more. 'I am aiming to win on Saturday, and win the following Saturday,' he said. 'Then you can come back and ask me the same question, and you will get the same answer.' He insisted his youth and inexperience were irrelevant. 'Age doesn't count,' he said. 'It's what you know about football that matters. I know I'm better than the 500 or so managers who have been sacked since the War. If they had known anything about football, they wouldn't have lost their jobs.'

The same day, the centre-half Alan Fox was sold to Bradford City, the one team in the league with a worse record than Hartlepools and Clough's first opponents. Fox aside, though, Clough insisted, 'There will be a place here for everyone who works hard. I want 100 per cent effort all the time, because football is just like life and hard work brings results.' That wasn't strictly true, and he soon set about reshaping the side, but there were other battles to be fought first, most notably over bringing in an assistant. In that first interview, he referred to Peter Taylor only obliquely, saying merely that he had somebody in mind to replace Peter Gordon.

First, though, there was the game at Valley Parade to be dealt with, a game that, had they lost 3–0, would have put them bottom. Clough brought in Simpkins in goal for John Small and at inside-left recalled his former Sunderland team-mate Willie McPheat, who had been dropped just four games after moving from Roker Park. Pools began on the defensive, but after twenty-one minutes the left-winger Jimmy Mulvaney was tripped in a promising position. He took the free-kick himself and Cliff Wright fired in Hartlepools's second away goal of the season. Mulvaney doubled Pools's advantage from a narrow angle after an Ashworth shot had been parried and, although Roy Ellam pulled one back, Mulvaney sealed the win with six minutes remaining after fine work by Ernie Phythian on the edge of the box. 'Pools greet manager with a win,' roared the *Mail*'s headline. 'Energetic forwards the masters in the mud.'

In the hours after accepting the Hartlepools job, Clough had realised he needed an ally, somebody with an in-depth knowledge of the game, somebody with whom he got on, somebody to spark off. As Shackleton told him, there was only one choice: Taylor, who was already developing a reputation for his knowledge of the game and players at all levels. 'I knew I needed him,' Clough said. 'I knew we were right together.' Alan Brown once met Taylor on holiday in Jersey and was pumped by him for information. He was so impressed, both by his thirst for knowledge and by the penetrating nature of Taylor's questions, that he claimed to have known then that Taylor would become a major force.

George Hardwick wondered whether he and Clough could have formed a similar partnership, but Clough and Taylor were a potent blend, a duo who had differing but complementary attributes yet shared a similar outlook. As far as Clough was concerned, there was nothing complicated about their chemistry. 'It's simple,' he wrote in his second autobiography. 'We were mates, the best of mates, both as players and later in management together.'

Clough was a hoarder, Taylor a gambler, and at their best they got the balance between the two right. 'So much of it was off the cuff, instinctive, but we knew about things like tactics, having been in the game so long,' Taylor told Pat Murphy. 'Our temperaments were right for what we each had to do. It never bothered me that it was always Clough and Taylor, rather than the other way round. From day one, I accepted he'd be more famous than me and I accepted that, preferred it. My strength was buying and selecting the right material, then Brian's man-management would shape the player.'

Taylor had left Middlesbrough in 1961 and, after a season with Port Vale that brought just one further appearance, he joined Burton Albion in May 1962. That December, he was named as manager, and he went on to have considerable success, winning the Southern League Cup. By the time he left, Burton were top of the Southern League. He and Clough had little contact after leaving Middlesbrough, apart from a cricket match in 1962, when Taylor organised a number of his friends in football to face the Nottingham Inland Revenue Cricket Club, for whom he played. Clough was part of the footballers' team, alongside the likes of David Pleat, Ian Storey-Moore, Tony Hateley, Peter Grumett and Jeff Astle. 'Our captain told us to let the all-stars get a good score and then we'd chase it,' Clive Wood, one of the Inland Revenue side, told Wendy Dickinson, Taylor's daughter, in her biography of her father. 'This young chap came in to bat at five for the all-stars . . . Our captain deliberately drops a catch that would have had him out. This lad stops the play and says, "If we're going to fucking play this game then let's play it fucking properly."' Needless to say, that young chap was Clough.

A few months later, after Clough had suffered the injury, Taylor had found him some work scouting. It was not a great success. Clough recommended only one player, a winger from Darlington called Carl Taylor; Peter Taylor signed him, but he made little impression at Burton.

Clough rang Taylor, told him he'd been offered the Hartlepools job and said he'd take it if Taylor agreed to be his assistant (actually, he'd already given Ord a verbal acceptance). They agreed to meet to discuss the offer at the Chase Hotel in York. Taylor was shocked by Clough's appearance, and later suggested it was just as well the opportunity had come just in time. 'His face reflected a dreadful year,' Taylor said. 'If it had been any longer, he'd have gone to pot. He was a no-hoper: jobless, boozing heavily, and on his way out. He'd been having a really rough time. One minute the world was at his feet, the next his career was at a dead-end. It was an overweight and careworn Brian Clough I was looking at. He had a young family to support and Hartlepool was the only hope.'

Taylor was tempted – it might only have been Hartlepools, but this was still league football – but he had the relative security of a three-year contract. Moving north would mean a pay-cut from £34 to £24 a week, as well as missing out on the £7 a week he received for coaching at Burton Technical College, and the bonus he got from Burton of a shilling for every paying spectator once the attendance at home games passed 2,300 (money he set aside for gambling). Money would become a major issue between the two of them, but Clough solved the initial problem by giving Taylor £200. The issue then was getting Ord, who knew nothing of Clough's intentions, to agree to them, something they managed – although the chairman was never happy with the situation – by designating Taylor as the trainer, that is, as Peter Gordon's replacement, and having him sit in the dug-out during matches with a bucket and a sponge. Ord helped out by putting them both up in semi-detached houses he owned on the Fens Estate in West Hartlepool, and charging below the going rate, although Clough soon moved out, paying £2,300 for a semi of his own.

For Taylor, though, it wasn't really about money, and even with Clough's unofficial signing-on bonus, he was out of pocket within six months. 'You may ask why a manager of a successful non-league club joins a struggling League side as assistant manager,' Taylor told the *Hartlepool Mail* the day he arrived. 'The answer is that I want success, and I know that under Brian Clough we will achieve that success. We were close friends at Middlesbrough, and I quickly learned to respect him both as a man and a professional. I joined this club because of the man, and I know that together we can, and will, make something of the challenge here.'

Clough's impact was enough that television cameras made their first appearance at the Victoria Ground for Clough's first home game, against Crewe Alexandra. Graham Matthews hit the bar early on for Crewe, but McPheat headed down a Wright cross for Phythian to put Pools ahead after fifteen minutes, and an overhead kick from Wright, after Phythian had headed down a Mulvaney cross, doubled their advantage before half-time. Peter Kane made it 2–1, but Phythian capitalised on a Mulvaney cross to add a third and then seized on an underhit Peter Leigh backpass and chipped Crewe's goalkeeper Willie Mailey for Wright to head in a fourth. Hartlepools were up to sixth bottom.

'We knew within a couple of weeks that he was going to be great,' said the goalkeeper Ken Simpkins. 'He couldn't change much because we didn't have a lot of money, but the way he talked and thought about the game, you could tell. He knew exactly what he wanted to do and he brought a new discipline. Geoff Twentyman we all thought had been a bit quiet. There was one game I remember at Aldershot when we came in 3–0 down at half-time and he just said, "Lads, we're not good enough." We ended up telling him he had to bollock us. Cloughie would have been shouting at us before we'd got off the pitch.'

When Pools beat Workington 3–1 in the FA Cup, several fans couldn't contain themselves, with delirious pitch invasions following each goal. When appeals over the Tannoy failed to shift celebrating fans, the referee threatened to call off the game. Clough's response was typically forthright, foreshadowing the action he later took against pitch-invaders at Nottingham Forest. 'The first youngster I catch on the pitch will get a boot in the bottom from me,' he said. 'We want the support and enthusiasm of these youngsters, but we don't want them on the pitch. We want them to shout and cheer as much as they can, so long as they do it on the right side of the wall.'

Perhaps recognising the difficulties that would lie ahead with Ord, Clough sought to surround himself with familiar faces and tried to bring in Jimmy Gordon, his old coach from Middlesbrough with whom he hadn't always had the most cordial relationship. Gordon was by then working with Blackburn in the First Division and although Clough turned up at his door, his son Simon in a carry-cot in his hand, to beg him to join the team he was putting together, he decided – for then – to stay put.

Hartlepools, after all, was a long, long way from the First Division. The club was in a dreadful state, but Clough and Taylor, fired with the novelty of it all and the sense that this could be the beginning of something extraordinary, threw themselves into the job. Clough had a tiny office, the roof of which leaked. The boardroom floor was covered in buckets to catch the drips when it rained. Clough finagled some of Sheffield Wednesday's cast-off training gear from Alan Brown, but it still wasn't enough. 'The only time everybody came early,' Clough said, 'was on a Monday. The kit would be dumped on a table and those who got there first got socks, shirts and shorts. The last two in got no socks or ripped shirts.'

The club secretary, Frank Perryman, was an accountant who, when needed, had to be contacted at his company offices. There was a secretary who came in twice a week to go through the mail, but Barbara ended up doing most of the typing. The corner of one terrace was ankle-deep in feathers because a previous manager had kept his bantams there, while the rickety wooden stand was such a wreck the board wished it would collapse. Perryman, a genial sort who seems to have regarded the decrepitude with resigned amusement, used to joke about the time the stand caught light and the chief fire officer had to apologise for the enthusiastic recruit who got the wrong idea and put the fire out.

In the absence of proper facilities, training took place on the beach at Seaton Carew. Players remember training suddenly becoming interesting, as Clough and Taylor kept changing things and insisting on work with the ball rather than simply having them slog through fitness work. Wright claimed that for the first time he found training 'enjoyable', some achievement on Seaton Carew beach which was, Clough said, 'the coldest place on earth when the wind's blowing in off the sea. You had to keep running just to keep the circulation going, even if you were fat and lazy like the goalkeeper, Simpkins – he was the fattest goalkeeper I've ever seen – even he had to keep going; all the blubber he had round him couldn't keep out the cold.'

Clough, aware that even that could be turned to the club's advantage, invited press photographers to Seaton Carew, and in those early weeks the *Mail* carried regular photographs of the players on the sand. Even more aware of the advantage of a good goalkeeper, Clough signed Les Green from Burton that November, Taylor making the approach through Maurice Edwards, a postmaster who had been an amateur at Burton and refereed friendly and youth games at the club. Edwards went on to become a regular scout for Clough and Taylor, his initial brief being to recommend players he spotted while refereeing matches.

'If I was a top-class manager I would be prepared to spend as much on a polished goalkeeper as on a man like Denis Law,' Taylor said. 'After all, a keeper's mistake can mean the difference between victory and defeat. One error on his part could cost a side promotion or send them slithering to relegation. He must be fearless, possess natural anticipation, and be a safe handler of the ball. But most important of all, he must not be a "liner". He must come off his line and take up the correct position to cut off the danger. Whoever said his is the easiest position is making a grave error of judgement.'

Taylor had managed Green at Burton, and was sure he met the criteria. Green was a notoriously bad timekeeper, but he lived opposite the Taylors on the Fens Estate. On match-days, Taylor would give him a lift to the ground and there were times when he would send his son, Phil, to throw pebbles at his window to wake him up.

Inevitably, Clough's style of management was informed by his own disappointment, the awareness that football was a precarious career and his determination that no player in his team should not make the most of their ability. 'The ability to play football for a living ...' he said, 'is a gift that should be cherished and relished by those who have it.'

Other than that, he had three major managerial influences. There were the two managers he had played under: Bob Dennison, whose *laissez-faire* policy he wanted to avoid, and Alan Brown, whose toughness and probity he wanted to emulate, even if he was doubtful of the merits of some of his training methods. Brown was a regular visitor to the FA's academy at Lilleshall, an institution Clough instinctively distrusted, although that may have been as much for the sense it gave of being part of the establishment as for the ideas generated there. For someone who thought so much about the game, Clough was remarkably disdainful of theory, of 'Subbuteo men being pushed around a felt pitch', and Brown's belief in the merits of shadow-play was just the sort of sophistry Clough despised (even if he did at times accept its usefulness). He would later – particularly at Forest – have players run through patches of nettles, an inland equivalent, perhaps, of Brown's insistence on running through the North Sea, but at Hartlepools the most obvious signs of Brown's influence were his dictatorial attitude and his insistence on short hair.

The figure who most shaped Clough in his early days, in fact, was somebody for whom he had never played, Taylor's guru Harry Storer. They first met in slightly strange circumstances after Taylor, Clough and Derek Stonehouse had taken a lift with Billy Day, who'd borrowed his brother's car, to go and watch a Cup tie at Nottingham Forest. They went first to visit Taylor's brother Donald, who lived in Nottingham. 'He worked for the Co-op,' Day said, 'and he was in distribution, a big warehouse, and it was arranged that we'd get some food, boxes of salmon, John West salmon, and we'd fill the boot up with this – Peter's idea because he was always a con merchant. John West salmon was scarce at the time – an automatic good sale.' They didn't have tickets for the game, but Taylor met Storer before kick-off, and the Derby manager was able to use his local influence to find the four places in the press box. After the game, they returned to Middlesbrough with their feet resting on crates of salmon that Taylor then sold around the streets. 'I think I lived on it for about three months,' said Day.

'[Storer] was blunt . . . able to destroy almost anyone verbally,' Taylor wrote in *With Clough By Taylor*. 'He was ruthless and often frightening, yet always fair. His strength was an enormous ability to want. He wanted to win, he wanted the truth. He wanted his own way which, in itself, was unusual in an era when directors lorded it over most clubs.' On one occasion, as a director tried to meddle, Storer asked what his profession was. The director said he was a brewer, at which Storer started offering advice on how best to make beer. The director was midway through rebuking his impertinence when he got the point.

Clough, like Storer, became noted for the sharpness of his put-downs. Storer once told a trainee hairdresser to whom he'd given a trial that he should sell his boots and buy another pair of scissors. His expertise in reading body language, meanwhile, was something that inspired Taylor similarly to study not just what a player said or did, but how he did it. Storer, essentially, believed players couldn't be trusted, but had constantly to be manipulated and cajoled, scrutinised for any sign of weakness; that became Clough and Taylor's method.

At some stage in Taylor's first season at Middlesbrough – presumably after his failed attempt to sell Clough to Storer's Derby, although it is hard to be sure of the chronology – he arranged for mentor and protégé to meet at a British Rail hotel. Clough recalled feeling nervous, partly because of the surroundings, which were grander than he was used to, and partly because of Storer's reputation, particularly as polished by Taylor. He was struck, though, by the way Storer 'took the trouble to talk to me as if I was a grown-up', and even more so by his first words (the assumption seeming to have been, even then, that Clough would at some stage become a manager). 'Don't ever forget,' Storer said, 'football is a world in which nobody ever says thank you.' Especially not directors, with whom Storer found himself in regular dispute. It was a lesson that was quickly reinforced.

Storer also told Clough that a manager had to take responsibility for everything at the club, from top to bottom, and that he shouldn't take criticism to heart because it was inevitable. Accepting it was part of the job of the manager, and part of the wider notion of courage with which Storer was obsessed. Before leaving for an away game, he said, a manager should look around the team bus and see how many hearts were there; if there were fewer than five, he believed, it wasn't worth setting off.

He also told Clough the story of how, the day after a game, he'd taken a player by the arm, led him back to the side of the pitch and asked him to show him the hole.

'What hole?' the confused player asked.

'The one you were hiding in for every minute yesterday.'

Above all else, Storer believed, players had to have the moral courage to fail and then go back and try again. Late in his career when he was scouting for Everton, Storer filed a one-word report on a player: 'coward'. Moral courage became a virtue Clough and Taylor came to look for in every player they signed.

Clough learned from Storer the need to 'make the difficult decisions quickly', as he put it in his autobiography. 'You never know how long you will survive, so the first three months are vital ... You need to set the ground rules ... you must establish your territory.' That applied not just to players, but also to directors, and Clough soon ran into problems with Ord.

Ord was, Clough said, 'one of the most evil men I've ever met.' He was a millionaire draper who had made his fortune during the war. He was only five feet tall, and seems to have had all the complexes stereotype suggested he should, flexing his authority whenever possible. He would regularly ring down to Clough's office at 4.55pm, cutting the line if anybody answered, just to make sure he and Taylor hadn't snuck off early. 'He used to sack managers like he was having fish and chips,' Clough said. 'He'd sold his business and football was the only power he had left, so he made everybody's life a misery. You just stayed away from him; he was a nasty little man, it was as simple as that.'

Any journalist who dared criticise Ord's team or the way he ran it would be banned from the ground, a bizarrely self-defeating point of principle for a club so desperately in need of support. He would invite players to his office and subject them to lengthy interviews, secretly taping the conversations so they could be used against players at a later date. Les Green told Wendy Dickinson of an occasion when Ord had burst into his house one Saturday evening and demanded that he 'spill the beans' on Clough and Taylor. When he said he knew nothing about them, Ord shouted, 'You bloody do!' at which Green told him to get out of his house. Ord pointed out that he owned the house, but Green was adamant that as he'd paid the rent, he had rights as a tenant, at which Ord left. John Curry, who later became a board member, remembered going to a dinner-dance given by Ord at which he accosted one of his employees – a notably tall, physically robust man –

and insisted, to the employee's obvious embarrassment, that he tell his guests how much Ord paid him.

Clough himself, of course, was not above underlining his authority, even if at that stage he rarely did it in such an unpleasant way; conflict was inevitable. When Ord sold his drapery business, the club became his life which meant, as Clough saw it, he was always poking around and interfering. Unsurprisingly, Clough soon told him to mind his own business and, equally unsurprisingly, that only antagonised Ord. 'His size annoyed me,' Clough said. 'He was a tiny man who drove a Rolls-Royce and when it passed down the street it looked like a car without a driver.'

The delirium of three wins soon came to an end, as Pools lost 2–1 at home to Halifax. They then went to Chester, where Clough opted for a defensive system with only McPheat and Phythian up front. Clough insisted it was 'the side's best performance since I arrived', and had McPheat not missed two chances they might have got something from the game. As it was, Pools lost 2–0. 'The first thing I learned,' Clough said, 'was that those in the dressing-room had so little talent. Poor lads – I couldn't give them a hard time because they had a big enough problem with their inability to play.' His first decision was simple: replace the players with new ones.

Making the decision was one thing; acting upon it something else. 'It's easy to be a good manager – all you have to do is sign good players,' Storer used to say, knowing full well that raising funds and persuading other clubs to release talent was hideously tough. A month after Clough's arrival, the club announced its financial results from the previous season, which showed Pools had made a loss of £19,792. That was mitigated by donations of £7,094 from the Auxiliary Association, but it still left the club £41,357 in the red. A 2–0 FA Cup win over Wrexham at least offered hope of a lucrative third-round tie, but Pools' situation was parlous. On 9 December, Clough approached the Auxiliary Association to beg for more money to finance further transfers.

Clough fielded his defensive formation again at Lincoln two days later, and Pools were eight minutes from taking a point; a 2–1 defeat, though, left them second bottom, and the early gains of the Clough reign had been wiped out. Had those first three wins, letter writers to the *Mail* began to ask, simply been the familiar bounce enjoyed by a new manager?

The nineteen-year-old outside-right Tony Parry had been bought from

Burton – for whom Taylor had signed him after seeing him playing for the Norman Cochrane Youth Club at Stapenhill – and after a few weeks in the reserves he made his debut at home to Colchester. 'It was chances, chances all the way for Pools,' wrote Sentinel, 'and they should have had the game tied up before the interval – but none of the forwards was able to get the ball in the net. Then Colchester, who had played a defensive game, scored on a breakaway in the seventy-sixth minute, and took away two points Pools could ill-afford to lose.'

Three days before Christmas, Ord and his son offered their resignations again. Whatever Clough thought in private, in public he was supportive. 'If he has left,' Clough told the *Mail*, 'it will be a great pity because there is no doubt that he kept the club going. Football is in a sorry state financially and it is essential for every club to have a man like Mr Ord.' Maybe at that stage that was genuinely how he felt, and subsequent events coloured his early memories of Ord; maybe he was simply aware that however difficult things were financially with Ord, they would be far worse without him. Ord eventually agreed to stay on 4 January, but only after a bitter board meeting that lasted an hour and three quarters and ended with the resignation of six other directors.

The two Christmas derbies against Darlington both ended in creditable 1–1 draws, but there was still an apologetic tone about the column Clough wrote for the *Mail* on New Year's Day, in which he took stock of his first two and a bit months of management. 'As a player I often smiled quietly at the stock phrases used by managers as they sought excuses to hide a bad run, a bad result or sometimes a bad buy,' he wrote. 'You know those phrases as well as I do. Some have said that the ball has been running badly. Some have said that the breaks never came. And there's the evergreen "it wasn't our day".' He vowed he would never resort to such clichés. 'I shall always pursue the practical reasons behind them,' he said. 'It's the best way ... indeed, it's the only way in football.'

So what were the practical reasons behind Hartlepools' predicament? 'Those three unforgettable wins in a row, immediately after my appointment, brought many comments,' Clough wrote. 'But I well remember saying at the time I had no magic wand. ... I must tell you that everything in the garden is not rosy. There are players who want to leave and I won't stand

125

in their way when the opportunity arises. I will not retain players who are unhappy with the club. I will not tolerate players who don't want to play for Hartlepools United. I don't want those who want to play the game any other way but mine. I want men who never complain about hard work. My job in 1966 is to get the club out of trouble.'

That job didn't start well: that afternoon Pools lost 6–1 at Tranmere, playing, Sentinel said, 'like novices, without method or mobility, without a plan and without discipline'. Clough responded by signing the right-back Brian Grant from Nottingham Forest, and Pools at last won again, goals from Peter Thompson and Phythian giving them a 2–0 win over Port Vale. Sentinel watched the game from the terraces, having found his way to the press box barred by Ord, although whether for his comments on the defeat at Tranmere or his reporting of the bloodbath of a board meeting wasn't clear. A 2–2 draw at Barnsley helped Pools up to third bottom, but still facing an application for re-election and still with major problems.

A lack of ability was only part of it. 'We inherited a real collection of renegades,' Taylor told Francis. 'Hartlepools was a clearing-house for every cast-off in the Football League – drinkers, gamblers, womanisers and fighters.' He recalled having to separate Les Green and one of the established hard-cases as they scrapped under a stand after Green had taken the management's side in a dispute.

Clough and Taylor quickly tried to impose a sense of order. Cliff Wright had been an apprentice at Middlesbrough and had cleaned Clough's boots. Instinctively he referred to him as 'Brian' rather than as 'boss', and after being warned twice for doing so, he was fined two weeks' wages when he made the mistake a third time. 'Cloughie put a barrier straight there and he had that authoritative air about him,' Wright said, 'while Pete was calm and jovial.'

Not that Taylor was without his hard side. One of the drinkers was Simpkins, who had once been good enough to play in goal for Wales Under-23, but who had put on weight and was notable at Hartlepools primarily for having once scored in a 3–2 win over Port Vale while playing at centre-forward during an injury crisis. Clough described him as 'tubby, unmarried, staying in digs and living the life of a rake'. Taylor found the pub where he spent his evenings drinking pints of Cameron's, and told him that if he ever caught him there again, he'd kill him. 'There was a few of us liked a drink, as you did in them days,' said Simpkins, 'but they soon quietened that down.'

Clough and Taylor never formally divided the workload; it just happened that they excelled at different sides of it. Clough was the front man, dealing with the media; while Taylor remained in the background with his telephone and his contacts book. That, though, is to oversimplify the relationship; as many have pointed out, their roles were never discrete. Clough may have appeared the dominant partner, but it was Storer's principles, and thus those of Taylor – keep clean sheets, build from the back – that informed those early days. And Taylor was funny; everybody who talks about him recalls his wry comments, delivered out of the side of his mouth, and the way he could transform Clough in seconds from rage to helpless laughter. When Clough described their partnership as being like Morecambe and Wise, it was he who was the straight-man. 'Pete,' Clough said, 'was the only bloke who could stick an arm round my shoulder and tell me – straightforwardly, mate to mate – that I was wrong, or right, or to shut up and just get on with my job.'

The two got on remarkably well, to the point that it wasn't until they got to Forest that they thought to ask for separate offices. They'd pick the team together on the day before games, disagreeing only rarely and, as both told it, backing down without fuss if the other clearly held his opinion more strongly. 'Clough had a bit about him,' said the Hartlepools coach Tommy Johnson. 'He knew what he wanted and to him a spade was a spade. Taylor went about his job in a quiet way. He was more to do with signing players and getting everybody going.'

Even then, Taylor used to take charge of training, although the influence of Alan Brown was clear. The team would line up against no opposition, and would practise passing and moving on their way to goal – an example of the 'shadow play' that would become an accepted method, but back then was regarded with suspicion even by Clough.

The FA Cup draw paired Pools with Huddersfield, then a Second Division side. Pools battled hard and even took the lead through Thompson after an Ashworth corner had hit the bar. Johnny Quigley levelled but Pools held out until four minutes from time when the referee deemed, despite Pools' protestations, that a header from Tony Leighton had gone in off the underside of the bar. Quigley then added a late third.

Simpkins made a number of fine saves, but the following Thursday, without explanation, he was transfer-listed. The following week, Les Green returned for a 'ninety-minute pounding' in a 4–1 defeat at Southport, but when Pools then beat Wrexham 4–2 they climbed to fourth bottom, the second of four teams tied on nineteen points. After a defeat at Luton and the postponement of a game against Bradford Park Avenue because of snow, though, they were back down to the foot of the table.

Finally, there came some good news in the boardroom as John Curry, a local caterer, was appointed as a director. He was the leader of the Conservative group on West Hartlepool Borough Council and far from a natural ally for Clough, but he would become a key figure in the battle against Ord. The short-term significance of his arrival, though, was to release funds to sign the centre-half John Gill from Mansfield, a player Taylor described as being 'terrifyingly tough'. The £4,000 Clough and Taylor paid for him represented more than half of their total spending at Pools. Gill made his debut in a windswept 3–0 win over Aldershot. 'It was a victory without colour; workmanlike, adequate, and efficient rather than blessed with any inspiration,' Sentinel wrote, 'but no less valuable for that'.

The result evidently moved Ord to magnanimity, and he allowed Sentinel back in the press box for a 2–0 win over Luton that lifted Pools out of the bottom four. Back-to-back defeats to Newport, though, pushed them back down to second bottom. Clough made bids for his former Middlesbrough team-mates Edwin Holliday, who was still at Ayresome, and Billy Day, who had moved on to Cambridge, and when both were rejected he signed John Bates, a twenty-two-year-old winger from Consett. At around that time Clough and Taylor received a letter complaining at the influx of new signings and how the players who'd been at the club when they arrived were being squeezed out. It was written in green ink and signed 'Percy Vere', but Taylor had little doubt it had been composed by Ord.

Pools picked up a useful point with a goalless draw at Port Vale, but the day was overshadowed by Clough's decision to impose a fourteen-day suspension on Stan Storton, who had missed just five games in the twenty-two months since signing from Darlington. The full-back was bemused by the decision. 'When the team was announced yesterday I asked why I had been dropped,' he told the *Mail*. 'I said I did not think I had played badly and was by no means the worst player in the side. I was offered no explanation and a few minutes after we finished talking the manager told me I was suspended. I asked why, but again was given no explanation. I am going to ask the club to release me from my contract ... I feel that I have been made a scapegoat and have been treated very unfairly. I was happy here last year, but now I want to get away as quickly as possible.'

Two days later, Nigel Clough was born in Sunderland Royal Infirmary, but the new arrival did little to mellow his father, and two days after that, hours before an away game at Chesterfield, he suspended Les Green for a week. Simpkins was restored to the side and saved a penalty as Pools showed great 'spirit' and fight to win 3–1 with late goals from Phythian and Parry. 'If I haven't got team spirit here, I've got nothing at all,' Clough said, in the nearest he came to explaining the two suspensions. 'On Monday at Port Vale, it was spirit and spirit alone that brought us a point. The players grafted and ran and spared nothing for me ... Since I came I have built up the spirit in the dressing-room until I really believe that it is now better than it has been for a long time. I have given a fair deal to every one of the players here at the moment ... What I don't like is when anyone tries to destroy what I have built up. And if I think that I am being hindered, that I am being stopped from doing my job, then I will not be slow to act. I have said before that if the players I have got will not give me one hundred per cent effort, I will play eleven who will.'

Hartlepools taught Clough about the economics and the politics of football, showed him, if Storer hadn't already convinced him, that dictatorship was the only reasonable means of governance, and also allowed his genius for publicity to flourish. Len Ashurst may have claimed that the drawl and the abrasive persona developed during his period of rehabilitation, but it was at Hartlepools that he became a master of manipulating the media, drawing an unprecedented amount of attention to a small, provincial club whose only realistic objective was survival. He secured a public service vehicles licence so he could drive the team coach. He never actually did so, but it drew publicity, and publicity drew fans. His work for the club went far beyond PR tricks. He canvassed door to door encouraging locals to come to support their local team. He helped unload the trucks bringing metal sheets to re-roof the stand, recalling Alan Brown mucking in to help with the construction of Burnley's new training complex. 'The steel came on the back of a lorry,' Clough remembered. 'The bloke knocked on the door and said, "Your steel's here." So I said, "Well, it's not much good on the truck – get it off." And he said he couldn't get it off by himself. I said I was the manager, and he said I'd have to get somebody. But there wasn't anybody, so I ended up getting a pair of his gloves on and getting down these great long girders.'

Finances were so tight Taylor would go round the dressing-room after games collecting tie-ups so they could be re-used the following week. Where other clubs would eat in a restaurant on the way back from away games, Hartlepools stopped off at a chip shop in Wetherby. If they did stop at a restaurant, Ord would hover by the tables during pudding to make sure directors paid for their meals. The league demanded that each game be played with a new ball, but Clough and Taylor circumvented that, Clough keeping the referee talking while Taylor replaced the new ball he'd inspected with a repolished one that had been used several times before.

At the same time, though, Clough realised how damaging it could be if the players began to think of themselves as representing an impoverished, downtrodden club. He made sure they always stayed in decent hotels on away trips and hated it when the newspapers made a fuss of players eating fish and chips in the street. He was fiercely protective of his squad. When a hotel manager told him his players were banned from the lounge because they smelled of liniment, Clough snapped back that his players bathed at least once a day and unless he received assurances that the other guests were as fastidious, he'd be moving them to another hotel. 'If we were away the night before an away game, we'd always go to the cinema,' Simpkins remembered. 'And you had to go. You couldn't say you fancied staying in the hotel. He treat us like schoolkids in a way. We didn't have to walk in lines, but we might as well have.'

Clough's gift for man-management soon became apparent. After his experiences at Middlesbrough, and aware of how the arrival of a fleet of new transfers could unsettle things, he and Taylor were concerned by the possibility of cliques developing, and so drew lots before every away trip to determine who was rooming with whom. Knowing how they themselves had sat up late playing cards, they insisted on an 11 o'clock curfew, and prowled the corridors to enforce it. 'It was properly organised at last,' Wright told Dickinson. 'We did things we'd never done before as players, like going off golfing together as a team. Brian took us round the factories. It was to boost team spirit, but it was also to show us footballers that if we didn't shape up, this was where we would be.'

Unity was key, and when a series of well-informed pieces in the *People* led Clough to believe there was a mole in the squad, he set out to trap him. He suspected Eric Phythian. Before a Friday night game, Clough took him aside and told him to give his all because scouts from Southampton and Portsmouth – wholly invented – were there to watch him. Phythian played superbly and, sure enough, the story appeared under Shackleton's byline that Sunday. Presented with the evidence, Phythian admitted that he liked to gamble and that Shackleton had got him through some cash-flow problems by paying him for information. Clough couldn't be too hard on Phythian, though, because he had a vital role to play, and not just as a muscular target-man: he also played the guitar, so Clough had him bring it on the coach to away games. 'We had a sing-song on the way back,' he said, 'built up team spirit like that.'

Pools slipped back to fourth bottom with a 3–1 defeat at Crewe, but by the beginning of April, there was a clear optimism about Clough, and he began talking buoyantly of the coming season, of how gates could touch 10,000 if only he could sign a few more players. Despite facing a schedule of three games in four days over Easter, he suspended Storton again.

Those matches couldn't have gone better. Mulvaney converted a Phythian cross with fifteen minutes remaining to seal a 2–1 win over Stockport, and goals for Fogarty and Thompson gave them a 2–0 victory over Notts County. Then, at Stockport on Easter Monday, with seconds remaining and the score level at 1–1, Mulvaney, as Sentinel described it, 'swooped on a ball in the penalty area, drove it against Mulhern and ran the rebound home'. Three wins out of three, and the pressure was off. Four defeats from the next five games carried the issue into May, but back-to-back home wins against Lincoln and Barrow saw Pools safe.

On 21 May, the final day of the 1965–66 season, Clough handed a debut to John McGovern in a 1–1 draw against Bradford City. He was the first apprentice ever to play for Hartlepool and, at sixteen years and 205 days, he became the youngest player in the league. More significantly, it marked

131

the beginning for a player who was almost as prominent in Clough's success as Taylor.

Clough and Taylor had first become aware of McGovern one Sunday morning the previous November when they watched a trial match hastily arranged by the part-time physio and youth coach Tommy Johnson, himself a former Middlesbrough player. 'We got everybody we thought had a chance together at the ground,' Johnson remembered. 'Clough and Taylor just wandered round the perimeter of the pitch, and when it was over, Clough came over to me and said he thought there were one or two who had potential, but that one of them really stood out: John McGovern. He was only a junior at the time, and didn't have anything obvious like pace or a ferocious shot – in fact he had a slightly strange gait, a waddling way of running – but he understood the game and could pass with both feet. And, of course, he progressed.' Fifteen years later, McGovern was lifting his second European Cup.

Signing him, though, proved rather more difficult than spotting him. The former was Clough's domain, the latter Taylor's. There have been countless directors over the years who doubted Taylor's worth, but if he'd done nothing other than identify McGovern as a potential great, he'd have proved his value; and, as Clough later acknowledged, McGovern was very much a Taylor spot.

'When I was working for the *Mail*, I did round-ups of the smaller clubs,' Doug Weatherall recalled. 'I spoke to Brian and a bit had been said about John McGovern who'd just got into the team. He told me to go and meet him and Peter Taylor at the Grand Hotel in Hartlepool. I was having a pint of Strongarm and I said to Clough that I'd looked at McGovern and I couldn't see what he saw in him. He said, "That's why I'm a manager and you're a reporter." Years later, Derby had just had a good victory at Newcastle, and the journalists were waiting in the foyer as usual. Brian got me into the dressing-room, said he liked to see his friends after a good win. He started talking about Willie Ormond, who was Scotland manager at the time, and said he'd probably been there to see Archie Gemmill, but nobody would mention John McGovern. I told him the story of the Grand Hotel, which he'd forgotten. Brian was highly amused and called Peter over and made me tell him the story. Then he revealed that it was Peter who'd seen something in McGovern; at the time he'd agreed with me.'

McGovern was captain of his school rugby and cricket teams, and had only started playing football a year earlier. He was still a junior, so couldn't be signed on professional terms, which left him prey to other clubs. At the beginning of the next season, Hartlepools played Middlesbrough in a friendly. 'I said to Stan Anderson, who was manager of Middlesbrough, that we had a junior we'd like to bring on at half-time,' Tommy Johnson said. 'He said that was fine, because they had one as well. Turned out it was the same player: McGovern. We got him in the end, though.'

It was a protracted process. Joyce McGovern, John's mother, wanted him to stay on at Henry Smith Grammar School, do his A-levels and become a PE teacher, even though he had rather let his studies slide and passed just two O-levels. Clough visited her regularly, telling her that the money her son earned would be a useful top-up to her pension, but she remained unconvinced. In the end, two things persuaded her. First was the attitude of the headmaster at Henry Smith, who disliked football and told McGovern he would have to give up his Sunday League games if he wanted to do A-levels; and second was McGovern's grandmother, who fell for Clough's charm and seemed delighted that someone so famous was happy to sit and drink tea with her. As a compromise, McGovern studied two mornings and two evenings a week at West Hartlepool Further Education College, but Joyce McGovern ended up losing out with her pension, as it fell from £4.10s to £2.10s because her son was in work. Clough promised to make up the difference, but the board vetoed his plan.

McGovern's father, a former paratrooper, had been killed in a road accident while working on the Volta Dam in Ghana when McGovern was eleven, and Clough became an odd kind of substitute. 'It was unnerving for a sixteen year old,' McGovern said, 'but when the fear subsided, I worshipped everything he did and said. As a young lad without a father, I was glad of someone to look up to and take orders from.'

Those orders weren't slow in coming. 'Sometimes he would say something to you in the manner of a parent talking to a small child,' McGovern said. On his first day, he recalled, he was told to stand up straight and have his hair cut. McGovern was in a band at the time, and deliberately styled himself on Mick Jagger but, reluctantly, he complied. Clough came to trust him so much that he ended up signing him a further three times; none of those negotiations was anything like as fraught as the first.

133

*

Pools finished seventh bottom, three points clear of an application for re-election 'I'm not joking when I say that if I live to be ninety and stay in football management for another forty years I will never experience a period so difficult and so worrying as the season which finished this week,' Clough wrote in an end-of-season column in the *Mail*. 'It was as bad as that. I came to Hartlepools United as a novice to the managerial side of the game, knowing a little, prepared to listen and learn a lot more. I knew there would be problems, but never dreamed they would be as constant and as complex as those that have arisen in the last nine months. Right away I am prepared to admit that I have not achieved what I hoped and what I said I would when I first came.

'The biggest obstacle was the lack of cash. The cupboard was almost bare, and with the players available it was impossible for the team to do any better than before I arrived. They were then second from bottom and that was NOT a false position.' Storton, Ashworth and Eric Harrison were all on the transfer list when Clough took the job, and told him his appointment didn't alter their desire to leave, but there were no buyers. 'This meant there was a deadlock, which was only broken by finding a couple of thousand pounds . . . to spend on three defenders [by which he meant three players whose job was to stop the opposition from scoring] – Les Green, Brian Grant and John Gill. In the final analysis these players, and the success of Brian Drysdale, stiffened the side just enough to ward off trouble . . . There were other difficulties, too, like getting the players to do what I wanted on the field. Only in the past few weeks have they started to play the plan as I really wanted them to.

'Off the field there was also trouble. I am not a manager who demands a detailed account of his players' behaviour every minute of the day and night. They can do what they like so long as they give what I ask for ninety minutes on Saturday afternoon. But I was forced to take measures merely to enforce a standard of discipline which is NORMAL at all clubs, and ended up suspending two players [Storton and Green] and fining another [the midfielder Bobby Brass].'

Clough concluded by acknowledging Taylor's input, a tribute that was certainly heart-felt, but which may also have been a warning to Ord that his trainer was an essential part of the club. 'No manager,' he wrote, 'can achieve success on his own – a glance at any of the top clubs is enough to prove this: Matt Busby, Bill Shankly, Don Revie, Alan Brown all have top-class "deputies" to share the load, and it is just as true at a small club like Hartlepools. Peter has been a great help – and, given the chance, we are both looking forward to a much happier time both for the club and our supporters, next season.'

Clough seems to have done his best to ignore the World Cup that summer, all too aware, presumably, that had it not been for the injury, he might, after two seasons in the First Division, have been in the England squad. He would become a stern critic of Alf Ramsey's supposed negativity, but as England won the World Cup, he didn't offer a single opinion on the subject to the *Hartlepool Mail*, instead focusing on reconstructing his squad. McPheat, Ashworth, Harrison, Bradley, Storton, Brass, Hamilton and Robertson were all discarded, while Clough signed Joe Livingstone, who had emerged at Middlesbrough just as he left, from Carlisle. In early July, he picked up four more players in one night at a pub in Nottinghamshire: the former Forest inside-forward Terry Bell, the Notts County duo of Tony Bircumshaw and John Sheridan and the Torquay outside-left Mick Somers.

The same month, West Hartlepool Council, who had bought the ground from the club in 1961, agreed to install floodlighting – leaving Chesterfield as the only league club without lights – but sought an increase on the £1,000-a-year rent they were charging. As Pools's accounts showed, they were in no position to pay, having made a loss of £13,428 for the previous season, leaving a deficit of £54,785.

For all the problems, though, Clough was bullish, and insisted Pools would finish in the top half of the table. The fans, who had quickly warmed to his forthrightness, tended to believe him. As a teenager, Alan Gillies would go to every Hartlepools home game. 'I used to wait for autographs,' he said. 'Taylor would always come out first with his family and hang around and chat to people. Clough would swagger out later, really arrogant, like a marching soldier, and he'd go through everybody, ignoring them. One day – I must have been fifteen – I decided I'd make sure I got his autograph. I went up to him, and said, "Can I have your autograph, please, Mr Clough?" But he just kept walking. So I followed him. He went through the ramshackle old gate, and turned left up the road towards his car. All the way I was rushing along trying to keep up, saying "Can I have your autograph please, Mr Clough?" And all the way he was ignoring me. Then he got to his car, got his keys out, grabbed my book and signed it, got in his car and drove off without saying anything. I think he was teaching me a lesson, that persistence matters.'

The anecdote is revealing for two reasons. It shows that, at that stage in his career, the influence of Alan Brown remained strong, and that Clough had not slipped into the wilful scruffiness – old tracksuits and jumpers – that would become increasingly characteristic through the seventies and eighties. But it also highlights Clough's messianic quality; no matter what he did, it was always assumed he was doing it for a reason, as though he existed on some higher plane and was constantly manipulating mortals, stimulating them to greater heights or dispensing nuggets of wisdom. Was Clough really trying to teach Gillies the value of determination, or was he just rushing to his car until eventually he got sick of the boy following him? Alan Peacock told a story of walking by the school next to Ayresome Park at break-time one day with Clough and another Middlesbrough team-mate. One of the pupils ran to the gate and asked for autographs; Peacock and the other player – he couldn't remember if it were Day or Holliday – signed, but Clough 'slapped him on the head and said, "You should be in bloody school or you'll end up like these two buggers."' Clough always liked to emphasise who was in charge.

'I got on really well with Cloughie and enjoyed playing under him,' said Somers. 'But if you stepped out of line you'd be in trouble. Even as a young man of 33 or 34, he was a disciplinarian. I lived in digs with four other players, and one of them was a lad who didn't always toe the line and used to like a drink. But Cloughie knew everything that went on, and he came up with a great way of stopping this lad from going out the night before matches. He'd come round to our house and go, "Come with me, young man" and he'd get him to spend the night babysitting for his children.' That 'lad' was presumably Tony Parry.

Optimism was an unusual feeling in Hartlepool, and it came as no great surprise when Pools started slowly with two draws. In the first of them, away at Aldershot, the goalkeeper Les Green played on despite breaking both thumb and collar-bone in the first half, a sign of the level of commitment Clough and Taylor had generated. What followed, though, was bizarre, an indication of how irrational and bloody-minded Clough could be. Back at Hartlepool, Green was strapped up at the hospital, but when Clough saw him in a sling, he drove him back there and insisted all the bandages be removed and forced Green to squeeze a sponge ball with his broken thumb.

That sense of denial around injuries was a recurring trait. During a training session at Derby a few years later, Barry Butlin fractured a cheekbone in a clash of heads. As he lay on the ground, Clough screamed at him to get up, insisting there was nothing wrong with him. Even after he'd been taken to hospital, Clough refused to believe there was anything the matter. When Butlin's wife turned up looking for her husband and mentioned an 'accident' to Clough he snapped, 'I'll tell you when there's been an accident.'

Ignoring all medical opinion, Clough made Green train, accused him of malingering and then, after doctors had confirmed he had to rest for two months, refused to speak to him, and broke with convention by denying Green his £10 a week first-team bonus. They had already fallen out when Clough ignored Green's pleas that his bus hadn't turned up and fined him for being late for training one morning, despite the fact that the only reason Green was taking the bus was that Clough had borrowed his car. It was after the injury, though, that a real coldness entered their relationship.

Pools beat Wrexham 2–1 before a 2–1 home defeat to Bradford Park Avenue, for whom Kevin Hector scored the winner. Clough, with a perversity that would become typical, insisted it was Pools's best performance since he had taken charge. Perhaps he meant it, or perhaps he was seeking merely to salve bruised morale; perhaps he was simply being deliberately contrary.

If it was intended to lift spirits, though, the comment failed, as Pools went down 2–0 at Southend. It was a sign of the changes Clough had wrought that only three of his starting eleven had played under the Southend manager Alvan Williams, who had left Hartlepools eighteen months earlier. 'Hartlepool to Southend is a hell of a long way,' Clough said in an interview in 2000. 'Now their ground's adjacent to a market square so we had to play on a Friday night. We went to Southend, lost and had to come all the way back. About half three in the morning the heaters broke down on the coach, because we had the cheapest coach. We came back to the ground, got back at about half past five, and we all had coats and gloves on. It was freezing.'

It's a telling image of the club's poverty, but there is, as so often with Clough anecdotes, a caveat, which is that that game took place on 2 September, and so it seems implausible it could have been as cold as he insisted it was. Perhaps he mixed it up with another away trip; perhaps it was just more exaggeration.

A home victory over a previously unbeaten Barrow side raised hopes, although Sentinel admitted it had been 'a lucky win'. 'I want the supporters to bear with us,' Clough said. 'I know the team is not perfect, but everyone knows the position – we just haven't got any money and that's that. We are hoping to buy another player, but this would be difficult at the moment. Therefore, we just have to make do with what we've got and stop grumbling, and that is why I want the supporters to support us and not be too critical.'

But three defeats in a row to Tranmere, Bradford City and Newport suggested this could be yet another season of struggle and with the early season optimism fast dissipating, directors held an emergency meeting with the Auxiliary Association on 21 September to discuss ways of raising money to sign more players. Given that Pools had only managed to pay Burton for Parry by playing a friendly against them and allowing them to keep all the gate receipts, seeking further expenditure was risky, perhaps reckless.

It was the return of a player already on Pools's books, though, that turned the season around: Jimmy Mulvaney. Recalled at inside-left for the visit of Exeter, he teed up Phythian for the first and then scored the third himself in a 3–1 win. Away to Barrow, Clough fielded Mulvaney as a lone forward, with Phythian retreating to left-half and Fogarty sweeping. By half-time, Pools were 2–0 down, at which Clough returned to a more orthodox formation. Seventeen minutes into the second half, Mulvaney met a Phythian cross with a diving header to make it 2–1. Somers soon cut a cross back for Phythian to level, and the big striker then added a third – Pools's third goal in seven minutes – finishing deliberately after Somers had picked him out with a free-kick.

Defeat at home to Crewe set Pools back, but when a Mulvaney equaliser capped a second-half fightback against a York side that was unbeaten at home, there was a definite sense of a club on the up. 'Underneath the surface hope probably lies a little thicker than usual, and ambition is certainly stronger,' Sentinel wrote. 'Critics say the side needs strengthening, which is true, and they add that there is little money to spend, so how can there be an improvement? ... The side is actually playing better than at any time last year ... They have been playing with more purpose away, and probably with a good deal less luck at home where some appalling finishing has cost them valuable points.'

Pools confirmed Sentinel's impression by thrashing Lincoln 5–0 at home, and when they then produced 'a technically faultless show with a goal in each half' to win 2–0 at Newport, the *Mail* headlined their report, 'Look out, top four'. They lost 1–0 at Chesterfield, but then beat Stockport, the league-leaders, as Phythian turned in a Mulvaney cross eight minutes from time.

On the field, things were going exceptionally well; off it, though, it was a rather different matter, as Ord was at pains to point out. 'We have no money, the cupboard is bare,' he said in an interview in the *Mail* on 5 November. 'We can't afford to buy unless we get some money from some-where, unless a fairy godmother appears. We have wasted a lot of money in the past and we are not going to do it again. Anyhow, we were forced to part with money then because we were in trouble. Now we are doing well, so why should we spend cash we haven't got ... We are really going for promotion this season. I would love to see the side go up, and I know we could hold our own in the Third Division. We can do this with the players we have on the staff now. In fact we would have been top of the league today but for some bad luck at home early in the season which cost us four points.

'The spirit is better than I have ever seen it ... All the players are really going for the manager – he's the one who should take the credit. He can put it over to the players in the dressing-room better than any manager I have ever seen, and I've seen a few. I'm sorry to say it, but he won't be staying with Hartlepools United. He's bound to finish up with a big club one day. The players have a lot of respect for him and that is why they are giving everything they have on the pitch. But it is not all one-way traffic, because the players get little extras in return. Once a week we spend a day on the golf course – it's an idea that's gone down really well and I think the players really appreciate it.'

At Rochdale that day, Pools were 3–0 down inside twenty minutes and, although they recovered to lose only 3–2, things were fairly evidently amiss in the boardroom. The following Thursday, a late-night board meeting was convened to discuss a bid from Southend for Phythian, but it ended with Ord resigning. Pools came from behind to draw against Southend, by then the league-leaders, at the weekend, but the game had been overshadowed by the appearance of Ord demanding the gate money as repayment for money he had put into the club. 'Including guarantees,' he said, 'the club owes me between £13,000 and £14,000 and I want it back. I am not fussy about returning to the board. I just want my money. It's as simple as that.' The *Mail* calculated that figure as being made up of £7,000 in cash and £6,000 in guarantees to the bank.

'I got the club out of trouble last week when it was threatened by a court order,' Ord went on. 'I settled the matter and then called the emergency board meeting on Thursday where I was criticised for not having the club's accountant present when a settlement was reached over the order. I was so sick that I walked out and said I wasn't coming back. I was prepared to go quietly and leave it at that, but the attitude of some of the directors has forced me to ask for my money and if necessary I will issue a writ. I haven't thought about the future yet. I don't know what I will do if Hartlepools United are forced out of existence because of my demands for the money. But I have the good of the club at heart. I want to see Hartlepools United flourish, not die.'

Ord had eventually been persuaded to accept a cheque for £1,100 to cover the cheque he had signed the previous Thursday to pay the wages of the players and staff, and he even said he would be happy to return to the club, but only on his own terms, by which he meant he and his son David would be the only directors. 'I want to emphasise,' he said, 'that I have no quarrel at all with the manager Brian Clough. He has done a wonderful job.' That wasn't how Clough saw it, and in his version of events, which was broadly corroborated by John Curry, Ord used that final board meeting to try to have him sacked.

Quite what precipitated the confrontation is hard to say, but for some reason Ord seems to have decided he had to rein in what he saw as his manager's excesses, including his use of Taylor as an assistant. In hindsight, of course, it looks a ludicrous moment of caprice – even if it did foreshadow what followed at Derby (but again, did events repeat themselves, or did Clough, in the telling of the tale, project later events onto earlier ones?) – but how could Ord have known that in five years the pairing he was binning would have won a most unlikely league championship with Derby, never mind what they would go on to do with Forest? History is written by the victors, and Ord, in this instance, was a very definite loser.

Tommy Johnson said he was 'all right', and Billy Day, Clough's former Middlesbrough team-mate, recalled him as a friendly punter at the betting-shop he later managed, forever bringing in cream-cakes for the staff, but most others seem to remember Ord as a mean-spirited bully, and the fact that after being forced out of the club he evicted Green from his home on the Fens Estate tends to support that view. Even so, it's easy to imagine him looking at the league table, seeing Hartlepools in mid-table in Division Four and, while acknowledging that was a significant improvement on what had gone before, wondering why he was paying for two managers when every other club seemed to get by with just one – and, quite possibly, wondering whether even one was worth the aggravation if he was as obstreperous as Clough. In that light, his earlier claim that Clough was destined for greater things might have been less a compliment than an attempt to persuade a bigger club to come in and take Clough off his hands.

As Taylor had stood by Clough during the round-robin debacle at Middlesbrough, so Clough stood by Taylor as Ord tried to oust him. When Ord decided his son was taking over responsibility for publicity, Clough told him to 'piss off'. Ord then announced that Clough and Taylor had been sacked, but they found in John Curry a willing ally. As he led a counter-attack, the board refused to ratify Ord's decision and he was forced to resign, with Curry being appointed chairman in his place.

The board met again on Tuesday, 15 November and Ernest Ord's res-ignation was accepted, with Curry replacing him as chairman, although Ord's son David remained on the board. Taylor saw victory in the battle with Ord as a key step. 'If ever we were destined for greatness,' he said, 'that was the moment. Beating Ord was equal to winning the European Cup. If we'd lost, we'd have gone our separate ways, but once we'd survived, I knew we could take any job, face any challenge.' A couple of days later, though, Ord turned up unannounced at Taylor's door. 'I've come to give you a warning,' he said. 'Your mate has finished me and one day he'll do the same to you.' At that he turned, walked down the path and drove off in his Rolls-Royce.

Besides which, there was the issue of the money Ord was owed. He demanded it back within seven days, which threatened the very existence of the club. Curry pointed out that the last official contact with the board had been at the emergency general meeting at which Ord had resigned, and there Ord had said he would not demand money back straightaway. 'It is true I did say at the emergency meeting that I would not press for the money, but the directors have so antagonised me since then by the rudeness with which I was received when I went to the ground last Saturday that I want my money back now . . .' Ord said. 'It's a weight off my mind to be finished with the club. If I do go back I will pay through the turnstiles. I don't want there to be any unpleasantness, because there has been enough already. I want to go out with a little dignity.'

As the club launched a public appeal for funds, Clough offered to give up his £2,000 a year salary and work for free until the crisis had passed. Although there were various insistences that he hadn't meant the gesture to be made public, that might have been a political move to raise awareness of the club's plight – for he never actually did work for free – but he also anonymously donated £1,000 from his testimonial fund.

The initial response was good. The West Hartlepool Schools Association presented a cheque for £20 collected by schoolboys. The RAF club arranged a dance and also donated a football to the club. Cerebos Food Ltd raised £12 with a collection from their workforce. A fishmonger Clough visited handed over £5.

Curry admitted it would need gates to rise to over 7,000 for the club to break even on matchdays, and outlined three reasons why the club needed cash: to reduce an overdraft that was costing £2,240 a year in interest; to settle outstanding accounts; and to strengthen the playing staff. 'The present situation has arisen because in the past large sums have been borrowed in an endeavour to improve the playing strength,' he explained. 'Unfortunately, this has merely hastened the financial crisis without achieving the success needed to improve the attendance and so recoup the expenditure. This decline has now been halted and there is now a marked improvement in both playing performance and attendances. Unfortunately the gradual improvement in attendances takes time to reflect in the finances, hence the concern over the present position.'

The donations kept arriving. Ron Trotter, a butcher and the president of the Hartlepools Chamber of Trade, bought a season ticket for five years, admitting he wouldn't use it because he worked on Saturdays and preferred golf anyway. A pensioner, John Clark, handed over 10 shillings.

Clough became the embodiment of the movement, and that weekend, the *Mail* offered a paean – of sorts – to him. 'When you first meet Brian Clough,' Sentinel wrote, 'you don't like him. When you have known him a week you can't help liking him. When you have known him a year you can't think why you did not like him in the first place . . . Clough is ruthless and ambitious; he has an iron will to win, a determination to succeed that he puts before everything else. That is precisely why Hartlepools United, with a team that cost next to nothing, and a reputation worth the same, are in the top half of the League with a chance of promotion. But his character is not as simple and straightforward as this. For with the tough exterior goes a sense of honesty and a complete frankness – and, as someone close to him described it "a heart of gold". His gesture this week in sacrificing his wages for the sake of Hartlepools United – a sincere offer and not an eye-catching publicity stunt that was only made public by the insistence of others – is proof enough of this. But there are other, smaller, revealing chinks: last season he suspended a player, then in the next breath lent him his car to go home.'

Taylor offered further testimony. 'People said I must have been mad, stupid, to throw up success and security to come here,' he said. 'But I will tell you why I came. Because of the man's complete integrity . . . They [the squad] are the best bunch of lads in the game. There's not many step out of line, but when they do he comes down hard on them and quickly. Then it's forgotten. That's how he is – no grudges, no malice, everything is brought out into the open. On top of that he's a soft touch. I've known him for ten years, and I've seen him listen to more sob stories and dip into his pocket more times than I can remember.'

Pools drew 0–0 at Notts County, and when they stopped off at a restaurant near Doncaster on the way back, the manager refused payment. As donations reached £3,000, the brewers JW Cameron and Co. promised £1,000 to sponsor a player's wages for a year. An FA Cup run would have helped, but that was ended by a 5–2 defeat at Shrewsbury. In the league, though, Pools's form, as though galvanised by the off-pitch battle, got better and better, and three wins in a row took them up to sixth after their best start for nine years.

Clough trawled the town, talking to any organisation he thought might be able to offer cash. The Rift House Club, for instance, handed over £120 to pay for a new roof on the Rink End stand. 'I simply went in, talked to the committee for fifteen minutes, they discussed what I had said and within ten minutes offered us £120,' Clough explained. 'I have been to several clubs already and I mean to go round to everyone and talk. It will take some time, but I am sure that if they will listen to me for a few minutes and let me outline just what we are doing here, they will be ready to help.'

He was a respected figure already, but his efforts took his popularity to new levels. 'In pubs, clubs, at dinners, at meetings, Clough has been speaking practically every day since the appeal fund was launched,' Sentinel wrote. 'He's never stopped. On top of this he has travelled miles arranging, organising, begging, pleading. And in his spare time he has managed the team as well.' At the end of the year, the *Mail* named Clough as Hartlepool's sportsman of the year alongside the British lightweight boxing champion Maurice Cullen.

Barbara Clough admitted her husband's efforts were taking a toll. 'He more often than not disappears in the morning and gets back just in time to take in the epilogue on TV,' she said. 'In the last five days he reckons he has seen his two small children for a total of an hour, and ruined an average of a meal a day for a month.'

Recognising the PR battle was lost, Ord, sniffily noting that 'it is obvious that the appeal to save the club is not meeting with the response which was originally expected', decided not to press for immediate payment, but the club's improved circumstances were made clear when Clough had a £3,000 bid for the Hull left-half Norman Corner turned down. He then picked up the centre-half Stan Aston from Burton, and three points from the back-to-back Christmas games against Brentford lifted Pools to fourth. 'It's the best we've played this season,' Clough said after a 2–1 win at Griffin Park. 'I've never seen eleven players give so much as they did in the second half. It was marvellous, but I didn't think it was going to last and I was convinced they would crack. We could have won by a lot more. We spent

75 per cent of the game on the attack and they didn't have one shot at goal. We went for a point, but we had so much of the ball that we couldn't help attacking.'

Momentum was lost, though, at the turn of the year as a 4–1 defeat at Wrexham was followed by a 2–1 home defeat by Southend in the first game played under the new floodlights and then by a 2–0 defeat at Tranmere. But after a 1–0 win over Bradford City, 7,988 turned up to see Pools beat Chester 3–2 in a Monday night game under floodlights, which seemed to confirm the wisdom of installing them.

With Sentinel protesting that the 'home side must surely have mortgaged their entire stock of luck for the season', Pools then lost 1–0 at Exeter. Taylor was so outraged that he was reported by the referee for dissent and warned by the FA, although it may be that he was prickly after one of what were still his rare rows with Clough. Don Taylor, Peter's brother, who was living in Plymouth, remembered driving to meet them in Taunton, where they were staying before the game. Having gone to bed early, he was woken at 11pm by Taylor looking for support in his demands for a £2 a week raise as Clough insisted the club couldn't afford it and that the board would never agree to it. The argument dragged on for four hours without ever reaching resolution.

Money was always the issue. Clough was notorious for his financial caution, certainly when compared to Taylor. Clough enjoyed the experience of racing, but was reluctant to bet. The jockey Sandy Gilroy became a friend of Clough's after being introduced to him at Catterick races. They would meet in the Bridge Hotel before racing began, have a couple of drinks, and then Gilroy would help smuggle him into the jockeys' section of the grandstand so he could avoid the worst of the crowds. 'I remember once telling him about a sure thing and saying "stick a tenner on it",' he said. 'So off he trots, and it won, but when he comes back he'd only put £2 on it. But that was Cloughie: cautious with his money. It wasn't just money either. He smoked Player's and I smoked Woodbines and he would always be cadging them off me. So I asked him if he liked them so much why he never bought a packet himself, and he said he couldn't let people think he smoked Woodbines. He was always getting cigarettes off people, never getting his own out. We'd take the mickey out of him about that. But he was good company, and after the racing was finished we'd go back to the

145

Bridge and get stuck into the drink and a few games of three-card brag. Jockeys and footballers loved a drink and a gamble in those days; some games they'd be playing for hundreds of pounds. Not Cloughie, of course. It was just the drink and a few pennies with him.'

Taylor often told the story of how he took Clough to Redcar races one August bank holiday. After much encouragement, Clough was eventually persuaded to venture 10 shillings on a 7–2 shot. When it won, he put his winnings in his pocket and refused to bet again.

Pools ended Crewe's five-month unbeaten home record and drew at home to Barnsley. When Clough signed Albert Broadbent for £3,000 from Bradford Park Avenue, he said he would bank on promotion if he could also bring in Corner from Hull. Football fans, though, are never entirely happy, and that Saturday the *Mail*'s sports edition printed a letter from W. Richardson of Middleton Road. He acknowledged Clough as Pools's 'best manager since Fred Westgarth' – having taken Pools to the fourth round of the FA Cup and then died after being taken ill during a third-round FA Cup defeat to Manchester United in 1957, Westgarth remained a cult figure – but 'as a team selector I've got my doubts as to his ability. . . . Bell gets the top-match rating in a Sunday national newspaper. Bell scores a wonderful goal. Bell is described in Monday's newspaper as a great football player. Who gets the boot the next match? Why, of course, Bell.' Richardson wanted Wright dropped for 'slowing down the play'. As the significant roles played in his later teams by Alan Hinton and John Robertson showed, though, Clough was far more concerned by a winger's technical than his physical attributes.

Clough, of course, cared nothing for the opinions of far more highly regarded experts than Mr Richardson, but his selection was vindicated anyway as Wright scored one and made one in a 4–2 win over York. They lost at Lincoln, but victories over Barnsley and Chesterfield had Pools up to sixth by mid-March. They beat Luton and lost unluckily at Chester, but subsequent wins over Luton and Rochdale took Pools to within a point of the promotion places.

Behind the scenes, there were further problems. Clough had been switching between Green and Simpkins all season, with the disappointed player usually responding by demanding a transfer. By the end of March, Clough was so irritated by Simpkins's lack of fitness that he put him on a special diet and told him he'd be fined if his weight exceeded fifteen stones. Almost as soon as he'd done that, though, he cancelled Green's contract. 'This is an internal matter between the club and the player, but it would be true to say that this action has been taken because of disciplinary reasons,' Clough said. 'All that I am prepared to say is that I demand certain standards of behaviour and discipline on and off the pitch . . . I have not arrived at this decision easily. Green is without doubt the best goalkeeper in the Fourth Division and we can ill afford to lose him.'

What the issue was remains a mystery. 'Nobody knew,' said Simpkins. 'It was a personal thing between the two of them. Green was Peter's man. He'd brought him from Burton Albion and I think Cloughie always thought he was a bit short.'

Pools promptly lost four of their next six games, and finished the season eighth. That felt like a disappointment, but it was their best finish since 1957, when the team that Westgarth had created came second in the Third Division North. On 1 May, Pools completed an aggregate win over Gateshead in the final of the Durham Senior Cup, and Clough had his first trophy as a manager. 'It's been hard here and at times I've been on the point of packing it all in, things have been so difficult,' he said, but the job he had done was recognised beyond Cleveland, and he was named Manager of Tomorrow by readers of the *Football League Review*.

For Clough, though, that tomorrow would not lie at Hartlepools. The side he had put together went on to win promotion under Angus McLean the following season, but by then Clough and Taylor were gone.

A Poor Fish and the Comedians

However significant the victory over Ord may have been, it brought only short-term relief. The fundamental problem that Hartlepools was a small, impoverished club remained and, perhaps jarred into action by how close he had come to losing everything, Taylor was still keen to move on. He had none of the sentimental attachment to the north-east that Clough did and, understandably, sought an improvement in his salary. Taylor spoke regularly with Len Shackleton and he asked him to try to find him and Clough another position.

Shackleton found it at Derby County, a club that, while certainly bigger than Hartlepools, was still something of a backwater. Clough may have made appeals to a golden past as he looked to generate support and belief, but it was certainly not a case of simply waking a slumbering giant. The combination of Raich Carter and Peter Doherty, both of whom had by good chance been stationed at nearby Loughborough during the war, helped Derby to the FA Cup in 1946, and the club twice broke the British transfer record to bring in Billy Steel and Johnny Morris to replace them. That led them to fourth in 1948 and third a year later, but the success could not be sustained and in 1953 Derby were relegated. Two years later, they slipped into the third flight for the first time in their history. Harry Storer took them back into the Second Division in 1957 before being replaced by Tim Ward.

Ward was, by all accounts, a thoroughly decent man, but under him the club stagnated, largely because of a lack of investment. 'The shortage of money has been frustrating,' he said. 'The trouble with this club is that you can't put a threepenny stamp on a letter without consulting the board personally. I was told that money was available, but I could never get an answer when I asked how much.'

Clough would never wait for an answer. Ward's geniality, in the end, was probably his failing as a manager. 'He disliked confrontation, which in some walks of life might be a virtue, but made managing and handling directors difficult if not impossible,' George Edwards, a long-time football writer for the *Derby Evening Telegraph*, wrote in his memoir, *Right Time, Right Place*. 'He seemed to run the team rather as if it was a 1950s boys' club and was only really happy with players unlikely to rock the boat.'

It was one of the rare occasions when Ward made a stand that led to his departure. He insisted on signing the twenty-one-year-old Kevin Hector from Bradford Park Avenue and, in September 1966, finally persuaded the board to release £20,000 to buy him. Clough had been a fan long before he arrived at Derby. John McGovern recalled sitting on the bench next to Clough at Hartlepools and Clough telling him that when he moved on, he was going to take McGovern, Hector and one other player from the division with him. In that, Ward saved Clough a job.

Hector proved his worth instantly, playing brilliantly on debut as Derby beat Huddersfield 4–3. Just over 15,000 saw that game; a further 3,000 turned out four days later as Derby drew 2–2 with Ipswich Town, and for the next home game, a 5–1 win over Millwall, the attendance was 22,949. Sam Longson, Derby's chairman, began to claim credit for the deal, even though Ward had been complaining for weeks before the deal was done about the board's reluctance to spend such a sum on a player unproven above the Third Division North. Expectations were raised, but Derby remained inconsistent and finished the season seventeenth. Ward's contract was set to expire that summer and when he found out it was not to be renewed, he resigned. The trainer Ralph Hann and the chief scout Sam Crooks, one of Derby's greats as a player, were also forced out in what George Edwards termed 'the most remarkable clean sweep in Rams' history'.

'We have nothing against any of these men personally,' Longson said, 'but football is a ruthless game. It is success that counts and we have not had success. Ralph has been a wonderful servant to Derby County for many years, but he has had a good innings and the time had come for a new face.'

Ward didn't go quietly, speaking of his time at the club as 'the five toughest and most frustrating years of my life' before lashing out at the board. 'Naturally I am disappointed that things have ended this way, but I am not really surprised,' he said. 'The club wanted success at all costs, but I have not been given the tools to do the job. There have been a long string of frustrations, notably over transfers. I have not had the power to act without reference to the board over the smallest matters and this has meant many chances being lost. I recently told the board I could get a player for about £10,000 and was told to offer £3,000. Nobody can build a team like that. There is potential in Derby for a great team, but under the present set-up I see no chance of an improvement. Indeed, had I known what I know now, I would not have taken the job. Mr Walters was chairman when I came and I expected him to keep the position. Then came this business of changing chairman every two years, which means there has been no continuity.'

The fans seemed broadly to agree, several hundred gathering on Shaftesbury Crescent after the final game of the 1966–67 season, a 1–1 draw against Plymouth, and chanting, 'Sack the board and bring back Ward.' Contributors to the letters page of the *Derby Evening Telegraph* were similarly supportive of the outgoing manager. 'Tim Ward out! Ralph Hann out! Sammy Crooks out!' wrote Supporter of Edale Close, Allestree. 'Is there any possibility of the present directors getting out? Who is going to be the next poor fish to satisfy the inability of this bunch of comedians?'

A 'virile young supporter' of Repton asked, 'What can any manager or trainer achieve when they are submerged beneath antiquated government at boardroom level? When team-building is stifled by lack of a bold financial policy and a steadfast refusal to listen to or adopt the manager's advice?' A 'disgusted supporter' of Breaston claimed that 'even Matt Busby' would fail under the Derby set-up. 'Ex-Rams fan' of Littleover Lane, meanwhile, accused the board of wanting a 'yes-man'. That certainly wasn't what they got.

As the board debated Ward's successor, Len Shackleton approached Longson and suggested Clough. 'Brian hadn't applied and no one had mentioned him in discussion,' Longson wrote in his diary, 'but I knew instinctively that this was the name I'd been searching for. I was so excited I couldn't sleep that night.' He remembered seeing Clough playing for Sunderland at the Baseball Ground, directing all around him, and recognised in that memory the sort of self-confident organiser he felt the club needed. The other directors, though, were less impressed when he set up a meeting at Scotch Corner.

'They thought I was out of my mind,' Longson wrote. 'Not only weren't they very impressed by the young man whose success as a manager had been confined to Division Four, but I was telling them *they* were to meet *him*.' One said the only manager he'd bother to go and meet would be Matt Busby; in that context, Clough's hang-up about directors was easy to understand.

That created an impasse that was broken only when Shackleton, quite dishonestly, told Longson that West Bromwich Albion were also interested in Clough, and that if he didn't hurry up he'd lose his man. Longson, described by Clough as 'a blunt, plain-speaking millionaire who ... had the kind of voice that could shake stone from quarry walls', had made his fortune in road haulage, having pioneered carrying milk to Manchester by lorry rather than train, and wasn't somebody to let the indecisiveness of others stand in his way. He persuaded three other directors – Sydney Bradley, Harry Paine and Bob Kirkland – to join him, and drove north in his Rolls-Royce. Over lunch, Clough talked non-stop about his achievements at Hartlepools, the limitations there and how he yearned for a bigger challenge. Before the main course arrived – Clough was evidently used to starters by then – Longson had offered him a contract.

Superficially, it seemed like the beginning of a beautiful relationship, and for a while perhaps it was, yet there were warning signs right from the start, and not just because Clough, gloomily predicting the future, told Longson that at least one of the club's seven directors would want him gone within a month.

Ultimately, nobody would feel satisfied by that meeting. Longson would be wrong-footed by the fact Clough hadn't mentioned to him that he intended to bring Taylor as his number two. Shackleton would feel aggrieved Longson neither thanked him nor paid for his lunch. After Derby had won the title, Clough sent him a tin of biscuits and a box of chocolates for Christmas each year, but the gifts stopped after Clough had departed. Longson said that he'd assumed Shackleton had been paid by Clough and Taylor given he'd effectively acted as their agent.

And Clough wasn't entirely convinced he wanted to move. He was always the conservative one of the duo, and regularly had to be persuaded by Taylor to take risks. He was also, it seems, reluctant to leave the north-east, where he'd lived all his life with the exception of his time doing National Service. Taylor and Clough went with their families to the Royal Hotel in Scarborough to talk the move over, which they did over three days in the snooker-room.

Taylor, optimistic as ever, had insisted throughout the season that Hartlepools were on the verge of promotion; if that were so, Clough asked, why would they leave, especially having won the battle against Ord? Just as Clough had an attachment to the north-east, though, so Taylor had an attachment to the east Midlands. He had been a regular at the Baseball Ground in the days immediately after the war, and had watched the likes of Carter, Doherty, Crooks and Jackie Stamps as Derby enjoyed their brief golden age. He remembered the ground packed to bursting, and was convinced they could bring the crowds back, could re-inspire a town with a football tradition far greater than that of Hartlepool. Harry Storer, intriguingly, advised them not to take the job, telling Taylor that 'the composition of the board is a scandal – and I've told them so'.

Eventually Clough was persuaded, and set off to Derby with Barbara and the three children to finalise the deal. Seemingly believing it was just a question of signing the contract – even though he had yet to mention that he wanted Taylor with him – he left them in Normanton Park playing on the swings while he set off to meet the board. It was early evening by the time he returned, the directors having reacted badly to his demand for an assistant. Fortunately, Longson had just sold his haulage business for around £500,000 and was infatuated with Clough. In the end he offered him a salary of £5,000, Taylor £2,500, and promised to make £70,000 available for transfer spending. Clough later insisted it was his focus on how he and Taylor had left Hartlepools 'solvent' that was the decisive factor.

'The offer from Derby was a good one, but money is not the reason for moving,' Clough told the *Hartlepool Mail*. 'If I'm going to stay in this game, I might as well have a real go at it and that's just what I'm doing . . . It won't come immediately, but I'm confident that, given two seasons, we can achieve something . . . All the lessons I have learned at Hartlepools will hold good. My approach will be the same and so will my demands. The problems in this game are very much the same whether you are at Liverpool or Hartlepool.'

If his autobiography is to be believed, having agreed the deal, Clough immediately set about flexing his muscles, telling the board that he didn't want a part-timer playing for the club. When they asked who he meant, he pointed out that the centre-forward Ian Buxton had it written into his contract that he could play for Derbyshire in the County Championship and then, when the cricket season was over, take a two-week break before joining up with the football club in September. By then, Clough said, the tone for the season was set. He wanted Buxton to be told to turn up for pre-season training, or not bother at all. In a sense the issue was academic as Clough and Taylor soon sold Buxton to Luton Town: the point was rather to let the board know that Clough wanted things done Clough's way; he was not going to fret diffidently as Ward had done.

'This is a new era for Derby,' Longson announced. 'Our supporters are starved of success – we are too. We aren't specialists at football, but we are successful businessmen and it is up to us to do something to put the club on its feet. We are now in a terrible state and we are looking to Mr Clough to bring us success again, although we realise we cannot expect results immediately. He will be in charge, just as Mr Ward was.' When Clough was in charge, though, he really was in charge.

As though to prove that, he drew up a rule book known as the 'Player's Ticket'. There were the obvious strictures about punctuality, but Clough also prohibited players from going to dances later in the week than a Tuesday (or a Wednesday if they had special dispensation from the manager), assuming there was no midweek game. They were banned from riding motorcycles, from smoking at the ground or in the dressing-rooms during training and, mystifyingly and unrealistically, from having any connection with 'licensed premises'. This was the controlling Clough – not dissimilar to Revie – demanding obedience and absolute commitment.

Clough had the photographs of Steve Bloomer, Raich Carter and Peter Doherty that lined the corridors at the Baseball Ground taken down, insisting the focus had to be on the future rather than a distant past. As with so much, Clough was praised for an act that in others prompted great controversy. When Gary Megson, who briefly played for Clough, took over at Nottingham Forest, he had the photographs of Clough's successes taken down, and was instantly accused of betrayal. Roy Keane, meanwhile, although a Clough disciple in many ways, had photographs of Sunderland's triumphs put up around the training ground during his time as manager on Wearside to remind players of the club's traditions.

The next step in his policy of taking control was to get the directors' wives on his side. He introduced himself to each one individually, charming them to the extent that 'they were competing with each other for the prize of being in charge in the tea-room'. He similarly set about getting the press on his side, inviting George Edwards of the *Derby Evening Telegraph* and Neil Hallom, who worked for Raymond's, a local news agency, to the ground in his first week in charge and telling them that while he didn't expect biased reports or favours, he did want publicity. He soon began to use that to pressure the board.

The players' first meeting with their new management team was characteristically memorable. They waited nervously in the dressing-room, aware that Clough and Taylor both had a reputation for fieriness and that they had proved themselves willing at Hartlepools to make radical changes to the squad. The door crashed open, and the two walked in. After a few moments of nervous silence, Bobby Saxton, the club captain, stood up and introduced himself, making the mistake of calling Clough by his first name. 'I'm "Boss" not "Brian",' he snapped, 'and I'll decide who's club captain.'

153

Clough and Taylor began work with the squad on a pre-season tour of Germany. Things began badly, as Clough suggested convening in the swimming pool at 10.30am. He turned up in his trunks with a towel slung over his shoulder to find half his squad huddled in the shallow end. To his disbelief, he realised they couldn't swim. Even more seriously, they couldn't play football either, or at least not to his standards. During the first game of the tour Clough turned to Longson and asked what he expected him to do. Longson replied that it was in his hands, at which Clough announced he'd like to sack the lot.

Clough gathered the players on their return from Germany – where they had remained unbeaten – and told them they could not expect improved contracts after finishing sixth-bottom of the league. 'I'll fight tooth and nail to get these lads good wages when they do their stuff,' he told the *Evening Telegraph*. 'But they are well paid already and if they don't produce the results they needn't bother asking. My players have got to die for Derby County and die for me. Anything less will not be good enough. We're not running a holiday camp down here, we're out to build a winning team – and for the time being, results will come before everything, including entertaining the public. There will be no place for loafers. The players will have to work hard, but the sort of lads I want won't mind that. There are bound to be staff changes. Players who won't fight can go. After all, these men can get me the sack ... but I'll make sure they're sacked first, even if it's only the day before.' They had two months, he said, in which to prove themselves.

And so began a major overhaul of the club, on and off the pitch, not that Clough minded that. As he pointed out in his autobiography, 'Taylor and I were at our best and fired with the greatest enthusiasm when we were dismantling teams and rebuilding them, rather than maintaining standards already set.'

The board had often promised Ward money for transfers, only to equivocate when it actually came to completing deals; Clough and Taylor were determined they wouldn't be thwarted in the same way. Clough began to hint to the press that new signings were imminent, creating a mood of expectation that pressured the board into action. At the same time, Taylor talked about how it would take time to get things right, and how important it was to source good youngsters. Having softened the board up, he then struck a decisive blow by asking Edwards to write a piece praising the directors for recognising that new signings were necessary. The board were trapped, and as others shuffled into the background, Longson, who had money and was prepared to release it – and who enjoyed the attention – came increasingly into the foreground.

A sign of Clough's ambition came with a 'massive' bid for the Derby-born striker Tony Hateley, who was unsettled at Chelsea. He instead joined Liverpool for £100,000. After that, when the first signing came, a week before the start of the season, though, many were underwhelmed. In *Right Place, Right Time*, Edwards admitted his confusion when he found out that Clough had spent £21,000 on a nineteen-year-old reserve forward from Sunderland who wasn't a great goal-scorer, wasn't particularly tall and wasn't particularly quick. John O'Hare, though, had other qualities. 'O'Hare was the gentlest of men,' Clough wrote in his autobiography, 'but also, on the field, one of the bravest, because he always received the ball with his back to the defender. People used to say that he had weaknesses in his game. Absolute balls! O'Hare could receive and control a ball on his thigh, his chest, his head, his ankles or his knees. And he had a heart as big as a bucket.' In other words, he had the moral courage Storer demanded.

Others might have been reluctant to leave a First Division club for Derby, but Clough offered O'Hare £40 a week, £15 more than he had had been on and, besides, O'Hare believed Clough when he told him that the clubs would pass each other as Derby went up and Sunderland went down; as it was, they overlapped in the First Division by a season. 'Clough was a much more aggressive person than when I last knew him,' O'Hare said. 'He was confident and outspoken. I felt it was only a matter of time.'

The season began positively, an own-goal and strikes for Hector and O'Hare securing a 3–2 win over Charlton. 'It was far from being a great performance, but it was a promising one,' Edwards wrote, but Clough and Taylor's revamp of the club had only just begun. Taylor wasn't at that first game; he was in Devon standing behind the goal watching Torquay play Tranmere and trying not to be recognised. Taylor had noticed Tranmere's nineteen-year-old centre-back Roy McFarland playing against Hartlepools in 1966 and regarded him as 'an uncut diamond'. Watching him mark Torquay's Jim Fryatt, an experienced and awkward centre-forward, Taylor was convinced. 'The kid never lost his composure,'

Taylor wrote, 'and I noted again his cultured left foot and his ruthlessness.'

Clough and Taylor went to Tranmere the following Friday, ostensibly to watch their match against Reading, but in reality to sign McFarland as a replacement for Bobby Saxton. Other managers were also circling, and Clough and Taylor realised they had to be both subtle and decisive. There were numerous representatives of other clubs in the guest-room after the game, so Clough and Taylor waited until they saw Dave Russell, the Tranmere manager, leave for the gents. Clough followed him, and by the time they returned negotiations were already well under way.

Clough initially offered £12,000, which Russell laughed off as derisory. Clough agreed and suggested doubling the fee, but claimed he would have to ask Longson's permission to go over £20,000. He picked up the phone, dialled his own number, and improvised a pretend argument with Longson, eventually winning his supposed approval to go to £24,000. Actually, they could probably have gone as high as £49,000, the amount left in the kitty Longson had provided, but Russell was won over by Clough's theatrics and agreed, giving Clough and Taylor permission to speak to the player.

He had assumed they would wait until the following morning, but Clough and Taylor were gripped by the thrill of the chase and perhaps a little paranoid, and insisted on setting off straightaway. Russell reluctantly agreed and, after driving a short distance in the wrong direction to put off would-be pursuers, led them through the Mersey tunnel to the terraced house McFarland shared with his parents.

It was after midnight when they arrived. McFarland was in bed and had to be woken by his father. He wasn't even sure he wanted to be a professional footballer, let alone to sign for Derby in his pyjamas, and asked for time to think. Clough, though, was adamant he wasn't leaving without a decision one way or the other. Eventually McFarland's father, who remembered Clough scoring at Anfield, suggested that Clough and Taylor must really want him to have made such an effort and created such a fuss, and McFarland signed the forms Clough had brought with him. He woke up thinking he'd made the biggest mistake of his life, a feeling that was only strengthened that afternoon as he watched Liverpool, the team he supported and for whom he dreamed of playing, beat Newcastle 6–0 at Anfield. 'I couldn't believe I'd been so stupid,' he said. 'Derby County – who were they? One more day and I'd never have signed for Derby.' By luck or by judgement, Clough and Taylor had got the timing just right; although the edge was presumably taken off any triumphalism as Derby went down 1–0 at Crystal Palace that afternoon. 'Rams never created a chance', the headline in the *Evening Telegraph* acknowledged.

McFarland suffered badly from homesickness in his first months at the club, and travelled back to Merseyside every weekend. Clough and Taylor helped him settle, though, by lodging him with the long-serving right-back Ron Webster, who had only recently married Doreen. Taylor would ask how his parents were getting on and encourage him to send money back to them, while Clough sent them a letter telling them how well their son was progressing, something McFarland only discovered several years later. This was the other side of Clough: beneath the brashness, there was genuine concern for those he respected.

Clough had decided the first thing to get right was the spine – goalkeeper, centre-half, centre-forward – and if that was right, the rest would follow. He had signed a centre-forward and a centre-half, but was happy enough with Reg Matthews, who had played in goal five times for England. Taylor had been a squad-mate of Matthews under Storer at Coventry and insisted he was 'the bravest player on the staff'. Clough warmed to him as a result and, after realising he was persistently late for team-meetings because he was sneaking off for a cigarette in the toilets, gave him dispensation to smoke in front of the other players on the grounds that he was the only England international among them. 'There are many players,' Clough wrote in *Walking on Water*, 'who can get away with a certain lack of ability because they are particularly courageous. Very few, if any, can get away with not being brave at all, however talented they might be. Ability will never blossom if a lad is too frightened to have the ball.'

Negotiating down the fee for McFarland left money in the pot for a third major signing, and he arrived at the end of September. By then, Derby seemed to be cruising to promotion. McFarland gave what Edwards described as 'a display of remarkably mature defending' on his debut in a 3–1 win at Rotherham. Aston Villa were then beaten by the same scoreline, but the game was overshadowed by the death, the day before, of Harry Storer. He had played over 250 games for Derby and managed them for eight years, as well as making over 300 first-class appearances for

Derbyshire, helping them to their only County Championship in his final season. He had been one of Derbyshire's greatest all-round sportsmen, but at least by the time he went, aged sixty-nine, he had seen Derby appoint the two men who would take his philosophy and make it more successful than he could have imagined. Clough visited Storer's widow, Kathy, and ensured that whenever she wanted to watch games at the Baseball Ground she'd be picked up, given a meal, looked after and driven home again after the game.

Derby played well in a 3–2 defeat at Norwich, then beat QPR and Plymouth 1–0 in the league. They returned to Hartlepools in the League Cup and won 4–0, but Clough and Taylor felt they needed to add bite to the midfield, and decided Willie Carlin was the man to provide it. They had first spotted him playing for Carlisle when they were at Hartlepools, and from the moment they arrived at Derby, they had had him in mind. Any potential deal, though, was complicated by the fact that, after leaving the Baseball Ground, Tim Ward had taken over at Carlisle. Taylor had gone so far as to ring Carlin to tap him up. Carlin was keen, so Taylor told him to tell Ward he wanted First Division football. A few days later, Taylor made a formal bid, and then called Carlin back, suggesting he should go and see Ward. He did and Ward told him that no First Division club had made an approach. He admitted a Second Division side had come in, but dismissed them as 'rubbish', and ended up refusing to allow Carlin permission to speak to Clough, even though he had promised to outbid any other suitors by £10,000. Dissatisfaction, though, had been sown in Carlin's mind, and when Sheffield United came in with a £45,000 bid, he left. Clough was furious. 'Carlisle have sold a player for a certain fee when, for all they know, we were prepared to top it,' he said.

Hector scored three and O'Hare two in a 5–1 win at Cardiff. 'Let it be said from the outset,' Brian McDermott wrote in the *Evening Telegraph*, 'that this was a splendid team effort – precisely plotted, astutely executed. But let it also be said, before the superlatives are vastly overworked, that this was very much a Cardiff side ripe for defeat.'

Still, the rebuilding went on. Clough's first two signings had been gifted young players who showed the sort of physical courage for which Clough had been noted in his playing days. His third was rather different. Alan Hinton had played three times for England and, having developed at

Wolverhampton Wanderers, was an established player at Nottingham Forest. Few doubted his ability, but a reputation for shirking physical challenges had earned him the nickname 'Gladys'. Clough didn't care: Hinton 'had pace and used his excellent left foot to hit shots and crosses with equal accuracy'. Hinton was actually right-footed, but at Wolves Stan Cullis had made him train with a plimsoll on his right foot and a boot on his left until he became equally adept on either side.

The deal was done at the Baseball Ground at midnight. Forest's chairman, Tony Wood, had been having a drink in the Bridgford Hotel when Clough telephoned, and rushed straight over, confirming Clough's suspicion that Forest were keen to be rid of a player they felt, even at twenty-four, was past his best. Wood demanded £30,000, but Clough, seemingly for reasons of mischief as much as anything else, told him that Hinton wanted £1,000 for himself – he didn't – and asked if it could come off the fee. Wood agreed and, Clough said, went round 'boasting he'd offloaded a passenger'.

According to Taylor, after the signing, a director asked him what colour Hinton's handbag was; four years later, Hinton was top-scorer as Derby won the league. 'If we'd wanted a centre-forward who was six feet tall and ran like a sprinter we wouldn't have signed John O'Hare,' he said. 'If we'd wanted a winger who could tackle, we wouldn't have signed Alan Hinton. We signed him because he is a highly-talented footballer.' Hinton also, Clough insisted, had that most vital ingredient: moral courage.

The signing of Hinton took Clough £4,000 over budget, but given his first three signings went on to make a total of 1,154 appearances for the club, the excess could probably be justified, particularly when Buxton was sold to Luton for £10,000. Hinton made his debut in a 4–1 home win over Rotherham. The crowd was up to 28,251, and with seven wins in nine games Derby lay fourth in the table, a point behind the leaders QPR. Even as fans began talking excitedly of promotion, though, Taylor was gloomy and Edwards remembered him insisting Derby were not playing as well as results suggested and claiming relegation was a serious possibility.

Results gradually tailed off. After a 1–0 home defeat to Portsmouth – 'a tactical success based on tough tackling, good covering and a philosophy of safety first,' Edwards said – Clough gave the players the Monday off, saying they looked tired and pressured by the unaccustomed publicity. The following week, at home to Millwall, Derby were 3–0 down at half-time, but salvaged a point with two goals in the final three minutes.

Only then did Clough get round to signing a three-year contract, snubbing an offer from Coventry to replace Jimmy Hill. Whether that was an early sign of his willingness to use threats to leave to get his own way or not is difficult to say. At the time, at least, he insisted not. 'It is the same contract that has been lying in the safe for three months,' he said. 'It is simply that I have never got round to signing it.' Perhaps significantly, perhaps merely coincidentally, on the same day Derby signed the forward Ritchie Barker from Burton (for whom Taylor had signed him from Matlock). That Wednesday, Edwards described Derby as 'brilliant' in a 3–1 win over Birmingham City.

Defeats at Ipswich and Bolton dampened thoughts of promotion. 'Something of the ground that has to be made up before Derby County can even begin thinking in terms of First Division football was painfully revealed ...' Edwards wrote, at the end of October, criticising Derby's 'rank bad defending'. They didn't win again in the league until mid-December, by which time Clough and Taylor had been called in to see Longson and the vice-chairman Sydney Bradley to explain why things were going wrong and why their investment was not paying off.

Most galling was a 1–0 home defeat to Ward's Carlisle. 'It was a bitter pill, maybe the bitterest, but we are in a transitional period,' Longson said, showing a sense of perspective rare in directors. Three days later, Derby achieved a rather more meaningful victory over Carlisle as they faced FA charges of having made an illegal approach for Carlin and were cleared within twenty minutes.

The reshaping of the team continued all season. Perhaps Clough and Taylor's most bizarre attempt to shake the side up came in the attempt to sign Ken Wagstaff from Hull. Taylor felt Hector lacked 'devil', and saw in Wagstaff a pugnacious, energetic striker with an impressive goals record. Clough offered Hector – for whom he had turned down an £80,000 bid from Nottingham Forest – in a straight swap, and went so far as to suggest Wagstaff should go on strike to try to force a move, but Hull remained adamant they weren't selling, which in the end was probably for the best for Clough and Taylor, not that they would ever admit it.

After a 3–0 defeat at Hull, in which Edwards described Derby as 'lacking completely both confidence and zest', Clough signed Arthur Stewart, an experienced wing-half, from Glentoran for £10,000. He made his debut in a 4–2 defeat at home to Middlesbrough. Clough was angry enough to bring the players in on the Sunday: he made them run ten laps, said nothing about the game, and sent them home. It seemed to work: Derby followed up a 1–1 draw against Blackpool with a hard-working 2–1 victory away at Charlton, but over Christmas Derby drew at home to Crystal Palace and then lost 3–0 at Blackburn.

The year ended with a 2–2 draw in the return against Blackburn, stretching Derby's run without a home win to five games. 'The Baseball Ground bogey continues . . .' Edwards wrote, 'but it surely can't go on much longer and surely won't.' Derby, he insisted, were playing far better than they had been at the end of November, but they ended 1967 in twelfth – nine points off promotion and ten off relegation.

When Derby then lost 2–1 at Aston Villa thanks to 'two moments of shoddy defending', the letters pages of the *Derby Evening Telegraph* began to suggest a mounting dissatisfaction. S.W. Tracey of 70 Grange Avenue, Derby, having seen Hinton play superbly in the reserve team, complained that the policy of passing down the middle meant that the winger wasn't getting the service he needed, and pointed out that on heavy ground games tend to be won on the firmer turf of the flanks. A. Pennington of Long Eaton, meanwhile, advised Clough to sign an inside forward, ideally 'Lincoln City's inside-forward [Roger] Holmes'.

Only the League Cup provided relief. A 5–4 win over Darlington in the quarter-final had set up a semi-final against Don Revie's Leeds United, the first time Clough the manager had faced the man who would become his great rival. *The Damned Utd* made great play of Clough preparing to face Revie, and of the subsequent snub that supposedly ignited their feud, but there is no evidence of any such incident. With over 3,000 fans making the trip from Leeds for the first leg, Derby took record receipts of £9,248, and enjoyed a morale-boosting night. 'The great Leeds United side bent, buckled but did not quite break in last night's League Cup semi-final first leg at the Baseball Ground,' Edwards wrote. 'Leeds were reduced to a set of very ordinary mortals by a fighting Derby side.' They didn't win, though. Bobby Saxton had replaced the Cup-tied McFarland at centre-half and he 'had a rush of blood to the head in the sixty-fourth minute and handled a

161

[Jimmy] Greenhoff corner'. Giles converted the penalty, and Saxton was sold to Plymouth for £12,000 ten days later.

Phil Waller played at centre-half in the second leg, and when Hector scored from an O'Hare cross, Derby were level on aggregate. Ron Belfitt equalised on the night following a scramble from a free-kick. Further goals from Eddie Gray and Belfitt effectively decided the game and Stewart's late goal for Derby meant little. That was Derby's third defeat to Leeds in the space of a fortnight, as between the two legs they went down 2–0 at Elland Road in the FA Cup. 'Fighting Rams go out with honour', claimed the headline in the *Evening Telegraph*. Testing themselves against the best, Derby were found lacking, but only just; and to put up such a fight in three successive games suggested that they weren't that far from being a seriously competitive team.

In the league, though, Derby remained inconsistent. They won 4–3 at Plymouth, but then lost 4–3 at home to Cardiff and 3–2 at Portsmouth. By the end of February, relegation was a realistic, if still distant, threat.

Most troublingly, Derby had taken just three points from their previous six home games. 'I have played on a lot of Fourth Division pitches where the surface is better,' McFarland said at a supporters' meeting. 'This may be part of the reason why we are not doing well at home.' It was, of course, the same for both sides, but the onus is always on the home team to create the play, and that is significantly harder on a muddy pitch, particularly for a team like Derby who, even then, were more patient and methodical, less direct, in approach than many of the sides in the Second Division.

Just as McFarland voiced that concern, though, Derby thrashed QPR 4–0. For most of the game, Edwards wrote, 'the defenders were chasing shadows and the forwards battering themselves against a defence in which Webster and McFarland were in tremendous form.' Hector put Derby ahead from a Hinton cross as O'Hare dummied, Hinton lashed in after Ron Springett had dropped a cross, Stewart got the third from the edge of the box, then Hector helped on a Hinton ball for McFarland to score his first goal for the club.

A 1–1 draw at Millwall followed, but Clough still wasn't happy, as he made clear in a meeting at the King's Hall. For once, his tone was cautious, as though the difficulty of the task, the constant set-backs, were beginning to get him down. 'My greatest disappointment since coming to Derby has been the results of the team over the last three months,' he said. 'I can answer most questions, but this is one I hesitate on for there is no obvious reason why we have not done a lot better.'

The respite those three points brought was brief. Clough handed a debut to the seventeen-year-old John Robson at home to Ipswich. Robson exemplified Taylor's willingness to consider any player, no matter how obscure their background. Taylor had gone to the north-east to look at another player and then, unimpressed, had wandered off to look at a game taking place on an adjoining pitch, where he saw Robson, in those days a clean-cut wing-half. After an elaborate charade in which he berated Derby's north-eastern scout for having dragged him to Newcastle on a wild-goose chase, Taylor signed him within twenty-four hours of seeing him for the first time.

Robson would become Derby's regular full-back, but he made his debut at right-half as Derby lost 3–2 to Ipswich. Nerves were mounting. They gave what Edwards called a 'very poor display' in drawing with Norwich, then went down 3–1 at Huddersfield. 'Changes due after this shocker', said the headline in the *Evening Telegraph*. 'A few more such performances,' Edwards added, 'and they will be spending the summer preparing for a spell in Division Three.'

The assumption often is that the early days at Derby were characterised by a sense of enthusiasm and mounting belief, but there were problems that went beyond results. The early months were marked by 'a hostile atmosphere backstage', as Clough termed it, with hate letters arriving from people who believed Tim Ward should never have been replaced. Ward, 'a dear, kindly man', almost certainly had nothing to do with it and, despite the bitterness he clearly felt towards the club, would probably have been horrified to find out what was going on, but there were those who belonged to the same Lodge, the same Round Table or the same Rotary Club who resented his removal. One of them, Fred Walters, Clough suggested, 'even seemed pleased at our initial lack of success'. On Saturdays, when the games were finished, he would bellow down the corridor from the board-room, letting everybody know what position Derby had fallen to.

Even those without an anti-Clough agenda caused problems. The vice-chairman, Ken Turner, who also sat on the committee at Derbyshire County Cricket Club, had, Clough said, 'a typically amateurish approach despite a charming personality'. He suggested McFarland should train in a weighted belt so that he'd feel light when he played without it on a Saturday and so be able to leap even higher. 'Although I didn't swear much in those days, I seem to recall one or two unfamiliar little words slipping out,' Clough said.

Heeding the call of the *Evening Telegraph*, for the home game against Bolton Clough dropped Matthews for Colin Boulton, whom he had suspended less than a fortnight earlier for failing to turn up at a reserve game, and shuffled nine of the outfield players into new positions. Only McFarland, whom Clough had taken to hailing as the finest centre-half in the country, retained his position. The result, Edwards said, was 'hardly a feast of soccer brilliance', but it was 'a vast improvement', and Derby won 2–1.

They lost at Birmingham, but then beat Bristol City 3–1, with two goals for Ritchie Barker 'who can look like a selling-plater one minute and a Derby winner the next', as Edwards put it, to take his tally to twelve in twenty games. And that, fortunately, was enough to preserve Derby as they drew three and lost three of their final six games of the season. Again, it was their home form that was of particular concern. Brian McDermott spoke of 'a second-half performance of inexplicable incompetence' in a 2–1 defeat to Hull, and they lost the final game of the season 3–1 to Blackpool at the Baseball Ground, a match in which the full-back Jim Walker, signed from Northwich Victoria after impressing Taylor in one of Derby's regular Sunday trials, made his debut. It was typical of Taylor's willingness to back his judgement against the orthodoxy that Walker was twenty-two, way beyond the age at which players should, according to convention, have made their breakthrough.

In Tim Ward's final season, Derby had finished seventeenth. Clough had vowed that he would take the club forward, but in his first season they finished eighteenth, and that after significant expenditure: little wonder there was anxiety in the boardroom. Reflecting on the season as a whole, Edwards suggested that Derby's main problem was that away sides always seemed to dominate midfield at the Baseball Ground.

As soon as the season was over, Clough and Taylor began further reconstruction. Clough had become convinced that Matthews' 'old reflexes had gone a bit', which, given his conviction that the importance of goalkeepers was often overlooked, was a major worry. 'I've never fathomed why top keepers don't cost as much as top strikers,' he said. 'A save can be as important as a goal, but a mistake by a keeper is often more costly than a miss by his team-mate at the opposite end of the field.'

Matthews, then aged thirty-five, was released. As a replacement, Clough and Taylor settled, slightly surprisingly, on Les Green. He had followed Taylor from Burton to Hartlepools and had joined Bob Stokoe's Rochdale after being sacked for a breach of club discipline. Green was a great fan of Taylor – 'Talking to Pete about football was like talking to Einstein about science,' he told Edwards – while Taylor described him as one of the top half-dozen goalkeepers in the country. Taylor insisted Green and Clough should make up, and after they had, he signed for a fee the *Evening Telegraph* described as approaching five figures. 'He was not the tallest,' Clough said, 'but he had long arms and incredibly big hands.' He was also noted as a great organiser of a defence.

Not everybody was convinced by Clough and Taylor and shortly after the end of the season, the attacking midfielder Alan Durban asked to be placed on the transfer list. 'I have not been enjoying my game recently and this is unusual,' he said. 'I know the crowd at the Baseball Ground have been after me quite a bit, but I have no real complaint on that score. That sort of thing doesn't really bother me and at least it stopped them getting at somebody else.' He would, of course, stay, and become an integral part of Derby's success. The road to success is never straight and easy, and holding on to Durban was another potential derailment Clough avoided.

Others, fortunately, were more positive than Durban. Clough, as he had been at Hartlepools, was central to the marketing of the club, and signed letters sent to every season-ticket holder outlining his plans for the coming season and explaining why price rises were necessary. Despite the increased cost, by the beginning of July the club was reporting record sales of season tickets, which gives some indication of how impressive Derby's football had been at times the previous season. Clough raised further cash with the sale of Mick Hopkinson to Mansfield for £6,000 and then, on 23 July, came confirmation of a startling new arrival.

Of all Clough's signings, perhaps none was so significant as that of Dave Mackay. Certainly none became so romanticised in the retelling; Clough was not averse to polishing his own legend. As Clough told it, Taylor was scanning the list of young players at the club when he announced they needed experience, and told Clough to go and sign Dave Mackay, whom Eusébio had described as 'the finest wing-half I ever played against', but who was, at thirty-three, leaving Tottenham to become player-manager at Hearts. Clough was initially incredulous. 'Go and try,' Taylor supposedly told him. 'You've pulled off bigger things than this.' Clough's version of the story then has him jumping in his car and driving down to London, although there seems a general consensus that he travelled in Longson's white Rolls-Royce rather than in his own Rover.

In his autobiography, Clough speaks of arriving at White Hart Lane, wandering in, and Bill Nicholson, the Tottenham manager, emerging before him. Clough asked to speak to Mackay, at which Nicholson told him it was too late and the deal with Hearts was agreed. Clough said he still wanted to speak to him, at which Nicholson's phone rang and he disappeared, leaving Clough to hang around in a corridor waiting for Mackay to return from training (itself an odd detail, given it was the close-season). Clough told Tony Francis a slightly different story. 'They treated me like a leper,' he said. 'Kept me hanging around in the corridor for ages and had me travelling to and from the training ground.'

Eventually Mackay arrived, strode over and shook Clough's hand. Clough was struck by how old Mackay looked – the player was six months older than the manager – but went ahead and told him he wanted him to join Derby. Mackay replied that he was going to Hearts, so Clough suggested he went and had a bath, and they could have a chat afterwards. Washed and changed, Mackay returned and took Clough into the players' lounge. 'Everything was immaculate,' Clough wrote in his autobiography. '[There were] women running all over the place making cups of tea and sandwiches.' This was revelatory: Middlesbrough had had only a snooker table; Sunderland and Hartlepools not even that – although again the suspicion must be that Clough exaggerated how overawed he was to emphasise the scale of his achievement in persuading Mackay to sign.

As they chatted, Mackay said he couldn't come for £10,000, at which Clough told him he could probably raise £10,000 if that was what it took. Mackay demurred, and they chatted some more. Clough asked what sum he would come for, to which Mackay replied £15,000. Clough said he couldn't get that, but that he might be able to manage £14,000, to be paid as a signing-on fee over three-years. Mackay accepted. 'I'm not sure whether I've ever matched the feeling of total elation that swept me along the return car journey north,' Clough said. 'I kept telling myself I'd nailed it . . . I hadn't just signed a player, I'd recruited a kind of institution . . . I never made a more effective signing in my entire managerial career.' When he got back to Derby, Taylor told him he hadn't thought he'd had a prayer.

The next part of the plan, as Clough told it, was to persuade Mackay that he'd be playing not as a wing-half but as a sweeper. Clough's version of events had he and Taylor in a room with Mackay seated between them. Taylor said he wanted him to play sweeper; Mackay said he couldn't do it. Clough said that in McFarland they already had the best centre-half in the league, so they wanted Mackay to drop off and play behind him. According to Clough, Mackay argued against the move for twenty minutes before eventually being broken down and agreeing to give it a try.

The account Mackay gave was rather less dramatic. Spurs finished seventh in 1967–68 and he was aware that his abilities were waning. After a 4–0 reverse against Arsenal – Tottenham's heaviest defeat since 1959 – Mackay began to contemplate retirement. A 3–1 defeat to Manchester City, the eventual champions, in the penultimate game of the season confirmed his decision to retire. 'As I traipsed off the pitch, I knew I was no longer good enough to play well in the top flight,' he wrote in his autobiography. 'Age and two broken legs had made me sluggish. I was one of the reasons why Tottenham were not as good and, if I had been manager, I would have dropped me and put me out to grass.'

The following Monday, Mackay went to see Nicholson and told him he was retiring. Nicholson tried to talk him out of it, saying he felt he had a couple of seasons left, but Mackay was adamant. The following Saturday, he played his final game for Spurs in a 2–1 defeat at Molineux. Ideally, Mackay would have become Nicholson's assistant, but Eddie Bailey was fulfilling that role. During the close-season, though, Nicholson called Mackay in and told him John Harvey, the manager of Hearts, wanted to stand down and have Mackay replace him as player-manager. Mackay was keen to return to Edinburgh, but insisted he was always reluctant to go back to Tynecastle as a player because he couldn't bear the thought of 'middle-aged men standing on the terraces, saying to their sons, "See that fat guy out there huffing and puffing? He used to be Dave Mackay.""

He was still deliberating, and had delayed his departure for Edinburgh for a week to see if there was any interest from English clubs, when Clough rang him at the tie shop he ran near White Hart Lane. Mackay had played against Clough in that Under-23 international at Birmingham, but other than that he knew little of him. Clough told Mackay he saw him as part of the great side he was building at Derby, but admitted he hadn't spoken to Nicholson. Mackay expressed cautious interest, until he looked up where Derby had finished the previous season. When he saw they'd been eight-eenth, he thought 'he must be bonkers'.

It was only then, Mackay said, that Clough drove down to London. He explained his project as they walked around the pitch at White Hart Lane – so not in the players' lounge – and it was then that Clough suggested deploying him as a sweeper. He was not to be a *libero* in the free-roving Franz Beckenbauer sense of the term, but a central defender who let the other centre-back compete for crosses and high passes, seeking to pick up loose balls and intercept, and with licence to step a few paces out from the back line to initiate attacks. Mackay immediately, he said, recognised the role as a way of prolonging his career. 'His enthusiasm was infectious,' Mackay said, 'and his confidence shocking.' Given his doubts as to the level at which he could continue to play, it also helped that 'Derby supporters didn't know me from Adam and therefore we owed each other nothing.' The *Evening Telegraph*, meanwhile, suggested Clough made two separate trips to London to complete the deal.

Whatever the precise details, what is clear is that the £5,000 Derby ended up paying Spurs for Mackay represented an extraordinary piece of business, even with the £14,000 signing-on fee. Clough's handling of a player who effectively outranked him was subtle, and evidence that, in the early days at least, his handling of players extended beyond intimidation. 'Clough introduced me to a world of four-letter insults, slamming doors and even an underlying hint of physical violence,' Mackay said, but Clough didn't try to dominate him and made a point of asking his opinion at half-time. He allowed him to skip training sessions if he felt like it, rearranged the first practice of the week for Tuesday afternoons to give Mackay time to get up from his London home and spared his ageing limbs by calling him over for a chat while other players were running laps.

Mackay's contribution was not just in what he did, but in the example he set. 'We felt unbeatable and it all stemmed from Dave,' Clough said. 'He brought a swagger to the team, to the whole club.' Not that the directors were necessarily convinced. Shortly after Mackay had signed, one of them commented to Clough that he was the most expensive player in the league. Clough replied that he was probably the best.

The signings aside, the other big change that summer was Longson's decision – perhaps not entirely his own – to retire as chairman, and his replacement by Sydney Bradley. It might have seemed little more than committee-room shuffling, but it would have great significance in Clough's eventual departure from Derby.

Mackay's first appearance came in a friendly at St Johnstone. Derby lost 1–0 and Mackay missed their best chance. 'Mackay had plenty of advice for his new colleagues, directing operations with a quick word of command,' Edwards wrote. 'Throughout, Mackay coasted, and was content to remain in defence except for one sortie.'

That game also saw Derby switch from a W-M formation to a back four, with Mackay operating alongside McFarland in the centre of defence, something that prompted soul-searching about whether a move to 4–2–4 – and, as it turned out, often 4–3–3 – meant a season of defensive football. Edwards described it as 'a system which places massive responsibility on the two midfield players. These players, at present, are Arthur Stewart and Alan Durban, one of whom has yet to show the flair for the job and the other of whom is on the transfer list at his own request.' Jimmy Walker provided another option in the role, but as Edwards said, he remained relatively undeveloped: he 'has a long way to go before he can be regarded as an inside-forward capable of driving a team towards the top'.

The switch, though, was telling, not merely because it showed Clough addressing the problems Derby had faced in at times being over-run in midfield, but also because it exposes as nonsense the often-voiced claim, one he himself was happy to propagate, that he was a coach who didn't deal in tactics.

Clough was always scathing of those guilty of what he saw as 'over-complicating' the game, and regularly used the term 'tactics' dismissively, but with him it seems to have had specifically negative connotations; to have referred to stopping the opposition rather than how his own side played. 'Tactics,' he insisted in *Walking on Water*, 'played very little part in my method of management. I concentrated ninety per cent on how my team played, in preference to wondering about how the opposition would set out their stall.'

He may have thought tactics was a dirty word, something fit for only Italians or Don Revie, but the idea he just sent eleven players out on the field and hoped for the best is absurd. Although he usually feigned indifference to the opposition, there were times when he took specific action to counter them; Durban, for instance, spoke of a game against Wolves when he was given specific instructions to cut out the supply from Mike Bailey to the left-winger David Wagstaffe.

Taylor always insisted that he and Clough did coach, just not necessarily on the training field. His own philosophy of the game, as for so many of his generation, was shaped by seeing England humiliated 6–3 by Hungary at Wembley in 1953, but he was also impressed by the attacking full-backs employed by Brazilian sides he saw in occasional friendlies. His ideas were essentially a development of those Jimmy Hogan had taken to Budapest during the First World War, which had been transported around the world by a series of Hungarian coaches from the late thirties. 'The ability to command space is vital in a good defensive system,' Taylor explained in a lengthy interview in the *Guardian*. 'By that I mean that a player who is on his own when the opposition has the ball must be poised and capable of assessing whether he should commit himself or funnel back. [Igor] Netto of Russia was the first player I noticed with this. Dave Mackay has it, so have Bobby Moore and Terry Hennessey ... Then there is the ability to play the ball accurately. At Derby everybody has it. It is essential because the game has got to flow. We do not ask our players to lick a man except in tight situations. We believe in playing football right from the back. We do not want our forwards to have a service of high and hard balls out of defence which are impossible to control.'

Taylor and Clough discussed tactics all the time – what else, after all, could those long chats at Middlesbrough have been about? – and one of their great gifts was their ability to boil that down into simple instructions. They didn't believe in drawing diagrams on blackboards, and they certainly didn't, as Revie did, hand out dossiers on the opposition. 'Telling them how to play,' Taylor said, 'took no time. To O'Hare it was: "Hold the ball no matter how hard they whack you." To Hector: "Watch O'Hare. You've got to be ready when he slips that ball to you." And to Hinton we didn't say any more than: "Stay wide."' Durban recalled being told he was responsible for his area of the pitch, advice that, in itself, was enough to make him sit in and protect the right-back rather than charging all over the field looking for glory. It seems basic, and each individual component was, but multiply those components together and the total was devastatingly effective.

During games, it was simply a question of reinforcing those messages. 'I'd shout reminders,' Clough said, 'adjustments when they occasionally got themselves out of position, which is easy to do in the heat of the moment. I'd emphasise the need to keep the ball and pass it forward whenever possible.' It sounds simple – it was simple – but it was also a clear tactical manifesto.

The pair were quick to act if they felt a player wasn't obeying tactical advice. After signing John McGovern, for instance, Clough felt he was running with the ball too much and holding on to it too long. He took him aside at the training ground and made him do several sprints around the corner flag running with the ball at his feet. Then he made him do them again, but this time without the ball. 'Which is easier?' he asked. McGovern replied that, of course, it was easier without. 'Then pass the bloody ball more this Saturday and you'll run a lot easier,' Clough replied.

Clough's sides may not have practised set-plays, whether attacking or defensive, but he was a great evangelist for his philosophy of the game, which is tactics by another name. 'A team,' he insisted, 'blossoms only when it has the ball. Flowers need the rain – it's a vital ingredient. Common sense tells you that the main ingredient in football is the ball itself.'

In terms of coaching, Clough's approach was about common sense, about stripping the game down to its simplest components; it was his psychological ploys that made him unique. Alan Durban, who credited Clough with turning him from 'a very mediocre midfield player' into the captain of Wales, said Clough made football the most important thing in the players' lives, whereas previously they'd spent their afternoons playing snooker or golf or selling insurance. He made sure training never became a chore, and was quite prepared to stop sessions after quarter of an hour if he felt it had gone well. Clough still trained with the players, still changed with them, still engaged in the banter; at first, management was a way of prolonging the sense of camaraderie and belonging he'd felt as a player. His memory was prodigious, and he would often stop a session to admonish a player for a mistake, backing up his advice by detailing a similar error he'd made in a game, often several weeks earlier.

The first signs that the new approach may be successful came in two further pre-season friendlies at the Baseball Ground, the first against Sunderland of the First Division, and the second a return game against St Johnstone. Both were won 2–1; Edwards was impressed by the apparent solidity of the defence against Sunderland, and although Derby were 'far less convincing' against St Johnstone, the back-line again 'performed most creditably'.

On the eve of the season, Clough insisted there were 'two reasons' for Derby fans to be positive: Mackay and Green. 'These two are not just good players, they are exactly the types needed by Derby County,' he said. 'I am confident [the players remaining from last season] will play better partly because they are a season more experienced and, of course, because they have better players around them.' He was still looking for two further players, he told the *Evening Telegraph*, but he still thought Derby could expect 'a vast improvement. And I mean vast.'

That improvement was far from apparent from the opening game of the season, in which Green immediately proved his worth, making a string of fine saves in a 1–1 draw away at Blackburn. Derby's equaliser came as McFarland headed in a Hinton corner; it would become a very familiar mode of attack. After a 3–0 win over Chesterfield in the League Cup there came further encouragement in a 1–1 draw at home to Blackpool. The game, Edwards said, 'bubbled over with skill and energy' and he predicted a positive season for both sides.

Three days later, though, Derby went down 2–0 at Sheffield United, undone, as the headline in the *Evening Telegraph* had it, by 'Carlin craft'. 'Credit Brian Clough with knowing a good inside-forward when he sees one!' said Edwards. 'For it was wee Willie Carlin, the man Mr Clough tried to sign last season, who guided Sheffield United to a deserved 2–0 win.'

Accepting the validity of Edwards's pre-season concern that Derby lacked the midfielders to operate with a 4–2–4, Clough stepped up his search for new players. A fee of £80,000 was agreed with Leicester for the wing-half

Graham Cross, but the player vacillated. Sick of waiting, Clough decided a fortnight later not to pursue the move, saying he wouldn't sign Cross if he crawled from Leicester and begged to join Derby. Given his own indecisiveness in the face of major moves, he might have been more sympathetic.

It was the 'shortcomings in midfield' that cost Derby in their fourth league game of the season, a 2–0 defeat away to Huddersfield. While others despaired, though, it was then, Clough claimed in his first autobiography, that he became sure Derby were destined for greatness. It was a moment that to others may not have seemed especially significant, but as Roy Keane would later explain, one of Clough's great gifts as a manager was his ability to pinpoint the moments that turned games. In this case, the key moment came as Mackay calmly played the ball out of trouble, turning defence into attack as somebody on the bench urged him to whack it clear. Taylor turned and explained it was just that ability to retain possession for which Derby had bought Mackay.

It was not quite so simple as that, though, and after the Huddersfield game, looking for somebody to protect the ball-players in the side, Clough and Taylor went out and, a year after their first attempt, bought Willie Carlin, who had scored against them for Sheffield United. 'Taylor and I believed in balance as well as talent – and Carlin, a belligerent aggressive little Scouser, gave us just what we needed in midfield,' Clough said.

When the Sheffield United manager Arthur Rowley called him into his office after training, Carlin assumed the club wanted to discuss his mortgage. He was happy at the club, and initially refused even to speak to Clough. Rowley, though, persuaded him it would be rude not even to talk to him, even if it were just to turn him down. Clough's enthusiasm gained further ground, and Carlin agreed to go home and discuss a potential move with his wife. Clough was scornful, asking who wore the trousers in their relationship. Carlin remained adamant, so Clough insisted he get in his Rover and drove him home.

Carlin had assumed his wife Marie would be reluctant to move house again, but when he walked in and asked her if she fancied leaving for Derby, she asked, 'Now or tomorrow?' Clough, seeing an opening, immediately set about charming her, discussing, as Carlin put it, 'carpets, curtains, furniture, the kids' rather than football. The next day, Carlin travelled to Derby to finalise his contract. It was only as he took the train back to Sheffield that it occurred to him to buy a paper and check where his new side lay in the table. To his horror, he realised they were fourth from bottom. Again, that is the story as Clough tells it; according to the scout Maurice Edwards, Taylor had actually tapped up Carlin before the game, doing everything he could to maintain secrecy having already been charged once with making an illegal approach to Carlin while he was at Carlisle.

As soon as the signing was complete, Taylor rang Edwards and asked him to place bets for both him and Clough on Derby winning the division: £60 each way, to which Edwards added £120 of his own money. Others were less convinced by Carlin's usefulness. By chance, Edwards ran in to Rowley at Wolverhampton races a couple of days later and found him drinking a bottle of Moët in celebration at having 'got one over on Cloughie' by offloading an over-aggressive and slow midfielder who couldn't keep his mouth shut. Much the same story, of course, was told about the signing of Hinton. Perhaps Clough did pull the same trick twice, or perhaps he just reused the anecdote.

Carlin made his debut in a scrappy 2–2 draw against Hull, for whom Wagstaff, inevitably, scored. A day later, Derby had a third bid for the St Johnstone winger Kenny Aird turned down, at which Clough decided to withdraw from the pursuit.

Slowly, the turnaround began. Carlin's influence was clear against Oxford at home when, despite a bout of flu, he 'just would not stay out of the game. Almost everything stemmed from this non-stop grafter, whose ability to win the ball in tackles with men much taller and stronger than himself bears comparison with that of Bobby Collins.' Carlin and Durban combined to set O'Hare through for the first after fifteen minutes, and then Carlin cleverly held the ball up, bursting through the Oxford line as they tried to play offside before laying in the charging McFarland to fire in off the post. After a 2–0 win, the *Evening Telegraph* concluded that 'Carlin gives Rams that missing zip'.

It was in a League Cup tie against Stockport that Derby really found their rhythm, Hinton scoring four, two of them penalties, in a 5–1 win. They beat Aston Villa 3–1 without playing particularly well and then Clough added the final key ingredient, agreeing a £7,000 fee with Hartlepools for the eighteen-year-old John McGovern. He arrived without great fanfare. Clough had told the squad to expect a new signing who would 'play for

Scotland before he's twenty-one'. Even with the warning, Mackay was taken by surprise. 'That afternoon,' he said, 'a boy with fair hair and a neat side-parting arrived at the ground on a push-bike. As he approached us, I guessed he was a rather bold, adolescent autograph hunter.'

'He couldn't run and often looked ungainly,' Clough said, 'but he would always stand up straight, he would always strive to get and to pass the ball, and he would do that whether the team was losing 3–0 on a filthy night at Walsall or winning 4–0 on a sunny afternoon at Wembley.' Clough recalled a director asking why he'd signed 'a sparrow-footed, innocuous frail weakling', but McGovern was just the sort of player Clough loved. His odd running style, in fact, had nothing to do with his feet, but was down to a muscle that was missing from his left shoulder, something that wasn't diagnosed until McGovern was twenty-eight, by which time he felt there was little point in corrective surgery.

With McFarland's form good enough to earn a call-up to the England Under-23 squad, Derby's defence became formidable. After a 0–0 draw at Bristol City, the mood of optimism was such that 250 fans had to be turned away from the following home game, a 1–0 win over Fulham. With the team unchanged for the fifth game running, a Durban volley gave Derby a 1–0 win over Millwall. Mackay was evidently enjoying himself. On the coach to away games, he would ask who Derby were playing and whether they had anybody he'd heard of.

The good form continued as Derby went to Chelsea in the third round of the League Cup, and not merely held them to a goalless draw, but restricted them to a single chance. Clough was worried that the replay might prove a distraction as they went to Bolton in the league, but having found their rhythm his side showed no sign of losing it. 'For long periods,' Edwards wrote, 'the Rams took Bolton to pieces.' When Barker opened the scoring from a Hinton cross after sixteen minutes, it seemed so inevitable that the home fans applauded it. Then Jimmy Walker 'picked up a loose clearance twenty-five yards out and set off into the penalty area. Three defenders went to him but he left them flat-footed with remarkable close control, before lashing a shot into the top corner.' It was his first league goal and Clough, who usually frowned on celebration, danced a jig along the touchline.

The replay against Chelsea was, Edwards said, 'the most dramatic and exciting game of football I have ever seen'. The headline in the *Evening Telegraph* called it 'the finest night for years as Rams take Chelsea apart'. 'Imagine a boxer staggering around the ring, battered, bewildered, not knowing which way to turn and finally sinking to the floor,' Edwards began. 'That was Chelsea at the Baseball Ground last night – played to death – thoroughly and completely taken apart by a Derby County scaling new heights. The Rams were a goal down until the seventy-seventh minute. Then, inevitably, Chelsea went under as wave after wave of white shirts hit them time and again. And they were not just outfought – they were outskilled.'

The away side had gone ahead after twenty-six minutes through Alan Birchenall. Minds perhaps went back to the defeat to Leeds the previous season when Derby had more than held their own but succumbed to a needless penalty. This time, though, taking their lead from Mackay, who seemed unfazed by the set-back, Derby poured forward with no loss of belief. 'You did quite often get the feeling that with Dave in the team you just couldn't lose,' Hinton said. 'When things were going wrong you just had to look across at him, fists clenched, urging everybody on.'

'Derby's clockwork interpassing,' Edwards wrote, 'the ball flashing from man to man in extraordinary fashion, had Chelsea chasing shadows in midfield.' The equaliser came thirteen minutes from time. 'Carlin,' said Edwards, 'with whom Chelsea simply never got to grips, raced through the middle and suddenly backheeled the ball. Mackay, following up, hit a thirty-yarder which dipped late and deceived Bonetti completely.'

Six minutes later, with the atmosphere throbbing, Walker burst through on the left and crossed for Durban to head in, and four minutes after that, O'Hare got a touch to Robson's cross, and Hector reached the loose ball ahead of Peter Bonetti to make it 3–1. It was then, Mackay said, 'that I realised Brian Clough was not a complete fantasist and that this team I had joined was becoming a bit special.'

That win was a clear sign of Derby's improvement, and in retrospect can be seen as a signal of what was to come, but at the time the victory heralded a wobble. Derby drew 0–0 at Middlesbrough, but the eleven-match unbeaten run came to an end with a 1–0 defeat at Hull.

Derby were 'patchy and not always convincing' in beating Preston 1–0 at home and then went to Everton in the fourth round of the League Cup.

Perhaps the thought of that game had been a distraction, for Derby found their form again, restricting their First Division opponents to set up another replay at the Baseball Ground, where the tightness of the stands to the pitch meant that the atmosphere could, as Mackay put it, at times feel 'more like a cockpit that a football stadium'. Tickets had sold out by 1.30pm on the day of sale and the enthusiasm was justified as Hector took Walker's cross on the half-hour, turned and lashed a shot that deflected in off Brian Labone for the only goal. It wasn't as emphatic a performance as the win over Chelsea, but then Everton were a better team. Most importantly, Derby were in the quarter-final.

That autumn, Duncan Revie, Don's son, went to the Baseball Ground to watch Derby, his father having called the club to arrange tickets for him and a friend. Clough made a point of meeting them, taking them to the directors' lounge and giving them a Coke. Clough told Duncan that his father was the greatest manager of all time, and chatted away until about ten to three. That is significant for two reasons: for one thing, it suggests that at that stage Clough felt respect rather than distaste for Revie, and for another it indicates just how little time he needed with his players immediately before a game to prepare them.

In the league, Derby outclassed Portsmouth to win 1–0 at Fratton Park, then beat Birmingham 1–0 at home to move to within a point of the leaders, Middlesbrough. They also, though, lost Hinton to injury, something that had a profound impact on their League Cup quarter-final. Against Swindon Town of the Third Division, they looked jaded, and drew 0–0, frustrated by lower-division opponents just as they had frustrated Chelsea and Everton away from home. Hinton was still injured for the replay, and with O'Hare ruled out with a bout of flu, Derby were flat. They were also unlucky, the only goal of the game coming as Don Rogers returned a ball into the box and saw it loop in off Robson's shoulder.

Clough, who usually made a virtue of consistency of selection, brought in McGovern for his debut against Charlton in the next league fixture. The mood of fretful expectation had so intensified that there were jeers even as Derby won a scrappy game 2–1 to go second in the table. Draws against Cardiff and Carlisle only added to the anxiety, and when the publication of financial results from the previous season showed a loss of only £1,980 –

a remarkable figure given £61,100 had been spent on transfers – Clough began to consider a new signing to lift the mood.

Hinton's return to full fitness brought immediate improvement, as he set up goals for Carlin and McFarland – with a corner – in a 2–1 win in muddy conditions at Crystal Palace. The problems, though, hadn't gone away, and it took a McFarland header from a Mackay cross three minutes into injury time to salvage a draw from a home game with Norwich. A goalless draw at Preston followed. Clough, determined to instil the sense of relaxation he felt was necessary for players to perform at their best, took the squad to Bisham Abbey for a break before the Christmas programme. It would become a regular retreat.

The players, though, weren't allowed to become too comfortable. Ritchie Barker was sold to Notts County and Hector was fined £10 for saying in a Sunday newspaper that he would leave Derby if they were not promoted. Clough insisted the fine wasn't about what was said, but that anything had been said at all. Having used the newspapers to fight his battles from his Middlesbrough days, Clough, more than most, knew how unsanctioned player comments could destabilise a club.

The approach seemed to work. On the Saturday before Christmas, with Robson in for the injured Mackay, Derby found themselves a goal down at home to Portsmouth, but rallied superbly. Hector levelled from a Hinton cross just before the hour, then Hector fired the winner as everybody else half-stopped in anticipation of a penalty for a foul on O'Hare. As others faltered, Derby, suddenly, were top.

Then, on Boxing Day, came what was arguably the most important game that season. It may have been the Chelsea match that lived in the memory, that lifted spirits and stimulated the belief that Derby were worthy of a place in the First Division, but the game that in practical terms really set them on their way was against second-placed Middlesbrough. With 33,481, the biggest crowd of the season at the Baseball Ground, packing in, it was, Edwards said, a great occasion rather than a great game. The Hinton–McFarland combination had Derby ahead from a nineteenth-minute corner, but John Hickton levelled from the penalty spot and put Middlesbrough ahead just before half-time after charging down a Webster clearance. Derby controlled the second half and pulled level on seventy minutes through a

Hinton penalty. Five minutes later he scored the winner, converting a cross from Carlin, and Derby were three points clear.

Keen to avoid complacency, Clough let it be known he was keen to sign the Leicester full-back David Nish, and although Derby then went out of the FA Cup to Burnley, they beat Bury 2–0, then produced a superb performance in drawing 1–1 at Birmingham, whom Edwards described as the 'latest side to be given a football lesson by Derby County. At times the Rams mocked them. The swift inter-changing of positions and deft ball control pulled men out of position so easily that a hatful of goals seemed certain.'

By mid-January, Derby were four points clear of Millwall with a game in hand and Edwards's tone was undeniably jubilant. A 2–0 defeat at Charlton had him warning that poor finishing could yet cost Derby promotion, but then came one of those moments of Clough perversity that was hailed as genius.

Away at Bury, with Derby leading 1–0 through a John O'Hare goal, Mackay was knocked out by a flailing arm from George Jones midway through the first half. Clough opted not to use his substitute, instead playing on with ten men until half-time so see if Mackay could continue. When it became clear that Mackay would have to be replaced, Walker finally came on, McGovern dropped in to sweeper and Derby won 1–0. Edwards saw the delay in making the change as an impressive show of faith that had boosted the morale of those who remained, but had it gone wrong, it could easily have been seen as indecisiveness or even an over-reliance on Mackay; a sign that Clough would rather play with ten men for twenty-five minutes than risk seventy with eleven but no Mackay. It was the sort of gamble in which he delighted – and it is easy to imagine Bury being unsettled by the thought that they would have to take advantage before Mackay returned – and in those days, they tended to come off. There is a sense with Clough's early period of management that the self-belief he radiated was so absolute that his players regarded anything he did as an act of eccentric brilliance and were inspired accordingly.

Concerned both by the relative slimness of the squad and Derby's occa-sional wastefulness in front of goal, Clough decided Derby needed a striker to bolster confidence. He and Taylor, with typical disregard of consensus, settled on Frank Wignall, a twenty-nine-year-old forward then at Wolves.

He was experienced, had played twice for England and had averaged a little better than a goal every three games over a career spent largely at Nottingham Forest, but it was generally believed that he was past it. And besides, with O'Hare and Hector in the side, there was the issue of where he would play. 'Hopefully he won't have to,' Taylor said, but he made forty-five appearances over the next four seasons.

Derby beat Blackburn 4–2 but were still 'sloppy' and, with Carlin absent with a knee injury, went down 1–0 at home to Crystal Palace. The importance of Carlin's aggression in midfield to Derby's surge was such that they lost only once that season when he played and was fully fit, and it is indicative of Clough's vision of what his side needed to have balance that he had attempted to sign him a year earlier.

Carlin was given a few days off and when he turned up at the Baseball Ground for training on the Thursday, he found Clough had taken the players to Blackpool for a three-day break before their fixture at Bloomfield Road on the Saturday. It was a typical Clough trick, so focused on relaxation that the players spent the day before the game crashing into each other in dodgems rather than training. Carlin followed in Longson's Rolls-Royce, and declared himself fit enough to play. Early on, though, he took a whack on the knee and, incapacitated, hardly touched the ball. He focused instead on running about directing the play, and as Hinton converted an eighty-sixth-minute penalty to win the game 3–2, earned the rare accolade of a handshake from Clough at the final whistle.

At Carlisle, Derby were in 'exhilarating form' and were unlucky only to draw, but the point carried them two points clear of Middlesbrough in second and four clear of third-placed Cardiff who had played a game more. McFarland headed in a Hinton corner to give them a 1–0 win over Huddersfield, and the charge was on. Derby won 2–0 at Oxford and 1–0 at Aston Villa. 'In the end it was an anti-climax because Aston Villa were out of their class,' Edwards wrote. 'Their massed choirs of supporters stood in numbed silence throughout the second half as Derby County extracted full pleasure from humiliating inferior opposition.'

When Wignall's first goal for the club gave them a 1–0 win at Fulham, Derby were six points clear. That meant a win at home to Bolton would secure promotion on the first weekend in April. Hector ran on to a long ball from the goalkeeper Les Green to smash them in front after twenty-one minutes, and Wignall added a second just before half-time as McFarland chested a Mackay free-kick into his path. Bolton pulled one back soon after the break, but that only jolted Derby into fluidity. O'Hare latched onto a lofted ball from Hector to make it 3–1, Hector and O'Hare combined for Carlin to add a fourth, before McFarland, on his twenty-first birthday, rounded off a 5–1 win.

'What a triumph from Brian Clough and Peter Taylor, who joined this club that was dead on its feet just sixteen months ago, took it by the scruff of the neck and shook professionalism into it,' Edwards exulted. 'And what a triumph too for former chairman Sam Longson, the man chiefly responsible for bringing the Clough–Taylor duo to the Baseball Ground.'

Clough described it as being 'like his first Christmas', a moment he would never forget and that would forever remain among the sweetest of his memories, but Edwards noted a reserve. '"Well, that's phase one completed," commented Mr Clough, strangely quiet as his players sang, joked and toasted each other in champagne,' he wrote. 'And it was perhaps significant that within half-an-hour of the Rams having beaten Bolton 5–1, Mr Clough was meeting the parents of two thirteen-year-old triallists and that Mr Taylor missed the celebrations to watch players elsewhere. Promotion, they feel, is merely a stepping stone to greater things.' Clough, certainly, seems to have been intent on keeping the focus on what was to come in the First Division. 'We won't set 'em alight up there, but we might surprise a few people,' he said. 'We shan't score many goals, but I hope we won't concede many either.'

All that remained was for Derby to romp through their remaining four games of the season, sealing the title after 1–0 victories over Sheffield United and Millwall, before Clough released the reins for emphatic wins over Norwich and Bristol City. Mackay won the Football Writers' Player of the Year award jointly with Tony Book – an astonishing achievement for a player from the Second Division – and, on 18 April, the *Evening Telegraph* announced that Clough and Taylor had both agreed new five-year contracts. Derby County seemed vibrant with optimism.

Problems, though, were brewing. The first sour note came when Clough sent the players to Mallorca for a ten-day end-of-season break, as Carlin, Green, McGovern and Robson were arrested on charges of damaging a car, with an additional allegation of physical assault against the driver. All four had their passports confiscated, and Carlin, McGovern and Robson subsequently appeared in court.

Clough, with his characteristic suspicion of foreigners, was dismissive. 'I have been to Spain quite often and I can believe anything of the police over there,' he said. 'They'll have you if you spit the wrong way.' Basing his version of events on what Taylor had told him, he explained that 'the lads were walking down the middle of the road late at night and a car came racing at them and almost knocked them flying'. McGovern and Robson were acquitted after Carlin admitted kicking the car. He was fined 500 pesetas (£3 10s), plus damages of 2,500 pesetas (£15) and legal costs of 1,100 pesetas (£6 10s). Marie Carlin blamed Clough, saying 'there would have been no trouble if the wives had been allowed to go'.

That wasn't the only incident on the trip. Les Green had to rescue Jimmy Walker, who got out of his depth while swimming off the beach, and then Derby were fined by the FA for having broken a regulation that prevented clubs taking their players on holiday unless the provision to do so had been stipulated in their contracts. Had they played a game, they would have been all right as the trip would have been classed as a tour. Clough had little time for what he regarded as nit-picking pettiness, and tended just to ignore rules he didn't like. This was a warning, but he paid no heed and a year later his refusal to do things as the authorities demanded would have more serious consequences.

The First Rebellion

By the start of the new season, Clough and Taylor still hadn't signed their contracts, an early indication of troubles to come. Clough later claimed it was because the chairman, Sydney Bradley, hadn't had the contracts drawn up. 'If I took as long to do my job as the directors have to sort this out,' he said, 'Derby County would be in rack and ruin.' Perhaps that was the case, although Clough tended to be slow to sign contracts, whether because he was a prevaricator or a procrastinator is hard to tell.

It would be several months, though, before it emerged that the new deals hadn't been signed and for most fans the mood was unprecedentedly optimistic as they prepared for Derby's first season in the top flight for sixteen years. An indication of Derby's heightened ambitions came with the construction of the Ley Stand, at a cost of £230,000, increasing the capacity of the Baseball Ground to 41,000. As with most things at the club at the time, it seems to have been done almost on a whim – specifically Clough's whim – without any great advanced planning. Building work had already started when the club applied to the council for a loan of £75,000. It was granted, but Alderman C.E.J. Andrews admitted to have begun work without guaranteed finance was 'a little strange'.

According to Clough in his autobiography, when the plans for the new stand were drawn up, it became apparent that Derby required an extra eighteen inches of land from the Ley factory that backed on to the Baseball Ground. Clough negotiated with the factory, securing the extra space in return for a new fence, naming rights and a handful of complimentary season tickets.

As he had at Hartlepools, where it had been a necessity, Clough followed the Alan Brown model and involved himself in all aspects of running the club, even sweeping down the terraces on a Sunday morning when the mood took him. His willingness to perform menial chores irritated Taylor, but far more significant was the way his grander schemes irritated the directors. Some were concerned merely with protecting their power base, but there were other worries, which would be borne out at the end of the following season.

As the players reported back to begin 'commando-style' training in Colwick Woods, Clough appointed Jimmy Gordon as trainer. Given Gordon had been one of his sternest critics while trainer at Middlesbrough, that came as a surprise to everybody, even after the approach at Hartlepools, not least Gordon himself, who was by then quite happily employed at Blackburn. It made sense that Clough, in his first job, should have sought to surround himself with familiar faces, but turning to Gordon even when he was established suggested just how highly he rated him, for all their differences.

When Clough telephoned him, Gordon's first thought was that he wanted to sign Keith Newton. Hearing that Clough wanted *him*, Gordon pointed out that all they'd ever done was argue; that, Clough replied, was precisely why he wanted him.

'He was military, everything was spot on,' the Middlesbrough winger Billy Day remembered. 'No wonder Clough took him on. You could trust him with anything and what he said stood, with international players and everyone.' Brian Phillips was just as big a fan. 'He told you everything that he should tell you,' he said. 'If you were a bit slow or not doing this or that. He watched you while you were training and he could see if there was anything wrong with you. He's one bloke I would never criticise. He was a man.'

Gordon agreed to allow Clough to come and visit him, and so became yet another figure who came on board with Clough despite serious reservations. 'It was against all my principles to join him,' he told Francis. 'I didn't like him . . . neither was I a fan of Peter Taylor.' It took five hours, but eventually Gordon cracked. In the end, it wasn't Clough's charm – Gordon had presumably seen enough of that at Middlesbrough – but money that persuaded him, as Derby offered a £1,000 interest-free deposit on his new house. 'He was just the same then,' Gordon said. 'Impatient, wanting to put everything right overnight, not just football but the world. As a coach, I used to pull him apart for getting caught offside and only thinking about scoring goals himself. But he had this incredible eye for putting the ball in the back of the net.'

The move immediately created discord as Jack Burkitt, who had held the post, resigned at what he perceived as a demotion, although Clough insisted he was simply looking to add numbers to his backroom staff. In the long run it probably didn't much matter, but it was another off-key note in a summer that was full of them. Another came in Derby's first pre-season friendly as Wignall was sent off during a brawl in a 3–3 draw at Fortuna Cologne. 'I'm blazing,' said Clough. 'It was a stupid thing to do. It's no good saying sorry after the event. There is simply no excuse for what he did.'

Derby slowly improved over the rest of the tour and as ticket sales broke £200,000 and Werder Bremen were thrashed 6–0 in a home friendly, Edwards felt the need to temper what he saw as unrealistic optimism. 'The days when a promoted team could race straight to the championship have gone since the super league within Division One formed with Liverpool and Leeds at the spearhead,' he wrote in the *Derby Evening Telegraph*, insisting that eleventh would be 'a brilliant achievement at the first attempt'.

Clough, meanwhile, vowed there would be no change of approach, while warning fans that that would mean the emphasis was still on clean sheets.

'We shall stick to our 4–3–3 because we spent a long time perfecting it,' he said. 'But there will be times, obviously, when we shall be under a lot of pressure and have everybody back ... Our aim, always, will be to keep a clean sheet. The question of entertaining people comes fairly low on our list of priorities at the moment. The job in hand is to consolidate our place in the First Division.' He rejected, though, the notion that that meant Derby would be playing negative football. 'Football can't be negative if you pick up points,' he said. 'You draw 0–0 away by defending and you get one point. That's not negative. We are not going to become a kick and rush team or anything like that. I thought we were good to watch at the end of last season, but the prime aim was still to stop the opposition from scoring.'

Sure enough, Derby began with a goalless draw at home to Burnley, in which they were on top for most of the game but took the point only after Green had saved a late penalty from Frank Casper. At Ipswich the following Wednesday, Derby were, Edwards wrote, 'at first cautious, then confident and finally almost arrogant.' They won 1–0, McFarland heading the only goal from a Hinton corner. Clough, oddly, didn't turn up for a post-match drink with John Cobbold, the Ipswich chairman, sending Taylor to say he was tired and preferred to wait on the bus. It may be that there was nothing sinister about it, but it could be seen as a sign of Clough becoming increasingly erratic. Now he was in the First Division, he had no need to court controversy; it followed him around.

A Hector winner was disallowed in a 1–1 draw at Coventry because Carlin, standing yards away, was offside, and Derby then beat Ipswich 3–1, a game the *Evening Telegraph* summed up with the one-word headline, 'Ffficiency'. Clough criticised his players for a supposed lack of effort, a theme he pursued after a 0–0 draw with Stoke.

After the stick came the carrot and Clough described his side's response as 'tremendous' as they drew 1–1 at Wolves, a result that left them fifth in the table. A 2–0 win at West Brom secured Clough the Bell's Manager of the Month award; it was the first of many.

Derby beat Hartlepools in the League Cup and then came the first real test, at home to Everton, one of the only other two unbeaten sides in the division. Clough said before the game that it would be won and lost in midfield, where Durban, McGovern and Carlin met Colin Harvey, Howard Kendall and Alan Ball. He was right. McGovern effectively neutralised Ball, allowing Derby to control possession. O'Hare headed in Hinton's tenth corner of the match after thirty-nine minutes, and then Hector flicked in another Hinton corner at the near post. That may make it sound as though Derby were a side that relied on set-plays, but the corner that produced the second goal stemmed from a move that featured eight players and ended with Webster overlapping on the right from full-back. Kendall pulled one back after a McGovern slip, but Derby were worth their 2–1 win. 'O'Hare was out of this world,' Clough said. 'And John McGovern's ability to lay the ball anywhere first time with either foot is fabulous. We laid the ball, laid it there, checked out, laid it again. It was wonderful.'

They beat Southampton 3–0 and Newcastle 1–0, despite McFarland struggling with a groin injury, Hinton suffering a cold and a thigh injury, Durban having a bad knee and Mackay taking the goal-kicks because Green had a bruised foot. Watching Newcastle struggle against Derby's defence, Edwards said, 'was like watching fish in a keep net, threshing wildly and exhausting themselves'. After ten matches Derby were top, and had conceded only four goals.

It was what followed, though, that really startled the rest of the division as Tottenham went to the Baseball Ground and were hammered 5–0. 'Two ghastly defensive errors gave Derby their first two goals,' Paul Fitzpatrick wrote in the *Guardian*, 'but thereafter they were destroyed by some of the most exciting and ruthlessly brilliant football that one has seen in a long time. Derby could hardly be faulted. Their defence, revolving around the massive command of McFarland and the authority of Mackay, seems capable of containing the best. Carlin was an inspired and inspiring master of midfield; O'Hare gave [Mike] England a nightmare of a match; Hector was irrepressible; Hinton with his savage shooting and powerful running continually erupted like some minor volcano.'

Durban, retrieving the ball after being tackled by England, put Derby ahead after fifteen minutes and Hector capitalised on more defensive uncertainty five minutes later. The game's defining moment, though, came two minutes after that. 'Greaves, with hardly room to move, swivelled beautifully, timed the ball perfectly on the volley, and sent it hurtling towards what seemed an inevitable destination,' Fitzpatrick wrote. 'But Green saved spectacularly. That, possibly, was the psychologically crushing blow for

Tottenham. They were already two goals down, and if you cannot score with those sort of shots, can you score at all?'

Dave Mackay called it the best save he'd ever seen: 'It was like somebody firing a rifle in your direction and you effortlessly catching the bullet.' Within a minute, Carlin had headed in a corner to make it 3–0. Carlin and Durban created a fourth for O'Hare before Durban finished things off with a 'nonchalant header' from Hector's cross. 'We used to play two-touch football in training most days,' Carlin said, 'and we beat them by playing two-touch football for ninety minutes.' This was proof that the Clough method could produce astonishing results at the very highest level. 'They humiliated us,' the Tottenham manager Bill Nicholson admitted. 'They are very talented and they don't just run, they know when to run and where.'

A first defeat was lurking, and it came at Sheffield Wednesday. Edwards was quick to point out that Derby had still had the better of a 1–0 reverse and Clough was again named Bell's Manager of the Month, adding another cheque for £50 and another gallon of Scotch.

Their momentum, though, had been checked, and after a 2–0 win at home against Manchester United, Derby went down 3–1 at home to Coventry. 'Coventry,' Edwards wrote, 'played efficient, hard football and the Rams did not always show the combative spirit necessary.' Worse was what happened off the pitch. There had been minor incidents of crowd trouble all season, usually involving away supporters – although twenty-one fans watched the United game in stockinged feet having had their steel-capped boots confiscated – but here Derby suffered its first real outbreak of hooliganism. Derby fans smashed the windows of the Coventry team coach and were involved in a series of skirmishes with police. As Edwards reflected, they had thought Derby fans were better than that, but their comparatively good behaviour turned out merely to have been an illusion conjured by a series of positive results. Clough remained oddly silent, although he would later become vociferous in his attacks on the troublemakers.

Derby's form drifted through October, as they took one point from three games. They struggled to deal with the power of Leeds and the goals, both controversial, came in a five-minute spell before half-time. The first followed a throw-in that was flagged as a foul throw by the linesman but not given by the referee, while Allan Clarke looked – to Derby eyes at least – offside as he scored the second.

Clough finally brought in the additional coach he'd been seeking when he appointed John Sheridan at the end of October and immediately there was a flickering of the old form. Hinton scored a brilliant volley as Derby beat Crystal Palace 3–0 in a League Cup third-round replay, and they then hammered Liverpool 4–0 to record their first league win in a month, Hector scoring twice. 'To lose to that team is no disgrace,' said the Liverpool manager Bill Shankly.

It was, though, only a fleeting return to form, and with McFarland badly hampered by his groin injury and everybody else having an off-day, Derby were beaten 4–0 at Arsenal. Clough was furious, and there was silence on the coach from Highbury to St Pancras. Usually the players would have had a beer in the station bar, but Clough instead had them sit in the Great Northern Hotel, stewing on the defeat. As they got on the train there was such a subdued mood that the players were reluctant even to pick up a menu in the dining car for fear of provoking Clough. Taylor, finally, sidled up to Clough, and said something that drew a snort of involuntary laughter. Soon, Edwards detailed, the whole carriage was laughing and when they reached Derby Clough took the players into the Midland Hotel for a couple of drinks. Quite apart from his capacity to spot players and his tactical nous, Taylor's ability to lift Clough was a key factor in their partnership.

The optimism of early season was fraying. As Derby drew 0–0 at home to Manchester United in the fourth round of the League Cup, an away fan was beaten up and stabbed by five locals. Even more alarmingly, dangerous crushes developed outside and it became apparent that construction of the Ley Stand had cut access to the popular end. The *Evening Telegraph* that week was deluged with complaints from other fans who discovered that, following an administrative error, they weren't able to take up seats to which vouchers in their season tickets should have entitled them. That Derby lacked professional long-term planning and organisation had been apparent for some time; here the potential dangers of that became clear.

Two days later, Derby's twenty-two-year-old secretary Malcolm Bramley resigned. Blaming long hours and a lack of assistance, he insisted criticism of arrangements for the United game were only a minor factor in his decision. That weekend Derby won 3–0 against Sunderland, who were bottom of the table and sinking fast, but that was a brief respite.

The following Wednesday, as Derby prepared for the replay against United at Old Trafford, Sydney Bradley was forced to call a 'crisis meeting' with Clough. Reports had appeared a few days earlier suggesting Barcelona wanted to hire Clough to replace Josep Seguer as head coach and when Bradley appeared to hint Clough himself may have been the source of the reports, Clough threatened to quit. They emerged from the meeting insisting the whole matter was the result of 'a misunderstanding', but it was only then that it was made public that neither Clough nor Taylor had signed the contracts they had been offered six months earlier. That night, after Hector had missed two fine chances, George Best, having played 'like a man in a dream', according to Edwards, hit the post and Kidd knocked in the rebound to put Derby out of the League Cup.

The next day, as if to prove the rumours had substance, George Sturrup, an agent for Barcelona, made contact with Clough and revealed they would offer £8,000 a year, tax free. 'That sounds absolutely ideal and I should be a fool not to follow the thing up,' Clough said, insisting that there was no chance of him signing the contract he'd been offered by Derby, which was believed to be worth £40,000 gross over five years. 'There's as much chance of me signing it,' he said, 'as of me joining the Apollo 12 spacemen on the moon.'

The bad news kept on coming. That Saturday the directors' report to shareholders for the year ending on 31 July 1969 was leaked to the *Evening Telegraph*, which highlighted several major concerns. Five members of the board between them had bought 701 shares originally issued in 1896 but forfeited in 1926. 'These shares,' the *Evening Telegraph* explained, 'were reissued on the basis of the payment of the amount of the unpaid calls on each share – which means that all were bought at less than their £1 face value. They may have been used at last year's annual meeting to oppose the bid of Mr Cyril Addey to gain a seat on the board.' Take that figure of 701 off the total declared votes for each candidate and Addey would have been elected by six votes. In a sense, the issue was academic, given Addey died a fortnight later after a short illness, but the details add to the picture of a club beset by intrigue and boardroom in-fighting, which Clough was quick to attempt to exploit.

There were also two financial issues that demanded explanation. One unnamed member of staff had received 'emoluments' of between £10,000 and £12,500, while there was a discrepancy of £3,000 between the face value of season tickets sold and the £183,906 entered in the accounts. These were serious issues and they would have major consequences. That afternoon, Derby were guilty of a series of 'defensive blunders' as they lost 3–0 at West Ham.

When Derby then lost the east Midlands derby 2–0 at home to Nottingham Forest, it meant they had failed to score in five of their previous six games. Taylor, though, was more concerned about the other end of the pitch. 'If necessary we must start again from scratch,' he said. 'We have temporarily forgotten the art of defending. If necessary we must start playing as tight as possible for 0–0 draws like we did at one stage last season.'

The back-to-basics approach had an immediate impact. 'One heard last week's reports of Baseball Ground pep talks, liberally laced with words not to be found in the dictionary,' Edwards wrote. 'One player I met had all the symptoms of somebody suffering from severe shock, even to the glazed-over eyes after one of these talks. The effect was quite astonishing.' Derby not merely frustrated Crystal Palace at Selhurst Park, dominating possession, but Hector, holding off two defenders, smacked in the winner.

There remained, though, the issue of Clough and Taylor's contracts and on Tuesday, 9 December 1969, they met with Bradley and his deputy Ken Turner, who was scheduled to take over as chairman in June. The dispute, Clough insisted, was not over his salary but over club policy, which he felt was lacking in ambition. Eventually, after five hours of talks, minor changes in the contract – assumed to concern incentives – were agreed, with Clough and Taylor promising to sign them at the board-meeting the following Thursday. Asked what his target was for Derby over the coming five years, Clough was characteristically sanguine. 'We want to win everything. The sky is the limit.' It later emerged that a consortium of businessmen had wanted him to front a takeover of Sunderland.

Just as Clough and Taylor's contracts were resolved, along came another off-field problem as the FA and the Football League launched a probe into the club's finances, although whether it was a spot check or prompted by the missing £3,000 was never clear. In his diaries, Longson insisted the sum was not missing but had simply not been properly recorded, which was certainly in keeping with the general way things were run. Players had not been registered, money – including £2,000 to Mackay for writing his column in the programme – had been paid without being recorded, there was no system for the sale of season tickets and petty cash was paid without chits.

No sooner had the investigation been launched than there was another outcry over the supply of Cup tickets, with 900 fans who had vouchers for seats for the FA Cup fourth-round tie against Sheffield United having to stand because the away side took up the full allocation of twenty-five per cent to which they were entitled under competition rules. Derby won the game 3–0, as O'Hare, who had been the focus for some of the fans' frustration as their impressive start petered out, scored twice to take his tally to eight goals in five games. The Cup run, though, ended in a dreary 1–0 defeat at QPR in the fifth round.

Derby were well beaten 1–0 at Manchester United at which, with the season drifting, Clough acted. His solution to wandering form was straightforward: he made a signing. Just as the arrival of Frank Wignall the previous February had given Derby renewed zest for the run-in, so the signing of Terry Hennessey for £110,000 from Nottingham Forest galvanised them in 1970, his versatility offering both cover for McFarland, who was still struggling with the groin problem he'd had all season, and an extra option in midfield. Hennessey was another Clough player who didn't look much like a footballer: he was bald from his mid-twenties, never especially slim, and with his creased face could easily have passed for a couple of decades older than he was. He could pass a ball and read the game, though, and fulfilled the niche Clough asked him to. Injuries blighted the tail-end of his career and he was forced to retire in 1973, aged thirty, having made sixty-three league appearances for Derby.

It was as a right-half that Hennessey made his debut against Chelsea alongside Durban and Carlin. Having gone 2–0 down, Derby salvaged a draw with two goals in the final twelve minutes, a point that left them tenth, the achievements of early season all but forgotten. Clough fielded the same midfield at Burnley, where Derby conceded after eighty-nine minutes, but managed a draw as O'Hare levelled in injury-time.

Two late comebacks at least spoke of tenacity and Clough rewarded his players by taking them to Guernsey for a break. While they were away, it became apparent that Derby would face Football Association charges over

191

a number of financial irregularities, most notably their failure to register a reserve-team player as a professional, making the wages he was earning illegal. Clough seems to have regarded the whole affair as a minor administrative matter and his players returned refreshed to face Arsenal. Twice Derby went behind, but they came back to win 3–2.

Others might have stuck with the same line-up, but Clough deployed Hennessey as a centre-back with Mackay sweeping for the trip to Liverpool the following week. Hennessey got the opener, heading in a Hinton free-kick, and a 2–0 win was sealed from a breakaway that began with Ron Webster and ended with Hector crossing for O'Hare to volley in. The confidence was back and Derby were flowing again. A 3–0 win over West Ham lifted Derby to fourth, although they had played more games than many of their rivals. The sense of off-field unease remained, though, as reports surfaced that Taylor was considering setting out on his own. In itself, it was a rumour, a vague news story on a slow day, but it was another drip of unrest in a growing puddle.

Clough, though, was in his pomp, enjoying one of those periods in which whatever he tried came off. Dropping Hector for the return east Midlands derby at Nottingham Forest was unorthodox and would have drawn derision had it failed, but the introduction of Wignall upset Forest's marking structure. Just as significantly, Forest's hard-man, Sammy Chapman, who had recently become the first Forest player sent off in thirty-two years, came out second best in an early clash with Wignall and had to be substituted. Derby went on to win 3–1.

Taylor was linked with the Birmingham City job, which had fallen vacant after Stan Cullis's departure. He insisted he could never work without Clough, which seemed reassuring for Derby fans, until it emerged that Birmingham wanted them both.

A 3–1 win over Crystal Palace meant Derby were unbeaten in seven matches since Hennessey's arrival, the last five of them won. The *Evening Telegraph* was so upbeat that it published two six-page souvenir supplements detailing the 'Race for Europe'. Derby's position improved further as a McFarland header gave them a 1–0 win at Manchester City, and they drew 1–1 at Sunderland.

The visit of Leeds on Easter Monday promised to be a climactic test, but Leeds, with an eye on their forthcoming European Cup semi-final against

Celtic, played a reserve side. Forty years on, that may be standard practice, but in 1970 it was seen as scandalous, bringing a £5,000 fine from the League and adding to Clough's distaste for Leeds. The *Evening Telegraph* blasted the selection as 'a let-down', while Edwards called it 'a farce'. The Baseball Ground was sold out, the gates locked twenty minutes before kick-off; it was later joked that that was just to stop people walking out when they saw the Leeds line-up. Amid the fury, though, there was a positive, which was a relatively simple game: Derby won 4–1 to go third and all but guarantee qualification for the Fairs Cup.

It was rapidly becoming apparent, though, that qualifying for the Fairs Cup might be an irrelevance. That week, Derby sent a delegation to an FA–Football League commission into their alleged financial malpractice. The previous season, Manchester United had been fined £7,000 and banned from Europe for a year for a similar offence. Remarkably, Clough was not in attendance. 'In view of the gravity of the situation,' Edwards wrote, 'and Mr Clough's record as a convincing speaker, this is a staggering omission.'

That Saturday, goals from Wignall and Hennessey gave Derby a 2–0 win over Wolves, securing them a place in Europe. Five days later, it was taken away as the commission announced its sentence. While acknowledging there was 'no question of fraud or dishonesty against any person now or formerly connected with the club', it fined Derby £10,000 and banned them from European competition for a season.

'This young manager had arrived like a whirlwind,' Sam Longson wrote in his diary. 'We were all under his spell. Unfortunately for the club, he took more and more control both on and off the field. I had to work overtime to explain to him that a football club is a limited company subject to company law. It is also subject to the rules and regulations of the Football Association and the Football League Chaos was abounding inside the ground. The young man [Malcolm Bramley] to whom Brian had given the vital backstage job of secretary and his staff of three part-timers were run off their feet. I could see we were heading for trouble. Brian had a free hand in running most aspects of the club and it was becoming increasingly apparent to me that the time had come to separate the duties of team management and general administration.'

There is no reason to believe there was anything more sinister going on than the club growing faster than its infrastructure, but if anybody had wanted to take advantage of the administrative fog, the opportunity was certainly there. Clough blamed the directors, insisting administration was their preserve, which was true up to a point, but Longson was surely right when he insisted that Clough 'must take his share of the responsibility'. Clough and Taylor, though, immediately sought further talks with Bradley about their future.

On the playing side, all that remained was to see whether Derby could break their record for points won during the season. To do so, they needed to win away at Southampton on the final day of the season, and when McGovern put them ahead with two minutes remaining they looked well set. Tony Byrne, though, levelled in the final minute and so Derby had to be content with fourth place and equalling the tally of fifty-three set in 1948–49.

In terms of the club's future, though, the season's key battle was only just beginning. Sam Longson, forced into retirement a year earlier, returned, breathing fire and demanding the resignation of three directors – Harry Payne, Ken Turner and Bob Kirkland – for their part in the financial mismanagement. At the same time, a group of rebel shareholders, led by Mike Keeling, the owner of a local removals firm, attacked the board in general. Longson insisted he was not allied to them, but Bradley responded by demanding his resignation.

A week after the end of the season, the Birmingham chairman Clifford Coombes told the *Evening Telegraph* that he was about to go on a three-week cruise and was sure that by the time he returned Clough and Taylor would have been appointed. 'It is incredible,' Longson said, 'that we should be in danger of losing Peter and Brian to a struggling Second Division club and even more incredible that my colleagues on the board do not seem worried whether they leave or not. Mr Turner, who has been running the club for the last six months [something that was denied by Bradley], has disappeared for a holiday I believe. This is terrible when we are facing the biggest crisis in our history.'

Bradley responded by insisting he would resign if Clough left, which he did not expect. Payne, Turner and Bob Kirkland all refused to resign, at which Longson called 'an extraordinary meeting to have these three men removed from the board. I am going to seek legal advice. I don't know what support I have from other shareholders, but I think there is plenty there from people who do not want to see Peter and Brian leave.' With a minimum notice period of twenty-one days for an EGM to be called, that meant the situation could have dragged on until mid-May.

The following Monday, though, Payne resigned, saying he wanted 'a complete rest from football'. Three days later, Turner and Kirkland also quit; they too declined to blame Longson's ultimatum. Turner, who had been on the board since 1961, was scheduled to replace Bradley that summer; Kirkland, who had been there since 1964, would have succeeded him in 1972. The board was thus reduced to just four members: Longson, Bradley, the club president Robertson King and Fred Walters. 'The ball is now in Brian's court,' said Longson. 'I hope that when he considers what has happened in the past fortnight he will scotch these rumours about moving once and for all.'

It was then, according to Don Shaw, who would come to prominence as leader of the Protest Movement that sought to reinstate Clough at Derby after his resignation, that Longson did a deal with Clough promising him a free hand if he supported his bid to return as chairman. Quite what the details of any agreement were it is impossible at this remove to know, but it is almost inconceivable that there was not some dialogue between Clough and Longson before the former chairman launched his attack. Finally, on 5 May, Clough committed to Derby, but only after receiving an assurance that either the Normanton or the Osmaston stand would be replaced and that money would be made available for one more major signing. The club took the opportunity to announce price rises to help fund the development.

Or had he committed? Two days later the Greek football federation made an enquiry to see if Clough fancied managing their national side. As ever, Clough showed early interest, but he was deeply parochial at heart and after making a painful joke about how many 'draculas, I mean drachmas' the Greeks were offering, decided there were 'too many snags'.

Keeling was appointed to the board, as were Bill Rudd, a clerk in a firm of solicitors, and Bob Innes, a chartered auctioneer and estate agent, at which Clough and Taylor finally did commit their futures to Derby. Longson soon succeeded Bradley and had the stipulation that chairmen could only serve a maximum of two years removed from the club regulations. How involved Clough was in the plot it is hard to be sure, but he had ousted one chairman at Hartlepools and he certainly benefited in the short-term from Longson's accession. At Hartlepools, though, Clough's relationship with the new chairman never had time to go wrong; at Derby the revolution was the beginning of the end.

At first there was real affection between Clough and Longson, even if Clough did call him 'an old twit' in private while praising him in print. Although not an Ernest Ord figure who revelled in the exertion of his power, in business Longson – after selling his haulage firm, he still owned a hire-purchase company, two farms with a dairy herd and a raspberry plantation – had a reputation for ruthlessness and was notorious for sacking employees for the slightest breach. He was tough and thorough and so determined not be cheated that on one occasion he sat up till three in the morning in a lorry park to spy on a driver he suspected of siphoning petrol from the tank. When he caught him red-handed, he dismissed him on the spot.

Derby County, though, was Longson's weak spot. It is inconceivable he would have allowed any of his other businesses to have been run as haphazardly as Derby was, indulging Clough way beyond the allowances that might usually be made for a figure of such brilliance who had had such success. Reflecting on the events leading to his resignation from Derby, Clough commented that if you gave directors an inch they'd take a yard, but the reverse was surely at least as true.

That is not to suggest, though, that – at first at least – there was anything cynical in Clough's response to Longson. Rather they had, as Clough put it, 'a genuine, close friendship'. He happily borrowed his Rolls-Royce and drove his Mercedes as though it were his own. When things were getting on top of him at the training ground, Clough would ring Longson, saying he couldn't 'talk to any of the other buggers here'. Longson, meanwhile, carried a photo of Clough around in his wallet. He had three daughters and both parties were well aware of the role Clough had come to play; in his diaries Longson openly acknowledged that Clough was 'like a son to me'. Longson bought his children presents, would take a leg of lamb around on Sundays and let Clough use his cottage on Anglesey for holidays. Intriguingly, Longson also praised Clough's business acumen and the way he managed to balance the books.

*

The other major change that summer, again one that would contribute to Clough's downfall, was the arrival of Stuart Webb. After the fiasco of the financial negligence, Clough decided he needed to bolster his administrative staff and, on Jimmy Gordon's recommendation, turned to Webb, assistant secretary at Preston North End, to become Derby's new assistant secretary. The decision, of course, should have been Longson's, but he was on holiday when Clough, having booked Webb and his wife Josie into the Midland Hotel, took him to a board meeting and presented him as the new assistant secretary. Clough insisted he was merely seizing the opportunity while it was there, as he had with countless players, but although the other board members – Rudd, Innes and Keeling – went along with it, Longson was understandably 'extremely annoyed' that Clough had so undermined him by making an appointment without his consent.

Quite why Clough should have pushed through Webb's appointment is baffling. Perhaps he was simply impatient, or perhaps he was again, as he had in his first dealings with the board over Ian Buxton, asserting his authority. What is clear is that if he thought Webb would be a yes-man who would strengthen his position within the club, he was mistaken.

A mutual distrust was soon established. Webb said he was always unsure of Clough, whom he described as having 'at least five different personalities'. Clough, meanwhile, soon took a dislike to Webb, revelling in the *Times* football correspondent Geoffrey Green's description of him as 'that most perfect of polished penguins', a reference to his dapper appearance.

His suspicions, he felt, were confirmed by an incident on a tour of Spain when Jack Kirkland challenged Webb to a swimming race, both men putting £5 on the result. Webb swept into an early lead, but mysteriously allowed Kirkland, who was swimming in glasses, to overhaul him. As far as Clough was concerned, that marked Webb out as an untrustworthy figure who 'tended to play both ends against the middle'. Clough insisted that amid the poisonous atmosphere that overwhelmed Derby, Webb 'was never a major problem', but there was, according to Longson, at least one occasion when Clough threatened to quit if Webb weren't sacked.

Banned from playing games abroad, Derby accepted an invitation to play in the Watney Cup, a pre-season knockout tournament featuring two teams from each of the four divisions. To get the players in the right mood, Taylor showed the squad a film of their 2–1 win away to Everton the previous season, an indication of the sort of football – seizing control of the midfield before becoming more expansive – at which he and Clough were aiming.

Away at Fulham of the Third Division in the first round, Derby opted not for midfield domination but for a 4–2–4, and soon went 3–1 down. The replacement of Hinton with McGovern and a switch to 4–3–3, though, turned the game and Derby went on to win 5–3 in extra-time. McGovern then scored the only goal with a swerving drive as Derby beat Sheffield United in the semi-final. That set up a final against the other First Division entrant, Manchester United.

Derby were superb. 'Rams humiliate feeble United,' the headline in the *Evening Telegraph* roared, and while a critic may point out that three of the goals in their 4–1 win came from free-kicks, Edwards stressed that Derby had 'hammered in shot after shot'. Later, when he won the Anglo-Scottish Cup with Forest, Clough insisted winning anything, however small, was a key step because it persuaded the players they were champions, but here he was concerned the success might breed overconfidence.

Even more of a concern was the serious crowd trouble that marred the event. There were running fights in the street involving hundreds of fans, a milk float and a hot dog stand were overturned, and the bar of the Baseball Hotel was closed after suffering 'indescribable' damage, while a barman was hospitalised after being hit by a flying glass. Away fans attacked home fans after the opening goal, and after the game a car was burnt out, other vehicles were overturned, windows were smashed and bottles and stones were hurled at buses. A United fan was later jailed for four months after repeatedly kicking a prone policeman in the ribs.

In the week before the start of the 1970–71 season, Taylor admitted to major doubts, warning fans not to expect a repeat of the previous year's performance. 'There will be times,' he said, 'when we have top men out injured and those are the matches that worry me. I can't stand another season like last one, worrying every time a player went down that he might be badly hurt and asking men to play when they were far from fully fit. The other top clubs don't have this. Chelsea, Everton and Leeds have squads of sixteen or seventeen and even with two or three injuries can fill in without being weakened too much.' That may have been intended as a typical managerial plea for more funds for more players, but his fears would soon be borne out.

Clough and Longson were far more bullish. The chairman spoke of how he'd found that 'life begins at seventy . . . the influence of Peter Taylor and Brian Clough has given me a new lease of life', while the manager insisted, 'I have never seen players so supremely prepared for a season.' Edwards predicted another top-four finish. 'It seems certain,' he wrote, 'that the Rams will again have one of the best defensive records in the division . . . The question mark remains against the ability of the forwards to pick up vital goals away from home.'

Given the build-up, the season-opener at Chelsea was an immense disappointment. Although O'Hare gave Derby the lead after a neat combination between Hinton and Hector, Ian Hutchinson levelled with a looping header after seventy-four minutes, and then nudged John Robson out of the way to head the winner. Criticising Derby's lethargy, Edwards wrote that 'Chelsea and Derby County performed like middle-of-the-table teams for much of Saturday's match at Stamford Bridge and the result was a game that was something of a non-event.'

Two goals for McGovern – the first deflected, the second rattled in off the bar from twenty-five yards – plus Durban and O'Hare goals from Hinton corners gave Derby a 4–2 win at Wolves, all six goals coming in the first thirty-one minutes. It was a start, but it was hardly the controlled football to which Clough and Taylor aspired. Both at Derby and Forest, their first priority was to take control of midfield, and then to pick opponents off; it was about close, neat passing, never squandering possession, patiently waiting for spaces to open up. At the same time, both sides broke quickly, and Clough had a clear preference for centre-forwards – John O'Hare, Roger Davies, Tony Woodcock, Trevor Francis, Garry Birtles and perhaps most obviously, his son Nigel – who could receive the ball to feet and turn quickly. Put simply, Clough expected that if space opened for a controlled pass to a forward who had just one defender behind him, that forward should either win a free-kick – the physical courage to take a whack from behind was a prerequisite – or work a shooting opportunity.

Derby 'performed only moderately well' in beating Stoke City 2–0, and Green was the hero in an uninspired 2–0 win over Ipswich. Six points from four games was decent enough, but the side's deficiencies were evident.

A run of three games without a win culminated in a 2–1 home defeat to Newcastle, a performance Edwards described as Derby's 'worst since they returned to the First Division'. After six games, Derby had conceded ten goals; the previous season they hadn't let in their tenth goal until the fifteenth match. The defensive worries got worse during a 3–1 victory over Halifax in the League Cup as McFarland was carried off with a pulled hamstring.

Without either McFarland or Hennessey, Derby lost 4–0 at Southampton, and Taylor's gloomy words about the slenderness of the squad seemed grimly prescient. The injury crisis worsened and Derby faced the bottom club, Burnley, without McFarland, Hennessey, Webster and McGovern, who withdrew with illness on the day of the game. Durban sustained a leg injury during the match, but at least it was won, Hinton getting the only goal of a scruffy contest.

Clough responded in familiar fashion and made a new signing. He and Taylor felt they needed more pace in midfield and, hearing their thoughts, Webb recommended signing Archie Gemmill from his former club, Preston. Derby paid £64,000, but as with all Clough signings at the time, the deal couldn't go through without an anecdote. Gemmill had all but agreed a move to Everton, in a deal that would have netted a signing-on fee of £5,000 and increased his salary from £60 a week to £225, with an additional £25 added each year over the course of a four-year contract. His wife, Betty, was pregnant and reasoning that Everton was close enough they wouldn't have to move, they were already dreaming of taking their child for walks along the promenade at Lytham and on the rollercoaster at Blackpool.

Gemmill only met Clough because his manager, Alan Ball (the father of the England World Cup-winner) told him he had to out of politeness, but Betty was opposed even to that, having seen Clough on television and taken a dislike to his aggressive manner. As he walked in, Clough told her she looked 'radiant' and said he'd heard she hated him. She replied that she hated the man called Clough she saw on television.

After a couple of hours of negotiation, twice interrupted by calls from Everton (although they had to call next door because Gemmill, by his own admission, was too parsimonious to own a telephone; his neighbour came in saying 'his mother' needed to speak to him), Gemmill said he wanted to think it over and would make a decision the following morning – 'the first evidence,' as Clough put it, 'that Archie Gemmill could be an awkward little shit.'

As with the McFarland signing, though, Clough didn't like the idea of leaving his quarry overnight, particularly not as Everton were known to be hovering, and so said that he'd sleep, in his account, on the sofa or, in Gemmill's, in his car. (Again, Clough's version of events played up the brazenness of his behaviour.) Gemmill's wife took pity on him and, as she made up the spare room, Clough washed up the dinner plates. He signed Gemmill over bacon and eggs the following morning; two decades later the child Betty Gemmill was carrying, Scot, would also play for Clough. So persuasive was Clough's vision for the club, that Gemmill accepted terms of £70 a week, with no signing-on fee, merely a colour television and the promise of a new carpet for his front room.

'As a player,' Clough went on in his autobiography, 'he was superb. As a man, I'm not sure who disliked him more – those who worked with him or those who played against him.' Initially, Gemmill was a player who liked to run with the ball rather than distribute it quickly – a 'headless chicken' Durban said – but within a couple of months he'd adapted, apparently after Clough advised him to 'give it to Hinton and run past him'.

Gemmill made his debut at West Brom and had 'a splendid match', but two defensive lapses cost Derby and they lost 2–1. There was further encouragement in a 1–1 draw against a Tottenham side that had won its previous six games, but points were still being frittered, and there was an awareness even by October that the season would be about nothing more than treading water.

Having won just one of their previous nine games in the league, Clough continued to attempt to restructure the squad, missing out on Henry Newton, who preferred to join Everton from Nottingham Forest, and selling the thirty-year-old Carlin to Leicester for £40,000. 'There's no pleasure in parting with a player who has given good service,' Taylor said, 'but the decisions have to be made … I considered that Willie was over the top, I thought Leicester's offer was reasonable and, being realistic, money in the bank was more useful than a veteran midfield player in our reserves.'

McFarland and Hennessey returned for the visit of Leeds, who won 1–0, and then, 'still labouring', Derby went out of the League Cup at Coventry and lost 2–0 at Arsenal. 'After Derby County supporters had waited weeks in the expectation that a full side would automatically begin to climb the table, the last three results have been, to say the least, depressing,' Edwards wrote. 'Well as the Rams defended for much of the Arsenal game, it was not only confidence but aggression that was missing.' Even worse, Taylor was taken ill on the coach on the way to the game, early warning of a heart problem, although at the time he dismissed it as a bad case of indigestion.

Clough resorted to his other tactic when things were going badly, and took the squad off to Mallorca. A goalless draw at home to Liverpool on their return was, Edwards said, a 'first step back towards respectability'. A 1–1 draw at Manchester City – Mackay's 500th club match – had Taylor proclaiming them 'the Derby County of last season' and at last, on 21 November, they won again, goals from O'Hare and McFarland setting up a 2–0 win over Blackpool. It came at a cost, though, Durban suffering a serious ankle injury and Hinton breaking a bone in his foot.

Derby's form, though, remained inconsistent and for Clough, the Boxing Day fixture against Manchester United came as the final straw. It was an extraordinary game, played on a snow-dusted pitch that made the white ball at times impossible to see. Mackay fired in a free-kick to put Derby ahead in the third minute and when Wignall added a second before half-time Derby seemed comfortable against demoralised opponents. But then Green was caught out of position as Willie Morgan crossed, allowing Law to nod in. Moments later, the goalkeeper parried a David Sadler header from Bobby Charlton's corner and George Best prodded in. With thick black mud mingling with the snow, an unmarked Law then gave United the lead from another corner, the ball bouncing tamely past Green. Hector levelled following a clever pass from Gemmill, and laid in Gemmill to make it 4–3, but when Green misjudged another Charlton corner, Brian Kidd nodded in the equaliser. It wasn't enough to save Wilf McGuinness, though, and he was sacked as United manager three days later.

'The present side is not good enough,' Clough admitted afterwards. 'There are individuals who are playing brilliantly and individuals who are throwing points away. This was a superb match from a spectator's point of view, but many more like this and I'll get the sack ... Of course, it's an indictment of me. There were mistakes being made that you would not have seen at schoolboy level. We could have gone 3–0, 4–0 up. But this was like our early Second Division days – looking a good side, but conceding goals and losing.'

One particular individual stood out. 'Les Green, inevitably, takes the major share of the blame for this defensive debacle,' Edwards wrote. 'Largely as a result of Green's goalkeeping errors, United, without playing particularly well, suddenly found themselves 3–2 up.'

Taylor operated a policy that he described as 'observe and replace', the aim being constantly to rejuvenate the squad and to jettison any player whose standards were slipping. 'It's as important in football as in the stock market to sell at the right time,' Taylor said. 'Brian and I are noted for our signings, but it shouldn't be overlooked that we picked up some handy fees through selling. It's an unpopular part of management, but it has to be done.' It was a mentality that meant there could be no sentimentality, and that performance against United was the end of Green. 'Worry off the field shows itself on the field,' Taylor said, 'and damages our aim of a maximum performance on match days, so it's a crime against your team to retain a problem.'

The goalkeeper and Clough had never really got on, and tensions had arisen the previous summer when Clough had banned Green from touring Australia with England A, saying he wanted him to spend the close-season resting. On Christmas Eve, Green asked to borrow £100 to buy Christmas presents for his children. Taylor told Edwards he knew he was 'in trouble with gambling debts and [was] being chased by a woman' and so kept an even closer eye on him than usual. The United game persuaded him that Green was 'shot'.

At half-time, Taylor saw Green shaking, and mentioned his concerns to Clough. His second-half 'stinker', as Taylor referred to it, sealed his fate. Green never played for the club again. 'After about six months of being mucked about and not knowing where I was with the club,' Green said. 'I went to Brian's office and told him I wanted to sort everything out once and for all.' Clough, though, was in no mood to listen. 'You can't talk to me,' he said. 'I'm Jesus Christ.'

'I chose the wrong time because he was knocking back the brandies,' Green went on. 'He shouted and swore at me to get out so I shoved him and he fell off his chair. I just turned round and walked out.' Clough had taken to heart Storer's complaint that directors never said thank you, but then his players could probably have said much the same about him.

Colin Boulton returned in place of Green for the FA Cup third-round tie away to Chester, in which 'extra class beat enthusiasm' and Derby won 2–1. Taylor's health, though, was worsening, and after being diagnosed with a heart murmur the night before a league game against Wolves, he was advised to take a few weeks off. Clough arranged for his admission to Derby Royal Infirmary but, during Taylor's six weeks away from the club, he went to visit him only once. Clough, since at least the time of his own injury and possibly before, had always had an oddly detached attitude to illness, preferring not to get too close but, still, his distance here seems strange and perhaps highlights that, for all the talk of their great friendship, he and Taylor didn't really have a relationship beyond football. After all, after Clough had left Middlesbrough, he and Taylor had barely kept in contact until they began working together at Hartlepools.

Sitting at home, reading the papers and watching television, Taylor's perspective began to change. Clough was, he acknowledged, 'a TV natural' but, he wrote, 'I began to feel he was abusing the platform while, at the same time, the programme bosses were exploiting him. It seemed he was being urged into ever-greater controversies and it was inevitable that Brian and the unvarnished truth would create enemies in high places.'

Clough appointed a temporary replacement, choosing one of Derby's scouts, George Pycroft. Taylor was suspicious, and fretted that he was being eased out. Taylor and Pycroft had been friends since their schooldays and Pycroft had scouted for Taylor when he was manager of Burton, but they had a major falling-out over a scouting trip Pycroft made to watch Kevin Keegan the previous September, nine months before Liverpool signed him. Pycroft liked what he saw, and told Derby that Keegan was a player they should do everything in their power to sign.

Taylor, though, was always reluctant to act on anyone else's recommendations, as though fearing that to acknowledge somebody else may have spotted a talent would be to undermine his own position, and had written off Keegan after watching him in an away game at Southend (although he also sent Maurice Edwards to watch him; he, too, was unimpressed). When Liverpool signed him for £35,000 the following May, Taylor commented that 'Shanks has dropped a clanger'. It later emerged that Clough had himself been to watch Keegan and had thought him a talent, but had decided not to act because signing players was Taylor's department.

When Taylor returned after the illness, he distrusted Pycroft, who ended up being sacked and replaced by Maurice Edwards. Pycroft's letter of dismissal was written by Clough, and cited the fact that Longson had seen him at home games rather than looking for players, but Pycroft always maintained it had been dictated by Taylor who, he said, had never forgiven him for the embarrassment of the Keegan affair. 'Taylor,' George Edwards wrote, 'was justifiably confident in his judgement of players, yet there was always a sense of insecurity lurking behind the easy laugh and the wise-crack. He was a heavy smoker and a serial worrier.'

The upturn in form Taylor had identified more than a month earlier had been disrupted by further injuries, but slowly, even while results remained patchy, Derby continued to improve through January 1971. They played well against Wolves, but lost 2–1 to a late Bobby Gould winner. Finally the breakthrough came at Ipswich, as O'Hare scored the goal in a 1–0 win.

Then came dreadful news, for the town and the country. Egged on by the then-minister of technology, Tony Benn, Rolls-Royce, one of Derby's largest employers, had signed a fixed-price deal with the American Lockheed Corporation in the late sixties to make engines for the new RB-211 Tristar airbus. It soon became apparent that the deadlines for completion had been over-optimistic and that the penalties for missing them far too harsh. Even a £20million bail-out from Benn's Industrial Reorganisation Commission couldn't halt the descent, and by February 1971, it had run up debts of £110million in production losses, far more than the cost price in the contract. On 4 February, Rolls-Royce called in the receivers. As a leader in the *Times* put it, it was a 'shattering blow to both international prestige and industrial confidence'.

It also had severe consequences for Derby. 'When the colder economic winds started to blow by the early 1970s Derby had not diversified its industrial structure as had Nottingham and had been much slower to build up service industries . . .' Maxwell Craven wrote in his history of the town. 'With the contraction of the railway industry, an unpalatable reality for decades (kept at bay by government subsidies), changes in household heating methods which killed the demand for stoves and grates . . . a whole sector of Derby's industrial base shrank quite rapidly. The real impact of this was emphasised by the sudden collapse of Rolls-Royce in 1971. Thousands of people were pitched out of work from a firm which almost everyone believed would go on forever and in which they assumed their working futures lay.' Although it was subsequently reconstituted under public ownership, it was significantly slimmed down.

The club's immediate problem was the opposite; rather than suffering an unimagined collapse, it struggled because nobody had expected such progress. 'Success,' Webb said, 'had caught the club cold. The books were in utter disarray. Nothing seemed to be accounted for.' Money was commonly kept in waste-paper baskets, precipitating a bizarre scandal, the truth of which seems irretrievably lost. In Francis's biography of Clough, he describes how, in the absence of a proper box-office, takings from ticket-sales for an FA Cup tie against Wolves had to be kept in waste-paper bins. When one of the bins disappeared, Webb threatened to call the police, at which Clough came forward to say that he'd been looking after it.

Clough's version, as relayed in his autobiography, is rather different. He said he was leaving the ground one day at 5pm and went through the general office to say goodbye. He saw a large waste-paper basket propping open a door, containing, he estimated, between £7,000 and £10,000. 'I thought, "I know this lot are under pressure in here, but this is bloody ridiculous." We operated one of the most open, accessible grounds in football. Anybody could walk in and wander all over the place. Surely even an understaffed office couldn't leave a fortune just lying around.'

So he took it and waited for quarter of an hour to see if anybody would notice the money's disappearance. When they hadn't, he returned to the office to find it locked up for the night, so he took the money home. He returned it to Webb the next day, 'telling him this couldn't go on. Webby seemed relieved, I think because he had an idea a lot of cash had gone missing. He certainly thanked me profusely.'

The same tensions were there a few months later, after Webb had been promoted to secretary, when he and Clough clashed over the key to the safe. Webb went out to lunch and gave the key to his assistant, a seventeen-year-old called Michael Dunford, telling him to give it to no one. Clough sent his own secretary to collect the key, but Dunford refused to hand it over. Clough rang Dunford and demanded the key, but Dunford still refused, at which Clough sacked him. Webb reinstated him the following morning after receiving a complaint from Dunford's father, a special constable, but again the question was raised over why Clough wanted the key. Given it would have been obvious who was responsible had any money gone missing, the dispute was presumably about power, but it seems an odd fight to have picked. The most charitable interpretation, perhaps, is that Clough was trying to interfere in matters that were – by law – Webb's responsibility.

The Cup tie itself, played on a typical Baseball Ground mudbath, was won, O'Hare flicking in a last-minute winner. Confirmation of Derby's growing stature came as McFarland became Derby's first England international for almost twenty years, making his debut in a 1–0 win over Malta.

Wins over West Ham and Crystal Palace perhaps gave Clough additional confidence. With Mackay starting to show signs of age and McFarland and Hennessey both regular injury victims, he had decided he needed additional central defensive cover and circumvented Longson to sign Colin Todd from Sunderland for a British record fee of £175,000. A couple of days earlier, presumably to throw other potential suitors off the scent, he had dismissed him as 'a bread-and-butter player'.

In Clough's version of the tale, he bought him almost on a whim, then sent a telegram to Longson, who was on holiday, saying, 'Just bought you another great player, Colin Todd. We're almost bankrupt. Love Brian.' Had that been what happened, of course, it would have been outrageous and Longson would have been within his rights to sack Clough on the spot. In the frequent retelling, presumably, the truth became eroded to emphasise Clough's audacity and his refusal to bow before – even the most reasonable – authority. 'Our judgement of players was beyond doubt or reproach,' he wrote in his autobiography. 'We had nothing to prove in that department and I didn't feel the need even to consult the chairman or directors.'

Todd himself was unaware of any controversy until much later. 'I'd played about 170 games when the phone rang at home and it was Alan Brown, the Sunderland manager,' he remembered. 'He said, "Colin, I've got someone to meet you down at my house, can you come down?" So, I went down never having any idea of who it might be, you rattle your brain thinking who it might be. When I knocked on the door, Alan Brown said,

"We've agreed to let you go, this football club has agreed to pay the money and it's Brian Clough." And I walk in and it's Cloughie.

'The only thing we spoke about was football. What he was going to do for Derby County, they were on their way, he was going to take them to glory, and we never spoke about a contract. It was inspirational, I was just twenty-two and that was one of the reasons I wanted to leave for somewhere because I had that ambition. At the time, you look at Derby County and they weren't one of the biggest clubs, but they were going to be a successful club. What he put to me in football terms was everything that I wanted to hear.

'I had to go down on the next morning to his office, we didn't speak about money, he just said, "This is what you're going to get" and I signed the forms. That was it. There was no haggling or anything like that. That's how powerful a man he was. The wages were nothing really, in those days you could equate them to ordinary people, nothing substantial like you get today. Most importantly, I wanted to play for the man. I knew what he was like at youth level. I had no hesitation in signing for him. The wife was in awe of him as well. He said, "Right, young man, your wife's your problem: sort her out – you're coming with me." She had to go to the hotel, the trainer and his wife took her there, while I went off with Cloughie.'

Longson had actually agreed in principle to the signing of Todd before he headed off for the Caribbean and was amused to receive Clough's telegram (the actual words of which read 'Signed you another good player, Todd. Running short of cash, Brian'). It was only later, when he bumped into the Coventry chairman Derrick Robins and the Crystal Palace chairman Arthur Waite, who were staying in the same hotel, that he learned the extent of the fee and resentment sprouted.

'How could any manager go out and spend that sort of money without even a word to the chairman?' he wrote in his diary. 'I was bitterly disappointed that Brian had taken on both Stuart Webb and now Colin Todd without discussing finance. I felt the incidents destroyed something between Brian and myself, a sort of unspoken trust. I don't think the relationship between us, once seemingly untarnishable, was ever quite the same again.' His reaction, of course, was totally reasonable and understandable, particularly given what had happened with Webb. Yet it is telling that the fury followed a conversation with two other chairmen; Clough always insisted that his relationship with Longson fell apart because of the interference of others. Of course, it would be natural for Longson to be shocked by the size of the fee, by Clough acting as if the money were his rather than the club's, but it seems equally possible that what wounded him was other chairman wondering how he could let his young manager act in such a way.

Undaunted by the chairman's hurt feelings, Derby marched on. O'Hare scored the only goal in a drab win at Blackpool, and then Todd made his debut at home to an Arsenal side pressing for the double, replacing Durban, a much more attacking presence, and playing at right-half. Clough often liked a defensive figure in his midfield three, reasoning that the extra cover freed Gemmill to push forward and join the attack: this was the 'balance' of which he regularly spoke. The game was a classic of Clough's philosophy. 'Derby first bustled Arsenal out of their stride ...' Edwards wrote, 'then, their confidence suddenly back in abundance, settled down to control the game and outwit opponents who rarely looked championship calibre and, in the end, were lucky to restrict the score to 2–0.' McFarland, who had a superb game marking Radford, got the first, finishing off after Hector had headed a Hinton free-kick back across the face of goal, and then Hector beat Bob Wilson at his near post after a smart ball inside the full-back from O'Hare.

That was five wins in a row and a charge for Europe remained a vague possibility. Leeds, though, were on hand to stifle those ambitions. As so often when Clough and Revie met, there was controversy, an air of mutual suspicion hanging over the confrontation. With several players suffering flu, Revie appealed to the League for the game to be postponed. The League rejected his plea and, given only Allan Clarke missed the game, probably rightly so. From Clough's point of view, this was just more chicanery from the masters of the art. Peter Lorimer got the only goal and, typically, there was an element of doubt about it, Clough believing he had handled in the build-up.

With nothing left to play for, Derby's good form withered. The fans became restive, and McGovern was a particular target for abuse at a testimonial for Ron Webster. Another defeat followed, 2–1 in the east Midlands derby against Nottingham Forest. 'For most of last night's home match ... they were almost embarrassingly superior,' Edwards wrote, 'but their failure to create scoring chances and their capacity for giving away gift goals cost them two more points.' Making a point to the moaners – one he underlined in an angry interview in the *Evening Telegraph* – Clough selected an unchanged side against Huddersfield, and was rewarded with a 3–2 win.

A 2–1 defeat at Tottenham followed but, Edwards said, 'There were signs . . . that Derby are not far from being a good side,' a view that was confirmed when they won 2–1 at Manchester United.

The season drifted to a conclusion, before finishing as it had begun with rival gangs clashing in the streets as Derby beat West Brom 2–0. It was Mackay's last game for the club, having agreed a £20,000 move to Swindon, where he had been appointed as player-manager a few weeks earlier, staying only so he could play every game in a league season for the first time in his career. Even two minutes from the end, Edwards reported, in a meaningless game that was already won, he was directing his team-mates about and his departure was characteristically understated, as he waved briefly to the crowd and then ran off down the tunnel. The squad presented him with a portable radio, an oddly prosaic farewell gift after a magnificent three seasons. He would be back, though, and sooner than anyone expected.

After such an impressive first season in the First Division, to finish only ninth in 1970–71 was a little disappointing, but the mood that summer was still one of optimism, as improvements to the stadium continued. £60,000 was invested in adding 1,500 new seats to the Osmaston Stand, and then a more ambitious proposal was unveiled to buy up property behind the Normanton Stand so it could be rebuilt and the pitch extended, something Clough felt was necessary to help Derby break down sides who came to the Baseball Ground and defended deep and in numbers. With season-ticket sales hitting a British record of £225,000 and the waiting list topping 2,500, the need for a larger stadium was obvious.

Those would have been extraordinary figures at any time, but they were particularly striking given the economic gloom that hung over the town. Where all else failed, Derby County demonstrated what could be achieved with hard work and visionary management. It wouldn't be an exaggeration to say that, in troubled times, Derby clung to its football club because it had nothing else; Clough became far more than a football manager; he was a bright young leader whose brash confidence gave hope for the future.

Where the old certainties had failed, he offered a new approach. 'There was a vibrancy about the town and club,' said Gemmill; 'a sense of excitement and anticipation you could almost taste.'

The club's awareness of its commercial potential was seen as the kit was changed, the black shorts being switched for navy, with red rather than black numbers. An away kit of yellow shirts and blue shorts was unveiled, with Longson doing little to dampen a predictable outrage by insisting the move hadn't been taken to squeeze more money out of fans, but because he felt the club should model its kit on England and Brazil. Revie, of course, had changed Leeds's kit from yellow and blue to all-white to mimic Real Madrid; Derby's change was not so radical, although accusations of a sell-out were fuelled by the fact that Derby happened to have moved to the colours of Texaco, who were sponsoring a pan-British tournament Derby had entered and had bought significant advertising space at the ground.

As the moulding of the squad went on, Green, Wignall and John Richardson were placed on the transfer list, while Derby pursued Jeff Astle, a chase that ended when Don Howe was appointed manager of West Brom and insisted his centre-forward would not be leaving. Green eventually joined the South African side Durban City in the first week of the season. Clough, surprisingly, had made no effort to replace him, meaning Derby's only goalkeeping cover was the sixteen-year-old apprentice John Turner. Only at the end of September did Clough move to rectify that – an odd omission given his insistence on the necessity of a good goalkeeper – and even then the player he picked to be a reserve was Graham Moseley, a seventeen-year-old signed from Blackburn for £20,000. That made him the most expensive seventeen-year-old in the English game, but he soon succumbed to the Clough regimen, having his shoulder-length hair trimmed between joining Derby and making his debut for the reserves two days later.

The team prepared for the 1971–72 season with a tour of West Germany and the Netherlands, beating Schalke 04, Werder Bremen and Go Ahead. Clough experimented with Hector playing behind O'Hare and Wignall, and he revelled in the additional space the role allowed him. The week before the season began, Derby beat Schalke 2–0 at the Baseball Ground with a performance Edwards described as 'methodical'.

Perhaps stung by what had happened the previous season, Clough was far less aggressively optimistic this time round – possibly as part of an attempt to pressure Longson into releasing further funds. He insisted the squad was too small for a title challenge and spoke of the problems of having to pick players whom he knew were carrying injuries. He then hit out at the fans who had criticised McGovern, saying he, O'Hare, McFarland and Hinton were the best players at the club. Certainly they were the players who most embodied Clough's vision of football: McFarland the tough centre-back who was dominant in the air but could pass a ball; McGovern the understated midfield reader of the game, always in the right place, always giving the ball simply and economically; O'Hare the centre-forward who could hold off defenders and retain possession with his back to goal; and Hinton, the left-winger whose crosses, particularly from set-plays, were Derby's main creative threat. His corners were vital; with a great individual, a flair player to unpick defences, there had to be a means to convert possession into chances: the dead-ball link-up of Hinton and McFarland offered exactly that threat.

Given how well Derby usually performed against Manchester United, the season didn't begin especially auspiciously. 'They were never at their best, because they lacked calmness, control and poise,' Edwards wrote. 'This was never a polished display. But they did enough to suggest that the high hopes many have for them this season are not misplaced.' An equaliser from Wignall earned a 2–2 draw.

There was a similarly unsatisfactory feel as Derby beat West Ham 2–0, O'Hare and Wignall scoring in the opening eight minutes before the game petered out. A 2–0 win away at Leicester suggested a side clicking into form as Gemmill and McGovern took control of midfield before the game was settled by Hector and a Hinton penalty. McGovern's role, Gemmill insisted, was key. McGovern, he said, 'would always cover for me when I went on runs and the enormous amount of work he got through in ninety minutes was never truly appreciated by either the public or the press. The number of tackles and interceptions John made is astonishing and he very rarely gave the ball away ... John's unselfish holding role meant Alan Durban and I could get forward at every opportunity.'

Momentum was checked by successive 2–2 draws against Coventry and Southampton, and Derby were 'anxious' in a goalless draw at Ipswich. They were, though, still unbeaten, and when McGovern again dominated Alan

Ball as they won 2–0 at Everton, there were signs, Edwards said, of Derby 'now opening the throttle'. That continued at home to Stoke, Hinton setting up the first two with set-plays and then scoring the third before Gemmill capped a fine passing move in a 4–0 win.

A new signing arrived the following week, although Roger Davies was perhaps not a player of the stature Clough might have been hoping for. He was tall and gangly and, frankly, didn't look much like a top-class footballer, but he had moments of genuine quality. Although he was capable of missing the simplest of chances, he was effective, and fulfilled the role Clough and Taylor saw for him, as a forward who could hold the ball up. In his way, Davies was a typical Taylor signing, scouted at Worcester City and picked up despite being a month shy of his twenty-first birthday, and so well past the point at which convention said he should have made his breakthrough. As Torquay, Millwall, Coventry and Arsenal all suddenly expressed an interest, his fee rose to £14,000, but Taylor was confident enough in his judgement to advise Clough to pay it. As Clough and Taylor arrived back at the Baseball Ground having completed his signing, they were met by Longson, who told them he thought £14,000 was a lot for a non-league player. 'A professional,' Taylor wrote, 'ought not to be needled by criticism from an amateur, but I allowed the timing of Sam's remark and the sarcasm of his tone to get under my skin.' The relationship between board and management was beginning to fray.

After a 1–1 draw against Chelsea, Derby were third in the table, three points behind Sheffield United and one behind Manchester United. A dour West Brom held them to a goalless draw at home and, of course, there was always Leeds to check any momentum, a Lorimer double putting Derby out of the League Cup after a replay. Clough had an excellent record at Newcastle and it continued as Hinton got the only goal in a comfortable 1–0 win. 'The temptation,' Gerard Mortimer wrote in the *Evening Telegraph*, 'is to abandon all restraint and laud this as the best performance of the season.' Yet Clough was uneasy – or perhaps saw his opportunity after a good result – and the following week he launched a campaign for more funds and further investment. This time, though, his target wasn't the board but the fans. 'I've said before that we need two more players before we can hope to win the title,' he said. 'The trouble is when we find one or both and if they become available, will we be able to afford them? Obviously we are looking as hard as ever. But if a star man came on the market we could be outbid by a club who are wealthier than us through getting bigger crowds.' At the time, despite the waiting list for seated season tickets, Derby were only filling around three-quarters of their 40,000-capacity ground and it's not hard to discern Clough's frustration that, having taken Derby from Second Division no-hopers to title contenders in the space of four seasons, he wasn't getting rather better support.

There was a sense that, although they were unbeaten, Derby hadn't quite clicked, that they weren't quite performing as well as they should have been, and that was only heightened by a 2–2 draw at home to Tottenham, about both of whose goals Derby felt aggrieved. There had been a suggestion of offside about the first, while their late equaliser seemed to have stemmed from a foul on Boulton. 'To occasionally fail to beat a team you largely outplay is forgivable and can be put down to bad luck,' Mortimer wrote, 'but when it happens as often as it does to Derby, then there must be genuine grounds for supposing something is wrong with the side.'

The unbeaten record didn't last much longer, as Derby were outplayed by the league-leaders Manchester United at Old Trafford and were fortunate to go down by only a George Best goal. The home game against Arsenal that followed took on increased importance: as Sir Alex Ferguson would say much later, what matters is less a bad result than how a side responds to it, and Derby reacted with their best home performance of the season. With Durban, McGovern and Gemmill running midfield Derby went ahead as O'Hare turned in a Gemmill cross and, although George Graham levelled after Boulton had misjudged a cross from George Armstrong, Hinton gave them a 2–1 win after a generous penalty award just before half-time. Steve Powell came off the bench in the second half to make his debut, becoming, at sixteen years and thirty-three days, the youngest player to play for Derby in a League match and helping to answer those critics – Revie foremost among them – who suggested Derby were a club who had bought their way to the top.

Slowly, Derby began to find their rhythm. They beat Nottingham Forest 2–0 away, and then overwhelmed Crystal Place 3–0 to move to within a point of United at the top of the table. Todd followed McFarland into the England squad, but just as it seemed the club had climbed another rung, two Boulton errors and a string of missed chances, most notably from Hector, resulted in a 2–1 defeat at Wolves.

Derby responded by beating Sheffield United 3–0, Hinton scoring twice from the penalty spot. 'For half an hour we played football that no side in the country could have contained,' Clough said. 'Some of our passing was miraculous.' But then they lost 2–1 at Huddersfield, their third defeat in four away matches. 'Defeat was to a large extent self-inflicted,' Mortimer said. Clough erupted.

After the game, Longson went down to the dressing-room, found Clough subjecting his players to a tirade of profanity and quietly slipped out. The next Monday, Clough asked him why he'd walked away, to which Longson replied that he didn't think Clough should speak to his players like that. Clough was scornful, and Longson was forced in the end to accept that Clough's method worked. 'Even though he used to pull players to pieces and shout at them something terrible,' Longson wrote, 'most of them spoke well of him. He made sure they were properly paid and looked after. His technique in the dressing-room was to hypnotise people. That's the only way I can think of describing it. He'd break their will-power, then put them under the influence.' Clough, similarly, believed he had something approaching psychic powers, insisting that he could sit on the bench and, without saying anything, make players turn and look at him.

He seems to have been rather more popular with the players at Derby than he was at Forest, where there are numerous stories of players seeing him walking towards them down a corridor and diving into doorways to avoid him; George Edwards, certainly, says he couldn't imagine any Derby player being forced into similar evasive action. Maybe Clough became increasingly capricious and ferocious as he aged, or maybe a younger generation of players simply found his volatility harder to deal with.

'It was the man-management,' Todd said. 'That's how he got the team to relax, to bond together. Every Friday night, home game, we were at the Midland Hotel. We knew what the routine was, every Friday we'd have our meal at 7 o'clock, then we'd go to our room, have a game of cards, a few beers. Anyway, this one night I went straight to my room, straight to bed. No sooner did I get to my bed, the phone rang and Clough said, "Hey, young man, get your arse down here, would you?" I went down, he said, "You know the format, you've got to get some beers down you, because

215

you're going to sweat tomorrow." We always used to meet in the foyer at 10.30 the next morning and walk up to the Baseball Ground. And that was every home game! There's no right way, there's no wrong way, is there? That was the right way for Brian Clough in that era.

'The respect he had for the players, the respect the players had for him, it was unbelievable. They would do anything for that man. A lot of players were a little bit frightened of him. He used to pick on me something terrible. He used to pick on David Nish. There were other ones there – McFarland – wouldn't say anything to him.'

Back at home, Derby were back on form, beating Manchester City, who had title ambitions of their own. Hinton converted another penalty after the increasingly influential McGovern had been tripped, and his crosses also laid on goals for Webster – a rarity, but a fine header after a determined late run – and Durban to give Derby a 3–0 lead after thirty-eight minutes. City pulled one back, but it hardly mattered.

After a 3–2 defeat at Liverpool, Clough took his players to Greece for four days, where they lost 3–1 to Olympiakos in a token friendly but, more importantly, relaxed and recharged. They returned to beat Everton 2–0. Leeds, though, lay in wait, and an early strike by Eddie Gray followed by two goals for Lorimer secured a 3–0 win. 'Leeds United have a nasty habit of reminding Derby County of how far they have to go,' Edwards wrote, and 1971 ended with Derby still looking some way short of being genuine championship challengers.

During the run of poor away results, Clough attacked his players for not being prepared to match their opponents physically, but the result of their efforts to rectify that seemed to be a loss of fluency at home. They began the new year with an anxious display against Chelsea, enlivened only by a dart and explosive shot from Gemmill that provided the game's solitary goal. The increased aggression, though, showed its worth at Southampton, as Derby matched their opponents for muscularity and came from behind to win 2–1, Robson being involved in the build-up to both goals.

A Hector double saw off Shrewsbury in the Cup, before Clough made another signing. Many of his buys were unexpected, but his decision to sign Tony Parry, by then converted into a centre-back, from Hartlepools for £2,500 seemed inexplicable, at least from a footballing point of view.

Clough made some half-hearted claim that Parry, a powerful natural athlete but no great technician, was better than most of the players at the club, and the scout Maurice Edwards later claimed that there were 'high hopes' for him until an incident while drunk on a post-season trip to Mallorca brought his time at the club to an end. It was fairly obvious, though, that Clough was doing his former club a favour, something John Curry, who remained as chairman, pretty much admitted. 'We are very sorry to see him [Parry] go,' he said, 'but it was necessary. The financial position is critical and though the sale will not solve all our problems it will go a long way towards easing them.'

When he felt it was deserved, Clough could be extremely loyal. The question, though, was whether he should have been so loyal with other people's money. Longson recorded in his diary that he was forever having to defend Clough's signings from other directors – the £110,000 he spent on Hennessey and the £14,000 on Davies coming in for particular criticism (presumably their less-than-sleek appearances contributed to the board's suspicion about their ability) – but if he was shelling out £2,500 of Derby's money to repay an old favour the directors had reason to be suspicious.

Derby twice came from behind to draw 3–3 with West Ham – although again there was the sense that they shouldn't have twice fallen behind in the first place – then Robson got the only goal at home to Coventry after a one-two with Gemmill. Durban hit a hat-trick as Notts County were thrashed 6–0 in the FA Cup, and then came a trip to Highbury. Before the match, Clough described it as 'the most important match of the season for us. We are third in the league, but a bad result at Highbury could endanger our prospects of playing in European competitions next season.' Significantly, he didn't mention the possibility of the championship, and if he really thought it out of reach, the game seemed to confirm his view. 'Derby had only a little less of the game than Arsenal,' Edwards wrote, 'but in their periods of superiority never threatened with the power and resolution of their opponents.' Arsenal won 2–0.

Back at home, where the miners' strike and the imposition of a three-day week had only made the economic situation of the town even more precarious, form returned and, with McGovern dominant, Derby hammered Forest to leave them five points adrift at the bottom. 'Saturday's 4–0 victory evoked no exultant scenes from Rams supporters,' wrote Mortimer.

'They cheered and filed away, almost embarrassed by the ease with which Derby had shredded Forest and at watching the pathetic wreck of what was once a good side shamble a step nearer to inevitable relegation.'

The embarrassment, though, would soon be Clough's. Derby twice drew against Arsenal in the FA Cup. Then came the incident that suggested he had begun to believe his own hype, that he felt he could flout and ignore authority and bend circumstance to whatever he wanted it to be. That was his tragedy; Ian Storey-Moore's is that, to later generations at least, he is remembered far more for being the McGuffin in the series of events at which Clough's hubris finally exploded than for his undoubted footballing ability.

Storey-Moore was a quick, direct left-winger who, despite expectations he would go on to better things, had hung around at Nottingham Forest until he was twenty-eight. Eventually, almost two years after he had won his solitary England cap, Manchester United made a bid of £200,000 for him. Matt Gillies, Forest's manager, accepted and he, Storey-Moore, the United manager Frank O'Farrell, and the Forest secretary Ken Smales met at the Edwalton Hall hotel in Nottingham to finalise the deal. Storey-Moore failed to agree terms, at which Clough, kept up to date by one of his many spies, pounced, ringing the hotel and telling Storey-Moore to stay where he was. He obeyed, while Smales and Gillies, having agreed to allow Clough to speak to the player, drove off. Why they did so has never been satisfactorily explained, for if they were reluctant to deal with the manager of their local rivals, as they later claimed, where was the logic in letting him talk to Storey-Moore at all? And, frankly, with Forest adrift at the bottom of the table, were they really in any position to dictate terms anyway?

Clough arrived and, as he had with countless other signings, persuaded Storey-Moore that Derby were destined for greatness and that he would play a key role in it. Convinced that Derby represented a better move than United, who were going through their awkward transition after Matt Busby's retirement and had fallen away in the title race, Storey-Moore signed the transfer papers. So did Webb, but Smales refused, meaning Storey-Moore technically remained a Forest player.

Smales went further, calling Longson to warn him that there'd be trouble if Clough pressed on. Clough, of course, was not somebody to be distracted by protocol or red tape – or what anybody else felt. He reassured Longson that Storey-Moore was keen on the deal and, just to make sure the winger remained keen, took him to meet the Derby squad at the Midland Hotel and booked a room for him to stay in that night. The next day, Storey-Moore was paraded around the Baseball Ground as a new signing and watched Derby come from behind to beat Wolves from the directors' box. That night, his wife joined him in the Midland. 'I hadn't bargained for the shit that hit the fan after that,' Clough later admitted.

Forest refused to confirm the deal and on the Monday, frustrated and in limbo, Storey-Moore went home to Bingham. Clough remained bullish. 'As far as we are concerned, we have signed Moore and I am not really concerned what any other party might feel . . .' he told the *Evening Telegraph*. 'I am absolutely staggered and distressed at the performance of Nottingham Forest Football Club this morning. They are depriving the game of the dignity it deserves.' As soon as Storey-Moore left Derby, O'Farrell and Busby, who had stayed on at Old Trafford as a director, visited his house, carrying a large bouquet for his wife. Eventually Storey-Moore agreed personal terms and signed for United.

Clough was furious and rattled off a four-page telegram to Football League secretary Alan Hardaker, pointing out that Gillies had given him permission to discuss terms with Storey-Moore. Longson, appalled by the hectoring tone Clough had taken, sent another telegram apologising. Derby, nonetheless, were fined £5,000, while Clough was warned 'as to the manner in which any future negotiations regarding the transfer of players are carried out'.

'You couldn't mess with Manchester United, the great Matt Busby's club, in those days,' Clough said, although given United had been fined and banned from Europe for a season over financial irregularities the year before Derby had, there is little evidence the football authorities went soft on United. More significant than the fine, though, was the damage it did to the relationship between Clough, who remained happy to flout authority at every turn, and Longson, who was becoming increasingly concerned both about his own standing within the game and about the possible impact on Derby County of repeatedly falling foul of the administrators. It also – perhaps – turned Clough against Busby, and certainly made Longson very aware of the risks of upsetting Busby, which was to have significance in the events that led to Clough's eventual resignation.

Clough's relationship with Longson had already begun to deteriorate, something for which each blamed the other. While Clough was certainly provocative, there was also something delusional about Longson's self-regard. His diaries show how he revelled in the role of saviour of the club, describing encounters with fans who would stop him on the way to games to exchange a few words, always calling him 'Sam'. Clough later blamed himself for stoking Longson's ego – something that was against Storer's rules for dealing with directors. Taylor would joke that the team was so good that even Longson could manage it. The problem was that Longson began to believe him.

Regardless of the off-field issues, Derby rumbled on. The style of play, Gemmill explained in his autobiography, was simple. 'When we lost possession,' he said, 'everybody was expected to get behind the ball as swiftly as possible to make it difficult for the opposition to play through us. When we regained the ball, it was a case of all hands to the pump going forward, getting as many white shirts into the opposing penalty area as we could . . . We played a disciplined 4–4–2 and it helped that Alan Hinton, as well as our two front men . . . was a natural goalscorer.'

They held Tottenham comfortably at White Hart Lane, and were gifted a win as Hector capitalised on a mix-up between Pat Jennings and Mike England and was pulled down by the goalkeeper. Hinton, inevitably, converted the penalty. A rare error from McGovern, under-hitting a backpass that stuck in the mud, handed Arsenal a 1–0 win in a second replay in the FA Cup, something that was probably a blessing in terms of the title race, removing one of the distractions that ultimately undermined Leeds. When they swept Leicester aside 3–0, Derby were up to second, five points behind Manchester City with two games in hand, one ahead of Leeds, who had played a game fewer, and two ahead of Liverpool, who had played a game more.

For the first time, the *Evening Telegraph* began to contemplate – in the vaguest terms – the possibility that Derby could be champions, but it was not a belief many fans seemed to share. Although the power-cuts brought about by the miners' strike and general economic unrest probably played a part, it still seems bizarre that Derby's game against Ipswich the following Wednesday attracted their lowest gate of the season, just 26,738 turning out to see Hector score the only goal, running on to a long kick from

Boulton. The *Evening Telegraph* described the attendance as 'disgraceful' and it's fair to assume that even if that wasn't a direct quote from Clough, he shared the sentiment.

Derby played what Mortimer termed 'controlled football' to draw at Stoke, a Durban free-kick cancelling out a penalty from Jimmy Greenhoff. Walker was a key figure again at Crystal Palace the following Tuesday. Gemmill missed an early penalty, but Walker slammed in the only goal after a Hennessey shot had been blocked. That left Derby a point behind City with eight games remaining; Leeds were a point further back with a game in hand and Liverpool two behind having played the same number of games as Derby.

Three of those remaining games were against other sides in the top four, the first of them against Leeds on Easter Saturday. For once, Derby got the better of their nemeses. McGovern won the battle with Johnny Giles in midfield and, as Mortimer described it, 'Derby County, brilliant, indefatigable and utterly ruthless, did not so much beat Leeds at the Baseball Ground as massacre them.' Robson hustled Billy Bremner out of possession and crossed for O'Hare to head the first after sixteen minutes, and an own-goal from Norman Hunter, unable to get out of the way after Gary Sprake had saved an O'Hare shot, completed a 2–0 win.

The gain, though, was soon lost, as a dogged Newcastle held out for a 1–0 win at the Baseball Ground on Easter Monday. Clough and Taylor kept the players back in the dressing-room for two hours after the game. 'There was no panic,' Taylor insisted. 'The disappointment of a home defeat must never overshadow our reading of a match. There are no excuses from us. Newcastle came to defend, they defended as a team and they did it better than most sides who have come here this season.'

A goalless draw on a hard, bumpy surface at West Brom in a game ruined by high winds was enough to take Derby top, a point ahead of Leeds and two clear of Liverpool and Manchester City having played a game more than all of them. They began nervously at Sheffield United, but took a twelfth-minute lead, Gemmill forcing in after John Hope, the Sheffield United goalkeeper, had palmed away a Hector cross under pressure from Durban. Durban headed in a Hinton corner six minutes later, and Derby were safe. Hector glanced in his 200th league goal from a Hinton cross and then laid in Hector for a late fourth to take Derby to their highest-ever points tally in the First Division.

That week should have been full of excitement and anticipation for the visit of Huddersfield; after all, this was a situation Derby had never experienced before. Instead, it was dominated by intrigue and yet more boardroom wrangling. Derrick Robins, the Coventry chairman, had approached Clough the week before about the possibility of replacing Noel Cantwell at Highfield Road. Clough, his relationship with Longson fractured, perhaps irreparably broken, decided to accept and he, Taylor and Gordon all submitted their resignations. On Tuesday, 11 April, those resignations were accepted by the board.

There were rumours, of course, but that matters had gone as far as that only became public much later, and the front page of the *Evening Telegraph* that night led with more upheaval at the club, as the executors of the late O.J. Jackson, the second-largest shareholders, sold two-thirds of their shares – 2,434 – to Jack Kirkland, the brother of Bob Kirkland, who had resigned following Longson's putsch in 1970. At the same time, Jack Kirkland also bought 370 of the 375 shares held by Harry Payne, who had resigned with Bob Kirkland. That meant Jack Kirkland held 2,804 shares, making him the second largest shareholder behind the Bass brewery, which retained 3,000, but had always maintained a strict policy of non-involvement.

'I have been a season-ticket holder for a long time and I have bought these shares because I am a great fan of the Rams,' Kirkland said, insisting he had no desire to wrest control of the club from Longson. The chairman, though, seeing his coaching staff resign en masse and the brother of one of his rivals accumulating shares, was rattled. 'I thought the executors would let the board know before taking important action like this,' he said. 'Perhaps now it is as well the small shareholders know what is going on. Should anybody else be thinking of selling we would obviously like to be kept in the picture. We have never sought a position in which one person, via a majority holding, could control the club. That is not a desirable situation.'

That night, Clough and Taylor went to Longson's house with Mike Keeling, indicating that they may be prepared to stay if Derby offered more money. Perhaps Clough's approach was heavy-handed, and perhaps the board may have hoped for rather more loyalty having largely backed their management team over transfers, but at that stage there seemed nothing particularly reprehensible about Clough's actions. The board promptly agreed to the pay-rises. A day later, though, Longson discovered the late-night visit had been a charade. Robins, tiring of Clough's delaying tactics, had withdrawn the offer, sending Coventry's assistant secretary Richard Dennison (the son of the former Middlesbrough manager Bob Dennison, who briefly took over as caretaker) to deliver the rejection to Clough personally. The same afternoon, Dennison reported the withdrawal of the offer to Webb who, knowing nothing of the meeting at Longson's house and occupied by Kirkland's manoeuvring, saw no reason to inform him until the following day. By then, the pay-rises had already been confirmed. Longson, understandably, was 'furious'.

Although Clough always hammed up approaches from other clubs, there had been genuine interest from Coventry, Birmingham and Barcelona, and at least part of the reason he rejected those offers was that he demanded complete control, something he couldn't be guaranteed anywhere apart from Derby. That began to be challenged when Kirkland rejoined the board. He questioned Taylor at every opportunity, demanding to know where he had been and what he had been doing. Taylor met him for the first time at Doncaster races and 'disliked him immediately ... He wanted to dictate and dominate, although he had not been in football for five minutes.'

As Taylor became increasingly depressed, Clough became increasingly angry (although given he was criticising Taylor in board meetings, he was surely partly to blame) and Longson became increasingly convinced that Derby's success was not down to either his manager or his assistant manager but to him.

Two goals from Hinton corners – one for McFarland and one for O'Hare – and a Hector strike following a series of blocked shots gave Derby a 3–0 win over Huddersfield and ensured European football for the following season. Derby had fifty-six points from forty games, Manchester City fifty-five from forty, Liverpool fifty-four from thirty-nine and Leeds fifty-three from thirty-eight. The following Wednesday, City lost 2–1 at Ipswich, giving Derby breathing space ahead of their game at Maine Road, although the title was still in Leeds's hands.

The signing of Rodney Marsh is commonly blamed for disrupting the balance of City's side towards the end of that season, but he was the difference against Derby, scoring one and winning a penalty that Francis Lee converted in a 2–0 win. That was City's last game of the season, and left them a point clear of Derby, who had one game left, and Liverpool, who had two to go, and two clear of Leeds, who also had two games still to play.

Before their final game, against Liverpool, though, Derby had a Cup final to win. The Texaco Cup, featuring the top English, Scottish and Irish sides who had not qualified for Europe, had been dragging on all season. Derby had seen off Dundee United, Stoke and Newcastle the previous autumn to set up a final against Airdrieonians. The first leg of the final had been held in January, with Derby securing a 0–0 draw. Three months later, they completed the job, Roger Davies scoring his first for the club in a 2–1 victory.

On the morning of the Liverpool match, Monday, 1 May, there was good news and bad news. Clough and Taylor had both agreed new five-year deals, but plans to rebuild the Normanton Stand were shelved. 'This was put off because we could not get permission to go ahead straight away,' Longson explained. 'What I can say is that we will build a new stand as soon as possible. There is a chance, however, that it might be a better proposition and more feasible to redevelop the main stand first, depending on decisions taken by local authorities. You can see from all this that we are not lagging behind the management.' That final sentence is surely telling: why even mention it unless the accusation had been made? Clough, almost certainly, had accused the board of lacking ambition during his negotiations. 'I even did plans to buy all the houses on the opposite side of the ground [to the Ley Stand],' he wrote in his autobiography. 'We had the money. We could have grown into something special, but the directors couldn't cope.'

McFarland started against Liverpool, despite having – to Alf Ramsey's fury – withdrawn from the England side that lost 3–1 to West Germany at Wembley in the first leg of the European Championship quarter-final two days earlier. Powell, still only sixteen, replaced Webster, and had an excellent game in a generally anxious display. Hector had an early drive tipped against the bar by Ray Clemence, but then Keegan possibly should have had a penalty when he seemed to be fouled by Boulton. The only goal came seventeen minutes into the second half, Gemmill twisting to create an opening and slipping through a pass that Durban dummied, leaving McGovern to score. Derby were top, but few gave them much hope, with bookmakers pricing them at 8–1 to be champions. Leeds needed only to draw at Wolves to win the title; and if they slipped up Liverpool's superior goal difference meant a win for them at Arsenal would give them the championship.

Leeds beat Arsenal in the FA Cup final that Saturday and faced their final game of the season two days later. 'There were allegations of attempted bribery by Leeds, supposed offers of cash for a penalty,' Clough wrote in his autobiography. 'Some of the claims were legally disproved later and Revie threatened writs, although I never did hear whether he disproved them.' Clough leaves the story hanging, and the implication is obvious; if the allegations had been disproved, of course, even to mention them is, at best, mischievous.

The allegations were made by the Wolves defender Bernard Shaw – who stressed the approach did not come from anybody at the club – and were serious enough for the Football Association to refer them to the Director of Public Prosecutions. They were never 'disproved', as Clough said; rather insufficient evidence was found to pursue the claims.

Others, of course – notably Bob Stokoe, Malcolm Allison and Frank McLintock – made similar allegations at various times against Revie, while the Leeds goalkeeper Gary Sprake admitted to having acted as a go-between to fix games against Wolves and Nottingham Forest – although he later retracted his accusation, and later still withdrew his retraction – but in this specific case, no action was taken and it may even be that the furore motivated Wolves to extra effort for fear they would be perceived as having rolled over. It's not even clear whether Clough really believed the accusations or whether his claims were born of a desire for controversy (after all, certain other stories in the book were rapidly withdrawn after publication), a loathing for Revie or, more generously, a genuine fear that he might have tried to fix the game.

That said, Clough certainly did believe that Revie had been guilty of manipulating match officials at various times, and it was probably that that turned rivalry into dislike (there are suggestions that the antipathy was born in Revie's supposedly dismissive attitude towards Clough after a Leeds

BRIAN CLOUGH: NOBODY EVER SAYS THANK YOU

game at Derby, but accounts are conflicting and there is no agreement on which match that might have been). The story Clough told was of going to watch a game at Elland Road – frustratingly nobody seems able to recall when or who Leeds were playing – and going to see Revie in his office afterwards. By chance, he had been sitting in a position in which he could not be seen from the door. The referee had come by and, unaware Revie had company, had asked if his performance had been all right. In Clough's account, Revie had looked flustered, muttered 'marvellous' and then shooed the referee away. It's hard to place exactly when that happened – assuming it did happen – but clearly sometime between Duncan Revie's visit to the Baseball Ground in 1968 and the final game of the 1971–72 season.

Clough sent his players – apart from Todd and McFarland, who were on England duty – to Mallorca with Taylor and went to the Scilly Isles with his parents, Barbara and the children. As Clough followed the game on the radio, the players hung around the bar of the Bahia hotel in Cala Millor. 'You could tell with Peter that he was nervous,' Todd said. 'He was smoking those cigars all the time.' About quarter of an hour from time, a porter called Taylor to take a phone-call in the foyer. When he didn't return, the players drifted out and found him listening to a British journalist giving updates from Molineux.

Leeds, exhausted, found Wolves, who had lost their previous four games, unexpectedly defiant – the curse, perhaps, of being quite so disliked – on a heavy pitch at Molineux. Richards had already gone close, when, three minutes before half-time, Shaw's cross skidded off Giles to Munro, who beat Harvey from close range. At Highbury, Emlyn Hughes had hit the bar for Liverpool, Keegan's attempted overhead follow-up drifting a foot wide, but it remained goalless. At half-time, Derby were still on course for the title.

After the break, Leeds were relentless. Twice Lorimer put good headed chances wide, Parkes saved from Giles and Clarke, while McAlle and Hegan, Eric Todd wrote in the *Guardian*, 'performed miracles of salvage'. And then, midway through the half, Richards sent Dougan clear, and he steered his finish past the advancing Harvey: 2–0, and with Liverpool still being held at Arsenal, Derby were twenty-three minutes from the title.

Leeds rallied immediately, Giles and Madeley combining to set up Bremner, but the equaliser wouldn't come, despite a protracted late siege

226

that saw everybody apart from Harvey in the Wolves half. Twice Shaw seemed to handle in the box and Clarke also might have had a penalty, but this time the referee, Mr W. Gow of Swansea, did Leeds no favours.

In fact, the refereeing on that final evening could not have been more favourable to Derby. With two minutes left at Highbury, John Toshack had the ball in the net, a goal that, had it stood, would have won the title for Liverpool. It did not stand, though: ruled out for offside. 'I do not think the goal was offside,' said Shankly. 'Toshack came from nowhere to put the ball in. The linesman did not flag, but the referee took no notice.'

In Spain, Derby's players and staff fretfully watched Taylor. 'He was ashen white,' Maurice Edwards recalled. 'Suddenly he raised his free arm in the air and shouted, "We've won it! We've won it!" The place erupted.'

In the Scillies, Clough bought champagne for everybody in the hotel restaurant. 'It's incredible,' he said. 'I do not believe in miracles, but one has occurred tonight. I believe they played four-and-a-half minutes of injury-time at Molineux – it seemed like four-and-a-half years to me. For a team and a town like Derby to win the title is a credit to all concerned. This has given me far more pleasure than I can adequately express. It makes you appreciate what a job you and your players have done. And my players have given blood this season.'

Others might have been disappointed to have won the championship in such an apparently anti-climactic way, waiting for others to fail rather than winning a game themselves, but not Clough. 'It was nice that Mam and Dad were there to share the moment,' he said; nice, given his evident desire to prove himself to his mother, that she was there at the moment of his first great triumph. 'Mam was never carried away by what she considered the important things in life,' he wrote in *Walking on Water*. 'She probably got more satisfaction from seeing her washing blowing in the wind before anybody else's in Valley Road on a Monday morning than she got from the championship pennant fluttering above the Baseball Ground. But I think she was pleased that day I became manager of the English league champions. I think I detected an extra little sparkle in her eyes as we sipped champagne and enjoyed the moment.'

He bought them a bungalow, which they moved into only reluctantly, and added a fridge, the first time they had had such a luxury. His mother, though, determinedly set against excess to the last, refused to turn it on over the winter, saying it was a waste of money to use it when the weather was cold.

While some, such as Michael Carey in the *Guardian*, praised Clough's 'realism', his 'honesty, with his directors, with his players and above all with himself', some of the coverage of Derby's success, Clough said, made him 'seethe'. 'Fools in newspapers and on television,' he said, 'tried to make out a case that we'd won it by default ... A full league season never has produced false or unworthy champions and never will.'

Leeds players, frustrated by having come so close so often and been thwarted again, and this time by their self-declared nemesis, were particularly scathing. 'It was easy for Derby,' said Norman Hunter. 'They were sunning themselves while we sweated blood. We were forced to play Wolves on the Monday after the Cup final. We could only field half a team. Derby were a good side but, if we'd had a fair crack of the whip, we'd have done the double.' The way Derby had dismantled Leeds on Easter Saturday was probably the best riposte.

Shankly, frustrated as he was by the disallowing of Toshack's late header, was rather more gracious. 'I don't take anything away from Leeds when I say Derby are a better all-round team,' he said. 'Derby play hard, aggressive football and are prepared to attack and defend with great power. The only consolation I have is that Derby are the best team we have played this season and they have won the championship.'

Clough had done at Derby what Shankly had done at Liverpool – and what Revie had done at Leeds – in taking a provincial club from the Second Division to the title. In the summer of 1972, there seemed no reason it should be Liverpool rather than either Leeds or Derby who would go on to dominate the decade. Clough, though, would play a part in the decline of the other two.

III

1972–1974

'Ceux qui n'ont jamais souffert ne savent rien;
ils ne connaissent ni les biens ni les maux;
ils ignorent les hommes; ils s'ignorent eux-mêmes.'*

(François Fénelon, *Les Aventures de Télémaque*)

* 'Those who have never suffered know nothing;
they know neither goods nor evils;
they are ignorant of men; they are ignorant of themselves.'

The Bitter Taste of Glory

Derby were champions, but there was little glee about the Baseball Ground. As the *Evening Telegraph* excitedly contemplated Derby's first season in Europe, the situation behind the scenes continued to deteriorate. Derby had arranged a pre-season trip to the Netherlands and West Germany, on which Clough expected to be able to take Barbara and the children. When Longson refused to pay for them, Clough refused to go, and Taylor ended up leading the team alone. Clough subsequently claimed – in public at least – that he had opted not to go because he needed to be at his desk to make a signing or two, but he had always gone on pre-season tours before, and the fact he pulled out late the night before the players left – that his decision was, as Gerard Mortimer called it, 'a bombshell' – is surely an indication his absence wasn't part of a calmly thought-out plan.

Not that it seemed to matter, as Derby impressed in drawing with Den Haag and beating Willem II and Schalke 04. On the day of that final game in Gelsenkirchen, the FA announced that Colin Todd was to be banned from international football until after the 1974 World Cup for having turned down a call-up to play for England's Under-23 side at the end of the previous season, insisting he was exhausted and going on holiday to Mallorca with his family instead. Clough saw the punishment as evidence that Derby were being victimised and, given the penalty was imposed in the same week that the sanctions over the Ian Storey-Moore transfer were announced, it is easy to understand why he might have felt persecuted. Harsh as the sentence may have appeared, though, the FA handed a similar ban to Chelsea's Alan Hudson for the same offence at the same time. Both were later commuted.

Other, more concrete, concerns arose with Derby's final pre-season game as they were beaten 2–1 at home by Den Haag. The report in the *Evening Telegraph* suggested it would help to suppress any complacency about the challenge of defending the Championship, but if anything the problem seemed to be the opposite. Derby were too fretful, and Clough and Taylor were concerned that the momentum they had generated should not be lost; given how well pre-season had gone generally, that suggests they were aware of deep-lying problems at the club, issues that went far beyond the players, but served to undermine their morale. It was not, Mortimer wrote, that Derby had played badly against Den Haag, but they had been unusually sloppy at the back. It was to become a familiar refrain; after all the arrogance and the confidence, doubt had begun to set in.

Tony Francis remembered being on a club trip to Spain and observing as an apparently contented Clough watched his squad jogging along the beach. It was, Clough said, a great life that he had. A couple of days later, though, he was admitting to crippling anxiety. 'Most of the time,' he said, 'I feel as if I'm hanging on by my fingertips. I like to be right and most of the time I think I am right, but I'm not infallible. I constantly doubt my ability to manage. I think it's the bloke who doesn't question himself who goes wrong. If Hitler had sat down and thought for a minute that he was wrong we wouldn't be here today. He'd have sorted himself out and made the right moves.' It was, of course, typical of Clough, having admitted his insecurity, then immediately to suggest that if only he'd been in charge, Germany would have won the War. Whether it was Bob Dennison, Don Revie or Hitler, Clough was always convinced he'd have done it better. As he once commented, 'Rome wasn't built in a day – but I wasn't on that particular job.' At that stage at least, the bravado was always there, waiting to leap in and smother the doubts.

It wasn't just himself he doubted. Clough began to question how few young players Taylor was delivering; his talent, he felt, was in spotting untapped potential in players who were already fully formed, rather than in players who were still developing. It seems that in the previous year or so, Clough had started to wonder whether Taylor might be losing his touch, wondering, perhaps, whether he could go it alone.

Steve Powell, who had made his debut for Derby as a sixteen-year-old, was a case in point. He had been the captain of England Boys, but Taylor for some reason had refused to watch him, until the scout Maurice Edwards tipped him off that Powell was thinking of joining Chelsea. A practice match was arranged with several Derby first-teamers in which Powell was brilliant; he was signed immediately. 'My strong impression,' Edwards wrote, 'was that Clough and Taylor fell out about this shambolic episode in quite a big way.'

Taylor's method, in as much as there was one, wasn't geared to youth development. 'You deal in hard facts and you must never back hunches,' he said. 'Watch a player in different conditions, not just at home, but in tough away matches when they'll be under pressure. And you never bid for somebody on the basis of what they might do, always what you know they can do.' At times he could be insensitive and while watching junior games would dismiss players after a few minutes, only for Clough to insist they be given at least until half-time, for the sake of their feelings if nothing else.

That Powell, having signed, had performed so admirably in the final game of a Championship season only strengthened Clough's doubts, but at that stage the Clough and Taylor partnership, whatever fissures were developing under the surface, was still capable of functioning well. Durban recalled going in that summer to ask for a raise from £80 to £100 a week, thinking that was reasonable given Derby would be playing European football. Clough offered instead to double his appearance money, which Durban read as a sign that he wouldn't be playing so frequently. After his confidence had been shaken, though, Taylor weighed in, accusing Clough of being ungrateful to a loyal player. As they argued between them – presumably a staged row – they compromised on raising Durban's wages to £88 a week, which he swiftly accepted.

Derby's start to their title defence was indifferent, justifying Clough's fears. Derby looked 'tense' in drawing 1–1 at Southampton, and were then held to a goalless draw at Crystal Palace: 'a poor game and a very disappointing display,' George Edwards said. At home to Chelsea, Mortimer wrote that 'only for about twenty minutes in the second half did Derby County play football as the football world knows that they can'; they lost 2–1. A home game against Manchester City provided a first win, Walker scoring the only goal after a Hector shot had been saved, while Powell was excellent. With Powell, Robson and Webster, plus Todd able to step across if required and Daniel in the reserves, Clough's options at full-back seemed plentiful, but he wanted more.

Perversity had become almost a prerequisite for Clough signings, as though after his unorthodox success in buying McFarland, Mackay and Gemmill, he had similarly to assert himself with every deal he did. Clough

233

drove to Filbert Street, where Leicester City's directors were holding their final board meeting before the start of the season. He hadn't phoned ahead, let alone made an appointment, and burst in, demanding to buy their left-back, David Nish. Leicester's chairman, Len Shipman, told him fairly bluntly to get out, at which Clough, with what was apparently a mocking graciousness, agreed to wait outside until they were finished. When they had, Clough agreed a fee of £250,000. It was a British record figure, all the more extraordinary in being paid for a full-back with no international experience. Taylor, though, had been impressed by the way Santos's full-backs pressed forward in a friendly against Sheffield Wednesday, and saw in Nish something of the same buccaneering spirit, somebody who could offer attacking width from deep. 'Nish was anything but intimidating in the tackle,' he said, 'but I didn't care.' Nish had already said he would be keen on the move after being approached earlier in the summer by Maurice Edwards shortly before the final of the Burton and District Tennis Championships, which he won – the sort of tapping-up at which Clough and Taylor excelled.

That same day, the wife of Doug Weatherall, the journalist who had worked with Clough in the north-east, had open heart surgery at a hospital in Shotley Bridge. 'Edna came to all wired up,' Weatherall said, 'and there beside the bed was a lovely bunch of roses. It was a very thoughtful thing, but what made it especially so was to do it while he was spending the biggest fee in the history of British football buying David Nish. If I'd been under that sort of pressure would I have had the thoughtfulness to send flowers, even if it was just asking my secretary? I don't think so.'

Longson knew nothing of any of it. The fee, he felt, could have been reduced by negotiation, but what made it worse was that Shipman, as well as being chairman of Leicester, was president of the Football League. Clough may have cared nothing for the hierarchy of the game, but Longson did. 'Such was my respect for Brian,' he wrote, 'that I was prepared to bite my tongue and swallow as best I could the irritations that were cropping up.' His patience, though, was running out.

It might have run out even faster had Longson known that Clough had also made an unsanctioned £400,000 bid to sign Bobby Moore from West Ham United, something that emerged several months later in a conversation between Webb and his West Ham counterpart Eddie Chapman. Ron Greenwood, then the West Ham manager, confirmed the story in his autobiography, describing how Clough, having tapped up Moore, then made bids for both him and Trevor Brooking, responding to Greenwood's insistence they weren't for sale by repeatedly increasing his bid.

Nish made his debut at Norwich, but Derby were, Mortimer said, 'harried and hustled', and lost 1–0. They went down by the same score at Everton, with Taylor insisting it was Derby's best performance of the season, and if that engendered optimism, it was fanned by a 2–1 home win over Liverpool.

The mood, having been restive, should have been one of relief, but Clough came out fighting, saying the fans who had criticised the team made him 'sick', prompting a flurry of complaints in the *Evening Telegraph*. 'I admit Mr Clough that you have done wonders for Derby County,' wrote 'Disgruntled Season-Ticket Holder', 'but it is noticeable that the attendance has fallen at the Baseball Ground since you have allowed your mouth to try to control the footballing world.' It evidently wasn't just Longson and the FA who were tiring of Clough's persistent outrageousness and insistence on igniting controversies at every turn. For three days, the *Evening Telegraph's* letters page addressed nothing else. 'Why is Clough so determined to repeatedly bite the hand that feeds him?' asked Richard Beale of Wirksworth. 'We never expected the George Best-like tantrums of last few weeks.'

Even for somebody of Clough's abrasiveness, it was some feat for a manager who had just led a side to their first ever title to draw such criticism from his own fans only a month into the following season. It was surely a political error: with the fans behind him, the board would have been powerless to act against him; once the fans began to turn, Clough became isolated, even if the players supported him.

Derby struggled through a 1–0 win over Dave Mackay's Swindon Town in the League Cup, but when they lost 2–1 at West Brom, they had just six points and six goals from eight games; the league title defence was effectively over before it had begun. As preparation for their first European Cup tie, against the Yugoslav champions Željezničar, it was far from ideal, but there was also a sense that the game had become a distraction and that the season was almost on hold until it was done.

When the occasion finally arrived, Derby rose to it, putting on what Edwards described as a 'magnificent display'. McFarland met a Hinton free-kick to put Derby ahead six minutes before half-time and, with Hennessey dominant, they controlled the game thereafter, Gemmill converting a Hector centre to make it 2–0. 'We worried them,' Clough said, 'because of the pace, the precision and the skill with which we play.'

A 1–0 win over a 'robust' Birmingham was followed by a 3–0 defeat at a struggling Manchester United, prompting an outburst from George Edwards, who revealed that Clough had only been able to spend thirty minutes on the training field with his players in the week leading up to the game. There were few details, but readers were left in little doubt as to just how serious the situation at the club had become. 'Problems behind the scenes, childish vendettas that would not be tolerated in any other industry, are eating away at the heart of Derby County,' Edwards wrote. 'Saturday afternoon, the big match, is no longer the highlight of the week, but merely light relief after six days of mischief . . . of scurrilous backbiting and football politics. And this was never more obvious than after the Rams had been beaten 3–0 away on Saturday by a team who, for half an hour, were the worst Derby have met since promotion.'

Early goals from Hinton and O'Hare in Sarajevo ensured Derby completed a 4–1 aggregate win over Željezničar, but they were unconvincing in beating Tottenham 2–1 and then drew 0–0 at home to Chelsea in the League Cup. There was a dreadful inevitability about the trip to Leeds that followed. Clough, surprisingly, left out Hennessey, bringing Peter Daniel, a reserve full-back who had barely played in two years, into midfield and the result was a 5–0 defeat. Derby had always, as Edwards said, had an 'Elland Road inferiority complex', but this time it was 'embarrassing to watch them at times'.

That defeat came at just the wrong time, sapping the confidence of a side that was already beginning to wobble. In the League Cup at Chelsea, Derby played what Mortimer described as 'some glorious football', had a goal ruled out and were denied at least one penalty. Chelsea, though, made the most of 'a very limited number of incursions' and won 3–2. 'The problem of the management now is to prevent them losing faith in their style,' Mortimer wrote. 'This kind of football has brought them rich rewards in the past. Currently the Rams are getting nowhere fast, but the players must maintain their belief in themselves.'

They kept up their form at home to Leicester, only the excellence of Peter Shilton preventing them winning more comfortably than 2–1, but then suffered a sixth successive away defeat at Ipswich. 'The whole structure is tottering and there is an uneasy feeling that if, for any reason, Colin Todd were out of the side, it would collapse,' Mortimer wrote.

The European Cup, though, provided a release, particularly when the opponents were as glamorous as Benfica. Clough went to scout them, and when he came back he didn't dare tell his players how 'bad' they'd been for fear it would breed complacency. Still, he decided to take action to combat Benfica's superior technical ability. Following the plan first pursued when Wolves beat Honvéd in a mudbath in 1954, he snuck into the Baseball Ground the night before the game and watered the pitch with two fireman's hoses. In *Walking on Water*, Clough suggests this was a regular occurrence, and he usually left the water running for twenty minutes. That night, though, he fell asleep and 'woke up drenched and with enough water on that ground to have staged an Olympic diving event'. At the game, Stanley Rous, the English head of Fifa, ticked him off for such obvious gamesmanship.

Like so many Clough anecdotes, though, it doesn't quite hold up and not just because Maurice Edwards remembers the Baseball Ground being locked until 5pm on the day of the game to allow the groundsman – not Clough – to water the pitch. 'They were what I call Fancy Dans who like to knock the ball around without any pressure, but don't like away games too much especially on a cold evening on a tight little pitch like the Baseball Ground,' Clough told Pat Murphy. 'I wanted them to get bogged down in the heavy conditions. They were, and we pissed all over them.' Yet Clough prided himself on the way his teams retained possession; why make that harder to do against an opponent he believed to be technically inferior to his side? Watering the pitch in moderation to make the surface slicker makes sense for a passing side, but even if he did regularly do that, why hide it? And if he did deliberately soak the pitch, where does that leave Clough's regular diatribes about playing the game in the right way?

Still, whatever the underfoot conditions, Derby were excellent. Before kick-off Taylor ran through a number of Benfica's players, making inconsequential comments about them, then screwed up his piece of paper and said, 'There's nothing to worry about with this lot.' Derby responded with their best performance of the season. 'Derby have struggled in the league, but last night they went to town,' wrote Edwards. 'They took on opposition whose reputation borders on the legendary and beat them out of sight before the tea had been made for half-time.' McFarland got the first from a Hinton corner, Hector lashed in after McFarland had headed down another Hinton delivery, and McGovern made it 3–0 after Hector had won another aerial ball.

Sheffield United were beaten 2–1 at home and, having had clauses restricting their contact with the media removed, Clough and Taylor signed new five-year contracts; things seemed to be looking up. As soon as Derby played away, though, everything unravelled again, and they lost 4–0 at Manchester City. With Gemmill, O'Hare and Hector all rested, 'they made elementary mistakes in defence, attacked with hope but not the slightest conviction, and looked a very moderate team indeed.'

With those three back, though, Derby produced a fine defensive display to draw 0–0 away to Benfica. 'We were in the dark for twenty minutes,' Clough said in his autobiography. 'They came at us from every conceivable angle. There was only one way to describe their superiority – they pissed on us. We couldn't get a kick, but we hung on and the game remained goalless.'

After the game, the players went out for a celebratory meal in Lisbon, during which Clough stood up and shouted, 'Hey, Toddy! I don't like you and I don't like your missus either!' It was, it seems, at attempt to rile Todd whom, Clough felt, was 'too good to be bloody true'. Learning from Ord, he and Taylor investigated the backgrounds of players, trying to find their weaknesses and their secrets – gambling, drinking, womanising. Todd, it seemed, had none, and that meant Clough had no hold over him. Todd was hurt by the abuse, particularly that directed at his wife, Jenny, and went to see Clough the following day.

'It got a bit personal,' Todd said. 'When I first signed for Derby, I was a very quiet lad. On the training ground, he'd kick me from behind and this went on for about two weeks. This morning I had [had] enough and I gave him some verbal. He just stood there laughing, He'd achieved what he was looking for, he got the reaction he wanted. From that day on I stood up for myself. This Benfica thing, he was having a dig at me, he wasn't having a dig at the wife. He wanted a reaction from me. Well, he didn't get it on the night, but the following day I went down to the ground, went into his office and said, "Hey gaffer, I don't mind you having a go at me, but when it gets personal I think you're totally wrong." I'd no sooner come out of the office than he'd got up to my house and presented my wife with a bouquet of flowers. He treated everybody different and I was a quiet, unassuming lad who used to do my job and probably get nine out of ten every Saturday. He wanted a change, some direction. That's how he did it. I became more aggressive.'

In the end, Clough and Taylor did discover Todd's weakness. It wasn't anything especially major, but he did occasionally gamble, and when he'd run up a £700 debt with Whittaker's, the bookmakers near the ground, Clough and Taylor challenged him over it. 'He was very clever with that,' Todd said. 'I was sitting at home and the phone rang. It was Brian, He said, "Can you please come down to the stadium?"

'He said, "Any idea what it's about?" It was towards the end of the season.

'I said, "Probably I've won some trophy or something." He said, "Well, come down to the stadium and bring your wife with you."

'So we get into the room and there's him, Peter Taylor and Mike Keeling, one of the directors. He said, "Any idea why you're down?"

'I said, "It can only be football related, probably because I've won a trophy?"

'"No, it's nothing to do with that," he said. "You've got a problem over the road." Now, over the road there was a betting shop. He said, "Well you owe the betting shop money, don't you?" I said, "Yeah." He said, "I'll tell you now, we're going to pay that money. One of the directors is going to pay it for you, but I tell you, if you ever do it again, you'll be kicked out of this football club." Anyway, there was method in his madness, if you can call that madness. When I got outside that office, I got the biggest bollocking of the lot. From the wife. If I'd only have been on my own, I'd probably have kept on doing it. With the wife there, well, it was very astute. That was it, it taught me a lesson.'

After a 2–2 draw with Crystal Palace, in what Edwards described as a 'miserable, unattractive and exceedingly dull match', Derby slipped to sixteenth. A Hector double gave them their first away win of the season at West Ham, though, and with confidence returning, Derby thrashed Arsenal 5–0, all the goals coming in a twenty-six-minute period as Bob Wilson, on his return after a cartilage operation, couldn't get to grips with Hinton's crossing. That put Derby nine points behind the leaders Liverpool, and when they then won 2–1 at Wolves, they were only two points off fourth.

With no European action until March, the surge of form continued. After a 1–0 win at Norwich early in 1971, the *Evening Telegraph* still suggested the title was possible; that might have been fanciful, but European qualification, certainly, was within reach and came closer when, switching to a 4–4–2, they frustrated Liverpool, drawing 1–1 at Anfield. There was further positive news in the club's accounts. Derby had announced profits of £87,000 for the previous season, and Barry Butlin and John Robson were sold for a total of £150,000 towards the end of 1972. Whatever other concerns the directors may have had, money shouldn't have been one of them, even with the outlay on Nish.

On the surface all seemed well, but relations between Clough and Taylor were worsening. Taylor became increasingly upset by the perks Clough was receiving, something exacerbated when he learned from Webb that Clough had a habit of 'murdering him' in board meetings, belittling his contributions. Against that background, is it any wonder that certain members of the board began to wonder exactly what they were paying Taylor for? 'Taylor,' Longson wrote, 'was unable to conceal his envy and jealousy of his more illustrious partner.'

Things reached crisis point when Taylor, after a furious row with Clough over his perks, went home complaining of 'chestiness'. Ten days later, he had still not reappeared. Clough, having lost patience with his truculence, went to Longson's house and demanded he sack Taylor, who had, he said, become impossible to work with. When Longson refused, Clough became so agitated that, 'shaking with rage and shouting "I'm getting nowhere with you buggers",' he spilled a large Scotch on the kitchen floor. As details of the friction dripped into the public domain, both Clough and Taylor gave interviews to the *Evening Telegraph* insisting it was nothing to worry about. 'We have had arguments since the first day we met,' Taylor said. 'Part of our success can be put down to the fact that we can sort out our differences.'

Their relationship, though, was deteriorating, success having emphasised the extent to which Clough was seen as the dominant partner. Longson's diaries make relatively little reference to Taylor, whom he evidently regarded as a junior figure. It was Clough, he said, who had the 'wisdom', something that came increasingly to rile Taylor, particularly as Longson lavished more and more gifts – a suede coat, a waste-disposal unit – on Clough. In 1971, he had given him shares in Derby County as a Christmas present and, at one point, he had even contemplated bequeathing Clough his remaining business interests in his will.

Eventually, Longson increased Clough's salary by £5,000; Taylor, meanwhile, got nothing, and only found out about the rise eighteen months later when, by chance, he saw the contract lying on Webb's desk. He was appalled. As Taylor saw it, he'd had a heart attack trying to manage the team while Clough was off gallivanting on television, and this was his thanks. He sought out Longson and when he demanded an explanation, the only response he got was to be asked how he had found out; it wasn't, in other words, an oversight, but there had been a deliberate attempt to keep the rise a secret. 'I'd thought I could trust him with my life,' Taylor reflected later, after his final break-up with Clough, 'but already I was having doubts.'

Taylor was at least as insecure as Clough, probably more so – by the time he got to Forest he was ordering players to mention his name in interviews to try to ensure he took some of the credit – and he had an acute awareness of the value of things, but even if he had had a more self-confident personality, his increasing sense of alienation would have been understandable. 'I was so choked over the perks Brian was getting,' he said, 'that I couldn't face the celebrations when we won the title.'

At Hartlepools, the pair had agreed that any bonuses or external earnings should be divided equally between them, something on which Clough had clearly reneged. The issue became even more divisive, as Taylor demanded a cut of the money Clough was taking for television work, pointing out that he was having to do more and more work with the players as Clough was away so often. Things had got so bad that even in the run-in to winning the championship, Taylor had considered leaving. In February 1972, he had received an offer from Frank O'Farrell to become his number two at Manchester United, and had decided to accept when the United board rejected O'Farrell's proposal, apparently because Busby was worried that Clough would mount a campaign against United in the media.

Yet on the pitch, Derby seemed to have found their rhythm. They beat West Brom 2–0, and then drew 1–1 at home to Tottenham in the FA Cup, Davies scoring an eighty-fifth-minute equaliser. The replay was one of the most memorable games played under Clough, one of the days on which

241

he was at his most Cloughish. Derby were unlucky to be 2–0 down at half-time to goals from Martin Chivers and Alan Gilzean. Hennessey was struggling but, speaking so the whole dressing-room could hear, Clough begged him to stay on, saying 'We've only got Ally on the bench.' Alan Durban was furious, but when he did replace Hennessey, he was inspired. Hector pulled one back with a looping shot that went in off the post, only for Mike England to make it 3–1 from the penalty spot after McGovern had handled in the box, a harsh call that prompted a furious reaction from a cluster of Derby players that was out of keeping with Clough's insistence on respecting the referee. Davies, though, struck twice in the final twelve minutes – the first swept through a crowd from the edge of the box, the second a brilliant flick-up and volley from O'Hare's cutback. 'Justice,' Barry Davies said in commentary, 'is seen to be done.'

As the Spurs management raced onto the pitch at the final whistle to give advice, Clough and Taylor sat unmoved in the dugout, and, as Davies powered in a header and then flicked on for Hector to score, Derby won 5–3. Back then, their refusal to leave the bench was seen as confidence, an indication they knew the game was won; eighteen years later when Clough did something similar at the 1991 FA Cup final, he was condemned for it. Managerial quirks are almost always judged by their success rather than by any internal logic: the same act can be hailed as genius one day, and dismissed as perversity the next. It could be, of course, that the skill is in selecting the right time to play the trick, but it's hard not to wonder whether the quirks are at times irrelevant. Or perhaps Clough's aura at the time was such that whatever he did would inspire his players: for nothing begets success like success.

Davies completed his hat-trick from a Hector corner to give Derby the lead two minutes into the second period of extra-time, and Hector ran on to a long clearance to round off the win with six minutes remaining. 'Quite honestly we were lucky that Derby only scored five goals,' said the Tottenham manager Bill Nicholson. 'In fact we were lucky all the way through, so lucky that I thought we would win. We had all the breaks and for so long Derby couldn't get the ball in the net, but they just kept playing quite superlative football. It was a brilliant performance and although we were humiliated I am bound to say that justice was done.'

That, though, was the high point. With injuries taking their toll on a squad that was probably still two or three players light, Derby lost at Birmingham and at home to Stoke, and it soon became clear that their minds were on the FA Cup and the European Cup, even if Boulton was banned for two games for rubbing his dirty glove into the face of the referee after a 3–2 defeat to Leeds. That match had shown just how deep the antipathy between the sides had become, featuring fifty-five fouls, two disputed penalties and about a fortnight of sniping between the two managers afterwards.

That antipathy resurfaced when the sides met again in the sixth round of the Cup. Revie, in a startlingly frank interview in the *Evening Telegraph* before the game, revealed the depth of his antipathy to Clough. 'It all boils down to the fact that I dislike the way Clough repeatedly knocks other personalities in the game . . . .' he said, 'especially rival managers.' Clough missed the game, spending the afternoon with his mother, who was by then gravely ill. A Peter Lorimer goal on the half hour was enough to give Leeds the win.

That meant Derby's only hope of success was in Europe, and their form there seemed far more certain. The resolve on which Clough insisted had returned to an extent in Czechoslovakia as Derby lost 1–0 to Spartak Trnava in the European Cup quarter-final. Colin Todd had been excellent, but he was dispossessed by Kamil Majerník, who laid in František Horvath to score. After a 0–0 draw at Leicester, O'Hare was brilliant in a midfield role as Derby overturned the first-leg deficit against Spartak Trnava. Gemmill won possession and fed McGovern to cross for Hector to score the first, and the forward added his second with a smart volley to make it 2–1 on aggregate.

Derby's league form remained poor, though, a run of three points from seven games meaning their hopes of Uefa Cup qualification were fading fast, even if a switch to 4–4–2 brought a 1–0 win at Arsenal. The European Cup, and a semi-final against Juventus, dominated the fixture list and, it seemed, Derby's thinking. It was arguably the biggest game Derby ever played in; it was certainly the bitterest disappointment.

Things began to go wrong the night before the game. The Derby squad was booked into a hotel in the hills outside Turin, while the staff and press stayed in the centre. Stuart Webb had arranged a dinner at a restaurant in the city, at which Clough was to be the guest speaker. When the time for them to leave came around, though, Clough was still in his tracksuit playing cards. Taylor tried to hurry him up, at which point the two had a public row that ended with each storming off to his own room and neither making it to the dinner.

Presumably because of that disagreement, the two hadn't discussed the team before Clough announced it in the dressing-room the following day. As he read it out, it included a major surprise, with Tony Parry named in midfield instead of Alan Durban. Taylor told him it was absurd to field a player with so little experience at the highest level in such a big game and convinced Clough to change his mind. Neither incident was catastrophic, but they can only have had a destabilising effect.

Worse, though, was what was going on outside the dressing-room. John Charles, a former Leeds and Juventus player who still commanded huge respect in Turin and was on the trip in an ambassadorial capacity, warned the Derby staff before kick-off that the Juve substitute Helmut Haller, who had scored against England for West Germany in the 1966 World Cup final, had twice been into the room of the referee, his compatriot Gerhard Schulenberg.

At half-time, as the players left the field, Taylor realised that Haller, rather than going into the dressing-room with his team-mates, had followed Schulenberg. He hurried after them and, claiming, quite falsely, to speak German, asked if they minded him listening to their conversation. 'Haller jabbed me in the ribs with his elbow and, while I was gasping for air, some heavies grabbed hold of me,' he said. 'I heard John Charles shouting to me to hold on to my passport. I've never been so scared in my life.'

Taylor, it should be said, was not immune to paranoia and it could be that there was nothing more sinister going on than one German making sure a fellow German was being looked after. Given the other circumstantial evidence, though, it's easy to see why Clough was convinced something was seriously amiss. 'Juventus bought the referee,' he said. 'Of that there is no shadow of a doubt. I was cheated. Taylor was nearly arrested and two players were booked for next to nothing.'

Those two players were McFarland and Gemmill, the only two Derby players carrying yellow cards into the game; both were suspended as a result and missed the home leg. It's easy for conspiracy theories to develop in hindsight, but the British press was suspicious from the start. Frank

Clough in the *Sun* wrote that Derby 'were the victims of some of the most amazing refereeing I have ever seen', while in the *Mail*, Jeff Farmer described the bookings as 'scandalous'.

'Gemmill had his name taken for a trip on [Giuseppe] Furino, retaliation after Furino's elbow had smashed into his face,' Mortimer wrote. 'Herr Schulenburg failed to see the original offence, so the booking of Gemmill at least had a certain justification from his point of view. McFarland's booking was totally absurd. He went up to challenge [Antonello] Cuccureddu for a high ball and the two heads clashed. For that, and only that, he was cautioned . . . it looked like a put-up job.'

Clough had no doubts. 'I'd heard lurid tales of bribery, corruption, the bending of match officials in Italy . . .' he wrote in his autobiography, 'but I'd never before seen what struck me as clear evidence. I went barmy.' That night he emerged from the dressing-room and faced a throng of Italian journalists. 'No cheating bastards will I talk to,' he said. 'I will not talk to any cheating bastards.' Brian Glanville, doyen of the British press and fluent in Italian, initially feigned incomprehension when the journalists asked what Clough had said, but Clough wanted his point to get across: 'Tell 'em what I said, Brian!'

'The curious thing about that game . . .' Glanville wrote, 'was that though strange and suspicious things may have happened, Juventus won it fairly and squarely on the field.' José Altafini put Juventus ahead from Pietro Anastasi's cross after twenty-eight minutes, but O'Hare laid in Hector to level. The introduction of Haller lifted Juventus, and Franco Causio restored their lead after Derby had twice failed to clear crosses midway through the second half. He later hit the post, and Altafini added a third seven minutes from time.

A few days before the second leg, Clough's outrage over what had happened in Turin was fanned as the Portuguese referee who was scheduled to take charge of the second leg, Francisco Marques Lobo, revealed he'd been offered $5,000 and a car if Juventus won. Uefa subsequently investigated and exonerated Juventus, ruling that the bribe was the work of the notorious Hungarian fixer Dezso Solti, whom the commission ruled to have been acting independently. The Wolves defender Bernard Shaw, of course, had similarly insisted when he was approached ahead of his side's decisive game against Leeds that it was not anybody connected with the club who had made contact; for those looking to fix matches, the use of an intermediary was an obvious ploy. That's not to say either Leeds or Juventus were necessarily guilty; merely that the involvement of a third party is hardly a defence. Glanville, who conducted a thorough investigation the following year, turned up a letter signed by Solti on behalf of Juventus in 1971. Little wonder Clough showed such scorn for authority when, as he saw it, it so often acted with such pusillanimity.

At the Baseball Ground, it's generally agreed, Lobo refereed fairly. He awarded Derby a fifty-seventh-minute penalty after Luciano Spinosi had fouled Hector, but Hinton missed, and six minutes later sent off Davies after he had butted his marker Francesco Morini, with whom he had been tangling all night. Clough called it a 'disgrace' but he was referring to the assault rather than the decision. The game ended 0–0 and Derby were out.

That night, according to Clough, a bad day became a terrible one. 'It was 11.30 that same evening, and I was in bed with Barbara when I heard the phone ringing downstairs,' Clough wrote in his first autobiography. 'When I picked it up my brother Joe's voice was hushed and brave, but what he said hit me like a sledgehammer: "We've lost our mam."'

She had had cancer for some time, and had never really recovered after falling ill on the trip to the Scillies the previous year. Clough had been back to Middlesbrough to see her, had rubbed her lips with an ice-cube when she asked for a drink. 'Nothing,' he wrote, 'prepared me for the news she had gone.' He remembered her in her woolly hat, the way she hung out the washing, how she looked standing by the mangle and leading the kids to church. Had he had her faith, that may have offered some comfort, but he didn't. 'I'm sure there is no afterlife,' he wrote. 'The loss of mam was final.'

That has become the accepted version, but the strange thing is that it didn't happen that day at all. Sal Clough did, as Clough said, die on his thirty-eighth birthday, but that was 21 March, the day Derby beat Spartak Trnava. That night had shown Clough at his most selfless. He had known his mother was near the end, and yet he went out of his way to ensure that Gordon Turner, a former Luton player who suffered motor neurone disease, was looked after at the ground. He had met Turner while playing for the Football League, and had been reintroduced by Colin Lawrence, who would become a great friend. The harshness Clough could demonstrate was all the more shocking, all the less explicable, because there was a genuinely warm and generous heart beneath.

The Juventus game happened a little over a month after his mother's death, but the fact that he linked two events he clearly recalled with vividness and pain is surely significant. In the twenty years that separated the game and writing about it, his grief at the loss of his mother and his disgust at what he perceived as Juventus's cheating became entwined until they were inseparable.

Success for Clough was always partly about satisfying his mother; over the course of five weeks in 1973, it's possible to see the European Cup in particular becoming about honouring her. His thought processes, of course, are unknowable, but it's surely not too great a stretch to suggest that when she died on the night of the quarter-final, Clough made a pledge to himself, whether consciously or not, to win the European Cup for her.

When he was then denied in that quest, and denied by what he saw as cheating, he was unable to restrain himself. In the rest of his career, Clough never criticised a referee in public as he had in Turin, even when Forest were thwarted by a corrupt official against Anderlecht in the Uefa Cup in 1984, but the game against Juventus was for him about more than football; they had cheated not just Derby County, but his mother, and so over time the two events were elided, and the European Cup became his grail, winning it his way of living up to what he believed his mother's expectations to be, his way, even, of making up for that stain he could never wash out: that of having failed his eleven-plus. 'I don't have any O levels,' he said in that 1993 interview with the BBC, reiterating what had become a familiar theme, that his European Cup and Championship medals were his O-levels and A-levels.

The only thing left to play for that season was qualification for the Uefa Cup, something that was still possible thanks to the archaic rule – a hangover from the Fairs Cup – that stipulated no more than one team from the same city could enter in any one season. After beating Everton and Ipswich, Derby went into their final game, against Wolves, knowing a win would secure seventh spot. With Arsenal and West Ham missing out because Tottenham had won the League Cup, that meant Uefa Cup qualification providing Leeds took up a slot in the Cup-Winners' Cup by winning either the FA Cup or that season's Cup-Winners' Cup, the finals of both of which they'd reached.

Derby fulfilled their part of the deal, two goals from Davies and another from McFarland securing a 3–0 win, but Leeds were always there to thwart Clough, even if they had to lose to do so. Sunderland beat them in the FA Cup final, and AC Milan in the Cup-Winners' Cup, so Leeds took the final Uefa Cup slot and Derby ended the season with nothing. Bad would soon become worse.

Sam Longson is not a figure well-served by history. With hindsight, knowing what Clough went on to achieve, getting rid of him looks like a cata-strophically awful decision, like the publishers who turned down J.K. Rowling, or the Decca executive who rejected the Beatles. In fact, in some ways it was worse, for Clough and Taylor had already achieved huge success at Derby; it wasn't a case of Longson not being able to recognise the talent waiting to blossom; having watched them lead Derby from the lower reaches of the Second Division to the semi-finals of the European Cup, Longson was well aware of what Clough and Taylor could do. Having worked with them for five seasons, though, he was also well aware of the strife they brought.

At one point the previous season, Longson had been hospitalised with a nervous illness, brought on, he said, after Alan Hardaker told him that in future the club could face punishment for its manager's public pro-nouncements. 'It was like walking a tightrope,' he wrote. 'We had been left in no doubt that, if Brian stepped over the mark again, it would be regarded as the responsibility of the club. But it had become clear by now that we had little influence over him.'

Hardaker and Shipman were friends of Longson and he had no desire to upset them. More seriously, it is clear from his diaries that he believed that following the fine for administrative negligence there was a genuine threat of the club being relegated, perhaps even expelled from the league should they step out of line again. 'I only regret that no official warning was issued by the League to back up what we were left to say in private to Brian,' he wrote.

From then on, though, Longson seems to have been looking for an excuse to sack Clough, and he found it when Clough took a part-time job with London Weekend Television's *On the Ball* programme. He had toyed with accepting a £16,000 salary to replace Jimmy Hill as the programme's anchor, but decided against leaving football. At first Derby agreed to the compromise arrangement, but as Clough began going to London on a Wednesday or a Thursday every week, and Taylor was twice sent to cover for him at board meetings, Longson had his opportunity. 'His absences,' Longson wrote, 'did not comply with his undertaking not to allow outside commitments to interfere with club duties ... It could hardly be argued that for a manager to be away on Wednesday or Thursday was the best way of preparing a team for a Saturday match. In addition, he was travelling to London again on Sundays to contribute comments and analyses.'

Clough, with a degree of justification, insisted there were double stand-ards at work, arguing that the directors had as good as insisted he had to sit on ITV's panel providing analysis on games at the 1970 World Cup. Not, presumably, that Clough needed much persuading. He had, anyway, changed, familiarity with television and notoriety stimulating the less pleas-ant side of his personality: 'His early and very likeable forthright self-confidence had to some extent evolved into a bumptious arrogance,' as Edwards put it. Perhaps that was the result of early success: as Tony Francis said in a BBC documentary, what made him difficult to work with wasn't his genius per se but his recognition of his genius, and his awareness that because of it he could get away with things others couldn't. 'All the confidence I had experienced as a goalscorer of exceptional quality was flooding through my veins again,' Clough wrote in his autobiography. 'I realised I could be as a manager what I had been as a player – the best in the business.'

Or perhaps, as Taylor would later hint, it was fear that having reached that level again, it could all be taken away again, an insecurity that mani-fested itself in an exaggeration of the characteristics that had led him to success, coupled with a desire, perhaps unconscious, to belittle others. Or perhaps it was the drinking, itself probably a symptom of the fear that everything for which he had worked, the team he had built and the life he had created for himself and his family, could be swept away as easily as his playing career had been.

How much Clough was drinking at that time remains uncertain, for he was good at hiding the problem. Even at the end of his managerial career, when his face was ravaged and the issue was clear, there were those who knew him prepared to swear they'd never seen Clough drunk, and one of the principal complaints directed at *The Damned Utd* was that it overplayed Clough's alcoholism as it was at the time. Yet Clough admitted he'd had a problem as he tried to recover from the knee injury at Sunderland, Webb clearly had concerns even while Clough was at Derby, and in *Clough's War*, Don Shaw's memoir of his time leading the movement to have Clough reinstated at the Baseball Ground, the author recounts an incident at Walsall's ground, a post-match meal where Clough has the whole Brighton first team abstaining.

What brought the dream to an end, Clough said, was 'a combination of my ego, Taylor's pride, and the stubbornness of an old man who wanted to be seen running his club and regaining control of his outrageous, outspoken manager'. In the face of Longson's provocation, Taylor, not surprisingly, backed Clough, despite the apparent cooling in their relationship, maintaining that the promotion of the club on television was part of a manager's job. Webb remembered them at that time constantly bickering, and occasionally engaging in blazing rows, although he admitted he wondered at times how much of their apparent antipathy was an act, part of the hypnotist's show that somehow kept the players performing to the maximum. Even if a frostiness had entered the marriage, though, it's revealing that Taylor still felt his first loyalty was to his partner and closed ranks against outside threats.

Whatever frustrations both might have expressed, there seems to have been awareness on the part of both Clough and Taylor that they needed the other man. 'When Clough hesitated, it was Taylor who nudged him forward,' George Edwards wrote. 'When Clough's impulsiveness bubbled over it was Taylor's restraining hand on his shoulder.' More than anything, Taylor had the capacity to lift Clough out of the dark moods to which he was prone. Taylor, Edwards said, 'was just incredibly funny – a sort of amalgam of Tommy Cooper, Les Dawson and Spike Milligan. Almost everything was a corner-of-the-mouth aside, delivered with a slight sideways tilt of the head.'

Bizarre and nonsensical as his demands may seem in retrospect, it's easy to have sympathy with Longson, who saw his manager disappearing for substantial periods and using that time away to make his life more difficult.

To an extent, Clough came to acknowledge that he was to blame. 'I was good value for newspapers,' he wrote in his autobiography, 'because I blew my own trumpet – too often and too loud, I now realise – which made good copy for journalists.'

Generally, though, it was easier to blame Longson. 'When a club mushrooms like Derby did,' Clough wrote, 'there's a lot of envy, jealousy and bullshit. Longson suddenly found himself in boardrooms where he'd never been allowed in before, let alone welcomed as chairman.' On one occasion, on a pre-season tour when Derby happened to be staying near West Ham, Clough recalled, Longson asked for an introduction to Bobby Moore. Geoff Hurst and Martin Peters were there as well, but 'he said he only wanted to meet Bobby Moore. I don't think he'd heard of the other two!'

That was palpably untrue, but even if the jibe was intended as a joke by Clough, the image it presents is the image of Longson that the world has accepted, a bumbling figure suddenly drunk on the celebrity to which football had introduced him. It is utterly unfair. This was a man who had built up his business interests to become a millionaire; there was nothing bumbling about him. As others dithered, he was the one who had had the foresight to offer Clough the manager's job in the first place. And while Derby's promotion and title success raised Longson's standing in the game, he had already served as a director for thirteen years before Clough arrived, much of which he'd spent as the club's representative on the Football League board. He'd been to ten European Cup finals and, as a consequence, was acquainted with many of the game's hierarchy, not merely in England but in Europe. Clough's antics, he wrote in his diary, far from opening doors, actually meant people deliberately avoided him.

By 1973, Clough was out of control, a wilfully controversial figure who attacked anybody and everybody in his newspaper columns and his television appearances, which became so popular that his nasal drawl became a staple for television impressionists. By a quirk of coincidence, Mike Yarwood was appearing in Derby in the week Clough resigned, which led to the editor of the women's page of the *Evening Telegraph* calling Clough to ask his opinion of the impressionist on the day he submitted his resignation.

Clough, as he admitted in his first autobiography, 'loved' the notoriety.

As he noted in his second, it blinded him. 'I didn't recognise the danger,' he said. 'I was like the twenty-year-old pilot in the war who went up in a Spitfire to take on half a dozen German fighter planes. I didn't know the meaning of fear ... You don't see the possible pitfalls when you're thirty. When you get into your fifties and sixties, you don't see anything else ...'

Gradually Longson tired of going round clearing up the mess Clough had left. There were only so many times he could smile awkwardly, mutter 'he's a lad' and hope to get away with it. Clough, though, was too carried away by notions of his own omnipotence to heed Longson's warnings and seemed almost to relish provoking him further.

Not that Longson was blameless, on one occasion throwing a tantrum in the directors' box after being handed a newspaper that bore the headline 'The Man at the Helm', beneath which was printed a photograph of Clough. At some level, he clearly had bought into the misguided notion that he was the messiah, rather than merely the man who had brought the messiah to Derby.

In his diaries, Longson admits he contemplated getting rid of Clough and replacing him with Taylor. 'The more I considered the idea,' he wrote, 'the better it looked ... The big stumbling block was Peter Taylor's loyalty to Brian.' According to Taylor, Longson twice tried to persuade him to replace Clough. On one occasion, he pulled up outside Taylor's house in his Mercedes and offered him the job outright. Taylor refused and imme-diately told Clough what had happened.

A few weeks later, Taylor said, Longson returned and asked him to write out his own contract. Taylor again turned him down without a second thought. Longson, though, insisted in his diary that he had resisted the temptation to offer Taylor the job. When challenged on the discrepancy by Francis, he said that he went to see Taylor after his ten-day absence to ask why he wasn't at work and to test how deep his resentment towards Clough ran. 'I didn't want him as manager,' he said. 'He completely misinterpreted the reason behind my visit.'

That summer Leeds were found guilty of 'persistent misconduct on the field' during a particularly unpleasant game against Birmingham City the previous season and given a suspended £3,000 fine. Clough, remembering the £10,000 fine and the European ban Derby had received for their administrative misconduct, and perhaps hoping that a similar ban would lead to Derby taking Leeds's place in the Uefa Cup, laid into Revie's side in the *Sunday Express*. Worse – at least as far as Longson was concerned – he then went on to attack what he saw as the weakness of the game's administrators. 'The Football Association,' he wrote, 'should have instantly relegated Don Revie's team after branding them as one of the dirtiest clubs in Britain. As it is, the befuddled minds of the men who run the game have missed the most marvellous chance of cleaning up soccer in one swoop. By "fining" Leeds and Birmingham £3,000 they have allowed the "bad boys" to laugh at authority.

'No wonder Don Revie was smiling broadly as he left the disciplinary commission's hearing in London. I looked at his happy face smiling at me out of my newspaper in Spain. It just about spoiled my holiday to read that the £3,000 fine has been suspended until the end of the coming season . . . If the FA had fined Don Revie £3,000 and sent his football club into the Second Division, they would have cured many of the ills of the game at a stroke . . .'

Clough's issue with Leeds and Revie had gone beyond the ideological to become personal, but that was of less concern than the line in which he said that 'the trouble with soccer's disciplinary system, is that those who sit in judgement, being officials of other clubs, might well have a vested interest'. As Clough was charged with bringing the game into disrepute, Longson was sure that Derby were, as he put it in his diaries, 'for the high jump'. Had Clough been found guilty, he could theoretically have been facing a three-year ban. As it was, Clough was cleared, but by then it was largely academic as he'd resigned several days earlier. 'The attack on Leeds was the last straw for me,' Longson wrote. 'I was sick and tired of the whole business. If Clough wanted to quit the game to give himself freedom to speak his mind on any subject under the sun, I told him I wouldn't stand in his way.'

The season had actually begun promisingly, on the pitch at least. A McGovern goal was enough to convert an excellent performance against Chelsea into a win, although the afternoon was marred by running battles on the pitch after the game, which carried on into the streets outside. Temporary fences were erected in time for the midweek match against Manchester City, in which a Hinton free-kick gave Derby another 1–0 win.

253

They nearly had another at Birmingham, where they absorbed pressure and should have had a penalty when Hector was tripped by Kenny Burns and had to settle for a 0–0. After the defensive laxity of the previous season, Clough seemed determined his side should have a solid base, which, as Mortimer observed, left him open to charges of hypocrisy. 'Brian Clough,' he wrote, 'the man who castigates [Ramsey] so thoroughly for negative tactics, seems to have crossed the floor of the house.'

A thirty-yarder from Phil Thompson and a Kevin Keegan penalty saw Derby suffer their first defeat of the season, 2–0 at Liverpool, and they then produced what Mortimer described as their worst performance under Clough in labouring to a 2–1 win against an Everton side reduced by injury to ten men for an hour. Never somebody to be misled by a result, Clough had the players in for a lengthy post-mortem on the Sunday. Reassured that the problems had been solved, he kept the same side for the visit of Liverpool and was rewarded with a 3–1 win. A draw at Burnley and a 1–0 defeat to a Coventry side who unsettled Derby with their pace, though, checked any sense of momentum. Clough sold Durban to Shrewsbury for £12,000 and, on 22 September, bought Henry Newton for £90,000 from Everton, five years after he'd first tried to sign him. That suggests that, at least then, things weren't too bad behind the scenes; no manager, surely, would spend so much money if he were planning to quit.

Hector hit a hat-trick in a 6–2 win over Southampton, taking him beyond Jack Parry's post-war scoring record, but Derby were inconsistent, poor on the road and prone to not taking advantage when they did control games. Longson, perhaps seeing a repeat of the previous season's frustrations and reasoning Clough was no guarantor of success, went on the attack. He told Clough that in future he would have to apply for permission before appearing on television and that all newspaper articles would have to be submitted to the board for approval before publication. That was part one of a two-pronged strategy: the other was to lock the drinks cabinet in Clough's office. Harry Storer had faced a similar sanction just before he was forced out as manager but, on this occasion, Webb insisted, the directors 'locked his cabinet because they were concerned about the amount of drink Brian and Peter were getting through. Brian was drinking heavily. His office doubled as the boardroom. There was a bar with a constant supply of bottles. He'd have a couple of Scotches first thing in the morning and entertain his friends until late in the night.'

Clough insisted in his autobiography that he had merely used the cabinet to entertain journalists, recalling how delighted Longson had been to be introduced to David Coleman, among others. 'Trouble was,' he added, 'nobody was that interested in what he had to say.'

Taylor, though, acknowledged there was a problem. 'We were both drinking to excess,' he said. 'It was a temptation because it was always available. Sometimes I'd take a bottle home. Having said that, Brian's drinking wasn't a problem to me. If I saw him overdoing it, I only had to say "You've had enough," and he'd stop. In any case, he could hold it well.'

Holding your booze well, though, tends to be a sign of practice and, according to Jimmy Gordon, Longson could not have devised a better way of needling Clough. 'Standing between Clough and the bottle was deadly,' he said. 'We knew there'd be hell to pay. The boss couldn't operate unless there was champagne around.'

The following day, Clough phoned Longson and – with what the chairman described as 'urgency' in his voice – asked him to go to the training ground to meet him. When Longson got to Matlock, Clough asked for permission to sack Webb for having locked the drinks cabinet. Longson told him the secretary had been acting on his instructions; at that, Clough must have known that either he or Longson would have to go. Their separation happened the following week.

On 10 October, Poland played the Netherlands in Amsterdam as a warm-up for their World Cup qualifier against England at Wembley. Clough was to be on the ITV panel for that qualifier and decided going to watch Poland in Amsterdam would be useful research. He asked Longson for permission to go to the game with Taylor. Longson agreed, so long as the time off was regarded as part of Clough's holiday and he paid for the trip himself. On 11 October, Longson reported to the board that Clough had nonetheless submitted a bill for the trip; Derby did not pay it.

More significantly, Longson put a motion before the board to have Clough sacked. He did not have sufficient backing from other directors, though, and Clough stayed on, feeling an acute sense of betrayal. 'Beware the "friendly grandfather",' he cautioned in his autobiography. 'Beware the ambitious chairman who will "give anything for success". Beware the knife behind the smile.'

On 13 October, Derby went to Old Trafford to face Manchester United. Hector scored early and although Brian Kidd and Tony Young both hit the bar, Derby held on for their first away win of the season. Despite the problems they'd had, that was good enough to leave Derby third, with ten points from seven games, Derby's best start to a First Division season under Clough and Taylor. They also had, Taylor estimated, around £250,000 in the bank.

It should have been a time of celebration and optimism, but it was their last game in charge of the club. Unusually, Barbara, whom Clough reckoned had only been to ten matches in the previous ten years, was there and, unwittingly, became a central player in one of the two incidents that precipitated the furore. Clough had been scathing of Busby and made little secret that he resented the way the former United manager had – as he saw it – used his reputation to secure the signing of Storey-Moore. The ill-feeling had been inflamed earlier that afternoon when it became apparent that United had not provided seats for the wives of the Derby players and managerial staff, although it remains unclear whether United were to blame and the problem was, anyway, soon resolved. Longson believed he had seen him direct a V-sign at Busby in the directors' box; Clough insisted he was merely waving to Barbara, although Wendy Dickinson, Taylor's daughter, wrote that Clough admitted to Taylor that he had made the gesture but that it was aimed at Longson. At this remove, there is no way to be sure one way or the other, but that a septuagenarian was fretting about whether a thirty-eight-year-old had flicked a V-sign at a sixty-four-year-old (or perhaps a seventy-one-year-old) suggests the depths of petti-ness to which the situation at Derby had sunk.

After the game, Taylor, pointing out that victories at Old Trafford didn't happen every season, suggested they should go up to the boardroom. Clough agreed – reluctantly, he claimed in his autobiography. Louis Edwards, the Manchester United chairman, opened a bottle of champagne and they stood around chatting awkwardly with a handful of directors. After a few minutes, an uncomfortable Taylor decided to leave, but as he looked around the room before going, he caught the eye of Jack Kirkland, who beckoned him over. Kirkland had been a critic of the board and had been invited to join largely because Longson believed it was better to have him on the inside, rather than casting stones from without. 'He stopped criticising the directors once he became one of them,' Clough noted. 'Then he turned his nasty attention to us.'

Kirkland, it is widely accepted, had an anti-Clough agenda. Wendy Dickinson cites what she terms an 'impeccable source' as saying he only returned to the board in order to 'get Clough'. Perhaps he was trying to avenge his brother, ousted when Clough had backed Longson's return as chairman, but as George Edwards said, 'What motivated him is hard to fathom because no normal person would want to be remembered for driving Derby County's most successful ever managerial team out of the club, but he tackled the job with relish.' Whether he influenced Longson against Clough, whether Longson used him to push the anti-Clough line in board meetings, or whether it was a combination of the two, Kirkland was at the centre of the rift between the board and the management, and it came to a head that day at Old Trafford.

Taylor went to speak to Kirkland and was, Clough noted, unusually quiet afterwards. Later, on the coach home, Taylor told Clough what had been said. Kirkland had asked him to see him on the Monday morning because he wanted to know exactly what his job at the club was supposed to be. If what Webb had said about Clough 'murdering' Taylor in board meetings was true, a share of the responsibility for the fracture was his.

As far as Taylor was concerned, that was it. He had been publicly belittled after a great result and he 'was adamant – he was off'. As Longson was writing his letter formalising the restrictions on Clough's media commitments, three other directors arrived at his house to tell him that Clough and Taylor could no longer work with him. Twice before Clough had ousted club chairmen, and he seems to have assumed he could do so again. Longson, though, responded by listing his grievances with Clough and Taylor.

That night, Clough and Longson had an angry telephone conversation. When, on the Sunday, Longson refused to lift the ban on media work, Clough resigned, on behalf of himself and Taylor, selling the story to the *Mail* for £1,500. He demanded an immediate emergency board meeting, but Longson refused to drive to the Baseball Ground from his home outside Derby. Instead, he said, he wanted their resignations in writing and called a board meeting for the following morning. 'Deep down,' Clough wrote in his autobiography, 'I thought our resignations would be rejected immediately, or that the board would have a rethink and eventually call us back.'

Clough sought to rally support. He turned first to Philip Whitehead, a friend and the local MP, who advised him not to resign unless he really meant it, because that was precisely what Longson wanted him to do. Clough then had Keeling, his closest ally on the board, arrange a meeting with the club president, Sir Robertson King, in a pub in Borrowash. He was, Clough said, 'a trustworthy man, one of the old school, one of the gentlemen of the game. Tweed suit, waistcoat, walking-stick . . .' He also warned against walking out, but resignation had become one of Clough's principal weapons. He asked King to take over as chairman, saying he would withdraw his resignation if Longson left the board. It was a solution Keeling favoured, but King was reluctant.

Clough began the morning of the board meeting by opening a shop a few miles out of town and then visiting some elderly patients in hospital. Gradually, news of his resignation spread, and the first protests began to be heard. Demonstrators began to gather outside the Baseball Ground and a group of night-shift workers from the Rolls-Royce factory telephoned to ask the board to do everything they could to find a solution.

The directors met to discuss their best course of action as Clough and Taylor waited in the lobby outside the boardroom. Eventually, they were called in, at which Clough accused Longson of being narrow-minded, saying he would withdraw the resignation only if the restrictions on his media commitments were thrown out and Longson left. He then outlined the progress Derby had made under him and Taylor. Longson, though, was sure he had the backing of the rest of the board, and told Clough that he'd had the club's lawyers go through his and Taylor's contracts. 'Don't even think of a settlement,' he said. 'You're getting nowt.' Eventually the resignations were put to a vote. King and Keeling voted against, but the rest of the board voted to accept them. 'Put your car keys on the table and leave,' Longson said to Clough and Taylor as the meeting wrapped up.

Rather than leaving, though, Clough and Taylor headed along to the executive lounge, where the television cameras were waiting. At one point he and Longson were both addressing the media at the same time from different ends of the room, a situation that played into Clough's hands, because he was so much more charismatic and so much more at ease in front of the cameras.

'You're going to be disappointed,' Longson said, adopting an uneasy, joking tone that was wholly inappropriate. 'My statements are going to be brief. I don't know why I'm smiling because this is a very sad time for me. I hope you don't portray me as a smiling, elated chairman. . . . It is not a fight between Brian and myself and Peter. It is a fight between right and wrong. Through his television appearances and writing, Brian has not done the image of Derby any good.'

Eventually, as Longson stuttered and hesitated in what Michael Carey in the *Guardian* described as a 'totally inadequate press conference', Kirkland dragged him away to spare him further humiliation. 'It surprises me a little,' Clough said, revelling in Longson's discomfort, 'that people who want to stop me putting two words together can't put them together themselves. There are a million reasons why I have resigned and you have just been talking to one of them because he slammed the telephone down on me twice last week. My feeling is now one of nausea. I feel embarrassed for the chairman and deeply ashamed for Derby County.

'I'll tell you why I'm going. My knees and elbows are sore from all the crawling that Peter and I have been forced to do these last three months. Only two things have kept us here for so long. First and foremost, the players; secondly, the supporters. They haven't always agreed with us, but they've always gone along with what we've tried to do. Before the Sunderland game last week, while we were talking to the chairman, other directors were going through our contracts. They were looking for ways in which they could find fault.'

It was a brilliant performance, made to look all the more so by Longson's hesitancy. Clough was a plotter and a manipulator, but he made it seem as though he were the victim, an innocent brought down by the machinations of grey men in the boardroom. By the time he finally decided to leave, the board had resumed discussions on what was to be done next. Clough, picking up a jug of water, made for the boardroom door, but Taylor restrained him before he could throw it over anyone and they left, as a final gesture of defiance, in a club Mercedes. Later that week, the club cancelled the insurance on the club cars and then, in a moment of staggering pettiness, informed the police the pair were driving without appropriate cover. A friendly policeman, fortunately, called Clough and Taylor to warn them.

Taylor was less comfortable in front of the cameras, but he had his say in the *Evening Telegraph*. 'It's the little things that rankle,' he said. 'You could say that they shouldn't, but when they come thick and fast it's very difficult to live with. Our home life is suffering. Why should our wives have to put up with that? We can't communicate with the board and the chairman puts the phone down on Brian. It's a ridiculous situation. Don't think it's easy for us to go. We have our homes here, our children are either working or being educated here. But we just can't put up with this any longer. We have to go like men, not wait until they've cut all the ground from under our feet. We think we're the best. We think, sooner or later, we'll outdo Revie because there are two of us.' It's surely indicative of how personal that rivalry had become that even in the moment of crisis, Taylor was fretting about whether or not he and Clough would be able to match Revie's achievements: it wasn't about putting right the wrong of Turin and winning the European Cup, or about regaining the Championship; it was about asserting themselves over Revie.

Roy McFarland was at the Hendon Hall hotel with the England squad preparing for a World Cup qualifier against Poland at Wembley when Clough resigned. He learned of his manager's departure when he walked into the television lounge and Alan Ball showed him the story on the back page of the *Evening Standard*. He sought out the three other Derby players in the squad – Kevin Hector, David Nish and Colin Todd – and after a series of phone-calls to players back in Derby, it was decided they should take no action until after the game. 'It came as a bitter blow to us, a massive blow to us, because we never saw anything untoward going on,' said Todd. 'If there was, he hid it very well.' At the training ground, Alan Hinton had paraded up and down with a tea urn on his head saying, 'This is the only bloody cup we'll win from now on.' As captain, McFarland spoke to the *Derby Evening Telegraph*. 'God knows what will happen without him,' he said. 'This might lead to terrible upheaval.'

Weirdly, when the England players walked out at Wembley the following evening, Clough was there to greet them in the centre-circle, shaking hands and preparing for his job as a pundit for ITV. His judgement, it's fair to say, wasn't at its best that night. He dismissed Poland's unorthodox goalkeeper Jan Tomaszewski as 'a clown', then watched him pull off a series of saves –

some brilliant, some lucky – as England, needing a win to qualify for the World Cup, could only draw 1–1. After the game, McFarland was so depressed he decided not to stay in the hotel with the rest of the squad but drove straight back to Derby.

Players and fans were horrified. 'The spirit we had after we had beaten Manchester United was as good as it has ever been and we have a lot to thank Brian and Peter for,' said Hinton. 'They brought me here when I was ready to pack up the game and they have given me the best six years of my life. They can knock you down and pick you up again to play at your best. That's a skill. I know Brian is difficult, but all good men are difficult. Wherever they go, players will want to follow them.'

As the players considered their options, the fans acted. On the day Clough went, a side column in the *Derby Evening Telegraph* reported that Don Shaw, 'the well-known local playwright', was looking to form an action group with the aim of having Clough reinstated. That evening, he was a guest on Radio Derby with three football writers debating the crisis; all four were pro-Clough, as was every call the studio took that evening. Shaw, a scriptwriter for a number of television series including *Z-Cars*, had been in Israel researching a film when the Yom Kippur War forced him home. With time on his hands, he threw himself into the protest.

The following day, Longson began to fight back, explaining just how serious Clough's battle with football's administrators had become. 'We will go into the Second Division with our heads held high,' he told the *Evening Telegraph*, 'rather than win Division One wondering if the club will be expelled from the Football League.'

In the same article, though, Bill Holmes, the manager of a brewery in Burton, warned fans just how serious losing Clough could be. 'This is a mortal blow for Derby County and a crime against football . . .' he said. 'As a manager and a man he is unique and if Derby hitches its wagon to his star he will make its name ring around the world. But if he and Peter Taylor are allowed to go, they will leave a vacuum which will never be filled and Derby football fans can prepare themselves now for a decline into mediocrity.'

That evening, the night of the England game, the protestors arranged to meet in the lounge bar of the Crest Hotel. So many turned up that the meeting had to be moved into the wedding reception room, but to Shaw's disappointment, Mike Keeling wasn't there. Perhaps there was nothing especially significant in that, but given he had become a Clough confidant, his non-appearance could be taken as the first indication of Clough's ambivalence towards what was christened that night as the 'Derby County Protest Movement'. Shaw was elected leader; Holmes was named as chief advisor on strategy; and John McGuinness, a local health-club owner, became the hands-on activist, somebody with time and contacts. It was decided that a further meeting should be held the following night at the Grand Theatre on Babington Lane.

A bucket passed round at that meeting raised £150.53 and a vote was taken to march and demonstrate, both inside and outside the ground, at Derby's match against Leicester that Saturday. Keeling was absent again, but a figure who arrived late and sat in the back row wearing a cap and a raincoat with the collar upraised drew suspicion. As McGuiness, a muscular Irishman with a withered leg, lurched towards him to determine whether he was a spy for the board, the figure scarpered. When Shaw returned home to Etwall, a village just outside Derby, though, the figure was sitting in a car waiting for him; it turned out to be Clough, who seems to have relished the cloak-and-dagger element to the whole affair. He and Shaw drove deeper into the countryside, Clough admitting he was disappointed Keeling had resigned, removing a key ally on the board. According to Shaw, Clough told him to target the director Sydney Bradley, saying, 'He's a little man with a little mind. Scare him and it might spread.'

The letters page of the *Evening Telegraph* was abuzz, with the vast majority of correspondents supportive of Clough, and even those who recognised his faults for the most part wrote begging the board to find a compromise that would allow Clough and Taylor to resume their positions. There were some dissenters, though. 'An Observer' was 'glad to see the back of Mr Clough': 'In many ways he has brought the club bad publicity with his outspoken attitude. He must be a very greedy man to wish to hold two posts and the end product must be for Derby County to suffer. The performance on the field has suffered in recent months and I am sure that a part-time manager must have an adverse affect on the team's performances.'

That Wednesday, Derby reserves played a Central League fixture at Nottingham Forest. The Derby board turned up en masse, something that was highly unusual for a second-team game. Each approached a member of the Forest board, Jack Kirkland going to Stuart Dryden. 'He warned me, "Don't ever have Brian Clough at your club – he'll ruin everything,"' Dryden told Tony Francis. 'It was an odd thing to say because I'd never met Kirkland or Clough, and Forest had never given any indication that they were considering such a move. When I spoke to the rest of our committee afterwards, each reported that he'd had a similar warning from a Derby director. That's how nervous they were of seeing him set up shop down the road.' Fourteen months later, their worst fears were realised.

Longson, meanwhile, continued his counter-attack through the press, with an astonishing statement in the *Evening Telegraph*. 'The time has now come,' he said, 'that the supporters of Derby County and in fact everyone concerned with football should hear my side. Just over two years ago, I was appointed chairman for the second time and I found that a new secretary had been appointed. On getting in touch with him I found that we had a secretary who was capable of carrying out the administration of the club. I therefore got the board to agree that he should be put in complete charge of the administration. Mr Clough did not take too kindly to this move and criticised it in many ways. His first reaction was since I did not agree that he should take his family on the pre-season tour, he declined to go himself and failed therefore to fulfil his managerial duties. This was a very difficult situation.'

That was the first time the truth of Clough's no-show on the tour to West Germany and the Netherlands had been revealed. Longson outlined the dispute over expenses for the trip to Amsterdam, and went on to explain that he had received a number of letters from the Football Association and the Football League that warned of the consequences if Clough persisted in his attacks on other managers, players and officials. 'I begged the manager to refrain before the club got into very serious trouble,' Longson said. 'He still persisted in this field and also ventured still further into television media. Events occurred that, to the board, got near to a breach of Football League regulations and in the interests of Derby County I felt that any infringement of the FA and League rules would not, this time, be settled by a fine, but could mean the club being expelled from the Football League and the directors severely censured.

'When he stated that he was thinking of taking the ATV post just vacated by Jimmy Hill, I publicly stated that he would have to make up his mind whether he was carrying on as manager of Derby County or taking this post. He stated later that he was not going to take the post, he was staying as manager of Derby County. It came to our notice that he had taken a post with ATV, called it a different name, "freelance commentator", and that he had taken a programme on a Saturday called *On the Ball*.

'This necessitated him travelling down to London for these recordings and he was absent from two board meetings because of these appointments. The board naturally was very concerned and asked him to give an account of these commitments and also reminded him of the clause in his contract which required him, amongst other things, to give his whole time and attention to the affairs of the club.

'I received a letter from the manager dated 24 September 1973, in which he stated that he had decided that to avoid any further confusion or misunderstanding regarding television, radio or newspaper work, he would not utter one single word to any of these media unless permission had first been obtained. Not for the first time by any means, he failed to keep his understanding. There followed letters, phone calls where he stated that both Peter Taylor and himself would go and not smear the board if we would agree to some form of compensation and also give them their club cars. He also stated that he would sell one of the first team pool of players to provide the money for the compensation. We, of course, did not agree to this action as a board.

'We, therefore, informed him that unless he gave us in writing the particulars we required, the board would take a very serious view of it. I say at this stage that we did not bar him from television, we merely asked that he must seek the board's permission before taking any work and that he must honour his contract.

'While the manager states that this has all blown up in the last few weeks, he is right in some respects that I would rather say it has been going on for two years and has come to a head in the last few weeks. Things have moved on rather quickly this last week or so, and he has embarked on a tyranny of abuse on myself and co-directors, but I am afraid that on receiving his letter of resignation we had no alternative but to accept. I have had in the past many letters of resignation from him and many threats of leaving. He has said many times that Derby is not big enough for him.

'In the case of Coventry City, I was blackmailed into giving the manager a £5,000-a-year rise and the assistant manager £3,000.

'The board and I have always met his demands and I myself very generously. The manager's and assistant manager's salary for last year came to over £40,000. This was without their television and press fees. He was allowed to carry on his activities from the club's offices, using all facilities, telephones, stationery and staff.

'At the present point of time he is already due to appear before an FA Disciplinary Commission on serious charges due to press attacks on the FA and, even as late as last Saturday, at Old Trafford, he is alleged to have made what is now called "the Harvey Smith gesture" to Mr Edwards, chairman of United, and to Sir Matt Busby, a director.

'The manager came up to the boardroom and denied having done this. An official of the Football League told me at Wembley last night that Sir Matt Busby was under no illusion as to what took place.

'Mr Clough has often insulted the supporters of Derby to the embarrassment of the board and has often stated that he owes no loyalty to Derby, which is too small for him.

'Nobody regrets the present situation more than I do. I brought him here, I have glorified [sic] in his success and I leave it with the supporters of Derby County to judge me and my board.

'Hysteria is prevalent at present with some supporters. This is a position that he has created. It has been reported to me that he is receiving a considerable sum of money from the *Daily Mail* for a series of articles. Whether this is true or not, I cannot say. All in all, I say enough is enough.'

The explanation stung Clough, who hit back. 'Expenses are submitted for approval. They are initialled and sanctioned or they are thrown in the bin,' he said. 'In six-and-a-half years I have only had one claim rejected. If I am guilty, why am I not in jail and why was I not sacked? If they [Longson's allegations] are true I would not be finished as a manager. I would be finished as a man – never able to set foot on a football ground again.'

He launched a libel action, which the board settled out of court for, Clough said, £17,500. Given his legal fees totalled between £12,500 and £15,000, any satisfaction he drew from the victory could only have come, not from financial gain, but from the embarrassment he caused Derby, for whom the total cost of the case, he estimated, came to £41,000. Longson, whose judgement by this stage seems to have been clouded by his desire for revenge on Clough, opposed the settlement, and laid a cheque for £20,000 before George Hardy, his successor as chairman, offering to pay all legal fees necessary to fight the action. Hardy, keen to move on and unwilling to expose any further the bitterness that had lain in the club's heart, threw it back.

That Saturday, about one thousand demonstrators gathered in Tenant Street off Derby Market Place and, headed by the Ilkeston Town brass band and a Womble keen to promote the new television programme, set off for the Baseball Ground, numbers swelling to three thousand by the time they got there. Inside the ground, Shaw waited for Clough to make an appearance. He had wanted him to parade around the pitch, but Clough, fearing he may be dragged away by stewards, decided simply to take a seat in the stands. 'We had built up a terrific rapport with the fans and I wanted to say cheerio to them,' Clough said. 'I suppose in the back of my mind there was a feeling that my appearance might spark enough of a reaction to bring about our eventual reinstatement.'

It became one of the iconic images of Clough's career, as he stood alongside the directors' box taking the applause of the crowd, but Shaw, at least initially, felt the move had backfired. At first, standing amid a mass of people, Clough couldn't be identified and the cheers for him were localised. Bradley then urged Longson to stand and take the applause, and by the time the cheering had spread, it seemed the ovation was for him (although surely he wasn't so deluded as to believe that was the case).

Jimmy Gordon had taken temporary charge of the team and urged them to win for Clough and Taylor. They emerged only four minutes before kick-off, registering their own protest by raising thoughts of a boycott, but played superbly and won 2–1. Clough left soon after kick-off, driving to London to be interviewed by Michael Parkinson.

He arrived slightly late following a puncture, but that didn't affect his performance. He was as teasing as ever, mocking directors as a breed, and vowing that Longson wouldn't drive him out of Derby. 'I'm not leaving the town,' he said. 'I would go back [to the club] under one condition – the people who run Derby would have to be replaced by people of integrity.'

There was, though, just a moment when the mask slipped, and a more vulnerable Clough was revealed beneath the belligerent public persona as Parkinson asked him about his parents. 'I was very close to me mam and dad,' he said. 'Very, very close. Me mam died nine to ten months ago, and this could have caused quite an upheaval with me, in actual fact, which I'm not aware of. I'm not quite sure if I've recovered from me mam dying.' That, surely, explains a lot, not just in terms of Clough's behaviour that year, but also in terms of his obsession with the European Cup, from which her death could not be separated.

A week after the resignations, Shaw attended a meeting of the players at the Kedlestone Hotel at which they decided not to strike. Instead, a delegation of players went to the ground to deliver a letter to the directors explaining their feelings. 'During the events of the last week,' it read, 'we the undersigned players have kept our feelings within the dressing-room. However, at this time, we are unanimous in our support and respect for Mr Clough and Mr Taylor and ask that they are reinstated as manager and assistant manager of this club. Nobody can say we have acted on the spur of the moment or are just being emotional.' It was signed by every member of the squad apart from Henry Newton, who'd been away in Liverpool on business.

Clough said he was 'staggered' by their response and thanked the players for 'restoring my faith in human nature', and the players resolved to present their case to the board personally. The board, though, had already appointed a successor, but had promised not to reveal his identity until the following morning, and so refused to meet the players. That enraged them even further and, seeing the lights on in the boardroom at the Baseball Ground, the players came to the conclusion that a board-meeting was in progress. Demanding to speak to the directors, they staged a sit-in.

In fact, only Jack Kirkland and Stuart Webb were at the stadium and, alarmed by the prospect of confrontation, they locked themselves in the boardroom. Kirkland ended up urinating in a champagne bucket rather than risking a dash to the toilet. Eventually, as afternoon stretched into evening, they made a break for it, but ran into Colin Boulton and Ronnie Webster, who had been posted by their cars. As the players hammered on the car roofs, Kirkland and Webb sped off, Kirkland shouting out of the window that they'd have a new manager in the morning.

Longson had initially approached Bobby Robson as a potential successor to Clough, but he preferred to stay at Ipswich. His next target was Dave Mackay, who by then had left Swindon to replace Matt Gillies at Nottingham Forest. Longson, Bradley, Kirkland and Webb drew up a four-year contract and phoned the other two directors, Bill Rudd and Bob Innes, for their approval. Rudd offered the first sign that the board wasn't entirely united behind Longson. 'Bill Rudd was now saying he would consider taking Brian and Peter back if Brian was prepared to give an undertaking to toe the line,' Longson wrote. 'To say I was shattered is an understatement.'

Keeling, meanwhile, was trying to muster support to have Clough and Taylor reinstated, something that would surely have been easier had he not resigned his position on the board. Clough, in an admission that his bluff had failed, even offered to stop his columns and his television work if he could come back, but Longson was not for turning.

Mackay was watching Forest reserves at the City Ground when Longson approached him. 'He said I was the only man in the country who could replace Brian Clough at Derby County Football Club and he was right,' Mackay said. 'I was under no illusions. I knew I was only being offered the post because there was no other person who might be able to unite the fans, players and board behind the club in the midst of this mass revolt.' Mackay, though, insisted on taking charge of Forest's home game against Hull before making the move.

Hearing an appointment was imminent, McFarland realised that Mackay was the only realistic candidate and so called him at the City Ground half an hour before kick-off. He warned him about the rebellious mood of the players, at which Mackay swore at him and asked why he should turn down the best job in England just because the players were unhappy. Henry Newton then made a similar call and received a similar response.

After Mackay had been appointed, the players met at the Newton Park Hotel near Repton. That was probably the high point of the protest. With wives and children also there and a great spirit of bonhomie prevailing, helped no doubt by the alcohol Clough provided, it was suggested that everybody should decamp to Spain, and that the players should train in a local park, effectively boycotting the club. In the cold light of sobriety, though, both ideas were rejected, much to the relief of Terry Hennessey, Derby's PFA representative, who warned that any such action could place the players in breach of contract. He remained a conciliatory presence throughout the conflict, as did Jimmy Gordon, who openly backed Mackay, and asked the players to consider the impact of strikes and the possibility of subsequent suspension for young players like Powell.

Shaw and McGuinness met Bradley and Keeling, who had unsuccessfully tried to persuade Jack Kirkland to stimulate a boardroom plot against Longson. The Protest Movement instituted a wave of letters and phone calls to directors. Longson alleged the calls contained threats to expose financial misdemeanours and accused the Protest Movement of having tried to convince players to throw games.

After the PFA had effectively warned the players against striking, Clough asked Shaw to tell the players he would call off the protest if they asked him to. That offer was reported in the newspapers on the morning of 1 November. Clough, by then, was moving on, albeit in a hesitant, unconvincing way. The first club to approach Clough, oddly, was Forest, seeking a replacement for Mackay, although their interest was never official. Dryden, then only a committee member, met Clough and Taylor at a friend's office in Nottingham, explaining that they were looking to re-energise the club. Clough was reluctant to act without a firm offer, so Dryden suggested he should call the club at 11am the following day to ask about the vacancy. The thought of not having to leave his house in Derby appealed to Clough, but he never made the call.

At half-time during Brighton's defeat to Hereford United on 27 October, their chairman, Mike Bamber, received a call from Keeling, telling him to drive back through London and to meet Clough at the Waldorf Hotel, where Clough was staying while doing some work for LWT. With the Brighton players sat outside on the bus, Bamber met Clough, who then arranged a further meeting at the Midland Hotel in Derby.

He and Harry Bloom travelled north and were kept waiting for two hours by Clough who turned up wearing what Bamber described as 'a scruffy old tracksuit'. Brighton offered more than Clough had been on at Derby and when Bamber and Bloom left, the deal seemed all but done. Taylor was keen to get going again, but Clough got cold feet and rang Taylor in the early hours to tell him he didn't think he could go through with the move. Taylor was furious and ended up slamming the phone down. 'He'd backed out for the same reasons he always backed out,' he said. 'He wanted all the fuss and publicity and people chasing after him but, it didn't matter which club it was, he never wanted to go anywhere.' Clough changed his mind again, and went to see Bamber to finalise details; this time, Taylor refused to go with him. Whatever else Clough was thinking, he was aware of the precariousness of his position. With an FA disrepute charge still hanging over him for his *Sunday Express* column condemning the punishments handed out to Leeds, there was a real possibility of a lengthy ban; Clough needed a job before the hearing to guarantee an income in the event of a suspension.

They met again on 1 November and, that lunchtime, Clough called Shaw and asked him whether he should take the job. Shaw at first couldn't believe he would even consider the Third Division – and Brighton were impoverished even by Third Division standards, not having a training ground but practising in a park in Hove – and assumed the call must be a prank, but then Taylor came on the line. In *Clough's War*, Shaw describes how at a loss he felt, how he wanted time to think it over; Clough gave him none. 'I can't tell you what to do,' Shaw said eventually. 'It's your career. You have to do what you think is right.'

Clough took the job, but later told Shaw – how truthfully it is impossible to say – that he'd wished he'd said no and given him an excuse not to take it. In his autobiography, though, Clough suggested he had recognised it was time to move on. 'The fires were still burning in Derby,' he wrote, 'the protests surrounding our resignations raged on, but the flames were beginning to die down a little and it was obvious to anyone but a complete idiot that there was no immediate way back for us.' That seems to hint at a degree of contempt for the Protest Movement, a sense that they were fantasists whose enthusiasm Clough felt unable to betray. Perhaps that is to over-read an offhand comment in a book that, for all its moments of genuine poignancy and insight, is also peppered with scattergun opinions, but there was certainly an ambivalence in Clough's attitude to the Movement.

Having spoken to Clough, Shaw rang George Edwards and that night the story of Clough's move to Brighton appeared on the back of the *Evening Telegraph*. A few minutes later, McFarland called Shaw and asked him to end the protest. Shaw wondered whether 'his taut tone and his formality' was an indication he was being pressured into the decision, but McFarland was adamant. Shaw asked him and the players to attend one final meeting at the King's Hall the following evening. McFarland conferred with some-body – Shaw believes Mackay – then agreed.

'It looked like peace at last,' Longson wrote in his diaries, 'but the tinder-dry atmosphere needed only the faintest spark to blow the whole thing up again. It got more than that. It got a flash of lightning in the form of Brian.' Specifically, in his performance at the King's Hall. The meeting was packed. Shaw spoke first and explained that he didn't speak for the Movement as a whole and apologised for having made the offer – on Clough's instruction – to stop the protest. Then, impersonating Clough's accent, he joked he'd only agreed to take over Brighton because of the direct railway line to Derby. At that, Barbara Clough led in the players' wives. They didn't stay long, but it was enough to express their support for the protest.

Clough himself arrived ten minutes later. His eyes, Shaw said, 'had a faraway look' and he for once seems to have struggled for articulacy. 'If you watch football for another forty years I don't think you will ever see more character, more intelligence and more talent on one field,' Clough said, before stressing that, even though he had accepted the Brighton job he wasn't moving from Derby. As the audience began chanting, 'Board Out!', though, apparently responding to a cautionary word from Taylor, he urged the Protest Movement to accede to McFarland's wishes. Taylor then led a tearful Clough away, urging everybody to 'calm down a bit'. As they went the crowd sang Clough's name. 'They thought Clough was as good as back,' Shaw wrote. 'But I couldn't shake the look on Taylor's face from my mind.'

Clough's future was even less clear than it had been before. He seemed both unable to sever his ties with Derby and yet unwilling to take decisive action that might win him his job back. Shaw admits he felt like a pawn in a game he didn't understand and became resentful towards Clough; the most sympathetic reason he could find for Clough's hesitation was a fear that if he did call the strike one or more players would disobey him, and the image of his authority would be shattered. Clough then called with his own semi-explanation, saying that he'd only taken the Brighton job so he wouldn't be tempted by a bigger offer; Mike Bamber, he insisted, knew the situation and would release him should the Derby job become available again. 'He was thought to be honest to the point of hurting people with his blunt and uncompromising plain-speaking,' Shaw said. 'He was never considered devious. But his manipulation of Longson and directors from other clubs and countries presented another picture.' Perhaps there was something more Machiavellian about Clough than is often accepted, but it may equally have been that Clough didn't know what he wanted; Steve Hodge recalled that one of Clough's favourite phrases was 'if you're not sure what to do, do nowt, sleep on it'; there were times when he seemed petrified by indecision. He had, for instance, been stricken by doubt before leaving Hartlepools. Then, it had been Taylor who had convinced him to leave; this time Taylor seems to have been far more willing than Clough to accept that their time at Derby was over.

Clough's own explanation for not calling the strike, given in his first autobiography, was rather simpler. 'I didn't want to be part of anything that would embarrass [the players] or in any way jeopardise their careers,' he wrote.

After the phone call, Shaw arranged that they should meet with Keeling and McGuinness at McGuinness's house in Twyford. As they toured his gym, Clough abruptly challenged McGuinness and asked if he were going into business with Webb. McGuinness denied that he was, to which Clough replied by asking if a quid pro quo could be arranged; if Webb could be persuaded to support Clough's return. Shaw was bewildered, and Clough later admitted that he'd made up the accusation, reasoning that if McGuinness had been in league with the board, he would have waited a couple of days and then returned to say that Webb had agreed to a deal, thus shutting down the Protest Movement and causing them to lose momentum. The level of paranoia that suggests is bizarrely disproportionate; this, after all, was a provincial football club they were squabbling over, not control of a government or a vast multi-national corporation. If Shaw is to be believed, Clough at the time saw demons at every turn, and spoke of how he liked 'to go home at night and lock the door'.

'He was impetuous,' Shaw wrote, 'but he was also a planner and a plotter, manipulative as well as scheming.' Suspecting Clough himself may be undermining the Protest Movement and so keeping him out of the loop, Shaw arranged a meeting with McGuinness and the players for Sunday, 4 November to discuss strike action. That Saturday, though, McFarland told them that two players weren't prepared to strike, and admitted that he felt 'fed up' with the way the issue was dragging on. The same day, Shaw called Clough, ostensibly to let him know that Bill Holmes, one of the three leaders of the Protest Movement, would be interviewed on Anglia Television the following day.

A little later, Clough rang back and told Shaw to expect a surprise. After about half an hour, Keeling and Clough arrived at Shaw's house in Keeling's Mercedes and drove him to a hotel in Newton Solney. It was raining heavily, but as Clough led them into the bar, Shaw realised he wasn't wearing any shoes. When he pointed that out, Clough took off his wet socks and dried them by the fire. Clough then revealed that Holmes was a Forest fan and that ATV planned to spring that on him during the interview. From his speech – not to mention his lack of footwear – Shaw was sure Clough had been drinking. That said, it seems Clough had a habit of taking off his shoes (or not putting his shoes on) in the rain; Stuart Dryden also told of an occasion when Clough turned up at a country pub on a wet day in his stocking feet.

Shaw rang Holmes repeatedly to warn him, but that night he couldn't get through. The following morning, he waited till 10am to call him, but by then Holmes had already left home. The interview was a disaster, not just because Holmes's Forest leanings were exposed, but because Gary Newbon, who was conducting the interview, had been briefed – presumably by Longson – on the breakdown of relations within the club. Presented with the detail of numerous internal controversies, Holmes was left floundering. Later that afternoon, Clough and Keeling met Shaw at the Kedleston Hotel, and told him that Longson had hired a private investigator to dig up whatever he could on the leaders of the Protest Movement. Again, the response seems weirdly disproportionate.

Realising the momentum was turning against them, the Protest Movement opted for decisive action. All twelve members of the committee wrote to journalists and sought television and radio interviews to try to mitigate the damage done by Holmes's appearance on ATV, plans were drawn up for another march to the ground, and Operation Snowball was launched, by which the players would be called with the message 'Snowball' to tell them the strike was underway. Again, the use of a code name seems to hint at a love of intrigue for intrigue's sake. That said, this was a time when the Heath government was asking the security services to bug union meetings – they refused – while the Watergate scandal was less than a year away; conspiracy and paranoia were very much in vogue.

273

The End of the Pier

With hindsight, Clough's spell at Brighton looks an aberration, a strange exile akin to the time Napoleon spent on Elba, regrouping, recharging and plotting before the next real challenge came along. Bamber said Clough 'had his heart in it for a while' and Clough insisted 'I was sincere', but he never really seemed committed to his new club, as he continued to live in Derby and became increasingly involved with political campaigning for Phillip Whitehead, the local Labour MP. Even Clough later admitted he should have moved south. 'I was manager of Brighton for about nine months,' he said, 'and I'm convinced eight of them were spent on the M1. I was attempting to live in Derby and work on the South Coast. And that's about as daft as trying to mine coal without going down the pit shaft.' Perhaps the surest sign of his lack of commitment for Brighton was that he never fell out with Bamber; he never cared enough to get into a scrap.

That said, there were moments of friction. Bamber arranged to meet Clough in his office after his first day of training. Clough arrived in his tracksuit and boots and sat down claiming to be exhausted after his first physical exercise in three weeks. Clough was dry, though, and outside it was raining. When Bamber pointed out the discrepancy Clough took out his fury on an eighteen-year-old winger called Tony Towner who had the misfortune to be leaning against a wall as Clough left Bamber's office, telling him that in future he expected him to stand up straight when he walked past.

Clough arrived with typical swagger. 'It's tougher here than at Hartlepools where they didn't expect anything,' he said. 'Now we have a reputation, but there are no fairies at the bottom of Brighton pier. There are only sixteen professionals here. Only one goalkeeper, one trainer, one secretary, one groundsman; in fact one of everything. That puts Peter and me in the majority, for they have two managers.'

Brian Powney, Brighton's goalkeeper, had some forewarning of what to expect, having met McGovern on holiday in Mallorca a year earlier. 'I asked him what Cloughie was like, not ever dreaming he would come to Brighton,' he remembered. 'He said that he was hard, but fair, that he was an arrogant and self-opinionated man, but he gave me the impression that if Clough had asked him, he'd have jumped over Beachy Head for him. All the players at Brighton at the time were sad to see Pat [Saward, Clough's predecessor] go. He'd done well and most of us thought he was a good manager, but when we heard Clough and Taylor were coming, we were very excited."

When Clough and Taylor first met the players, they were appalled by their casual attitude, the way they joked about the club's plight. Clough thrust out his chin, encouraging them to punch it to prove that they were 'capable of positive action'. 'I think people were nervous, probably in awe of the man, I don't think *they* saw it as short term,' remembered the forward Ken Beamish. 'On the first night we met him, at a hotel in Lewes, you could sense that some of the lads were nervous. We were all supposed to meet up for dinner, but Brian turned up after the players had eaten. He welcomed himself to the club and then asked everybody if they'd have a drink with him. He went round the table and ordered drinks for everybody.'

Essentially, as Bamber admitted, Clough's spell as manager became an extended publicity stunt for the club: the crowd for his first game, a goalless draw against York, was 16,500, around three times Brighton's average that season. The club took gate receipts of £6,500 for that game; up from an average of £2,700. Clough didn't know the names of the players, but seemed generally encouraged. 'They played well enough to have won,' he said. 'I would have liked to see them win, but York aren't exactly the worst side in the Third Division, though I've not seen much of it. The No 10 for us [Lammie Robertson] got in good positions. There was a lot of effort on goal, but I would rather have been the away side. York were lifted by coming here: the crowd and everything. Our lads were very nervous to begin with. They left some of their strength in the dressing-room. I thought our No 5 [Norman Gall] was superb, especially in the first half. His heading was as good as I've seen. He headed the ball remarkably well by Third Division standards.'

Yet even in that game, one of the main problems of Clough's time at Brighton began to emerge. The forward Barry Bridges had said before kick-off that 'the lads are playing for their jobs, let's be clear about that. Every mistake and they'll be sneaking a look up at the stands.' That sense of unease was pervasive. 'The man who made the first error, [George] Ley, belting the ball into touch from the kick-off,' Brian James noted in the *Sunday Times*, 'seemed to shrink visibly.'

Clough and Barbara looked at a number of houses, and eventually settled on one that was still under construction in Hove. While it was being built, Clough stayed at the Courtlands Hotel, travelling back to Derby on a Saturday after games, and taking an early train back to Brighton on a Monday morning. Given his devotion to his family, the 'feeling of isolation', as he described it, didn't suit Clough. 'It didn't matter how much I was cosseted,' he said. 'Somehow, even the best doesn't taste as good as it should when you're eating alone.'

In their managerial life, he had rarely socialised with Taylor, but the fact that they seem not to have spent much time together even in the relatively alien surroundings of Brighton perhaps indicates the cooling of their relationship.

Clough spent his spare time listlessly visiting the cinema, where the manager insisted he shouldn't pay, while Bamber would try to entertain him by taking him to the shows he was putting on. On one occasion, he was invited by Bamber to go and see Les Dawson in his dressing-room. Wandering along a corridor back-stage, Clough saw him sitting by a low table nursing a half. He introduced himself, at which Dawson snapped, 'I'm bloody working.' Far from being offended, Clough understood, and insisted he felt the same when directors came to visit him or the team in the dressing-room before games. He even refused to allow Neil Kinnock into the dressing-room at Anfield on the anniversary of Hillsborough.

Brighton came from 2–0 down to draw at Huddersfield and then, with Pat Hilton heading the only goal with twelve minutes remaining, won their first game under Clough at Walsall. John Vinicombe of the *Evening Argus* walked into the dressing-room after the game and found Clough on his knees on the floor, unfastening a player's boot-laces. 'They put on a shirt,' Clough said, 'and they look at you to make sure they're doing it right.'

Certain players were unimpressed. 'I came off, got to the dressing-room and sat down with my cup of tea,' Powney recalled. 'Next thing I know, Brian Clough is on his hands and knees undoing my boots. That was him, it was always over the top in demonstrations. He was undoing the laces of my boots for me.' Given Clough relegated Powney to second choice as soon as he could, perhaps there is a little bitterness in his retelling of what happened at Brighton, but he certainly wasn't the only player who felt the same way.

Don Shaw, Mike Keeling, Roger Davies and Colin Boulton went from

Derby to watch that game at Huddersfield. The four ate with Clough and the players at the team hotel and, in *Clough's War*, Shaw observed that, for once, Clough didn't have a drink in front of him. John Sheridan, the assistant coach, came over with a request from the players that they be allowed alcohol. Clough refused. Shaw realised that nobody at the table was drinking and wondered whether Clough were trying to kick the booze and couldn't bear to see anybody else with alcohol.

The Protest Movement began to be taken more seriously after a piece in the *Sunday Times* at the beginning of November that suggested that Clough was poised to return to Derby – a little over a week after taking the Brighton job. Clough angrily denied the reports when pressed on them by the *Brighton Evening Argus's* football reporter, John Vinicombe. 'I have met this man Shaw on two occasions,' he said. 'There are so many hangers-on that it is difficult to know who is who ... they are all over the place. But I am Brighton's manager and I just want to get on with the job.' Was he lying to sound more committed? Or was he really so dismissive of Shaw's efforts? By Shaw's account, they had met on at least six occasions and had spoken frequently, most notably when Clough telephoned him to ask if he should take the Brighton job in the first place. Perhaps the contempt Clough's words suggest was genuine and he really did resent the interference of an outsider; after all, if he'd wanted to call a strike, he could have done so quite easily, without any need to mobilise the fans. Whether Shaw was aware of that interview or not, it was hardly surprising that he came to distrust Clough, leading to the farcical situation of him trying to secure the reinstatement of a man who seemed at best ambivalent about being reappointed.

Shaw, still trying to keep his activity secret from Clough, visited Todd and Gemmill at home to explain what Operation Snowball entailed. Both were concerned that the players weren't unanimously behind the strike, but both agreed that the issue should be put to a vote and agreed to abide by a majority decision. While he was speaking to Gemmill, Clough arrived, and rebuked Shaw for speaking to the players without his consent. As Shaw tells it in *Clough's War*, there was an element of farce about that period, with Clough repeatedly popping up unexpectedly, foreshadowing the quasi-omniscience he would later demonstrate at Forest. Clough repeatedly asked Gemmill if he would strike to have him reinstated; Gemmill repeatedly replied that he would if Clough asked him to. With Clough unwilling to issue a direct order, they reached an impasse and Clough left telling Shaw to carry on with the protest, but not to involve the players; a fudge that kept Clough's name centre-stage but that was never likely to bring enough pressure to bear to see him reappointed, which – bearing in mind Taylor's comments about his vacillation before taking the Brighton job – was perhaps just what he wanted.

A meeting of the squad was called for the following night at the health club owned by Shaw's co-conspirator McGuinness, but again Clough somehow found out about it and the meeting was cancelled. Clough's attitude to the protest may have seemed equivocal, but Barbara called the players' wives and had them bring their husbands to yet another meeting.

Brighton had gone a fourth game unbeaten under Clough, drawing 0–0 with Chesterfield. Clough's behaviour, though, was becoming increasingly erratic and the physio Bert Parker was banned from attending matches after protesting when Ken Beamish was forced back onto the field despite having damaged an ankle. 'I had an ankle injury all week and pre-match I had an injection, what I assumed to be a painkiller,' Beamish remembered. 'I went down to play the game from the start and I lasted ten minutes. I couldn't run. The injection didn't work. I played on, I played about fifteen–twenty minutes maybe, but I just couldn't run. It was too painful. I signalled to the bench that I was struggling, but I was made to carry on. It didn't anger me, I just thought it was strange, but there were lots of little things that we found strange, things we hadn't experienced before.

'Stevie Piper had a similar problem. He got an injury in the first half of a game. We saw him at half-time and there a huge lump on his hip. For all the world, it looked like a tennis ball. He'd come off, but was put back on and he was still there at full-time. Afterwards, he wasn't allowed to leave the ground on crutches, and the lad was in a lot of pain. You never argued with the gentleman though, you never took him to task about things. You would be admonished in no uncertain terms if you did. No one even tried, we just took him for what he was and went down the route of just getting on with it. There were problems with the medical staff and all sorts.'

It wasn't just those carrying injuries who were affected. 'I think he hated physiotherapists,' said Powney. 'We at the time had a very good physiotherapist, he was a private guy, but he used to do our physio because,

Hartlepools: Clough cycles to the Victoria Ground … and raises awareness at a local school (*Northern Echo*).

Early days at Derby – the green jumper is still a long way away (PA).

The days of plenty: Dave Mackay lifts the 1970 Watney's Cup, Clough's first trophy as a manager … and John McGovern (out of shot) beats Liverpool's Ray Clemence to score the goal that wins the league title in 1972 (both PA).

The dream turns sour: Derby's directors became concerned by Clough's extra-curricular activities – here he's seen in a Staffordshire nightclub, and Alan Hinton misses a penalty against Juventus in the 1972–73 European Cup semi-final (both PA).

The day of the resignations: Clough seems very relaxed after he and Taylor face the media outside the Baseball Ground (both PA).

Clough sneaks in to the Baseball Ground for the game against Leicester and takes the acclaim of the crowd, while Sam Longson tries to pretend the applause is for him (both PA).

Glum times at Brighton.
Between Clough and
Taylor is the chairman,
Mike Bamber (PA).

Clough at Heathrow, having broken a
holiday in Mallorca to negotiate with
Leeds (PA).

The damp first day at Elland Road. Clough pushes through the media scrum and then, with his two sons standing beside him, shakes hands with Manny Cussins (both PA).

Despite the rumours of dressing-room unrest, Clough looks happy enough taking training at Leeds, but he was never comfortable in the Elland Road dug-out (both PA).

let's face it, trainers in those days were sponge-men. That's all they knew. Bert Parker was a qualified physiotherapist with a good business in Hove and he would be at our ground on match days. He knew his job backwards, he was a great physio. When Clough arrived, Bert Parker tried to introduce himself and he literally told Parker that he didn't want to know him, didn't want to see him again and to get out of the ground. And that broke Parker's heart. He was a very loyal club man and he was such a gentleman. It really upset him and it upset the players because after that we didn't have a good physio.'

That draw seems to have persuaded Clough just how radically his squad needed restructuring, and on the day of the aborted Protest Movement meeting at the health club he returned to Derby to ask Mackay if there were any Reserve or A-team players he could sign for Brighton. Even for Clough, this was an act of outrageous chutzpah, but Mackay responded calmly, asking Clough to get on with his job at Brighton and leave him to get on with managing Derby. He told Clough that, given he could have the Protest Movement disbanded with a word, what he was doing was unfair. Clough, apparently, replied that he was out to get Longson and Webb; he seems to have regarded Mackay as unfortunate collateral damage in his attempt to embarrass the club.

Mackay told the squad that anyone who wanted to could leave. Although numerous players were clearly unhappy at Clough's departure, none was prepared to take that step, particularly when it still seemed possible that Clough could return. Mackay, anyway, was keen to keep the team together and didn't waver even when the QPR manager Gordon Jago offered £250,000 for any three of Todd, McFarland, Nish and Gemmill.

At Barbara's meeting, she asked the wives to offer support when the Movement gathered the following Saturday at the Pennine Hotel. After weeks of talking without much progress, that rallying cry at least provoked a reaction, with John O'Hare adamant he didn't want his wife to be 'used' in that way. He then said that the players would already have gone on strike had Clough not wrong-footed them by taking the Brighton job. O'Hare and his wife left, at which Clough – at last – explained his logic to the players. 'It makes no difference to my commitment to you,' he said. 'There's most of you want to go on strike. There's some who are worried about it. But I can't be seen to lead it. It's up to you. If you want me back it's up to you.'

Had a vote been taken then, Shaw insisted, it would have been in favour of a strike, but it wasn't. Instead Barbara typed up a letter to Mackay, which every player still there signed. 'We the undersigned players,' it read, 'refuse to report to Derby County Football Club until 1pm on Saturday, 24 November for the following reasons – (a) dissatisfaction with the present management and (b) the refusal to reinstate Brian Clough and Peter Taylor.' Francis wrote that the letter was never sent because the contents had been leaked; Shaw believed it was sent and that Mackay read it, then threw it straight in the bin, not even bothering to show it to Longson or Webb. In the end it hardly mattered, for the contents were known and Mackay told the players that if any arrived as late as 1pm he'd play the reserves in that afternoon's game against Leeds.

Finally, McGuinness called Shaw and told him he was about to launch Snowball. Shaw went to the health club – giving a password to gain access through the back door – and slowly the players joined them. Just as the meeting had begun, though, Clough burst in, using the front door, which McGuinness had insisted was locked. Clough sent the players home, took out three bottles of Marston's Brown Ale, handed two to McGuinness and Shaw and told them to go to Tommy Mason, a reserve, and get him to take the reserves out on strike; the first team, Clough reasoned, would surely follow.

Shaw remained bemused and in *Clough's War*, written thirty-six years after the event, he was still unable to provide a satisfactory explanation either for how Clough knew about the meeting, or how he had managed to pass through a locked door. He briefly suspected McGuinness of having kept Clough informed, but reasoned that Peter Taylor, who was in regular contact with the players and so knew of their movements, was a more likely saboteur, sick of Derby – and perhaps also of Clough's politicking – and happy with his new life on the south coast.

Whether Taylor was deliberately undermining Shaw and McGuinness is unclear, but speaking to Tony Francis he expressed clear reservations about the protest. 'The players were thunderstruck, but they got carried away with the media and the public,' he said. 'They were loyal to us, but I wasn't sure how much I wanted their loyalty in a situation like that. I told Brian we weren't ever going back so we should stop misleading people. He knew it was a loser from the start. All sorts of businessmen were jumping on the bandwagon, trying to promote themselves.'

Suspicious of everybody, and Clough in particular, Shaw nonetheless delivered the message to Tommy Mason, but too late. By the time Mason tried to mobilise the reserves, Mackay had taken decisive action. He called the players into his office one by one, explained that Clough wasn't coming back, that the protest was undermining the club and that they were losing win-bonuses as a result. McFarland symbolically shook Mackay's hand in the dressing-room and the protest was over. Derby drew 0–0 against Leeds that afternoon and rallied to finish third that season – although they had slipped to as low as fifteenth at one point – and the year after they went on to win the title.

That same afternoon, Brighton faced Walton & Hersham in the FA Cup. The non-leaguers kicked off, knocking the ball to Dave Bassett, the future Wimbledon and Sheffield United manager. He whacked a long ball forward and, with the goalkeeper Brian Powney distracted by Russell Perkins, the ball bounced in. The goal was mysteriously disallowed, and Brighton survived for a replay. It might have been better if they hadn't.

'We could have got stuffed there,' said Powney. 'But we didn't see Cloughie from after that game on the Saturday until the replay on the Wednesday. He turned up about an hour before kick-off, ranted and raved, called most of us crap because we didn't win up there. There was no constructive tactics discussed, no confidence building, none of this. Just get out there and do the business. But the fact was, everybody, including myself, was suffering from lack of confidence, lack of self-esteem and, to a certain extent, fear. Whatever you did for the guy, it wasn't going to be good enough. You didn't know what you had to do. When a new manager comes in you expect him to change things, to build things, but basically he wasn't interested in being constructive, he wanted to demolish things. He wanted to destroy people, to destroy players.'

As Gall was deceived by a flick-on from a twentieth-minute corner, Perkins, a schoolmaster, 'got down like an old man with lumbago to head the simplest of goals,' as Vinicombe put it. Clive Foskett, a joiner who worked for the Natural History Museum, then hit a hat-trick in the last eight minutes as Walton & Hersham won 4–0. 'Yesterday's display was too bad to be true,' wrote Vinicombe. 'Some players gave everything; others did not. . . . Until Clough and assistant Peter Taylor move permanently to Brighton, the full impact of their presence will not be felt by the players. The side have yet to score at home under Clough. When Albion were without a manager for a short time, they hammered Southport 4–0. That was just over a month ago . . . Has the arrival of a man so steeped in success and possessing such a reputation, suddenly caused the players to seize up? A goal blight of 270 minutes at the Goldstone is a curious state of affairs and in the context of this debacle pinpoints the structural weakness of the side. Albion lost to Walton primarily because the midfield was found wanting.'

Clough was scathing of his side. 'When I came here I knew virtually nothing about the Third Division,' he said. 'I assumed the club must have some good players having only recently been in the Second. But when I had a chance of really assessing what we had, I was shocked. I was shocked not only at the standard here, but at what appears to be the norm in the Third Division. So far I cannot say I have seen many players who can play.'

'It was the start of what was setting in to Brighton at the time,' said Powney. 'Cloughie used to manage by fear. He wanted to manage Brighton by fear. What he did at Derby or Forest, I don't know, I wasn't there, but when he came to Brighton, he'd had a bluff double-bluffed at Derby. He didn't want to leave Derby. He loved Derby, loved the players. When he came to Brighton, we weren't Derby players, we weren't his players, we were somebody else's players. He resented it, he'd lost his bluff game at Derby, he was visibly depressed. I know he was drinking. I used to smell it on him. You'd have to get close to notice it, but whenever I went into his office, which wasn't often – maybe two or three times in his stay – there was always a bottle on the go. Scotch or brandy. I got the feeling he was very much a brandy man.

'He didn't want to be in the Third Division, he didn't want to be with a struggling side, a side with no confidence. Instead of building confidence and self-esteem, he destroyed it. He would lash out in bad temper – sometimes it could have been alcohol-fuelled, I don't know – sometimes he would just rant and rant and rant, but there was never any real constructive confidence-building or esteem-building exercise with the club. They

[Clough and Taylor] were both pretty much the same. They'd just rant. They must have had something, they did it at Forest, they did it at Derby, but they didn't do it at Brighton because they just didn't want to be there.'

It got worse. The following Saturday, Brighton lost 8–2 at home to a Bristol Rovers side forced to wear Brighton's new away kit because ITV felt their usual red-and-white change shirts weren't sufficiently different from the home team's blue-and-white . 'One end of the ground was frozen, thirty yards from the goal-line at the bottom end of the Goldstone Ground, which created havoc,' Beamish remembered, 'but Bristol Rovers absolutely battered us. They used to call us "Brian Clough's Brighton" and I do recall after that game that he admonished the press for calling them that. He said, "It's Brighton." I don't know if he was doing it for his own reputation.'

By any measure, it was a shambolic performance. Clough exploded. He sent the women from the post-match press conference, ordered that all microphones be turned off, then laid into his side. 'The team didn't have enough heart to fill a thimble,' he said. 'I feel ashamed for Brighton – the town and the club. I feel sick. This was the worst day of my football life.'

His hurt at least suggested some level of emotional investment in the club, unless he was merely concerned for his own reputation, but not all were convinced that expressing it so candidly was the best policy. 'The danger at the Goldstone is that the cure prescribed by Mr Clough might kill the patient,' Vinicombe observed in the *Argus*. 'That Albion were ailing before Clough took over is beyond doubt. But has the latest emetic proved too much of a purgative?' The defeats to Walton & Hersham and Bristol Rovers, Vinicombe continued, were 'frightening in portent ... the consequences of failure by a club so heavily in the red do not bear thinking about ... To rebuild is his task and in view of the massive structural weaknesses, he has to demolish the very foundations of the side and begin afresh. In the process Albion will lose more matches, but never, let it be hoped, surrender as they did against Rovers.'

The following day, Clough fulfilled a pre-existing agreement to appear on ITV with Brian Moore. Moore introduced him by saying there'd been an office debate as to whether he'd turn up or not. 'Then they don't know me,' Clough replied, the picture of confident defiance. 'It was a terrible night ... I've got my family down at Brighton trying to house-hunt and being on the receiving end of eight goals is not very easy. But you get up the next morning, the sun was shining, and here I am, wanting to talk football.'

He was unapologetic about his attack on his players. 'Things went wrong right from the start of the match,' he said, 'and this got on top of them, plus our Cup exit last Wednesday, and they just caved in. They were raw, and they just couldn't cope with this kind of pressure.' They lacked, in other words, the moral courage that Clough demanded as a minimum. 'They've got to have more spirit and more heart to play professional football than they showed.'

Much later, in his second autobiography, Clough acknowledged his reputation may have been counterproductive. 'It was not just because we had a terrible team with players who couldn't play,' he wrote. 'It was because they were petrified of me.' There were those who said that was how Clough liked it, that he managed by fear, but that, Clough said, was 'the biggest load of crap I have ever heard in my life'. It might have suited him to terrify players to ensure their compliance, but once he had, it was all about relaxation. At that point, Brighton's players were stuck in the first stage.

Vinicombe went into more detail about his concerns in his column in the *Argus* that Thursday. Recalling how Pat Saward's attack on Norman Gall had precipitated a run of eleven straight defeats the previous season, he urged Clough to 'stop the tongue-lashing'. 'We are sure it is not lost on Clough that he is stuck with the present players for some little time to come and must depend on them if the club is to stay up,' he said. 'There are very real signs that morale has been sapped by saying everything in public ... It was not Clough's team that fell to Walton, or trembled before the onslaught of Rovers. But it is Clough's job to motivate the players he inherited.'

Clough himself acknowledged the problem. 'I have become larger than life, larger than the players, larger than Brighton,' he said. 'This is not right. If I don't come down to their level, we will all perish.' Larger, perhaps, also than Taylor, who seems to feature far less prominently in the memories of Brighton players than he did in those of Derby or later Forest; oddly so, given he was the one with whom they had day-to-day contact. Clough tended only to be seen on match-days; players had no chance to get used to him and, intimidated by him, went into games in just the state of anxiety Clough sought to avoid. 'There is no doubt Clough knows what he is talking about,' Vinicombe went on, 'but there is the danger of impact being muffled by the sound.'

The mood of Brighton supporters, though, at least as expressed through the *Argus's* letters page, was overwhelmingly pro-Clough. 'I am all in favour of Clough telling off his players in public,' wrote C.G. Hickson of Shirley Drive, Hove. 'It is the only way. Some of the players would have difficulty in getting into park teams. John Vinicombe must take some of the blame for the present position of the Albion. He should have suggested to the board months ago to strengthen the team. There are only about three players worthy to be called players. We have got a good manager; now support him.'

Quite why it was a local journalist's fault that the board hadn't realised the team needed strengthening he never explained. Happily, the rebuilding began that week. As the loan spell of the reserve goalkeeper Ron Hillyard expired, he returned to York, and to replace him Clough brought in Peter Grummitt, a Sheffield Wednesday goalkeeper with whom he had played cricket against Taylor's Inland Revenue side. He then spent £20,000 to sign the central defender Ken Goodeve from Luton Town.

Both made their debuts at Tranmere in a 4–1 defeat. 'The scoreline does not tell the story' the headline in the *Argus* insisted, while Vinicombe wrote that 'an indifferent Tranmere accepted four chances out of six'. Nonetheless, sixteen goals conceded in three successive games was hardly a positive sign, something that may have emboldened Longson ahead of Derby's Annual General Meeting; had Clough inspired Brighton to brilliance, it would have been rather harder to justify his position.

In a gesture that is hard to construe as anything other than rabble-rousing, Clough had sold his shares in Derby to members of the Protest Movement, with the money going to charity. That enabled the protestors to go to the club's Annual General Meeting. Mackay spoke of being unable to turn anywhere in Derby without seeing the letters BBC – 'Bring Back Clough' – scrawled on walls, printed on bumper stickers, or on posters pasted in windows, and yet it is an indication of how the protest was running out of momentum that their petition calling for Clough's reinstatement bore only 7,000 names.

Longson produced a counter-petition of 22,000, and opened with an attack on the Protest Movement. 'You haven't done Derby County any good by all this,' he said. 'It is so silly. Nor have you done your champion Brian Clough any good. His image has suffered so much that it will take years for him to get back his respect. I deplore the action of the players. I wouldn't say they were encouraged, but I wouldn't say they were discouraged either. The Movement was tampering with the livelihood of the club. That was disgraceful and disgusting. Your attacks on Dave Mackay have been out-rageous. Dave has proved himself to be a man of courage. They should knight me for what I have done. I have had letters from all over the world backing me up, but you people only stand for the ruination of the constitution of football.'

It was an impressive start, but as the meeting became increasingly fractious Longson became so discombobulated he picked up his micro-phone and held it to his ear as though it were a telephone. Losing patience at a series of interruptions, he told Keeling that, 'I have four men here who will pick you up, throw you down the stairs and into the street.' After a further interruption, he turned to the protestors and told them, 'I am being advised to call for the police to have you thrown out.'

What Clough made of it all is anyone's guess, but if he still thought a return to Derby was possible, he was acting with extraordinary irre-sponsibility, continuing to spend Brighton's money. Two days after the meeting, he and Taylor signed the left-back Harry Wilson and midfielder Ronnie Welch from Burnley for £70,000. With the three-day week having been introduced as a response to the energy crisis precipitated by a com-bination of the Yom Kippur War and the miners' strike, they didn't trust the post and so, rather than sending a telex and hoping the mailed docu-ments would arrive the following day, the two drove to the League head-quarters at Lytham. They arrived, though, at 5.15pm, quarter of an hour after the deadline, so neither was eligible for the following day's game against Watford.

Brighton lost 1–0, but Clough detected 'more heart and greater con-fidence'. All four new signings played at home against Aldershot on Boxing Day, but in front of 14,769, their second highest crowd of the season, Brighton ran into a 'better organised and more determined' opponent and lost 1–0. 'Albion can have no complaints,' Vinicombe wrote. 'Indeed they were fortunate to escape so lightly.' The defeat left Brighton fifth bottom, only a place above the relegation zone.

That was probably the lowest moment. The crowd for the home game against Plymouth three days later was 3,500 down, but among the players 'there was,' Vinicombe said, 'a good deal more eagerness for the ball and a noticably higher work-rate.' With the help of a deflection off Ernie Machin, Beamish turned in Towner's low cross for the game's only goal to record Clough's first home win.

Gall and Grummitt then excelled in a goalless draw at second-placed Bournemouth, before a stunning second-half performance at Charlton, who had been seventh at kick-off, brought Ronnie Howell a hat-trick in seventeen minutes and a 4–0 win. Bamber went down to the dressing-room to congratulate Howell, and found Clough berating him. 'It was brilliant psychology,' Bamber said. 'I loved watching the pair of them [Clough and Taylor] at work. The players were in absolute awe of him. Before a match Brian ranted and raved, then Peter came in and quietened them down.' Clough then refused to let any of the players speak to the press, and ran off to catch a train without answering any questions himself. Perhaps that too was brilliant psychology, in terms of keeping players grounded, but it lent an oddly sour note to the *Argus*'s coverage, and Clough opened himself up to the accusation that if he didn't have time to speak to the press, he was determined nobody else should do so and deflect the glory either.

That too had an impact on morale, as Beamish remembered. 'We went to Charlton away and won 4–0 and he kept us in the dressing-room and a young lad, Howell his name was, a real Cockney, he scored a hat-trick,' Beamish said. 'Brian wouldn't let him talk to the press. The players were full of the joys of spring, we were all bubbling and excited, the lad who scored the hat-trick was on cloud nine and the press wanted him, but Brian stopped him talking.'

With the three-day week forcing the League to lift its restrictions on when games could be played, Brighton faced Rochdale on a Sunday and drew almost 19,000 for a 2–1 win. Fears of relegation were fading and there was a sense that a similar turnaround to that which Clough had effected at Hartlepools and Derby had begun. The following Sunday, though, Clough missed a 1–1 draw at Cambridge to fly to New York to watch the Muhammad Ali–Joe Frazier fight. 'Whatever the result at Madison Square Garden it can hardly be as dramatic as Albion's point-winner, scored by Micky Brown in the second minute of injury-time,' Vinicombe wrote pointedly, while the *Argus's* postbag, having been so in support of Clough when Vinicombe had questioned his public criticism of players, turned critical: how, it was asked, could a manager justify missing a game to go and watch a boxing match? From then on it was difficult to shake the perception that Clough wasn't committed to Brighton and that affected his relationship with Taylor.

The good run came to an end with a 2–1 defeat at Port Vale, even though the home side had John Woodward sent off with half an hour remaining. Clough responded with characteristic rage. 'The days of passing the buck at Brighton are over,' he said the following Thursday, an odd statement for somebody who, ten days earlier, had been off in New York as his side had drawn with Cambridge. 'It is going to be D-day for these players and from now on supporters are going to see action.'

It was home form, Clough said, that was the biggest problem. Brighton might have beaten Rochdale in their last game at the Goldstone Ground but, he insisted, the performance was 'criminal' and his players were lacking in 'moral courage'. 'We have now got the problem of facing a home match,' he said. 'At every club we have been connected with this has never been a problem, players have looked forward to playing in front of their own supporters. But I don't think our lot do. And the reason is that they don't accept responsibility. They duck out of it. They are exposed before their home crowd and they don't like this.' Just in case anybody hadn't got the message, he went on: 'There is a gale blowing through this club and the players concerned are about to feel the draught.'

Derek Dougan, the head of the PFA and one of Clough's colleagues on ITV's punditry panel for the 1970 World Cup, hit back. 'This sort of thing takes footballers back to the days when they were chattels,' he said. 'I'm bewildered to know what Brian Clough expects to achieve by this.' What Brighton achieved was a 1–1 draw with Grimsby. 'More things were right for us today than for a long time,' Clough said.

Brighton then came from 2–0 down to draw at Halifax, suggesting there was at least some spirit in the side, but Clough was off again, canvassing for Phillip Whitehead, the Labour candidate for Derby North. It had been widely predicted that Whitehead would lose his seat, but he held it with a majority of 1,200. Clough gave two speeches during the campaign, at

Beaufort and Brakensdale schools, and seems genuinely to have tried to direct the debate away from his possible return to Derby, and towards Whitehead, who later described Clough as having drawn people out to vote like the Pied Piper.

Clough's politics were heartfelt but not necessarily consistent. He was vehemently and instinctively anti-Conservative, particularly where Margaret Thatcher was concerned. He upbraided his mother for showing Tory literature in the window of the house in Valley Road and tore down election posters in Derby. Yet he contributed to the explicitly Conservative *Express* and supported the Hartlepools chairman John Curry, the leader of the Conservative Group on West Hartlepool Borough Council, during local elections. In that instance, personal loyalty seems to have overridden ideological concerns. During the strike of 1972, though, he handed out free tickets for matches to miners and he marched with unions during the strikes of the early eighties, suggesting a genuine commitment.

Similarly, after Nottingham Forest's European Cup semi-final victory over FC Cologne, Clough took out a front-page advert in the *Derby Evening Telegraph* saying 'Clough supports Phillip Whitehead'. Technically that was against election law – as if Clough cared for such things – which prevents anybody but party agents spending money on advertising. To get round the issue, Clough made a £100 donation to party funds, then took out another similar advert a week later.

There is nothing necessarily contradictory between being wealthy and being a Labour Party supporter, but there were times when Clough's tone seemed hypocritical. Campaigning for Whitehead in the 1979 election, for instance, he addressed a gathering at St Anne's church hall, railing against the dangers and debilitating influence of wealth and privilege. He attacked the Conservative candidate, Sally Oppenheim, for having, as he put it, 'more gold on her fingers than Fort Knox'; all the while, his Mercedes was parked outside. Nonetheless, Whitehead was impressed by Clough's political instincts – honed, perhaps, by his boardroom battles – and his ability to think on his feet, although his regular swearing caused consternation.

Despite his evident interest, Clough didn't join the Labour Party until April 1986. There had been persistent rumours about him standing for election long before then, but given prospective MPs have to have been party members for at least twelve months before standing, none had much substance. The closest Clough came was in Richmond in 1964. Richard Hoyle, a local farmer, had stood in the 1951 and 1955 elections and lost by 15,000 votes each time, but he was president of the general management committee of the Richmond Division of the Labour Party. He remembered Clough and his father-in-law, Harry Blackburn, popping into Middlesbrough Bowls Club for a drink, and decided he'd be perfect to try to woo any voters who had been left floating by the Liberals' decision not to field a candidate in that constituency. Clough, who'd been injured for six months and knew his future in football was far from secure, met Hoyle at a pub in Northallerton and seems seriously to have considered standing. Alan Brown, though, persuaded Clough to stick to football, advice he later acknowledged was 'very shrewd'. There were rumours Clough might stand on an anti-Thatcherite ticket in Loughborough and Stretford in the eighties, but there was never anything more than a tentative sounding out to see whether he may be interested.

Clough's absences perhaps spoke of a growing frustration with the lack of ability he found at Brighton, something he as good as admitted in an interview with the *Express* at the beginning of February. 'The players have shirked all moral responsibilities and have not even attempted to learn their trade,' Clough said.

An anonymous player hit back. 'We had this fairly stormy meeting,' he said, 'but we never dreamed the manager would launch an attack like this against us. I don't think Clough has tried to get to know us.' Another asked what gave Clough the right to question the players' professionalism. 'How can he say all that,' he asked, 'when he flies off to America the day before a match and doesn't reappear until the day before the next match?'

Yet the absences didn't seem negatively to affect Brighton. 'We just got on with it,' said Beamish. 'There wasn't any lack of endeavour or anything like that. Some new lads were brought in, one from Blackpool, a couple from Burnley, but as a unit we just got on with it. We put our lot in and if it worked, it worked, if it didn't, it didn't. I played most of the games, but we never saw much of Clough. We saw him on match-day and Friday. I never felt any bond with him. A couple of the lads did, Piper and Towner, they really came to the fore as individuals and players, there was a link there somewhere for them to improve the way that they did, but the rest of us, we just got on with our football.'

Brighton signed the defender Paul Fuschillo and the midfielder Billy McEwan from Blackpool for a combined £15,000 and produced what Vinicombe called 'their best performance of the season' in beating Blackburn 3–0, the veteran forward Barry Bridges scoring twice. The day before polling day, Brighton came from behind to beat Wrexham at home and the following Sunday, as the party leaders attempted to thrash out a solution to an election that had produced no overall majority, a Ken Beamish goal was enough to secure a win at Aldershot as both sides had a man sent off. 'Superb,' said Clough, despite the dismissal of Fuschillo.

When they then came from behind to beat Hereford, Brighton had picked up eighteen points from their previous twelve games, and there was even over-optimistic talk of a late surge for promotion. Just as it seemed the Clough magic was taking effect, though, he raised further questions about his commitment by going to Iran to talk to the Shah's representatives about taking charge of the national team. Clough travelled to Tehran with Billy Wainwright and Vince Wilson, who ghosted his column for the *Sunday Mirror*, and was treated lavishly, with huge banquets and a visit to the Shah's stable. On other occasions, Clough cynically used offers from other employers to pressure his board, but on this occasion he insisted he was sincere and checked out schooling possibilities with both the British Embassy in Iran and the former foreign secretary George Brown, whom he met at a pub in Belper. Despite an offer of more than double his salary at Brighton, though, Clough decided he couldn't face leaving Britain, although the reason he offered the press was typically mischievous. 'Of course I wanted to go to Iran,' he said, 'but the board vetoed the move. But I'm not saying I'm not happy here.'

Perhaps that wouldn't have destabilised Brighton, but that Saturday Grummitt fractured his pelvis in a 1–0 defeat to Shrewsbury. Although a 2–1 win over Port Vale lifted them to ninth, Brighton never really recovered from losing their goalkeeper. Defeats to Huddersfield, Wrexham and York followed, quashing any thoughts of promotion, which, in any case, had only ever been a remote possibility.

Powney, the only goalkeeper remaining at the club, broke two fingers diving at a forward's feet in the game at York. 'I strapped the fingers together and that was it,' he recalled. 'It was a bit difficult to punch the ball, to say the least. My little finger was dislocated, but they put that back. They didn't have to talk me into it. I had to play. I was the only goalkeeper apart from the youth-team goalkeeper. When he called me in to his office, he was sitting there with Taylor. As soon as I walked into the office, he offered me a brandy. It was a Friday before a game and I was a pretty decent pro. I never used to drink on a Thursday or a Friday, but he offers me this brandy. Cloughie and Taylor were into their brandy and their scotches. I said no, that I was fine and he went on and said, "You're going to have to play."

'I said, "OK, fine, it's down to you. I can't guarantee that I'm going to be able to perform as well as I can with a broken hand."

'"Oh that's all right," he said. "Don't worry about that."

'That's Cloughie, you see. Clough wasn't interested in anybody else's opinions, you could plead your case, he wasn't interested. Didn't listen. You either did what Cloughie said or you went.'

Clough's faith in his goalkeeper was rewarded with a 4–1 win over Cambridge. As Abba won the 1974 Eurovision Song Contest at the Pavilion, a couple of miles from the Goldstone, Powney remained in goal for a 2–1 win over Walsall, and two Beamish goals gave them a 2–0 win over Southend. Three wins in a row ensured a mid-table finish, but there was little left to play for, and after defeats to Chesterfield, Southend and Tranmere, Clough admitted 'we are looking forward to the close season'.

Even before the summer, though, things around the club began to change. In the final week of the season, John Sheridan, the coach, quit for 'personal reasons', and Clough signed the winger Ian Mellor and the defenders Andy Rollings and Steve Govier from Norwich for £60,000, taking Albion's spending under him to £172,000. His final game came, appropriately enough, against the opponent with whom his reign at Brighton would always be associated, Bristol Rovers. Lammie Robertson gave Brighton the lead and Rovers, who had already secured promotion, were fortunate to steal a point with a late penalty.

'From the worst start in living memory, the players found their self-respect, and Clough showed compassion,' Vinicombe wrote looking back on the season, but Clough wasn't minded to be forgiving when Mick Brown, Pat Hilton and Terry Norton were caught in the Goldstone Ground in the early hours of the following Wednesday. High spirits after Hilton's birthday celebrations, in which Piper was also implicated, had led to the misguided prank of breaking in to the stadium; all three were sacked, while Piper got away with a fine.

Beamish was also offloaded, sold to Blackburn in Clough's characteristically brutal style. 'I was still under contract,' he said. 'My last game was Bristol Rovers away and I never spoke to Brian Clough from that day to this. Funnily enough, it was one of my neighbours who told me I was on the transfer list. He'd heard it on local radio. It was a couple of days later that Gordon Lee came to me and said that he'd been given permission to talk to me.

'You just follow your route in football. It's just part and parcel of the game. I was married with a young daughter and my wife was a bit bemused, to say the least. I'd played all the games outside of that ankle injury. I'd scored a few goals for them, it was a bit of a surprise. Normally, they pull you into the office, give you an indication of where your future lies, but that didn't happen. And then my neighbour, who'd been coming up to me all the time saying, "Have you heard anything? Have you heard anything?" comes over and says he's heard on Radio Brighton that I'm on the list. I'd have preferred a phone call from Brian, a conversation with someone at the club, the manager, the assistant manager. Just for one of them to say that it's come to an end, we've decided to let you go.

'I should have known. We played in a testimonial against a London XI and a couple of days after that we were going to Torremolinos for an end-of-season gathering. As a regular player, I fully anticipated being on the trip. However, we were told that the list of players being taken abroad would be on the notice board in the dressing-room after the testimonial game. So we get in at full-time, the list is up and there was a whole group of us not on it, regular players who had played throughout the season. Maybe that was a sign that I wasn't going to stay in Brighton for much longer.' Still, a player surely shouldn't be expected to read signs; Clough complained constantly about directors, but he could be as callous as the worst of them at times.

More signings followed: Fred Binney came from Exeter for £20,000 plus Templeman and Robertson, then came Gerry Clarke and Rick Marlowe – an indication surely that, at that stage, Clough saw his future at Brighton.

By the time the job offer from Leeds arrived in the July, Clough and Taylor's spending totalled almost £250,000.

Yet the news of Clough's departure didn't come as a great surprise to the players. 'I think it was down to a certain amount of greed by Cloughie and Taylor,' said Powney. 'They were out of work, out of a job and I don't think either of them ever intended to stay at Brighton. I think they came for a short stay. Cloughie proved that, he never moved down to Brighton, we never saw him apart from match days, apart from the very odd occasion in midweek, and it was very odd. He would come down and say, "it's going to be a practice match" and that was it. He never coached us, he never trained us. There was no individual or collective training at all. There were no tactics, we only saw him for an hour before kick-off. I think it was pretty obvious right from the start. The first game they were in charge, he never came into the dressing after the game. The next time we saw him was the following Saturday at an away game. We had no relationship, nobody ever built a relationship with Clough at Brighton.

'Mike Bamber, who I quite liked as a chairman, was very much into famous people. He loved rubbing shoulders with famous people. He used to have a nightclub which had all the big cabaret stars, Bruce Forsyth, Des O'Connor, he'd bring them down to the ground, come into the dressing-room, you'd see them in the stands. Taylor and Clough were big news at Derby and I think he went out of his way to rub shoulders with them. As soon as they came it was obvious there were going to be huge problems because they were not interested in Brighton, in the Brighton players, in the Brighton fans, or whatever was going on in Brighton. In fact, Cloughie hated Southerners. He had no time for them. "Effing Southerners" he called them. That was Cloughie.

'The season ended, I left the club, Cloughie and Taylor were still there. In that close season, he went to Leeds. I was surprised he'd gone. I was surprised because he hated Leeds and Leeds hated him, especially the fans. That was common knowledge. But I wasn't surprised he left Brighton. He didn't want to be there, that was obvious. And I think if it was any other club than Leeds, Peter Taylor would have gone as well, but Taylor knew what was going to happen; he knew that the fans didn't want Cloughie there and, at the end of the day, if the fans don't want you, you can't survive. Taylor sussed that.

'Taylor wasn't a football manager, he was a below-stairs back-up man. Apparently, he was great at spotting players, but his team talks, when he did them, were pathetic. There was no detail, go out there, do this do that, nothing constructive, nothing on tactics. Nothing in detail about their team. With all due respect, that Brighton team was the biggest joke ever and I was there for fourteen years. And there were one or two dodgy managers while I was there. When Pat left, we were sorry to lose him, but everyone was excited. Cor, Brian Clough from Derby! And, of course, when he came down, all that was dashed.

'He offered one or two a drink, he came late, one or two of his usual clichés, got to earn your corn, the usual thing, For those of you lucky enough to be here next year, that sort of thing. Players are looking at each other thinking, do we really need this?

'I didn't like him as a man and I didn't like him as a manager.'

Powney, though, was one of those Clough off-loaded; not the sort of player or personality with whom he could work. While it seems fairly clear that Clough, unlike Taylor, was never committed to Brighton, his start at the club – early problems followed by a resurgence towards the end of his first season – mirrors almost exactly what had happened at Hartlepools and Derby and what would happen at Nottingham Forest. Who knows what might have happened had he stayed a year or two more?

Clough's time at Brighton was no great success, but neither was it the unmitigated disaster it is often presented as.

Forty-four Days

The sixties had seen two clubs rise from the Second Division to domination of the First under the aegis of a great manager. What Bill Shankly achieved at Liverpool, Don Revie did at Leeds. Both led provincial sides to promotion, both stamped their personality on the club, both won six major trophies – Shankly three League championships, two FA Cups and a Uefa Cup; Revie two League championships, an FA Cup, a League Cup and two Fairs Cups – and both left their positions in 1974. Where the history of the clubs diverged was in the successors they chose: Liverpool favoured an internal appointment, promoted Bob Paisley and went on to become even more dominant, both domestically and in Europe; Leeds went external and appointed Brian Clough. By the end of the seventies, Clough and Paisley had between them won five European Cups in a row, while Leeds were scrapping against a relegation that finally arrived in 1982.

When Revie took over in March 1961, the club was moribund. At his first meeting with the players he told them that Leeds was a 'dead club', that discipline was poor, training outdated and the attitude slapdash. He said half of them looked as though they didn't want to be there and that they would be got rid of. In its own way it was as devastating as the introductory speech Clough would later give, although the context was very different.

Progress came slowly. Only a win on the final day of the following season saved them from relegation to the Third Division. Once Revie's plans began to work, though, success came rapidly. With Jack Charlton and Bobby Collins as the dominant figures, Revie promoted the likes of Gary Sprake, Paul Reaney, Norman Hunter and Billy Bremner from the youth set-up, and signed Johnny Giles from Manchester United. He fostered a ferocious team spirit, which extended to bingo nights and sessions of carpet bowls, something that drew derision from those on the outside. He would massage his players himself, and encouraged them to go to him with any personal problems; classes were laid on to provide practical advice on such matters as dining out, checking in to hotels and replying to toasts. 'In addition,' Revie explained in the *1970 Park Drive Book of Football*, 'there is the emphasis upon religious advice if they want it and talks on girlfriends, male and female fans, etc'.

Revie's mother had died when he was twelve and he had moved to Leicester City four years later, where he'd become noted for his seriousness, his abstention from cigarettes and alcohol, and his rigid focus on self-improvement. Family life had effectively passed him by, and it was almost as though he sought to create at Elland Road a family he'd never had. The players 'were his children ... and their children his grandchildren,' as a close friend quoted by Andrew Mourant in his biography of Revie put it. Clough, by contrast, had revelled in his family upbringing, and was so devoted to his wife and children that at times he seemed to resent football for preventing him spending more time with them.

There was, though, a darker side. Although they mellowed towards the end of Revie's reign, there was an undeniable streak of cynicism that ran through Leeds. Clough's reaction to it may have been hysterical, but they did waste time, they did harangue referees and they were quite prepared to indulge in the physical side of the game, as was seen, most notoriously, in the 1970 FA Cup final and its replay, in which Leeds and Chelsea hacked lumps out of each other in a pair of extraordinarily violent games. Revie's motto was 'keep fighting'. He had it emblazoned in the dressing-room and his players followed the advice.

'Like a lot of teams,' Giles admitted, 'we believed that gamesmanship and manipulation were part of the professional game.' Leeds, though, he insisted, were far from alone. 'Do you think Leeds went and bullied everybody? How do you go to Chelsea and bully Chopper Harris, Eddie McCreadie, Peter Osgood. Or at Everton – Jimmy Gabriel, Johnny Morrissey. Same at Burnley – Gordon Harris, Brian O'Neil, Andy Lochhead. We were meant to be bullying all these? We were no angels, don't get me wrong. The first thing, in England, was to say: "We've got to get into this lot."' After all, even Clough had picked Frank Wignall with the express intention of taking Sammy Chapman out of the game in one Derby match against Forest. 'The culture of the game was different in the sixties and seventies – but it was accepted,' Giles went on. 'It was tough – and it wasn't right. But it wasn't Leeds against a gang of angels. We were involved in some rough matches. But not every week. It was occasionally. Look at the videos where we played Manchester United or Southampton and it was some of the best football I've seen anywhere.'

Then, of course, there were the allegations of match-fixing. Clough was convinced Revie had paid off opponents and referees, rumours that, although never proven, were common in the game at the time. It should be said that nothing was ever confirmed, and players of the time – Sprake excepted – deny the claims, but they were so widespread and credible that figures as respected as Ted Croker, the FA secretary, and Sir Matt Busby seemed to believe they had substance. Then again, if Revie was fixing games, he did it astonishingly badly, regularly losing trophies at the last.

The combination of gamesmanship, dirtiness and success made Leeds deeply unpopular and, strangely, they seemed to get their comeuppance with a run of bad luck at crucial moments, and defeats in finals. For all the trophies they did win, they probably should have won more, losing in the Cup-Winners' Cup final, the Fairs Cup final and three FA Cup finals, as well as finishing second in the league on four occasions. The unluckier they were, the more superstitious Revie became. He believed Elland Road had been cursed by gypsies, insisted on wearing his lucky blue suit, took a rabbit's foot into the dug-out with him and would walk to the same set of traffic lights before every home game. Clough was predictably scathing, and it sat oddly with Revie's intense rationalism in other matters, most notably the dossiers he prepared on opposing players. Predictably, they too drew Clough's scorn; he insisted they only served to confuse players and make them apprehensive. Whatever doubts there may have been about his methods, though, Revie's success was undeniable. After winning promotion in 1964, Leeds didn't finish outside the top four until Revie accepted the FA's offer to replace Alf Ramsey as England manager in 1974.

Replacing Revie was always going to be difficult. Most within the club assumed the job would go to Giles, and on 1 July, the *Yorkshire Evening Post* ran with the headline 'Giles set to succeed Revie'. He had been a guest of the Brazilians at the World Cup in West Germany, but returned to Yorkshire before the end of the tournament, prompting speculation he was ready to take over. Two days later, the sports editor, Mike Casey, urged the board to 'Give Johnny the Job' as the headline on his piece had it. 'The little Irishman has all the qualifications for a job which demands stamina, enthusiasm, ambition, physical and mental fitness, self-confidence, an ability to work with players and directors, and, above all, intelligence.'

Giles played down the speculation, but that Saturday, 6 July, he admitted that Revie had offered him the position and that he had accepted it the previous Tuesday. At the same time, though, Percy Woodward, Leeds's vice-chairman, confirmed the job was being advertised nationally 'to give as many people as possible a chance to apply'. Did that mean, then, he was asked, that Revie had exceeded his authority? 'I agree entirely,' he said. 'The first I knew of Giles being suggested was when I read it in the newspapers. It's not for a manager who is leaving to invite his successor. I can't go out and choose a successor. It's a decision for the board and it's a pity such a nice fellow as Giles has been involved in this way.' Giles, meanwhile, gave the classic politician's answer. 'I will not be applying for the position when it is advertised,' he said. 'That is different from saying I do not wish to be manager of Leeds United.'

Fans polled by the *Post* agreed that if it weren't to be Giles then it should be Bremner. Alf Ramsey had been slashed to evens favourite with a Leeds bookie, and there was also support for Jack Charlton, who had become manager of Middlesbrough after leaving Leeds the previous summer, and Freddie Goodwin, a former Leeds player then in charge of Birmingham. The *Post*'s piece ended with an odd post-script: 'FOOTNOTE: The man no one tipped as manager? Brian Clough.' Were the jungle drums already beating? Or did the *Post* feel it was such a ludicrous proposition it made a comic pay-off? Did readers chortle at the absurdity?

Choosing between a selection of Leeds legends, past and present, perhaps, was impossible, but the decision to turn to Clough was still bewildering. His attacks on Leeds had gone beyond anything English football had seen before; given the context, and the absence of the twenty-four-hour media to project the smallest molehill as a towering peak, his feud with Revie was probably the bitterest in English football history. 'Clough is the last man I would like to be stranded on a desert island with,' Revie had once said.

If it had just been the column in the *Sunday Express* that had led indirectly to his resignation from Derby, the issue may just about have been soluble; after all, most managers say things to unsettle opponents. Even then, though, the nature of the club, the way Revie had built it into a self-supporting family, meant they were an unusually close-knit group of players, insular, set in their ways and suspicious of outsiders. And Clough couldn't have been more of an outsider. His battle with Revie was a long-running, persistent dispute of such consuming intensity that at one point even Harold Wilson was caught up in the fall-out.

Wilson was one of five hundred guests at a dinner given in honour of Peter Lorimer in January 1973, when Clough was still manager of Derby. For some reason – inexplicable in retrospect – Clough had been booked as a guest speaker. Lorimer was presented with Yorkshire Television's Sports Personality of the Year award, and then left to prepare for a Cup replay Leeds were playing against Manchester United the following day. A couple of speeches acknowledging his contribution to Leeds followed, after which Clough stood up to speak. 'I have sat here now for approximately two-and-a-half hours,' he started, 'and I am not replying to anything or anybody until I have had a wee. And I'm being very serious – you get on your bloody feet and go to the toilet, you get a beer, and then if you've not got to get up early in the morning, get back and listen.' When he finally got back, having – according to his autobiography – been waylaid by somebody who wanted to talk to him about Edward Heath's love of sailing, impoliteness rapidly became outright offensiveness. 'I've come along to pay tribute to sport,' he said. 'I've come along to pay tribute to Peter Lorimer ... Despite the fact he falls as many times when he hasn't been kicked, despite the fact he protests as many times when he has nothing to protest about ...'

He got little further, as the room erupted. Battling the hubbub, Clough called Bremner 'a little cheat', called for Leeds to be docked points for their cynicism and, for the first time, made his crack about Eddie Gray having so many injuries that he'd have been put down if he'd been a racehorse. As members of the audience tried to shout him down, Clough accused them of being cowards, attacking him from a position of strength in a crowd. When one heckler began to make a coherent point, Clough harangued him for being 'a mumbler' and disappeared on a bizarre tangent about Britain becoming 'a nation of mumblers'.

Through a mixture of rudeness and weirdness, Clough had ruined what had been intended as a night of celebration; Yorkshire Television refused to show any of his speech when they aired highlights of the evening. Although he eventually sent a bunch of flowers to Mary Wilson, Harold's wife, to apologise, Clough initially insisted he couldn't see what all the fuss was about. 'They didn't tell me beforehand it was being filmed,' he said – although it's not clear why it would have been less offensive had he known – 'they didn't brief me on what I could and could not say and, in future, if they want a puppet to get up and say something to please everybody in the room I suggest they invite Basil Brush.'

Despite the history, by 15 July, Clough had emerged as a serious candidate to replace Revie. 'His forthright approach,' Don Warters noted in the *Post*, 'is a quality which has more than once made him an unpopular and controversial figure in the world of football, but it is also one which some people can admire – especially Yorkshiremen.' A day later, and Clough was understood to be at the head of a shortlist of four managers, which, it later emerged, comprised Ian St John, then the Motherwell manager, Ipswich's Bobby Robson and the Bolton manager Jimmy Armfield.

Lorimer and Hunter both insisted they would have no problems in working with Clough, but the suspicion he faced was made clear by a petition against his appointment organised by two season ticket-holders, George Hindle and David Ross. The Leeds United Supporters Club formally dissociated itself from the campaign, but in his first night of collecting signatures, Hindle gathered 400 names. 'My sole concern is for the good of Leeds United,' Hindle said, insisting he was concerned about 'bad publicity that might follow if he becomes manager'.

Finally, on 22 July, the news was announced, although not with the fanfare club and manager might have liked. 'Brighton to sue Leeds United in Brian Clough sensation,' roared the *Post's* headline, reporting Bamber's fury that Leeds had made an 'illegal approach' by contacting Clough without first seeking permission. After negotiations between the directors of both clubs, a compensation package of £75,000 plus a friendly match between the clubs had been agreed, Bamber said, only for the Leeds chairman Manny Cussins subsequently to withdraw from the deal. Cussins denied having shaken hands on anything and dismissed Bamber's claims as 'lies'.

Clough admitted he was concerned by the reception he may get. 'I'm coming home to Yorkshire,' he said. 'I was born in Middlesbrough, the same as Don Revie, and I'm coming to do a job. That job is to keep Leeds United at the top of the tree. I know there's been a lot of anti-Clough talk in the West Riding, but it doesn't worry me. All right, I've spoken my mind more than once, but that's because I'm honest. I like to get things out into the open. That's the way I live. I can't change that. But what my critics overlook is the good things I say about people.'

For all his criticism of the club and of Revie, Clough was well aware how good a team they were. 'They were a wonderful side who set a wonderful example for the most part,' he wrote in *Walking on Water.* 'In fact, I had the impression that Leeds could have been more dazzling still had Revie been less systematic and allowed them off that tight rein of his.' Although that sounds like just another of his many jibes at Revie, Clough does seem to have had a genuine respect for Leeds, while noting that, 'their cynicism, their intimidation of referees and the over-physical element of their game … undermined public respect for what they achieved.' The 'dirty Leeds' tag that still overshadows the quality of their football, Clough said, was 'a shame, but … also a kind of justice'.

The players were generally supportive of Revie's nomination of Giles, but he seems never particularly to have wanted the job. He was thirty-four and felt he still had plenty to offer as a player, but was persuaded by family and friends that if the job was offered it was too good to turn down. It never was, seemingly because the board believed Giles would return to Ireland following the collapse of his insurance business.

Having decided against an internal appointment, the board felt that they needed a big personality to take over, and who had a bigger personality than Clough? 'We wanted a manager who was as big as the players,' Cussins said. 'Someone with experience and a proven winner. It was my decision to go for him. I was impressed with the display of loyalty from the team and the fans when he walked out on Derby. It has to be a special person to inspire devotion like that. What Brian had said about Leeds wasn't a problem. If he soft-pedalled, I was certain he'd win everyone round. I liked him a lot. In fact, I preferred him to Don Revie.'

That hints at a lingering sense of ill-feeling towards Revie. Giles noted in his autobiography that there had been constant friction between Revie and the board: Revie felt he wasn't being paid enough – and despite his success, he was far from financially secure when the FA made their approach – while the board, like directors everywhere, couldn't understand why Revie got all the credit or why he could be so abrupt with them: refusing to stop for fish and chips on the way home from a game, for instance, or objecting to the delay when a director cleared wine he had bought on a European trip through customs.

That resentment was inflamed by his reaction after being named England manager. After he'd been appointed, the FA had given him six weeks to carry on working with Leeds while the club found a successor, but Revie cleared his desk immediately. It sounds absurd, but it may be that Cussins turned to Clough in part to spite Revie.

Clough and Taylor, accompanied by Bamber, met with Cussins and the Leeds director Bob Roberts at the Courtlands Hotel in Hove. Unbeknown to Clough, Taylor had already agreed with Bamber that he would stay. Clough shook hands with Cussins on a deal, at which Taylor announced that he wouldn't join him. Clough and Cussins were both furious, and the meeting broke up. Cussins spoke to Bamber on the stairs, asking whether he thought Clough could handle the job on his own, when Clough bounded past him, and addressed a clutch of journalists who had assembled in the lobby. The negotiations had, in theory, been conducted in secret; only

Clough seems to have known the media would be there. 'Gentlemen,' he told them, 'I've just been appointed manager of Leeds United.' At that stage nothing had formally been agreed, and given Taylor's reluctance to move it may never have been, but after that Cussins felt he couldn't back out.

Taylor's decision not to move itself bears some investigation. Initially Leeds had offered £40,000 a year for Clough and Taylor combined. Clough ended up on £22,000, £10,000 more than he was on at Derby, so it's safe to assume that whatever the precise breakdown, Taylor would have been getting around double what he was on at Brighton. Logically, money shouldn't have been a problem, and even in his second autobiography, Clough was insisting that 'money would have got Pete to Leeds', but Taylor complained about the lack of perks and help moving. He had moved into a seafront apartment in Brighton and his daughter had found a job as a journalist there, so moving involved far greater upheaval for him than for Clough, but it may be that he simply saw the problems ahead. Besides which, the relationship between Clough and Taylor had been strained by their time in Brighton. 'The break started at Derby,' Taylor told the *Argus*, explaining his decision to stay after Clough had accepted the Leeds job. 'Brian was bitter about the Derby episode and I think it affected his performance at Brighton.' Clough had never left Derby, and working in Leeds meant he could live back at home without the long, lonely nights in a hotel, but as he admitted in his autobiography, there was one thing that Leeds could give him that no other English team could. 'Our experiences at Derby, particularly the rotten way in which we were eliminated at the hands of Juventus, wouldn't allow me to forget the European Cup,' he said. 'I wanted another crack at it as soon as possible, and Leeds offered that chance on a plate.' He also had the opportunity to take Revie's side and make them his own, and by so doing make Revie's legacy his own; had he won the European Cup with Leeds, then he would have been able to argue that he had capped Revie's achievement. Revie would never have become merely Clough's precursor, just as at Liverpool Bill Shankly is not simply the man who prepared the way for Bob Paisley, but neither would he have stood alone as the one man who made Leeds great. His decision to take the job was far less perplexing than Leeds's decision to offer it to him.

Having forced Cussins's hand over the deal, which suggested impressive levels of political nous, Clough proceeded to make a series of grave errors.

Almost everything he did from then until his departure from Leeds was wrong. His first mistake was almost incomprehensibly crass: he had broken a family holiday to negotiate with Cussins, and having sealed the agreement, he returned immediately to Cala Millor. When the players reassembled for pre-season training, Clough was still away, and dissent was allowed to fester. 'Cloughie was out of order,' said Allan Clarke. 'Pre-season training is a vital part of the season, especially if you've just taken over a new club. As a player, the one man you wanted to see at the training ground was the manager.'

Clough's only act to reach out to players he'd regularly criticised and insulted was to send a telegram to Bremner, who was one of a number of players whose contracts were up for renewal. He told him it was 'an honour to manage Leeds' and asked Bremner and his wife to join him in Mallorca. Bremner refused. 'This,' Lorimer suggested to Phil Rostron in *We Are the Damned United*, 'was no doubt his way of letting everybody know he wasn't daunted by the task at hand. "Leeds? So what?"' Perhaps it was, and it certainly added to the sense that Clough came looking for confrontation. It seems just as likely, though, that Clough wasn't consciously sending out a message at all, and simply didn't realise how his decision would look. He was, after all, devoted to his family – he was an opponent of Sunday football, for instance, because it reduced his time with them – and enjoyed, and seemed to need, his holidays. But whatever the reason, it was an appalling miscalculation.

In his absence – not that it's clear he could have prevented the ill-feeling – an unsettling row developed over the refusal of players to speak at a civic reception given to celebrate their league title. Bremner, who as captain came in for the most criticism, explained that he'd had no idea he'd be expected to give a speech. As the Lord Mayor, Joan de Carteret, put it, 'because of the atmosphere which this unfortunate incident created, the indoor speaking programme was abandoned,' and a number of letters in the *Post* asked whether Leeds players had come to take the fans for granted. It wasn't a major incident, but it ensured pre-season began in an atmosphere of irritation.

When he did finally turn up, Clough just made things worse. As he drove into the car park, 'a man, heavily-built, red-faced and aggressive' – Clough assumed he was a fan – ran up and accused him of being late. As the media scrum that surrounded him became unruly, Clough snapped, turning to Cussins and asking whether this was any way to run a club. Clough seems to have anticipated trouble, taking Simon and Nigel with him, presumably to try to soften the atmosphere. It didn't work: 'it was like walking into an ambush,' he said.

Perhaps in anticipating trouble, though, Clough invited it. Even taking his sons with him suggested an insecurity, that he felt he needed a human shield. 'One of the many misconceptions about Clough's days at Leeds,' Giles wrote in his autobiography, 'is that we were lying in wait for him, conspiring against him, doing all we could to ensure that he failed. This is to misunderstand the huge level of self-interest in footballers, who may regard the arrival of a new manager as an odd appointment, even a completely mad appointment, but who ultimately want to keep winning things. If he fails, they are hardly going to succeed.'

The players waited for Clough to address them, but by the time he made his long awaited entrance, training was already underway. He joined in a five-a-side, but gave no talk, said nothing about his plans. The same day, Les Cocker, who had been Revie's trainer, announced he was quitting the club to join Revie with England. It was not an auspicious beginning, as the *Post* noted, seeing ill-omen in the heavy rain.

Revie had not been a particularly hard taskmaster, and often allowed senior players to work out their own training regimes. Clough, similarly, both as a player and as manager, felt that it was best for players not to expend too much energy between matches. At Leeds, though, perhaps misled by Revie's dossiers into thinking he had been a stickler for time on the training pitch and that the players expected to be drilled to exhaustion, Clough imposed extra sessions. 'Revie had us running up hills forwards,' Paul Reaney commented. 'Clough had us doing it backwards.' Then again, at Derby and later at Forest, Clough and Taylor had pursued a policy of rigorous pre-season training to build up a basic level of fitness, followed by comparatively little physical work during the season; although players complained, had he been there longer, the policy may have proved its value.

On his second day at the club, Clough arranged a practice match on the training ground behind the West Stand. He was again late, and so the players kicked off without him. When he did turn up, with Nigel and

305

Simon, he barely glanced at the game, preferring instead to kick a ball about with his sons on an adjoining pitch.

Taylor had refused to join Clough, but one other member of his Derby backroom staff did heed the call, Jimmy Gordon agreeing to leave the Baseball Ground for Elland Road. 'Brian could be in trouble and I could help him,' Gordon told Dave Mackay as he left. For a man who professed not to like Clough, Gordon was remarkably loyal.

The players seem initially to have been mystified by Clough's brusqueness, the distance he placed between them and him, but that bewilderment hardened into resentment at the pre-season get-together at The Mansion in Roundhay, a smart dinner at which players and their families mingled with directors. For Revie, such events had played a critical part in building up the family atmosphere around the club, of creating a sense that they were all in it together. Clough arrived two hours late, wearing a tracksuit, which was perceived as being a deliberate snub, a way of asserting that he had no time for such things, for Revie or his methods. When he presented the Players' Player of the Year award to David Harvey, he muttered, 'How the fuck you've won this, I'll never know.'

Clough was habitually late to training as well, so most days began with Gordon sending the players on laps of the pitch until he turned up. 'You'd sit and wait for his arrival and wait and wait and wait,' Eddie Gray said, admitting it soon became 'irksome' and added to a general sense that 'Clough was lowering our professional standards'. Perhaps that was a consequence of driving in from Derby most days, but it was hardly a move likely to improve morale among players who knew they'd be fined if they were late. At best it was unprofessional; at worst contemptuous. 'I don't know what point he was trying to make,' Gray went on, 'but I do know we had gone from a well-drilled professional outfit to something of a holiday camp.' Yet at the same time the likes of Reaney thought Clough was pushing them too hard; if the players were mystified by Clough's capriciousness it is hardly surprising.

Clough's changing attitude to punctuality is revealing. At ICI, at Middlesbrough and at Sunderland, he had regularly arrived at the final second, but he was always on time. Alan Brown, Clough said, 'spent half his time trying to catch me arriving late because I wasn't a good timekeeper. I'd get there at five to ten – training was at ten o'clock – and he used to walk down the stairs. By the time he got there I'd be changed, and he'd say, "One of these days I'm going to get you."' Clough asserted his independence and conveyed the impression he had better things to do, but within the limits imposed by the club; he didn't allow his poor timekeeping to become self-indulgent.

At Hartlepools, Ernest Ord's phone calls had ensured Clough was in his office when he was supposed to be. Understandably, he chafed at that and perhaps, as he kept Mike Bamber or the LWT cameramen waiting, he was asserting his authority, his disregard for those he was meeting. That was certainly how it was seen at Leeds. But perhaps it wasn't as volitional as that; perhaps it was simply that the more he drank, the harder it was for Clough to stick to a timetable. The two aspects are not discrete: the more he became Clough the public figure, Clough the personality, the more leeway he had to be brusque or disrespectful, the more his audience demanded it; but the more he felt the need to live up to the image, to match past achievements, the greater the pressure, and the more drink became a comfort.

It was only after a week, on Friday, 2 August, that Clough gave his notorious first team-talk, seemingly after Bremner had suggested it might be beneficial to get everybody together. Given that at Hartlepools and Derby, Clough had loved meetings, had done everything he could to get the players together to foster team-spirit, his reluctance to do so at Leeds itself suggests a trepidation on his part; for once, he seemed to shy away from a confrontation.

When the meeting at last came, it marked the beginning of the end. Before it, Giles said, the players had still been reasonably positive, if a little puzzled; afterwards, there was a sense there was no going back, that already Clough's reign had entered its final phase. In Lorimer's account, he began by saying he hadn't addressed the players earlier because he'd wanted to spend some time observing, making up his own mind about things, which seemed reasonable enough. Most, including Eddie Gray, said Clough opened with the word, 'Gentlemen . . .' – a common Cloughism – but Giles insisted that is a later invention and that he actually began his notorious address, 'Right, you fucking lot . . .'

The exact words don't really matter; accounts of the details vary, but the gist remains the same. What followed had nothing to do with any observations Clough may have made over the preceding few days. 'The first thing you can do for me,' Clough said, 'is throw your medals in the bin because you've never won anything fairly; you've done it by cheating.' Understandably, the reaction was one of outrage. 'That hurt,' Peter Lorimer said. 'The physical emphasis in our game had gone. We'd matured into a very good footballing side. Clough had no right to talk to us like that. Who the hell did he think he was? We'd won more things than he ever had.'

Clough then went round each player individually. It began benignly enough. 'You scored eighteen goals,' he said to Allan Clarke. 'I want nineteen this season.' Clarke was impressed; here was the positive Clough, the Clough who dreamed, as he later admitted, not just of matching Revie's achievement of lifting the Championship, but of 'winning it better'.

But as Clough turned to the other players, the comments became increasingly insulting. He turned to Giles, whom he assumed, as Revie's anointed successor, would be the centre of any dissent. 'You're a dirty bastard,' he told him. 'You go over the ball.' As he turned to his next victim, Clough muttered, 'It's not my fault you didn't get the job.' Giles was far from impressed. 'The man cut his own throat,' he said. 'He arrived with entirely the wrong attitude, immediately on the defensive as if expecting the players to dislike him. His remedy was to be bad-mannered, and there's no way we were standing for that.'

Norman Hunter was next. 'No one in the game likes you,' Clough said, 'and I know you want to be liked.' Hunter replied that he was an established international and didn't care what anybody else thought, least of all Clough. Finally, he came to Eddie Gray, telling him that he'd had so many injuries that if he were a racehorse he'd have been shot. As Gray pointed out, Clough of all people should have understood the frustration of the injured footballer. Here again, Clough's double standards are exposed: he felt justified in making a calculated jibe at a player who had suffered a string of injuries, but nursed a lifelong grudge against Bob Stokoe for an offhand comment made about his injury on the spur of the moment.

'I honestly thought a bit of friendly stick might have melted the ice,' Clough said, 'but I couldn't have been more wrong.' Friendly stick might have done; telling players they'd cheated their way to success and then picking each apart individually certainly didn't. Referring to the insults as 'banter', as Clough did in his autobiography, is the last resort of somebody who knows they've gone too far. Giles described the atmosphere as being like that of a headmaster chastising a group of unruly schoolchildren. Perhaps that was an attempt to crush the players' egos, to 'break their will-power, then put them under the influence' as Longson had described it, but these weren't impressionable dreamers such as he'd managed at Hartlepools and Derby. 'They weren't threatened, any of them, because they felt they were bigger than me,' Clough said. 'When I went to Derby and Brighton, everybody looked up to me. When I went to Leeds, the boot was on the other foot.' They were players with a history of success and Clough's words did nothing but offend them and harden their resolve against him. 'I realised it was an act he was putting on because he was insecure,' Giles said. 'His way was to knock you down. Once you submitted to his will you were OK. He was as good as gold then. The trouble was he couldn't crush any of us.' In his autobiography, Giles said that for a long time he'd thought that if that meeting hadn't happened, if Clough had been able to stick it out for three months, he might still have been a success; as the years went by, though, he came to conclude that it could never have worked: 'We were coming from different planets.'

Selecting Clarke as his player to praise backfired as well, if Giles is to be believed. After Clarke had joined from Leicester in 1969, 'it was a hell of a job getting him to knuckle down and realise he was just another player.' With Clough puffing him up, 'he started strutting about the place again.' Compounding the error, Clough then told Gordon McQueen, another player the Leeds collective had felt the need to 'knock that ego stuff out of', that he was planning to build the club around him.

Although it was Clarke with whom Clough ended up getting on best, he believed it was the forward who had 'whacked' him from behind in the first training session in which he participated. 'There was no obvious laughter,' he wrote in his first autobiography, 'nothing out loud. But I could sense that every single one of them was hiding a smile of satisfaction.' Clough's watch flew off his wrist and seemed to have been lost until the groundsman mysteriously returned it a week later.

The assault continued in an interview with Austin Mitchell on Yorkshire TV that evening. 'They've not been good champions in the sense of wearing the crown remarkably well,' he said. 'I think they could have been a bit more loved. I'm going to bring a bit of warmth, a little bit more honesty and a little bit more of me into the set-up, I hope.'

The club, he felt, had to undergo a process of deReviefication, a policy at which Clough hinted with reference to the most notorious of Revie's superstitions. 'I had great fears of that bloody suit of his – you know, the one he's had thirteen years,' he said. 'I thought if that's there, that's going straight in the bin, not just because it's old, but because it'll smell.' The suit wasn't there, but other signs of his predecessor were. Revie's spirit still haunted the club, so much so that Clough got rid of his desk and other office furniture, an act that prompted his secretary, who had been Revie's secretary, to resign. Oddly the furniture had some revenge, the name-plate Clough fixed to the office door refusing to stay in place. At least, though, it was only Revie's spirit; at the Baseball Ground it had been Clough himself haunting his successor, Dave Mackay. Clough believed Revie was in touch with the players, but he wasn't mobilising them to launch a counter-revolution.

Startling a secretary into resignation was one thing; the coaching staff were something else. Clough accused Syd Owen of being 'truculent and obstructive', but then, on that first day, Clough had told him that he didn't think he was the right man for the job. Maurice Lindley, who'd been Revie's assistant, he said was 'a master of the art of looking busy' without actually doing anything. 'It was as if nobody wanted to let me in on how things had been done and achieved in the past,' Clough wrote. 'It was if they wanted to keep it a secret.'

And the players, of course, were another thing again, not least because, irrespective of the new manager's desire to impose himself, there was a need for new blood. For a side that had just won the title, Leeds were not in the greatest shape when Clough arrived. The squad was ageing, and the contracts of eight (or perhaps as many as twelve; there seems no agreement on the exact figure) senior players were up for renewal. Clough, in fact, had suggested Leeds were 'on the turn' as early as August 1972; given they went on to win the title that season, and reached the final of the FA Cup and the European Cup-Winners' Cup, and then won the league the following season, he was fairly evidently premature, but his later complaints that they were an ageing side in desperate need of rejuvenation were not some *post-hoc* rationalisation for what had gone wrong. After he'd replaced Clough, Jimmy Armfield said he had the hardest job of any Leeds manager because he was the one who had to tell Bremner, Hunter and Giles that they were finished, while Eddie Gray suggested the reason Revie left was precisely because he couldn't face dismantling the side he'd built.

For Clough, though, even drawing attention to the age of the players, calling then the 'Over-Thirties Club', proved an error because, combined with his general disparaging remarks about their abilities, it planted the idea that he was looking to move them on. 'We just went out there to play the game and get the game out of the way,' Lorimer said, 'because we thought, "This guy doesn't rate us. He's going to piss us all off and get rid of us all."'

Clough's first game, a friendly away at Huddersfield, came the day after his notorious address. Harvey and Yorath were both unavailable with flu, while Jordan and Eddie Gray both had groin injuries. Again, it was nothing too serious, but the absentees were part of a general background discontent, a sense that circumstances, great and small, were conspiring against Clough. Phil Summerhill put Huddersfield ahead, but Giles levelled before half-time and Mick Bates, back after a cartilage operation, scored the winner.

Tony Collins, the scout, urged Clough not to change too much too quickly, but Clough was determined to find a better goalkeeper than Harvey – a little oddly given how well he'd played the previous season. Selling him was not a popular move, but it was one that would probably have been accepted; again, though, the way Clough went about it was ham-fisted, and Harvey only found out Clough was looking to move him on when he saw on television that Leeds had made a bid to sign Peter Shilton.

Clough was prepared to sell Terry Cooper, and he thought Norman Hunter, by then thirty, was past it and wanted to replace him with Colin Todd. His biggest problem, though, was Giles. He tried to sell him to Spurs where, in Clough's mind at least, he could have been groomed as a successor to Bill Nicholson; Giles turned down the move.

With other players he was more positive. Terry Yorath was on £125 a week, but shortly before leaving Revie had promised he would double that. Unsure how to approach Clough, Yorath went to Maurice Lindley, only to find Clough in the room. He explained the situation, at which Clough asked why he thought he was worth £250 a week. He explained that he'd played thirty-five matches the previous season for a team that had won the championship. Clough asked if the chairman knew about Revie's promise and when Yorath said that he did, Clough promised to sort it out. Ten days later, Yorath had heard nothing, so returned to Clough, who told him that the chairman had said he knew nothing about it. Before Yorath could react, though, Clough said that he thought the chairman was a liar and that he could have his money.

'There were lots of strands to that little episode,' Yorath told Rostron. 'Firstly the man has been at a new club for no time at all and already he's calling the chairman a liar. Next, if you want to undermine the confidence of a young player, then delaying such an important issue so long is probably the right way to go about it. And further, more positively, it showed he could be persuaded to do the right thing.' It could be added that by delaying and by making the claim about the chairman, Clough made clear that Yorath was getting the pay-rise because of him, not because of Revie, and suggested that he was the players' friend against the untrustworthy directors. Again, though, it may be that because Clough manipulated so often, people attributed deeper motives to him than were really there: it may be that Clough was telling the truth and Revie really hadn't let Cussins know or that Cussins did lie, and that he took so long to tell Yorath because, given everything else that was going on, sorting out an improved contract for a back-up midfielder wasn't a priority.

The background grumbling continued. Clough provoked another row by preventing a visiting party from the USA from touring the ground because double training meant the dressing-rooms were constantly in use; it seemed almost as though he were picking fights because he felt he had to win some. After a friendly against Aston Villa, Hunter congratulated Giles on a pass he had played in the build-up to a goal from Clarke. Clough butted in. 'Never mind the pass,' he said, 'what about the way Clarkey stuck it in?' Giles interpreted that as 'a pathetic attempt to make me look small' and perhaps it was. But could it not equally have been Clough revelling in the striker's art, perhaps making a jokey reference to his own past as a striker as he did so? From the outside, the exchange sounds like the nervous new kid at school blurting out a self-deprecating comment that misjudges the tone horribly and ends up confirming his position as an outsider.

His first signing, similarly, seemed either to misunderstand what the club was about, or to aim at upsetting the Revie ethos. Duncan McKenzie, who'd effectively gone on strike to engineer a move away from Nottingham Forest, was an undoubtedly fine player, but his inconsistency and flamboyance could hardly have been more alien to the Leeds philosophy.

The fans remained unconvinced by Clough, and one of the four football special trains scheduled to take fans from Leeds to London for the Charity Shield against Liverpool was cancelled for lack of interest. Club officials blamed the time of year and people being on holiday, but a number of fans said they were boycotting the game, disillusioned by Clough's apparent desire to sell club favourites. There were internal issues as well. The Thursday before the Charity Shield, Yorath, Frank Gray, Madeley and Clarke all met Clough individually in his office, prompting speculation in the *Post* that they might be putting in transfer requests. Everything was unstable and uncertain.

The Charity Shield that year had been given a higher profile than ever before by the decision to switch the game to Wembley and to broadcast it live on television for the first time. It was also to be Shankly's farewell, his final game in charge of Liverpool. The week before the game, Clough rang Revie and asked if he too wanted to lead the side out at Wembley. Revie declined. That might have been a touching gesture from Clough, an acknowledgement of the debt of gratitude the club owed to Revie, but he admitted he made the offer more because he didn't feel 'the remotest connection to the team' than through any desire to honour Revie. That said, he did develop a habit of giving his honorific roles, particularly at Wembley, to others, whether through generosity, insecurity or instinctive contrariness was never clear.

As Clough himself acknowledged, the contrast was painful: on one side Shankly, marching out for the final time, with his Liverpool team proud behind him, and to their right, Clough, his anxiety evident in an aborted attempt at small-talk, followed by as surly a looking group of players as there can ever have been.

Almost immediately, it became apparent that the game was a friendly in name only. Tommy Smith clattered Allan Clarke early and was booked, then Norman Hunter tripped Steve Heighway and the tone was set. Phil Boersma put Liverpool ahead after nineteen minutes, following in after Harvey had saved from Keegan, and they seemed to have few problems against a flat Leeds. The second half, though, brought a new attitude. Giles,

313

irritated by how close Keegan had got in tracking him across the top of his own box – 'he was all over me with his arms and legs, which I hated' – turned sharply, swinging a right fist as he did so and punching Keegan in the face. He was booked, but he should surely have been sent off, as he later admitted. Liverpool messed up the free-kick and as it was cleared further trouble flared off the ball between Keegan and Bremner.

The referee, Bob Matthewson, sent both off, to Keegan's disbelief. 'Oh come off it Bob, man,' he can be lip-read as saying. 'I've not done fuck all and I've been hit twice.' In what can be seen in those two incidents, Keegan certainly appears the victim, but Giles insisted he had been in 'a peculiar mood' all game. Both took off their shirts and threw them down as they went off, and both were subsequently summoned to appear before an FA commission. 'Keegan could have been the man of the match,' Geoffrey Green wrote in *The Times*. 'Leeds patently realised this by half-time and seemed intent on eliminating him fair means or foul. They chose the unfair method, finally goading the little Liverpool man into hot-headed retaliation.' Clough admitted he regarded Keegan as 'a victim' and said he understood his 'anger and frustration'.

Leeds levelled on seventy minutes, Trevor Cherry heading in Lorimer's cross, taking the game to extra-time and then a penalty shoot-out, which Liverpool won after Harvey blasted Leeds's sixth kick over. The Bremner–Keegan clash took the headlines, but arguably the fact a goalkeeper was taking a penalty was more significant, particularly given Clough had effectively brought it about by ordering McKenzie not to take one: he was seen as Clough's man, and Clough dreaded the consequences if he should be the one who missed. Those doubts that had infected Clough in his final months at Derby were haunting him even more.

After the game, Hunter said he was concerned by the way Leeds had been exposed at corners. Clough's response was to tell the players that they were professional footballers and so should be able to sort out such issues for themselves. That, and Clough's continuing insistence that he never practised set-plays, seems remarkable given they were one of Derby's great strengths, and perhaps suggests just how important Mackay and then McFarland had been in organising things at Derby.

That was just part of what the Leeds players came to see as Clough's lackadaisical tactical approach. After Revie's obsessive, paranoid mindset, it was not inconceivable that the players may have relished being let off the leash – just as Ajax only truly blossomed (then faded) after the *laissez-faire* Ştefan Kovács replaced the disciplinarian Rinus Michels. Arguably Revie had already begun that process – leaving his successor to deal with the consequences – but Clough's refusal to offer even the most basic tactical instructions left his players bewildered.

The pressure was starting to tell on Clough. While he looked for a house, McKenzie was staying, as Clough was, in the Dragonara Hotel. The Tuesday after the Charity Shield, Leeds played a testimonial for Ted Bates in South-ampton. They flew back that night and McKenzie went to his room, only to receive a call from Clough in the early hours, telling him to get down to reception in five minutes. Clough met him there and berated him for having been drunk on the plane. McKenzie argued that he'd had nothing more than two tonic waters. Clough accepted that, but insisted that McKenzie stay with him for a pot of tea, at which McKenzie realised that he just wanted somebody to talk to. Clough told him that outsiders didn't realise what a big job it was, breaking up a squad full of thirty-somethings. He asked him to be his spy in the camp, and probed him on what other players had revealed to him. McKenzie replied that he was still getting to know his team-mates and so their conversation rarely stretched to more than small talk. 'In fact,' he said, 'the talk was of nothing but Clough. They began to think everything he did was wrong.'

Clough himself was all too aware of the climate of suspicion. Later that week, as he lay sleepless in the hotel, he called Taylor's number in Brighton. Lill answered. Clough was in tears, admitted he'd made a terrible mistake and claimed there was a conspiracy against him. He said he'd give anything to have Taylor alongside him again, but asked Lill not to wake him. Taylor did wake, though, and took the phone. Clough begged him to join him, saying that together they could do the job, but that alone he had no chance. Taylor, though, remained loyal to Mike Bamber.

Leeds opened their league season at Stoke, an away trip they rarely relished. A couple of hours before kick-off, Clough rounded up the players at the team hotel, and took them for a walk. When they reached a motorway, Clough led them to the central reservation, sat them down, and began his team-talk. He'd barely started when it began to rain, at which the players, despite Clough's efforts to keep them sitting where they were, stood up and returned to their hotel. Not surprisingly, the incident provoked further dissent and was seen, Lorimer said, as another example of Clough treating the players with 'disdain and contempt'.

Injuries ruled out Clarke and Jones, meaning Clough had to field McKenzie as a partner for Jordan before he was probably physically ready and, according to Warters's report in the *Post*, it was, as much as anything, an inability to take chances that cost Leeds. 'We played enough football in the first half to have won three matches,' Clough claimed. 'In the first half we could have been 3–0 up.' As it was, it was goalless at half-time, and Stoke went ahead five minutes into the second half with a thirty-yard drive from John Mahoney. McKenzie had a great chance to level, as Lorimer found him with a right-wing cross three yards out, but the ball stuck between his feet and he ended up scuffing his shot into the goalkeeper John Farmer. Madeley went close with two close-range efforts, Lorimer and Giles hit shots narrowly wide and Farmer made an excellent save from a Giles free-kick. With four minutes to go, a Jimmy Greenhoff shot deflected off Cherry and past Harvey; two minutes later John Ritchie added a third and Clough had begun with a 3–0 defeat.

Desperate for familiar faces, Clough signed McGovern and O'Hare, both of whom had slipped into Derby's reserves after his departure. Not surprisingly, they were seen as Clough's men and were greeted with suspicion by players and – more particularly – by fans.

For all the problems, Clough was still welcomed by the majority of fans for his first home game, against QPR, which suggests that, difficult as things were, his failure was not inevitable. Missing seven players because of suspension and injury, Leeds, according to Warters, 'lacked rhythm'. They lost 1–0 thanks to an error from Harvey, who allowed a thirty-yard drive from Gerry Francis to squirm through his grasp. 'The ball must have kicked at the last minute,' Harvey said. 'Mick Bates said it definitely swerved to the right very late, but I should have got my body behind it. It's the worst mistake in my career.'

Clough's former Sunderland team-mate Stan Anderson was the assistant manager at QPR. The two bumped into each other that night at Clough's hotel. Clough complained about Leeds's luck, to which Anderson replied that he'd be all right. 'I'm not sure about that,' he remembered Clough replying. 'I don't think I'll be here too long.'

A team meeting was called at which there was abundant evidence of disintegrating morale. McKenzie recalled sitting in the front row, hearing Syd Owen sitting at the back dismissing what Clough was saying as 'rubbish'; if he could hear, he realised, so too could everybody else, including the manager. Clough, meanwhile, became increasingly eccentric and took to carrying a brush around with him that he would suddenly brandish and order everybody to stand to attention.

The players became openly sceptical of Clough, asking O'Hare and McGovern what he'd been like at Derby. 'They thought he knew nothing about the game and couldn't understand how he ever won the league title,' O'Hare said. 'Bremner and Giles were the most inquisitive. They couldn't fathom his casual approach to the job.' Later on, though, Giles came to appreciate the Clough method. 'By not dwelling too much on the technicalities of the game, he didn't complicate it,' he said. 'Like Matt Busby, he had the courage to allow his players the freedom to take responsibility and to express themselves.'

At the time, though, Giles was openly sceptical, adding to the constant politicking to create an atmosphere of suspicion that unnerved McGovern. 'When he spoke to us at Derby,' he said, 'players would stop in their tracks and listen. At Leeds they just walked away and ignored him.'

Clough was still convinced the team was past its best and determined to carry on with the rebuilding work, but he accepted that there were key tactical elements he had misread: it was Giles rather than Bremner who ran the midfield and Hunter had greater influence than he'd acknowledged. For all his doubts about the side, it was still essentially the team that had won the title losing only four games the season before, and once Clough had gone, Jimmy Armfield was able to coax them to the final of the European Cup.

Understandably, Leeds bore 'an air of anxiety', as Warters put it, for the home game against Birmingham City. McKenzie, Jordan, Cooper and Bates were all out injured, with Bremner suspended, but Clarke returned from suspension, Hunter came back into the centre of defence with Cherry reverting to full-back. Leeds began 'in a way which suggested they might swamp the Blues with powerful attacking play . . . yet, when that much-needed early goal failed to materialise, United lapsed into a state of near nervous tension.' After an hour, though, they at last had a stroke of luck, the ball squirting out of a challenge between Joe Gallagher and O'Hare, and cannoning off the referee John Williams into the path of Clarke, who pounced. The big positive was the form of O'Hare who, according to Warters, 'remained calm and showed touches of class'.

The win inspired confidence and Leeds were much improved the following Tuesday at QPR. 'Fears that Leeds United's crown is slipping were dispelled by the champions in an exhilarating display,' wrote Mike Casey in a breathless report in the *Yorkshire Post*. 'Playing with zest and confidence, two qualities lacking in their previous games under new management, United were full value for their 1–1 draw in an action-packed thriller.' Yorath was effective in marking Francis, and put Leeds ahead after twenty-one minutes, lobbing Phil Parkes after O'Hare had beaten him and Terry Mancini to an aerial ball on the edge of the box. Leeds had much the better of the remainder of the first half, but Don Givens levelled two minutes after half-time and later hit the post. Clarke had an effort cleared off the line, but the game ended in an encouraging draw.

Later that week came the disciplinary hearing into Bremner's sending-off in the Charity Shield. Clough travelled to it with Don Shaw – whatever strain there had been in their relations evidently passed – by which time his dissatisfaction with the job was obvious. 'I hate managing them, but what can I do?' he asked. Oddly, Clough didn't speak on Bremner's behalf, instead handing that responsibility to Maurice Lindley, which hardly suggested a manager backing his captain to the hilt.

The hearing suspended Bremner until the end of September and imposed a £500 fine, which Clough insisted Bremner pay out of his own pocket. Bremner pointed out that Revie had always made sure the club paid the players' fines, to which Clough replied, 'Don's not here any more.' Jimmy Gordon witnessed the exchange and realised from the look on Bremner's face that Clough had no chance.

Yet Clough went out of his way to get Bremner onside. As the captain served his suspension, Clough made a point of including him in team-talks, sat next to him on the coach, and asked him to act as assistant-manager at a reserve game to report back on the form of McKenzie and Jordan. Bremner refused, citing a prior engagement. As a way of reaching out to the squad, though, even the attempts to forge an alliance with Bremner were misguided. 'Because he was our captain,' Giles said, 'Clough got the impression that the other players followed him. He couldn't have been more wrong. We spent most of our time trying to avoid Billy. He had the respect of the team as a player, but he had a terrible temper, he was a heavy smoker and he could drink.'

The semblance of form shown at Loftus Road was maintained in the first half against Manchester City the following Saturday, Warters noting that 'the champions looked to be approaching the form which took them to the title last season'. Mike Summerbee put City ahead after seven minutes, but with Leeds continuing 'to play attractive football', Clarke ran on to a John McGovern clearance to level half an hour later. But City stifled Giles, and with McGovern struggling to impose himself, the home side took control after half-time, Colin Bell slamming in the winner twelve minutes into the second half.

Hope may have been provided the following Thursday as Leeds reserves, featuring eight players with first-team experience, hammered Blackburn 3–0. 'The approach, the application, the link-up and the workout were all absolutely superb,' Clough said, but the quality of the performance was overshadowed by the death at the ground shortly before the game of Harry Reynolds, the chairman who had appointed Revie. That era was irrevocably at an end. The next day, unthinkably, bookmakers offered Leeds at 10–1 to be relegated.

After three defeats in five games – only one fewer than they'd suffered in the whole of the previous season – Leeds fans began to turn and Clough was booed by a large section of the crowd at Elland Road for the home game against Luton. That seemed to bother him less than the crowd's reaction to the performance of McGovern who, Warters wrote, 'had what must have been his worst first-team game'. Clough was understandably protective. 'To say the crowd gave him some stick is the understatement of the season,' he said. 'Their attitude to him sickened me. But though he is a boy in stature, he is a man out there on the pitch and he won't allow it to destroy his game.'

Having gone ahead through Clarke, Leeds were pegged back by Barry Butlin, who had played under Clough at Derby. After the game, as Clough went to speak to the press, he met Butlin. Putting his arm around him, he told the assembled journalists, 'This is who you want to write about after that wonderful goal. He deserves it.' He was bullish about Leeds's hopes.

'It was a question of confidence,' he said, 'and the confidence is down to me. I instil it or destroy it and I have not been able to instil it as yet. If we had stayed at 1–0 for a time against Luton and then got another one, we would have blossomed.'

The draw left Leeds second bottom, but, outwardly at least, Clough remained defiant. 'Do people really believe I would go out and destroy something for the sake of destroying it?' he asked in a front-page piece in the *Post*. 'I am getting the full support of the players. I have never been so convinced of anything in my life as that.'

Others were less sure. 'He had an obsession about cutting us down to size and building us up again in his own image,' said Eddie Gray. 'I think Brian came to Leeds with a bit of a complex, and that complex was Don. He didn't want anything connected with Don round and about him.'

Either way, the impact on the club was disastrous. 'We didn't even look like winning a match,' Lorimer told Phil Rostron in *We Are the Damned United*. 'There was a simple reason; nobody was going to play for Brian Clough.' Not being inspired by him, though, is not the same as deliberately underperforming to try to force Clough out, as some have suggested. 'Our professional pride wouldn't allow us to play below our best,' Hunter insisted. 'I'd never experienced a run like it. We played our butts off and things just didn't go for us. I remember that Manchester City game in particular. We played some super stuff that day and still got beaten.'

McKenzie, though, suspected several players had slipped into a grey area, something that wasn't outright sabotage, but wasn't full commitment either. 'There was no malicious intent to play below our best,' he said, 'but some players refused to accept responsibility for our predicament. If they had acted like mature pros we'd never have been in that mess.' Trying to isolate the culprits is tough. Clough assumed that Giles would have been the centre of discontent, yet he picked him for all six matches, which hardly suggests a player performing below par. 'I played really well for him,' Giles wrote in his autobiography, admitting he felt oddly conflicted towards Clough. 'I actually felt there was some chemistry developing between us towards the end,' he went on, 'which gave me some inkling of the genius which the man undoubtedly possessed.'

Clough seems to have projected his own feeling of persecution onto

McGovern, as though it were the midfielder rather than him who was loathed and under pressure and suggested players were deliberately under- or over-hitting passes to him to make him look bad. That is something they all vehemently deny, and most seem to have sympathised with the position into which McGovern and O'Hare – 'smashing lads' according to Lorimer – had been thrust. 'But McGovern and O'Hare,' Lorimer went on, 'frankly were not good enough to get into our team and, further, I think they knew they were not good enough to get into our team. Certainly it was evident to the crowd.'

More importantly, it was evident to the directors that something was badly amiss. The board was divided three to two in favour of Clough. Cussins and Roberts, having been there at the appointment, supported him, as did Sydney Simon. Sam Bolton and Percy Woodward, though, had been sceptical from the start. When Roberts went on holiday to Mallorca, Bolton and Woodward struck, calling on Cussins at home and telling him that Clough had to go. 'I didn't think it was right to sack him,' Cussins said, 'but Leeds is a democratic institution. There was nothing I could do.' There was: he could have contacted Roberts, or at least have urged Woodward and Bolton to wait until he returned. How 'democratic' was it, after all, to wait for a fifth of the electorate to be away before calling a vote? Instead, the manoeuvring to depose Clough occurred in a meeting so secret even Keith Archer, the club secretary, didn't know about it, so no minutes were taken. If the account Cussins gave was accurate, the infamous players' court that enacted the coup against Clough was little more than skilful PR on the part of Sam Bolton.

That something was seriously wrong first became apparent on Monday, 9 September, when Clough was called into a meeting to be told that the board had vetoed the sale of Cooper to Nottingham Forest, with whom Clough had agreed a £75,000 fee. 'The situation is beautiful and clear,' Clough said after that meeting. 'We have to get on with it on the field. That is my job and the players' and that will solve everything. The board wanted to be informed on everything that goes on within the club and rightly so. The bid from Forest was not high enough. I feel Terry is more valuable than that, also he can do Leeds some good. There was no pressure from the board on me to withdraw from the Forest deal.'

The report of the meeting in the *Post*, though, was sceptical, and hinted at a mounting sense of crisis. 'Leeds chairman Mr Manny Cussins had what he described as "a satisfactory" meeting with the players at Elland Road today, following the club's decision to reverse the decision to sell Terry Cooper,' wrote Warters. 'Before going into the meeting, Mr Cussins said: "I know there is no unhappiness among the players. All I want to do is to find out if any of them have problems."'

Cussins went on to say that no players were up for sale. 'Rumours that there was unhappiness at the club,' Warters added, 'were scotched by United manager Brian Clough who said he had the full backing of the players.' But there were rumours, and rumours that were serious enough for both Cussins and Clough to feel the need to deny them.

Fans, at least as they were represented on the letters page, were divided. Most seemed generally supportive of Clough and unsettled by the booing, but others made clear their opposition to the signings of McGovern and O'Hare. 'Come off it, Mr Clough!' wrote L. Gregan of Dewsbury Road. 'We supporters can criticise players if we like. We are used to world-class players at Elland Road and when we think players are below that standard we are entitled to have a go. Perhaps Mr Clough can explain why he has spent £375,000 on new players who are no better than those in the reserves?'

The following day, a squad meeting was called in the players' lounge. After the previous day's board-meeting, Clough must have had a good idea of what was coming. Bolton, chairing, said that he'd heard of unrest among the players, of dissatisfaction with Clough, and asked to know more. At first, nobody was willing to break cover, then Clough, with what some claim was a notable lack of enthusiasm, suggested they should try to forget the previous few weeks and start over. Throughout the meeting he remained calm, displaying none of the rage that might have been expected. Perhaps he was stunned, perhaps he was resigned to the fact the battle was lost; perhaps he knew what was coming and was already planning how best to negotiate the pay-off his impetuousness had denied him at Derby.

One of players – nobody seems quite able to agree who – asked why Clough had ever been appointed given his long-standing antipathy to the club. 'It wasn't just me who appointed him, boys,' Cussins replied. Giles then suggested that the players couldn't be expected to speak freely in front of Clough. He didn't need a second invitation to leave. On his way out, Clough passed Gordon and told him that he was going to resign, but that he'd make sure his (Gordon's) job was safe. Gordon replied that he had no intention of staying without Clough.

Back in the meeting, Giles and Hunter admitted they found it tough to work with Clough after what he'd said to them in that first team-talk. Others questioned Clough's methods. Jordan, McQueen, Yorath and Frank Gray remained silent. Reaney did nothing other than to murmur to McGovern that the whole process was wrong. McGovern, O'Hare and McKenzie understandably kept out of it. Nobody spoke in Clough's defence. For Bolton, that was ideal: the coup could be passed off as player revolt. Even Paul Madeley, widely regarded as the model professional and the most level-headed player at the club, spoke out. 'What the players are trying to say, Mr Bolton,' he said, 'is that he's no good.' A couple of players have since spoken of how Bolton seemed to 'revel' in the criticism, egging the players on to greater condemnation. It was, Giles insisted, 'a sham'; he felt the board wanted the players to criticise Clough in front of him so they could claim to have been left with no alternative. After all, if they had simply been assessing the players' mood, they could have called them in privately. Bolton and Cussins concluded the meeting by saying they would 'look into' the players' concerns; in reality, their conclusions had been drawn long before.

There was talk in the press afterwards of a 'gang of four' players – presumably Bremner, Madeley, Giles and Hunter – who had plotted to take down Clough, while Clough told Maurice Edwards, his chief scout at Derby, he believed seven senior players, guided by Revie, were undermining him, but there seems no concrete evidence of any coherent plan. Clough's claims, in fact, and his assertion he had a mole who was keeping him informed – presumably McKenzie, although he was a reluctant informant if he was one at all – seem evidence of his paranoia and his love of intrigue, perhaps influenced by what had happened at Derby, rather than anything more substantial.

'It's rubbish to suggest there was a faction bent on destroying Clough,' Hunter told Francis. 'What motive would we have had? I don't deny I wasn't one of his greatest fans, but if anyone was doing the ganging up it was the directors. None of us had any secret meetings with the board that I'm aware. They knew they'd dropped a clanger and used the players to get rid of him. ' Jimmy Armfield, who replaced Clough, found his transfer dealings hampered by Clough's pay-off, but recalls no great sense of resentment from the players towards Clough and maintains that the players at no stage tried to assert any sort of power over him.

Even Bremner, most seem to agree, was resentful rather than scheming, and was nowhere near as hostile to Clough as has often been made out. 'We've been the fall-guys for Clough's sacking for all these years, but it wasn't true,' he said when, many years later, he broke his silence on what had happened in the meeting. 'Players don't sack managers, but it was convenient to use us. We only had one meeting about him, and that was on his last day when Manny Cussins and Sam Bolton were looking for us to do their work for them.'

There was still time for one further game, a League Cup tie away to Huddersfield Town of the Third Division. Revie, perhaps tipped off that something was going on behind the scenes, was there to see it, but his appearance did not stoke the dissent. On the contrary, the fans seemed more supportive of Clough than they had been the previous Saturday, and a number chanted his name, perhaps encouraged he had omitted McGovern and O'Hare, dropped for Bates and Jordan. But then word got around that Revie was there, sitting in the directors' box in his sheepskin coat, watching Madeley, Hunter and Clarke in his role as England manager. Suddenly it was his name that was being chanted.

It had been at Huddersfield that Clough had felt his Derby side was on the brink of something extraordinary and it was there that he experienced his last game in charge of Leeds. He ended it leaping from the bench 'with fist clenched in triumphant salute', as Warters saw it, but that unusually emotional act was in itself indicative of how badly things had gone.

The referee, Pat Partridge, was to do Clough's Forest team an almighty favour with a penalty in the League Cup four seasons later, but here, after Lorimer had converted from the spot after nine minutes, he ordered a retake for encroachment by Clarke. The retaken kick hit Terry Poole on the foot as he dived towards the corner, and the ball spun away to safety. 'That is the sort of thing that happens when a team is going through a bad patch like we are,' said Lorimer. 'The keeper dives the wrong way and still manages to save it. It did not worry me really, because I thought at that stage we were playing well enough to win.'

Warters even saw evidence that the 'clear-the-air' talks had had the desired effect, noting a renewed determination, even if there was a lack of 'flair and poise'. But Huddersfield, driven on by a 15,000 crowd, by some distance their biggest of the season, rose to the derby atmosphere. Clough said he'd never seen a Third Division team run as much, and after a series of chances at both ends, it was Alan Gowling who struck, beating Hunter and McQueen before hitting a rising shot past Harvey to give Huddersfield a seventy-eighth-minute lead. At that, Revie stood up and left.

It would have been a particularly ignominious way for Clough to depart, but Lorimer at least spared him that, thrashing a last-minute shot from a narrow angle past Poole to take the tie to a replay. Clough leapt from the bench and punched the air, a rare show of emotion that is hard to explain. Did he think there was still time, that the equaliser and probable victory in a replay would be enough to spare him? That, at least, suggests that he wanted to be spared. Perhaps he was simply relieved that his final game would not be a humiliation; or perhaps it was simply an instinctive, if uncharacteristic, reaction to an important late goal.

If he'd thought it would save him, it didn't. Whether the board were determined to be rid of Clough or not, what the players had said clearly, at the very least, encouraged them to act swiftly, before the European Cup campaign got under way the following week. That night, when the squad arrived back at Elland Road, Clough was told the chairman wanted a word. He drove to Cussins's house in Alwoodley and there he was told he would be leaving the club.

Clarke had got on with Clough better than most of the Leeds players – 'he offered me some warmth and comfort,' Clough said – and he felt uncomfortable about the way Clough had been savaged. 'I said nothing [in the meeting] because I was so angry I might have done something I regretted,' he said. After talking things over with his wife, he telephoned Clough, only to find that he was at Cussins's home, presumably discussing the terms of his departure. He left a message asking to see Clough at the ground the following day. He then dissociated himself from the views of the other players, and told Cussins that he was making a mistake, that it was treachery to listen to players with axes to grind.

On the Thursday afternoon, fifty-three days after he had been appointed and forty-four days after he had actually taken charge, Clough formally parted company with Leeds. This time, unlike at Derby, he wasn't alone, but had with him Colin Lawrence, who advised Clough to bring in Charles Dodsworth, a solicitor from York, to negotiate his pay-off. In his autobiography, Clough described Dodsworth carrying out the negotiation. In fact, Dodsworth only acted for him in reaching a settlement with Brighton. He was on holiday in France when Clough left Leeds, and so his firm brought in another Leeds company, Jobbings, Fawcett and Grove, to act on Clough's behalf. In *Clough & Revie*, Roger Hermiston convincingly argues that the man who actually acted for Clough that day was David Somersall Creasey, who died in 2009.

Creasey's son Julian told Hermiston how Cussins and Woodward didn't bother with a lawyer, believing they could settle Clough's pay-off themselves. They drank gin and tonics throughout the afternoon, becoming increasingly tipsy while Clough and Creasey stuck to water and tea. 'They,' Julian Creasey said, 'just didn't appreciate the whack they were going to take.'

In the room next door to the office where Clough finalised his compensation, Hunter was meeting his testimonial committee. As he left, Clough popped his head round the door. 'Make as much money as you can for him,' he said cheerily, his mood radically improved by the size of his pay-off. 'He's been a good pro for this club.' Clough later tried to sign him for Nottingham Forest.

On the steps outside Elland Road, Clough grinned and made jokes, presumably unable to believe his luck, while Cussins shuffled about looking awkward. 'What has been done is for the good of the club,' the chairman said. 'The club and the happiness of the players must come first. Nothing can be successful unless the staff is happy.' A journalist asked if it was true that it had been the players who had got rid of Clough. 'We've been spoilt by Don Revie,' Cussins replied. Clough would say merely that it was 'a very sad day for Leeds and for football'.

The director Arthur Haddock told the *Post* that the board was concerned that Clough had spent £380,000 without consultation, but given that had seemingly been resolved at the Monday meeting, it sounded like an excuse, perhaps trying to remind the public of the reasons Clough had left Derby.

Roberts was still in Mallorca and was appalled by the decision. 'It's absolutely shocking,' he said. 'Clough hasn't had a chance. He's not been there five minutes. If there was a crisis, they could at least have asked me to return. I'm sorry I wasn't there to take part in discussions, but I have not heard a thing from Leeds. I still think we got the right man and it's a loss to Leeds in my opinion.'

Gordon was similarly strident in his defence of Clough, placing the blame on the players. 'Some of the things the players said about Clough's capabilities were so wrong, how he kept his temper or his head on occasions I do not know,' he said. 'If the players could not accept Brian Clough then I cannot accept them and they cannot accept me. ... If you had asked me three days ago if there had been any unrest I would have said no. Everything appeared to be running smoothly, but, of course, we were not getting the results we wanted.'

The players themselves, meanwhile, were just glad it was over. 'They say Cloughie was at Leeds for forty-four days, but in reality it was more like twenty,' Harvey told Rostron. 'He was there so rarely that no one really had the chance to get to know him, and, from what I saw of him throughout his career, I'm at least grateful for that small mercy.'

In his second autobiography, Clough acknowledged that the decision to get rid of him 'was no real surprise in view of the way I tackled the job, trying to do in minutes what should have taken months, maybe even years ... I reckon they actually hated my guts. Reflection tells me that the biggest mistake of all was my eagerness to accept the job in the first place. Leeds weren't for me and I wasn't for them.' That eagerness, of course, was, as he admitted, bound up with his desire to win the European Cup, to put right the wrongs of those months in early 1973 when he lost his mother and was, as he saw it, cheated out of the competition by Juventus. The trophy had become to him as Moby Dick was to Captain Ahab: it had hurt him, maimed him psychologically, and he needed his revenge.

The admission that he erred in accepting the job raises another issue: at what stage did Clough decide that he wanted out? By the end, Eddie Gray said, 'It must have been a relief to Clough when he and Leeds parted company. It had been a case of him picking a team, us going out there and getting beaten ... him picking a team, us going out there and getting beaten. And there he was. The biggest certainty was that he was going and, from our perspective, the sooner the better.'

John Wray, who covered Leeds for the *Bradford Evening Argus*, recalled agreeing to spend his day-off helping Clough go house-hunting. He arrived at the hotel to find Clough wearing a tracksuit-top and shorts, drinking a beer and watching the cricket on television. Clough suggested Wray help himself to a beer and watch a few overs; several hours and several pints later, they decided it was too late to bother. Although Clough's fondness for both drink and cricket means he may just have got settled in front of the television, Wray wondered whether he knew that he would be there too short a time to make it worthwhile finding a house, wondered even whether Clough may have deliberately engineered his own dismissal. Almost whatever Clough was doing, people around him suspected an ulterior motive.

Although Clough hadn't signed his contract, Leeds honoured it. He initially agreed a pay-off of around £25,000, but signed nothing. Creasey negotiated it up to somewhere around £100,000 after tax and ensured he was allowed to keep his club Mercedes. Clough also secured Jimmy Gordon an assurance from the club that it would pay his tax; the £3,500 he received allowed him to pay off his mortgage, and he too was allowed to keep his club car.

As though unable to believe what he'd pulled off, the next day Clough drove back to Leeds from Derby to pay in the cheque, having been told that the quickest way to get a cheque passed is to present it at the issuing bank. He paid off the mortgage on the house he lived in on Ferrers Way and moved into a much larger property in Quarndon. 'Leeds,' Clough said, 'provided me with the financial security to ensure that I could insist on doing the job my way. For the first time in my life, if I didn't like anything that was going on, I could turn round and say "Fuck you, I'm off".' At Derby, of course, he'd said that quite often; after the Leeds pay-out, though, he could mean it.

Perhaps the most surprising aspect of the whole affair was how supportive of Clough the *Post*'s letters page was. Of course, letter-writers are not necessarily a representative selection, but the anger with which so many complained of the decision to get rid of Clough gives the lie to the idea that Leeds fans were set against him from the beginning. 'Brian Clough needed time – years and not just months,' wrote B. Richardson of Barwick-in-Elmet. 'The present team, without doubt, was on the slide before Don Revie left and the rebuilding might take two or three years.'

Others saw a more worrying trend. 'I am afraid football has got to the state where players are dictating all the terms,' wrote K. Fleming of Morley, whose disgust at that development led him to drastic action. 'Because of the circumstances I shall cease to be a pools agent and, at the first opportunity, sell my season ticket.'

After leaving Elland Road, Clough went to the studios of Yorkshire Television, where, alongside Revie – whom he later said he hadn't realised would be there – he was interviewed by Austin Mitchell. It is, quite rightly, regarded as a stunning piece of television. There is a prevailing belief that Clough won the debate, that he verbally skipped around a lumbering Revie, landing blow after blow, but he did not. Clough, of course, was the more telegenic presence, slim and dapper in a pale grey suit, smiling frequently, while Revie was more ponderous, occasionally struggling to find the right word. In Kennedy's first televised debate with Nixon before the 1960 presidential election, it was widely perceived by those who'd listened on the radio that Nixon had won, whereas those who had watched on television were convinced by the slick presentation of Kennedy. Just as Nixon suffered for his sweaty, shuffling appearance, so Revie, perhaps, was disadvantaged by his lugubrious demeanour, by having, as Arthur Hopcraft memorably put it, 'an outdoors face as though he lives permanently in a keen wind'. Listen to the words, though, and there was a sincerity and intelligence to Revie, who raised numerous points that Clough, for all his glib plausibility, wasn't able to answer.

Clough began by expressing his regret and sadness for what happened, but things soon moved from the orthodox platitudes as Mitchell asked when Clough had realised it wasn't going to work out – astutely hinting that Clough might have foreseen his dismissal several days in advance. 'Oh! I didn't realise it at all,' Clough insisted. 'I was always convinced, right up to tonight, that it was going to work out, that it was inevitable. To replace the best manager on record in the Football League, then obviously Leeds had to get somebody that was, you know, slightly special. I don't want to be blasé, conceited, but I'm not sure who they could have got to improve on Don's record.'

Immediately, even before he was asked, Clough turned the conversation to his relationship with Revie, an indication both that part of his motivation for taking the job was to surpass him and also how he had found Revie's influence at every turn.

'You were the best man for the job, you thought?' Mitchell asked.

'I believed I was, and obviously the Leeds board did,' Clough replied.

'Well, why didn't it work out? What was the single thing that went wrong?'

'Results! In seven weeks there is not a lot of time to become established when you have taken over the job of a man who has been there ten, fifteen years and he has been regarded as the King Pin, the father figure, as the man that has made everything tick. It is impossible, utterly impossible to replace that type of thing. If the results had gone a bit better then obviously it would have been easier. But due to circumstances, due to the fact there were inherited suspensions and little Billy was sent off and banned for a long time, and Paul Madeley's injury and that type of thing, the results were not as good as they should have been.'

That assessment is hard to dispute: replacing Revie was always going to be a hugely difficult task, but it was rendered more so by circumstances. Events, as Harold Macmillan noted, are the bane of any leader with a plan, but Revie, while acknowledging how tough his successor was always going to find it, was not inclined to be sympathetic. 'I basically think that they [the present squad] are good enough to win a trophy this season,' he said. 'Last season we had an awful lot of injuries and suspensions and we played without four, five or six players right from the first match. I knew the players. I know how to handle them and I juggled them about, but he didn't have the time to do that. But the players are there and they are dedicated professionals and I had no trouble with them for thirteen-and-a-half years.'

'In saying that the team was good enough,' Mitchell said, 'you are making a criticism of Brian Clough. Do you think Brian Clough was the man for the job?'

Revie was hesitant. 'My personal opinion I stated at the time before Brian took the job,' he said. 'I won't call him Clough because I would not take him down like that, because I think it is a sad night for anybody to get the sack as a manager in any football job – in any job. I openly stated, before anybody took the job, when I took the England job, that I thought Johnny Giles was the man for the job. Only because he knew our system, he knew how I worked, he knew how the staff worked and he knew how the players reacted to things. He knew everything. He travelled all over Europe with us. He played in matches. A great player, a great thinker on the game and I recommended him to Leeds because . . .'

Mitchell, to Revie's apparent dismay, interpreted that as a suggestion Clough wasn't the right man to carry on the legacy. Clough's response was enigmatic to the point of incoherence and, as he rocked back, cheeks red, quiff askew, eyes slightly glassy, it's hard not to wonder how much he may have had to drink before the programme. 'That's a very difficult question,' he said. 'It's like saying if religion goes out of our way of life, who takes over from who?'

Mitchell decided a gloss was necessary. 'You're saying your style is very different from his style,' he said. 'When the players are used to Don Revie's style it might have been upsetting.'

'My style's not different at all, in the sense that I wanted success and I believed I could deliver it,' Clough said. 'My methods are ninety-nine per cent, or ninety per cent, the same as Mr Revie's. Management is ninety per cent the same right throughout the country, irrespective of who the manager is. It is the extra ten per cent that's the special bit.'

'Over the years,' Mitchell said, 'Leeds United have almost been like a family – like sons of Don Revie. Now didn't you go in and upset them, unsettle them by going in for a big buying policy?'

Clough, though, denied that had been his policy, saying McKenzie was back-up for Eddie Gray, that O'Hare was cover for Mick Jones, whom he had been led to believe would be out till at least February. 'So the buying,' he explained, 'was not buying in a sense.'

'You don't think it was unsettling for the players?'

'Oh, it could have been slightly upsetting because they'd been there so long, and one or two of them are getting on for thirty-two, thirty-three, possibly even thirty-four.'

Mitchell turned to Revie. 'Would you have gone in for this kind of buying, or would you have worked in more cautiously?' he asked.

'Well, first of all let me answer Brian's question. Now about them getting old, and about injuries and one thing and another: as I said already, we had this all last season. But what you must remember is this, that team was written off by the press and television in 1970 when we missed three

331

tournaments, in '71, in '72 and in '73, when we lost against Sunderland and then AC Milan, they all said, that's it, they're finished; they are too old and this, that and the other. As last season, with all these injuries and all these suspensions to Allan Clarke and Norman Hunter and all these people, we only lost four matches out of forty-two and won the championship and they went twenty-nine matches at the beginning of the season without defeat.'

Mitchell, sensing blood, sought clarification. 'Are you saying that Brian's buying was not necessary?' he asked.

Revie, though was determined to be diplomatic. 'No, no Austin, please, please give me a chance . . .'

Clough, seeing an opportunity, jumped in. 'That was incredible, what the man is saying . . .' but Mitchell insisted Revie be allowed to finish, with the result that Clough looked a little shrill, opportunistic.

'I would have given them three months to settle down and play as they are capable of playing,' Revie said.

By that stage the two were turned to face each other, and Mitchell became almost a spare part.

'Don, even with Billy's eight-match suspension?' asked Clough.

'Yes, I would have had Terry Yorath, Mick Bates, I'd have had Joe Jordan, I'd have had Frankie Gray. You had four world-class players there in the making. Well, I juggled about last year, Frankie Gray, whether you think Frankie's a good player or not . . .'

'Well, world-class, you said.'

'Well, I think world-class if he'd got the chance. Brian, I think he could be world-class. And I think I'd play Terry Yorath up front, this is what I'm saying. You didn't get the chance to see them. I knew them. I played Terry Yorath up front alongside Joe Jordan. I played Terry Yorath midfield. I played him at full-back, I played him at sweeper. I played Mick Bates up front. I played Frankie Gray up front and inside-left. Now these players I thought should have had a chance.'

'Don, Don. Why didn't they get a chance? Terry had a tummy bug, enteritis, I think they call it, and he was out, he was in bed, for ten days.'

'Yes, but you still had Joe Jordan and Mick Bates and Frankie Gray you didn't play at all, Brian. Now I feel that the unsettling part came when you didn't give these lads a chance and quite rightly, the manager has got to stand or fall by his decisions, every time. When he is going to buy, or when he is going to make a team selection or what he is going to have, he has got to stand or fall by what he says and what he does. And Brian decided to go in the market and whether it was unsettling to the players I don't know.'

Which raised the question, asked by Mitchell, of whether the players had been giving their all. 'The team don't dictate that much,' Clough said. 'The team can have a vote of confidence or that type of thing. The teams are the be all and end all regarding results on the field. But regarding the confidence – it is essential to have the confidence – the men who make the decisions are directors in football.'

'But are you sure that the team was playing its best for you?' Mitchell repeated; his role in making the viewing compelling should not be underestimated.

'Oh, that is absolutely certain,' said Clough.

'With results like that?'

'Of course they were playing their best; they could not do anything else. It was second nature to them.'

Revie interjected, he and Clough for once on the same side in defending the honour of the players. 'Let me ask you a question,' Revie said to Mitchell. 'How long have you lived in Leeds?' He'd been there five years, Mitchell said, and he'd never seen Leeds start a season as badly.

'But have you ever seen the Leeds United team not trying?' Revie went on. 'They might have sad times and they might miss open goals, but never ever accuse or insinuate that a Leeds United side never tries. They might have a bad game, they might miss open goals, they might do bad things, but never not try.'

Mitchell, though, was too good an interviewer to allow a blanket defence of the players' professionalism to deflect from the rumours that it was the players who had deposed Clough. 'There have been claims that there was in fact a vote of confidence, or something amounting to that, passed by the players,' he said. 'Is that correct?'

'It is correct,' Clough said.

'How did you react to that?'

'Oh, I wanted to be sick,' said Clough. 'If you had a vote of no confidence

333

with the people you work with I would assume you would react exactly the same. I felt sick.'

'What was the main reason for that, do you think?'

'I don't know what the main reason was. I think the fact that I didn't have time to get to know them, and this type of thing. I do believe honestly that whoever had walked in would have had the same thing, plus the fact that all the other incidentals went against us – i.e. results and that type of thing.'

Mitchell asked Revie what he thought about the vote. 'I honestly feel,' he said, 'knowing Leeds players as long as I have known them, they must have had a very good reason to do that. With respect to Brian I must say what I feel about Leeds United players. They must have had a very good reason to do that. Why I don't know . . .'

'Whatever the reasons, do you condone players acting in that fashion? Does it make a manager's job impossible?' Mitchell asked.

'No, I do not condone players doing that in any club, because I think it is totally wrong and I think directors are wrong to listen to it. But I can't understand why, if Leeds United players voted a no confidence vote in you Brian . . .'

'Not exactly a vote, but the feeling was there, yes,' Clough said. 'No, vote is a very strong word, but the feeling was definitely there.'

But whose fault was that? As Mitchell pointed out, Clough, by attacking Revie so persistently before he joined Leeds, and then again in an interview on Yorkshire Television after taking over, had effectively created a climate of confrontation. 'Now if you were asking me now did I make mistakes, the answer is yes,' Clough admitted. 'I'm not infallible. I definitely made mistakes. Having said that, when you say that I criticised Don Revie about unsigned contracts, I stated the fact that there were, when I took over, eleven contracts not signed. Now, if it was Don's fault, if it was the chairman's fault, if it was the players' fault – that is immaterial for this particular argument. There were eleven contracts not signed. That is fact.'

Revie, it turned out, had been furious about Clough's claims. 'I phoned you up that night,' he said to Mitchell, 'and asked you if I could face Brian the following night and I got no reply. Talking about the eleven contracts that were not signed, all the contracts were basically agreed in the minutes for the directors for what each player was going to get.

Brian is possibly right that the contracts were not signed; not by eleven – I would say by five or six. All these things were agreed in the minutes. All the players have signed blank contracts for me in thirteen-and-a-half years and I have never had one scrap of trouble ... Now on that same programme Brian said there was no warmth in the club. Now that really shook me.'

'Did I say no warmth?' Clough asked.

'You said no warmth in Leeds United. Now that was the closest ... relationship between players and managers and staff [anybody] has ever had.'

Clough was evidently shaken by Revie's anger, and backtracked unconvincingly. 'Did I say no warmth between me and them – or did I say no warmth ...'

'No, you said no warmth in the club, Brian.'

'I don't remember. I did say that obviously the warmth you generated between you and the players ... that can't be taken away?'

'Never!'

Given they seemed to agree on so many fundamentals, Mitchell asked, how did the antipathy between them develop? 'When I was manager of Derby County,' Clough said, 'I was in direct conflict with Don Revie and his Leeds side. Naturally I didn't get on with him because invariably they were above us. That's the flippant answer. I believe in a different concept of football to Don. I believe that it can be played slightly different to the way Don plays it and get the same results. Now that might be aiming for Utopia and it might mean me being a little bit stupid, but that is the way I am. I am a little bit stupid regarding this type of thing. I am a little bit of an idealist. I do believe in fairies and that is my outlook. Now Don's is slightly different and his record proves over results that perhaps he is right. But having said that I want to be like me and obviously he wants to be like him.'

'I think that – truthfully – Brian is a fool to himself,' said Revie. 'I honestly feel that he's criticised Matt Busby, Bertie Mee, me personally, Norman Hunter, Peter Lorimer, Billy Bremner, Peter Storey, he's criticised so many people in the game, whose record stand to be seen. This is his style, and if he wants to do it in that style, fair enough, but I think that is totally, totally wrong for the game of professional football. He says about honesty and things like this, but when you talk about honesty, if honesty's going to destroy the game, then you're in all kinds of trouble.'

'Aaaah,' Clough interjected, sarcastic, knowing. The camera cut to him and, frankly, as he rocked backwards in his chair, he looked drunk. Producers on the show confirmed he had been drinking champagne most of the afternoon.

'I think you're doing the game a great disservice,' Revie went on.

Mitchell asked Clough if he were 'too ready to shoot your mouth off', but before he could answer, Revie insisted on finishing his point.

'You talk about winning the championship better or differently,' he said, his right arm gesturing towards Clough, who was turned to his left, staring at him intently. What followed could have been scripted by Strindberg; it was perhaps the most mesmerising conversation about football ever recorded on British television, a double-header fascinating both in its surface detail and for the hostility that flickered constantly beneath.

'Our record,' Revie said, 'is there to be seen for eleven years. The first four or five years, I've always said, we played for results. The last four or five years, we've been the most entertaining side by crowd entertainment. Topping charts in the national newspapers and on television.'

'Also Don,' said Clough, 'the disciplinary charts.'

'The disciplinary charts?'

'You topped that.'

'We've topped that once.'

'You topped it for the last two or three years.'

'No, no, no, that's not true. It wasn't one hundred per cent right, I would agree. It wasn't one hundred per cent right, discipline on the field. But last year we straightened it out.'

'Well it was, it was. You were the top.'

'You see, Brian, you talked about coming to take the Leeds job, yet you had all these things and all these worries about stepping into my shoes and one thing and another.'

'Which I had.'

'Yes, you had. But why, why did you come from Brighton to Leeds to take over when you criticised us so much, and said we should be in the Second Division, and that we should do this and we should do that? Why did you take the job?'

'Because I thought it was the best job in the country.'

'Of course it was the best job in the country.'

'I was taking over the League champions.'

'Yes, you took over the League champions. You took over the best bunch of players you've ever seen.'

'I didn't know the players, Don. I didn't know them intimately like you. But I knew you were the League champions and I was taking over the League champions. I wanted to have a crack at the European Cup this year. I think it was near and dear to your heart also.'

Revie nodded in agreement.

'I wanted to win it, and I wanted to do something you hadn't done. Now when I said that – I think I said it to Trevor Cherry – he said, "What can you do that the Boss hasn't done?" You were the Boss; he was referring to you. And I said, I want to win the League, but I want to win it better. There was no other reply to that question, because you had won the league.'

'Yes, but there is no way to win it better.'

'Why not? It was the only hope I'd got.'

'We only lost four matches.'

'Well. I could only lose three.'

'No, no, no.'

'I couldn't give any other answer, and I wanted to win the European Cup. I believe that just a fraction, just a fraction, Don – I don't know this because I haven't spoken to you – but I believe it was just a fraction whether you took the England job, or had another shot at the European Cup.'

'That is totally true. Because I was so involved with the players and everybody at Elland Road.'

'Good lad! Now I wanted to do that and I wanted to do it better than you. You can understand that, can't you?'

'Yes, and I think if you'd have said that to our players then you'd have got the message across.'

'I couldn't say that to "our players" as you say, I couldn't say that to our players just as a bald statement. You see when I went in there, there was friction, there was unhappiness because you had left unsigned contracts.'

'No, no. When you walked in did you have a meeting the first day with them—?'

'No.'

'Why?'

'Because I didn't think it was necessary to have a meeting the very first day.'

'So you were taking over as manager of a new club and you did not call your players and your coaching staff and the office staff together. You did not introduce yourself and meet them, tell them exactly what you felt and what you wanted to try and do.'

'Don, the first day I walked in I'd come back from holiday and I did two hours training with them.'

'Irrespective of what you did, I feel—'

'I was out on the field with them.'

'Right. You went out on the field. My immediate reaction to any job – the same with the Football Association – I got seventy people together and we had a cocktail party and I introduced myself . . .'

'That is your way . . .'

'Yes, but I talked about Ramsey's record. I said how great Ramsey was, with his record as a professional man. I never got close to Ramsey. He was a cold man, but as a professional man . . .'

'I think you are.'

'A cold man? Don't ask our players that or they'll laugh their socks off.'

'That's opinion.'

'That's my opinion. But Alf Ramsey, I thought he did a good job, and I thought it was important to me to introduce myself to everybody in the Football Association offices, and I thought it was your duty to walk into Leeds United's ground with everybody saying, "Well, Brian Clough's arriving today, we'd love to meet him."'

'Yes, but you didn't have a training session.'

'No, no, no, Brian. Training sessions on your first day didn't mean anything.'

'Why?'

'How could a training session overcome not meeting everybody in the club?'

'It couldn't overcome it.'

'It would have taken you ten minutes to get everybody together as a group and say, "I'm pleased to meet you, I'm pleased to come."'

'I walked into the dressing-rooms and shook hands with Billy Bremner the very first—'

Revie interrupted again, perhaps aware he'd isolated a weakness. After all, addressing the staff on the first day would seem natural for a manager in any walk of life. Perhaps Revie didn't quite realise the full implication of what he was saying; if he did, it suggests a ruthlessness bordering on the cruel, because the impression created, after all the talk of Clough's unease at replacing such a big figure, was that he hadn't had a meeting because he was scared. As Lorimer had pointed out, taking his sons with him itself indicated Clough's insecurity.

'Now Brian,' Revie went on, 'don't hedge, why didn't you get everybody together?'

'Because I didn't think it was necessary.'

'Why?'

'Because I thought I would do it more subtly instead of having everybody bang, bang, bang. They were all on edge. I was on edge.'

'So you could have put them at ease.'

'No, hang on. Talk to them? I took their shirts off their backs when they'd finished training.'

'I used to do that, and massage them on Thursday.'

'Of course. Well that was my approach, of course.'

'But you didn't meet everybody the first day.'

'I shook hands and said hello, met them . . .'

'Everybody? Did you go to the laundry ladies and the office staff?'

'Oh, no, I'm sorry . . .'

'Did you go to the groundsmen?'

'I didn't have time to do that Don, it was the players . . .'

'You must have had time . . .'

Mitchell, at last, intervened and turned the conversation back to the board. 'I don't believe they've done Leeds United a service,' Clough said. 'I don't care whether it was me or whoever it was. I'm talking about a manager. I don't believe they've done football a service. I think they've struck a blow to send us back to the Dark Ages. I think if the Football Association who employ Mr Revie sack him if he loses his first match, they will set football back thirty years or fifty years. In turn, I believe that Leeds perhaps have done that a little bit also. Manny Cussins was under a lot of pressure; he was my chairman. If he didn't stand up to it as much as he should have done that's a matter of debate. He was under a lot of pressure and today when the final decision was made – and it was a board decision – he then made it right with me regarding a lot of things.'

Specifically, of course, Cussins made it right with Clough by arranging his pay-off, which gave Clough financial security and ensured that the weeks and months of joblessness were not as daunting as they would otherwise have been.

'What's going to happen now to Brian Clough?' Mitchell asked.

'Oh, a million things will happen to Brian Clough,' Clough said. 'I'm going to have forty-eight hours or three days or I don't know. Please don't think I'm being flippant. I've had many ambitions in life and one of the ambitions is, and I wanted this when I was manager of Leeds and manager of Derby, I wanted to coach the England Youth.' He wagged a thumb in Revie's direction. 'I just might apply for the job to this guy.'

'Well, aren't you going to be in a very difficult situation because after the argument with Derby, you left Brighton under a cloud and now this with Leeds,' Mitchell said. 'Who's going to touch you with a barge pole?'

'Well, I think many, many people will touch me with a barge pole because the whole country knows, including Leeds ... and you've heard it from Don's own mouth tonight ... I do not think six weeks is enough even to find out where the local butcher's shop is.'

The lack of coherency perhaps suggested Clough's uncertainty, his awareness that Mitchell was right, that having left three jobs in such a short space of time, other clubs would be wary.

'What happens to Leeds now?' Mitchell asked.

'Well, obviously they'll prosper,' Clough said. 'I hope they'll prosper. Despite the fact that I've only been involved with them seven weeks you've got to hope they prosper. I hope everybody in football prospers. I hope Leeds go on to win the European Cup.'

Mitchell turned to Revie and began to ask him where he thought Clough could go from there, only for Clough to interrupt, calling Mitchell 'a terrible man' for cutting him off when he was talking about the European Cup. It was, frankly, a bizarre interjection: at face value, it suggested the European Cup was so sacred – or at least that Clough's quest for it was so profoundly rooted – that it could only be discussed in reverential terms; more realistically, it probably just suggested Clough's frazzled, alcohol-fuelled state of mind.

'If Leeds United players have had a meeting with Brian and the chairman,' Revie said sadly, 'there must have been something totally wrong.'

For Leeds's first game after Clough's departure, away to Burnley, the team was picked by Lindley, Owen and Bremner, which may have been what prompted the outburst from Clough on ITV's *On the Ball* programme in which he accused Bremner of having tried to run the club. 'When Bremner called me boss,' he said, 'it meant nothing. He'd got to call me boss and believe it. What Bremner has to establish is that he is not the manager of Leeds United. I was.' Bremner said the remarks were 'ridiculous'. Leeds lost that game 2–1 but they got their season back on track the following week with successive home wins. FC Zurich were hammered 4–1 in the European Cup, and Leeds then thrashed Sheffield United 5–1. They went on to finish ninth in the table, as Dave Mackay's Derby won the title, and reached the European Cup final where they were beaten by Bayern Munich amid some highly controversial refereeing.

At that stage, with the two clubs he'd left in such acrimonious circumstances apparently in rude health, Clough was in retreat. Who, after all, would want to take a risk on somebody so volatile? The following season, Derby finished fourth and Leeds fifth, but, thereafter, the decline set in. Derby have never been so high since, while it would be another fifteen years before Leeds again experienced such success. Had Clough's goal been to destroy Leeds, he could hardly have done so more effectively. There is nothing to suggest that was his aim, but, in later years, the way he reiterated the fact that he had won two European Cups and Leeds none suggested he enjoyed it.

IV

1975–1982

et in arcadia ego

(title of two paintings by Nicolas Poussin)

Reborn Again

Clough had his money and with it a sense of security, but the experience of Leeds had chastened him. He had been at the top, won a league title and reached a European Cup semi-final, and he had through his own recklessness thrown it away. He had lingered, hoping for a reprieve that Derby had denied him. Perhaps even then he had assumed greatness was his for the taking, but what happened at Leeds had shown how elusive glory could be. For the first time in his life since his eleven-plus he had failed and, while circumstances had been difficult, at least some of the responsibility was his. When he arrived at Nottingham Forest in 1975, he was somebody who had already seen two great chances of footballing success disappear, and, perhaps for the first time in his managerial career, he was truly aware how few chances a man gets. After his injury, for all the work he had put in, there was no way back as a player; after a similarly traumatic experience at Leeds, management gave him another chance. Money was one thing, but what Clough really wanted was glory.

Having finalised his settlement at Leeds, Clough returned to Derby, changed his ex-directory number and became a semi-recluse, spending most of his time indoors. Taylor believed that the only football he saw between his departure from Leeds and his appointment at Forest was Stoke City's goalless draw away to Ajax in the Uefa Cup. Then, fourteen months after he'd first tried to get him, Stuart Dryden was delegated by the Forest board to approach him again. This time, Clough was ready, and after a perfunctory interview with senior members of the Forest board, he was appointed on 6 January 1975. 'There was a sense of shock when he arrived,' remembered the journalist Richard Williams, a Forest fan who grew up in Nottingham, 'because he was so closely associated with Derby and because it was so out of character for Forest, which was essentially run like a golf club at the time, to go for such a high-profile and controversial character. There was a feeling in football he was damaged goods, but for Forest there was a sense of exhilaration that they were trying something different.'

The glory after which Clough lusted seemed an awfully long way away. Forest were thirteenth in Division Two, crowds had fallen to 12,000, and a general sense of disillusionment hung over the City Ground. Johnny Carey's 'fizz-it-about' side had finished as runners-up in 1967, but after Carey's departure in 1968, Forest went through five managers in the seven years before Clough's appointment. It seems unthinkable now, but at the time the *Evening Post* seemed to regard County as the bigger side: their match reports were longer, and tended to be positioned higher up the page. 'They were probably of equal standing,' said Steve Hodge, who would soon join Forest as a youth player, but who at the time went to home games with his father and grandfather. 'We knew Clough had done well at Derby County, and we thought things would improve with him in charge, but I don't think anybody – not even him – really imagined how well it would go.'

A cartoon in the *Express* showed Clough walking down the Trent to take over; in fact he arrived in a manner less dramatic but almost as significant: in the Mercedes he'd been given by Leeds. Perhaps it seemed incongruous at an impoverished club, but it demonstrated Clough was somebody of substance, reminded players and fans that he was somebody who had known success and showed the directors that he was at least their financial equal – and therefore not somebody who could be browbeaten with financial threats. 'I've left the human race,' he said, 'and rejoined the rat race. Hope is all I can offer.'

As at Derby, Clough's presence alone was enough to energise the fans, and £4,000 of season tickets were sold in the first twelve days after his appointment. Others, though, responded less positively to Clough's reputation. The outgoing manager, Allan Brown (not the Alan Brown who had been Clough's manager at Sunderland) was openly sceptical. 'The board want Clough,' he said. 'Good luck to them.' Four directors threatened to resign when Clough's name was first suggested before being talked round, and even the chairman, Jim Willmer, wasn't convinced, troubled both by the experience of various Derby chairmen and by the stories about Clough's temper. His unease is clear from the photograph in the *Nottingham Evening Post* that showed him greeting Clough with a handshake and an apparently terrified grin. 'He's an energetic young man with an exciting background,' Willmer said, which as welcomes go sounds distinctly equivocal. Clough's arrival, though, was not the main story on the front page: that, in a worrying indication of the pressures facing football, told of how the local magistrate's court had met on a Saturday for the first time two days earlier to deal with outbreaks of hooliganism during Forest's 1–1 draw in the FA Cup third round against Tottenham Hotspur.

It wasn't just the pay-off from Leeds that gave Clough freedom. The structure of Nottingham Forest meant it was far easier for him to become the dominant figure and impose his will than it had been in any of his previous jobs. Forest were not a limited company, but had members, just over 200 of them, who paid a nominal sum and elected a committee to run the business side of things. When Clough arrived, the key personality was Brian Appleby, a QC, whom Clough predictably took against. His contemptuous attitude towards the committee was obvious from his report to the chairman in 1977, which consisted simply of two photographs: the League Cup and the League Championship trophy.

Although Clough relished the independence, he protested it was unfair that the committee enjoyed their privileges when they contributed nothing to the club beyond their membership fee. The structure also meant that the financial well-being of the club was almost entirely dependent on results and the number of fans who could be drawn through the turnstiles; benefactors could not be attracted by the possibility of wielding power on the board. Even after the club's constitution was amended following the second European Cup success in an attempt to provide a more streamlined and modern structure, the directors and shareholders, of whom there were 209, owned a single share each.

For a club that prided itself on its gentlemanliness, Clough was a change of pace. Forest had once banned all advertising at the ground; it was a club Walter Winterbottom had said everybody wanted to manage. Willmer was unsure whether Clough really fitted. 'We don't want success at any price,' he told his successor, Brian Appleby. 'Set him on and you'll live to regret it.'

Clough himself was unsparing in his analysis of Forest's recent past. He noted the speed at which Carey's side had been sold off – a process he had hastened by signing Terry Hennessey and trying to buy Ian Storey-Moore and Henry Newton – and the lack of return on investment since: '£1 million of failure', as he summed it up. 'There is only one thing in the club's favour, now,' he went on. 'And that's me.' Chastened he may have been after the Leeds experience, but humble he was not. Nor had he lost his gift for publicity, selling a ghosted article to a newspaper on the day of his appointment and using the money to buy a new cooker for the club. 'The old one was knackered,' he said, before making a predictable joke about picking it for the first team.

As ever, Clough was exaggerating. Under Brown, Forest had narrowly missed out on promotion the previous season and they'd been 3–1 up after seventy minutes of an FA Cup quarter-final replay away to Newcastle when home fans rioted, Newcastle winning the rearranged game 1–0. The squad included at least some of the raw material Clough would mould to greatness: Viv Anderson, Ian Bowyer, Tony Woodcock, Martin O'Neill and John Robertson, even if those last two were on the transfer list. 'Everything boils down to the players,' Brown said. 'They are the people who make a manager a success or not. A lot of the problems came from the Newcastle Cup-ties. We did not get the breaks and I'm sure that cost us promotion last season. The pressure was only felt after one or two bad results, but I was still sure I could have brought success.'

Appleby took over as chairman from Willmer and appointed Stuart Dryden as his deputy, allowing him to deal with Clough so he himself could retain a plausible deniability. He may have been suspicious of Clough, and probably didn't like him, but he recognised that Clough 'gave a transfusion of life to a dying club'.

Clough's first task was to assemble his back-room staff. John McSeveney and Bill Anderson went by the end of January as Clough sought to bring in his own people. With Taylor committed to Brighton, he turned again to Jimmy Gordon. After leaving Leeds, Gordon had lived on the dole for two months before joining Rolls-Royce in Derby. Mike Keeling, the director who'd quit the Derby board in protest at Clough's departure, invited him to a post-Christmas party. It was there that Clough met Gordon and asked if he'd like to get back into football. Gordon phoned him the next day to accept the offer. 'I wondered about the quality of the team when I joined,' he said. 'There were some very ordinary players.'

Clough's first game was the FA Cup third-round replay away at Tottenham. 'The lads all know that everybody is starting from scratch with everything to prove,' said Barry Butlin, who had joined Forest from Luton. 'Brian Clough has the ability to make an average player good and a good player great.'

Clough soon began imposing himself. Having been given a day off the day after Clough's appointment, the players stayed at Bisham Abbey prior to the game. 'We're all having lunch and then he comes over,' Woodcock recalled. '"Young man," he says. "Young man, here's my room key. In front of the door there's a pair of shoes. Give 'em a good polish up because I want to look my best for the game tomorrow."

'Now, I'm twenty years old. Should I stand up for myself? "I'm having my lunch, boss," I said, but I'd already finished.

'"I might be fucking daft, young man," he said, "but I'm not blind."

'So I looked down the table at all the seasoned pros for guidance and nothing came back. Then, finally, one fella called George Lyall looked back at me and nodded, as if I should go. So off I went.' When Woodcock got back, Jimmy Gordon made a point of telling him that Clough had made Gordon McQueen do the same at Leeds. That was typical of how they operated: Clough abrasive, Gordon conciliatory.

On the pitch, Clough's impact was immediate, Forest taking the lead through Neil Martin then holding out with a combination of courage and good fortune. Clough, though, was realistic. 'It would be foolish to say we are going places just yet,' he said. 'There are a lot of things to work on and my main aim is to get us playing to a pattern and a rhythm.'

His first league game, away to Fulham, produced a similar result, Butlin getting the only goal after Martin had seized on a weak throw-out from the goalkeeper Peter Mellor. 'I was pleased,' Clough said, 'not so much because of the win but from the signs we were playing to a pattern.' It was still early, though, for such a positive interpretation and reality began to encroach in Clough's first home game as manager, against Leyton Orient. Paul Richardson scored twice in the last five minutes to salvage a 2–2 draw but, as the *Post* noted, it had been 'a fortunate point'. Clough admitted the side was even worse than he'd expected and later said he wondered if he'd 'dropped a bollock' – although, of course, it was in his interests to exaggerate how bad things had been when he took over.

Richardson played on the left side of midfield and, when he was ruled out for the FA Cup fourth-round tie against Fulham, Clough turned to

John Robertson. 'Some of our players couldn't play, some couldn't kick the ball from A to B and several couldn't head it to save their lives,' said Clough. And yet it was Robertson who was on the transfer list. Clough admitted he could understand why. 'He was fat, often unshaven, dressed like a tramp, and smoked one fag after another,' he wrote in his autobiography. 'He was a late-nighter and used to eat all the wrong things.' Something, though, persuaded Clough to persevere with him.

Forest drew 0–0 at Craven Cottage, but Clough said he was 'delighted with the display', while John Lawson wrote in the *Post* that 'the Reds produced some of the best football seen from them this season'. A failure to take chances, though, was a recurring theme and Forest lost 2–0 at Oldham the following Saturday despite dominating for long periods. Twice more Forest drew with Fulham, before they finally went down 2–1 in a third replay, ending a thirteen-year unbeaten home record in the FA Cup. 'In a way,' Clough said, 'I'm glad we are out. Now we can get down to some hard work in the league.'

It was much needed, the other league game Forest managed to fit in between their Cup marathon ending in a 3–2 defeat to Bolton at the City Ground. 'A team frittering away home points with Forest's regularity,' Lawson wrote ominously, 'must ask questions about their ability to float on top of the relegation zone.'

Clough, in a slightly odd move, went back to Derby and addressed members of the Protest Movement, astonishingly still going well over a year after he'd left Derby, apparently trying to encourage them to come and support Forest, something that would at any time have required a remarkable leap of faith, and a ranking of personal-over-club loyalty, but particularly when Derby were on their way to clinching the title under Dave Mackay. When Forest then drew 1–1 at York, relegation seemed a serious threat, and so Clough did what he usually did when under pressure – he bought three players.

First came Bert Bowery, a nineteen-year-old forward signed for a nominal fee from Worksop Town, and then came two more predictable names as John O'Hare and John McGovern were bought from Leeds for the bargain price of £70,000 – around half what Leeds had paid Derby for them. 'There is no deal I could possibly have done,' Clough said, 'which would have given Forest better value or me more pleasure. They have skill and character and as far as Forest are concerned the price we paid was robbery. I've bought them to teach the others how to play.'

O'Hare had been expecting the call. He took a fifty per cent pay cut and had to sell his house to finance the move, but was glad of the escape from Leeds, where he had only played seven league games. He too found Clough changed. 'To the Forest lads,' he told Murphy, 'he was brash enough, but we'd known him when he'd been really full of himself. He wasn't breezing around so much, picking on anyone for the hell of it. He was more subdued. I think it took him some time to get his confidence back after Leeds.'

Anderson, certainly, didn't see much reserve in Clough. 'I sat on the bench sometimes and he'd be verbally abusing certain players, absolutely hammering them for everything. We'd walk in at half-time and I'd think, "Oooh dear, this could be nasty." We'd get into the dressing-room and he'd walk up to his victim and say, "Well done, lad. Keep it going!"

'I'd be sitting there thinking, "What? You've been calling him a shithouse for forty-five minutes."

'He'd be there giving it, "You keep that going, son. You'll do for me" and the fella would go out for the second half on cloud nine.'

Woodcock similarly remembered not just how Clough could slaughter a player, but how inspiring he could be. 'If he said, "Young man, you are a credit to the game," you knew you were all right,' he said. 'That was a big thing for me. Not a credit to the club, not a credit to him: a credit to the game. I'd walk out swelling with pride after that.'

McGovern made his debut in a 0–0 home draw with Cardiff. He too noted that Clough 'had lost some of that fantastic energy', but there were still signs that, as in the early days at Brighton, he might be falling into the trap of intimidating rather than inspiring his players. 'Pretty soon they were terrified of Clough,' Gordon said. 'I acted as the go-between, trying to calm some of their shattered nerves.'

Forest drew at Oxford and lost 3–2 to Aston Villa, despite O'Hare scoring on his home debut. As the threat of relegation increased, self-doubt began to gnaw at Clough, something apparent from the justificatory tone of an interview he gave the *Evening Post* published the morning of an away game at Sunderland. 'The problems,' he explained, 'began at this club long before I arrived. There is no way that my coming here could have had an adverse effect on the performance of players. In fact, I'm convinced results would have been a lot worse than they have been. Things were in such a state that I would not have banked on the side taking points at places like York and Oxford.'

Clough showed a clear awareness of the pattern – upsurge, slump, steady progress – that had been established at Hartlepools, Derby and Brighton, although the validity of his explanation for that pattern is debatable. 'When I arrived I expected to be able to lift the players initially,' he said. 'And that happened with the wins at Tottenham and Fulham. But since then the players have dropped down to their own level, and it is a case of trying to lift them again. I don't think there is any question of the players being frightened of me. The problems that exist at this club have got a deep root and it will take time to sort them out. The situation we are now in did not develop from when I took over. It goes back to the first day of the season when Forest drew 0–0 with Bristol City.'

True as all that might have been, though, a goalless draw at Roker Park meant Forest had won just one of nine league games under Clough. It wasn't just results that were frustrating him; his restructuring of the squad was proving difficult. Ron Webster decided against a £30,000 move from Derby, while attempts to send Martin O'Neill and Tommy Jackson on loan to Lincoln and Preston broke down.

Clough saw signs of that elusive 'pattern' of play – the domination of midfield followed by rhythmical passing to which McGovern was essential – in a 1–0 home defeat to Manchester United, and a seventy-eighth-minute equaliser from Butlin earned a 2–2 draw against Notts County. It was obvious, though, that significant spending was required and with that in mind the 200 or so members were called upon to raise £25,000, with fans encouraged to loan the club £50 interest free for a three-year term.

Finally, on April Fools' Day, came a first home win, ending a fifteen-match run without a victory, George Lyall scoring the only goal from the penalty spot against Sheffield Wednesday. Not that the performance was any reason for great optimism. 'Dismal show,' roared the headline in the *Nottingham Evening Post*, while Lawson wrote that 'if things don't improve at the City Ground, recent relegation fights will be recreated in twelve months' time'. The win, though, eased the immediate threat of relegation. A 'slack defensive display' led to a 4–2 defeat at Bristol Rovers, but a goalless draw at home to Southampton all but ensured survival. Forest finished sixteenth, four places – but six points – above the relegation zone. Brighton, meanwhile, finished nineteenth in the Third Division, just four points above the relegation zone.

For Clough, those first months had been largely about gathering information. Based on his observations, he gave Neil Martin, Steve Baines and Tommy Jackson free transfers in the summer. When Manchester United picked up Jackson, Forest's board publicly questioned Clough; he, though, was adamant that Jackson 'couldn't play'.

Neither, unfortunately, Clough maintained, could many of the others. 'Forest could have been relegated the season I took charge for one basic reason,' he said. 'We were crap.' He estimated it would take £500,000 to get them promoted, but by the end of the season the appeal to members had raised just £3,000, with only twenty-one of the 200 plus contributing anything; it wasn't the last time Clough would be frustrated by the apparent apathy of the Nottingham public. Later that summer, Forest announced a loss of £77,618, something Willmer blamed on a lack of income from home games. His target, he said, was regular gates of over 20,000.

Forest didn't have much of a budget for transfer spending, but that didn't mean Clough couldn't bring players in. A couple of weeks after the end of the season, Clough got a phone call from the journalist Doug Weatherall to tell him that Frank Clark had been given a free transfer by Newcastle. He would turn thirty-two that September, but Weatherall was certain he had two or three seasons left in him at a high level, as were various Newcastle players who, led by Malcolm Macdonald, protested against the decision to release him. Clark was already in talks with Doncaster, managed by Clough's former Sunderland team-mate Stan Anderson. Weatherall approached Clark, told him Clough wanted a word and, the following day, he signed for Forest. 'If you ever wanted an intelligent footballer it was him,' said Anderson. 'He wasn't the fastest, but his reading of the game made him a class player. When Newcastle, for whatever reason, decided to let him go, I was straight on to him. I was prepared to give him any money he wanted, but Cloughie nipped in. Clark rang me to explain and I told him he had to go to Forest. He couldn't turn down an opportunity like that.'

Clark himself was a figure reinvigorated by the new challenge. 'That's the genius of Clough,' Appleby said. 'He rekindled their pride and their thirst for the game.' Clough had known Clark could play football; what he hadn't known was that he could also play the guitar. As well as being a very fine full-back, Clark took on the role Ernie Phythian had at Hartlepools, helping while away long coach journeys with his music. Morale desperately needed lifting. 'The playing staff at Forest is as low as it has ever been,' Clough admitted. 'I have got to stop the rot and get us back to the position the club once held.'

That meant a lot of hard work. 'People have a bit of a misconception that the players never trained,' Clark said. 'Pre-season was very hard. The first pre-season I did [at Forest] took my breath away. We'd have been away for ten weeks, came back. Not many of them had done anything in the close season, and we just ran for the first week. Ran to the point that by the end of the week we could hardly walk. It was crazy, but that's what we did. It's what everybody did. We used to go to Wollaton Park – lots of lakes and hills.

'At that time people like Alan Hill, who had to finish playing because of his shoulder, were still bloody fit. He could run for ever. He used to be up the front making sure the pace was set properly. Jimmy Gordon used to supervise it. Jimmy was a real old-style trainer. It was hard. Two sessions a day. We used to have sandwiches and a cup of tea at some catering facilities near the university there.

'Hilly would set off and we'd get warmed up properly, run for a few minutes, then he'd pick the pace up, then it would be hard then we'd jog. It was interval training but we didn't call it that. It was hard but it was good. Then a bit of ball work in the afternoons. That was certainly the first week. We were glad of the weekend off because by then we could hardly walk, even those who had done a bit over the summer.'

Three players – Robertson, Bowyer and O'Neill – were so doubtful about the club's position that they had not re-signed their contracts by the time the team left for its pre-season tour of West Germany and were left behind.

The tour itself went relatively well, yielding two wins and a draw before a 9–0 demolition of the amateurs of Ingolstadt. Clough, though, seemed in oddly gloomy mood. 'I am no miracle worker and people were mistaken if they thought I could come here and bring about an improvement overnight,' he said in the *Evening Post*'s pre-season supplement. 'I suppose that when we beat Tottenham in the Cup in my first game and then went to Fulham and got another victory, supporters were looking ahead to better things. But after the initial reaction to my arrival the players found their true level again.' The irony, of course, is that several of those players would be European champions four years later.

Perhaps he was seeking to provoke a reaction, perhaps he genuinely believed he was working with inferior players, but that wasn't a one-off bout of pessimism. 'The last thing I want to be guilty of is kidding the people of Nottingham into thinking we have a chance of bringing First Division football to this city this coming season,' he said the Saturday before the season started. 'If I thought that I would be the first to stand on the Council House roof and let everyone hear. But the only promise I can give at this stage is that I, and everyone else connected with the club, will give everything in the hope of laying foundations for a future promotion effort.'

The season began well enough, with a 2–0 home win over Plymouth. 'Forest leave judges divided', said the headline in the *Evening Post*, but a 7–2 aggregate victory over Rotherham in the League Cup and a 1–1 draw at Portsmouth must have begun to sway the doubters. Then, in mid-August, came another signing. Clough had been interested in the winger Terry Curran – a quick, cultured player – the previous season, but had been put off by Doncaster's £140,000 asking price. He knew, though, that Curran's contract would expire at the end of the season, so decided to wait and pick him up in the summer, telling Curran's brother, Alex, of his plan so he could warn Curran not to sign a new contract.

When Stan Anderson, already aggrieved at having lost Clark to Forest, discovered Curran was refusing to sign, he rang Clough to protest that he'd tapped him up. Clough said that he hadn't spoken to Curran – which was technically true – but was reluctant to sign him immediately, worried about the fuss it would cause. Doncaster, though, stopped Curran's summer wages and, with nothing to live on, Curran asked Clough to make his move. Clough instead had Maurice Edwards, who had scouted for him at Derby, pay Curran for seven weeks, reimbursing him through fabricated expenses claims. For all his later claims of financial probity, he was happy enough to bend the law when the cause seemed justified. Clough eventually picked

355

up Curran for £50,000 plus the goalkeeper Dennis Peacock and the forward Ian Miller.

Still, the squad wasn't good enough to sustain a run of form and Forest lost to Notts County, Les Bradd scoring an eighty-ninth-minute winner. 'I am now getting together a side that stands a chance in the Second Division,' Clough insisted. They drew 0–0 against Chelsea, beat Plymouth in the League Cup, with a late goal from Bowyer, then lost 2–1 at home to Hull City. 'We were that far . . .' Clough said, holding thumb and forefinger close together, 'from a really big breakthrough . . . At one time we looked like the best side in the Second Division, but it all went wrong. Basically it was because the defence, which has played so well in the previous games, stopped doing their job and conceded two goals they should never have conceded.'

With Birmingham again suggesting they had an interest in Clough, Forest went to Oxford and recorded their first away win since January, despite Bowyer having to play much of the second half in goal after John Middleton had been stretchered off. But Forest still lacked consistency and the general exasperation they and their fans felt was evident in John Lawson's match report after a 2–1 home defeat to Charlton. 'Their failure to make a tangible impression led to frustration and the outcome was a performance that eventually lacked ideas and, at times, motivation,' he wrote.

Two Middleton errors saw Forest lose 2–1 at home to Bolton, although even the Bolton assistant coach, George Mulhall, a former team-mate of Clough's at Sunderland, admitted Forest could have been 4–0 up by half-time. Clough hit out at fans who had taken to criticising McGovern, whose qualities remained more visible to his manager than to spectators. 'I'd rather have my problems than Bolton's,' he insisted.

But then Forest lost 4–2 at Bristol Rovers, went out of the League Cup at Manchester City and drew at home to Fulham; every pace forward seemed to be followed by a three-quarter pace back. Forest beat Southampton, but after successive goalless draws against Luton and Oldham, another appeal went out to fans to help raise funds for transfers. 'It's time people stopped moaning and did something more positive to help Brian Clough get together a successful team,' said Roy Truman, a miner and a life-long Forest fan.

Gradually, though, the pattern by which Clough was so obsessed began to reveal itself. McGovern and Chapman were exceptional in a 1–0 home win over Bristol City, one of the promotion favourites, and after a 3–0 win at Southampton, their manager Lawrie McMenemy said, 'Forest will certainly be up there fighting it out at the end of the season.'

They beat York 1–0 and drew 1–1 with Orient, before heading off to the Persian Gulf for four days. Forest became famous for such breaks, of which they were pioneers, and it may be that in the long term they were beneficial, but in the short term they often seemed counter-productive. Having been on such a promising run, Forest were 'colourless', Lawson said, in three successive defeats. Bert Bowery scored twice on his debut as Forest won 4–1 at Blackburn to at least take something from the Christmas programme, but their problems scoring goals were evident again as they drew 0–0 at home to Peterborough in the third round of the FA Cup. They lost the replay 1–0, despite controlling possession. 'If I'd been playing even at my age, we would still be in the Cup ...' Clough said. 'We created so many chances that it seemed a goal must come but I could not believe the way we threw goalscoring opportunities away. I could have guaranteed us still being in the Cup if I had been able to get out on the park.'

The misery continued. Forest lost 1–0 at Hull, at which Lawson decided somebody had to be blamed, and it might as well be the board. 'The time would seem overdue for the club to back their faith in manager Brian Clough, and make transfer cash available to him,' he wrote, and as so often it's hard not to wonder whether the opinion was his own, or whether Clough was directing him. After a 3–1 home defeat to Chelsea, Lawson raised the stakes and suggested relegation was a possibility.

That threat, never entirely serious, soon receded as Curran hit form, scoring in three successive games that brought five points; a triumph for Clough's man-management. 'Things did not work out for me when I first joined Forest, but since coming back into the side I'm really enjoying my football,' Curran said. 'I feel as if I have got something to prove to the boss because he said a lot of nice things about me while I was not doing well.'

Clough, while expressing reservations over the defending, said he 'saw a spark' in a 4–3 win at Oldham and after a draw at Carlisle and back-to-back wins over Fulham and Sunderland, the *Post*'s headline boldly claimed that the 'Reds [could] open next season's champagne'. Given it was still mid-March, that demonstrates how little Forest had left to play for that season, but it also suggests that either Lawson, or Clough speaking through

Lawson, felt the foundations were in place even before the arrival of Peter Taylor.

A defeat at York checked the optimism to an extent, but Forest finished the season on a run of eight straight home wins and, more importantly, made permanent the loan signing of Colin Barrett from Manchester City. He'd been recommended by Maurice Edwards after he'd been sent to watch Tommy Booth in a City reserve game, and cost only £30,000, but proved a key figure in the two seasons that followed.

Clough released eight players at the end of the season and picked up the twenty-one-year-old defender Steve Wignall on loan from Doncaster. He signed the right-sided midfielder Sean Haslegrave from Stoke for £35,000 – suggesting he was considering moving Curran to centre-forward – and made an abortive attempt to sign the Newcastle centre-back Pat Howard. The man Clough really wanted, though, was Taylor, and after Brighton had finished a place off promotion, he pounced.

Taylor had gone to see Maurice Edwards at his post office to collect winnings from some bets he'd put on for him, and had seemed in low spirits, despite having finished fourth. Taylor said that he felt he couldn't really rely on any of the non-playing staff, and asked Edwards again to be his assistant manager. Edwards refused, but suggested Clough would probably welcome Taylor back. Taylor replied that he would willingly link up with Clough again, but that he was unwilling to make the first move. Edwards let Clough know.

A couple of days later, Clough called Dryden and asked him to meet him for a drink at Widmerpool Cricket Club, where Clough had been playing in a testimonial match. Duncan McKenzie was also playing, and Dryden wondered whether Clough may be trying to sign him. As they sat outside the pavilion, Clough, still wearing his whites, mentioned almost casually that he was going to Cala Millor to 'fetch Taylor'. Three days later, Clough phoned from Mallorca with the news that he'd been successful, but asked Dryden to be discreet as Taylor felt he had let down Bamber and wanted to explain personally his reasons for leaving. He may have felt a personal responsibility to the Brighton chairman, but Taylor was also well aware that his future lay with Clough, even if they had barely spoken for two years. 'We both knew we were banging our heads against a brick wall on our own,' he said. 'Together we could do any job. There was no point delaying.'

Taylor's arrival was the spark that ignited Forest. Almost immediately, he began predicting great things for Forest. Clough asked him to ease up, saying that by creating unrealistic expectations, he was putting a noose around both their necks. Taylor, though, was unrepentant. 'If I'd toned it down,' he said. 'I don't think either of us would have been so successful. Predicting was part of it. Infecting people with my optimism so that they believed they could conquer the world.' When he arrived, Appleby asked him if he thought promotion within three years was a realisable goal; within three years they'd won the European Cup.

Clough told him to go through the squad and assess it, binning anybody he thought wasn't good enough. Taylor was ruthless. He decided John Middleton, the keeper, who was widely regarded as an England prospect, wasn't up to it – although it took a year to replace him – and that Sammy Chapman 'had shot it'. On the other hand, he liked Robertson, who had been at the club since 1970 and of whom most despaired. He may have become a regular, but even Clough warned Taylor that Robertson was a lost cause. Taylor, though, took him aside after a game on a pre-season tour of West Germany. Standing by the hotel pool, he accused him of 'living out of a frying pan' and called him a disgrace to his profession. 'You've fallen into the gutter, socially and professionally,' Taylor went on. 'You must either climb out or vanish from the game.' Robertson was left on the bench for the next game, but did well after coming on in the second half, showing that, if nothing else, he at least had the moral courage Clough and Taylor demanded. 'Brian and Pete saved my career,' Robertson said. 'I was wasting away at Forest. The life was nice and easy until Pete took me apart. After that, Brian helped me an awful lot by watching every aspect of my play and pulling me up on little things. No great mystique, just good common sense.'

Clough made him throw away a pair of suede shoes that he persisted in wearing weeks after he'd spilled cooking fat on them, and encouraged others in the dressing-room to mock Robertson's appearance, all with the aim of smartening him up, both on and off the pitch. 'I didn't give Robertson any of his extraordinary abilities to manoeuvre and deliver a ball,' Clough said. 'All I did was offer him the chance to use them.' He felt Robertson offloaded the ball too quickly, and encouraged him to consider his options. 'He had the ability to hold it, to have a look, and to dart into space if it opened up. We simply told him to use that ability, to take his time and not to rush into trouble.'

The Clough approach didn't work for everybody, though. Shortly before Taylor arrived, as Clough outlined his plans for the coming season, with stories about how he wanted to rebuild the squad flying around, O'Neill chipped in. 'So does that mean we'll still be here next season?' he asked. Clough stared at him, and a frostiness entered their relationship that never left. 'Looking back,' O'Neill told Francis, 'if there was one time in my career when I wished I'd shut my big mouth, that was it.'

O'Neill, with his university education and his ready way with words, was never likely to appeal to Clough, who demanded subservience. Clough seems to have regarded him as something of a smart Alec, and gave O'Neill even less praise than he handed out to most players. 'I believe that's where their psychology went wrong,' O'Neill said. 'If they'd given me more encouragement they could have got twenty per cent more out of me. In fact I played my best football at Norwich after leaving Forest.'

That pre-season tour of West Germany went well, four victories following an initial defeat. Forest's preparations for the new season, Clough said, were 'ideal', and they soon proved it in the Anglo-Scottish Cup, as the Texaco Cup had become known. Only the brilliance of Peter Wells, deputising for Middleton, earned a goalless draw against Notts County in Forest's opening game, but they then beat West Brom 3–2 and Bristol City 4–2 to qualify for the knockout stage.

That high-scoring pattern, at least by Clough's standards, was continued in the first game of the league season as Curran scored one and laid on the equaliser for O'Hare in a 2–2 draw at Fulham. 'There's not a more exciting sight in the country than seeing Curran pick the ball up in his own half and go past people as if they weren't there,' Clough said, but he was rather less happy with his defence. 'Fourteen-year-olds would not have allowed those goals to go in. It was criminal we should only draw and the defence was to blame.'

A little more than three thousand season tickets had been sold before the first home game, against Bristol City, up around 300 on the previous year, a sign of the optimism bred by those eight successive home wins.

That run, though, came to an immediate end with a 1–1 draw against Charlton. 'The reality of how hard it will be to rise out of the Second Division was rammed home to Nottingham Forest's supporters at the City Ground last night,' Lawson wrote. It was soon rammed home a little harder, with a 3–1 home defeat to Wolves.

Martin O'Neill made his first start of the season in the League Cup away at Walsall and impressed, scoring twice in a 4–2 victory. League form, though, remained indifferent, but performances in the Anglo-Scottish Cup, the tournament Clough had scorned at Derby, kept morale up. The quarter-final had particular significance for Clough as it came against Kilmarnock, who were managed by Willie Fernie, one of the instigators of the round-robin at Middlesbrough. Gordon Smith put Kilmarnock ahead from the penalty spot just after the hour in the first leg at the City Ground, but Robertson smacked in a Curran corner on the half-volley six minutes later and as the Killie keeper Jim Stewart misjudged another corner soon after, Chapman gave Forest a lead to take to Scotland a fortnight later. At Rugby Park, Ian Fallis struck either side of half-time to give Killie the aggregate lead, but the introduction of O'Neill and a switch to 4–4–2 shifted the game back in Forest's favour. Curran followed in a blocked O'Hare shot to take the game to extra-time and, on 104 minutes, O'Hare laid in Curran for winner

Taylor, perhaps reasoning that age was beginning to sap at O'Hare, or at least at his willingness to take a hammering, wanted a forward who could hold the ball up and settled on the Birmingham striker Peter Withe, whom he had tried to sign for Brighton the previous summer. He was coming up to twenty five and had had an odd career, starting out with Southport and Barrow and having stints in South Africa and the USA. For Wolves and Birmingham he made, in total, only fifty-two league starts. There was little pedigree and, as Clough said in his autobiography, 'he looked destined to become one of the game's angry and disillusioned drifters complaining that he would have made the grade if only somebody had been bright enough to spot what he could do.' Fortunately, he was spotted by Taylor and, given his chance, he seized it. O'Hare, meanwhile, became a handy reserve, particularly as he had the intelligence to play in midfield if need be.

There was a sense that a 1–1 draw in the League at Southampton and a 3–0 home defeat to Coventry didn't give a true impression of how well

Forest had played, something Carlisle discovered as they were hammered 5–1 on Withe's debut, the new man prodding in the final goal. The tinkering, though, went on and, as September drew to a close, Clough made two vital loan deals – one in, one out. Tony Woodcock, at the time a diffident left-sided midfield player – Clough told him he was too lazy to be a midfielder and not brave enough to be a forward – was sent first to Lincoln and then to Doncaster, while Larry Lloyd was brought in, initially on a one-month loan, to answer Taylor's call for a defender 'with a bit of bite'. Lloyd had a reputation for being difficult, had just had a back operation and, by his own admission, was 'giving it the big-time Charlie' at Highfield Road, where he had played only forty games over the previous two seasons. Clough and Taylor, though, were – just about – able to quash his rebelliousness, even if Lloyd and Clough never really got on. 'I think you're a brilliant manager,' Lloyd once told him. 'But if you walked into a pub, I'd walk straight out.' That was a recurring theme: to many Clough was an unlikable man, and yet he somehow goaded them into playing to their maximum.

Lloyd's debut came at Hull, for whom Bremner, on his debut, scored the only goal with a floated free-kick that eluded everybody. The *Evening Post* described it as 'a freak win' as Curran missed three sitters. Lloyd impressed – 'he did not put a foot wrong,' Clough said; 'he won the ball in the air, was solid on the ground and had the composure to play it out of defence' – but his inclusion was controversial because it meant the omission of Sammy Chapman, the captain and a player Clough claimed in his first autobiography was 'a crowd favourite'. Fans of the era, though, seem to remember him as a limited player given a certain licence because he was local; Lloyd was so evidently superior that the transition was never challenged.

'We have not got too many captaincy contenders in our side when Sammy is missing,' Clough said. 'I have talked to Frank Clark about the job in the past and he said he didn't fancy it. Ian Bowyer came into the reckoning, but I decided to give the responsibility to John [McGovern]. He's only twenty-six, but he's come through the kind of crises in his career that would have finished any lesser characters. He was not everybody's favourite at Derby, but he proved the doubters wrong and when he found himself unwanted at Leeds, he battled on. Now he's giving everything for

Forest.' The problem was, though, that by making McGovern captain in place of Chapman, Clough again made him a target for dissatisfied fans, who took his appointment about as well as Leeds fans had taken him replacing Bremner.

Those dissenting voices, though, were kept in check by McGovern's first home match as captain, a 6–1 win over Sheffield United that lifted Forest into the top four. 'Now we have got there we are going to stay,' Clough said. 'There is only one way for us to travel ... and that is up. I was delighted with the way we played against Sheffield and for ten-minute periods during the match we produced the kind of football that would have stretched First Division defences. I am not getting carried away by saying that, but it was a very encouraging display.'

It was followed immediately, though, by an away defeat as Forest went down 1–0 to Blackpool, who were managed by the man Clough had replaced at the City Ground, Allan Brown. 'It is becoming monotonous to see them virtually dominate away games and fail to get the rewards their dominance deserves,' Lawson noted.

The good home form continued with a 5–2 win over Burnley, although Curran suffered a serious knee injury in that game. 'Promotion,' said Clough, watching him hobble across the car park on crutches, 'has just limped out of the door.' A 2–1 win over Ayr United in the first leg of the Anglo-Scottish semi-final suggested he may have been exaggerating, but the subsequent 1–0 defeat at Oldham, without the injured Curran and with Lloyd's loan deal having ended, was, Lawson said, the worst performance of the season.

Again, it was the Anglo-Scottish Cup that showed the way. Graham Taylor, then the manager of Lincoln, had begun to pester Clough about signing Woodcock. Wondering if he were missing something, Clough sent Maurice Edwards to watch him at Doncaster, and he reported back that somewhere on his travels Woodcock had been transformed into an intelligent centre-forward. 'I'd have bought him in ten seconds if I'd been able to,' Anderson said. 'He was a bit unlucky. We were in a bad run when he came to us – if he'd come four weeks earlier we were playing much more confidently, but we lost a couple of players to injury and I think in the end he was quite glad to get back.'

Having recalled him, Clough fielded Woodcock alongside Withe in the away leg at Ayr. He played well, dovetailing immediately with Withe, both players scoring in a 2–0 win. He retained his place for the 3–0 win over Blackburn that followed, setting up two, and from then on his place in the side was secure.

Woodcock got the only goal as Forest finally won an away game at Leyton Orient the following week, although the match was at least as notable for a delegation of around one hundred Sunderland fans who approached Clough to beg him to take over as manager at Roker Park, where Bob Stokoe had been forced to resign through ill health. One fan, the seventy-nine-year-old Joseph Briggs, was allowed to speak to Clough directly. 'I told him I fully understand his feelings,' said Clough, a comment that was ambiguous enough to send fresh anxiety through Forest fans and members.

It was fanned as Alan Hill, who had been appointed on Gordon's recommendation as a youth coach, quit unexpectedly. The official reason given was that he was taking over a pub in Bunny, a village to the south of Nottingham, but there were rumours of a falling-out with Taylor, who had apparently misconstrued comments Hill had made in a radio phone-in in which he'd referred to him as 'the icing on the cake'; quite why Taylor was so upset by that is unclear, but it hints at the insecurity that had undermined his relationship with George Pycroft at Derby. Hill wasn't really replaced until the following October, when Ron Fenton was added to the coaching staff about a month after being sacked as manager of Notts County. When Dave Mackay was then dismissed by Derby after a run of two wins in thirteen games, anxiety about Clough's future became panic. Colin Murphy was appointed to replace him, but he was widely seen as nothing more than a stop-gap.

On the pitch, meanwhile, Forest cantered along. After a 1–1 draw with Chelsea, Peter Bonetti said that Forest were, alongside Bolton, the best side they'd faced that season, and with O'Hare returning from an elbow injury to play in midfield, Forest won 3–0 at Cardiff. Lloyd finally signed for £250,000 at the beginning of December, his return coming in a 4–2 victory over his former side Bristol Rovers. Just as all seemed to be going well, though, Clough turned on Forest's fans, complaining that the attendance was down about a quarter on the 27,000 who had turned out for the Chelsea game. 'It's about time supporters came in numbers to see us,' he said, 'not the opposition.' Forest's inability to draw vast crowds and the attendant restrictions that placed on finances were a constant source of irritation and would later become a serious obstacle to success.

Forest won at Millwall, whose manager Gordon Jago said he was sure they would be promoted, and then rounded off their Anglo-Scottish Cup success by drawing 1–1 at Leyton Orient before beating them 4–0 at home in the space of forty-eight hours to complete an oddly anti-climactic 5–1 aggregate victory in the final. It might not have seemed much at the time, but in retrospect Clough always insisted that winning the Anglo-Scottish Cup in 1976–77 was crucial. Anderson, Clark, McGovern, Lloyd, Bowyer, Robertson, O'Neill and Woodcock all played at some point over the two legs of the final and would be key players in the run to the European Cup two seasons later. It was Forest's first silverware of any kind since winning the FA Cup in 1959. 'Our lot,' Clough said, 'tasted champagne and found that they liked it.' Winning something, however insignificant, gave his side self-belief, and over the sixteen months that followed they enjoyed an astonishing run of success.

In the immediate aftermath of the win, though, the mood was one of frustration. It took an eighty-eighth minute equaliser from Barrett to salvage a point at home to Plymouth, and Forest then had the better of a 1–1 draw at Bolton, themselves strong promotion contenders. 'It was like playing Liverpool,' said the Bolton manager Ian Greaves. 'Forest were so well organised and competitive they are bound to remain a force.'

Defeat at Charlton ended the unbeaten run at twelve games, and Forest went out of the FA Cup to Southampton in the fourth round. Something, evidently, was awry. Three goals in the last seven minutes against Fulham gave Forest a flattering victory, but they were then beaten 2–1 at Wolves, a game that left Taylor furious. 'Brian and I let them know where they stood, because we will not tolerate lacklustre performances like that,' he said. 'The players have performed heroics so far this season and we told them the tragedy of letting all the good work count for nothing in the run-in to the end of the season. We know where the problems lie and if players do not apply themselves in the way we demand they will be replaced. Some of them think tomorrow will do, but they are in for a rude awakening.'

The players headed off to Torremolinos for five days and on their return they went down 2–1 at home to Luton. Amid 'steadily increasing scepticism' about the prospects of promotion, Lawson reported, they 'lacked the vital flair and spark that made them such a formidable outfit for much of the first half of the season'. Forest were 'ragged' and trailing 1–0 when a game against Southampton was abandoned for fog. Given how the mist rolled in off the Trent, that wasn't an especially unusual occurrence, but it would have a decisive impact on the season.

Then came the news that Forest fans had dreaded, as Derby made one final approach to get Clough back to the Baseball Ground.

On a tour of Sweden, George Hardy worked on three other directors, Bob Innes, Arthur Atkins and Richard Moore, encouraging them to back him in an approach to Clough. Longson was still opposed, but Hardy reasoned that a four-to-one boardroom majority would be enough. All three of the others were initially keen, but the night they returned from Sweden, Moore changed his mind. Hardy proceeded anyway.

He sounded out John McGuinness, who got in touch with his co-leader of the Protest Movement, Don Shaw. He called Clough and met him at the Kedlestone Hotel. Clough, Shaw noted in *Clough's War*, drank vodka, his efforts to dry out evidently over. Shaw asked whether he really wanted to return or whether he was, once again, toying with a board. Clough had spoken regularly of how much he had missed Derby and insisted he was sincere. He and Taylor met Hardy and Webb at Hardy's house and then, after the Forest chairman Brian Appleby had given permission, more formally at the Riverside Hotel in Branston. Hardy initially offered Clough a salary of £17,000 – the same as he was on at Forest – but he demanded an additional £5,000. Once that had been agreed, he began to negotiate about cars and bonuses, something on which Hardy could not make decisions without the backing of the board. As the alcohol flowed, though, Clough and especially Taylor warmed to the idea and at 10pm they shook hands on a deal and opened a celebratory bottle of champagne. As they left, Taylor pretended to limp, jokingly hinting that he needed an automatic car.

Clough said he would clear his desk at Forest and call Hardy the next day to arrange a press conference to announce his return. The next morning, though, Clough woke with a hangover and reconsidered, unsure if he could face working with Longson and Webb again. Taylor remained keen. 'I was born in Nottingham,' he told Francis, 'but I always felt more at home in

Derby. I love the place, love the people and love the club. I would have gone back in a flash. If we'd stayed in the first place, Derby would have won the European Cup long before Forest did.'

Clough was also worried that Derby might be relegated, whereas Forest looked like going up and had momentum. In the end, after discussing his reservations with Taylor and Appleby, Clough decided he couldn't go. 'I was never seriously tempted to return to the Baseball Ground,' Clough claimed in his autobiography, which begs the question of why he bothered with the negotiations. Appleby suggested that he might have been messing with Derby, flirting with them to settle old scores, but Dryden wondered whether Appleby might have been keen to see Clough leave. 'He saw Clough and Taylor as riff-raff,' Dryden told Francis. 'The best at their jobs, but riff-raff. He and Brian hated each other.'

When Appleby had arrived at the City Ground that morning, 21 February, his first words had been, 'has he gone yet?' He may have had his doubts about Clough, but Forest fans didn't. Appleby was a QC and was defending a murder case at the time. When the case adjourned at midday, the defendant tugged at his sleeve and begged him not to let Clough leave the City Ground.

At the Baseball Ground, meanwhile, the directors waited nervously as the realisation dawned that something was amiss. Eventually, midway through the afternoon, Clough called to say he was on his way. When he reached the stadium, he asked to speak to Hardy alone. He told him that he would take the job only if Longson and Webb were both dismissed. Hardy, panicking, raised his pay offer, but Clough wouldn't budge. That night, he called Clough and offered him £50,000 to reconsider, suggesting he split it with Taylor as he saw fit. Clough again refused, and it was only several weeks later that Taylor found out about the offer. Clough admitted he had considered taking the full £50,000 himself and going it alone, and ended up at Taylor's house begging forgiveness. Taylor gave it, but the incident further undermined his trust in Clough. Bewilderingly, Clough claimed in his autobiography – contrary to everybody else's recollection – that Taylor conducted the negotiations against his will and tried to railroad him into taking the job by arranging a press conference.

Taylor insisted the intention had never been to embarrass Derby, even if that was, for Clough, a useful side-effect. 'I know that's what everyone thinks,' he said, 'but I for one could never do that to Derby. It wasn't revenge. It just happened that way.' Hardy, though, was less certain, believing he had been 'strung along' and asking why, if Clough had problems with Webb and Longson, he hadn't mentioned it at the Riverside Hotel the night before. Clough, unconvincingly, then said he had been put off by the initial offer of a £17,000 salary, saying it suggested a lack of commitment. Clough also claimed that Taylor used the saga to persuade the Forest board to cancel a £5,000 debt he owed them, having borrowed money to buy a house after taking the job.

In the *Evening Post*, Clough said the reason he'd stayed was Dryden. 'When I was out of work only one man came for me and that was Stuart Dryden,' he explained. 'I don't know whether he remembers that, but I certainly do ... and always will. There has been a lot of worry and heartache in my life and that's the way it has been this week, but at times like this you have to think of the people who have stood by you. I don't know why it is that people always want me when I'm in work. Only Forest came in for me after I was sacked by Leeds. If I had been unemployed this week, I would have crawled down the road to the Baseball Ground, but it was not my choosing that they came for me when they did. I have always wanted to go back every single day since I left. I was so flattered and elated that I experienced every possible emotion. That is why I took so long to say no.'

Doing little to head off allegations that he just enjoyed toying with Derby, though, Clough then advised Colin Murphy to 'take them for all you can get' and, after Murphy was finally sacked a little under a year later, returned to negotiate his pay-off. Not long after, Clough persuaded Tommy Docherty, who succeeded Murphy, to bring his Derby side to the City Ground to play a testimonial for Taylor and him; he then insisted Derby pay their players' appearance money.

Curran returned after four months out through injury to score the only goal in a 1–0 win at Hereford, but Taylor was so concerned by the performance that he brought the players in the following morning to analyse their weaknesses. They were exposed by a 1–1 draw against Carlisle and then a 2–1 home defeat to Notts County that left their city rivals looking the more likely promotion candidates. On transfer deadline day, Clough returned to Derby to try to sign Archie Gemmill, reportedly offering

£50,000 and possibly Woodcock in part exchange, but Derby, not surprisingly, were reluctant to have any dealings with him.

Woodcock scored in a 2–0 win over Hull, a game in which a twenty-year-old Garry Birtles made his debut. He had been working as a carpet-fitter when he was signed from Long Eaton United for £2,000, after being recommended by Maurice Edwards. He became a classic Taylor signing, bought despite severe reservations on the part of Clough, who had been to see him play after hearing a rumour linking him – inaccurately – with Manchester United. 'The Bovril was better than he was,' he said. Taylor, though, arranged a month-long trial. Forest's coaching staff felt Birtles lacked the strength to play at centre-forward so used him in midfield, where his lack of stamina – hardly surprising for an amateur – counted against him. The reports weren't positive, but in the final week of the trial, Taylor, paying on the gate so he could watch alone, without distraction, went to see him play for the reserves at Coventry. He was poor, and Taylor was on the verge of writing him off when, as he wrote, 'Birtles evaded a defender's challenge by dummying to go one way, dragging the ball back with the sole of his left foot and changing direction in an instant.' That was enough for Taylor to sanction the signing.

Never having met his team-mates, Birtles was thrown in to that game against Hull as a midfielder. 'If I ever play you in midfield again,' Clough said to him after the game, 'tell the chairman to give me the sack.' In fact, it was eighteen months until he played him anywhere again, but he developed into the classic Clough front-man: all work-rate and efficiency, few frills.

Forest were set back again by a 2–0 defeat at Sheffield United, in which they had had most of the ball and done most of the attacking. 'We did everything right up to their penalty area,' Clough said, 'but there was no one prepared to risk getting hurt for the sake of a goal.' To have a chance of promotion, Lawson wrote gloomily, Forest had to win each of their next three games, all of which were at home. They did just that, one of them a 2–1 win in the rearranged match against Southampton, the initial abandonment a stroke of fortune that would prove crucial. Victories over Burnley and Bolton and a 1–1 draw against Notts County left Forest third, two points behind Wolves, who had two games in hand, and Chelsea, and level with County who had played a game more.

The loss of Curran earlier in the season had forced a tactical tweak. As at Derby, Clough favoured a lopsided 4–4–2, with one winger pushed high, the other tucked in as an auxiliary midfielder. Robertson, because of his lack of pace, had always been seen as a midfielder rather than a winger, with Curran used as the orthodox winger on the right. In Curran's absence, Clough had little option but to advance Robertson on the left, with O'Neill tucked in on the right. It took time for the system to gel but, once it did, it became apparent that Robertson's crossing ability more than outweighed his lack of pace and that he was far more effective as a winger than in midfield.

'We played 4–4–2, played it in to feet as much as possible,' said Frank Clark. 'There's a misconception about Brian that his teams were intricate and built everything up from the back, but more often than not, Shilton would kick it, get it to the front men and we would play off there. If Shilton could roll it out and I could knock it to Robbo that was fine, because our plan was to play it to Robbo, but we never knocked it around at the back.

'We all knew our roles and he never changed it to the point that he would play a square peg in a round hole rather than change the system. His philosophy was that he might not be too comfortable there but the other ten are because they're doing exactly the same thing that they've been doing all season. So, for instance, he would play John O'Hare, who wasn't very mobile, instead of Martin O'Neill on the right.

'He had front players who were taught two things repeatedly: either get hold of the ball and turn with it if you can and run at the defenders or get hold of the ball and set a midfield player up. If any of the front players flicked it on first time, unless they were in the penalty area, he would go berserk. He was obsessed with front players getting hold of the ball. Everything fired off that. And that's why, of course, he loved his son, because that's what his son did.'

The defence was left largely to sort itself out. 'We never did any work as a back four,' said Clark, 'but I sussed it out that when the opposition had the ball I always had to be a yard in front of Burns and Lloyd so I was ready if they did step up or if they didn't because sometimes they went and sometimes they didn't. It was a zonal marking system defensively for corners. He always believed in that. Get your position, and when it comes in, you just head it out.'

*

Forest's momentum was checked as they lost 2–1 at Chelsea, prompting an outburst in which Clough decried the dressing-room as 'a pigsty'. They then went down 1–0 at Cardiff, after which the Bolton manager Ian Greaves, whose side held the edge in the race for the third promotion slot, said he had never seen Forest play so badly. Clough was furious. 'The players are going out there on Wednesday to face the music,' he said before a home game against Oldham. 'They took all the credit when we won five successive matches – now they can take the stick. I know people are shouting for the likes of Terry Curran to be brought into the side, but I am not bringing him or any other reserve player in to get the brunt end of the criticism. The only players I want under the microscope are the ones who didn't create a thing against Cardiff on Saturday. The only exception is Peter Withe. I cannot tolerate him any longer because I just don't know when he is going to see ninety minutes out.'

It was hard not to see in the outbursts a manager under pressure, the memories of so many missed promotions with Middlesbrough and Sunderland, perhaps, playing on his mind. Withe had gone off with an injured back against Cardiff, but despite Clough's frustration, he was included against Oldham as Forest won 3–0. That left them third, a point clear of County and two ahead of Bolton, who had two games in hand.

Three points from away games at Bristol Rovers and Plymouth kept Forest in third and when Jon Moore headed a Robertson cross into his own net to give Forest a 1–0 win over Millwall in their final game of the season, Bolton needed five points from their last three games to clamber above Forest and deny them the final promotion place.

In the first of them, they beat Cardiff 2–1. The second, at home to Wolves, the side, of course, whose victory over Leeds had given Derby the title five years earlier, came as the Forest squad flew off to Mallorca for a post-season holiday. The pilot announced the half-time score, but then lost radio contact and promotion was confirmed only when Clough rang Stuart Dryden's wife from Palma Airport and found that Wolves had won 1–0. Fans gathered in Nottingham's Old Market Square to celebrate.

It had not perhaps been the most convincing promotion, but it was then that Clough and Taylor really got to work. Going up helped eliminate some of the doubts, restoring the bounce to Clough; when Duncan Hamilton, for several years the *Evening Post's* main football writer and the author of *Provided You Don't Kiss Me*, first met him in 1977, he remembers being struck by Clough's confidence, the sense he had of his destiny. Clough had seen what an ungrateful game football could be, how a dream could be destroyed at the twist of a knee or the whim of a director. And, as he had pointed out after rejecting Derby, when a manager wasn't succeeding, was out of the limelight, he was soon forgotten. By taking Forest up he had, at the very least, another success, proof that what he had done at Derby wasn't a fluke, but more than that, he had another chance at the highest level.

The main practical issue was to improve the squad. Taylor immediately said he wanted three new players: Kenny Burns, Archie Gemmill and Peter Shilton. Clough, meanwhile, was aiming even higher: he wanted a new stand, and threatened to leave if Forest didn't grant him one. There was an innate caution in the Forest boardroom, for two reasons. They'd signed Jim Baxter from Sunderland in 1967 for £100,000, but after he had disappointed on the pitch and caused disharmony off it, they found him difficult to offload and ended up letting him return to Rangers on a free transfer years later leaving a significant financial burden; and the main stand had burned down at half-time of a game against Leeds in 1968, costing £330,000 to replace. Having seen what a drain debt could be, prudence had become the guiding philosophy. With takings for a First Division season estimated at £650,000, though, the banks agreed to lend Forest up to £450,000 for transfer spending.

The first of those new players to arrive was Kenny Burns. At Birmingham, he'd developed a fiery reputation and was rumoured to have a gambling problem. Taylor, though, had Maurice Edwards trail him to Perry Barr dog-track and his local pub. He reported back that his gambling was only small-time and that he drank only sparingly. 'He was a lamb underneath,' Taylor said. 'People had completely the wrong impression of him.' Nonetheless when he turned up at a motorway services to meet Clough before signing, he was driving a car that – Clough claimed – was neither taxed nor insured. 'He was a bit of a lad, but Peter could handle him,' Clough said.

He was proved right, but the initial signs weren't promising. 'We played a pre-season game near Wolfsburg,' Clark recalled, 'and when you played these amateur sides you played in a park. The game was part of a beer festival. Kenny and Larry weren't playing. Kenny's the new boy at the club so he wants to show how big he is. At the side of this park, away from the main tent, was a kiosk that sold beer. They spend the whole game behind this kiosk and by the end of the game Kenny's gone because he's trying to keep up with Larry. After the game we're invited to this beer tent – long trestle tables, and it's chicken and chips and a pint of beer. So we're all there at one table and Brian and Peter and Brian's family are all there at a different table. By the time Burnsy's meal comes he's really gone. The waitress has just put his chicken and chips down when he collapses into it. So we're all thinking, "Oh Christ. What's going to happen?" So me and Larry and Ian Bowyer manage to pick him up and haul him outside and pretend he's OK, and we lay him down outside the tent. We manage to get him back to the hotel, and there's nothing said for about two weeks. Then they [Clough and Taylor] got hold of him and frightened him to death, telling him he'd be out of the club if he ever did that again.'

Before taking Burns to the City Ground to sign the transfer forms, Clough took him to a sweet-pea exhibition. They were his favourite flower, he explained, although his purpose in taking Burns there was surely less to share his delight in horticulture than to unsettle him, to make clear that life at a Clough club was different. He encouraged Burns to shave, to dress better and to bring his wife to the ground. When he did, Clough made a fuss of her. 'It was a case of demonstrating decent behaviour to a lad who had come from a rough background and who had few standards,' Clough said.

Even more surprising than Clough and Taylor's decision to sign Burns was how they planned to use him. At Birmingham he had been a forward – and, with nineteen goals the previous season, a successful one – but Taylor saw him being of use at the other end of the pitch. 'I suspected that Burns didn't relish life up front,' he said. 'The running didn't suit his lazy nature. What's more, we desperately needed a sweeper alongside Larry Lloyd, and I visualised Burns turning into a Scottish Bobby Moore because he was as skilful as Moore and more ruthless.' A year later, Burns was named the Football Writers' Player of the Year. 'He was a player everybody detested when he was at Birmingham,' said the journalist Richard Williams. 'But Clough turned him into a cultured centre-back, and he probably became the greatest player at Forest.' The partnership replicated that of

Roy McFarland and either Dave McKay or Colin Todd at Derby: Lloyd the hard man, winning balls in the air; Burns the more composed, hard in the tackle but also capable of passing a ball. 'Burns was the best player in that Forest side,' Richard Williams said. 'A really top-class defender who was good with the ball.'

Curran's return to full fitness presented Clough and Taylor with a dilemma: could they accommodate both him and Robertson in the same side without diminishing Robertson's effectiveness? They toyed with the idea of a 4–2–4, but the fluidity of the midfield, with Robertson high on the left and O'Neill on the right in a friendly against Shepshed Charterhouse that August persuaded them that was the way they had to go. Curran never played for Forest in the First Division, and Robertson became their first-choice wide man. He was not an orthodox winger in the sense of hugging the touchline and concentrating on beating his full-back, but became effectively a playmaker, albeit one who operated on the left rather than in the centre. 'Keep giving it to the fat man,' became a regular refrain from the bench. O'Neill's function, much to his frustration, became effectively to win the ball and feed it outside for the overlapping Viv Anderson.

The 1977–78 season began with a trip to Everton, who were regarded as serious title challengers. They may have been weakened by injury, but Goodison Park was an intimidating place to start. As the players sat in the dressing-room before kick-off, O'Neill remembers how they 'felt about two-feet tall'. But Taylor came in and performed a ten-minute routine of jokes and anecdotes so funny that many of the players were still laughing as they went out onto the pitch. 'I would far rather,' Clough said in his second autobiography, 'have my players rolling about the dressing-room floor laughing than have them trying to fathom a list of instructions and tactics before they went out and played a match.'

Everton dominated early, but Withe, who'd been a major doubt after breaking his nose against Wacker Innsbruck in pre-season, scored from a corner and Forest quickly settled. Robertson doubled their lead from another corner as the Everton goalkeeper George Wood spilled Woodcock's cross and, although Jim Pearson pulled one back shortly before half-time, Forest held their nerve and sealed the game thirteen minutes from time as O'Neill followed in after Wood had parried Robertson's drive. Duncan

McKenzie, by then playing for Everton, said he couldn't believe how composed they were, but nobody predicted what was to follow. 'Brian Clough is quite a subdued fellow these days,' said the report in the *Guardian*. 'The Nottingham Forest manager did not get carried away by his team's demonstration of their abilities on their return to the First Division after five years, and neither should anyone else. One cannot go overboard yet ... they have the element of surprise at the moment. However, the skills of players such as Tony Woodcock and John Robertson are quickly going to be recognised by more competent defenders than those on display at Goodison Park. When that happens, Forest should be prepared for hard times.'

It was Withe, though, that defenders struggled to contain in the opening weeks of the season, as he scored three in two games in victories over Bristol City and Derby. After three matches Forest were the only team with a one hundred per cent record, and a 5–0 win over West Ham in the League Cup, Robertson setting up four of the five goals, suggested a team at the top of its form.

An away game at Arsenal brought a measure of perspective. 'It was,' Lawson wrote, 'like returning from a holiday and waking up to the realities of everyday life.' Bowyer hit the post and Pat Jennings made a number of fine saves, but Forest lost 3–0. A furious Clough fined Burns and Lloyd for onfield offences missed by the referee, something that was typical of his increasing insistence on playing the game his way. Later in the season, Burns found an envelope containing a fine – a 'red tree' as Forest players came to know them, because the club badge was stamped on the corner – waiting for him at half-time because he'd played a square ball across his own penalty area.

Clough was angered not just by individual transgressions but by the performance as a whole. 'Not much was said after the match, but then on Monday we gathered in one of the guest rooms at the ground where we normally have our team talks,' Bowyer recalled. 'For well over an hour the verbal battle raged. It was a real ding-dong. Each individual was analysed as well as the team. It wasn't all one way. We were given the chance to put our point of view, but the message from the boss was that we had not done ourselves justice and we had not competed as we should. Anybody who felt complacent before he went into that room came out of it completely humble, and it was really that hour of words that set us up for the rest of the season.'

The meeting was only part of it; there were still two signings to be brought in. The need for a new goalkeeper had intensified after a County Cup game against Notts County during the summer when Middleton allowed a shot from the halfway line to slip through his hands. As far as Taylor was concerned there was only one replacement: Peter Shilton, with whom he'd been obsessed since seeing him as a teenager playing for Leicester's reserve side. 'I admired his bravery, his handling and his temperament,' Taylor said, 'but was impressed most of all . . . [by his] mastery of positional play and marshalling defences.'

Stoke had paid £325,000 in 1974 to sign Shilton from Leicester, but after relegation it was fairly clear they would look to offload him. Clough repeatedly claimed that, unsure how a player of Shilton's stature would respond to an offer from a newly promoted club with seemingly limited prospects, he waited to approach him until after Stoke had played their first game of the season away at Mansfield. To see Shilton at Field Mill, Clough said in his autobiography, was like seeing Richard Burton in *Coronation Street*. Not that he did see Shilton at Field Mill. On the day Stoke lost at Mansfield, Clough was at Goodison Park, watching Forest beat Everton. Away games at Mansfield and Millwall may have helped persuade Shilton that he needed to get away from Stoke, but there was necessity as well as psychology about the timing of Clough's approach.

Clough was driving Dryden along the M1 to see Forest's reserves at Liverpool when he told him he'd set up a meeting at Anfield with the chairman of Stoke. With Appleby nowhere to be found, Dryden went ahead and authorised a £270,000 fee. That, though, was only the start of the negotiations. Shilton had agreed a £400 a week deal with Stoke, but had it index-linked, which meant that with inflation rampant he soon became the highest-paid player in the league. He was also one of the first players to start using an agent, something Clough hated. When they first turned up for contract talks, Clough hid behind the door and tripped up Shilton's two representatives, Jon Holmes and Jeff Pointon, with a squash racquet as they came in. As they made their case for more money – Shilton was on £22,000 a year at Stoke, but Forest were offering only £15,000 – Clough sat looking bored, whacking the racquet against his leg. After about three hours, he announced they were getting nowhere and left. A couple of days later Clough called Shilton and said he wanted to see him alone in a hotel near his home. When he got there, Clough and Taylor were waiting with champagne and the deal was swiftly concluded, as Shilton accepted £20,000 a year and gave up on the loyalty bonus for which his advisers had apparently been holding out.

As ever, there were murmurings from the board. Given Shilton hadn't managed to keep Stoke up, was he actually that good? Clough spoke of how a board member – of whom there were always plenty about waiting to be cast as straw men in his diatribes against the idiocy of directors – had asked why they were spending so much on somebody who might not be involved for eighty-five minutes of every game. The attitude, Clough maintained, was 'blinkered and barmy' and, to his mind, was proved to be so by the end of the season: 'Shilton won us that title,' he said. 'He was the difference.'

Certainly his arrival coincided with an immediate stiffening of Forest's defence. Between the fee being agreed and the contract being signed, Forest beat Wolves 3–2, racing into a 3–0 lead before a late wobble. That meant that in five league games, Middleton had conceded six goals. Shilton didn't concede his sixth goal until his fourteenth game and by the end of the season he and Forest had broken defensive records. 'With Shilton in goal,' Clough told Hamilton, 'it gave everyone more confidence. It spread through the side . . . The defenders felt safer, and the forwards thought if we could nick a goal, there was more than an evens chance that the opposition wouldn't score at the other end.' Shilton was also a model professional, something Clough acknowledged with what was probably the highest compliment he could pay. Alan Brown, he said, would have told the other players to be more like Shilton.

It was Shilton, too, who gave rise to Clough's trademark green jersey. He was giving Shilton a rollicking when the goalkeeper's green number one shirt caught his attention. 'There's only one number one around here,' he said, 'and it's not you.' Thereafter, he started turning up to training and matches wearing a green sweater or sweatshirt.

Shilton made his debut in a 2–0 win over Aston Villa that left Forest level at the top with Liverpool and Manchester City. The third of Taylor's targets joined the following week, Gemmill moving from Derby for £20,000 plus John Middleton. Clough was at a civic dinner when the deal was confirmed. The soup had just been served when the waiter told him he had a phone call. By the time he returned, rubbing his hands gleefully and announcing that he'd got him, everybody else was on their dessert. Clough sat down and complained that his soup was cold.

With the squad as Clough and Taylor wanted it, the results kept coming. The rest of the world seemed to expect Forest to slip up at any moment, but they won 3–0 at Leicester and drew 1–1 against Norwich. 'They had Justin Fashanu, who was quite tough,' Clark remembered. 'He used to knock people about. He had a real ding-dong with Lloyd and Burnsy. The game's going on and I'm pushed not too far forward. All of a sudden there's a great roar from the crowd, I look around, and there's Lloyd and Fashanu flat out in the centre-circle. So I ran over to Lloydy who looks up and says, "I'm all right. I just hit Fashanu and I thought I'd better dive myself."'

Clough, who would happily fine players for hitting square passes, took no action. He became more idealistic as time went by, and Forest's horizons became more limited, but at that stage Clough was essentially a pragmatist. 'He had a philosophy on how to play the game,' Clark said, 'but that's because he thought that was the best way to win the game. Winning was everything to him.'

Forest beat Ipswich 4–0 to go two points clear at the top, Withe scoring every goal and so becoming the first Forest player to hit four in a game since Nocker West in 1907. A goalless draw at West Ham suggested a stubbornness and a durability, and Forest's position as serious title challengers was confirmed at home against Manchester City. Brian Kidd gave City a twenty-first-minute lead, but Woodcock levelled thirteen minutes later after a dazzling run and cross from Robertson and then, with four minutes remaining, Gemmill linked with Robertson to set up Withe to score the winner with a deflected shot.

Not for the first time, Clough chose a moment of apparent success to make an unpopular point. He had been angered when only five thousand fans turned out in September for Liam O'Kane's testimonial against Leicester, and even more so when Paul Richardson's testimonial was cancelled for fear it would make a loss, and that irritation bubbled over after the win against City. 'I don't know how much longer I can stand for the Nottingham public,' Clough said. 'They couldn't possibly have had a bigger attraction than Saturday's game. There should have been 40,000 inside the ground on Saturday with more knocking on the door trying to get in. Someone came up to me ... and complained he could not get a seat for the game despite being a regular supporter.

'My answer to him or anybody else who asks the question is to point to the unsold season tickets we still have down here. The club have dropped the price of season tickets and if they drop them one penny more I'm walking out the front door. What also bothers me is when we were battling it out – and I mean battling – with Manchester City, all our Trent End supporters could do was chant abuse at visiting fans. These people who stand behind the goal are among the most privileged in the land because for forty-five minutes of every home match they can watch the world's best goalkeeper at work. Instead of coming out with filth they should be getting behind the side. It was so quiet at times you would have thought we were back in the Second Division. It's about time they willed us to victory.'

It was then that, with the backing of the sports minister Dennis Howells, Clough launched his anti-swearing campaign, erecting a sign in front of the Trent End that urges, 'Gentlemen! No swearing, please!' It was, of course, somewhat rich coming from a man who swore so frequently at journalists and players, but Clough was oddly effective, not necessarily in cutting out bad language, but in calming the worst excesses of Forest's hooligan fringe. John Lawson, certainly, in *Forest 1865–1978* gives Clough credit for having taken on the thugs.

There was little Clough could do, though, about the fact that Forest's attendances were so much lower than those of bigger clubs. Was there, perhaps, in his complaints already a recognition that his demands for a new stand were misguided? Did Clough, even then, begin to see what the financial consequences could be? Even if that weren't the case, attacking his own fans seemed an odd move; perhaps it was best to issue his criticism from a position of strength, but the complaint fitted a general pattern by which Clough soured the moment of triumph, almost as if he had to make sure he didn't enjoy success too much.

That season, though, it kept coming. The former Arsenal goalkeeper Bob Wilson, by then working at the BBC, had suggested before an away game at QPR that Forest tended not to play well on trips to London. If he was basing that on their performance at Arsenal, of course, then Wilson was justified – and Forest had lost at Chelsea and Charlton the previous season – but Clough took umbrage. 'He expressed an opinion that put him up there to be shot at – and I'm doing the shooting,' Clough said. 'If I make wrong decisions I could find myself out of work. But will someone at the BBC get rid of Bob Wilson for not getting things right?' A more convincing refutation came on the pitch, as Forest produced what Peter Taylor described as their best performance since the opening day of the season to win 2–0. 'We're ready to take on anyone in Europe at the moment, never mind in England,' Taylor said, presciently. 'I was in Germany for a few days earlier last week and I saw eight continental sides either live or on television. They included Hamburg, Borussia Mönchengladbach and Anderlecht and I'm telling you we need have absolutely no worries about taking on the cream.'

With Shilton Cup-tied, Chris Woods, at seventeen, made his debut in a 4–0 League Cup win over Notts County. Viv Anderson's surges from full-back had become a familiar attacking ploy for Forest, but he had only scored once in the league for the club before a trip to Middlesbrough. There he got two in a 4–0 win, both with powerful drives; the balance of Clough's side, its range of goalscoring options, was becoming increasingly obvious as Forest climbed four points clear of Liverpool in second.

Forest may have been top of the table, but a bigger job had become available that June as Don Revie resigned as England coach to take a lucrative post as manager of the United Arab Emirates. 'I'm glad Don Revie went – he should have gone years ago,' Clough said, failing utterly to hide his glee at the vitriol directed at Revie by those who felt he had betrayed his country.

Ron Greenwood assumed temporary control, overseeing a win over Italy that wasn't quite enough to get England to the 1978 World Cup, and that December the FA interviewed candidates to take the job permanently. Of the main candidates to replace Revie – Greenwood, Clough, Lawrie McMenemy, Jack Charlton and Dave Sexton – only Clough had won the league. Clough had largely toned down the controversialism at Forest, but shortly before the interview he came out with a spectacularly mistimed attack, criticising West Brom for failing to offer their manager Ronnie Allen a contract, pursuing a well-worn theme about the insecurity of a manager's life. The chairman of West Brom at the time was Bert Millichip, who would later succeed Harold Thompson at the FA, and who was becoming increasingly influential at Lancaster Gate.

Thompson, a chemistry professor who numbered Margaret Thatcher among his former pupils, was opposed even to giving Clough an interview. Clough had little time for him either, referring to his fellow Yorkshireman as 'a stroppy, know-it-all bugger', but he did have one great advantage: he had been a remorseless critic of Revie, who by then had been suspended from football-related activities for ten years by the FA for 'bringing the game into disrepute'. Although the ban was subsequently overturned by the courts, the FA remained furious at what they saw as his treachery. Revie's departure had been, David Miller wrote in the *Express*, 'a pathetic defection to Mammon'. Those who had experienced the sort of poverty Revie had in his childhood might have been more sympathetic of his desire to secure his family's financial future, but Miller was representative of the football establishment. Given the criticism directed at Revie following defeats to Italy, the Netherlands and Scotland, and memories of the unceremonious way in which Alf Ramsey's England reign had been ended, there was something sanctimonious about the condemnation; had he not jumped, Revie would almost certainly have been sacked anyway following the World Cup qualifying campaign.

Clough himself, of course, was happy enough to add his own voice to the hail of abuse. 'He has left us wearing a black armband for football,' he wrote in the *Sunday Mirror*. 'I'm carrying a millstone round my neck. I'm a professional man and he has sold me short by quitting England when he did. He has sold football short. What's worse, he has sold himself short.'

From somebody who habitually claimed it was only 'professional' to consider any offer, they were words of the deepest hypocrisy. Clough would probably have enjoyed sticking the boot in to his old rival anyway, but here there was further reason to be vocal in expressing his outrage; the more he distanced himself from Revie, the greater his prospects for succeeding him for a second time, only this time at national rather than club level.

The day Forest confirmed Clough had been approached about the vacancy, they lost 1–0 at Chelsea. Clough promptly called on Forest fans to persuade him to stay, a piece of emotional blackmail that showed his political acuity and led to £3,000 of additional season-ticket sales the following week. When Stuart Pearson headed in a Sammy McIlroy cross to give Manchester United the lead in Forest's next game, it perhaps seemed that the long-awaited slide had begun. But Burns lashed the equaliser four minutes into the second half after McGovern's shot had been blocked and, with sixteen minutes to go, McGovern and Robertson combined to release Withe, whose chipped cross was headed in by Gemmill. As Forest continued to dominate, Robertson then had a penalty saved by Paddy Roche. 'We may have produced more exciting performances, like the one against Ipswich, but this was us at our best,' said Clough. 'It was so good that had we transported the whole thing off to Brazil, they would have written songs about it.'

Then came Clough's return to Leeds. 'Just another game,' he insisted, but Paul Madeley admitted it was something special. Either way, Clough's Elland Road jinx was at work again, Ray Hankin getting the only goal as Leeds won 1–0. Clough took his side to Israel for three days, but they were poor on their return, drawing 0–0 at home to West Brom. Although Forest were still a point clear of Everton at the top of the table, Woodcock and Withe were without a goal between them in six weeks and there was a sense that the pressure was perhaps beginning to tell on Clough.

How much became apparent after a 4–2 win over Aston Villa in the League Cup. Furious at the reporting of the West Brom game, his post-match press conference was startlingly succinct. 'I want nothing to do with the fucking press,' he said. 'I have finished with the fuckers. They are a shower and they stink in my opinion.' He stood up and left, and returned a minute later to repeat the same message; again, it's hard to avoid the thought that somebody who so freely dished out opinions in the press might have been rather more tolerant of the opinions of others.

Withe had broken his drought in that win over Villa, and Woodcock ended his in a 2–0 win at Birmingham, although the more significant contribution was probably the superb save Shilton made from Trevor Francis with the score at 1–0. After their wobble, Forest were back in their rhythm.

The candidates for the England job were interviewed on 4 December. Even as he waited to face the panel, Clough couldn't control himself. Looking at a series of photos of England players, he told Ted Croker, the FA secretary, that the new England kit – the Admiral version with the red and blue panels on the shoulders introduced as part of a deal inspired by Revie – was 'hideous'. Croker, with a classically diplomatic evasion, suggested that the FA had to move with the times, to which Clough replied that 'a Rolls-Royce is always a Rolls-Royce'.

Clough knew that if he was to have a chance, the interview had to go perfectly, and as far as he was concerned it did. He returned to Nottingham and told Taylor, 'It went brilliantly. If it's straight, we've got it.' Peter Swales later confirmed that Clough had given the best interview, but Greenwood had impressed as caretaker and that, allied to the controversy Clough would inevitably have brought, led the committee to give him the job on a permanent basis.

In retrospect, overlooking Clough has been portrayed as a dreadful error on the part of the FA, a short-sighted decision rooted in committee-room cravenness, and he is regularly referred to as the greatest manager England never had. Even at the time, he was the popular choice, with Greenwood perceived as being the dull, safe option. But that is unfair. At the time, Clough had won only one league title, five years previously, and his European successes were in the future. His Forest side were top of the table, but with less than half the season gone. Just as pertinent as his two promotions was the fact that he'd fallen out with just about everybody who'd ever employed him.

And besides, as Dick Wragg, the vice-chairman of the selection committee pointed out, being manager of England wasn't like being manager of a club. 'It wasn't just a football job,' he said. 'It was a question of international diplomacy. We needed someone to restore the good name of the FA [after Revie's unseemly departure]. Clough wasn't that man. He never was, nor could be, a diplomat. He was too abrasive for his own good.' As a club manager, Clough's bouts of xenophobia – he once told Austrian journalists, for instance, that it was a disgrace the way they'd lain down for Hitler – could be written off as eccentric and abrasive good humour. For an England manager to say such things, though, would have been a very different matter. Clough might have promised to stop, but whether he'd really have wanted to, whether he'd have been able to, is doubtful. 'Often the England manager has long spells when he has little to do constructively and is out of contact with his players,' Croker wrote in his autobiography. 'He becomes more of an administrator ... Diplomacy is a quality that is required and that has not figured too highly with Brian Clough.'

Greenwood, by contrast, was a diplomat. He had won a Cup-Winners' Cup with West Ham and his spell as England caretaker manager, steadying the ship after Revie's departure, had been a qualified success. That win over Italy persuaded Greenwood he might like the job, and it persuaded the FA that he could do it. With a legal battle with Revie ongoing, a safe pair of hands was a necessity. That doesn't make the interview process 'bent' as Clough later described it; it just makes it sensible. Although Clough raged against Greenwood's supposed underachievement with England, it was only goal difference that prevented England from qualifying for the 1978 World Cup, the damage having been done under Revie. They then qualified for the 1980 European Championship with ease, dropping only a point, and although they were poor at those finals and only scraped into the 1982 World Cup, they were unbeaten in Spain, eliminated on goal difference in the second group phase. Greenwood's record was unspectacular, but it bears comparison with any other England manager apart from Ramsey.

As Clough had left the interview room, he'd said that he would do anything he could to help England, that he would take on any role. It was intended, he later admitted, as a way of proving his commitment, but the FA took his words at face value and offered him the role of youth-team manager, working alongside Ken Burton. Clough never took the role seriously, and later claimed to have been outraged that he'd even been given what he described as 'a bucket-and-sponge job', which perhaps proved Wragg's point; tact was alien to Clough's personality. A more serious drawback was that it clashed with being manager of Forest; there were occasions when Clough and Taylor would prepare the team, but then be unable to watch the match because it was scheduled at the same time as a Forest game.

Taylor said the highlight of the job was a free day after a youth tournament in Las Palmas when he dragged Clough to the beach early, they fell asleep, and woke to find themselves surrounded by nudists. That aside, the experience was largely one of rows. On that same trip, Clough fell out with FA councillors who objected to being kept waiting in the lobby of a hotel while he and Taylor finished a team talk. Then, during the first game, Clough and Taylor arrived in the dressing-room at half-time to find the team doctor, Professor Frank O'Gorman, and John Bayliss, a veteran administrator, slicing the oranges. Clough threw them out, leaving both fuming. England won the tournament, beating the USSR in the final, but Burton resigned immediately afterwards, complaining that Clough and Taylor took all the credit when, as far as he was concerned, they were merely figureheads.

'A coach called Ken Burton was in charge,' Clough wrote in his auto-biography. 'At least, he thought he was until Taylor and I stepped in!' So Clough was bruised by being offered the job, and then brutally insensitive to the man he was supposed to be working alongside; again, the contrast between the thinness of his own skin and the armour-plated hide required by those around him is obvious. Perhaps there was, as Clough claimed, a negativity about the atmosphere around the squad and a surfeit of hangers-on, but this shows Clough at his worst: arrogant, bombastic, disrespectful to those who were there before him doing a job he clearly felt beneath him and who would continue to do it long after he had flounced off. The one mitigation, of course, is that his behaviour brought success.

Clough and Taylor resigned after a year, saying it was distracting them from Forest; had they not walked, they would almost certainly have been pushed anyway.

In the chapter on the issue in his autobiography, Clough comes across as incredibly childish. He opens by saying 'when the FA get into their stride, they make the Mafia look like kindergarten material', which is – obviously – untrue, but just the sort of overstatement that made him so popular among the media; this is Clough as the embarrassing drunken uncle at the wedding, guaranteed to say something entertaining in its ridiculousness. Even leaving facts out of it, it doesn't work as a metaphor: had the FA given the job to one of their own, to Allen Wade or to Charles Hughes, perhaps, Clough's accusation that they kept it in the family would have been justified. But they didn't, they gave it to Greenwood, who for all Clough's bleating about the merits of their respective CVs, was the one coach on the shortlist who had any experience of international football.

'People wonder what kind of an England manager Cloughie would have turned out to be,' Clough wrote. 'There's only one answer – a bloody good one.' So far, so standard in his rabble-rousing. 'We would have been one of the most positive, exciting England sides of all time if I'd been in charge,' he went on, an astonishing statement given how defensive his sides could be, particularly in European competition. 'They did not,' he continued, 'want an England manager who told the Japanese: "If you can make watch-sized televisions, it's about time you learned how to grow grass."' No they didn't, and a good thing too, partly because it doesn't make sense (it was presumably a reference to the heavily sanded pitch on which his side lost the 1980 Intercontinental Cup to Nacional in Tokyo) and partly because it's blindly xenophobic.

The chapter ends with one of the self-serving, self-pitying paragraphs so common in sporting autobiographies. 'Life had its compensations for the rejected, would-be England manager,' he wrote. 'He just went away to win the League championship and a couple of European Cups. And sometimes he reflected on the meaningless charade of an interview at FA headquarters. And thought: "Sod 'em."' Most people manage to be rejected in job interviews without letting their disappointment ferment into a lifelong feud with the body that rejected them. If the autobiography really is an accurate representation of Clough's motivations, he seems to have seen himself surrounded by foes who needed smiting; little wonder Taylor later spoke of Clough's tremendous 'loneliness'.

The obsession with the England job continued. When Bobby Robson replaced Greenwood in 1982, Clough became an outspoken critic, and such was the public clamour for Robson to be sacked – fuelled by Clough's criticism – that he even offered to resign to allow Clough to take over. Having been denied much of an international career as a player, Clough seems to have been desperate to have some role in international football as a manager and volunteered to take Scotland to the 1986 World Cup after the death of Jock Stein – although, again, it may be that the offer was made at least in part as a way of pressuring the Forest board.

After Graham Taylor was appointed to replace Howard Wilkinson as England B coach a year later, Clough admitted to being 'green with envy'. 'I now know what an actor feels like after missing out on a part he was ready to play,' he wrote in his column in the *Evening Post*. 'I'd have loved Bobby Robson to have phoned up and asked me to take charge. He could have rung me at midnight – and reversed the charges.' Perhaps recognising that time was running out, Clough volunteered to go to the 1990 World Cup to assess England's group-stage opponents (an odd and contradictory step for a man so insistent that he didn't care what the opposition did). He even offered to pay his own way to Italy, but Robson – understandably – ignored him and instead took the Ipswich manager John Lyall.

Two days before Greenwood was formally appointed, Forest beat Coventry, but it was Manchester United who would bear the full force of Clough's fury. Lloyd had broken a bone in his foot, so before the trip to Old Trafford, Clough signed a replacement, bringing in David Needham from QPR for £150,000. He had been a popular figure at Notts County, and Taylor, who admired his capacity to pass the ball under pressure, had toyed with signing him at Derby as cover for McFarland, but he had never settled in London, continuing to live in a cottage in Leicestershire. Moving to Forest allowed him to return to a lifestyle he enjoyed, while giving QPR a £50,000 profit.

Needham's debut came at Old Trafford in what was probably the defining performance of Forest's season. United had been the better side early on, but Forest took the lead midway through the first half as a Woodcock shot hit the post, cannoned off Brian Greenhoff and went in. Five minutes later Robertson seized on a long clearance from Shilton and crossed for Woodcock to add a second. From then on Forest were in total control. Robertson sidestepped Paddy Roche to add a third from Gemmill's through-ball eight minutes after half-time, before Gemmill laid in Woodcock for a late fourth. 'In terms of a performance it maintained our improvement,' said Clough, as understated in victory as ever. 'But it does not need me to tell anyone that we could have had a hatful. I lost count of the number of times we played people clear but failed to take advantage. It was a massacre and could so easily have been a result of incredible proportions. But we should not complain too much.'

'They don't play with eleven men,' said Dave Sexton, the United manager. 'They seem to have sixteen or seventeen. When they attack, about seven of them come at you, and when they are defending, there are about nine of them.'

Throughout that season, Hamilton said, Clough showed not the slightest sign of doubt, merely an irritation that it was taking Forest so long to get the respect he felt they deserved. Perhaps that was understandable; after all, Derby had enjoyed a similarly impressive start in their first season up, only to fade away around the New Year before taking fourth with a late rally – the pattern was well established. With the win at Old Trafford, though, the world woke up to just how good Forest were. Clough, who had always had an animus against United, and whose last game as manager of Derby had been at Old Trafford, felt a particular satisfaction. 'We showed all the clever clogs in the media that we were good enough to win the title,' he said. 'I enjoyed that.'

'A question many people were pondering afterwards was whether Forest were so good because United were so poor,' wrote Paul Fitzpatrick in the *Guardian*. 'United were wretched, as bad as one can recall, but to seek in any way to diminish Forest's performance would be unforgivable. Observers with long memories of Old Trafford football would say they were the best side seen on the ground for many a long year. They will not be surprised if Forest win the championship, rather if they don't. There has been a widely held feeling that Forest's success so far has been slightly phoney, based on doubtful virtues that would eventually be exposed. But there was nothing false about Forest.'

In the *Times*, Tom German was just as effusive. 'Those who have doubts should be prepared to shed them now,' he wrote. 'Nottingham Forest are equipped to win the championship and assuredly will if the exciting style which demolished and demoralised Manchester United sets their standard for the second half of the season ... They switched the ball around with speed and dexterity, channelling men forward to join the attack at exhilarating pace. Robertson and O'Neill gave Manchester a roasting on the flanks, while Woodcock and Withe were so shrewdly mobile they fooled Manchester's central defenders in so many directions that, by the end, they were as bemused as the man in the middle in some particularly impish game of blind man's bluff.'

In the crowd at Old Trafford that day was the Scotland manager Ally MacLeod, who excitedly announced that all of Forest's Scottish players would be in his squad for the World Cup the following summer. A photographer, seeing an easy money-spinner, set up a photograph of the four – Burns, McGovern, Gemmill and Robertson – wearing hired kilts. It was never used: when MacLeod announced his squad, there was no place for McGovern. He later admitted he hadn't realised he was Scottish, a confession that goes some way to explaining why one of the most garlanded players of his generation never won an international cap, and perhaps why Scotland underperformed so miserably in Argentina.

That was one darker note, but there was also a longer shadow. In some ways – certainly stylistically – that game marked a high for Forest that was never repeated. Success was still something fresh and new, an aspiration coming within reach, rather than a miser's narcotic to be clung to with increasing desperation, and that was reflected in the sense of fun about their play. That night, though, Taylor approached Appleby and said, 'I hope you've enjoyed the football you've seen this season because you won't see us play like that again.' When Clough's sides had been successful in the past, it had almost always been because of their solidity, but after that game at Old Trafford the focus shifted even more to the maintenance of clean sheets. 'Winning became the only thought,' Taylor said. 'We were obsessed with defence. Looking back, I think we overdid it. People called us "boring", but I think that was unjustified. We would never tolerate the long ball. It was all about possession and a team that doesn't give the ball away can't be boring.' That isn't entirely true; there is always something admirable about teams who hold the ball, but that doesn't make them entertaining; even Arsène Wenger, somebody who might be expected to evangelise possession football, was moved to describe Barcelona's control of games as 'sterile domination'.

Just how good a result it had been at Old Trafford was brought into perspective as United beat second-placed Everton 6-2 on Boxing Day. Forest drew 1-1 with Liverpool, and then went to Newcastle and won 2-0 as Everton were beaten 3-1 by Leeds. By New Year, Forest were five points clear of Everton and Arsenal with Liverpool a point further back.

That gave Forest the breathing space to endure a slight wobble, and they did quaver slightly after a 3-1 win at Bristol City, drawing against both Everton and Derby. Even then, though, they were four points clear, and a clinical 3-0 victory over Bury in the League Cup quarter-final suggested a team dusting itself down for the final assault. 'Now we are back to our best and I just can't see anyone stopping us,' said Gemmill.

Arsenal were beaten 2-0, Shilton proving his worth with an excellent save from Alan Sunderland two minutes before Needham, a regular goal-threat from set-plays, opened the scoring. Thereafter, only the brilliance of Jennings kept the score down. Forest were relentless. After a 2-0 win over Wolves the players had a whip-round for the groundsman, Mervyn Davies, to thank him for getting the game on despite torrential rain and thus easing potential fixture congestion later in the season.

With Forest still going strong in three competitions, that fear was well-grounded and the pundits who had written Forest off before Christmas began talking of a possible Treble. Taylor, though, was already looking beyond domestic trophies. 'The competition that really excites me is the European Cup,' he said. 'It's the Cup of Cups and while we are enjoying all the success we are having at the moment, that's the big one as far as we are concerned.'

Leeds were despatched in the League Cup semi-final, beaten 3–1 at Elland Road – a rare success for Clough at the ground – and 4–2 at the City Ground. 'They continue to crush anything in their path with a determination and skill that makes you think the unthinkable Treble is far more than a pipedream,' wrote John Lawson.

But then came an unexpected glitch that was largely self-inflicted, as Clough went on holiday with his family. Bill Nicholson had told him a story of how he'd stood at his daughter's wedding, watched her walk down the aisle and realised she'd grown up almost without him noticing because he was so focused on football; Clough seems to have determined it would never happen to him. He also believed that 'the breaks kept me from going stale'. His critics, of course, saw it as laziness. In truth, it was just another Clough quirk that in the good times looked like genius and in the bad times like insufferable perversity. Given his way of working, though, it's easy to understand why he felt the need at times to get away. 'No manager,' he insisted, 'can go into a dressing-room twice a week for ten months on the trot and pretend he's bubbling over about the next match.'

At Norwich, Forest swept into a 3–0 lead inside twenty-four minutes, but they ended up drawing 3–3, the first time Shilton had conceded more than one in a game for Forest. There were suggestions Gemmill and Barrett had clashed after the game and, when Forest drew 1–1 at home to QPR in an FA Cup fifth-round replay, Clough broke his holiday to return for the second replay. At half-time, his team-talk consisted of sticking his head into the dressing-room and shouting, 'You're playing crap when I should be on holiday.' He then slammed the door and walked away. After the game, when Forest had finally won 3–1, he briefly thanked the players and flew back to Spain. Two late goals saw off West Ham, but Forest's twenty-two-match unbeaten run came to an end with a 2–0 FA Cup quarter-final defeat at West Brom. Clough suggested his players were distracted by the thought of the League Cup final and said only O'Neill and the coach-driver were sure of their places for Wembley.

Forest were still far from their best as a Robertson penalty gave them a 1–0 win over Leicester that took them six points clear, and they weren't much better in the League Cup final against Liverpool. Clough had Nigel toss the coin to determine which side got to wear their home kit; Forest won that, but there was little other good news. Shilton, Gemmill and Needham were all Cup-tied, Barrett was injured, and McGovern struggled through with a groin problem. 'We were shelled for ninety minutes,' Clough admitted. Woods, at eighteen years and 124 days, was the youngest goalkeeper ever to play in a Wembley final, but he was probably Forest's best player, making a number of fine saves to keep the score at 0–0. 'He kept his cool,' wrote Lawson, 'revealed the immense natural talent that he possesses and stole the hearts of a Wembley crowd as well as headline acclaim.'

A photograph in Keith Mellor's pictorial history of the club shows Forest's fans at Wembley, brandishing a vast array of banners: 'Forest: Robbo make Phil Kneel'; 'Cloughie's walked on water, now for the Wembley turf'; and 'Nottingham Forest are Magic', an oddly banal slogan referencing the single produced by Forest and Paper Lace. Perhaps the knowledge of what was to come colours the perception, but the sense of excitement and anticipation almost radiates from the shot – this was Forest's first Wembley final since the 1959 FA Cup final, and the first of five they'd play in a little over two years.

Before the replay, at Old Trafford, Taylor took the players to Scarborough to stop them fretting, although the trip served a useful secondary function in helping him move some furniture up to an apartment he'd bought there. That contributed to the sense of Forest as a team of outsiders, emphasised that they were different from the establishment. As the players helped out as removal men and enjoyed a day by the sea, Clough and Taylor plotted how best to deal with Liverpool in the replay.

The injury to McGovern forced their hand and John O'Hare returned, with Robertson dropping into a deeper role. That gave Forest a more compact shape and helped them cut off the supply to Kenny Dalglish. The success of the patient approach confirmed in Clough and Taylor's minds its

391

effectiveness, and paved the way for their strategy in European competition.

Woods made early saves from Phil Neal and Dalglish, and Alan Kennedy had a goal ruled out for handball, but Robertson got the only goal of the game from the penalty spot after a trip by Phil Thompson on O'Hare. It was a cynical foul and, under the modern law would have been a clear red card, but replays showed that contact had been made just outside the box. 'I knew he was outside the area when I kicked him,' Thompson acknowledged. 'It was a professional foul.' Tommy Smith was furious. 'Is the referee [Pat Partidge] on their side tonight?' he asked. 'It's bloody ridiculous. He's given a penalty, he's disallowed a goal for us. It's terrible. He should be shot.' Few neutrals had much sympathy. 'Liverpool could have no complaint about the outcome,' wrote Norman Fox in the *Times* the following morning. 'They suffered for their errors on Saturday, and again last night. They dominated the greater part of both games, but were doggedly kept out of the Forest penalty area.'

That was the first major trophy, and with Forest five points clear at the top of the table, with two games in hand, the second already seemed inevitable – although, as Richard Williams pointed out, success was such a new sensation that at that stage 'nobody would have been confident of anything'. Forest beat Newcastle 2–0, drew 2–2 at Middlesbrough and beat Chelsea 3–1 to stand two points above Everton with three games in hand. When an eighty-sixth-minute Woodcock header from a Robertson cross saw off Aston Villa to leave them four points clear with four games in hand, Forest needed only six points from their final eight games to be sure of the title.

They drew 0–0 at Manchester City and 1–1 at home to Leeds, then beat QPR 1–0 with yet another Robertson penalty. That meant a point at Coventry would be enough to secure the championship with four games still to be played. Underlining how important he had been to their success, Shilton made an extraordinary save, clawing away a Mick Ferguson header, leaving the player shaking his head disbelievingly. 'I was only four yards out,' he said. 'I was sure it was a goal.' The game finished 0–0, and Forest had their title. 'The save from Ferguson was a good one, but I also remember the occasion the ball was tossed into our box and all I could see was blue shirts until Peter Shilton punched clear,' Clough said. 'They are the sort of things that make a goalkeeper outstanding – not just the saves he makes when people are bearing down on goal.'

It's hard to overstate the magnitude of what Clough had done. He became only the third manager in English history to win the league title with different sides (Kenny Dalglish later became the fourth), but even that fact, impressive as it is, does not quite capture just how extraordinary an achievement it was. Tom Watson led Sunderland then Liverpool to their first league titles, but both were self-evidently large, wealthy clubs waiting for a spark to ignite them. Herbert Chapman took Huddersfield and Arsenal to their first titles, but the latter at least, with its marble halls and London location, was a major club in waiting. Derby and Forest were not merely provincial sides without a league title to their names, but neither was even in the First Division when Clough took over. To lead one modest club to promotion and the league title would be remarkable, to do it twice in the space of a decade was barely credible.

While others celebrated, Clough, demonstrating that strangely diffident attitude to triumph, went home and spent the night with Barbara and the children. The next day, he was up early, selling the Sunday papers at his brother Gerry's newsagents in Bramcote. The big team celebration came after the season was over at a small fish restaurant in Cala Millor.

Inevitably, having crossed the line, there was a dip in performance, something abhorrent to Clough. Injuries meant Gemmill started the next match, away at Ipswich, up front alongside Withe. The game was dire, and at half-time Clough and Taylor, in Frank Clark's words, 'went berserk'. They decided to take Withe off. 'It could have been anybody,' Clough told him, 'but you were the worst.' Clark came off the bench, and assumed he would slot in at full-back with Ian Bowyer moving from left-back to play at centre-forward. But Clough instead insisted Clark should play alongside Gemmill. He and Allan Hunter, who already had his mind on the forthcoming FA Cup final, agreed to do their best to keep out of each other's way, but midway through the second half, a corner dropped at Clark's feet. 'The goal was gaping and it occurred to me that even I couldn't miss this one,' he said. He lashed it in for his only goal in a career that comprised 506 league games. Back then, Clough wasn't just a good manager, he was a lucky one.

The championship trophy was presented at the City Ground on an April afternoon before a 0–0 draw against Birmingham as fighting rolled incongruously along the East Stand. Clough kissed Appleby, walked briskly to the claret jug, barely acknowledging the crowd, and snatched it up into his arms. Half a pace behind strode Taylor, similarly dressed in a club blazer; as he half-raised his medal, he seemed almost embarrassed. Clough, glancing at his players, who were lined up as though awaiting a roll-call, half extended his hand towards Shilton in acknowledgement of his contribution.

That season, Forest conceded just twenty-four goals in the league and remained unbeaten at home. 'If I'd been a centre-forward,' Clough said, 'and I'd got past Burnsy and Lloydy, you've then got to get past Shilton, and Shilton came out and he used to cover the goal. When I played five-a-side with them I'd never pack it in till my side was winning, but to get past him with his huge shoulders – a magnificent body – was a killer.'

For all the early doubts of the directors, the signing of Shilton had been obviously vindicated. In fact, Clough's transfer spending as a whole was justified, not just by the two trophies, but by the club's accounts, which showed gate receipts totalling £1,119,000 and merchandising revenue of £118,000. There was also £223,000 from winning the League Cup and £91,000 from reaching the sixth round of the FA Cup. Forest appeared to be swimming in money. The impact of Clough's demand for a new stand remained a dormant spectre.

Victory in Europe

Evolution cannot stop. The curse of many great sides is to grow old or complacent together so that when rejuvenation becomes necessary players have to be replaced not in singles but by battalions. Clough had seen the dangers at Leeds, and he and Taylor were determined Forest should not slide down the same path; their concerns intensified as Forest failed to win any of their four games in pre-season.

They thrashed Ipswich 5–0 in the Charity Shield, with Robertson superb, but after a 1–0 friendly defeat at home to Porto, John Lawson admitted in the *Evening Post* to a 'concern' about Forest's capacity to defend their title. There was more than concern about a section of Forest fans, several of whom ran amok in the village of Teddington in Bedfordshire after being denied entry to a pub on the way to the Charity Shield. Many more were then involved in riots after the opening game of the season in which Forest drew 1–1 at home against a Tottenham side featuring their two new Argentinian signings, Ossie Ardiles and Ricky Villa. The sense of shock in the *Evening Post* was clear; there had been a sense that such scenes were the preserve of other clubs.

Concern about Forest's form rapidly became unease as Peter Withe was sold to Newcastle for £250,000 the following Monday, Taylor having decided during the game at Ipswich towards the end of the previous season that he'd gone stale. 'Some [fans] suggested that I sold him because he'd been doing too well and hogging the publicity,' Clough wrote in his auto-biography. That was surely untrue, and yet is telling because it suggests that even after winning promotion and the Championship in successive seasons there were some who were tiring of Clough's grandstanding. In fact, the deal showed Clough and Taylor at their best, astute at recognising when an offer for a player was too good to turn down. Even Longson had accepted that Clough was good at balancing the books. Withe's departure, though, left Forest with only Birtles and Steve Elliott as attacking options alongside Woodcock, both of them inexperienced.

It was Elliott who played against Coventry, hitting the post in a 0–0 draw. Goals became a major problem, as Forest's next three matches – one of them away to Oldham in the League Cup – finished goalless. Four did arrive in a fifteen-minute spell in the second leg against Oldham at the City Ground, but Forest still lacked fluency and conceded two late on. They went through to the third round of the League Cup, but Clough knew the performance was still well below par. 'I'm more depressed than ever . . .' he said. 'We just did not function at all and it was significant we got two of the goals from corners and another from a penalty.'

Birtles played instead of Elliott – just his second game for the club – in a 2–1 win over Arsenal, after which Clough told him he would play against Liverpool in the European Cup the following Wednesday. He fully justified that faith, scoring the first and laying on the second with two minutes remaining as Forest won 2–0. 'The matter of fact way in which Birtles swerved past [Jimmy] Case and Thompson,' David Lacey wrote in the *Guardian*, 'before centring for Woodcock to head down and Barrett to score rather summed up Forest's approach to the game. Some of the most vaunted attacks in Europe have simply dissolved against Liverpool's stifling organisation, but Clough's players have never been over-impressed by the

European champions and while the Trent End's chant of "Muppets are better than Scousers" was a little unkind, it did reflect the mood of the evening.' At 1–0, Liverpool had kept pressing for an equaliser rather than bunkering in and accepting a narrow defeat as they might have done against foreign opposition. 'Because it was Forest,' Thompson said, 'we began imagining that it was a league game in which we had to get a point.' It was a miscalculation that effectively lost them the tie.

Before the second leg, despite that second goal, a poll of First Division managers showed only three – Middlesbrough's John Neal, Bristol City's Alan Dicks and Chelsea's Ken Shellito – believed Forest would hold on at Anfield. That contributed to a sense of anxiety among the Forest players – surely not helped by Clough's comment that it would be 'like coming face to face with Rommel and his panzers' – so Clough took them to Scarborough to relax. They had a few bottles of Chablis with lunch, then took the coach to Anfield, where they produced, Lacey said, 'precisely the type of tight, containing game with which the European Cup winners of the past two years had frustrated so many opponents away from home.'

Clough made no great show of changing his tactics, did nothing different on the training pitch, but he did give certain players specific instructions. 'Minutes before we left the visitors' dressing-room at Anfield, the gaffer casually told me that I would be playing as an extra right-back, tucked in just in front of Viv Anderson,' Gemmill explained in his autobiography. 'The Boss explained quickly that Steve Heighway and Ray Kennedy both saw a lot of the ball and loved attacking down Liverpool's left flank, so he wanted Viv and me to keep a tight grip of things in that area.' It was simple and minimalist, rooted in Clough's basic theory that players, having been strategically selected to blend together, should broadly be given responsibility. However much he disliked the term, this was tactical advice he was imparting. It worked, a 0–0 draw securing a 2–0 aggregate victory.

The result reverberated around Europe. The Norwegian artist Harald Nygård caught the general tone perfectly, reflecting the notion of Forest as romantic renegades challenging the establishment by drawing Clough and his players as Robin Hood and his Merry Men – Clough as a crafty Robin, Taylor as a jovial Friar Tuck and Peter Shilton as a looming Little John.

For Clough there were only two frustrations. Juventus had won the Italian title in 1978 and, having neither forgiven nor forgotten, Clough would have loved nothing more than to beat them and gain revenge for what had happened in 1972. They, though, were beaten in the first round by Rangers. And progress in Europe was not matched by results at home; draws against Manchester United and Middlesbrough, although respectable enough in isolation, adding to the sense of a club treading water in the league.

That said, when a win at Aston Villa was followed by a home victory over Wolves, Forest had gone thirty-five league games unbeaten, a new league record. A 3–1 win at Bristol City maintained the run, but a day earlier there had been the first hint of a major upheaval ahead as Stuart Dryden was interviewed by police as part of an inquiry into the finances of Ruddington Post Office, which he ran.

It took some time for the full implication of that to be felt, but the unsettled mood perhaps contributed to Clough's more than usually abrasive behaviour in Athens as Forest faced AEK in the second round of the European Cup. 'The Reds faced everything – a hostile crowd, intimidatory tackling and an appalling penalty decision – to bring back a vital lead to the City Ground,' wrote Lawson in the *Evening Post*, although they had had the advantage of playing against ten men for seventy minutes after Milton Viera was sent off for swinging a left hook at Burns. 'Just what do we have to do to get our just deserts?' Clough asked. 'Everybody is so willing to write us off – but we just keep proving them wrong. Do we have to go 136 games without defeat before people accept that we are a good side? We did English football proud yet again, when back home they were writing us off because we were supposed to be not as good as Liverpool.'

Perhaps that frustration was justified – although given Liverpool had won two European Cups while Forest were midway through only their second tie, the media scepticism was surely understandable – but it's hard to interpret his bloody-mindedness as the squad left the hotel for the return journey as anything other than a desire to pick a fight. Lloyd reported for the bus in jeans and a sweatshirt, while everybody else was in club uniform – apart from Clough, that is, who turned up in tracksuit bottoms and the familiar green sweatshirt. Clough disappeared, came back ten minutes later in his blazer, and asked Lloyd why he was so scruffily dressed. Lloyd turned to McGovern, the club captain, to see if there'd been any instruction about blazers and he confirmed that there had not. Three times Clough demanded

Lloyd should get changed and each time Lloyd, whose blazer was at the bottom of his case, refused. It may have been, as Pat Murphy suggested, simply part of Clough's strategy of picking on somebody every couple of weeks to keep everybody on their toes, but it was also deeply unfair, and not far removed from bullying.

In Lloyd, he had picked an opponent who would fight back. That Friday, Clough flung an envelope stamped with a red tree at him. It contained the details of a £100 fine. In front of the rest of the squad, Lloyd said he had no intention of paying. As the row developed, Clough said he'd fine him £50 for each additional word he said. Lloyd told him he should make it £500 and he'd still have no intention of shutting up. Clough threatened to drop him for the following day's game at Ipswich, at which Lloyd said he'd turn to the PFA. He was, though, left out, and with Needham playing alongside Burns, Forest won 1–0. The following Monday, Lloyd stormed into Clough's office to demand a transfer, only to discover he'd gone to Spain for a week. By the time he returned, Lloyd had calmed down and paid the £100 fine. A few weeks after that, perhaps realising he'd gone a little too far, Clough sent flowers to Lloyd's wife. She returned them to the club, with a message telling Clough what he could do with them.

Clough's relationship with Lloyd, never easy anyway, was always strained after that. They almost came to blows after a defeat at Arsenal the following January after Taylor had accused Lloyd of 'bottling it' for Frank Stapleton's winner, while it got to the point that Jimmy Gordon would warn Lloyd if Clough was in one of his moods, knowing he would take it out on the biggest target he could find.

It was perhaps tantamount to an admission that he needed Lloyd onside that Clough made him captain in the absence of the injured McGovern for the home leg against AEK. Forest were superb, powerful and intelligent, relentless in their passing, with Gemmill, in particular, exceptional on the right side of midfield.

A lucky ricochet set Birtles clear and when his effort was well saved by Nikos Christidis, the corner was taken short to Gemmill. He whipped the ball across goal, and Needham dived to head a thirteenth-minute opener. Perhaps Forest could have eased off at that, but this was a night when they were certain in their superiority and without mercy. A Birtles run set up Woodcock, who rounded Christidis, only for Lakis Nikolaou to clear off the line. Then, on thirty-seven minutes, Gemmill slipped the ball in from the right for Bowyer, who made a diagonal run through midfield before feeding Robertson. He jinked by the full-back and sent over a perfect cross for Woodcock to head in. Two minutes later it was three: Anderson made an interception and seemed to handle as he clambered to his feet. The referee, though, allowed him to continue and he strode forward, skipped past Babis Intzoglou and, from twenty-five yards, curved a finish into the top corner with the outside of his right boot.

Woodcock should have had a penalty when he was tripped by Christidis, and Dušan Bajević pulled one back with a powerful header from Thomas Mavros's deep cross, but two Birtles goals in the space of six minutes underlined Forest's superiority. First he got over an awkward bounce as Needham nodded down a Gemmill chip, then he glanced in a Woodcock corner: 5–1 on the night, 7–2 on aggregate, and any sense around the rest of Europe that England's champions might not be so strong as in previous years was gone. 'I cannot think of any team capable of stopping them,' said AEK's coach, Ferenc Puskás.

Clough's former captain at Sunderland, Stan Anderson, who had managed AEK earlier in the decade, was at the game. 'I saw Brian afterwards and I started walking along with him,' he said. 'We got near the exit and we heard one of the gatekeepers chatting to his mate about the match. "Easy game that," he said. "They weren't much." And Brian gave him a right bollocking. He slaughtered the fella, and not in a quiet way. People were looking around – the fella must have felt about two feet tall.' Larry Lloyd, gatemen, it didn't matter; Clough would lay into them all.

Goalless draws against Southampton and Everton kept Forest unbeaten in the league. Over 50,000 packed in to see them beat Spurs 3–1 at White Hart Lane, with tickets exchanging hands for more than five times their face value. There was another 0–0 draw against QPR and a 1–0 win at Bolton before, after forty-two games, the unbeaten league run came to an end with a 2–0 defeat at Liverpool, both goals – one of them a penalty – being scored by Terry McDermott.

Clough would later describe the unbeaten run as his finest achievement, treasuring the silver salver presented to him by Dryden that detailed each game. The forty-two games featured twenty-one wins and twenty-one draws – as David Lacey noted in the *Guardian*, the 'classic ingredients for winning championships, two points at home and one away'. Just as telling, though, was that Forest scored only fifty-eight goals in those forty-two games; their football may have been, as Lacey described it, 'clean-cut' and 'positive', but it did not necessarily translate to goalmouth incident.

The final games of the year were played out against a background of irritation. It wasn't anything like as bad as the ill-feeling that had followed the championship success at Derby, but neither was Forest a happy club at the time. Clough was again linked with the manager's job at Sunderland after the departure of Jimmy Adamson for Leeds, at which he and Taylor admitted they'd seriously considered the offer from Derby the previous year because they feared the support at Forest was 'lukewarm'. Improved contracts presumably helped persuade them it was warm enough, but there was still friction with the board. Taylor, for instance, was furious with a suggestion from the club's commercial director John Carter that the club lottery had paid for Shilton, saying, 'I feel very strongly about this and the last thing I want is for the public to be misled.' Taylor insisted the main factor behind the signing was the success on the pitch. The financial difficulties Forest suffered in the early eighties would prove him sadly correct.

Two days before the defeat to Liverpool, Clough had tried to sign Charlie George. In some ways it was a typical Clough move. George had been weighing up whether to join West Brom or Southampton, both of whom had offered Derby £400,000, when Clough pounced. Over the course of an eight-minute conversation he seemed to have persuaded George to join Forest, but Derby refused to sell to their neighbours. 'It would be,' their chairman George Hardy said, 'a smack in the face for our supporters.' It's hard to believe Derby's board was not motivated by a desire to get their own back on Clough, but logic, at least, was on their side; George, they pointed out, had asked for a transfer because he wanted a move south. As Forest called in the League to arbitrate, and Clough raged at the 'horse-traders' at the Baseball Ground, the similarities to the Ian Storey-Moore case were clear. George ended up joining Southampton.

The League Cup, at least, was going well. After beating Oxford 5–0, Forest beat Derby 3–2, setting up a quarter-final against Brighton. Goals from McGovern, Robertson and Birtles gave them a comfortable 3–1 win, but even as the *Evening Post* was glorying in another semi-final, a back-page report was warning that unless crowds improved the plans for a new stand would have to be shelved.

Indifferent league form was redeemed only by the League Cup semifinal. Even that was settled by a 0–0 draw in the second leg, Forest having beaten Watford 3–1 at home. After a 3–1 league win at Middlesbrough, though, Clough vowed that Forest would be in the top two come the end of the season. Later that week, Forest signed Trevor Francis from Birmingham, breaking the transfer record to make him Britain's first £1million player.

A couple of months earlier, Clough had presented Francis with a Player of the Year trophy on behalf of the Midlands Football Writers. On stage, Clough told him off for having his hands in his pockets. Coming from somebody as scruffy as Clough, that was absurd, even if it did invoke the spirit of Alan Brown, but Francis meekly removed his hands from his pockets and said, 'Yes, sir.'

There remains some doubt as to what the fee actually was, with various estimates ranging from £975,000 to £999,999. Clough, for reasons he later admitted were irrational, didn't want Francis to be the first £1million player, but, of course, the distinction was academic and the media referred to him as such, as did the Birmingham manager Jim Smith, who was keen to make Birmingham fans think he'd got a good deal.

Having signed Francis, Clough gave him his Forest debut playing for the A-team on a parks pitch in front of forty fans. At half-time, he told him off for not wearing shin-pads, pointing out that he'd paid a lot for his legs and didn't want them damaged, and made him go and find a pair. It later turned out Francis's registration hadn't been completed, so Forest were fined £250 by the Football Association for fielding an ineligible player. Clough had already berated Francis for bringing his own soap and towel to training, rather than using those provided by the club. As Shilton said, that was typical of Clough's determination to prevent any player getting above themselves: 'He saw Trevor bringing in his own soap and towel as an affront to his utilitarian approach whereby every player was treated the same and accepted what was on offer, which helped foster the "all for one and one for all" attitude that was prevalent throughout the club.'

Clough, acting on his pro-union credentials, gave exclusive photographs of Francis to the *Nottingham News*, a new paper that had just been set up by journalists sacked by the *Nottingham Evening Post* after they'd gone on strike as part of a nationwide dispute over pay, one of whom was his friend John Lawson. Clough, it's claimed, encouraged other journalists to strike in support of their sacked colleagues and tried to ban the *Evening Post* from the City Ground. That move was blocked by the directors, but Trevor Frecknall, who became sports editor following the dismissals, was kicked out of the City Ground on his first day in the job, Clough pushing him through the door with a boot in his backside.

Clough went out of his way to be supportive of the *News*, subsidising trips to European games, supplying them with the first colour pictures of Francis for a centre-spread and visiting them at their offices on Low Pavement. Ever the contrarian, and perhaps recognising it made little sense to alienate the major paper in the city, Clough also agreed to contribute a column to the *Post* for free.

Francis was Cup-tied in the League Cup and ineligible until the semi-final of the European Cup, so Clough had him brew the tea. He and Taylor always had one doubt about Francis: his hunger. He had never been at rock-bottom, had been showered with praise and money since making his debut as a sixteen-year-old. What he hadn't done was win anything, so Taylor would wind him up by asking to see his medal. It would arrive soon enough.

Forest went out of the FA Cup to Arsenal, but their league form did improve and they won seven and drew six of their next thirteen games, including a 6–0 demolition of Chelsea. It was results in other competitions, though, that defined the season. First came the home leg of the European Cup quarter-final against Grasshoppers of Zurich. Clough banned live radio commentary of the game, looking to boost attendances. He remained, throughout his career, firmly opposed to the live televising of matches, but in this instance his block had a specific trigger as Forest, despite concerns over low attendances, decided they would go ahead and spend £2.5million on an 8,000-seater stand. It was, Dryden said, 'the biggest decision in the club's history'. He promised the investment would not affect transfer spending and said he thought the loan required to build it could be paid off in five years. He was wrong on both counts, and it would be a decade before the club could stand straight again, unburdened by the cost of its new stand.

*

Judging the difficulty of Forest's run to the European Cup final isn't easy with hindsight, but it certainly wasn't the most glamorous series of games. Grasshoppers, the Swiss champions, had put out Real Madrid on away goals in the previous round, but lacked the cachet to earn Forest the credit their performance probably deserved. Forest had begun well when, after eleven minutes, Bigi Meyer helped on a clearance with a flick of his right foot. Claudio Sulser ran on, had the benefit of the bounce in a challenge with Needham, and clipped a neat finish past Shilton. A 3–1 defeat in Madrid, followed by a 2–0 win in Zurich had been enough to see Grass-hoppers through the previous round, and at the time Forest must have feared something similar. McGovern had an effort cleared off the line by Johnny Hey as Grasshoppers failed to clear a Robertson corner before Forest levelled after thirty-two minutes. Then Woodcock turned superbly and the laid the ball inside to Birtles, who beat Roger Berbig from just inside the box.

The second half, though, showed Forest at their best, as they attacked in wave after wave of neat, precise football. Robertson made it 2–1 from the penalty spot after Yves Montandon had handled to prevent Birtles running on to another Woodcock flick, but that was how the score remained until the eighty-eighth minute. Birtles fired wide after Berbig had saved at the feet of Robertson; Robertson, having been fed by Gemmill, sent a diagonal shot across the face of goal; then O'Neill was denied by a point-blank save from the keeper after Woodcock had spun on a McGovern pass and chipped a cross to the back post. Shilton, having barely been involved, made an excellent save to his right to deny Sulser on the break, before the third finally arrived. Lloyd crossed from the right and when Birtles' header was headed out by Meyer, Gemmill smashed a first-time shot under the dive of Berbig, who was probably unsighted.

What was really impressive, though, was what followed. Gemmill clearly asked the referee how long there was to go. Other sides may have settled at 3–1, but not Forest. A corner was won on the right. Needham flicked it on, and Berbig tipped O'Neill's header against the bar and over. Berbig came for the corner that followed, missed it and when the ball came to Robertson at the back post, his shot was deflected wide. Robertson's delivery from the next corner was too short and was headed behind for a fourth set-play in succession. This time Robertson got it right, Lloyd got to the cross ahead of Berbig and nodded in a near-post header to make it 4–1 and settle the tie.

That made the second leg all but a formality, something all the more significant given Forest had a League Cup final to play four days before it. As the players boarded the coach heading to London, Clough worried that they'd looked nervous. On the journey south, they'd remained silent and tense. Given his insistence players should be relaxed, he decided something had to be done. 'Sometimes,' he said, 'you win matches in unusual places – often before you put a foot on the field.' The players checked in to the hotel at around 9.30pm, expecting to go straight to their rooms. Clough, though, told them to drop off their bags and come straight back down to reception. He took them into a partitioned-off part of the lounge, where a waiter arrived with a dozen bottles of champagne and a dozen jugs of orange juice. Archie Gemmill, who usually went to bed at nine, was furious, but Clough insisted none of them was leaving until they'd drunk the lot. O'Hare protested that he didn't like champagne, so Clough ordered twelve pints of bitter. Clough and Taylor then entertained them with stories of their time at Hartlepools, acting out various scenes to great hilarity. Far better, Clough believed, to be drunk than nervous.

Clough had requested that he and Taylor both be allowed to lead the team out at Wembley, and when that was denied, he sent Taylor to perform the pre-match formalities. He never seemed keen to perform that famous walk at Wembley, but the reasoning is unclear. Here, it may have been that he wanted to make a point to the Football League, but it could equally be seen as a gesture of enormous generosity, a desire to acknowledge Taylor's role. Or perhaps, contrary to the image he projected in public, there were times when the limelight troubled him.

Before the game, Alan Ball had said in a newspaper column that he didn't rate Clough as a manager. When he then put Southampton ahead in the first half, he celebrated by running down the touchline, waving at the two benches. Southampton's manager Lawrie McMenemy, in Pat Murphy's words, 'gave him a real lashing', knowing that the worst thing he could do was antagonise Clough.

Clough was actually very restrained in the dressing-room. 'We've come in thinking that he's going to go into one, but he didn't,' Woodcock said.

'He just sat us all down and got us quiet. Then he simply said, "Don't worry, boys. When you go out there for the second half, as soon as you get the ball, just pass it to a red shirt. Don't think about positioning; don't think about making chances, just give it to another red shirt." Now, we had players who followed their instructions closely and when we came out for the second half, that's all we did. We got the ball again; we passed it on again. Without even thinking about it, we found our natural game and stopped Southampton getting anywhere near us.'

It may be that their improved performance was perhaps more to do with their collective hangover wearing off than anything Clough had said, but the reminder to keep things simple coaxed Forest into their rhythm. That might be grist to the mill of those – Clough among them – who claim he was never overly bothered with tactics, but Clough's strength was always long-term strategy rather than specifics. The team shape was good; having assembled players with mutually complementary attributes the key then was to relax his side into playing within that system. Two goals for Birtles and a third from Woodcock turned the game before Nick Holmes pulled one back with two minutes remaining.

Having been denied in his attempt to subvert the pre-match protocol, Clough had his disruptive way afterwards, insisting that he and McMenemy should go up the thirty-nine steps to the Royal Box to collect medals with the players. Alan Hardaker, the secretary of the League and a man who lived and breathed decorum and tradition, was apoplectic, but found two empty boxes to hand over as though it were all part of the plan; not even Alf Ramsey had made it up the Royal Box as manager. It may have been self-aggrandisement that made Clough do it, possibly even a desire to see managers get their due reward – although by the end of the seventies that battle was surely won – but it seems just as likely that he was just being awkward because he enjoyed being awkward.

That night, shunning public celebrations as ever, Clough took the League Cup home, put it on top of his television set and looked at it while eating fish and chips. The next target was Europe.

The away leg in Zurich ended up being as simple as it had seemed it would be, but there were some anxious moments after Sulser had given Grasshoppers the lead with a fourth-minute penalty. O'Neill levelled, though, and Forest went through by a 5–2 aggregate.

The semi-final, against the Bundesliga champions FC Köln, was rather tougher. Without Burns or Anderson for the home leg, Forest soon fell behind, Roger van Gool scoring with a low shot that went in off the post. 'We were surprised how attacking they were,' Lloyd wrote in his autobiography. 'It was unusual for an away team to come at you.' A rapid break then led to Van Gool crossing for Dieter Müller to make it 2–0 after nineteen minutes. For the first time in the tournament, Forest faced the possibility of defeat, but they found an inner resolve. Bowyer hit the bar, then Needham knocked a Robertson cross back across goal for Birtles to pull one back. Needham headed against the woodwork, then Gemmill was forced off through injury. On came Frank Clark, allowing Bowyer to shift from full-back into midfield.

'Bomber', as he had been nicknamed from his earliest days as a forward, could play in pretty much any outfield position, and was a Clough stalwart. He also had a happy knack of scoring goals when they were needed most. Eight minutes into the second half, Birtles headed on a Robertson cross for Bowyer to equalise. When Robertson headed in a Birtles cross just after the hour, Forest seemed safe. It turned out, though, not to be a case of Bomber flattening the Germans, but, as just about every headline the next morning pointed out, of Forest being sunk by a Japanese sub, Yasuhiko Okudera coming off the bench to squeeze a shot under Shilton to make it 3–3.

The first leg had been, David Lacey wrote in the *Guardian*, 'a harrowing experience' for Forest, but Clough, immediately after the game, had insisted to his players that they weren't out of it. Lloyd described his 'performance' as 'brilliant', and Taylor kept up the assault before the second leg. He blamed 'certain individuals' in Forest's side for naivety, and insisted Köln wouldn't be in the top half of the First Division if they were an English side. That they had lost 5–1 to Bayern Munich the weekend before the second leg only added conviction to Taylor's words. He was so convinced that he placed £1,000 on Forest going through. With Burns and Anderson back, Forest 'absorbed some outstanding attacking football' as Lacey put it, in the first half and then, after Bowyer had stooped to head in after Birtles had flicked on a Robertson corner on sixty-five minutes 'played out the rest of the match with only fleeting qualms'.

Taylor had surrendered the league title after a 1–1 draw at Manchester United the previous week, and Forest finished as runners-up, having lost only three times all season. At the beginning of the season, Clough offered his side, who hadn't even bothered to negotiate extra payments for winning silverware the year before, bonuses of £25 a point up to fifty-three points, plus £1,000 for each point thereafter. He had reasoned that sixty points would be enough to take the title, but it proved a costly miscalculation. Forest did get sixty points – four fewer than the previous season when they had won the league by seven – but Liverpool finished on sixty-eight, meaning Forest paid out £100,000 in bonuses for coming second. It was not a mistake he made again, becoming notoriously tight even about the spending money to which players were entitled under a PFA agreement when on foreign trips.

After finishing the season with a 1–0 win at West Brom, Trevor Francis scoring the only goal, Forest had twelve days before the European Cup final, against Malmö in Munich. So as not to lose sharpness, a few days before the final Forest played in a testimonial at Southampton. McGovern went down injured and the referee, Clive Thomas, stopped the game. McGovern was clearly hurt, but sprang to his feet, and explained to a puzzled Thomas that if Clough had even the slightest doubt about his fitness, he wouldn't let him play in the final. Gemmill and O'Neill ended up both being dropped from the squad for Munich because Clough suspected they were injured, although both maintained they were fit. Gemmill made his displeasure known in forceful terms, which was probably a contributory factor in his sale to Birmingham that summer.

Taylor was even less impressed by Malmö than he had been by Köln. 'I went to see them and I couldn't believe my eyes,' he said. That troubled him almost more than if they'd been spectacularly good. 'They're such a bad side I'm worried,' he told Clough. 'We daren't let the lads know.'

Clark found out rather more than he should have, despite Clough's efforts to keep him in ignorance. 'My best friend was working in Sweden at the time – player-manager of a third-division club,' he said. 'He sent me a report over on Malmö in a letter, and I thought, "What should I do?" I mentioned it to [Clough] about a week before the game. "Chuck it in the bin," he said. "I don't want to hear it. We will beat them. We're too good for them."

'It was a good report: Malmö were a very ordinary team, but very, very well organised. They played this really well-disciplined offside trap and we found it hard to deal with. We never looked like losing the game, but we never showed what we could do. This lad said that the way to beat it was to hit diagonal balls. We couldn't have done it right to left for Robbo, but it would have been ideal from Trevor, running behind them without the ball and we could have chipped it over for him.'

Dismissive of Malmö as Taylor was, though, he wasn't quite as confident as he had been before the second leg of the semi-final. Clough and Taylor both had it written into their contracts that they'd receive a £5,000 bonus if they won the European Cup; both hedged by placing a £1,000 bet on Malmö at 6–4.

Seeing Birtles looking anxious as he got onto the bus to go to the stadium, Clough ordered him to have a shave. Birtles objected, saying he always played with a couple of days' growth, but Clough was adamant and loaned Birtles his own shaving kit. Only later did Birtles realise that it was a tactic to take his mind off the game: Clough would rather Birtles be cursing his manager and his cantankerous ways than worrying about the Malmö centre-backs. Clough then produced two crates of beer for the players to drink on the way to the ground, again easing their nerves.

It was a dreadful game, but Forest never looked in any danger, particularly after Malmö's sweeper Stefan Tapper had been forced off in the first half because of the pain from a broken toe suffered in training. The winner came just before half-time, and encapsulated the two ends of the Clough spectrum, as Robertson, the rough diamond he had uncovered and polished, crossed for the £1million forward Francis to head in at the back post. It was as comfortable a win as 1–0 can be; Taylor said if they'd been anywhere near their best they'd have won 6–0.

Even if there was a slightly anticlimactic air to the way they won it, the fact was that in two years Forest had gone from Division Two to being European champions, an unprecedented achievement; one that completed Clough's quest and one that had ramifications beyond sport. Thanks to D.H. Lawrence and Alan Sillitoe, Nottingham had a reputation as a dreary industrial city, founded on coal, lace and the Raleigh bicycle factory. Clough's Forest, and the success of the ice-dancers Jane Torvill and Christopher Dean, who won four successive world figure-skating championships from 1981 as well as taking gold at the Sarajevo Winter Olympics, began to change that. 'Lawrence and Sillitoe,' wrote Colin Griffin, assessing Nottingham's twentieth-century development in John Becket's history of the city, 'painted an unflattering picture of the city, an image quite different from the glamorous and vibrant one projected across the globe by world ice-skating champions Torvill and Dean, and by Brian Clough's European Cup-winning Nottingham Forest.'

Clough, though, again ruined the moment of celebration. 'Cloughie,' Lloyd recounted, 'came in and put the biggest dampener on it' by demanding the players hand over their medals. Only sixteen had been issued, and Clough wanted to have replicas made for members of the training staff and players who had missed the final, but whom he felt were entitled to them. Lloyd took his into the shower with him and Clark was similarly protective; after all, there was no guarantee that a player would get back an original rather than a replica. 'Some handed them over,' Lloyd wrote. 'Mugs. So there were half a dozen sitting in the middle of the table waiting for him to get his grubby hands on.'

One player was only too happy to hand his over. Gemmill, having sat fuming on the bench, threw his to the floor and told Clough he was welcome to it, an act that hastened his departure from the club as he railed about feeling 'let down' by Clough and Taylor.

It's difficult to assess just how bad the friction was. After all, most organisations are fractured by cliques and backbiting and moaning about the boss. It's unusual, though, for the ill-feeling to be quite so apparent at a time of such success. As Steve Archibald commented in a moment of surprisingly eloquent cynicism, 'team spirit is an illusion glimpsed in the moment of victory', and there is an odd sense that even as Forest won their first European Cup the decline had already begun. When Forest returned to the Olympic Stadium and were beaten 5–0 by Bayern Munich in a pre-season friendly, though, it was probably a sign something was amiss, even if Forest did go on to beat Botafogo and Dinamo Bucharest to win a tournament in Spain. Gemmill was sold to Birmingham for £150,000 – too good an offer to turn down for a thirty-two year old, Taylor said, although his public complaints at being left out for the European Cup final presumably didn't help. Woods, frustrated by a lack of first-team opportunities, was sold to QPR for £250,000 and Jim Montgomery, by then thirty-five, was signed to replace him.

Montgomery, who had spent two years at Birmingham after leaving

Sunderland in 1977, knew he was coming in as second-choice. 'Brian loved Shilton,' he said. 'If he hadn't married Barbara, he'd probably have married Peter Shilton.' Just how much became clear when Montgomery and his wife met Clough at the City Ground for preliminary talks. 'Brian was sitting there. He had his usual green jumper and squash racquet. He said, "Come and understudy Peter."

'My wife turned round and said, "He hasn't just come for cover, you know – he's come to take his place."

'I knew Cloughie, so I just sat there. Peter came in and he said, "Did you hear what Mrs Montgomery said there?" He told him and Peter just laughed, like. That's how much in awe he was of Peter Shilton. But my wife thought that about me as well. And I know for a fact . . . I could have done the job. But you just don't say that sort of thing to Peter Taylor and Brian Clough.'

The big summer signing, though, was Asa Hartford, bought from Manchester City for £500,000, filling the hole in the squad left by Gemmill. Clough said he would do the team 'a power of good'; and compared him to Tony Currie at Leeds, Liam Brady at Arsenal and Graeme Souness at Liverpool. He played only three times in a Forest career that lasted just sixty-three days, though, before he was sold to Everton. Forest won all three of those games, but he was offloaded on the grounds that his style didn't suit the club. Hartford's passing, Taylor explained, although accurate, was too short. With defences beginning to read Robertson, they needed somebody who could switch the ball rapidly from left to right to exploit the forward surges of Viv Anderson. 'We made a mistake,' Taylor said. 'You can call it bad management or good management getting rid of Asa so quickly. I prefer to call it good management.' Maurice Edwards suggested Forest were rushed into the deal by interest from Everton; whatever the reason, Hartford was Taylor's first real mistake at Forest, and perhaps a sign that the magic was beginning to fade.

Hartford later said he was glad to escape the 'rule of fear' that dominated at Forest. 'Even relaxing round a lunch table, players were terrified of saying anything that might upset Brian Clough,' he said. 'Nobody knew what mood he was going to be in; he liked to keep people on edge.' That unpredictability would grow more pronounced, but at that stage at least Taylor's view seems to have been that Hartford would have adapted to Clough had he stayed longer.

After all, others did. For years it was said that Clough ruled by fear; since when the players who stuck it out for longest have turned it on its head so the cliché has become that he didn't rule by fear despite what outsiders said. What Clough did was to dominate by force of personality, even when he wasn't there. His unpredictability prevented anything resembling complacency ever setting in, and he radiated an odd sense of omniscience, even omnipresence. When Dryden was charged over the inconsistencies in the post office accounts, for instance, Clough, despite being in the Canaries, was on the phone to offer support almost before he'd told his family. Numerous figures – perhaps most notably Don Shaw and Dean Saunders – have told of leaving a meeting with Clough, driving home, and finding him already sitting there waiting for them. In part, that was down to the network of spies he operated throughout Derby and Nottingham – landlords, taxi-drivers and members of the public who came to feel it their duty to phone the club if ever they saw players misbehaving; in part down to his doggedness when pursuing a target. He was indecisive at times, particularly where his own career was concerned, but when chasing a player he was relentless, never resting nor letting his quarry rest until a decision had been made. What is striking now, though, writing this book seven years after Clough's death, is how many people with whom he dealt still seem afraid of him. There are always people who don't want to speak for fear of causing offence, or because they don't want publicity, or because their memory is fading, but in the case of Clough there was something else, something more visceral; the closest comparison, perhaps, is those from the former Soviet Union who became so used to suppressing anything that might have been construed as a challenge to the regime that even half a century later they refuse to discuss events of the fifties and sixties.

After replacing Gemmill, with Barrett struggling with injury and Clark at last feeling his age and agreeing a move into coaching at Sunderland, the priority for Forest that summer was a left-back. Maurice Edwards, who was scouting for Forest in an unofficial capacity, was out for a drink with his wife Edna at a country pub when the sight of a jet passing overhead gave them the idea of going to East Midlands airport to watch the planes coming and going. In the bar there, Edwards bumped into Frank Gray, who was on his way to Tenerife. Edwards asked if he'd be interested in a move and

411

when Gray said he was, Edwards got in touch with Taylor. A £400,000 deal was done soon after Gray had returned.

Francis, meanwhile, flew off to the USA after the European Cup final to fulfil a pre-existing agreement to play in the NASL for Detroit Express. While there, to Clough's frustration, he suffered a groin injury; on his return, Clough refused to field him for the first six weeks of the season, something that eventually had to be resolved by the players' union.

Yet for all the background problems, Forest enjoyed their best start to a season under Clough. Hartford and Gray made their debuts in a 1–0 win at Ipswich, and they beat Stoke by the same score. Hartford was dropped and the result was increased fluency as Forest scored a total of nine goals in victories over Coventry and West Brom. In the League Cup, after a 1–1 draw in the first leg, Blackburn were thrashed 6–1 in the second. A goalless draw at home to Leeds meant Forest's first dropped points and hinted at a lack of midfield flair, but they were still top of the league, at least until a 3–1 defeat at Norwich and a 1–1 draw at Bristol City that began to signpost problems ahead. A 2–0 home win over the Swedish side Osters in the first round of the European Cup, meanwhile, was too perfunctory to lift the sense that the season was still to catch light.

Woodcock scored a hat-trick in a victory away to Middlesbrough in the League Cup as Forest, according to Trevor Frecknall in the *Evening Post*, 'finally hit the form of European champions'. It was timely, coming immediately before a game against the defending champions Liverpool, and Forest won that as well, Birtles getting the only goal as an O'Neill cross deflected off Phil Neal.

Results, though, couldn't disguise the background tensions, and they spilled over before the second leg against Osters, as Clough used a pre-match press conference to attack the board. 'I've been having a running battle with Forest's committee from the day I arrived,' he said. 'If they don't think that Peter Taylor and I are handling their affairs to the best of our ability, I suggest they get someone else. If they think anyone else can pay for a stand worth £2,500,000 and produce sides that win leagues for less than £30,000 a year, I wish they would give me the secret. If they wish to shake hands and part company they can do so with pleasure. We've been thinking of doing it for ages because, at this stage of our careers, Peter and I don't need any hassle. If the committee want hassle, let them have it with somebody else. I've been here nearly five years and it has been a pleasant stay, but I am quite capable of finding employment elsewhere.'

That might have been dismissed simply as Clough using his success to angle for more money, but Taylor chipped in, insisting that, as at Derby, what had changed was not he and Clough, but the directors. 'We are doing the job in exactly the same way as when we arrived,' he said, 'but we are now being questioned about the methods that got us success in the first place.'

Clough picked up the theme. 'I've never been in love with directors,' he said. 'Our chairman, Stuart Dryden, is fantastic, but he is outnumbered at the club, and in football generally. Unfortunately, the game attracts a certain percentage of people who are nobodies in their own walk of life and want to become somebodies though football. They are welcome to do that, but not on my back. Let them earn their own corn.'

Not surprisingly, Forest's board took offence, a 1–0 win and progress to the second round forgotten amid the furore. With Derek Pavis threatening to sue, Appleby called Clough in to his office and persuaded him to apologise. 'The trouble was that people expected him to be controversial and he went over the top,' Appleby said; for Clough, the descent into self-parody began early. Clough always blamed directors and, to an extent, the tendency has always been to accept that they were at fault, that Clough, the genius, should have been given more leeway. When a manager falls out with the directors at every club he works at, though, it becomes hard not to wonder whether the fault may have lain at least as much on Clough's side. Perhaps he even needed the sense of conflict; others, perhaps, as was the case with countless directors, would have been worn down by constant attrition, but Clough appeared to thrive on it. The battles seemed to motivate him; his autobiographies are littered with triumphant examples of him proving others wrong.

Francis returned for a home game against Wolves at the beginning of October and scored after two minutes of a 3–2 win. A draw at Stoke left Forest a point clear at the top, but they then lost at Manchester City. Worse followed, as Clough was called in to a meeting with the committee and told that he would have to sell if he wanted to buy. Given Forest had made a loss of £367,000 in the previous financial year, the gains of success in Europe largely offset by the purchase of Francis, while the cost of the new stand had spiralled to between £4m and £4.5m once interest repayments were taken into account, that was only logical, but newspaper reports immediately began linking Clough with a move to Aston Villa. Again, it's not hard to see Clough at work behind the scenes, making a few calls to make sure the message got out that he felt he needed to work with a budget, to remind the board that Forest needed him rather more than he needed them.

Forest beat Bolton 5–2, but then lost at Tottenham, after which Clough admitted he regretted selling Gemmill. He seemed also to regret signing Francis, judging by his reaction to what others described as a brilliant goal in a 2–0 home win over Ipswich. 'Trevor's just turned and whacked it,' Clough said, an oddly deflationary remark that recalled his less-than-enthusiastic response to a Johnny Giles pass in his early days at Leeds. He was in conflict with his board and needling key players; for all his talk of learning the lessons of Derby and Leeds, familiar issues were playing out again.

A 2–0 win at home over Argeş Piteşti in the second round of the European Cup followed by a 2–1 win in Romania – Piteşti, Clough observed, was like Middlesbrough without the glamour – took Forest's unbeaten run in European competition to thirteen games, breaking the record set in the late fifties by Real Madrid. That, though, couldn't hide domestic concerns. After a 4–1 defeat at Southampton, Clough admitted this side was some way short of the team of two years earlier. 'I am beginning to doubt the character of this side,' he said. 'Southampton played fluently and well, but the consistent team I once had would have eaten them alive.'

Woodcock was sold to Köln for £600,000, trebling his salary to £75,000 and so emphasising just how far behind Europe's elite Forest were financially. Forest's run of fifty-one home games unbeaten then came to an end against the bottom side, Brighton, and when they completed a miserable November by losing 4–1 at Derby, their chances of challenging for the league title already looked slim. Birtles got a late equaliser in a draw against Arsenal, but even that game was overshadowed by a dart thrown from the Trent End that hit the Arsenal keeper Pat Jennings.

Gloom and discontent pervaded the club. Desperate to shake things up, Clough spent £250,000 to sign Stan Bowles from QPR. Taylor had had the opportunity to sign Bowles for Derby in 1971, but had been put off by concerns about his consistency and his gambling habit. He hoped that, by thirty, he would have matured, but it was a move that, like so many signings Forest made at that time, didn't quite work out. Previously when they'd signed those with a reputation for being difficult, such as Burns and Lloyd, they'd, if not quelled their rebelliousness, at least got them pulling the same way as everybody else. Bowles never seemed quite part of the set-up, a sign perhaps that Clough and Taylor's capacity to mesmerise was waning.

Forest lost at Crystal Palace and Manchester United and when they beat Aston Villa on Boxing Day, it was their first win since 3 November. Their league form remained inconsistent, while there was a general sense around the club of things falling apart. Dryden appeared in court on 7 January, accused of eleven acts of theft, involving £118.35, and two charges of dishonestly obtaining £77.40 from the Post Office by falsely claiming to have paid a substitute while he was on holiday.

Clough was supportive throughout, calling Dryden from Canaries, where he was coaching the England youth team, as soon as the charge had been announced, then sitting in the public gallery for each day of the trial. It concluded on 16 January, with Dryden being convicted on four counts of illegally obtaining money from the Post Office and sentenced to six months in jail. When he was bailed pending an appeal, it was Clough who drove Dryden home. At his best, Clough could be ferociously loyal. As he would admit much later, one of the things he found hardest about football was that he couldn't always be loyal to players; that, once age had begun to sap at them, or if a large bid for them came in, he had to let them go. Taylor's observe-and-replace policy may have been effective, but it was also terribly cruel, and took a toll on both player and manager. In life, though, friendship knew no such restrictions.

Withe, Gemmill and Woodcock had all been the victims of that policy. The next seemed like being Martin O'Neill. Forest lifted the gloom to an extent with a 4–1 win over Leeds in the FA Cup, Frank Gray scoring in the first minute of his return to Elland Road, but on the coach home, Clough called O'Neill over and told him he was going to be the £250,000 makeweight in a £750,000 deal to sign the centre-forward Mick Ferguson from Coventry. The next day, Ferguson and his wife, the Coventry manager Gordon Milne and the Coventry secretary arrived at the City Ground to finalise the deal. Clough took Ferguson's wife out to lunch at an Italian

415

restaurant on Trent Bridge, leaving the others hanging around making awkward small talk. When Clough returned he and Taylor had a chat, and then Ferguson was called in to see them. Taylor told Ferguson that he should use the negotiations to force a raise out of Milne. Ferguson replied that he wanted to join Forest; Taylor told him that he was mistaken and pushed him out of the door to ask Milne for an improved contract.

With nobody quite knowing what was going on, O'Neill ended up watching an old film on television while Clough sat with his feet on the desk reminiscing about the forties. In the end, bored and wanting to go home, O'Neill signed the transfer form, told Clough that he'd done it and that he was off. Clough screamed at him, insisting that he shouldn't think he was going anywhere and should report for training the following day. Ferguson, in the end, was sent home and told to await a telephone call that never came. Taylor said that he thought the deal hadn't gone through because of a poor medical report, but when pressed by Francis, couldn't remember the day in question – an indication of how, in their world, the bizarre became mundane and of just how chaotic the running of the club had become. Clough and Taylor had always cut corners, of course, and their unorthodoxy had never previously mattered; here, though, perhaps was evidence that something was not right. What, after all, was gained by involving O'Neill, Ferguson and Milne in such a pantomime? The likeliest explanation is indecisiveness: that one or other of Clough and Taylor decided they wanted to sign Ferguson, and the other vetoed it at the last minute. O'Neill ended up staying until the end of the following season.

On the outside, though, Clough remained as seductive a figure as ever, as he proved that January as he put his skills of persuasion to use in rather more serious circumstances. A forty-seven-year-old widow called Barbara Taylor had been moved to the Nottingham Hospice after refusing to eat. She had shrunk to four-and-a-half stones and had rejected the pleas of both doctors and clergymen to start eating again. The hospice chairman turned to Clough as a last resort. He spoke to Mrs Taylor on the phone and over the course of half an hour managed to convince her to stop starving herself. 'He has given me the will to go on living,' she said. 'I have never felt such tenderness.' This was the other side of Clough's irascibility; he could be immensely charming, and was prepared to put his charisma to very good use.

Clough was generally sentimental about the very young and the very old. He clearly loved the company of his own children, taking them with him wherever possible, and regularly taking time off work during school holidays. He was as solicitous as any father could be and George Edwards remembered how he would fuss them, making sure, for instance, that Nigel always wore a balaclava as soon as the weather turned remotely cold. Various players remember how attached Clough was to their children; Paul Hart, for instance, described his children, who were three and seven when he joined Forest in 1983, as 'worshipping' Clough. He would also drop off baskets of fruit at the Derbyshire Children's Hospital on his way home from the ground, and Edwards recalled him weeping having seen a report on television about starving children in Ethiopia. When a local journalist in Nottingham asked if she could do a bucket collection for Romanian orphans, he rang up and pledged £1,000, half from himself and half from the directors. He could be short with autograph hunters, but when two youngsters from Sunderland approached him in a hotel, he not only spent time chatting to them, but on hearing they had a difficult home life invited them to visit him at home every now and again, and paid for a new pair of glasses for one of the boys.

As Clough and Taylor continued their attempts to add a little flair to the side, Charlie George was signed on a month's loan, but his only real contribution came in the European Super Cup final against Barcelona. The Cup-Winners' Cup winners were on a reported bonus of £1,750 per man to win the tie, something else that emphasised the impoverished situation of Forest, who couldn't offer any bonus at all. George got the only goal in a 1–0 win at home, but it was away where Forest again demonstrated their formidable powers of resilience. Gray brought down Allan Simonsen to concede a penalty, from which Carlos Roberto equalised. Forest then missed a penalty of their own, before Burns headed the winner from close range as Lloyd flicked on a Robertson corner shortly before half-time.

Forest's domestic form also showed some signs of revival, with wins over West Brom and Leeds, but it was a series of games against Liverpool that defined the season on the home front. The League Cup had continued to offer hope even when Forest were at their least impressive. They beat West Ham after a replay in the quarter-final to set up a meeting with Liverpool

417

in the last four. The first leg, at the City Ground, was tight and looked like ending goalless when Ray Clemence conceded a last-minute penalty for a foul on Birtles. Robertson converted.

Four days later, the sides met again at the City Ground, in the fourth round of the FA Cup. This time Liverpool won 2–0. Then came the second leg of the League Cup semi-final. Robertson gave Forest the lead at Anfield with another penalty and although David Fairclough scored in the final minute, Clough was through to his third successive final in the competition. A week after that, they met at Anfield in the league, two goals in the final twelve minutes sealing a 2–0 win for Liverpool. Taylor was all too aware of what he had seen. 'Although we have won two and drawn one of our recent five games with Liverpool,' he said, 'there is an obvious gap between us. But give us six months and the gap will be closed.' If anything, after six months, it was even wider.

Francis scored a hat-trick as Forest beat Manchester City 4–0, but in their last game before European competition resumed they lost 1–0 at home to Bolton. Forest had been 'outrun and outfought', David Stapleton wrote in the *Evening Post*, and Clough was furious, bringing the players in for extra training on the Sunday and accusing them of 'putting perks before pride'.

His rage failed to lift his side, though, and Stapleton described them as 'insipid' against Dynamo Berlin in the first leg of their quarter-final. Frank Terletzki played a long ball down the left to Hans-Jürgen Riediger, who drifted through two challenges before smashing a shot past Shilton. Francis missed a good chance with eight minutes remaining, and Forest lost 1–0, with only memories of the Köln game the previous season to give them any hope. With the financial situation precarious, the defeat hit Forest particularly hard, and there was widespread speculation that Francis would be sold to try to make ends meet.

Although they then beat Tottenham 4–0 in the league – having played against ten men for almost an hour after Paul Miller was sent off – the uncertainty was far from ideal preparation for the League Cup final against Wolves. Clough took his side to Jersey to try to distance them from the rumours, but there was further disruption to Forest's usual routine for finals as Wolves beat them to booking their preferred hotel just outside London. Clough hit back, sending the players' wives and children to have a meal in the foyer of the Wolves hotel on the morning of the game. John Barnwell, the manager of Wolves, retaliated by keeping Clough waiting in the tunnel, but Clough was already on the bench, having again avoided the duty of leading the team out, this time allowing Jimmy Gordon to do it.

Wolves used Peter Daniel, who had been part of Clough's squad at Derby, on the right to negate Robertson, and unsettled Forest with a series of long balls. Had Lloyd been there, perhaps it wouldn't have been such an issue, but he was missing through suspension. In the end, Shilton and Needham collided in challenging for a long punt – Shilton said the ball, a new design neither side had ever used before, dipped suddenly in flight – leaving Andy Gray to tap in the game's only goal. Clough could be the harshest of critics, but he also understood when a player needed reassurance. 'There's no use in you cribbing about it,' he told Shilton. 'Get yourself off home, concentrate on what you're great at and get back to Wembley next year.'

With others, he was much tougher. Clough and Francis had never enjoyed the warmest of relationships. Clough didn't think he had the hardness to be a centre-forward, and so tended to field Francis on the right of midfield, even after Woodcock had been sold to Köln. After the defeat to Wolves, Clough made sure everybody knew how poorly he thought Francis had played. Francis protested at being singled out as the scapegoat, so Clough asked him where he'd like to play. He replied that he wanted to play as a centre-forward, alongside Birtles; for the second leg in Berlin, Clough granted him his request. 'Francis must aim for a lot more consistency,' Taylor said on the morning of the game, 'but we still have faith that he will prove our judgement correct in making him Britain's first £1million footballer.'

Whatever flaws they saw in Francis's game, he had at least turned up for the flight to East Germany, unlike Bowles, who mysteriously failed to show, something that as good as ended his Forest career.

That aside, though, the trip could hardly have gone better. As the teams crossed the car park that lay between the changing-rooms and the pitch, Forest's players walked with a conscious uprightness, their backs straight. That, Taylor believed, was enough to sow the first doubts in the minds of the Dynamo players, whose toughness he had begun to question after seeing them warm up in tights and gloves to combat the ferocious cold. Forest may have trailed from the first leg, but they gave the impression that they were confident they would win. 'I saw their team prepare to walk out for the start,' Taylor said, 'and they were so frightened they looked like zombies. They looked ready to freeze and from that moment I knew we were set for a win.'

The game is remembered for Forest's outstanding first half, as though they had charged out and swept Dynamo aside, but it wasn't like that at all, certainly not after Francis, getting to the ball just ahead of Bodo Rudwaleit, the Dynamo goalkeeper, as Needham flicked on a Lloyd free-kick, had levelled the aggregate scores after sixteen minutes. Gary Birtles, turning sharply, shot just wide from twenty-five yards soon after. That ability to roll a defender was characteristic of forwards who played under Clough: Francis and Woodcock were both excellent at it as well, and it was an essential part of the way Forest played, often playing with the midfield deep and playing longish low passes forward to the strikers. 'I liked having the defender right up against me,' Woodcock said. 'That way I always knew where he was and when the ball came to me, I knew where to go to get away from him. "That's what I used to do," Clough said to me. "That's what all good centre-forwards should do."'

The quarter of an hour that followed, though, was characterised by Dynamo pressure. Three long-range efforts flashed just wide and Shilton made a deceptively difficult save, changing direction and plunging to his right to push away a skiddy drive from Bernd Brillat.

To Forest's credit, they at least kept Dynamo at arm's length, and while John McGovern squandered possession more often than was normal, more important was probably his positioning. At the same time, Birtles and Francis held the ball up and offered a threat on the break, so Dynamo could never over-commit. It was Francis's ability on the turn that brought the second ten minutes before half-time as he swivelled in the box and lashed a shot in off the underside of the bar. Three minutes later, Robertson was tripped in the box by Michael Noack, and got up to send Rudwaleit the wrong way with the penalty.

The game seemed as good as won, and Clough, having made his players sit in silence through half-time to focus their minds, insisted after the game that he'd never been worried during the second half, but Frank Terletzki pulled one back from the penalty spot four minutes into the second half after Robertson had tripped Noack, and Ralf Strasser headed against the bar from a left-wing free-kick. If Dynamo had got another, to trail only on away goals, would Forest have been able to reverse the momentum? It's hard to believe they would, but Dynamo didn't get the second and so it didn't matter. Three goals in the opening forty minutes gave the performance a sense of the emphatic that perhaps wasn't merited, but to overturn a deficit in such difficult conditions was nonetheless an exceptional achievement.

There was still, though, Bowles to be dealt with. He claimed he hadn't turned up because of a fear of flying – something to which Clough could relate – but he was known still to be gambling regularly, while rumours had started to reach the management about Bowles's heavy drinking at home in Sheffield. Clough decided to cut his losses, and Bowles was sold that summer.

From then on, with the league title well out of reach, everything became about Europe. The win in Berlin may have flattered Forest, but their 2–0 victory at home to Ajax in the first leg of the semi-final certainly didn't. They were utterly in control, barely letting an Ajax side noted for its high offside line out of its own half. Robertson had already driven a low shot across the face of goal and O'Neill, laid in by Stan Bowles, had been thwarted by a brave save from Piet Schrijvers, when they took a thirty-fourth-minute lead. It was not, in truth, a goal in keeping with their performance, poked in from a couple of yards by Francis after Søren Lerby had misjudged a Robertson corner, jumping under the ball and unsighting Piet Wijnberg, who reacted late and couldn't get any purchase on his clearance off the line.

Anderson, overlapping from right-back, was a constant threat, and when his deep cross found Robertson at the back post, the ball was returned to the middle and only a smart save from Schrijvers prevented Burns from heading a second. The keeper, though, was at fault for the second, a goal that was, from an Ajax point of view, eminently preventable. Forest held possession well, but seemed to have run out of patience when Bowles looped an optimistic pass over the top. Francis ran on, and with Schrijvers seemingly assuming the ball would run out of play, hooked it back into the middle, where a panicking Kees Zwamborn handled. Robertson this time went right from the spot as Schrijvers dived the wrong way. Only a sharp low save from Schrijvers then prevented Francis, who had an excellent

421

game, adding a third, as he connected with a low cross from O'Neill.

Determined, as ever, to relax his team, Clough took them on a tour of Amsterdam's red-light district before the second leg. He had once, on a pre-season trip, taken them to a sex club; on this occasion he restricted himself to having Taylor perform a charade of trying to negotiate a group discount at a brothel. 'We used to treat Europe as a holiday,' Clough said, although for him it was a holiday with a profoundly serious objective. 'We'd go out on a Monday morning and be there in a couple of hours, away from the humdrum of the league. We would never train. We were fresh when we got on the field, fresh for success and fresh to win again on a Saturday.' In Amsterdam, freshness was Clough's watchword; he saw no point in making his players slog through gruelling training sessions two or three times a week.

It was in his attitude to training that the biggest different between the managerial styles of Clough and Alan Brown lay. 'Alan Brown did all the coaching,' said Montgomery. 'He was the first one to bring in shadow play, where you played eleven against nobody. You'd stop and start, have free-kicks and so on, going through certain movements. We did that religiously to the point where you'd got certain people knowing where to run in certain situations. Brian and Peter . . . up the river was a bowling green. Old Jimmy Gordon used to take the squad up there, we'd run a tree, walk a tree, run a tree, walk a tree, until we got to where we were going to play, and that was it. No warming up and warming down and all this. We get up there and get the five-a-side sorted and suddenly you'd see Peter and Brian up there with their dogs [at the time, Clough didn't have a dog, so presumably it was just Taylor with his], walking around, and on the odd occasion Brian would shout, "What are you bloody doing that for?" They'd walk around a couple of times and off they'd go. Just a five-a-side and that was it. Then we'd be down the other way and I'd stop behind with Peter Taylor and do crosses and shooting.' Forest's official training pitch was in the other direction down the river; according to Frank Clark, there were times when the park-keeper would chase them off the public pitch they weren't supposed to be using.

If there was no midweek game, Forest would train on a Tuesday and a Thursday, before a light session on a Friday after which the players would gather in the guest room at the ground. 'You could have a drink if you wanted,' Clark remembered, 'and we'd could be waiting there five minutes, or it could be an hour especially when Peter came. Then the two of them would come in, and they'd talk. It could be talk about anything. Might never mention the game the next day – could talk about something totally different. Peter could talk about going to the dogs, whether he'd won money, lost money; that kind of thing. And that was it. Off you go and they'd see us at two o'clock if it was a home game. We might not see them till 10 to 3. Sometimes he'd tell you the team on the Friday; sometimes he wouldn't.

'In the Second Division they'd tell us we were the best team in the division, say that they thought we could be promoted. I wasn't convinced, but they were – or they seemed – quietly confident. They never talked about who we were playing. They might talk about something that had happened in football that week. Or they might talk about something that had happened earlier in their careers. But they never, ever talked about the opposition.'

Anderson discovered just how comparatively unfit he was when he joined Arsenal, and was left behind on every training run. Sammy Chung, the former Wolves manager, once boasted to Clough that he could make Forest's fittest player sick within three minutes. Clough replied that when the League started awarding two points for that he'd give him a job.

Clough would go so far as to discourage his players from doing extra training. 'I didn't like having two days off at the start of the week,' Clark said. 'I was 31 and I'd got into my head from something I'd read about Muhammad Ali that if I wanted to keep training I needed to be training more, not less. So I'd go for a run myself on a Sunday morning and a Monday morning. He got to hear of this and he went berserk: "When I give you a fucking day off, you have a day off . . . " I tried to reason with him, but you couldn't really. And he never forgot. The first two seasons I never missed a game – played almost 100 consecutive games. And at the end of the second season he said, "Was I right?"'

In Amsterdam, Ajax were again disappointing, even if they did preserve an unbeaten home record in European competition stretching back to 1959. They 'failed by a considerable margin to approach the style of other teams who had so successfully represented them in the past', Norman Fox wrote

423

in the *Times*. 'They required unusual effort and something original to break through a defence that occasionally showed deficiencies on its edges, but was physically formidable in the middle, where McGovern and Bowyer regularly gave inspired support to Lloyd and Burns.'

Ruud Krol had been identified as the main danger, dictating the play from the back, but Forest allowed him possession and shut down his passing options, successfully stifling the game. Lerby headed in a sixty-seventh-minute corner and for a period after that, Fox reported, 'they clearly stretched the Forest side who briefly wavered. The gap was then perilously small, but Ajax did not have the experience and character to seize the opportunity.' Dogged and composed, Forest contained Ajax relatively comfortably. It may have been their first away defeat in the competition, but it hardly mattered: unthinkably, they were through to a second successive final.

This time their opponents were Hamburg, far tougher opposition than Malmö.

Well as Francis had played in a central role against Ajax, Clough moved him back to the right for the league game at Middlesbrough the following Saturday. Francis stormed into Clough's office to protest, and having made his case slammed the door on the way out. The next day he was summoned to a meeting with Taylor, and went with trepidation, expecting either a dressing-down or to be transfer-listed. Instead, Taylor made a joke about getting a carpenter in to fix the door, explained that he and Clough saw Francis's aggression as a positive and that he would play as a centre-forward from then on. For two weeks he did, but in a 4–0 win over Crystal Palace, he snapped an Achilles tendon, ruling him out of the European Cup final.

Clough banned him from travelling to the final in Madrid, something that hurt Francis, but was entirely consistent with Clough's phobia about injury and illness. For weeks afterwards, Clough ignored him, before finally summoning him to the City Ground just as he was about to set off for Plymouth to visit his parents. There Clough charmed him, gave him champagne and told him to take his parents out for lunch at his expense at a restaurant owned by a friend of his on Dartmoor.

Forest ended the league season with a 3–1 defeat to Wolves that left them fifth, having won only four away games all season. Taylor admitted the players were 'whacked'. Clough took the squad to Mallorca to wind down, but again Bowles failed to report at the airport. 'I do not know why Bowles is not here,' Clough said. 'He will need to have one hell of an excuse for him to retain any hope of getting away with this.'

If Bowles had had any hope of getting away with it, it disappeared the next day as he hit back at Clough, whom he described as 'a dictator'. He complained that he had only seen Clough three times at training since his arrival at the club, that he was impossible to speak to and that it had become a standing joke among his team-mates that he was only selected for home games. 'I couldn't stand it any more,' he said.

Those who were part of the inner circle, though, were devoted to Clough. They would, Jim Montgomery said, 'have died for him ... because he thought about them first.' Those on the outside may have seen Clough as a petty tyrant, but those on the inside insist that, at least back then, the public dressings-down were extremely rare. 'You never really heard Brian raise his voice,' said Montgomery. 'He's famous for pointing his finger, "You little bugger" and all that, but it wasn't ranting and raving or throwing pots and pans. He and Peter Taylor saw danger on the pitch and put it right. They knew exactly what system they played and everybody knew the system and knew what they had to do. And if they didn't, they were out and somebody else would come in.'

It was all about personal responsibility within the structure, a team-shape defined by its balance. 'Peter [Shilton] could marshall a defence,' explained Montgomery. 'Larry Lloyd could look at the midfield and identify problems, and he had front players who could see danger and fill in. He had Kenny Burns who could sit and fill in. There were always people filling holes. We didn't just have one captain on the field. We had a few. McGovern was a good player in his own right. He was influential in as much as people respected him. If they were asked to do something, they wouldn't argue.'

In Mallorca, McGovern, always a fitness obsessive, ran three miles each morning, but for the other players who had made it to Cala Millor, it was a time of almost complete rest, punctuated by drinking. 'No one who saw us stumbling around the streets of Mallorca in the early hours would have dreamed we were about to play the most important match of our lives,' said Anderson. It worked, but it was a high-risk strategy: O'Neill admitted they were exhausted by the end of the game and suggested Forest would have lost had Hamburg equalised to take the game to extra-time.

Lloyd had missed the Mallorca trip as he had treatment on an ankle injury suffered playing for England against Wales. He declared himself fit, but Clough was suspicious, and devised his own fitness test, whacking Lloyd on the ankle whenever he walked past him to see how he responded. 'It hurt – of course it did,' he said. 'But I didn't react.' Shilton, too, was a late doubt, straining his calf on the morning of the game, and playing only after a pain-killing injection. He had also been unsettled by the hardness of the pitches in Madrid, which made him wary of practising shot-stopping. He tried training with Jimmy Gordon on the lawn of the hotel, but the manager soon moved him on. Shilton complained to Clough, who pointed out a well-grassed traffic island and suggested he worked there. 'Jimmy and I dodged the cars and climbed on to the roundabout,' Shilton said. 'He put down two tracksuit tops as makeshift goalposts and I set to work . . . against a background noise of tooting horns from passing cars.'

Taylor predicted a 1–0 win, insisting that Hamburg's vaunted forward Horst Hrubesch was no use on the ground – 'he needs half an hour to turn round' – that Rudi Kargus, the goalkeeper, 'isn't worth two bob' and that Manny Kaltz, the right-back, wasn't happy when players attacked him. Hrubesch, as it turned out, was suffering an ankle injury and so only came on at half-time. Nonetheless, Taylor and Clough again had their £1,000 insurance bet against their £5,000 bonus.

In the tunnel before kick-off, Lloyd found himself standing next to Keegan, with whom he had played at Liverpool. He told him they'd arranged that Burns would mark him and that he was going to 'kick the shit out of him'. Keegan glanced up to see Burns removing his teeth, a fortuitous piece of timing that Burns believed unnerved him. 'Although Keegan began the game in his usual position up front,' Lloyd wrote, 'after four horrendous tackles from Kenny and a couple from yours truly, it wasn't long before he had shifted.' That is a slight exaggeration; only two free-kicks were given for fouls on Keegan in the first half, but the suggestion was that there was plenty going on off the ball.

Without Francis, Gary Mills played, becoming a fifth midfielder, which helped cut the supply to Keegan; a ploy that blasts yet another hole in the myth that Clough and Taylor somehow did not engage with tactics. 'Before the big European games,' said Montgomery, 'the only thing he'd talk about was if there was anybody with pace in the side. He'd talk a bit about them and put somebody specifically on them when they had the ball. If there was anybody breaking at pace from midfield, he'd have something in mind to counter that. Doubling up. Make sure you close him down, but that you've got a bit of cover in case he gets past you.'

The club doctor Mick Hutson sat on the bench that evening, and recalled Taylor and Clough constantly discussing the importance of squeezing the space between the back four and the midfield, seeing that as being key to stifling Keegan. Mills was rapid, having run in the All-England Schools 100m final and been capped at schoolboy level at both rugby and football. His energy and movement helped link Forest's midfield and attack, ensuring Birtles wasn't left too isolated. The centre-forward's, though, was a lonely role, particular after John O'Hare had come on for Mills midway through the second half. 'I've never seen a lad cover as much ground, willingly and unselfishly, as Birtles did that night,' Clough said.

Forest were on the back foot for most of the game, but for the most part were able to restrict Hamburg, although they were grateful to Shilton for two excellent saves in the first half, one to parry a Felix Magath free-kick, the other to push a low volley from Jürgen Milewski round the post. Between those two attempts, Forest took the lead with a rare attack. It began on half way on the far right, McGovern winning possession and laying the ball to Bowyer, who knocked it back for O'Neill. He drifted infield and fed Frank Gray who dummied to spread the ball left before charging at the heart of Hamburg's defence. As he was held up he let Mills take over, and he worked the ball left to Robertson. The winger had had a quiet game until then, largely watching Kaltz going charging past him, but as soon as he ran at the full-back, the truth of Taylor's criticism became apparent. Robertson gave it to Birtles, who stumbled, but managed to hook the ball back to Robertson, who from just outside a box clipped a low shot in off the inside of the post. It wasn't the cleanest strike, but it was clean enough.

From then on it was largely a matter of absorbing pressure. 'Everyone played like a hero,' said Clough. 'We had application, tenacity, dedication and pride ... We did everything right. We were forced to defend and did it magnificently. Granted there were some anxious moments, but I don't think we were lucky.' Kaltz smacked a long-range drive against a post and Shilton made one outstanding save, leaping back and to his left to palm a thirty-yarder from Peter Nogly over the bar, but so disciplined was Forest's defending that Hamburg's threat was reduced to long-range efforts. Brian Moore, commentating, was a bundle of anxiety for most of the second half, but Jack Charlton, giving a laconic masterclass of co-commentary alongside him, was dismissively confident that Forest would hold on from very soon after half-time; this, he clearly recognised, was a defensive display of exceptional intelligence and application. The game, perhaps because of the scoreline, has a reputation for dullness (and the previous year's final against Malmö certainly had been tedious); this, though, was a fascinating tactical battle, one won, paradoxically, by the manager who claimed never to give tactics a second thought.

Birtles, exhausted, but raising himself for a final sprint, might even have made it two in the final minute, but having charged by Nogly, he stumbled slightly allowing Kaltz to get back and check his counter. Shattered Forest may have been by the end, but they were victorious; Clough once again had won by gambling mental against physical preparedness. Perhaps it's cruel to raise the issue in a moment of triumph, but that Forest were forced to sit back and absorb pressure was perhaps indicative of their own waning powers. Clough did what he had to do with the resources available, but eighteen months on from the thrilling 4–0 victory over Manchester United, those resources were beginning to look a little threadbare.

Victories are often spoken of as being the platforms for greater things, the heralds of a new age. They rarely are; far more usually triumph comes not as the beginning but as the end of an era, and that was certainly how it was for Forest as they became the first side to win the European Cup more often than they had won their domestic league title. After that night in Madrid, it was never so good again, not for the club and not for Clough. In *Provided You Don't Kiss Me*, Hamilton describes a moment of incongruous poignancy after the final whistle, picturing Taylor standing outside the dressing-room in the Bernabéu thinking of future glories, while realising that the dream was already slipping away. 'I was a bit choked at the end,' said Clough. 'Peter and I walked down the tunnel after the whistle with the crowd noise still in the background. There was nobody else in the dressing-room and it gave us time to take in the victory. It was an emotional, satisfying moment for both of us after a season's slog.'

That, though, was only part of it. In the weeks leading up to the final,

Clough had been acting increasingly erratically. In Amsterdam before the second leg of the semi-final, for instance, as the squad left the hotel for a walk, Clough saw a group of teenage Forest fans minding their own business, walked over and deliberately and needlessly barged into them, shoving them out of the way. He would be so rude to waiters and hotel staff that it, according to O'Hare, made the players 'squirm'. 'Towards the end of my time there his behaviour was getting out of hand . . .' O'Hare told Francis. 'We hardly saw him. He'd walk down to the training ground, spend ten minutes there and disappear again. In a sense the club was being run by Jimmy Gordon. It got to the stage where everyone tried to avoid Brian. The players were frightened of him and so was the staff.'

That eccentricity was most clearly manifested immediately after the final, as Clough insisted the team should return to their hotel twenty-five miles outside of Madrid rather than meet up with their wives who were staying in the city centre. 'We came here together as a team and we stick together as a team,' Clough said – or at least that was how he reported the incident in his autobiography. 'I don't want any of you pissing off into town or anywhere else. We've won the European Cup together and we'll celebrate together.' Clough had soured triumphs before, but never quite so emphatically as this. Robertson protested, complaining until Clough threatened to knock his teeth out. In the end, eight players broke the curfew, taking taxis back into town to stay with their wives, then returning to be there for breakfast at eight, knowing there was no way Clough would be up that early if he'd been celebrating. It was a weirdly unsatisfactory end to Forest's period of greatness.

The End of the Affair

The summer of 1980 was no less turbulent, although Clough and Taylor did sign three-year contracts despite interest from Barcelona. There were arrivals: Ian Wallace came from Coventry for £1.3million and Raimondo Ponte from Grasshoppers for £180,000. Ponte was seen as a replacement for Gemmill, while the signing of Wallace was widely perceived as an indication Francis was on his way. Clough tried to sell him, still in plaster, to Barcelona for £1.5 million, but that deal fell through after three days of medical tests in Spain.

The bigger issue, though, was players seeking moves away from Forest. At the beginning of August, Birtles requested a transfer after what the *Evening Post* described as a 'stormy meeting' with Clough. He was angered by a piece Clough had written in a magazine. 'The time has come,' Clough had said, 'for Garry to take stock of what the game has done or more significantly what Forest have done for him. He really upset me a few weeks ago when he said he felt he should have had more than three weeks' holiday. He didn't say anything about wanting more time off before he shot off to Italy with England. I did not ask him to go to Italy. I did not ask him to be best man at Chris Woods's wedding when he returned. And I did not ask him to buy a bigger house. So as I am prone to do on occasions I went berserk with Garry and told him if he felt he was being hard done by he might be better off finding another club.'

The double-standard is breathtaking. Clough took more time off than any other top-flight manager. Mike Bamber, in particular, might have raised a wry smile, thinking back at Clough's regular absences to canvass in Derby, watch boxing in New York and negotiate with the Shah's representatives in Tehran. 'With Brian Clough, a player's view is hardly ever allowed to come out,' the *Evening Post* quoted 'a Birtles family member' as saying. 'Who ever heard Peter Withe's side of things when he was involved in his shock transfer to Newcastle two years ago?'

Robertson, meanwhile, was in dispute over pay, having not received the £25,000 he was due from his testimonial. That game had also prompted Clough finally to transfer-list Bowles when he protested at being left out for Bowyer, despite having initially been named on the team-sheet.

Adding to the players with specific gripes, there was a general background discontent provoked by a pre-season schedule that saw Forest play ten matches in Canada, the USA, Colombia, Ecuador, Ireland, the Netherlands and Switzerland. Clough, irritating his exhausted players even further, had stayed behind for the leg of the tour that took them to the Americas.

The warning signs were obvious. Forest were poor in pre-season, so bad against Bayern in a friendly in Amsterdam that the locals responded with a slow handclap. They played a testimonial in Dublin for the former Chelsea, Crystal Palace and West Brom full-back Paddy Mulligan, after which the *Sunday Times* accused Clough and Taylor of having taken an *ex gratia* payment to arrange the game. Clough and Taylor threatened to sue, at which the *Sunday Times* backed down and printed an apology – but only to Clough. Taylor, at least in his own mind, was made to look guilty by implication. A day before the season began, with an away game at Tottenham, there was talk of a walkout over bonuses. The mood was appalling and, not surprisingly, Forest lost 2–0.

In the few weeks that followed results held up reasonably well, and after that initial defeat, Forest went six games unbeaten in the league, putting five past both Stoke and Leicester. But the tensions had not disappeared, and after scoring twice in that latter game, Birtles reiterated his desire to leave.

Yet that was a time when it seemed there was nothing Clough couldn't do. Driving over Trent Bridge one day that September, Clough saw a crowd and so stopped. A twenty-seven-year-old, an epileptic and an alcoholic, was perched on the parapet, threatening to jump, and police were unable to pull him back in for fear of impaling him on the iron railings that line the bridge. Clough wandered over and chatted to the man for about five minutes, calming him down sufficiently that police were able to reach him. He was praised by both the police and eyewitnesses and the *Evening Post* named Clough their Citizen of the Month; it was the second life he had saved that year and he had come to seem oddly messianic. Even that, though, provoked discord: when Clough was presented with a radio by the *Evening Post* as a reward, Taylor bewilderingly demanded that Duncan Hamilton should give him one as well, a further indication of the jealousy that had begun to fester between him and Clough.

At first glance, the finances, like Forest's form, looked in reasonable shape. The club's football activities had yielded a £328,000 profit, commercial activities £443,000 and transfers £487,000, but season-ticket sales were down and Forest had spent £1.5million on transfers after the end of their financial year. With the repayments on the stand a continuing burden, Forest needed a European Cup run. They didn't get one.

CSKA Sofia was probably a tougher draw than was appreciated at the time, but there was little panic when Forest lost 1–0 in Bulgaria. There were suspicions Tsvetan Yonchev's winner was offside, and Robertson hit the post after a one-two with Wallace. At home, it was widely expected Forest would overwhelm CSKA. Instead they produced a performance that

Stapleton described as 'tame, indecisive' and when Needham slipped, Rudzhi Kerimov ran on to score the only goal of the game. Clough had speared the white whale but he could not command it, and it slipped away again; although history looked on his achievements with awe, in the present, satisfaction in football could only ever be transitory. And unlike Ahab, whom he, with his volcanic rages, in some way resembled, Clough was left to begin the pursuit anew.

There were practical considerations, too. 'I was very disappointed because I realised it would leave us with a major headache,' Forest's chairman Geoffrey McPherson admitted two years later. 'We were already spending money we thought would come from the semi-final and the final. We took no advantage at all from our period at the top. We were spending money faster than we were earning it. To bring economy to the club was a very considerable job.'

Defeats at Arsenal and at home to Manchester United left Forest six points behind the leaders, Ipswich, while the Birtles situation continued to deteriorate. Eventually he was told to stay away from the ground, and when he was called up for England, he had to send a taxi to collect his boots. He was eventually sold to Manchester United midway through October, after which Peter Ward was signed from Brighton to replace him.

When Ward arrived in Nottingham, he stayed with a woman who had babysat him as a child. Her son was the journalist Nick Harris, at the time a ten-year-old Southampton fan. 'I remember Cloughie came round twice to pick him up and take him house-hunting,' he said, 'which shows how hands-on he was with that kind of thing. The first time he came round, he pulled up and I went running out to the car wearing my Southampton scarf. He wound down the window and I asked for his autograph – which, actually, I'd already got a couple of times because he was always coming round schools and things in Nottingham.

'He said, "Young man, what is that thing around your neck?"

'I said, "It's my football scarf."

'"What team is that?" he asked. "Is that a Nottingham Forest scarf?"

'"No. It's Southampton."

'"Get that thing away from me," he shouted, wound up the window and refused to speak to me again.'

It's a barely explicable exchange: a joke about the wrong scarf would have been normal enough; to refuse to sign an autograph for somebody whose mother was doing the club a favour by putting up their new striker seems perverse. Perhaps it was, like so many of Clough's quirks, about asserting authority, about showing he was in control and could withhold or bestow favours on a whim; perhaps, though, it hinted that he didn't much care what Peter Ward thought of him.

Ominously, Taylor told the *Evening Post* that he and Clough had not fallen out over the Ward deal – as sure a sign as anything that they were not of one accord. The relationship between Clough and Taylor had never been smooth, but it took a decisive turn for the worse that autumn with the publication of Taylor's book *With Clough By Taylor*. Taylor made a half-hearted defence that he had every right to compose an autobiography, but it was so clearly a book about Clough that the front cover of the first edition featured a photograph of Clough in the dug-out, with Taylor slightly out of focus in the background, and opened with a chronology of Clough's career.

Clough initially claimed that contracts had already been signed and the book written when he first became aware of it, and he certainly could legitimately argue that his name and image – not to mention his achievements and thoughts – had been used to boost sales. It later turned out, though, that Clough, manipulative as ever, had found out about the book about a month before the advance publicity had begun and had kept quiet about it, waiting to see if Taylor would mention it; if he really had been as outraged about it as he said, he would surely not have waited to register his protest. Clough saw the book as a betrayal, and to an extent it was; Taylor perhaps felt he was entitled to make a bit of extra cash given he was always paid less that Clough, didn't supplement his income with media work, and, at least in the early days, was constantly having to justify his existence. That he kept the book secret, though, implies he felt a certain guilt about it, and is further evidence of his declining relationship with Clough.

Quite apart from the existence of the book, there was its content, which presumably had additional impact because Clough knew Taylor was a great reader of people and, therefore, probably accurate in his assessments. It portrayed Clough as somebody who hated being alone and covered a deep insecurity with arrogance and bombast.

433

In his own way, Taylor was just as insecure, but where Clough disguised his doubts with braggadocio, he had a variety of tics and nervous mannerisms. Taylor hated to be recognised, and if he were meeting with a journalist, he would often send him into the pub or restaurant first to check how many tables were occupied. Just because he didn't want publicity, though, didn't mean he didn't want credit, and Clough was somebody who tended to hog the plaudits. Don Shaw even suggested his relationship with Longson might not have disintegrated had Clough, after winning the title, at least acknowledged the support his chairman had provided and offered a word of thanks. As it was, he gloried alone.

There was also a darkness to Clough: a self-pitying streak that suggested depressive tendencies and manifested itself in his obsessive focus on failing his eleven-plus, his injury, the way chairmen treated him and the way Juventus had cheated him out of the European Cup. For a long time, Taylor was the antidote to that. 'When I walked into the office in the morning,' Taylor said, 'I was the one who got him laughing. It was my job to do it because no one else could. In the end he was asking for it. He needed me to get him out of his moods.' For somebody as outspokenly self-reliant as Clough, it's easy to see how that dependency could, over time, have become galling to him, Taylor becoming not merely the antidote to his dark moods, but also a reminder of his weakness in needing an antidote.

Taylor's own jealousy also emerged, as he asked why Clough never asked Bell's to supply a second bottle of Scotch when he was named Manager of the Month. Perhaps Taylor was due some of Clough's whisky, but the demand was typical of Taylor's determination to get what he felt he was owed – partly, it seems, through an insecurity about money and partly because he felt his contribution should be recognised. For a man on a reasonable, if not exorbitant, salary, his parsimony was extraordinary: he felt the *Evening Post* had secured serialisation rights for his book cheaply and so insisted Hamilton should place classified ads for his family for free. Clough, meanwhile, accused him of stealing bottles of wine from the team-bus.

Clough had also begun to wonder about Taylor's judgement, or at least, his energy. There had been a time when he'd be going to three or four games a week, always on the hunt for talent, but by the turn of the decade he rarely went to more than one. A radio reporter suggested to McPherson that he'd been impressed by a centre-forward he'd seen at Chester. McPherson passed the message to Clough who asked to Taylor to go and take a look. He was dismissive, though, and so, having written off Kevin Keegan, he also wrote off Ian Rush.

The discontent on the bench seeped onto the pitch. Graham Taylor's Watford, then in the Second Division, hammered Forest 4–1 in the League Cup and although Forest went seven games unbeaten in the league, climbing to third, Taylor admitted 'we're pushing our luck'.

'Just wait till we hit our stride,' said Clough, but they never did. As he announced he might stand against Winston Churchill, the former Prime Minister's grandson, in a by-election in Stretford (something he couldn't legally have done, given he wasn't a member of the Labour Party), Forest went down 2–0 at home to Birmingham. The headline in the *Post* described an 'abject display', while Hamilton pointed out that 'it's the effect on Forest's morale, not their current league position, that is both relevant and perturbing'.

Worse was to follow as they were 'flaccid' in losing 3–0 at home to Tottenham. Robertson, frustrated by the lack of progress in his pay talks, then submitted a second transfer request, which was again rejected by the board. Clough admitted he had a 'valid' argument for more money, but said it simply wasn't available. As Forest lost a third successive home game, 2–1 to Ipswich, Hamilton lamented that 'grey October has begat a black November'.

Clough turned to youth, and the performances of Mills, Bryn Gunn and Colin Walsh suggested the future may not be too gloomy, but Forest's league form remained inconsistent. The return of Francis after his Achilles injury brought fresh hope, but his first game back came at Valencia in the second leg of the European Super Cup final. Forest had won the first leg 2–1, but Fernando Moreno's fifty-first-minute goal gave Valencia an away-goals victory.

A 3–1 win over Sunderland and a 4–1 victory at Wolves suggested Forest might come again and when they drew 2–2 against Aston Villa just after Christmas 1980, Hamilton suggested Forest were the more likely league champions of the two. It was another prediction in the *Evening Post*, though, that proved more accurate as the astrologer Russell Grant forecast 'turbulent times' for Clough in the year to come.

Forest lost 1–0 to Nacional of Uruguay in the Intercontinental Cup final, having been the better side on a dreadful pitch in Tokyo. The spirit, it seemed, wasn't there any more, the fight had gone, and the break-up of the European Cup-winning team went on. Bowyer was sold to Sunderland for £250,000 and, after being left out of the team for a game against Stoke that ended up being postponed, O'Neill requested a transfer. He was sold to Norwich for £250,000 at the end of February, shortly after underlining his importance to the side by scoring twice in a 3–1 win over Arsenal. Lloyd left to become player-manager of Wigan, at which Jan Einar Aas, a Norwegian defender, was signed for £200,000 from Bayern Munich to replace him.

Clough then offered to re-sign Birtles from United, offering more than the £1.2million he'd received for him, a move that made little sense until an incident on the way back from a 1–0 FA Cup quarter-final replay defeat at Ipswich. 'Francis, who had limped out of the match with a calf injury, had apparently arranged for his car to be left in a lay-by en route to Nottingham,' Hamilton reported. 'The car was not there – but he was still put off the bus as arranged, effectively leaving him stranded.'

This was Clough at his worst, childish and crassly insensitive to the feelings of others, determined to make his point, whatever the cost. Francis, it became obvious, was on his way out of the club. A 1–1 draw away to Manchester United in mid-March saw Forest up to third, but any sense of well-being was illusory. They lost at West Brom and Southampton in successive away games, after which Shilton announced he would leave the club in the summer.

Clough's frustration led him to even greater extremes than usual. Between those two defeats, he was involved in an incident at a reserve game that led to charges being brought against him, although not until almost four years had passed. John Joseph Pye was one of Forest's 200 members and explained in his testimony that he had been looking for a telephone at half-time when he had inadvertently wandered into the foyer, where Clough was chatting to some apprentices. Clough demanded to know what he was doing there, refused to listen to his explanation, and dragged him bodily to the exit. Pye repeatedly sought an apology, and even set up a meeting with Clough and

McPherson that ended, he said, with Clough 'tapping me on the nose, threatening to sue me for every penny I had'.

Ten days after the reserve match, Clough saw Pye leaving the ground after a goalless draw with Liverpool in the league. Furious that he'd brought McPherson into what he saw as a private dispute, he approached him, verbally abused him, threw him to the ground four times, then dragged him to the directors' lounge where he tried to force an 'enormous' quantity of whisky down Pye's throat, despite his protestations that he was 'almost teetotal'. Clough ended up apologising, although Pye paid £750 towards Clough's costs. Again, the strangely bifurcated nature of Clough's personality is seen: on the one hand, the temper and the rapid recourse to violence; and, on the other, the magnetism that led a man who had a valid grievance to offer to pay for him to defend himself on a charge of which he admitted he was guilty. In that regard, Pye almost stands as a symbol for the Forest fans in general; whatever else was going on, by far the most important thing was the quality of football Forest were playing. The eighties might not have brought quite the success of the late seventies, but there was realism about Forest's stature and delight in their style.

The stalemate with Liverpool left Forest sixth. Wins over Wolves and Crystal Palace in their final four games of the season couldn't save them, and Forest finished outside the Uefa Cup qualification places. That would have been a blow anyway but, given their financial situation, it was devastating.

Forest took the dangerous route of trying to spend their way out of trouble. On 12 August, Mark Proctor, an energetic twenty-year-old midfielder, was signed from Middlesbrough for £425,000, plus an additional £75,000 if he played three times for England. He didn't. Six days later, though, came a far more startling signing, as Forest bought their second £1million player, bringing in Justin Fashanu from Norwich.

Fashanu had made his name with a brilliant volley for Norwich against Liverpool in February 1980 and was still only twenty when he joined Forest. The thought of a strike partnership with Francis was mouthwatering: two million-pound players, both of whom combined technical ability with physical presence. But there was still every suspicion that Francis, who had refused to sign a new contract, was on his way out and it soon became apparent that Fashanu was not going to settle in easily.

Three days after signing, Fashanu was sent off in a friendly in Spain, collecting a second yellow card by kicking the ball away after being fouled. He was the ninth English player sent off by Spanish referees in friendlies that summer – Burns had been the eighth, collecting a red card for dissent the day before, on Fashanu's debut – and so to an extent it was a matter of passing concern, evidence of the volatility of Spanish referees as much as English players. But it meant he had a suspension hanging over him (the FA would not ban him until receiving the referee's report from the Spanish FA, a process that took months), and it suggested from the start that his move to Nottingham was ill-omened.

Francis was used in the club's pre-season literature, modelling the new pin-stripe kit, which perhaps hinted that he wasn't as certain to leave as had been thought and, on the opening day of the 1981–82 season, he called on Clough to make him an offer. The forward underlined his value by scoring both goals in a 2–1 win over Southampton, a victory that, for the first time, brought three points. The new points system was designed to encourage more attacking play; there was a sense that it might count against teams like Forest and Liverpool, who were adept at closing games out.

Nonetheless, Forest then went to Old Trafford and drew 0–0. 'Forest's restyled side,' Hamilton wrote, 'have started to back up the summer rhetoric of their management; namely that a concerted title push is very feasible indeed.' His optimism didn't last long. Francis was sold to Manchester City for £1million the following Thursday and left with an interview that, if not a direct attack on Clough, certainly underlined the difficulties of playing under him. He revealed, for instance, that in the European Cup game away to Osters, he had had to find a public toilet to use because Clough wouldn't allow him in the dressing-room while he was speaking.

The sale of Francis made sense to the extent that his contract was expiring at the end of the season, the wage bill needed trimming to meet the interest repayments on the new stand and he was fairly evidently less than happy at the club, but it was still a huge blow to Forest's hopes of mounting a title challenge. Forest did make a profit for the year ending 31 May, but only because they'd sold Frank Gray back to Leeds for £400,000. Without European football, that position could only worsen. The departure of

Francis may have made financial sense, but it increased the pressure on Fashanu; whether he was intended to be Francis's replacement or not, that is how he came to be perceived – a huge burden for a player who was still only twenty.

Initially, he still looked promising. Forest lost 4–3 at Birmingham, Ian Wallace scoring a hat-trick. Even as Hamilton observed that the 'pressure is on' Fashanu, Wallace went out of his way to highlight his role in Forest's three goals. 'Every time Justin went for the ball he took two men with him,' he said. 'Because they were marking Justin very carefully, it gave me more room and a greater opportunity.'

The full nature of the pressure, though, became apparent as Forest then drew 0–0 against West Bromwich Albion. 'Frustrated Reds miss Francis fire' proclaimed the headline in the *Evening Post*. Forest won their next three games, but still Fashanu couldn't score. Worse, John Robertson was dropped for the home game against Stoke after saying he was looking for a transfer. He reiterated the demand after scoring in a 2–1 win over Brighton, at which it transpired that his first formal request lay unopened in Forest's office. Clough blamed a mix-up on the part of a secretary, who was suspended, but that did little to soothe Robertson's dissatisfaction.

Fashanu's first goal for the club finally came in a 1–1 draw with Middlesbrough on 10 October and, as the month came to an end, Forest were fifth. The reconstruction of the squad, though, continued as Kenny Burns was sold to Leeds for £400,000. Fashanu scored again in a 1–0 League Cup win at Blackburn, but it was the excellence of Shilton that secured Forest's passage to the quarter-final. A first home goal arrived in a 2–1 defeat to Arsenal and a third league strike in a 3–2 win at Sunderland, but the background hum of discontent continued as Clough threatened to shut the Trent End after a West Ham fan had his face slashed in violence that followed a goalless draw.

The German midfielder Jürgen Röber was signed from Bayern Munich for £250,000 and, as Needham suffered an injury, Willie Young was bought from Arsenal for £150,000. The fact he was thirty-one suggested something awry with Clough and Taylor's stated policy of rejuvenating the squad. Lloyd, who'd been persuaded to leave in the summer, was only a year older. As part of the transfer, Young was entitled to a removal allowance, which he spent on a riding school near Newark. Clough, demonstrating a self-defeating cussedness that would become increasingly familiar, refused to pay, saying the entitlement was for a house not for a business.

The ongoing problems over money left a number of players feeling frustrated and undervalued. The regular travel to play in friendlies to raise cash for the club would have been wearing enough, but what made it worse was that Clough refused to pay the players the full daily allowance they were entitled to under PFA regulations. When Young's protests got too much on a trip to Malaysia, he was stripped of the captaincy.

The strain was beginning to tell. Partly that was because of finances, but partly it was down to the self-imposed task of restructuring the squad. Clough later admitted it was undertaken too quickly, and he and Taylor began to worry about the age of players, something they'd never allowed to concern them previously. 'We lost our sense of proportion,' Clough said.

According to Maurice Edwards, Taylor's work-rate began to drop, although whether it was down to ill health or disillusionment and a disintegrating relationship with Clough was unclear. Either way, his recruitment became significantly less successful in the early eighties. Were Justin Fashanu or Ian Wallace really worth more than £1million? Was Peter Ward worth £500,000? Liverpool, whom Forest could conceivably have challenged as the dominant team of the age, tended to change their side one player at a time, often leaving the new signing in the reserves for several months to get used to the style of the club. Clough and Taylor, though, went for radical surgery, and it cost them. That said, Liverpool did not operate under the same financial constraints as Forest. When Forest won the title in 1977–78, the average gate was 36,000; four years later that figure had dropped to below 20,000.

As the relationship between Clough and Taylor worsened, Taylor took to calling Duncan Hamilton every weekend, sometimes on a Saturday evening straight after *Match of the Day*, sometimes on a Sunday morning, often calling from a payphone as though to evade those he thought might have been tapping his phone, trying to promote the players he had been responsible for bringing in – Fashanu, Wallace and Ward.

With the pressure intensifying, it was Clough who broke first. He spent 27 December at home, entertaining his brother Barry and Barry's wife Judy. Shortly after lunch he went outside to clear some snow and returned after a few minutes sweating heavily and complaining of chest pains. Barbara insisted he went for a check-up, but the Derby Royal Infirmary found nothing amiss, and advised only that he should take three weeks off. A subsequent visit to a Harley Street specialist produced a similar negative result and the same advice. Clough was kept under observation at the Infirmary and it was then that his real dependence on alcohol became apparent. At 2am on 29 December he rang home. Judy answered, fearing the worst, only to find Clough demanding champagne, insisting he had cleared it with the sister. Barry took him a bottle and sat in his room helping him finish it. 'Booze is part of the managerial scene, part and parcel of my business,' Clough wrote in his autobiography. 'Drink is readily available. It is always there if you want it. It is provided and it is free ... You have a drink with the chairman. The occasional journalist may be invited to join you. Friends and colleagues, particularly after a match, will sit and share a glass of champagne ... Because of its availability, if you are not very careful, drink becomes a habit which is extremely difficult to break.'

Stan Anderson, for instance, remembered going to a midweek game at Forest in the late seventies. 'It was a cold night,' he said, 'and before I went out to watch the game he gave me a tumbler of whisky and said, "Here, get that down you." There must have been a third of a bottle in there. Now I hated whisky, but he insisted, so I had a sip and put it down. Before we went out I realised it was all gone; he'd drunk it all.'

For a little over a fortnight Taylor was in charge and he too began to collapse under the strain, becoming increasingly paranoid. Believing Clough was somehow monitoring him, he began to claim that his office was bugged. Hamilton recalled him being particularly touchy around that time 'as if he had a permanent headache'.

A couple of days after Clough checked in to hospital, Ian Bowyer returned to the club for £45,000 – less than Sunderland still owed on the £250,000 they had paid for him – a tacit admission that the rebuilding work had been going on too quickly. Taylor's first game without Clough was an FA Cup tie against Second Division Wrexham; Forest lost 3–1. 'There are certain players in our side who are just not performing at home,' Taylor raged. 'They know who they are. I am not naming names. Suffice to say our creative output at home has been nil.' His one league game before Clough came back brought a 2–1 win over Birmingham.

Clough returned just in time to see Forest go out of the League Cup to Tottenham, and then lose 2–0 to Notts County, the first Nottingham derby played in the top-flight for fifty-six years. Everything was falling apart. Robertson, furious that, as he saw it, he was being asked to play too deep, at last had a transfer request accepted.

It remains unclear whether it were him to whom Taylor had been referring after the defeat to Wrexham. The more obvious candidate, Fashanu, felt moved to speak out after another poor performance in a 0–0 draw against Stoke. 'It's the worst spell I have ever had as a striker,' he said. 'I can understand that the supporters are becoming impatient. They have every right to be. I was bought to score goals and I've not done it. I can't seem to do much right at all. But I'm convinced that it'll come back.'

Clough, though, clearly felt he could be doing more to make his form return, as he made clear after a 2–1 defeat at West Brom. 'Our front men haven't been doing enough work,' he said and, four days after the game, both Fashanu and Wallace were transfer-listed, as was the ultimate symbol of the European Cup-winners, John McGovern. A night of the long knives might have been damaging enough, but what made it worse was that nobody seemed to know who was wielding them. Clough, it turned out, was in Spain on holiday, while McPherson, the chairman, was in New Zealand on business.

'Managerial masters Brian Clough and Peter Taylor are NOT at log-gerheads over the proposed sale of Justin Fashanu, John McGovern and Ian Wallace,' Hamilton wrote, the sort of story in which the 'not' only becomes less credible the more it is emphasised. 'Some people are trying to drive a wedge between us,' Taylor said. 'We have always worked as a partnership. What has happened this week is a policy that we have always adhered to. If something is not going right, then we go out to correct the fault.'

Who, though, were those people? Perhaps he meant Clough's hangers-on, who had increasingly come to annoy him, perhaps he meant muck-raking journalists, but the people who were doing most to drive a wedge between Clough and Taylor were Clough and Taylor themselves. That they had disagreed fundamentally over McGovern was made clear a month later when he was removed from the list. 'Some days we didn't see Clough, other days we didn't see Taylor,' McGovern said. 'They were drifting apart.'

As they did so, the atmosphere in the club was soured. McGovern, who had always been a fitness obsessive, became so disillusioned that he grew reluctant to go in to training. 'Players were getting away with murder in team meetings – any excuse to miss the next match,' he said. 'The magnetism and the buzz had gone.'

It was money, McGovern insisted, that lay at the heart of Forest's decline. 'It was like a cancer spreading through the club,' he said. 'Instead of looking forward to the next match, people were more interested in what their cut would be.' It was an attitude that had slowly filtered down from the top. Before kick-off in European games, Dryden remembered, he would usually spend around half an hour with Clough and Taylor haggling over their share of the gate receipts. 'Peter was very open about his earnings,' Dryden said, 'and it was uppermost in his mind most of the time. Brian was equally fond of money, but perhaps less obvious about it.'

Clough claimed in both autobiographies that he was not motivated by money; as George Edwards put it, John Sadler, Clough's ghostwriter, must have been 'laughing as he wrote the line'. 'Brian,' Edwards said, 'was a football man through and through and football is an Arthur Daley sport in which everybody is motivated by money.'

Clough was astute with his investments and had a particular fondness for newsagents. He bought one in West Bridgford from the director Frank Allcock for his son, Simon, and, understandably, switched the club's magazine and chocolate order for away games there. The chocolate bill suddenly shot up to £30 per trip, and he would buy a 1lb box of chocolates for the player's wives whenever Forest were on tour. Allcock queried it, not necessarily suggesting any wrongdoing, but wondering whether it wouldn't be cheaper to go to a wholesaler. Clough missed the board meeting at which he raised the issue, but at the next one he presented Allcock with a Mars bar and a KitKat. By making a joke of the order, Clough ensured it was laughed off and forgotten.

Hamilton remembers Clough sitting with newspapers, reading out the salaries of players and managers, pop-stars, actors and politicians in fascination, and suggested he was terrified of returning to a life of poverty. 'When you're brought up like that, always fretting about paying the bills, it colours how you feel about life, the way you regard money,' Clough said. 'I found that the only people who aren't obsessed with money are those with more than enough of it.' Revie, of course, had suffered similar insecurity, and in that regard they were both representative of the increasingly self-assertive and successful 'northern man', as Harold Wilson described himself. While their abilities and their earnings may have carried them out of the northern working-classes, certain neuroses remained.

Clough was concerned not just about money but about status. When Forest were struggling financially in the early eighties, his club Mercedes reached 75,000 miles and needed replacing. The board looked into the possibility of a sponsored car, and found a garage willing to offer a Ford Granada for free. Clough, though, insisted on a Mercedes, so a club with a £1m overdraft that was looking to save money wherever it could ended up paying £581 rental each month.

That was typical of his habit of following one rule while imposing another: he became a law unto himself. On one occasion, Forest's reserve team had to hire a coach from an outside contractor to go to a game at Leicester because Clough had commandeered the club bus to take his family on a trip to London. On another, Clough tried to persuade Elton John, at the time the chairman of Watford, to give a concert in Nottingham for his testimonial, offering in return two seats in the directors' box for a reserve game with the promise that Watford could sign any three players playing that night for cut-price deals. Even before the bungs scandal broke in the nineties, there was an abundance of evidence that Clough saw it as his right to use the club's resources to his own ends. Irregular it may have been, perhaps even illegal, but there are plenty who would argue that a bonus or two could be overlooked given the success he brought the club and the consequent joy and self-esteem he brought the city.

In the openly mercenary atmosphere of the early eighties, though, petty jealousies sprang up, as players squabbled over who was earning what, and there were arguments between those who had invested their money sensibly and those who had frittered it away. As the possibility of trophies receded, those disputes became ever more bitter. At one point, in a row over contracts and bonuses, Clough stormed out of the room, shouting, 'As far as I'm concerned the whole lot of you can bugger off.'

Clough, taking seriously his doctor's advice to rest, went to Cyprus for a fortnight. Forest, in Hamilton's words, 'put up only faltering resistance' in losing to Southampton. Fashanu was dropped for a goalless draw at Wolves and left out again as Forest won 1–0 at Brighton, where the nineteen-year-old Calvin Plummer made his debut. Those games were the start of an eight-game unbeaten run – although they didn't score more than a single goal in any of them – that lifted Forest to ninth in the table, six points behind the top three. Talk of a 'sprint for Europe' in the *Evening Post*, though, was soon dashed by back-to-back 1–0 home defeats to Everton and Wolves, and the season was drifting to its conclusion when Taylor quit.

Forest had just lost their fourth last game of the season, 1–0 at home to Manchester United, when Taylor walked into Clough's office and, with the phrase he had used to write off countless players, announced he was giving up. 'I've shot it,' he said. Clough said he wept when Taylor told him he had to go, but recognised the toll the job was taking and accepted his decision. He didn't, though, accept it without a fight and yet more of his opaque boardroom machinations. Whether he was unclear in his mind what he was doing, whether he was simply meddling or whether he was politicking towards a specific goal it is impossible to say.

As Taylor negotiated his pay-off with the chairman, Geoffrey McPherson, Clough threatened to resign as well. Taylor knew the club couldn't afford to pay them both off and feared a Clough scam, either to force him to stay or to boost his own salary. Clough later claimed he secured a £31,000 deal for Taylor, but Taylor was adamant that he negotiated it himself, and that it was for £25,000 plus his club car. At the time there was little animosity and they spent some time together that summer in Cala Millor, but it didn't take long for the sourness to set in.

At the time, Taylor blamed his departure on 'health and recent events', but much later, when questioned by Francis, he was scathing. He said that in that final year he'd stopped liking Clough, and that the differences that hadn't seemed to matter in the years of success came to rankle (the same, perhaps, could be said of the general relations between squad members). Critically, they'd lost their fabled ability to make each other laugh. Like McGovern, Taylor stopped enjoying football. 'I woke up each morning dreading the thought of work,' he said. 'I was irritable and tired. When that happens, you can't just carry on. Was it me who changed or Brian? I'm not sure. I just know there were sides to his character I could no longer come to terms with. His need for hangers-on was unbearable.'

445

It wasn't just Taylor who came to resent the outsiders who joined Clough's inner circle; it affected his family as well. At Derby, he had employed his brother Barry as an electrician, and he set up Gerald in a newsagents at Bramcote, but he fell out with Barry in a dispute over money that led to them exchanging blows and the police being called. Yet once he had paid off a £200 debt for Barry and paid for he and his wife Judy to have a holiday in Jersey. 'He went to great pains to build a protective circle around himself of people who wouldn't talk out of turn,' Judy told Francis. 'If he had kept it to the family, it would have been easier. As soon as the wall spread to include so-called friends, that's when it became weaker.'

At times, Taylor said, half a dozen or more of the inner circle – the likes of the former Derby director Mike Keeling, Colin Lawrence, who had helped him negotiate his pay-off from Leeds, and his gardener David Gregory – would turn up at the hotel while the Forest squad were having their pre-match talk, 'driving a wedge' – that phrase again – between him and Clough and loosening the focus of the squad. 'He seemed completely unable to cope without people running around after him: driving his car, running his errands, fetching his drinks and practically tying his shoelaces, while he sat back and ordered them around.'

Perhaps there was a touch of jealousy in Taylor's words: after all, in the past, he had been the only assistance Clough had needed, but his embarrassment at what Clough had become was understandable. Clough lapped up the publicity, and clearly took great delight in the fact that his social circle had come to include the likes of Geoff Boycott and Michael Parkinson. He revelled – at least some of the time — in being a celebrity, which sat uncomfortably with the image he liked to project of the simple Middlesbrough lad telling it like it was. Given his aversion to fame, it's hardly surprising that Taylor began to feel left out.

Clough, of course, was the exact opposite. He came to complain that Taylor never wanted to go out, and others said Taylor was a difficult man to get to know because of his aversion to socialising, which seems to have predated his horror of being recognised in public. Clough, though, loved being the centre of attention. He could have gone anywhere in the world for his holidays, but he kept going back to Cala Millor, kept sitting in the same cafe, because – particularly after Stuart Webb's travel business had made it a popular destination for holiday-makers from the east Midlands –

he knew there would be people there who knew who he was, who could be relied upon to point and stare and generate a buzz around him. 'If people don't recognise him,' Taylor said, 'he creates a fuss and makes sure they do.'

That had always been the case, but as Clough became more of a celebrity, the tendency grew more pronounced. Clough, Taylor complained, had 'become a media creation – a cardboard cut-out of the real Brian Clough. Many of the so-called brilliant one-liners were carefully rehearsed and geared to have the maximum effect. He was a great manipulator of the press. He and they fed off each other like leeches.' Becoming a self-parody is always a risk for those in the public eye, but particularly so for somebody whose image was as constructed as Clough's was.

Even the way Clough treated journalists came to sicken Taylor. Clough, of course, had once courted them, seeking publicity for Hartlepools and then Derby, but by the early eighties he knew the balance of power lay with him and he exploited it. Clough would make journalists wait for hours, and then treat them 'like children' when he finally did come to speak. At first, Taylor thought anybody who was prepared to put themselves through such humiliation probably deserved it, but 'after a while I began to wonder what motivated a person to behave so abominably towards others'.

The answer wasn't hard to find: it was about power. Some would excuse that by suggesting Clough was insecure – his obsession over failing his eleven-plus the most obvious manifestation of that, and his projection of a brash image perhaps being a symptom – but, as Taylor pointed out, others were insecure without acting so atrociously and Clough's behaviour only encouraged insecurity in others. Drink perhaps provides an explanation but not an excuse, and the colourful character he presented meant he remained a popular figure to the public at large, but it's hard to deny the fact that in the early eighties, Clough had become a monster, impossibly egotistical, falling out with all around him, even the man who had been his closest friend. 'Brian needed constantly to be number one,' Taylor said. 'Few of his friends had a normal relationship with him. Many of his associations were based on what each side could get out of it. He wouldn't tolerate anyone who answered back or posed a threat to his dominance.'

Where personal relationships faded, Clough's love of money, which had always been there, rose up in their place. 'Materialism had taken him over,'

447

Taylor said. 'His one thought from waking up in the morning to going to bed is "how can I make more money?"' Taylor said that it was the injury that introduced iron into Clough's soul. Fifteen years of management, the experience of the ingratitude of directors and fans, of the whole culture of the game of football, made it grow. He may have spoken to Woodcock and Anderson of the importance of being a credit to the game, and that strand of idealism was woven deep into his worldview, but football had hardened him; by the time Taylor walked out, his main priority was looking after himself. Football and Forest came after.

The public, of course, didn't care. They enjoyed the entertainment both of Clough's interviews and of the football his team played; and that, of course, raises an ugly question: without his unpredictability, his love of controversy and his larger-than-life image, could Clough have been as successful as he was? Or was that the 'mask' he later admitted having to don?

In that regard, an episode Ted Croker, the former secretary of the FA, recounted in his autobiography is telling. Justifying the decision not to appoint Clough as England manager, he wrote of having recently seen Clough on a television programme chaired by Gary Newbon about the failure of Midlands clubs in the 1985–86 season. 'Several other Midlands managers were present and Brian levelled unfair insults at both them and Newbon,' he said. 'Why he does this I cannot imagine. Possibly it is because he would not be so popular on television, radio and in Fleet Street if he was less provocative.'

That was the image; in less public circumstances, Clough could be a much more sympathetic figure. Croker and Clough were both called to give evidence at an Inland Revenue hearing into whether it was legitimate for Trevor Francis to trade not as an individual but as a limited liability company. 'We spent four hours together waiting to be called . . .' he wrote. 'We talked continuously about both the game and our families . . . he was much different from the strident, aggressive figure I had seen on television. I could see why he makes such an impression on younger players.'

Clough was, every player who spent more than a season or so under his management seems to agree, a master psychologist; was it, perhaps, that the monstrous image he created was the agent of that? That that was the way he – to use Sam Longson's terms again – 'dominated' and 'mesmerised' his players? Perhaps even the creation of the mask was a manifestation of his insecurity: as a younger man, as he said in his second autobiography, he'd been 'fearless', confident in his wit and his personality; later, as fear crept in, he constructed an exaggerated alternative self, just as boxers will commonly refer to the part of themselves that steps into the ring in the third person, before slipping back into the first when speaking about themselves in everyday life. He created the mask, a stylised, exaggerated construct of the brashness he projected as a young man as a means of self-assertion and self-protection, then grew into it.

Just as money began to dominate Clough's thoughts, Forest ran out – which might, of course, have been what brought the issue to the front of his mind. Taylor, standing in the corridor outside the dressing-room in the Bernabéu after Forest had beaten Hamburg, had wondered if things could ever be as good again. His resignation had provided the answer: they couldn't.

V

1982–2004

*'Wir kommen aus dem Dunkel und gehen ins Dunkel,
dazwischen liegen Erlebnisse.'**

(Thomas Mann, *Der Zauberberg*, chapter 6, section 8)

* We come from the darkness and we go into darkness,
between lie experiences.

Dangling Man

Together Brian Clough and Peter Taylor had won two promotions, two European Cups, two league titles and two League Cups. Clough alone would manage only two League Cups. The obvious conclusion, and the one Clough immediately feared people would draw, was that without Taylor he was a diminished figure. Perhaps he was, but there had always been two other parties in their relationship: Jimmy Gordon and money. The cash had left even before Taylor. It might not have matched what had happened in the seventies, and so perhaps always looked pallid by comparison, but what Clough achieved on extremely limited resources in the eighties was extraordinary.

Gordon, meanwhile, retired at the same time Taylor did, depriving Clough of the man who actually did his coaching on a day-to-day basis, and leaving him isolated. According to Ian Bowyer, at that time Clough would make sure that he walked out with the team before matches so it wasn't so obvious that he was alone. He kept up his pre-match routine, meanwhile, of playing squash. On non match-days, he often played Garry Birtles, who admitted he thought it politic not to win, but before a game he would play the club doctor, Mick Hutson. 'He was very competitive,' Hutson remembered. 'He couldn't move that freely because of his knee, so he'd take up a position in the middle of the court and use that big backside of his to get in your way. I could have called for a let, but if I had, we'd never have got a point played so I just ran round him.' They would finish their games at around 2.30, then Clough would have a shower before going to give his final motivational words to the players.

Winning the European Cup had given Forest an opportunity. They had money, a fine squad and a stadium that was beginning to take a leap into the modern age. That money, though, was squandered. Wallace and Ward never quite matched expectations; Fashanu came nowhere near. The fact that Forest averaged a goal a game and finished with only the eighteenth best attacking record of the twenty-two Division One teams in 1981–82 made clear where the squad's problems lay. As the reconstruction of the squad faltered and Forest finished only twelfth, failing to qualify for Europe, meeting the repayments on the Executive Stand became a debilitating burden. Football-related revenue had fallen £800,000 the previous season to £1,660,000; with no European football at all, that figure was only going to get worse.

Perhaps construction of the stand had been a gamble worth taking, an attempt to lure in more fans and allow Forest, if not to match the financial might of Liverpool or Manchester United, then at least to close the gap. As crowds dwindled, though – gate receipts for 1981–82 were down £102,000 on the previous season – it appeared increasingly as a folly, the moment when Clough flew too close to the sun. At one point, he subsequently claimed, he had to make the club an emergency loan of £35,000 to settle an outstanding debt to the Inland Revenue.

By June 1982, with over £1million still owed on the stand, Forest's overdraft had hit £1million, prompting three directors – Brian Appleby, Ian Loch and Leslie Burnham – to resign because they felt 'unable to accept terms of guarantee wanted by the bank for the club's overdraft'. The chairman Geoffrey McPherson admitted that to break even Forest needed crowds to go up from 18,000 to 22,000.

At the heart of it all was Fashanu, who was effectively the physical embodiment of that £1million overdraft. Goal statistics often don't tell the full story, but in this case his record of three league goals in thirty-one appearances did; he was offering little to the team and had he not been signed, Forest's bank balance would have been a comforting nil. By the end of his unhappy fifteen months at the club his confidence was so shot that he almost scored an own-goal from the halfway line in a reserve-team game. The deal was disastrous for Forest, not just because he failed adequately to replace Francis, whose position in the squad he effectively took, but because it was his signing, Clough always maintained, that finished off his relationship with Taylor. 'Justin,' Taylor said, 'didn't *want* to play football.'

Clough and Taylor had, between them, sorted out a number of troublesome characters, from Ken Simpkins at Hartlepools through Gemmill to Burns and Lloyd, but Fashanu was beyond them. 'He used to burst into tears if I said hello to him ...' Clough said. 'He had so many personal problems a platoon of agony aunts couldn't have sorted him out.'

Clough booked Fashanu into a nursing home to have an operation on his toes, which were, according to Clough, oddly shaped, but he didn't turn up. After games, Fashanu would throw his boots into the crowd; Clough had to tell him to stop because the club couldn't afford to keep providing new ones. He would park his jeep anywhere he fancied, and racked up, Clough estimated, between twenty and thirty unpaid parking tickets. When he announced he had found God, Clough was dismissive, asking if he could get God to sign some cheques for his unpaid bills.

Fashanu stood out. He had a personal masseur. He refused to use the club towels, preferring to bring in his own; Forest's first £1 million player had similarly brought his own towels at first, but had stopped when asked; their third insisted. On a trip to Spain, Clough was woken one night by a tremendous crash. He raced along the corridor to find Fashanu washing his bloodied hands in the wash-basin, his room-mate Viv Anderson cowering in apparent terror, and a large dent in the door. Fashanu, it turned out, had had a bad dream, during which he'd hurled himself at the exit.

None of that would have mattered had Fashanu been successful, but at Forest he wasn't. At one point he took to arranging extra shooting practice after training – which at least suggests the intent to improve was there – but, Steve Hodge recalled, 'these simple shooting drills turned into a nightmare for him … his shots continually few high and wide or were miscued.' His confidence, in other words, had deserted him utterly.

And then, of course, there was the homosexuality. 'That in itself didn't bother me too much,' Clough said. 'It was just that his shiftiness, combined with an articulate image that impressed the impressionable, made it difficult for me to accept Fashanu as genuine and one of us.' The claim it didn't bother him too much, though, rings uneasily with Clough's repeated use of the term 'poof' in his first autobiography. He decided, as he put it, to 'put him to the test'. He asked Fashanu where he'd go if he wanted to buy a loaf of bread. 'A baker's,' Fashanu replied. He asked him where he'd go if he wanted a leg of lamb. 'A butcher's,' Fashanu replied. 'So why do you keep going to that bloody poofs' club in town?' Clough asked. Fashanu shrugged. 'He knew what I meant,' Clough said. But what did he mean? Clough never explained explicitly, but the underlying homophobia, hardly uncommon at the time, is hard to miss. 'It wasn't long,' Clough went on, 'before I could stand no more of him.'

Matters came to a head on the final day of the 1981–82 season, when Fashanu, having been fined two weeks' wages for amassing ten cautions, withdrew from Forest's match away at Ipswich less than an hour before kick-off. An apoplectic Clough clipped him around the ear and, with options limited, handed a debut to the nineteen-year-old Hodge, who had impressed as a midfielder in the reserves. 'It had been drummed into me to receive the ball, get turned and run at the defender, and I tried to do that whenever I could,' he said, which pretty much sums up how Clough expected his forwards to play. Peter Davenport – who was himself only twenty and had made his debut less than a month earlier – scored a hat-trick, the third of them set up by Hodge, as Forest won 3–1. Hodge, exhausted, was substituted with five minutes remaining and, having been hugged by Clough, found his manager removing his boots for him. The good mood didn't last long, though, and Clough refused to allow Fashanu on the coach, leaving him to make his own way back to Nottingham.

Whether it was because of his experience with Fashanu, or because he no longer had Taylor alongside him, the type of player Clough signed changed. 'I didn't mind naughty boys,' Taylor said. 'Underneath many of them had hearts of gold. Gamblers and womanisers I could handle by feeding their vices if necessary. Booze was the biggest problem. That and drugs. You've no chance with them. Brian was different from me. He preferred the good lads.' And so, gradually, the make-up of Forest's team changed, from the rough-and-ready drinkers of the seventies to the good boys of the eighties with hair as neat as their passing.

Publicly at least, Clough remained sanguine as he approached the 1982–83 season, his first without Taylor and Gordon. 'Our main problems were centred around defence,' he said in a column in the *Evening Post*. That was a mystifying comment, given they'd had the fourth-best defensive record in the league the previous season. 'We thought we'd be alright in that direction. Ultimately it turned out to be our biggest headache. If Einar Aas returns, or Chris Fairclough comes through, and we find ourselves a left-back, we won't be in bad shape . . .' He also suggested that his patience with Justin Fashanu wasn't entirely exhausted, albeit in his usual abrasive way. 'He may still act like a baby at times – and he hasn't performed to the level that anyone expected him to – but he may get himself sorted out yet,' Clough said. 'It'll help when he moves out of that hotel he's lived in since last August.' As it was, he loaned Fashanu to Southampton before the season began.

That summer was largely spent offloading players in an attempt to balance the books. Needham was released, Röber sold to Leverkusen for £150,000 and McGovern joined Bolton as player-manager – symbolically the moment at which the team that had won the European Cup was no more. The biggest loss, though, was the sale of Shilton to Southampton for £400,000, which included a £100,000 signing-on fee. The sense of camaraderie in the dressing-room, Shilton said, had begun to fade and he had been irritated when Clough had him serve drinks to journalists at a press conference, something he felt was done 'not to indicate to them that there was an egalitarian policy at the club, but to show them that he was the boss and even England internationals did as he bade'.

Shilton's departure left Steve Sutton as the only goalkeeper on the books, so Clough signed Hans van Breukelen from Utrecht for £200,000. Crucially, his wages were far lower than Shilton's. The only other arrival before the start of the season was Colin Todd, signed from Birmingham to add defensive cover. 'It rekindled my career again,' Todd said. 'I was thirty-two and it was brilliant. It was as good as the first time – I knew what to expect now.' There was only one difference, but it was a profound one. 'The relationship between him and Peter Taylor was over,' Todd said. 'Something had happened, and it had soured Brian's mind. It was sad.'

Then there was the situation with Robertson who, after suffering an ankle injury early in the new year, had reluctantly settled down at Forest to try to get fit for the World Cup. 'John has been at this club for about fourteen years,' Clough wrote in the *Evening Post*. 'Ultimately I will have to find a replacement for him. I would like to delay that choice as long as possible. But the only way I can do that is if he starts to improve. For most of last season he didn't do himself or Forest justice. I've told him that if he doesn't get better, then he'll end up playing for Doncaster.' That may have been true, but it was an astonishing thing to have made public, particularly given the column was published on the day Scotland played their opening game of the World Cup, against New Zealand. The sense was that Robertson's patience with his manager was wearing thin anyway; if it snapped at that moment he could hardly be blamed.

There were problems with other players, too. Young, still frustrated by

Clough's refusal to pay him his removal allowance, snapped as Clough baited him at a restaurant in Torquay. He told Clough that if he wanted him to go along with his way of doing things, he should at least pay him what he was due by the terms of his contract. The row flared again in the bar later, as Young refused Clough's invitation to drink with him. Clough threatened to send him home the next day, to which Young replied that he'd have to physically drag him to the bus and lock him in if he expected him to go. As it was, Mike Keeling turned up and took Clough home the following day instead. In the old days, of course, after Clough had wound players up, Taylor and Gordon had calmed them down again; now there was only a bad cop.

For Steve Hodge, the overwhelming feeling was one of excitement, the thrill of a career just starting, and that outweighed any pressure of having to live up to the sides of the recent past. He admitted, though, 'There was a sense of starting again, the European Cup-winning team had broken up so quickly. There was only three of that side left when I made my debut, and we knew the club was skint because the new signings – Justin Fashanu, Ian Wallace and Peter Ward – hadn't worked out.'

Among more senior players, and among fans, disillusionment was rife. Forest won 2–1 at West Ham and then lost 3–0 at home to Manchester United as Todd was sent off for a deliberate handball. Even after Birtles was re-signed for £250,000 – a remarkable development given how seriously he and Clough had fallen out the previous season – only 13,079 turned out for the visit of Brighton, the lowest crowd since promotion, not even two-thirds of what was required to break even.

Those who were there saw Forest win 4–0, but they then shipped eight in two games, losing to Liverpool and Aston Villa, suggesting Clough had perhaps been right when he'd indentified the defence as the side's weakness. To make matters worse, Bowyer was sent off in the defeat to Villa – the rare indiscipline hinting at the upheaval behind the scenes – and Davenport was injured. Forest did beat Watford 2–0, but most of the headlines focused on Clough's attempts to chase a pitch-invader dressed as a clown. Farcical it may have been, but it foreshadowed a far graver incident to come five years later.

Forest puttered on, playing well at home and poorly away, and then came Taylor's second bombshell. Taylor going was one thing, but Taylor returning elsewhere was something else entirely. Only 186 days after announcing that he'd 'shot it', Taylor was back and, as far as Clough was concerned, in the worst possible place: at Derby. As a provocative gesture, it could hardly have been bettered. Not only would any success at Derby – which was admittedly unlikely, given the financial state of the club – have potentially drawn non-partisan fans to the Baseball Ground and perhaps hit the already declining attendances at the City Ground, but Clough lived in Derby: it was his retreat, his bolt-hole. Besides which, Clough was terrified that if he didn't drag Forest back towards success, and if Derby did begin to improve, Taylor's contribution to their partnership would be magnified.

Characteristically, he intervened, although – as so often – with what intent it is hard to say. The exact sequence of events remains unclear, but it seems Clough used Mike Keeling to get in touch with Stuart Webb, suggesting that he might be interested in a return to Derby. Webb, having been burned before, was doubtful and told Keeling that the job had already been offered to Taylor and that if Clough wanted to come back, the two of them would have to sort it out between themselves.

Taylor met Clough by the paddling pool on the banks of the Trent. He offered him significant money to return and Clough, who so often demanded instant decisions from others, asked, as was his wont, for time to consider the offer. Taylor agreed, having first secured a promise of secrecy from Clough. The next day, Taylor read of Clough's decision to reject the offer in a national newspaper that had paid for the story. 'I offered him the earth,' Taylor said, 'and he stabbed me in the back.' Their relationship had only one further notch to fall.

On the pitch, there was improvement, almost as though Taylor's return focused Clough's mind. A 2–0 win at Luton lifted Forest to seventh in a tightly bunched table in which five points separated the top twelve teams. Victory over Ipswich made a title challenge seem plausible and a 7–3 win over Watford in the League Cup suggested a side that had not merely hit its attacking rhythm, but had somehow captured the utopian spirit Clough had claimed to be seeking to impose at Leeds. After the final whistle, as Graham Taylor, the Watford manager, prepared to give his side a rollicking for having been so open, Clough came into the dressing-room and kissed him on both cheeks, congratulating him on such an exciting, attacking game of football. He then went round and kissed each player.

Peter Taylor was one ghost returned to haunt Clough; Fashanu was another. He had scored three times and looked generally sprightly in his loan spell at Southampton, but then, having been pencilled in to play for the A-side at Mansfield, disappeared before kick-off. Clough wanted him to play a couple of friendlies in Saudi Arabia so he could assess his form in his system, but visa complications meant he ended up playing for the reserves against Bradford instead.

Forest drew 1–1 at Southampton that Saturday, but the following Monday there was a row at the training ground as Fashanu turned up in contravention of a ban imposed by Clough the previous week. Fashanu said it was because he'd refused to go on loan to Derby – itself an interesting detail, because it suggests that at that stage, Clough was still looking to help Taylor out (or, viewed more cynically, to offload his biggest problem onto him). Fashanu turned to the PFA for support.

As the union was seeking some sort of arbitration, Norwich made a bid to re-sign Fashanu on loan, but asked that Forest should pay some of his £900 a week wages. Clough rejected the offer – or at least that's how the *Evening Post* reported it at the time. A later version, put about by Clough, had him keen to accept Norwich's offer only for Fashanu to say that, having sought God's advice, he had decided against returning. 'There's only one god in Nottingham,' Clough claimed to have replied, 'and he thinks you should go.'

That Thursday, Fashanu turned up again for training, bringing with him either his personal religious teacher or his masseur – nobody seems quite sure which. Clough ordered him to leave, but Fashanu refused. He had had boxing training, and there was a moment when it seemed he might punch his manager, but he backed down. Clough called the police and Fashanu was led away weeping. 'I can't imagine how he'd have coped at Middlesbrough in the fifties,' Clough said. The world had moved on; Clough perhaps hadn't. 'I am ready to serve out my suspension,' Fashanu told the *Evening Post*. 'Then I hope the manager will see that I am not trying to upstage him.'

That comment, surely, is telling and not just because it recalled some of the speculation about the reasons for Withe's departure four years earlier. Either Fashanu was as cunning and manipulative as Clough suggested, or that he felt Clough's hostility towards him had less to do with his individuality, his quirks, his homosexuality or his lack of form than his articulateness. Perhaps this was the O'Neill situation magnified by the fact that Fashanu was different, and offered little on the pitch, and that Clough no longer had Taylor as an ally. Clough essentially struggled to deal with those whom he could not browbeat, those who would stand up to him in an argument and had the intellectual capacity potentially to win.

'The basis of it is that Justin was at fault in regard to discipline,' the chairman Geoffrey McPherson explained the following day, announcing that Fashanu would be suspended until the following Friday. 'He did not report as he should have done for the Milk Cup tie against Watford. Because of that and other instances of general discipline, the manager suspended him for fourteen days on full pay. The manager's intention was, of course, to try to persuade Justin to obey the rules of the club. Unfortunately, Justin decided he would go down and train, to the embarrassment of the other players.'

Fashanu, it was reported, ripped up the letter from Ken Smales explaining the suspension. The following week, he won his appeal against the ban, but Clough had had enough, and at the beginning of December, Fashanu took a fifty per cent pay cut to move to Notts County for £150,000.

He never recaptured his early form, though, and was effectively ostracised by the game after revealing his homosexuality in 1990. He hanged himself in a lock-up in Shoreditch in 1998 believing, inaccurately, that Maryland police had issued a warrant for his arrest over an allegation of sexual assault by a seventeen-year-old.

A superb Ian Wallace winner at Sunderland lifted Forest to third. They were 'exceptional', according to Hamilton, in beating Manchester City 3–0, and even after losing 3–2 at Notts County, wins over Swansea and Norwich saw Forest third, behind Liverpool and Manchester United only on goal difference. Late goals from Birtles and Proctor secured a 4–2 win over Coventry on Boxing Day, but that was the high point. Clough dismissed his side as 'pathetic' after a 3–1 defeat at Everton, and draws against Sunderland and Brighton created daylight between Forest and the leaders.

The Clough–Taylor antipathy, meanwhile, was rumbling on. Clough claimed he did his best to be a good neighbour and pointed out that he had ended up at Taylor's house trying to get Viv Anderson and Mark Proctor to sign on loan for Derby. As so often, though, it was a gesture underlain by self-interest. Taylor said that he had made several attempts to loan players from Forest, only to see them end up at other clubs, when Clough arrived unexpectedly at his house in Widmerpool one evening with Anderson and Proctor. Both, it turned out, had been bundled into Clough's car under duress and neither had any intention of joining Derby. Even if they had, Taylor wouldn't have been able to afford their wages.

Anderson described the situation as 'embarrassing'. Clough, predictably, lost his temper, and told the players that if they wouldn't do as they were told, they would have to find their own way home. Both would have been more than happy to do that, just to get out of Taylor's house and away from a furious Clough, but neither was willing to risk provoking him further by telephoning for a taxi. So when Clough left the room, they made a break for it, running through Taylor's back garden, jumping the fence and stumbling through fields in the dark until they finally found a village pub from which they could safely ring for a cab. 'It was a joke,' Taylor said. 'He wasn't doing me any favours. He was just trying to unload two problem players. He had no time for Viv and he didn't get on too well with Mark.'

In one of the quirks of coincidence in which football delights, Forest were drawn against Derby, Clough against Taylor, in the third round of the FA Cup. For Clough, it was a disaster. That the game meant more to him than a cup tie would usually have done was obvious. He approached Young before kick-off and begged him to maintain his fine run of form. He left out Colin Todd on the grounds he might not be psychologically prepared to play against his former club – by which he probably meant Taylor – but then saw one former Forest player, Gary Mills, produce the game's outstanding performance by neutralising Robertson, and another, Archie Gemmill, open the scoring with a free-kick. Andy Hill completed a 2–0 win for Taylor's side in the final minutes.

Afterwards, Clough accused Young of having taken a bribe to throw the game. 'I'd never seen him under so much pressure,' Young said. Clough went on to accuse Young of not caring enough about the game and told him to 'fuck off and see your mate Taylor'. To spite his manager, Young did, and when Clough saw them shaking hands, he flipped. When Young got on the team-coach, Clough accosted him and then, his face puce, got off the team bus, ran round the back and, despite the presence of a number of fans, shouted through the window at Young that shaking Taylor's hand was the last thing he'd do for the club. Clough was then criticised in the press for failing to shake Taylor's hand, although Hamilton saw him go to Taylor's office after the game only to find it empty.

The defeat seemed to unsettle the whole club. Manchester United hammered Forest 4–0 in the League Cup and, with Robertson suffering a cartilage injury, their league form collapsed. When they lost at home to Southampton at the end of March, they had won just one of their previous thirteen games and had slumped to tenth in the table.

Robertson's return, though, prompted a sudden surge and, after winning six and drawing two of their next eight games – including a 1–0 win over the champions Liverpool – Forest went in to their final game of the season at Swansea knowing a win would guarantee a place in the Uefa Cup, and a draw would be enough if Manchester United beat Brighton in the FA Cup final. Goals from Wallace and Anderson and a Robertson penalty ensured a comfortable win, and Clough was able to set about restructuring his squad with a little extra financial leeway.

Einar Aas had been forced to retire with a groin strain, so Paul Hart was signed from Leeds for £60,000 as a replacement in central defence. Robertson, meanwhile, even at thirty – whatever Clough had said the previous season – had proved his immense value in the run-in. His contract expired that summer, but Clough – if his public pronouncements were an accurate guide, and they often weren't – seemingly expected him to stay. 'I'd consider resigning if we didn't get him [Robertson] to re-sign ...' he told the *Evening Post* that Thursday. 'He's the one player on our staff who can actually play a ball.'

By the Friday, as he set off on a 100-mile charity walk through the Yorkshire Dales, Clough was relaxed enough to discuss Taylor's position. 'I would have thought that the logical thing to do when Peter made up his mind that retirement wasn't for him, would have been to come back to Forest,' he said. 'I think pride may have stopped him ... The door was wide open for him – it still is. I certainly didn't feel let down when he left. I understood his reasons. So if he ever wants to change his mind then he only has to let me know.'

Was he really opening the door, offering to let bygones be bygones? Or was this Clough, the great manipulator, offering an ersatz olive branch in anticipation of what was to come, so that he would look like the injured party? The following day, Cup final day, came the final break with Taylor.

The Centurion Walk had been an event that saw Clough at his warmest and most demotic; on learning that it was the golden wedding anniversary of a blind man he had met, for instance, he insisted on going to his house and drinking tea with both husband and wife while the neighbours flocked round.

On the Saturday evening, Clough arrived at the pub where he was spending the night and spoke to Barbara on the phone. She told him that Taylor had signed Robertson. 'There was a minor explosion,' said the club doctor Mick Hutson, who accompanied Clough on the walk. Robertson was not merely still a useful player; he had become emblematic of what Clough had achieved at Forest, converting him from an overweight scruff idling in the reserves to a respected winger who scored the winning goal in the European Cup final. Shilton, Burns, Lloyd, Gemmill, Francis, McGovern and Woodcock had all left, but Clough saw Robertson as providing continuity with the past, a link from his champions to the side he was trying to build.

Yet it was Clough's fault that Robertson left, which perhaps made the hurt all the deeper. As Robertson was recovering from his cartilage injury, Clough had commented that it was 'a bad season for that to happen'; an astonishingly callous remark for somebody whose career had been ended by a knee injury. Robertson, understandably, began to wonder if Clough would use the injury as an excuse to offer him reduced terms and, sure enough, Clough told him at the end of the season that, Forest's finances being what they were, he might not be able to offer him as much as he had been on. As Clough headed off on his walk, Robertson was left a free agent, his future uncertain. Taylor offered him a deal, and Robertson took it. 'Things happened quickly, but Derby offered me a three-year contract as opposed to Forest's two,' Robertson explained in the *Evening Post*. 'I have been having talks with Forest for a while, but with my wife expecting a baby I didn't want any hassle.' Hassle, though, was what he got. His contract with Forest ran until 31 July, so technically he was their player until then. Clough initially stopped his pay, then fined him two weeks' wages for failing to make himself available for a pre-season tour of Canada.

Clough refused ever to use Taylor's forename again and the following season, when Forest's reserves failed to inflict on Derby the heavy defeat that most had predicted, Clough suspended Liam O'Kane, the coach he deemed responsible, for a week. In an attack on what Clough saw as Taylor's perfidiousness, he called him 'a rattlesnake'. Taylor responded by dismissing his outburst as 'poisonous, vicious, disgraceful ... unfortunately it is the sort of thing I have come to expect from a person I now regard with great distaste.'

Courtesy dictated that Taylor should have told Clough what was going on, but there was nothing in football's legal or moral code to say he should have informed him. Robertson later expressed regret that he hadn't fronted up to Clough, but it was Clough who had allowed his contract to run down, Clough who had generated an atmosphere in which players were afraid to approach their manager about such issues. Besides, given Clough's scams to get players – given the way he boasted of his cunning – it was monstrously hypocritical for him to blame Taylor for a simple sin of omission. 'I'd been breaking my neck to get Robbo to sign,' Clough later claimed, quite untruthfully, 'because I was trying to survive with a very inferior side to the ones we'd had. Thanks to Taylor, we'd wasted £3million on bad players, then he does that to me.'

Clough had his revenge, though. That July, as the transfer tribunal sat in the Great Western Hotel in Paddington, they didn't say a word to each other, Clough maintaining his air of outrage and insisting he'd found out about the treachery only on Cup final day. When he found himself approaching Taylor and the Derby delegates in a corridor, Clough performed a theatrical about-turn. He told the tribunal he'd resign if Robertson weren't forced to sign a new contract and railed against the 'dishonesty' of Taylor. Only much later did he admit that he'd had an 'inkling' of what was going long before that phone call on Cup final day.

'It upset me,' he told the *Evening Post* at the time, hamming up his hurt. 'But then I think the affair as a whole does not reflect too well on either Taylor or Robertson. It went on behind my back when all it needed was a five-second phone call to let me know what was happening ... When Taylor left Forest last April I negotiated a good settlement for him – because he said he wanted to retire – as if he were my own brother. By doing so I received a lot of criticism. But after what's happened – and the way it's happened – I feel deeply let down. In my opinion the way he [Robertson] decided to leave the club was an insult to everybody who contributed towards his testimonial.'

Robertson, presumably pretty upset himself, adroitly pointed out Clough's hypocrisy. 'Obviously, Brian Clough has helped me during my time with the club,' he said. 'He has done a lot for me, but he cannot deny that I have done my fair share too. He has said that he feels let down. But in the past I feel that he has let me down. He has passed comment about me, sometimes in front of millions of TV viewers, and those remarks have upset my wife and my family … That testimonial was granted to me for twelve years service to the club. I proved my loyalty by signing for another three seasons. As far as I am concerned, in leaving, I was only exercising my right as an individual to make my own choice. If Brian Clough thought I wasn't good enough in a year or so's time, would he be so concerned about my future then?' Of course he wouldn't; and having seen the culling of the team that won the European Cup, Robertson knew just how ruthless Clough could be.

Clough produced evidence – much to Robertson's surprise – that South-ampton and Luton (managed by Lawrie McMenemy and David Pleat, two of his closest friends in the game) had both made bids for the player the previous season. As a result, the tribunal set the fee at £135,000, far higher than Derby had anticipated. Because of that, they were unable to strengthen their defence, and far from mounting a promotion challenge, they ended up being relegated, fully five points from safety. Clough toasted their demise with a double whisky; Taylor had already gone by the time their fate was confirmed, having retired for a second and final time a month before the end of the season.

Robertson was initially banned from the City Ground, but as he proved ineffective in Derby's increasingly desperate battle against relegation, Clough relented and, after inviting him back to watch a game, he re-signed him. It seemed an odd decision, as Robertson by then looked as though he had, to use Taylor's phrase, 'shot it', and it seems plausible that Clough was at least partly motivated by a desire to succeed where Taylor had failed. As it turned out, he was unable to rehabilitate Robertson for a second time, and the winger played only a handful of games before being discarded.

Clough continued to attack Taylor in the papers, saying at one point that if he saw him on the A52, he would run him over. Taylor's family were in Scarborough when they saw that piece and, understandably, they were outraged; if Taylor had had any lingering respect for his 'mate', it disappeared then. 'No one,' he told Francis, 'will know how my wife and daughter suffered over those remarks. It hurt more than anything in all my years with Brian. He did it out of pure spite without a thought for the agonies I was going through trying to manage Derby.'

Although Clough came to regret the feud, he remained unapologetic. Discussing the issue in his first autobiography, Clough insisted that 'I don't have a problem with my conscience' and about a page later repeated, 'my conscience was untroubled'. Perhaps he was protesting too much, and perhaps he did come to see his reaction as disproportionate, but the sense of hurt and betrayal he felt at the time, however justified it was, was real enough.

The summer of 1983 was another one of trimming expenditure. Proctor went to Sunderland, having spent two months of the previous season on loan there, and Stuart Gray was sold to Barnsley for £40,000. Wallace and Anderson were both out of contract at the end of the season, and Clough spent much of the following year trying to persuade them to stay on reduced terms. By December, Clough had agreed to sell Van Breukelen to PSV for £175,000.

Inevitably the financial uncertainty had an impact on the team, which won only one of its five games on a pre-season trip to the Netherlands. The overdraft stood at £800,000, with £1 million still owed on the Executive Stand, so the board agreed that no bonuses could be offered for the Uefa Cup. Clough began to chafe at the financial restrictions placed on him, complaining that he had only £100,000 with which to try to replace the three players he had lost that summer. 'Brian,' the chairman Geoffrey McPherson noted, 'should remember that Forest's poor balance sheet reflects his own dealings, both in buying and selling players.'

The significance of the move was perhaps overlooked at the time, but that summer the Football League took a decision that would radically alter English football, and effectively ensured that, barring the arrival of a sugar-daddy, Forest and clubs of similar stature would be excluded from the elite for good. From the end of the First World War, twenty per cent of gate receipts were paid to the away club, which effectively meant those sides with bigger crowds were subsidising those with a smaller catchment area for the good of the league as a whole. In 1983, gate-sharing was done away with, drastically increasing the advantage bigger clubs, with larger grounds and attendances, had always had. From then on, whether they'd over-reached on the stand or not, Forest would always have been battling against the odds.

A 1–0 defeat at home to Southampton on the opening day of the season suggested the worst, but Peter Davenport struck with five minutes remaining at Old Trafford to secure a 2–1 win and inflict United's first home defeat in eighteen months. Even after a 1–0 defeat at Anfield, there was a high-class performance to reflect upon, and while Forest were a little fortunate in draw at Aston Villa and beat QPR, they soon found the rhythm that was so crucial to Clough's teams. And Clough himself still had his magical touch. Frustrated by Colin Walsh's form, he told him he had one more chance before being relegated to the A-team. He responded with a hat-trick in a 3–2 victory at Norwich.

Forest's game away at Tottenham at the beginning of October was the first league match to be shown live on television as part of the new deal; they almost didn't make it. Forest's coach got stuck in a tailback caused by roadworks, and as the players became increasingly anxious, Clough jumped off the bus, moved some cones and made Albert, the driver, take the coach down one of the restricted lanes. When a policeman pulled him over, Clough explained the situation and persuaded him to provide an escort. It got them there on time but, with Glenn Hoddle superb, Spurs won 2–1.

That checked Forest's surge and a 3–1 aggregate defeat to Wimbledon, then of the Third Division, in the League Cup demonstrated a vulnerability against aggressive direct sides that would become a familiar theme through the eighties. With the toughness of Burns and Lloyd it perhaps wouldn't have been an issue; for the clean-cut side Clough eventually preferred it certainly was. Desperately hunting for players to replace those offloaded, Clough brought in the 31-year-old Frans Thijssen from Ipswich, who added poise and quality to a midfield that – by Clough's standards – had become a little frantic.

That could hardly have been clearer than in his debut, a particularly hectic derby against Notts County. Goals from Wallace, Bowyer and Davenport had the game won before half-time. Fashanu was sent off after retaliating to a Hart challenge eleven minutes after the break, and David Hunt followed him for a hack at Hodge as he took the ball to the corner.

Clough had hated such time-wasting when performed by Leeds, and he was unsparing in his criticism of Hodge afterwards, more or less saying he'd got what he deserved. That said, when Garry Birtles ran the ball into the corner in the 1980 European Cup final, Clough raised no complaint.

Initially, though, Forest's league form remained inconsistent, and when a 4–1 defeat at Arsenal was followed by a 1–1 draw at home to Sunderland, Hamilton was left fretting in the *Evening Post* that victory was needed over PSV Eindhoven in the second round of the Uefa Cup to 'save the season'. Forest had made it through the first round with a victory over Vorwärts of Berlin that in its professionalism – a Van Breukelen-inspired 2–0 win at the City Ground followed by a stifling 1–0 win in East Germany – recalled the great Forest of five years earlier, but PSV were a different level of threat.

Davenport put Forest ahead shortly after half-time, before an exchange of controversial penalties allowed Walsh to score a late winner. With Van Breukelen injured, Sutton was superb at the City Ground – a relief after the way he had allowed Gary Rowell's shot to slither under him in the draw with Sunderland – and Davenport sealed the game ten minutes after half-time.

That set up a tie with Celtic, in an era in which Anglo-Scottish matches were a rarity. 'It was bitterly cold, and the pitch was frozen,' Paul Hart recalled. 'The gaffer looked at the pitch and he said he'd take a draw; he'd walk away with a 0–0.' That was exactly what they got. 'Celtic had quite a small side and they played well that night,' said Hart, while Clough admitted that 'quite frankly we were extremely lucky', acknowledging that Celtic had shown 'more commitment'. Given how poor Forest's away form had been domestically, few gave Forest much hope. 'Everybody, all the ex-Celtic players, were all saying that they'd murder us at home in front of 68,000 people,' Hart remembered.

The second leg was very different, and shows Clough at his inspirational best. After Forest had arrived at Glasgow airport on the Monday, Clough got the coach driver to drop the players at a pub owned by the Celtic manager David Hay. They had a couple of pints, with Clough telling the barman that Hay would sort out the bill. They then took the bus to Troon, where they were staying, most of the squad playing a round of golf before another few drinks with dinner. There was more golf the following morning. 'We had lunch out at Troon harbour, another glass of wine,' Hart said. Then there was a choice of more golf or a tour of Ibrox and a visit to a boys' club in Airdrie. 'We didn't train at all till the Wednesday, and even that was very light, just by the side of the golf course,' Hart went on. 'It was about an hour in to Glasgow and we had a quiz on the bus with Ian Bowyer firing questions at us. We still hadn't spoken about Celtic. About an hour before kick-off we walked out, went and stood in front of the Jungle. They were all baying for blood, and Bomber showed them 2–0 with his fingers.' Wigley laid on the opener for Hodge shortly after half-time, Davenport created a second for Walsh and even after a late goal from Murdo MacLeod, Forest were never in danger. 'The place was like a graveyard,' said Hart. 'That was a great win. 2–1 flattered them.'

Forest's league form remained frustrating, wins at home alternating with poor performances away. After a 3–2 defeat at Watford, in which Forest couldn't take advantage after George Reilly had been sent off, Clough snapped, isolating Van Breukelen, Kenny Swain and Anderson for blame, saying they 'let me down very badly'. His outburst had the desired effect and, with the Birtles–Davenport partnership flourishing, Forest won their next three games, including a first away league victory in three months at Birmingham. A victory over Liverpool on New Year's Eve would have taken Forest to within two points of the top, but they lost 1–0. It was a defeat that would prove decisive; Liverpool's lead at the end of the season was six points; had Forest won either of their games against the eventual champions, they would have finished level on points with them and Southampton.

Forest went out of the FA Cup in the third round for the third successive season, losing to Southampton, but three straight wins in the league lifted them to within three points of the top. The third of those victories came at Southampton and brought another assault from Clough on his board. He was furious that of nine directors only John Hickling had made the trip to the Dell, and attacked the chairman Maurice Roworth and the vice-chairman Derek Pavis in particular for their absence.

Only a last-minute Chris Hughton equaliser for Tottenham denied Forest a fourth straight victory, but they won 5–0 at West Brom. Forest scored five on four occasions that season, their precision on the counter-attack punishing any side that chased the game against them. Forest then faced an away game at QPR and, knowing his players were troubled by the plastic pitch at Loftus Road, made sure they left the hotel late, arriving only just in time for kick-off. With no time to warm up and start fretting about

Forest's chairman Jim Willmer looks tense as he welcomes Clough to
the City Ground (PA).

The double act: Clough and Taylor at work in Forest's dugout during
an FA Cup fifth-round replay v QPR (played, unusually, on a Thursday
night in March 1978 – Forest won 3–1; but then went out to West Brom
in the next round) (PA).

Clough and Kenny Burns (doing his famed impression of a cardboard cutout) lift the League Cup at Old Trafford in 1978 (PA).

Clough ponders the future in the waters of the Trent ... (Action Images).

... a new stand for starters ...
(*Nottingham Evening Post*).

'Football encourages you to have
a drink because of the strain and
the pressures you're under,' Clough
admitted. Here he cradles his Bell's
Manager of the Year award for
1978, presented the same day as
the Championship trophy (PA).

Clough, squash racquet in hand, introduces Trevor Francis to Forest, and the £1million man repays Clough's faith with the winner in the 1979 European Cup final against Malmö (PA and Getty Images).

Martin O'Neill in the mud in the final moments against Köln
(*Nottingham Evening Post*).

Madrid, 1980: Taylor thought Forest's second European Cup win was
just the start of an era of domination; it turned out to be the last trophy
he ever won (PA).

Nigel looking very much like his dad (left); and at the training ground with Terry Wilson, his dad, dog and squash racquet (John Sumpter at JLS photography/PA).

Clough expresses his displeasure at the Trent End jeers for the injured Charlie Nicholas (PA).

The final days: fans at the City Ground and Portman Road make
sure Clough knows just how much he'll be missed (both PA).

The end: Clough says a painful goodbye to the City Ground (PA).

the surface, Forest just got on with playing the game, which they won 1–0.

Clough dismissed suggestions Forest were good enough to win the title, and then turned on his players, making them come in to train on their day off. A 'handful' of players, he said, were to blame. 'Because of them, their mates had to come in for a training session when they could have been at home with their feet up,' he said. 'The reason was their attitude in training earlier this week was totally wrong. I have told them I won't stand for that happening.'

Did Clough see a slump in form coming, or did his cantankerousness provoke it? Either way, Forest's title challenge – not that it was one, according to Clough – disappeared over the fortnight that followed. Only an inspired performance from Van Breukelen salvaged a 1–1 draw at Sunderland and Forest then lost 1–0 at Arsenal.

A couple of days later, Forest were scheduled to fly to Dubai to play in a friendly. They had an early start and Clough was feeling, as he put it, 'delicate'. Things started to go wrong when Birtles started complaining about having to fly out for a meaningless game. Somewhere between Nottingham and east Midlands airport, Clough's patience ran out and he ordered Birtles off the coach. He then snapped at an autograph hunter in the departure lounge. The plane itself was packed and seemed unusually noisy, with children running up and down the aisle. When take-off was aborted, Clough lost his nerve completely and insisted he and the team were getting off. A stewardess tried to stop them, but Clough was adamant and a bus had to be brought to shuttle them to the terminal. The rest of the passengers eventually took off four hours late, which vindicated his decision, but to his irritation Birtles had got home before any of his team-mates.

The constant travel was one source of tension within the squad; another was the lack of bonuses for the Uefa Cup. With the quarter-final against Sturm Graz only a week away, the players stepped up their campaign and Clough reluctantly agreed to pay them £3,000 each if they beat the bottom side Wolves that weekend. Paul Hart scored an injury time-own goal, and Forest lost 1–0. The bonuses were gone and so too were Forest's chances of winning the league title.

Forest outclassed Sturm at home and should have finished the tie in the first leg, but ended up with only a Hart header to show for their domination. Before the second leg in Austria, Clough took his players for a walk by the river. To their amazement, he suddenly stepped off the path and started pounding a tree with his fists. 'He just leathered it,' remembered Paul Hart. 'I thought, "Bloody hell – that's going to hurt!" but he knew what he was doing.' With the players looking on incredulously, he proclaimed it was a 'punch tree' and expressed bemusement that they didn't know what he was talking about. When some then started, cautiously, hitting the trunk, they realised that it had soft bark and didn't hurt the fists; Clough's love and knowledge of horticulture was genuine, if esoteric.

The game took on added significance because of the date: 21 March, Clough's forty-ninth birthday and the twelfth anniversary of his mother's death. Thoughts of 1972 and the defeat to Juventus must have surfaced when the Soviet referee Romualdas Yuschka gave Sturm a controversial penalty just before half-time, after what appeared a dive by Bozo Bakota, who got up to convert and level the aggregate score. With no further goals in the second half, the game went into extra-time. At the final whistle, Clough remained on the bench, as he had in Derby's FA Cup win over Tottenham in 1973. 'He didn't speak to us,' Hodge said. 'That was his way: he said his piece and after that you were on your own. I don't think he did it for effect. It wasn't like today, where you see managers constantly talking, walking up and down the touchline looking for every angle.'

At half-time in extra-time, Clough was left shouting 'Come on lads! Come on lads!' constantly for a couple of minutes. 'He looked a little bit helpless,' Hodge said – a precursor, perhaps, to his notorious non-intervention in the 1991 FA Cup final. Nonetheless, with eight minutes remaining Yuschka generously decided Walter Hormann's aerial challenge on Hodge was illegal. As the Sturm fans seethed, Walsh knocked in the penalty.

That set up a semi-final against the defending champions, Anderlecht. With Birtles and Thijssen both out, Forest struggled to make headway until, after eighty-four minutes, Hodge steered in a Mills cross at the back post. Three minutes later, he added a second from Wigley's delivery and Forest had a significant advantage. In the away leg of Clough's first European Cup semi-final, Clough was sure he had been cheated; he felt just as certain after the away leg of his first Uefa Cup semi-final. This time, there was proof – although it didn't come till much later.

In 1997, Roger van den Stock revealed that his father, Constant, Anderlecht's president in the eighties, had paid £18,000 to the Spanish referee

Carlos Guruceta, who was killed in a car crash in 1987. Clough was suspicious even before the game. Oddly for somebody who spent so much of his free time in Mallorca, he was generally distrustful of Spaniards. 'From my experience the Spanish don't exactly love us,' he said beforehand. 'British teams often seem to have problems with them because they see our game as very physical, which it isn't.'

And Guruceta had history. He was notorious in Belgium for having sent off two Italians and awarded a controversial penalty to Standard Liège against Napoli in the Uefa Cup in 1979–80, and Hart remembered him for having sent off two of his Leeds team-mates in a pre-season tournament against Real Madrid two years earlier.

Enzo Scifo put Anderlecht ahead with a low drive from twenty-five yards after twenty minutes, by which time, at least in the memory of Van Breukelen, there was a feeling that borderline decisions were going against them. That said, Alex Czerniatinski had what appeared a valid goal ruled out for a mysterious offside, while Forest benefited from Guruceta's reluctance to show yellow cards. In fact, viewing footage of the game, the most striking aspect of the first half is not the referee's performance, but Clough, whose voice can clearly be heard on the effects microphone. None of what he can be heard shouting seems particularly sophisticated. 'Come on, come on, come on …' he shouted as Anderson took the ball down the line – recalling Hodge's description of him in Graz. 'That's lovely,' he said as Anderson laid the ball off. 'Fucking stand up,' he screamed as Hart lunged into a challenge and then, to somebody off camera as Forest defended a free-kick, 'Hurry up, hurry up, hurry up … what are you doing fucking walking?'

Although Clough can't be heard shouting at Guruceta, he made his feelings clear at half-time. As Guruceta blew his whistle for the end of the break, Anderlecht lined up promptly; Clough kept the dressing-room door closed. Twice more Guruceta blew his whistle, but only after he hammered on the door did Clough respond, poking his head round the door and saying, 'Did you want us?'

'We were still confident at that stage, bearing in mind we'd won every away game in Europe that year,' said Hart. 'It was 1–0 at half-time, but that wasn't a problem. We were used to grinding it out.' Forest were holding on when Swain was deemed to have tripped Kenneth Brylle, who got up to

473

convert the penalty. 'Ken was two yards from him,' Hart said. 'It was a disgrace.' Erwin Vandenbergh made it 3–0 with two minutes remaining, but in the final minute it seemed Hart had scored to win the tie on away goals. 'We got a corner and the ball flew past Ian Bowyer's ear to me,' Hart said. 'I took the defender under the ball and banged it. There was no contact. If I'd pushed him, his shoulders would have gone down, but nothing. The goalkeeper was gesticulating at the defenders, and if you look at the Belgian players' faces they all think they've conceded a goal. That's when we started to think something was up. I asked Ian whether he'd pushed someone and he said, "absolutely not".' The footage, unfortunately, isn't sharp enough to be definitive, but there's certainly no obvious offence.

Hamilton, as reasonable as ever, suggested Anderlecht might have won without the aid of the referee. 'If there was more than an element of doubt about those decisions,' he wrote, 'Anderlecht deservedly retained their firm grip on the trophy by turning in a performance which left no room for argument. Forest, it must be said, were completely overwhelmed by the brilliant Belgians.' Clough had recalled Van Breukelen after a finger injury, and Murphy suggested his tentativeness was a contributory factor in the first and third goals. Van Breukelen, though, also made a number of fine saves, and he was certain who was to blame, calling Guruceta a 'coward' and insisting Forest had been playing against 'twelve men'.

As the final whistle went, Clough made a point of shaking Guruceta's hand, presumably in an attempt to calm the Forest fans, who had reacted to the disallowing of Hart's goal with understandable fury. 'The gaffer was as quiet as a mouse afterwards,' Hart said. 'He knew something was going on. He'd been diddled. We'd all been diddled. I never won a medal.' Anderlecht went on to lose the final to Tottenham in a penalty shoot-out. After Roger van den Stock's revelations, Anderlecht were banned from Uefa competition for a season – the same penalty imposed on Clough's Derby for their financial irregularities in 1970.

Hart spoke of Clough's great 'resilience', of how, after a goalless draw at Stoke and a defeat at Leicester, he picked them up to win their final three games of the season, so they finished third and, with seventy-six goals they were the league's top-scorers. The Anderlecht game, though, cast a long shadow. Hamilton recalled him seeming exhausted after the game, reluctant to talk. 'I'd never seen him so flat after a defeat,' Hodge said. 'I think he really wanted to make his mark on Europe on his own. As Brian Clough, not Brian Clough and Peter Taylor.' And, yet again, the game of football had proved itself institutionally unfair. It doesn't excuse it, of course, but that endemic injustice perhaps explains why corruption was so part of the game at the time, why so many managers felt justified in taking what they could out of a game that kept cheating them.

What must have made that defeat all the more bitter was Clough's awareness that the club's financial position meant there was little hope of runs in Europe being a regular occurrence. 'I don't know how much longer we can match teams like [Liverpool and Manchester United] on crowds of 13,000,' he admitted. Although Clough persuaded Davenport to sign a new twelve-month contract, Wallace was sold to Brest for £100,000 and Anderson went to Arsenal for £250,000 that summer. The full-back later said he'd felt compelled to go because the players had not received Uefa Cup bonuses, despite promises from Clough and full houses against Celtic and Anderlecht. He had first become disillusioned by an incident on a tour of Israel three years earlier when he'd inadvertently been given the envelope containing Jimmy Gordon's spending money rather than his own. The players were unhappy anyway because Forest were paying them less than a third of what they were due, and that irritation was only increased when it turned out the coaching staff were getting twice as much as the players.

With Van Breukelen's transfer to PSV already agreed, there was a need for a new goalkeeper. Widzew Łódź sent a telex to Clough (or 'Mr Cough' as they called him) offering him Adam Młynarczyk and suggesting a meeting in Vienna to discuss the deal. Clough ignored them, and Młynarczyk ended up at Porto, where he won the European Cup in 1987. Clough instead picked up Hans Segers on a season-long loan from PSV.

The cut-backs had given Clough some flexibility in the transfer market, as the club declared a pre-tax profit of £402,000 for the previous season and a reduction in the overdraft to £747,000, and he also signed the young Scottish midfielder-cum-full-back Jim McInally from Celtic, the midfielder Gary Megson from Sheffield Wednesday, the Netherlands international Johnny Metgod from Real Madrid and, after Garry Birtles had suffered a serious back injury, the centre-forward Trevor Christie from Notts County.

He may have been less prepared to sign troublemakers than he had in the past, but Clough's underlying philosophy remained the same: buy

475

players who fitted together and gave the team a natural balance, then trust them to get on with it. 'He believed in his players,' said Hart. 'He bought them with the right character – he made the game simple. Do certain things and you win matches. He was a great, great coach, just not as we know coaches. Everybody knew their job, knew what to do and when to do it. At Leeds, sometimes I'd had to control the ball on the penalty spot. He just told me to head it and kick it away – anything else was a bonus. The midfielders had to play on the half-turn. The front men had to hold it. And everybody had to head it – not just free headers, but when there was a crowd of players – had to risk getting a clout.

'When I was there Forest were a counter-attacking side – the front men had a big job to do. We played 4–4–2 and you had to get it wide and get crosses in, then get across the near post because that's where most goals were scored. What he was saying was that he trusted us: do what he said and we'd win games; don't do what he said and you'd be out of the team. But this stuff about him ruling by fear was nonsense. It was the happiest club I've been at – great team spirit.' Only money, and Forest's comparative poverty, at times spoiled the mood.

Players may have arrived that summer, but the desperate quest for money had other, more direct effects on Forest's form. The Wednesday before the season began, Forest played a friendly in Athens against Panathinaikos – 'a first-class offer as far as cash is concerned', as Clough put it. The result, though, was that his players returned fatigued and were well beaten 3–1 by Sheffield Wednesday in their first game of the season. Clough admitted the side was nowhere near as good as it had been the previous year: 'How can we be?' he asked. 'We've lost the Dutch No 1 goalkeeper; an ex-England striker through injury; an international right-back and another experienced front player.'

His downbeat mood continued into that week's column in the *Evening Post* as he said he could understand why Viv Anderson had wanted to leave after twelve years, admitting that he too at times felt 'sick of the sight of the place'. At that, Forest suddenly hit a patch of purple form, goals from Metgod and Davenport giving them a 2–0 win over Arsenal, Davenport hitting a hat-trick in a 3–1 win over Sunderland, and Christie scoring three in a 5–0 win at Aston Villa.

A 3–0 defeat at QPR knocked Forest off the top of the table, but wins over Luton and Norwich and a draw at West Ham had them second. Clough, though, was still despondent. 'I celebrate my fiftieth birthday next March and at the moment I certainly don't envisage still being in the management game when I am sixty,' he wrote in his column. It turned out to be an accurate prediction. 'What's more, I reckon a lot of other managers in my position will feel exactly the same way. It's all down to the sheer intensity of the modern-day game. Believe me, it's overpowering. The sheer number of games in a season, the need to balance the books as well as win matches, and the demands for instant success are absolutely frightening.'

Again, it's hard to know whether his gloominess was prescient or whether it caused Forest's abrupt loss of form. They went out of the Uefa Cup in Belgium again, losing 1–0 on aggregate in the first round to Club Brugge. Again, there was a whiff of controversy, Davenport having a goal in the away leg ruled out for a debatable offside; had it stood, then, like the previous season, they would have gone through on away goals.

The league slump began with a 4–1 defeat at West Brom. 'I can't remember when I've seen a more pathetic, inept performance from us,' Clough said, and used his column in the *Evening Post* that week to pick the players apart one by one. They drew at Newcastle, lost to Liverpool and Southampton and went out of the League Cup at Sunderland. Defeat at home to Tottenham left Forest thirteenth in the table and by mid-November the FA Cup was the only tournament they had any chance of winning.

Forest signed the Australian defender Allan Davidson, and sold Megson to Newcastle for £110,000 without him ever starting for the club. Clough claimed at the time he had only bought him because he'd thought Bowyer was moving to Luton, but he later said Megson 'couldn't trap a bag of cement' and then that his intense nervousness before games – so intense he would vomit – unsettled the rest of the team.

The rot was stopped with a 3–1 win against Coventry, Segers's debut, but Forest remained desperately inconsistent. Metgod scored a last-minute winner as Forest came from 2–0 behind to beat Manchester United, but they then lost 5–0 to Everton. Clough was frustrated, which at times led to violent outbursts; on this occasion, though, it provoked generosity as he invited Jim McInally and Steve Hodge, both of whom were single, to have Christmas dinner at his house. Beneath the bluster and the irrationality, there was always a basic humanity. Clough worried about McInally, only recently arrived from Glasgow, and fretted that he didn't eat enough vegetables. On every away trip, Clough would hound him, popping up beside him at meals and badgering him to eat his greens. That Christmas, though, was the only time Clough, who seems to have been a talented cook, managed to make him eat sprouts.

Having made members of his team part of the family for Christmas, Clough made a member of the family part of the team on Boxing Day, giving his son Nigel his debut in a 2–0 win over Ipswich – poignantly on the twenty-second anniversary of the knee injury that had ended his career. 'I think he coped really well in every respect,' said Davenport. 'Nigel showed he can turn defenders, withstand a challenge and lay the ball off, even when someone is on his back.' That ability would become central to the way Forest played in the late eighties.

As a teenager, Nigel had played for AC Hunters, which was run by his son Simon, who might have been a player himself had it not been for a serious knee injury. At times he was singled out by opponents because of who his father was, and on one occasion an opposing goalkeeper was prosecuted and fined after throwing a cup of tea over him. He then played for Heanor Town and completed his A-levels before making his Forest debut. Certain ground rules were established. At the club, Nigel always called his father 'Boss', while his contracts were handled by Ron Fenton.

Perhaps seeing his son impress rekindled something in Clough: three days later, there came a moment of classic Cloughishness as the players came in after a poor first half against Aston Villa to find that their manager had locked the dressing-room door. Clough sent them back out and they stood around in the cold, clearly embarrassed, kicking the ball to one another. An improved second half brought a win.

Such moments of inspired unorthodoxy, though, were becoming increasingly rare. Wimbledon, having put Forest out of the League Cup the previous season, this time knocked them out of the FA Cup in the fourth round, leaving Forest with nothing to chase but European qualification.

Although Nigel Clough began to show his potential, and formed an effective partnership with Davenport, Forest spluttered on to finish ninth. As it turned out, the pursuit of a Uefa Cup slot was academic anyway, as

English clubs were banned from European competition following the disaster at Heysel.

Treading Water

With finances slowly improving – before signings were taken into account, Forest made a profit of £301,000 for 1984–85 – Clough, at last, had some money to spend but, as he pointed out, he needed it. His first signing that close season was the composed central midfielder Neil Webb, bought from Portsmouth for £250,000. On first meeting him, at a north London hotel towards the end of the previous season, Clough had taken him to a table where a number of Forest players were sitting, pointed at a couple of midfielders and told them that Webb could be taking their place. The next time they met, at the City Ground, Webb was still undecided as to whether he should leave Portsmouth. Clough told him to take a walk around the pitch and come back with a definite yes or no. Webb said yes, at which Clough opened a bottle of champagne. Webb demurred, explaining he didn't drink champagne, to which Clough replied, 'You do now.' He then took him to the Italian restaurant on Trent Bridge, and so charmed Webb that he signed a blank contract, trusting Clough to fill in the details later.

Clough was keen always to let new players know their place in the hierarchy straightaway and, shortly after joining, Webb was picked to play against Notts County in a County Cup final. When he sent a chip flying way over the bar after twenty minutes, Clough substituted him and berated him for not having passed to a team-mate who was better placed. Webb later said that Clough's main influence over his game was to stop him attempting the wonder-ball or wonder-shot at every opportunity.

As Swain went to Portsmouth, Clough strengthened his back four by bringing in Stuart Pearce and Ian Butterworth from Coventry for £450,000, and the winger Brian Rice arrived from Hibernian. There was probably more optimism at Forest at the start of the 1985–86 season than there had been since Taylor left, and when Clough boldly predicted that Kenny Dalglish, who had become player-manager of Liverpool after Joe Fagan's resignation, would find it difficult to combine both roles, it was widely perceived as a rallying cry, as evidence Clough felt this year Forest might be able to challenge again.

All of which made a 1–1 draw at Luton on the opening day all the more frustrating. When the players returned to the Kenilworth Road car park afterwards, they found the coach blocked in by another vehicle. Clough slipped into a rage, and sent an official to find the driver and get his keys. When he returned, Clough grabbed the keys and, rather than simply moving the offending car to another space, drove it into a side street round the corner. He returned with the keys in his hand and insisted the coach should set off. After a few yards, though, he relented, admitted he had effectively stolen the car, went back to it and drove it back into the car park. His mood swings were becoming wilder and wilder, and less and less focused on his team.

Forest's form was inconsistent as well, but generally poor, four defeats in their next five games leaving them third bottom. Webb was beginning to impose himself, although he rapidly ran into Clough's unreasonable side as Segers injured a knee in a 4–2 defeat at West Ham. When it became obvious the goalkeeper would have to go off, Webb volunteered to take his place. Some would have applauded the selflessness of the gesture, but Clough was furious and dropped him from the next game.

There was promise too in the performances of Forest's young players, most notably Nigel Clough, Peter Davenport and the rapid centre-back Des Walker, but too often, Clough said, his side lacked 'bottle'. A run of five straight wins through October and November at least eradicated any thought that relegation might be a serious possibility, but with no European qualification to play for – Clough, not surprisingly, repeatedly used his column in the *Nottingham Evening Post* to attack the Uefa ban – the season rapidly came to be about nothing but the cups.

Bolton were dismissed 7–0 over two legs in the League Cup – Clough even using Birtles as a centre-back in the second leg on the grounds that 'he needed a game and he's capable of heading a ball' – before Forest travelled to Derby for the third round. Metgod cancelled out an early penalty with a close-range header, and then Franz Carr, another of Forest's highly promising young talents, swept in Davenport's cross to make it 2–1. Hamilton spoke of the game having been 'a stage for Forest to demonstrate their character, composure and, above all, their class', but Clough remained grumpy, hammering his side for their attitude in the final twenty minutes and their reluctance to seek a more emphatic win. Perhaps that was typical

Clough contrariness, or perhaps he wanted Derby humiliated.

In the fifth round, Forest faced QPR, on whose plastic pitch – oddly given their close-passing style seemed perfectly adapted to the surface – they were never comfortable. Terry Fenwick gave QPR the lead with a penalty given for a foul probably committed outside the box, and although Nigel Clough equalised, two goals in the final three minutes put Forest out. Even worse, Davenport was sent off for throwing what Hamilton described as 'a limp punch' at Steve Wicks.

Forest's performance in the FA Cup was even more disappointing. They drew 1–1 at home to Blackburn, then a Second Division side, in the third round and, before the replay, Davenport submitted a transfer request, having been unsettled by a dressing-room row after he'd missed a penalty in a 1–1 draw against Liverpool just after Christmas. The implication was that Clough's moods were becoming increasingly difficult for players to deal with, a suggestion that was strengthened after the replay.

Forest lost 3–2 at Ewood Park and Clough, after haranguing his players as they got on the coach, refused to turn the lights on. If they were going to play like children, he said, he would treat them like children. Every few minutes during the journey he would stand up and berate the players further.

Perhaps his fury had the desired effect: Forest produced what the *Evening Post* called an 'Alice in Wonderland' performance to win 3–2 at Manchester United in their next game and lost only twice more that season, but those who had witnessed the outburst on the bus suggested Clough was wild, that this was another occasion on which his temper had taken over. Besides which, the twelve-game unbeaten run with which Forest completed the run-in was nowhere near as good as it may sound; seven of those games were drawn. Clough admitted only the form of Des Walker had salvaged the season. 'We could have gone through a catastrophic period, bearing in mind Chris Fairclough hasn't kicked a ball and I dropped the clanger of the year by letting Paul Hart go,' he wrote in his *Evening Post* column. 'But Walker's come through in his first full league season to carry us on his back. I honestly dread to think what sort of state we might have been in without him. He's been absolutely brilliant. It's no exaggeration to say he's been a cornerstone of our side for most of the last eight months.'

As well as the concerns about Clough's mood-swings, there were further

481

niggles with the board. A fortnight after the United game, the director Frank Allcock was forced to resign after it emerged that he had offered the former director Derek Pavis odds of 7–1 against Forest winning at Old Trafford as they travelled to the game. Pavis had been an earlier victim of Clough's manoeuvrings.

A typically abrasive self-made man, Pavis was one of the few to stand up to Clough. Where others were prepared effectively to give Clough a free hand, he questioned his record in the transfer market and criticised his outspokenness. Seeing a younger version of Longson – they even shared a similar gravelly way of speaking – Clough recognised the problems that could lie ahead if Pavis ever became chairman, so when he came up for re-election to the board, Clough was vociferous in his support for his opponent, a car dealer called John Smith. He lobbied shareholders and demanded that a photograph of Smith and the club car he was providing for Clough was printed on the back page of the *Evening Post*. Smith wanted to promote the club by dressing Clough up as Robin Hood; he baulked at that – perhaps recognising the uneasy similarities in their attitude to the riches of others – but Smith beat Pavis by five votes. Pavis, nonetheless, wrote Clough a letter on his retirement thanking him for all he had done for the club. There was that paradox again – even those he had actively fought often felt compelled to acknowledge Clough's achievements; like John Joseph Pye, he seemed captivated by Clough almost despite himself.

Allcock insisted the bet was nothing more than a light-hearted chat, but Clough, having sold the story to the *Mirror* and used it in his column in the programme, demanded his head. It would have been a strange over-reaction anyway, but what made it doubly odd was that Clough got on well enough with Allcock to have been on holiday with him in Mallorca two months earlier. It's hard not to be reminded of Taylor's claim that Clough woke up each morning working out how he could make more money: this was an easy fee from a newspaper, another dose of notoriety, and if a board member with whom he'd seemingly got on pretty well went down in the process, so be it.

Or perhaps, more charitably, it was all part of Clough's often impenetrable wider politicking. Earlier in the season he had been unusually flattering to Maurice Roworth, who had replaced McPherson as chairman, apologising to him through his column in the *Evening Post* after the club's poor start to the season and then accusing the other directors of offering their chairman insufficient support. If his ultimate goal, though, was to secure more transfer funds, he failed, and despite a significant reduction in the overdraft, he was asked to trim it further. McInally was the first to go, sold to Coventry, and in March, Davenport went to Manchester United for £575,000, having never re-settled following the row after the Liverpool game. Clough, at least in public, was opposed to the sale, but Roworth called it 'an offer we couldn't refuse'. At the end of the season, Robertson, Gunn and Bowyer were all released as Forest further cut their wage bill.

That season had, though, seen one other notable arrival. Clough would complain when Taylor brought his black Labrador to the stadium or the training ground, shying away if it jumped at him in greeting. But after Hans van Breukelen had retrieved his Schnauser from quarantine, Libby Clough decided she too wanted a dog. At Christmas 1985, Clough bought her a golden Labrador pup called Del Boy – he insisted on picking the runt of the litter – but he soon started taking it in to work with him. He would always insist it was his 'daughter's dog', but he doted on it, and would pretend to ask its advice on team selection. Later, he would look at the dog after finishing a Scotch and say, 'Don't tell me you want another one.'

As the pressure of juggling the team and finances increased, so Clough's dependence on alcohol worsened, even while those around him tried to deny the problem. 'He thinks he's indestructible,' Jimmy Gordon said in 1986. 'I know he likes a drink to help with the pressures of the job, but it's never interfered with his work that I know and I've never seen him drunk.' That sounds like blind faith, and Gordon had retired four years earlier, but perhaps it was true, at least at that stage. Perhaps Clough did need the alcohol just to keep going; perhaps it was not an inhibitor but a facilitator, as Churchill had argued it was for him. It could be argued that it wasn't alcohol that undermined Clough in the end, but the health problems his consumption of alcohol brought on. Perhaps Clough without alcohol would have been even worse; perhaps the problem was so not so much the booze as the fact that the pressures of the job caused Clough to seek solace in booze. Either way, by the mid-eighties he had become an erratic figure and he was probably fortunate to have, in Fenton, Hill, O'Kane and Gemmill, loyal lieutenants who could take the strain as Taylor and Gordon had once done.

Not that his assistants escaped his wrath. Clough would sometime share a bath with the players after the game and afterwards dust himself down in clouds of talcum powder. Once, on the bus on the way to a game in London, Liam O'Kane admitted that he'd forgotten to pack the talc, at which Clough had the bus pull into the next services and made O'Kane get off. He had to call his wife, get her to come and pick him up and drive him to the ground, where he handed over some freshly bought talc. 'That was extreme,' said Hodge, 'but he caught him in a bad mood, and he would sometimes make a big deal of it if people did something even slightly wrong. Then, another day, he'd buy somebody a watch for no reason. Maybe he cultivated the mood-swings at times, but he was a Jekyll-and-Hyde figure.'

That was typical of his disciplinarian tendencies, a seeming contradiction in someone so anti-authoritarian himself, but something first glimpsed in his delight at rebuking late-comers while head-boy at Marton Grove School. Duncan Hamilton recalled seeing him at youth-team games going to retrieve balls that had run off the pitch and then hurling them back at the groin of the player waiting to take the throw-in. 'I aim at the bollocks,' he said. 'It keeps 'em on their toes.' There was an ugly, bullying edge to him at times, a tendency to strike out indiscriminately at others as part of his self-assertion. Alongside that was a great spirit of generosity, both great and small. He would pay for children he saw queuing up to buy tickets, often adding a few pounds extra, and he once spontaneously paid for the wedding of a friend's son. He could savage people, or he could lavish great kindness upon them.

Numerous journalists have stories of being torn apart by Clough for something they wrote and being told they'd been banned from the City Ground for life, only for Clough to ring them a couple of days later to ask where they were. This was Clough, as Longson had described him, crushing the spirit of others until they responded to his will; and this, of course, was why he distrusted those who were different, those – like Giles, O'Neill and Fashanu – whom he could not break.

He made unpredictability a virtue. He punched a number of players. He would grab people by the crotch or he might kiss them. Sometimes it was simply a manifestation of his temper as, for instance, when he struck an angler across the back of the calves with his walking stick for the supposed crime of getting too close to Clough as he walked along the banks of the Trent. Most of it, though, at least in the early days before the booze added to his irascibility, was planned, part of a performance. It was about unsettling others in his company; it was about the assertion of his authority, which went beyond Alan Brown's tricks for preventing his stars getting above themselves, although he practised those as well. Like Brown, he would make established internationals brew the tea. He once publicly asked Lee Chapman, twenty-nine at the time, whether he had washed his hands after he'd been to the toilet.

If a player had a new shirt or a new suit, he would ask how much it cost and then tell them that that could provide for a family of eight, such as the one he'd grown up in; a way of reminding people what he'd achieved, how far he'd come. That habit of emphasising the toughness of his upbringing may help explain his animosity towards Revie, for Revie had achieved much the same as him having come from a poorer part of the same town.

In his column in the *Evening Post* that August 1986, Clough pointed out that his contract was due to expire the following June, and suggested he was considering not signing another one. That, of course, is a classic bargaining position, and one that Clough had occupied before, but there was a genuine sense of weariness in Clough's words as he threatened to walk away from the club, his outburst seemingly prompted by being outbid by Tottenham in his attempt to sign the centre-back Richard Gough from Dundee United. 'Believe me,' he said, 'it will happen, unless the financial burden of our club is lifted off my shoulders ... I can't build a side, win matches and do all the other things that First Division management entails – AND be a financial Einstein at the same time.'

The exact chain of cause and effect is difficult to trace and perhaps wasn't strictly linear anyway. The pressure made Clough more erratic and it made him drink, and the drinking made him more erratic, which added to the pressure. The culture of football, Clough acknowledged in an interview with Tyne Tees Television in 2000, was partly to blame for his increasing dependence on alcohol. 'It encourages you to have a drink because of the strain and the pressures you're under,' he said. 'When you finish something and it's over and it's been building up and you run your hands and say, "We haven't done badly today." You'd got a point away from home, then you put your feet up and have a drink. Joe Mercer said that to me after we'd won at City once. "You have your champagne," he said, "because you lose too many times in this game, so when you win, you enjoy it." You'd enjoy your success and you'd drown your sorrows.' The sense of bitterness towards the game, or at least the culture of the game, is unmistakable: the highs never lasted long enough; the lows were unbearably painful.

That summer, Clough went to visit Alan Hill at the Convent Hospital, where he was recovering after an operation on his leg. Clough asked a nurse if he could have a drink, and she replied that there was nowhere close that sold alcohol, but that Howard Noble, a City councillor, kept a bottle of Scotch in his room. Clough left Hill and went to visit Noble, eagerly accepting when he was offered a whisky. There was a sense by then not just that he enjoyed booze, not even that it perhaps relaxed him, but that he needed it.

For all that, and despite a 2–0 defeat at Everton on the opening day, the 1986–87 season started positively. 'We were rubbish,' Clough said after Forest's first home game, even though they beat Charlton 4–0. He dismissed his side as 'careless and inconsistent' after a 3–1 win at Southampton a couple of weeks later, but when they then beat Aston Villa 6–0, Birtles and Webb scoring two apiece, Forest were top of the table for the first time in two years. They celebrated by hammering Chelsea at Stamford Bridge, Webb and Birtles both getting hat-tricks in a 6–2 win. Clough insisted that the 1978 side would have kept a clean sheet.

With Chris Fairclough back after an eighteen-month absence, Forest did keep a clean sheet in their next game, at home to Arsenal, but again Clough wasn't happy. This time, though, his anger was directed not at his team but at Forest's fans for jeering Charlie Nicholas as he was stretchered from the field. He was so disgusted, he said, that he didn't want the Trent End to chant his name.

After a 1–1 draw at home to Manchester United, a title challenge still seemed realistic, but Forest were undone by a familiar failing – their away form. Norwich went top as Forest lost 3–1 at Leicester after Sutton was stretchered off and, when Forest lost to Oxford in their next away game, Clough called his side 'a disgrace', saying ten per cent had carried the rest all season. Further defeats at Coventry and Luton saw Forest drop to third. They won their next three in the league after that – and beat Bradford 5–0 in the League Cup as sixteen-year-old Lee Glover made his debut – but their title challenge unravelled with a run of six league games without a win over Christmas. Their cup hopes disappeared in the same slump, as they lost to Crystal Palace in the FA Cup – a fifth third-round exit in six years – and lost to Arsenal in the fifth round of the League Cup.

Oddly, it was in the middle of that run of poor form that Clough finally signed a new contract, committing to the club until May 1988, but it had been – by Forest's standards – another drab season. It finished with a 2–1 win over Newcastle that ensured they finished eighth, but saw Clough on the pitch after the final whistle helping police clear scuffling fans following a pitch invasion.

The summer of 1987 followed a familiar pattern of trying to keep players at the club. Paul Wilkinson had been brought in from Everton in March, which meant a free transfer for Birtles in May. Carr was on the transfer list, Clough said, because of the way his father had meddled in the club's attempts to negotiate a new contract – another indication of Clough's reluctance to deal with anybody who challenged him. Fairclough and Metgod were sold to Tottenham, Mills went to Notts County and so too did Alan Hill, taking up a role as youth administrator. In his early days at Forest, Clough had been a master at manipulating the market, had bought when he wanted and sold when he wanted; as Peter Taylor said, knowing when to let a player go was as important as knowing when to bring one in. By the mid-eighties, he was fire-fighting. The suspicion was increasingly that the constant struggle to balance the books wasn't the result of a misplaced gamble on the stand, but a permanent condition. Forest remained part of the elite, and perhaps the more optimistic of their fans believed a title challenge was possible, but they were severely handicapped by their finances, a disadvantage only Clough's genius – erratic as it had become – could temper. 'I was just too young for the European Cup successes,' said Dan Lawson, a regular in the Trent End in the eighties. 'And I suppose we sort of knew that we'd never get back to that level, but it didn't really matter. We were a regular top-six side and the lack of titles didn't matter because we had Clough. You only have to look at how things have gone since he left to see what he did for us. Everybody knew us because of our style of play, because of him. It was like with Clough different rules applied.'

Forest began the new season well enough, with wins over Charlton and Watford and a draw against Everton. They even spoiled Mirandinha's debut for Newcastle with a 1–0 win at St James' Park, but then threw away a two-goal lead to draw 3–3 at Southampton, and lost 4–3 at Chelsea, despite having led 2–0 and 3–1. As Hamilton noted after an Alan Smith goal had given Arsenal a 1–0 win at the City Ground, 'No one really needs to tell Nottingham Forest how much a trip into the transfer market is essential.'

Terry Wilson, Lee Glover and Steve Chettle all made their league debuts as teenagers that autumn, as Forest hit a run of form, winning five successive league games without conceding a goal. There was always a perception that Glover was one of Clough's favourites. 'He knew I came from a working-class, lower working-class background,' the forward remembered. 'We didn't have much in Corby apart from the steelworks. There were a lot of Scottish and Irish immigrants and he was a working-class icon because of his support for the Labour Party. When I was making my [league] debut at Charlton away, I was seventeen and really nervous. About five minutes before we went out, the gaffer said to me, "How are you feeling?" Then he added, "Glover, there is a lot of unemployment in Corby since the steel-works closed, isn't there?" I said yes. So he said, "Don't become another unemployed one." It was quite surreal, but it relieved all the pressure.'

More generally, though, Clough was far from happy. He called Ray Hough-ton 'inflexible and immature' for rejecting a move to Forest from Oxford, and fretted about home gates, accusing the Nottingham public of a lack of gratitude; it wasn't just directors, he felt, who didn't give him his due. The fourth of those wins came at home against Sheffield Wednesday, a game that drew an attendance of 17,685, of whom four thousand were away fans. 'Most of our rivals would have attracted 20,000 plus by getting the sort of results we've managed to achieve,' Clough said. 'What we got was our usual warm welcome back from the Nottingham public. Maybe things would change if we let them in for nothing – but I'm beginning to doubt it.' Perhaps the issue was financial – Nottingham, after all, had been hit as hard as anywhere by the miners' strike and its aftermath; perhaps it was the threat of hooliganism and general gloom that saw crowds across the country hit record lows in the mid-eighties, or perhaps it was simply that, despite what Lawson and other devotees may have said, there was a swathe of fans for whom style and Clough's charisma mattered less than success.

Clough must have known that Forest could never be a giant in the sense that Liverpool or United were, but perhaps it was only then, as the so-called Big Five – Liverpool, United, Everton, Tottenham and Arsenal, four of whom had won fewer European Cups than he had – began negotiating new television deals and agitating for a breakaway league, that he understood just how different the scale was. Little wonder Clough was so paranoid about games being broadcast live.

After beating Tottenham 3–0 with a performance of what Hamilton described as 'languid elegance', Clough insisted Forest, who were fourth, two points behind Liverpool having played two games more, were still in the title race. Forest promptly lost 3–0 to Manchester City in the third round of the League Cup – 'We didn't compete,' Clough said – but their league form held up. They drew at Manchester United, hammered Portsmouth 5–0 – 'dreadful' said Clough, his grumpiness after big wins now predictable. They lost at West Ham and drew at Wimbledon, but Nigel Clough scored a hat-trick between the eighty-first and eighty-fifth minutes as Forest beat QPR 4–0.

There were away wins at Oxford and Arsenal and a 4–1 demolition of Coventry in front of 31,000 on 28 December, a sign of how things could have been. The title challenge, though, fizzled out around New Year 1988, as defeats to Newcastle and Everton left Forest thirteen points behind the leaders Liverpool. As crowds fell again, Clough must have realised he was pushing against a glass ceiling.

That perhaps explains why he was so interested when Wales, seeking a replacement for Mike England, offered him a part-time role. With only four months remaining on his contract, Clough went through what Hamilton dismissed as 'a tiresome theatrical show' of threatening to quit if the Forest board didn't allow him to combine the two roles. The board, though, remained unmoved and Clough, having cried wolf once too often, was forced to backtrack while insisting 'I bitterly resent the decision'.

Clough's motives are never easy to determine, but it may be that he got what he wanted from the process anyway. It's impossible to know for sure, but it's been suggested that the whole dalliance was aimed at persuading Alan Hill to return from Notts County to run the youth set-up at Forest. Clough told Hill he would only take the Wales job if he would come as his assistant and, typically, gave him ten minutes to decide. Hill quit at Meadow Lane, but when he got to the City Ground for a press conference announcing Clough's involvement with Wales, he discovered Clough wasn't accepting the Welsh FA's offer after all. 'I said I'd already left Notts County,' Hill said, 'but he said he'd sort me out with a contract at Forest if he decided to stay.' In the end, it cost Forest £19,000 in compensation. County's chairman at the time was Derek Pavis; stealing one of his old rival's most valued staff must have given Clough additional satisfaction.

If that was what Clough was after, it was a rare moment of satisfaction in an otherwise frustrating spring. That season saw Dalglish's Liverpool at their very best, and Forest could only watch them disappearing into the distance, although they did inflict only Liverpool's second league defeat upon them at the beginning of April. That was the first of three matches between the sides in the space of eleven days. The final one proved Liverpool's superiority, their passing and movement superb as they thrashed Forest 5–0 at Anfield – the signature performance of a brilliant season. 'That was devastating,' said the journalist and Forest fan Richard Williams. 'That was when you realised how far ahead they were.'

The middle game was the FA Cup semi-final. Forest had comfortably overcome Halifax and Leyton Orient before beating Birmingham in the fifth round with a goal from Gary Crosby, a winger Clough had picked up from Grantham, where he'd been playing semi-professionally while working as a joiner, the previous December. They beat Arsenal in a fourth-successive away tie in the quarter-final, but two John Aldridge goals gave Liverpool victory at Hillsborough.

Forest did beat Sheffield Wednesday in the final to win the Mercantile Credit Trophy, a strange short-game tournament played over a weekend and featuring sides representing all four divisions, but that almost highlighted Forest's level; they were no longer a side that won European Cups, but one that won strange novelty events that nobody took too seriously. As Nigel Clough became the first Forest player in fourteen years to score twenty goals in a season, Forest finished third, but they were seventeen points adrift of Liverpool. Given Forest's budget, that was still a notable achievement, but it came without the consolation of European qualification. Clough, with few other options, signed a two-year contract at the end of the season.

The Last Hurrah

Realistically, the league was always going to be beyond Forest. Theirs was a gifted young squad, but they simply didn't have the resources to challenge

Liverpool, Arsenal and Manchester United over the course of a season. Winning the Mercantile Credit Trophy perhaps did for the Forest of the late eighties what winning the Anglo-Scottish Cup had done for the Forest of the late seventies, giving them a sense of self-belief and a taste for silverware. The economics of the game, the increasing importance of financial power in football as the decade went on, limited what was achievable, but Clough, at last, after eight years without a trophy, started winning again. By doing so, he proved that he could be successful without Peter Taylor.

With profits of £710,000 for 1987–88 and the final payment on the Executive Stand due the following July, Roworth insisted the club was in a better financial state than at any time since it won the European Cup and, for once, there were more arrivals that summer than departures. The forward Nigel Jemson and the midfielder Garry Parker had been signed in the March, Brian Laws was brought in from Middlesbrough and Steve Hodge re-signed from Tottenham for £575,000. Hans Segers left on loan for Genk and Kjetil Osvold, a Norwegian midfielder, who had made just seven starts after signing from Lillestrøm, was sold to PAOK, but Forest began the season with their strongest squad for at least five years.

Clough too seemed rejuvenated, his signing of Laws redolent in style if perhaps not stature of some of his coups of the past. 'I arrived at the ground, expecting to talk about how things would be played,' Laws said, 'and his first quote was, "Are you a good player or a bad player?" I replied that the fact he was trying to buy me meant I should fit in his team and he said, "I haven't seen you play, so if you're a good player, tell everyone I signed you. And if you're a crap player, tell everyone Ronnie Fenton signed you." I laughed. I wondered if it was him just being him, but it could be true.'

Clough was on similarly cantankerous form before the opening game of the season away against Norwich, stopping the coach about a mile from the ground and making his players walk there, between the crowds. Once it seemed that every unorthodox move he made came off; on this occasion, though, Forest were 2–0 down inside quarter of an hour and went on to lose 2–1. At half-time, pursuing his usual policy of letting a new signing know his place, Clough said to Hodge, 'When you get the ball, give it to Webb, because he's a good midfield player.'

Five successive draws rather killed any vague title aspirations before they'd begun, but victories over QPR and Liverpool steadied the ship – not that, in those days, the thought of relegation would ever have been taken seriously. With Sutton ill, Mark Crossley made his debut in goal against the champions. 'I was the fourth-choice keeper,' Crossley remembered. 'Hans Segers was out on loan, Paul Crichton was above me and Steve Sutton. The day before the game, Steve Sutton hadn't trained, but I thought he was just given a day off. Actually he was ill and it was kept from me. They had tried to get someone in as an emergency. I was only nineteen and had only been there a year. He called my dad and said, "Mark's playing, but don't tell him." I was living in digs with Tom and Olive, an old couple, and he told them, but told them not to tell me.

'He wined and dined my mum and dad. It was a 7.45pm kick off and I got to the ground at 5.30 as I always did. His head popped around the door at about 7 and said "Barnsley," – that was what he called me, along with a lot of other things – "get your kit on, you're playing" – and it was 7 for a 7.45 kick-off. We won 2–1 and after the game he took me into the referee's room, stole the match ball and told me to keep it. I still have it to this day.'

Typically, Clough didn't allow Crossley to get above himself – and equally typically, he merged family and club life and made his point heedless of the consequences. 'I played the next two games and I thought I'd arrived, so I picked my bag up and said, "See you on Monday." I took it for granted I'd get a day off. He said, "See you tomorrow, 9am at my house. Bring your boots and gloves." I didn't even know where he lived; I had to ask the groundsman. I knocked on his door and he opened it and said "thank you".

'I said, "What for?"

'He said, "For agreeing to play for Simon's team." It was in the Derbyshire Sunday League Division Five.

'I was picking dog shit and glass bottles out of the goal area. I heard a rumour that the team we played against complained to the league and got the result thrown out. We won 4–0 and I didn't have a great deal to do, but they realised I wasn't an amateur.'

Lee Chapman's arrival from Niort, after a protracted deal that was delayed until Niort had paid compensation to his former club, Sheffield Wednesday, added an attacking spearhead that helped turn Forest's possession into goals, and the result was that, after a run in which they won only one of eight games, it rapidly became obvious that Forest would finish at the very least in upper midtable. As it was, they again ended the season third, twelve points behind Arsenal and Liverpool.

It was the cups, though, in which Forest shone. They began the League Cup by beating Chester 6–0 at home and 4–0 away and then came from behind twice to beat Coventry 3–2 in the third round. That game, though, spoke of more than strength of character. Forest were without seven first-team players, something that in the past would almost certainly have derailed them. This, Clough said, was his strongest-ever squad.

Stuart Pearce became the first Forest player in three years to be sent off, as he committed two bookable fouls in the fourth-round tie away to Leicester, but Forest held out for a goalless draw. Paul Groves cancelled out Clough's opener in the replay, but Chapman ran on to Nigel Clough's chip to score the winner.

That set up a quarter-final against QPR, a game that seemed to show Clough's Forest at their best. They were neat and precise in possession, and won 5–2, Chapman scoring four. Clough's ability to taint a triumph, though, was spectacular and consistent. After the final whistle, Forest fans invaded the pitch to celebrate. Clough, walking slowly along the touchline towards the tunnel, reacted. 'I ran straight towards the tunnel to congratulate Lee Chapman who was just running off the pitch and as I had my arm round Lee Chapman, Brian Clough came from behind, clipped me round the ear, then kept on going, hitting other people,' said Paul Richardson, one of the fans involved. Clough threw a left hook at another fan, who made as though to retaliate, did a double take, realised who had punched him, and walked away. Clough grabbed a third by the jacket and threw him to one side. 'The stewards just stood back and let him get on with it,' Richardson went on.

In his first autobiography, Clough claimed that 'thirty or forty, maybe more' fans blocked his path to the tunnel and said he 'was having difficulty getting past them' which was what caused him to lose his temper. The television footage, though, is clear. Clough turned on to the pitch – that is, away from the tunnel – and, as he described it, 'clipped or belted two or three of them'. He only actually punched one fan, but he hit him so hard that he needed treatment on a wrist injury afterwards.

Roworth said the fans had deserved it, although it should be pointed out that this was an invasion rooted in over-exuberance rather than hooliganism, even if that didn't justify the sanctimonious interview Richardson gave at the time in which he said 'there was only one hooligan out there on that pitch and that was Brian Clough'.

The players were unaware anything was amiss until long after the final whistle. 'It was a normal game, even to the extent that at the end it was normal,' said Laws. 'We trotted off the pitch and, unknown to us, Cloughie was thumping supporters left, right and centre. He came into the dressing-room after the game and seemed his normal self. He went into the bath, stood up and said, "You've played well, you've played well."

'We had no idea what went on until we went into the players' lounge and saw it on the TV and said, "Oh my god, what's happened?" We thought that Cloughie had gone, that he couldn't recover from that. But he turned it around, made the supporters apologise for going on to the pitch.'

Roworth's backing for his manager was widely regarded as evidence that Clough was so powerful at Forest as to be practically unaccountable but, as the chairman pointed out, of 679 letters he'd received about the incident, 628, including one from the Labour Party leader Neil Kinnock, backed the manager. Clough didn't help matters, though, by telling the *Sun* the day after the incident that in the same circumstances he'd do the same again.

Two of the fans Clough had assaulted, Sean O'Hara and James McGowan, were slated to appear at the FA Commission hearing into the incident – speaking for the defence. Like Pye and Pavis before them, they seemed oddly conflicted between outrage at the offence, and love for Clough. In the end they weren't called, as the FA imposed a three-month touchline ban and fined Clough £5,000. In his autobiography, Clough staggeringly made out that he thought he'd been hard done by; the FA having its revenge on him again. In fact, Clough got off remarkably lightly and, as he acknowledged, Graham Kelly, the chief executive of the FA, did him an enormous favour by holding the hearing in Nottingham, where Clough could control access, rather than in London.

Both fans were offered money by newspapers for their stories, and encouraged to sue; both refused. Clough apologised publicly to the pair, and made them kiss him before a 4–0 win over Aston Villa that ended with the Trent End singing 'We love you Brian'. Clough also offered the two tickets to the League Cup final if Forest got there. Forest did make it, but O'Hara said he never received a ticket; Richardson, though, did. The Crown prosecutors in Nottingham, despite the clear television footage, decided there was insufficient evidence to mount a prosecution; three of the four police cameras, apparently, 'lacked clarity'. Meanwhile, Chief Superintendent Michael Holford, who had worked with Clough for fourteen years, said there'd been a sense of hostility in the air that night and he believed that was what Clough was reacting to. 'It is a big man who can apologise later and admit his mistake,' he said, in a somewhat liberal interpretation of events.

The police in general, arguably, seem to have gone out their way to protect Clough – giving credence to the suggestions made by residents of Derby that he was immune from parking regulations. Within twelve hours of the incident, Holford was saying no action would be taken unless there were 'specific complaints', while the *Police Gazette* came out forcefully in Clough's favour, offering what sounds suspiciously like a blueprint for vigilantism. 'Thank God there are Cloughies of this world,' its report said, 'who will not stand by and see standards eroded. The backbone seems to have been removed from so many members of society and nowadays far too many are willing to stand by, watch the wrongdoer and then harangue those who are prepared to challenge lawlessness.'

More significant than the punishments, though, was what the incident revealed about Clough. Other managers had been driven to emotional breakdown by misbehaving fans – Jack Charlton had wept in frustration as Sheffield Wednesday fans rioted against Oldham in 1979 – but none had started weighing in with fists. While the awe with which Forest fans regarded Clough was underlined by the refusal of fans to press charges, so too was exposed to the wider public the dark, violent, unpredictable side of Clough. 'I was not the worse for drink,' Clough insisted, but that was not the conclusion many drew.

Inevitably, Clough could not sit in the stand without generating further furore. The most notorious incident came in a 4–1 defeat at Wimbledon at the beginning of April, a match in which Nigel Clough suffered a shin injury following a challenge from Dennis Wise. Clough was watching from the directors' box and shouted so vociferously that a local policeman laid his hand on his shoulder to calm him down. Clough – not realising he was addressing a policeman, he said – told him to 'piss off', at which the policeman threatened to arrest him. In the end, Alan Hill talked him out of it, and a senior officer – recalled by Clough only as 'Wilson' – ended up taking Clough into the police control box. Wilson was a Dundee fan, so Clough introduced him after the game to Archie Gemmill, and as bonhomie blossomed a match ended up being arranged between the police forces of Wimbledon and Nottingham.

By then, Forest had already reached the League Cup final after a nervy semi-final against Bristol City. Paul Mardon had put the Third Division side ahead after Joe Jordan had knocked down a sixty-fifth-minute corner in the first leg at the City Ground, only for John Pender to turn the ball into his own net as he tried to prevent a Webb flick from reaching Nigel Clough with five minutes remaining. It was goalless after ninety minutes of the second leg, meaning Bristol City would have gone through on away goals had they held out through extra-time, but Parker found a winner.

Forest were also in the final of the Simod Cup, the tournament introduced to try to make up for revenues lost because of the European ban, having beaten Chelsea, Ipswich and Crystal Palace and, as they hit a fine run of form in the early part of the new year, they made progress in the FA Cup. Comfortable wins over Ipswich, Leeds and Watford set up a quarter-final away to Manchester United.

At Old Trafford, Garry Parker's forty-third-minute tap-in from Franz Carr's cross proved enough to win it, despite Manchester United claims that a second-half header from Brian McClair had crossed the line before Hodge hacked clear. By the time of the League Cup final, Forest were on course for a potential treble of domestic cups. 'We couldn't compete financially,' Hodge said, 'so the cups became our forte. I think Clough realised he wouldn't win the league again. He always told us the league was our bread and butter, but I think he was quite happy he could play his brand of football and be successful in the cups.'

The weekend before the League Cup final, Brian Laws was hospitalised for forty-eight hours, something that might explain Clough's irritability that day at Wimbledon. 'It was my first final,' Laws said. 'A few days before we were ready to go to London, I was having a glass of wine at home with my wife. I tripped with two wine glasses in my hand and cut my hand. I woke up in hospital with my hand in the air after having surgery. Cloughie was so angry, but he said, "I trust my players, will you be fit?"' I said yes, but the doctors said no. He got me into his office and threw a ball at me. I caught it. He said, "If you can take a throw in, you can play."'

Laws declared himself fit enough to play against the holders Luton at Wembley with thirty-six stitches in his hand. Despite his return there was disquiet among certain Forest players when Clough picked Lee Glover, widely perceived as one of his favourites, as substitute. That meant that if Forest won he would get a £10,000 bonus, while Brian Rice, who had played in five games on the way to the final, would get nothing.

Talk of bonuses, though, seemed academic in the first half. Forest were poor and fell behind after thirty-six minutes as Mick Harford headed in a Danny Wilson cross. 'Gentlemen,' Clough said at half-time. 'We are absolute crap. They are playing to the best of their abilities. Now my wife's in the stand, so are yours, so are your relations and friends and all these lovely people from Nottingham. So please – go out there and show them what you can really do.'

Nigel Clough levelled with a penalty after the Luton keeper Les Sealey had taken down Hodge as he ran on to a Webb through-ball. Rapid counterattacking, often funnelled through Clough, had become Forest's key method and they took the lead with a classic example: Webb cleared a Tim Breacker pass to Clough, he spread the ball wide for Tommy Gaynor and, when he crossed, Webb finished calmly. Gaynor then laid on the third for Nigel Clough, latching on to a ball from Pearce.

That gave Clough his seventh major trophy at club level, taking him beyond the six Revie had achieved. 'People had thought he was on the wane,' said Hodge, 'and we couldn't compete financially, so he was delighted to win a trophy.'

'It was,' Clough said, 'a beautiful day with lots of happy people watching a football match.' The banal phrasing was presumably another manifestation of Clough's habit of deflecting glory, but in the context of what happened six days later at Hillsborough, it sounds oddly chilling.

That, too, seemed a beautiful day, the sun shining on an FA Cup semifinal between Liverpool, the league champions, and a Forest side that had won sixteen of the twenty-one games it had played that year. What happened hardly needs repeating: ninety-six people killed, crushed as the central pens in the Leppings Lane End became overcrowded as a result

497

of poor stadium design and inadequate crowd control. The game was abandoned, Clough taking his players away long before they had been given official permission to leave.

In his first autobiography, Clough repeated despicable claims made in the *Sun* about the conduct of Liverpool fans that day, something that, frankly, defies explanation, given that the Taylor Report into the disaster had already shown them to be without foundation. This went far beyond his usual brashness into something far more disturbing; surely even Clough should have seen that the grief of the friends and relatives of the deceased and the horror of a city and club still coming to terms with the disaster were best left undisturbed. It is one thing to be insensitive when you're right; quite another when you're wrong, and particularly about something as obviously painful as Hillsborough. The pages were later expunged from the book, and Clough eventually retracted his claims in 2001. 'I now accept the investigations have made me realise I was misinformed,' he said. 'I wasn't trying to be vindictive or unsympathetic, but my opinion has altered over the years. It was never my intention to hurt anyone.' But he did, and badly, and it's hard not to see his allegations as a – severely misguided – example of the lust for publicity through controversy Taylor had identified fourteen years earlier.

At the time, at least to his own players, Clough was far more sympathetic. Forest's first game after the disaster came at Middlesbrough. During the minute's silence before kick-off, a group of Boro fans threw pies at Sutton and shouted obscenities. Sutton was so upset that he considered retiring from football, but Clough waited for him after the game, gave him a whisky and told him to spend as much time with his family as he needed before returning.

Forest's next game was the Simod Cup final, in which they completed the second part of their possible treble as Chapman scored twice in extra-time to secure a 4–3 victory over Everton. Two days before the final, the Forest players had asked what bonuses they would get if they won. Clough told them they'd get nothing, but when they won he gave them each a box of chocolates with a £10 note attached.

Then came the rearranged semi-final, for Forest an uncomfortable occasion in which, as pretty much every player has acknowledged, they felt like intruders on someone else's grief. 'My team just walked out of that dressing-room with intense expressions on every face and not the slightest sign of a smile,' Clough said. 'It was not a feeling of dread, more the feeling that "I'd rather not be doing this, I'd rather be sitting at home."'

Liverpool were comfortably the better side and won 3–1. Clough ended up raging at John Aldridge, who ruffled Brian Laws's hair after he'd scored an own-goal, and at Kenny Dalglish, a man with whom he had never got on, for suggesting after the match that only one team had really been motivated. It was probably true, Clough admitted, but he felt it was inappropriate for Dalglish to have said so. Three days after the semi-final, Liverpool played Forest again, and beat them 1–0 with an Aldridge penalty. Forest finished third and had a superb second half of the season, but the gulf to the top was clear.

Forest's reserve side won the Central League and their Under-18s won the Midland Youth Cup, which might have provided some reason for optimism, had it not been for the departure of Neil Webb for Manchester United for £1.2million, something that had seemed inevitable since the previous Christmas as he refused to sign a new contract. The reasons were obvious: United could offer him more money and a greater chance of success. The average gate at the City Ground the previous season had been 20,785, as opposed to 36,487 at Old Trafford; even in relatively good times financially, Forest couldn't help but be a selling club. John Sheridan was signed from Leeds for £650,000 to replace him.

Within their own parameters, the financial news seemed good. The final payment on the Executive Stand was made at the end of June – although more redevelopment was planned to comply with the recommendations of the Taylor Report – and by the start of the 1989–90 season, Forest had taken over £1million in season ticket sales, up twenty per cent on the previous year. They'd made a loss of £7,000, largely because of player acquisition, but turnover was up to £5.7million.

Sheridan missed the first match of the season, at home to Aston Villa, but few thought too much of it as a Parker equaliser earned a 1–1 draw. Clough called it 'a superb start'. As the previous year, though, Forest took time to get going. They won only one of their first seven games and although a spurt of successive victories over Charlton, Coventry and Wimbledon eased any relegation fears – although only the most pessimistic of fans would seriously have considered going down a possibility – they never looked like finishing higher than mid-table.

Again, it was the League Cup that provided salvation. Sheridan made his debut in the first leg of the second-round tie against Huddersfield, laying on the opening goal for Gary Crosby. Ken O'Doherty stabbed in an equaliser from a corner, though, leaving Forest with an awkward trip to Leeds Road. There they seemed comfortable at 3–1 up, but conceded twice late on and went through only on the away-goals rule.

After a goalless draw at Selhurst Park, Forest hammered Crystal Palace 5–0 in the third-round replay, Hodge scoring twice despite a groin injury that hampered him for much of the season. Sheridan could, perhaps, have played in place of him, but he had become a latter-day Asa Hartford, bought by Forest and discarded a few weeks later. Hartford stayed a shorter time, but at least was given three matches; Sheridan was picked only once, and never in the league. He had played 230 times for Leeds and that he subsequently played 199 times for Sheffield Wednesday, whom he joined later that week, suggests he was far from a turbulent character, but Clough decided he had a 'downbeat personality' and didn't want him lowering morale around the club. That his gloominess might have been caused by never getting a game seems not to have occurred to Clough. To the *Evening Post*, Clough said Sheridan didn't make the right forward runs, and noted he 'would play and pass and stand'. Hodge's description in his autobiography of a conversation he overhead between Clough and Ron Fenton similarly suggests his concern was more to do with ability than temperament. 'What have I signed him for?' Clough asked, despairingly. 'He can't tackle! He can't head! He can't run! What the fuck have I signed him for?'

Everton were eliminated 1–0 in the fourth round, Chapman getting the only goal after an indirect free-kick awarded against Neville Southall for time-wasting seven minutes from time, but the other cups were less kind. Aston Villa beat Forest in the ZDS Cup, as the Simod Cup had become, then Manchester United put Forest out of the FA Cup in the third round, the substitute Mark Robins getting the only goal and Terry Wilson having a late effort ruled out in the famous game that saved Alex Ferguson from the sack.

Given United's poor form in the build-up, that perhaps came as a shock, but what followed over the next week was far more surprising, as Lee

Chapman was sold to Leeds for £400,000 – a bafflingly low fee given that only two seasons later he would be the target-man in Leeds's title-winning side. Clough later explained that the decision had been forced on him: as he told it, Chapman had been badly advised when he had left Niort and so owed a significant amount of tax he could only afford to pay with a signing-on fee.

The nineteen-year-old Nigel Jemson, who had made his debut against Luton on Boxing Day after signing from Preston, offered an inexperienced alternative, but Clough opted for a more proven player later in January, paying Barnsley £700,000 for David Currie. He would be another Clough flop, managing just eight league games for the club. Toddi Orlygsson had arrived from the Icelandic side Akranes in the December, while Clough was openly chasing Gary McAllister as he sought to find a replacement for Neil Webb – the hole Sheridan was supposed to have filled – in midfield.

Forest continued to produce their best form in the League Cup. Crosby and Parker gave them a 2–0 lead against Tottenham, only for goals from Gary Lineker and Steve Sedgeley to take the tie to a replay at White Hart Lane, where Forest produced what David Lacey in the *Guardian* termed 'a marvellous display of passing, tackling and finishing'. Although Spurs took the lead, and levelled the scores at 2–2 just after the hour, Forest, Lacey said, 'were always ahead in thought if not in deed. There was nothing complicated about Forest's performance. It was the old Spurs push-and-run set in a modern context and given extra speed and vision.'

Nayim had Spurs ahead within the first minute, but 'Clough, Hodge and Crosby proceeded to dismantle the Tottenham defence with the easy assurance of men used to taking down scaffolding. So neat were their movements they did not even leave any builders' rubble.' Crosby and Clough combined to set up Hodge to level, and a rapid break involving Crosby and Parker created the opening for Jemson to twist past Sedgeley and give Forest a 2–1 half-time lead. Paul Stewart levelled, but within two minutes a Crosby cross had deflected for Hodge to knock in the winner. It was performances like that, as much as the entertainment of Clough's public pronouncements, that made neutrals warm to Forest, and it was perhaps all the more appreciated in an age in which the long-ball football of the likes of Watford, Wimbledon and Crystal Palace was making such strides.

Forest faced Coventry in the semi-final, with both legs televised live.

Clough was typically cussed and refused a request from ITV to delay kick-off until their coverage of Nelson Mandela's release from jail was finished, meaning the first few minutes of the game went unbroadcast. Nigel Clough put Forest ahead from a first-half penalty and, although Steve Livingston levelled after seventy-three minutes, Pearce smashed in the winner seven minutes later. A goalless draw at Highfield Road secured Forest's place at Wembley and earned Clough his twenty-second Manager of the Month award, equalling Bob Paisley's record.

After reaching the final, Forest's league form collapsed and they lost seven of their nine games in the build-up to Wembley. Even the final, against an Oldham side that also reached the semi-final of the FA Cup, and missed out on promotion as a result of their exertions in the cups, was anti-climactic. Forest won 1–0, but the goal that won it lacked drama or finesse, Jemson forcing the ball in at the second attempt just after half-time. Clough seemed exhausted by the win. 'They don't know how hard it is to win a trophy,' he said as he slumped in the bath afterwards, although it wasn't clear who he was talking about; perhaps the clutch of enemies he regularly accused of being ranged against him. Hodge recalled the mood on the bus on the way back to Nottingham being flat. 'Whereas the first year we'd had beer on the bus and lots of photos being taken, this time was deadpan with no real joy,' he wrote in his autobiography, *The Man with Maradona's Shirt*. 'The fans were happy – after all we'd just retained a trophy at Wembley – but for the players it was more a case of "job done".'

Forest's relief was evident in their final two matches of the season, as they climbed from twelfth, which would have been their worst finish under Clough, to ninth with a 4–0 win over Manchester United – their best performance of the season, even if United were distracted by thoughts of the FA Cup final – and a 3–0 win at Sheffield Wednesday. 'Maybe if we had not got to Wembley we would have won the league,' Fenton said.

Between those two games, Clough made his last great signing, picking up Roy Keane from Cobh Ramblers for £10,000. Aside from 'the Irishman', as Clough would always call him, though, his dealings that summer were erratic. Forest had money, having made a pre-tax profit of over £1million the previous season, but Clough's search for a midfielder was repeatedly thwarted. Jim Bett rejected a move from Aberdeen because his wife didn't want to relocate. Clough seemed close to signing Gary McAllister from

Leicester, but was late to his meeting with the player and, observing his cowboy boots, asked a series of pointed questions about his private life, persuading McAllister to join Leeds instead.

After the World Cup, there were persistent rumours linking Des Walker with multi-million-pound moves to Italy, all of which Clough rebuffed, and then there was Currie to be offloaded, something he did with a typical lack of sensitivity. 'I must have been daft to have signed you,' he told him, then asked whether he had bought a house yet. When Currie said that he was still looking, Clough replied, 'I wouldn't fucking bother if I were you.' He sold him to Oldham for £450,000.

The opening game of the 1990–91 season, at home to QPR, offered a worrying glimpse of the future. QPR played 4–3–3 and Forest were overrun in midfield. Hodge complained about it to Clough at half-time, but he didn't care; his sides played his way, and by that stage he refused to countenance change. It took a Jemson penalty to rescue a point. In the past, Forest had been financially outmuscled; here they were just outmuscled, perhaps even outthought. 'In pre-season,' Hodge said, 'we did a bit of shape work, three or four sessions of shadow play where you play against nobody – always in a 4–4–2. And that was it. Not once when I was there was the opposition mentioned in a team-talk.'

The refusal to practise set-pieces became an irritation among the squad. 'He used to love to beat Wimbledon and Palace, but he didn't do anything to make it happen,' Hodge said. 'You'd have the likes of Mark Bright, Eric Young and John Fashanu, or when you played Arsenal Steve Bould and Tony Adams, all giants bearing down on you in formation, and we did nothing to combat them. If you think there was one year we only lost the title by six points [1983–84], if we could have picked up a couple more wins by being a bit better at set-plays, well, maybe the championship wasn't so far out of reach.'

The following Tuesday, Forest were away to Liverpool. The first-team squad travelled on the Monday, after which it became apparent that Hodge, who was suffering from flu, would be unable to play. Clough decided to gamble on Keane, who had previously represented Forest only in an Under-21 tournament, in two pre-season games for the reserves and in one reserve league game in which he'd come off the bench with ten minutes remaining.

Clough picked him based on having seen him play twenty minutes against Sutton-in-Ashfield the week before.

Keane, who had been out drinking until 2am, found out he was expected to travel to Liverpool only on the morning of the match. Ronnie Fenton gave him and Phil Starbuck a lift from Nottingham to Liverpool, stopping at Clough's house to pick him up on the way. Keane was sent to ring the doorbell. As he got to the door, Clough emerged. 'He gave me a pint of milk,' Keane said. 'I said, "I don't like milk." He said, "You'd better drink it because I'm putting the bottles out." Trust me, I drank it.'

Assuming he was there for the experience, and feeling like a spare part, Keane began to help the kit-man lay out the shirts. Only then did Clough tell him to get the number six shirt because he was playing. Keane said he felt oddly calm as he walked out onto the pitch; only later did he realise how 'clever' Clough had been, placing him under no pressure. The next day, Clough came up to him in the dressing-room at the training ground and asked his name. After Keane had told him, he took off his shoes, which were muddy after a walk with Del Boy. 'Give those a clean for me, will you, Roy?' he said, a characteristic tactic to ensure Keane's feet stayed on the ground.

Forest lost that match 2–0, then drew 2–2 at Coventry in a game of four penalties – three of them against Forest – before beating Southampton 3–1. It was a typically indifferent start, in which the major positive seemed to be the form of Nigel Jemson, who had scored five goals. Typically, Clough decided it was then that he had to criticise the forward. 'Learn to play for your mates,' Clough wrote in his column in the *Evening Post*. 'He's got to be more aware of the lads around him. All the team play for him. Now he's got to do the same for them. I don't know whether he gets carried away a bit. Sometimes he doesn't seem to think. I'm sure he doesn't do it deliberately.'

Although Jemson's mother once wrote to Clough thanking him for looking after her boy, they often clashed, Clough saying the forward was the only player he'd ever met with a head bigger than his. Jemson's father was a police officer, but in Clough he found a far stricter disciplinarian. The biggest flashpoint came in a reserve game at Derby. Forest were leading, but were tiring when Clough sent Jemson on with ten minutes to go with instructions to play on the right and turn the ball into the corners whenever possible. Jemson, though, 'wanted the limelight', as Clough put it, and started cutting inside looking for goals. (It's not the point of the anecdote, but it does show up once again both the absurdity of Clough's claims never to have given tactical instruction and his pretence always to have played football 'the right way'; why was it right for Jemson to take the ball into the corners in a reserve game against Derby, but wrong for Hodge to do it in a league game against Notts County?) Forest hung on, but Clough, to use the term he used in his first autobiography, was 'blazing'. When he got in the dressing-room he ordered Jemson to stand up and, when he'd done so, asked him if he'd ever been punched in the stomach. When he said he hadn't, Clough 'clouted' him in the midriff.

Clough increasingly at that time used physical intimidation to impose his will on players. Dave Mackay had pointed out that even at Derby there was the threat of violence, but that season, Clough took to prowling the dressing-room with a tennis ball, pinging it at players as they were getting changed, apparently with the aim of keeping them alert. He also punched Keane for an errant backpass in a Cup replay against Crystal Palace. Before, his wit and his tongue – and perhaps a sense of underlying threat – had been enough; now he was turning more and more to his fists.

Forest were going nowhere in the league, but that September, Clough signed a three-year contract. It would be his last. On the final Saturday of the month, a Pearce screamer gave Forest a 1–0 win at Old Trafford, ending Manchester United's 100 per cent home start to the season. Seventeen years less two weeks earlier, Clough's Derby had won 1–0 at Old Trafford, and he and Taylor had celebrated in the boardroom, where Taylor's clash with Jack Kirkland had precipitated their departure.

Maybe Clough's mind was so hardened against Taylor that he didn't give those memories a second thought, but he certainly did six days later. Taylor was on holiday in Mallorca when he died, aged sixty-two. By then, he and Clough hadn't spoken for seven years. Ron Fenton telephoned Clough with the news, and he answered without a word, silently replacing the receiver.

Clough rang the family with his condolences and slipped in to the back of the funeral. Afterwards, Clough's attitude softened and he began once again to refer to Taylor as 'Pete' rather than by his surname, and to pay tribute to 'his brains' rather than criticising him for being 'lazy' and spending too much time reading the racing form. In his autobiography, Clough reflected movingly on the 'dreadful and needless waste' of those 'seven years of silence', and admitted that the signing of John Robertson seemed, with hindsight, 'a trivial, inconsequential thing' over which to have fallen out. He clearly regretted never having made an effort to build bridges, and in the long confessional interview he gave Hamilton after being awarded the freedom of the City of Nottingham he told him that his only regret was that 'my mate wasn't here with me'.

That Taylor's death hit Clough hard is undeniable. There are those, perhaps wishing to believe that the demons only seized him late, who say that Clough's real problems with alcohol were brought on by his grief but, while it almost certainly accelerated the issue, alcohol had been a regular part of his life since his injury, particularly in times of crisis. It's fair to assume that while much of his unpredictability was scripted, at least some of it, particularly from the mid-eighties onwards, was the result of the booze. His periods of poor timekeeping and unreliability – aspects that veer sharply from the Alan Brown template – certainly seem to have been caused by alcohol.

Even towards the end, when his dependence on alcohol had become obvious, even as his face became red and blotchy and his hands trembled, Clough tried to disguise the problem, hiding his bottle in the pocket of his tracksuit. He was aware it *was* a problem – aware very early – as was demonstrated by a deal he struck with Robertson after a 4–3 defeat to Liverpool in September 1982 that he would give up booze if the winger gave up cigarettes. He would then stalk Robertson, trying to catch him smoking so he could justify calling a night off and have a drink.

Journalists who worked with Clough in the eighties all remember mornings when he was clearly drinking to rid himself of a hangover, of morning meetings that couldn't start until those present had downed a couple of fingers of Scotch or brandy. Later, he switched to vodka, because the smell was harder to detect on his breath. His attempts to disguise his dependence were remarkably successful, perhaps because people simply didn't want to believe a man they idolised could be so afflicted. Even after Clough himself had admitted he had a problem, there were those who refused to believe it. The barman at his local in Quarndon, even, told Tony Francis he had never seen Clough drunk, and that, although he was a regular visitor, he tended to stick to mineral water.

*

Forest's first home game after Taylor's death was against Everton. Their players wore black armbands, but there was no minute's silence, something for which Forest were criticised. Roworth explained that Taylor had hated them, believing they distracted players, and the more fitting tribute was a 3–1 win – the same scoreline against the same opponents, of course, with which Forest had marked their return to Division One thirteen years earlier. A goalless draw at Chelsea lifted Forest to sixth, but that was as good as it got in the league.

Clough became an increasingly rare sight at the training ground, to the relief of the players. On one occasion he turned up just as the players had finished and burst into the dressing-room, sending the door crashing back against the wall. He went round each player and insulted them in turn. 'You've been crap since you got that new contract,' he told Pearce, who had signed a five-year deal in the October. 'Stop rabbiting to refs,' he told Jemson. 'Sign a new contract,' he told Sutton. 'Get a house in Nottingham or fuck off and play for Barnsley,' he told Crossley. For each player there was a different put-down, until finally he got to Keane. 'I love you, Irishman,' he said. 'It was his style of management; you had to expect the unexpected,' Crossley said. 'I played under him for six years and I never ever took anything for granted.'

Although he clashed with Clough repeatedly, Keane reciprocated his manager's affection and seems to have rated him as a manager even more highly than Sir Alex Ferguson. Certainly his own management style seemed informed by Clough's, not merely in the unexpected outbursts and the restraint in criticising referees, but also in more specific cases, as when he gave the teenage forward Martyn Waghorn his first-team debut for Sunderland in front of a packed Boxing Day crowd at home to Manchester United – surely an imitation of his own debut.

'He may have been a remote figure day to day on the training ground, but on match days his presence, and his eye for detail, made the difference,' Keane wrote in his autobiography. 'If you weren't doing your stuff, Clough would spot it. A seemingly innocuous mistake that led to a goal conceded three or four minutes later, a tackle missed, or a failure to make the right run, or pass, would be correctly identified as the cause of the goal . . . Every football match consists of a thousand little things which, added together, amount to the final score. The manager that can't spot the details in the forensic manner that Clough could is simply bluffing.'

In practice, that meant players had to take responsibility; there was no hiding-place. 'I remember a reserve-team game when I was only sixteen against Manchester United,' said Lee Glover. 'We conceded a goal. We didn't even know he was there, but he came in at half-time and said, "Who cost me a fucking goal?" Everyone sat there in silence until the left-back Brett Williams said, "He went past me." So then I said, "It was me." It was my fault, I knew it; I lost the ball. So he said, "Don't cost me another." And walked out with a smirk on his face. He knew it was me, but he just wanted to see.'

Laws was adamant that, for all his erratic behaviour, despite the problems with alcohol, Clough retained an iron control. 'Nothing got past Brian Clough. He ran the show from top to bottom. Anything and everything had to go through him.'

To an extent, it had to be like that, because nobody was ever allowed to rise up to challenge Clough. 'It was typical of him to put you on the back foot,' Laws said. 'From the first minute you met him, you couldn't be sure what his thoughts were, but it worked. It was part of his charms, the unpredictability was exciting. He was so good that the players didn't understand for months later. He was a psychologist. As an on-the-field coach he was down towards the bottom end of managers I worked with. He never did it. His style was instant, thought-provoking.

'He brought me off after twenty-five minutes once. There was a simple pass on to Nigel Clough, but I heard Neil Webb calling. I should have passed to Nigel, but I played it blind, Neil Webb lost it and a few minutes later it was in the back of our net. I knew instantly that he blamed me. Then I saw Cloughie standing there with the number two in his hand. He brought me off after twenty-five minutes against Manchester United and I wanted to kill him. The first thing he said in the dressing-room at half-time was, "Do you know why I brought you off?"

'I said, "Yeah, because I didn't pass to Nigel, I passed to Webby," and he said, "You're right. You're playing next week, now get out of my sight." It was dramatic, but it worked. That was his teaching tool, it was harsh, but it was fast. If he had taken me to one side on the training ground, it wouldn't have been as effective.'

That was part of the wider philosophy by which Clough encouraged players to take responsibility themselves; to that extent he remained less a tactician than a strategist, somebody who addressed the big picture and left the details to individuals. 'In my six years there, we never spoke about the opposition tactically,' Laws explained. 'We never practised corners or free-kicks, for or against. He never gave us jobs to do, who to mark. We talked to each other, organised ourselves. Now it is expected that managers and coaches will give you the organisation and practise set plays.

'We very rarely conceded crappy goals. We were probably well switched on. There are a lot of those players who have gone into management; we had good communication skills and we were students of the game. We talked about it rather than using the manager as an excuse. His signings were ones he thought would fit in his jigsaw. He had characters, not necessarily the best players, but people he thought would settle into his team.'

Again for Forest, it was the cups that offered the chance of glory. After beating Burnley and Plymouth, they faced Coventry in the fourth round of the League Cup. Coventry raced into a 4–0 lead, but Nigel Clough scored a hat-trick in an eight-minute spell as Forest clawed it back to 4–4. Just as it seemed Forest's unbeaten run in the competition might extend to a twenty-third game, though, Steve Livingstone scored the winner. Barnsley put Forest out of the ZDS, leaving Forest with only the FA Cup to play for.

The third-round draw paired Forest with Crystal Palace, one of the direct sides against whom Forest often struggled. Clough's public pronouncements, particularly in the day or two before or after games, should always be treated with a level of scepticism, but he hinted again that he was considering retirement. 'Palace will have an almighty cross to bear if I get knocked out,' he said on the morning of the match. 'It will mean I'll be staying around for another year to have another crack at winning the Cup.' Perhaps even then he was looking for a suitable way to bid farewell, and given the FA Cup was the one trophy he had never won, there could hardly have been a more fitting way for him to make his exit.

Forest drew 0–0 at Selhurst Park. They were 2–1 up in the replay when Keane played a backpass to Mark Crossley. He underhit it, and although

Crossley got to the ball, his clearance went to John Salako, who chipped him from fifty yards. As Keane walked in to the dressing-room after the game, Clough punched him in the face. 'Never play the ball back to the goalkeeper,' he shouted. Lying dazed on the floor, Keane could only nod his agreement. 'Knowing the pressure he was under,' Keane said in his autobiography, 'I didn't hold the incident against him.'

In the second replay, also played at the City Ground, Forest were 3–0 up when Hodge saw the substitute's board go up with his number on it. He trotted off, and had reached the touchline by the time he realised nobody was coming on to take his place. Clough claimed at the time he was protecting Hodge's calf. He later told Hodge, though, that it wasn't intended as a slight against him, but that he hated Palace's muscular approach and wanted to 'take the piss' out of them by playing with ten.

It almost certainly was, though, at least in part a slight against Hodge, with whom Clough had a protracted battle over a new contract throughout the latter part of the season. These were the 'situations', Hodge said, Clough deliberately created, creating provocations. It was Hodge's struggles with a calf injury that turned Clough against him – 'if he couldn't pick you on Saturday, it was like you didn't exist,' Hodge said – and suddenly he found himself the butt of Clough's digs.

Forest came from two down to draw at Newcastle in the fourth round, after which Hodge was relegated to the bench for an away game at Sunderland for 'not having held the ball'. Clough asked him in the second half if he fancied a run-out to which Hodge replied, 'It's up to you.' 'I know it's up to me,' Clough snapped. Angered by a 1–0 defeat, Clough made the players sit on the bus with the doors open, welcoming local children on to get autographs. The replay against Newcastle was rather easier, Forest winning 3–0.

Hodge scored the equaliser in a 1–1 draw against Southampton in the fifth round, but twisted his knee, keeping him out for six weeks, and further antagonising Clough. A Jemson hat-trick in the replay saw Forest through to the quarter-finals. Keane got the winner against Norwich in the quarter-final with a ferocious drive, and Forest beat West Ham 4–0 in the semi-final after Tony Gale had been sent off for a professional foul on Crosby. Suddenly inspired, Forest thrashed Chelsea 7–0 and Norwich 5–0 in the league.

Clough wouldn't pick Hodge, but he was called up for England's European Championship qualifier away Turkey at the beginning of May. He played the second half in a 1–0 win, but, when he returned, Clough still refused to select him for an away game at Spurs. Hodge sat in the stand for that game, for which Clough attacked him, insisting he'd told him to sit on the bench. By then, Hodge admitted, he was so sick of his manager he was counting down the days till he could leave.

Hodge, though, was then recalled for the final two league games of the season, a 2–1 win over Liverpool and a 4–3 win over Leeds. In contrast to the previous season, Forest's form had improved radically as they approached Wembley. Clough might have been expected to be jubilant, but Hamilton found him 'subdued and unimpressed ... hunched in his chair, his face grim'. He felt Forest had peaked too soon, and that the football they'd played over the previous month should have been saved for Wembley. The old Clough, surely, would have revelled in his side's good form; here, in abandoning reason – for think of the alternative; would Forest have been better off being hammered by Leeds? – and seeing gloomy portents in a bright performance, he resembled nobody so much as Revie.

That was just part of a more general pattern. There was something very odd about Clough's behaviour – even by his standards – around that final, almost as though he sensed the chance not merely of another trophy, but of something greater yet rather harder to define. The FA Cup, after all, had always eluded him, and his attempts to win it had taken on the sense of a quest. After years without fulfilment, Stanley Matthews had been carried by a similar sense of destiny to glory in the 1953 FA Cup final; 1991 felt as though it could be Clough's equivalent. Matthews, of course, had carried on, defying age to play on for another twelve years; for Clough it was far more likely to have been a curtain call. When Hamilton had first met Clough, a dozen years earlier, he had commented that he had never met anybody so gripped by a sense of his own destiny. Here, perhaps, Clough was facing up to the fact that this was a game that could determine his legacy and that this time, this late in his career, there might not be any second chances.

Returning from a trip to Spain to discover that Forest's reserves had lost three games out of four, and so had missed out on winning the Central League title for a third season out of four, Clough suspended their coach,

Archie Gemmill, calling the results 'unacceptable'. For anybody else to have picked a fight over something so essentially unimportant, particularly with somebody with whom he had worked for over a decade, would suggest a man driven beyond reason by pressure. Clough, of course, had always loved a confrontation; perhaps it was evenhis way of dealing with pressure.

Two days before the Cup final, Clough finally handed Hodge his new contract. It contained a rise, but such a small one that it only confirmed Hodge's determination to leave. For the trip to Wembley, Clough had Hodge rooming with Roy Keane. With the two competing for one place in the side, it was a situation, Keane said, that left both 'uneasy'. Did Clough really believe it would help, that somehow one would be inspired to over-perform? At times, it's hard to avoid the sense Clough enjoyed the role of a mischievous deity, setting off fireworks just because he could.

Forest trained at Burnham Beeches the day before the final. On the way back to the hotel, Clough came through the partition in the bus and threw a crumpled piece of paper at Pearce, telling him it was the team. Pearce glanced at Hodge and shook his head: Clough had decided to pick Keane, despite the doubts about his fitness. Nigel Jemson hadn't even made the bench and as he got back to the hotel, his eyes were welling. He got to the lift, at which Clough made him turn back to pose for a photograph with a fan.

Before the game, Clough was twitchy in the dressing-room, 'uncharacteristically nervous' according to Hodge, although Crossley remembers nothing out of the ordinary. 'He put the ball on a towel in the dressing-room and said, "God gave us grass to play football on." As the Forest and Tottenham sides walked out together, Clough, wearing a rosette proclaiming him 'the world's greatest grandad', looked notably red-faced and unsettled. The grandfatherly image was one he had fostered, always demanding 'a kiss for grandad' from mascots and then asking the child who their favourite players was, before invariably replying, 'Oh, he had a nightmare last week, he's not that good.'

Here, though, it could not disguise his anxiety. As they stepped out of the tunnel into the arena, he grabbed Terry Venables and they stepped out holding hands. He claimed it was merely a gesture of friendship, of managerial solidarity, but Hodge believed he was looking for comfort and Venables later revealed Clough had asked him to do it because he felt so nervous.

As the teams were presented to the Princess of Wales before kick-off, she paused and chatted to Clough for almost a minute. Given his professed socialism, he might have been expected to be scathing about her, but Clough had a tendency to be impressed by celebrity. He later described her as being like the smell of sweet peas in his garden and spoke of how 'they' – presumably some combination of the establishment and the media – 'crushed her'. 'I couldn't get her out of my mind for the first twenty minutes of the game,' he said. By then one of Britain's other great tragic celebrities of the nineties had already departed.

When Paul Gascoigne was wound up, he was terrifying. In the semi-final, he had charged out and, within four minutes, smashed a free-kick into the top corner from improbable range. This time, he charged out and committed what Clough described as 'two despicable fouls'. The first was a chest-high challenge on Garry Parker, the second a horrible scything foul on Gary Charles. Both were at least yellow cards, possibly reds, but the referee Roger Milford took no action beyond awarding free-kicks. From the second, as Lee Glover pulled a gap on the end of the wall, Stuart Pearce crashed in a free-kick to give Forest a sixteenth-minute lead.

Only then did it become apparent that there was something seriously wrong with Gascoigne, and as he was carried off on a stretcher, most observers feared they were seeing the end of one of England's great talents. From Clough, though, there was no sympathy. 'Any understanding or respect I had for Gascoigne disappeared that afternoon,' he wrote in his first autobiography. 'His actions, his sheer irresponsibility, did my game so much discredit; I was ashamed to be inside the stadium that day.' As Clough said, regardless of the fact the fouls were early in the game, irrespective of the occasion or the damage Gascoigne had done to himself, he should have been sent off. Roger Milford, Clough said, 'was a referee copping out of his responsibility'. Had Milford booked Gascoigne for the challenge on Parker, then the second foul may not even have happened.

Crossley saved a penalty from Gary Lineker ten minutes later, but Clough remained in the grip of a pessimistic fatalism. At half-time, he tapped Alan Hill on the knee and said, 'We're going to get done here.' Sure enough, ten minutes into the second half, Paul Allen laid in Paul Stewart to beat Crossley with an angled shot and equalise. It was still 1–1 at full-time.

After the final whistle, Venables strolled among his Tottenham players, geeing them up, offering tactical suggestions. With the Forest players gathering in a loose circle on the halfway line, the world waited for Clough to make his move. He didn't. He stayed on the bench, arms folded, and when he did finally get up, it was to go and joke with a nearby policeman. Perhaps this was simply Clough's instinctive perversity, doing the exact opposite of what everybody expected him to do, perhaps even, his critics would say, of drawing attention to himself precisely by shunning it so overtly. 'I felt he wanted to do it his way,' said Laws. 'It was crying out for more support on the pitch, but he felt he should let the players do the business. It wasn't to be. Nothing surprised you [in] what Cloughie did and for us that was normal. If he didn't do it, he didn't do it. He felt he didn't need to do anything, but looking back, he did.'

In the interview he gave to Hamilton on the day he was awarded the Freedom of the City of Nottingham, though, Clough suggested a rather more intriguing reason, hinting at the vulnerability Taylor had pinpointed nine years before. 'I thought we weren't going to win,' Clough said, 'and that somehow whatever we did that day wasn't going to be enough.'

That could be taken as a post-hoc rationalisation, a few memories of doubt drawn together in hindsight to creating a more general atmosphere of pessimism, were it not for Hill's recollection of Clough's gloominess. In his autobiography, Clough said he was worried that he might put too much pressure on the players, that seeing him before extra-time would remind them that this was the one trophy he hadn't won. It's easy, of course, to turn that round, and see Clough recognising perhaps a final chance not merely of completing the set of domestic medals, but of a meaningful trophy of any kind and feeling, as a result, a paralysing fear.

Hamilton wondered whether Clough, for once, didn't want the limelight, that he couldn't bear the thought of the cameras following his every move, of experts in the television studios trying to second-guess or lip-read what the master-motivator was saying. If he was right, that would suggest that Clough sensed the waning of his powers. Then again, when Clough had remained on the bench between the end of the ninety minutes and the beginning of extra-time in that FA Cup replay at White Hart Lane in 1973, everybody had said it was psychological genius. He'd done the same, too,

in the Uefa Cup against Sturm Graz in 1984, although on that occasion
Hodge had felt it made him look weak.

This time, it didn't work. Four minutes in to extra-time, Stewart flicked
on a Nayim corner and Des Walker, stretching in front of Mabbutt, headed
into his own net. 'Long before Walker headed the ball under, rather than
over, the bar,' the report in the *Evening Post* read, 'Forest were tragically
reminiscent of the boxer who leaves his hardest punches in the gym. The
overwhelming favourites were unrecognisable as the team that had scorched
its way through the First Division fixture list over the last month or so.'
Nigel Clough, in particular, was subdued, a critical factor given his centrality
to Forest's style of play.

His father remained unmoved, fatalistic till the end. This time, there was
no raging against the world, no twisting fate to his will, merely resignation.
He was never a ranter and a raver on the bench, but here his undemon-
strativeness was interpreted as resignation, perhaps even exhaustion. After
the game, his thoughts turned to his grandson, Stephen. 'When I go back
I'll raise my arms and smile,' he said. 'And he'll think the daft old beggar
won the Cup. He's not old enough to realise what really happened. But
when we go back next year and win it, hopefully he'll be able to forgive me
for lying to him.'

Had Forest won, it would have been the perfect opportunity for Clough
to retire; he hinted to Hamilton that he would have done and admitted in
his autobiography that he should have done. He could have gone out with
glory and dignity, lifting the one domestic trophy that had, until then,
eluded him. Whether he actually would have done so or not is another
matter. Hindsight suggests it would have been the right decision, but Pat
Murphy recalled a conversation the following January in which Clough
spoke of the promise of his young side and his belief that a raft of trophies
was just around the corner. That, certainly, perhaps inevitably, was the line
the *Evening Post* took. 'With cash in the bank and a young team,' wrote Ian
Edwards, 'there is no reason why the traditional promise to return cannot,
in Forest's case, be fulfilled. Age is on their side and so is talent.'

Nigel, though, has said since that there had been serious talk – as
opposed to contract-boosting rumours – of retirement for five years before
Clough finally went in 1993 and has suggested he thinks his father would
have taken the opportunity to step aside. Certainly that would explain his

outburst nineteen years later when asked about that Cup final. 'If you talk to any of the lads who played that day, they still feel very hard done to by the referee,' Nigel said. 'We still say now that [Gascoigne] left the field on a stretcher or in an ambulance – I don't care what – but without so much as a yellow card. Spurs could have been down to ten men early on . . . They were two of the worst challenges you will see on a football pitch. And it wasn't even a yellow card. Garry Parker had stud marks all down his chest. Roger Milford just gave him a little pat on the back and said, "I hope you're feeling better soon." And we lost the Cup.' And, more significantly, his father lost the chance of the perfect exit that would have spared him and perhaps Forest the trauma of relegation two years later.

And so Clough fought on in search of his glorious farewell. He would have one further chance, but that, too, would be spurned. That summer, once again, showed the diminishing of Clough's powers. For most of the decade he had been restricted in the transfer market by finances. Even with money, though, he didn't win the battles the way he had fifteen years earlier.

Clough was keen to sign Dean Saunders, who had decided to leave Derby after their relegation from the First Division. The negotiations were, frankly, bizarre. They met at Alan Hill's house, and when Clough arrived he was, according to Saunders, clearly drunk. Ignoring the forward, who was sat at one end of the room, he walked to the other, fell to his knees and crawled back, sniffing the ground as he did so. 'Good rug, that,' he said. A little later, after more orthodox chat about expectations, Clough asked whether Saunders liked flowers. When, uncertainly, he said he did, Clough dashed into the garden and began putting together a haphazard bouquet from various pots. As Hill tried to prevent him, he insisted this was what would clinch the deal. Saunders eventually negotiated his escape, but when he got home, about to tell his wife about his extraordinary afternoon, he found her shushing him and gesticulating to the front-room. Clough, somehow, had got there first. Saunders ended up joining Liverpool, with Clough raging that they'd offered £8,000 a week, to beat Forest's offer by £1,000. Following on from McAllister the previous summer, the trend was obvious: Clough's behaviour was increasingly off-putting to potential signings and, as a result, he was no longer winning his transfer battles.

Kingsley Black did sign from Luton, but he was very nearly put off, as

McAllister had been, by Clough's rudeness. First Clough had him stand back to back with him and, discovering the winger was a couple of inches shorter than him, made him take his shoes off. He then asked for his watch, which Black handed over. Clough pocketed it, and when Black asked for it back, Clough said he could have it after he'd signed. Clough then said he'd heard Black was a coward, and when the player bridled, asked him where he wanted to play. Black said he'd prefer a free role up front, to which Clough replied that that was a position for brave players.

It was all part of his process of psychologically testing players, of breaking them to his will, but as players sought and won greater and greater freedom, fewer and fewer were prepared to expose themselves to Clough's bracing approach. That, at least, is the gentle way to put it; it could equally be that, at the same time, Clough's eccentricities were becoming more and more unbearable. Even friends of his admitted that, by the late eighties, they dreaded attending any public event with him because they were never sure whether they'd get warm and charming Clough or offensive and sulking Clough. When he decided against attending the wedding of Dryden's daughter, instead sending his own daughter, Libby, Dryden admitted he was unsure whether to be dismayed at the slight from one of his closest friends or to be relieved that the day would not be ruined by Clough in the wrong mood.

That willingness to cause a scene had always been present. There was in Clough an anti-authoritarian streak that delighted in exposing hypocrisy – and, of course, he loved a row, especially when it was clear he was in the right. 'He was staying at Blackpool with his wife and as he was going down to dinner he got chatting with some bloke,' the *Mail*'s north-east football writer Doug Weatherall remembered. 'It turned out he was a Sunderland supporter and he hadn't been allowed into dinner with his wife because he hadn't had a tie with him. So Brian went upstairs to get a tie for him. But that wasn't the end of it. A while later, Hughie Green came in, and he wasn't wearing a tie. As soon as Brian saw this, he called the head waiter over and said, "Chuck him out; he's not wearing a tie." The waiter pointed out he was Hughie Green, but Brian said he had two choices: either chuck Hughie Green out, or go over to the Sunderland fan and apologise for being so rude to him. And he said if he didn't, he'd be facing the biggest row he'd ever known.'

That could be explained as a desire to stand up for the little man but, as he got older, Clough seemed to delight in being awkward for the sake of being awkward. Perhaps there was nothing particularly outrageous about him turning up to Sunday lunch at the Kedlestone Hotel in a rugby shirt and wellington boots but, at other times, his indifference to accepted standards of dress was calculated to cause a reaction. He went to watch the tennis at Wimbledon one year, for instance, wearing a tracksuit, telling anybody who would listen that it was simply the 'tools of the trade', much to the embarrassment of John McGovern, who was with him. On another occasion, Clough went to meet Dryden at the Victoria club, probably the smartest venue in Nottingham at the time. Neither was a member, so a friend of Dryden's signed them in, but ignoring the favour that had been done for him, Clough turned up in a green-and-white hooped shirt, shorts and trainers, and was followed by four taxis containing journalists who were desperate to sign him up as a columnist after his contract with the *Sunday Mirror* came to an end.

The effect on the players was, as Hodge put it, 'to keep them on their toes'. It's become a commonplace that Clough became an increasingly rare sight on the training ground through the eighties but while that may have been true of his final season or two, Hodge suggested that Clough didn't change during his time at the club. 'There was no set routine,' he said. 'You never knew if he'd be in, and you never knew what mood he'd be in or who'd get it. You had to be prepared, even if it was somebody else, you had to make sure you kept a straight face. He could be high or he could be low. Most of the time I think that was genuine, but sometimes, with contract negotiations, he maybe engineered a situation to make a point. He could be clever at times.'

That was what made him such a great motivator. 'He had ways of winding people up,' Hodge said. 'He knew people, he knew the right chord to strike and he used it to great effect. With young players, especially, when he knew you from an early age, he could get under your skin, which is probably why he produced so many great young players.'

And that, of course, is the key to the Clough enigma: it's impossible to know how much of his unpredictability was planned, the extent to which, as he got older, what had once been controlled bursts of temper (or perhaps, more accurately, 'temper') became uncontrolled, how much the image he projected became the reality.

So high were Clough's hopes for the 1991–92 season that he turned down Sampdoria's bid for £5million for Des Walker, even though, under the terms of his contract, it meant he had to let him go for £1.5million the following year. Darren Wassall, who was quick enough to beat Walker in training sprints, was emerging as a potential replacement, but he fell out with Clough following an incident in a reserve-team game at Rotherham. He came in at half-time complaining of an injured hand, at which Clough spat on it and rubbed it and said, 'that's better, now'. That followed another incident that had Wassall's mother writing a letter to the chairman complaining about supposed 'bullying', and when his contract expired the following summer, Wassall happily left for Derby.

Carr, who had been out of favour since his father's attempts to negotiate his contract, was sold to Newcastle for £250,000, and Hodge, with a sense of relief, went to Leeds. The winger Ian Woan had been signed from Runcorn towards the end of the previous season, as had Alan Mahood, a young forward of considerable promise bought with some fanfare from Greenock Morton for £300,000. Woan would become a regular, but Mahood suffered a knee injury, and by 1992 was back at Morton never having started a league game for Forest. The biggest signing of the summer, though, was Teddy Sheringham, bought for £2million from Millwall after Clough had missed out on Saunders. From his first day, Clough called him 'Edward', ignoring Sheringham's protestations that only his mother called him that. 'It was his way of introducing himself, of showing me straightaway who was the boss,' the forward said.

Clough insisted before the season that the title was a possibility, but there was little to support that in a fortunate opening-day win over Everton in which Nigel Clough played behind Sheringham and Jemson. An incident after the final whistle hinted at the problems to come. 'In the dressing-room plastic beakers of isotonic drinks had been lined up for us to grab immediately after the match to quickly replace the fluids we had lost,' Sheringham said. 'I traipsed into the dressing-room, totally shattered, and grabbed the first beaker I saw. I took a long swig, and

519

for the next ten seconds I couldn't breathe. It was a very large, barely diluted, vodka and orange.' Clough denied it was his, but Sheringham had no doubt.

Forest were much better away at Leeds, but lost 1–0 and that inconsistency continued with a 4–0 win at Notts County and then a 3–1 defeat at home to Tottenham in which Stuart Pearce was sent off for foul and abusive language. The experiment with Nigel Clough in the hole soon ended and by mid-September Jemson was so disillusioned by being asked to play on the left side of midfield that he left for Sheffield Wednesday. Parker, supplanted by Keane and Scot Gemmill, joined Aston Villa for £650,000 at the end of November.

Oldham were 'dismantled nut and bolt', as Hamilton put it after Forest's 3–1 win, but then began the slump. By the beginning of November, Forest were fourth bottom. A win over Coventry and a 5–1 thrashing of Crystal Palace eased the pressure, but it was a season in which Forest were constantly having to look over their shoulders in fear of a relegation battle. Yet the collective delusion was such that the *Evening Post* was still talking about the possibility of a title challenge at the beginning of December, by which time Forest were sixteen points off the lead. Four successive wins in March at least ensured they'd finish in the top half, but the warning signs were there.

The cups, though, helped add a lustre to what would otherwise have been a troubling season. After beating Wolves in the third round of the FA Cup, Forest faced Hereford in the fourth. Sheringham had been in a dreadful run of form, failing to score in eleven games, and becoming a target for the fans' frustration. He scored in a 2–0 win, at which Clough promptly dropped him for the league game against Sheffield United, not even naming him as a substitute. Instead, Sheringham was told to sit on the bench next to Clough, exactly as he had had John McGovern sit next to him at Hartlepools quarter of a century earlier. Listening to his manager during the game, Sheringham came to see the match as Clough saw it, something he later acknowledged was a far more effective means of education than calling him to his office and delivering a lecture. In particular, he said, he learned then just why it was so important for a centre-forward to hold the ball up when his side was under pressure, rather than trying to flick it on and risk losing possession. Some of the old magic, evidently, remained, although the fact Forest lost that game 5–2, their heaviest home defeat under Clough, perhaps suggests it was waning.

They beat Bristol City to reach the Cup quarter-final, but there they lost 1–0 to Portsmouth as Crossley dropped a John Beresford free-kick to gift Alan McLoughlin the winner. Clough reiterated the sentiment he'd expressed before the Palace game the previous season. 'Losing on Saturday had meant that I've had to reshape my thinking a little bit,' he said. 'I was definitely considering calling it a day this summer, getting my feet up and going for even longer walks.'

As it turned out, it was the League Cup that very nearly gave him the opportunity to bow out in glory. Forest thrashed Bolton 9–2 over two legs in the second round, beat Bristol Rovers in the third and edged past Southampton after a replay to set up an away quarter-final against Crystal Palace. Forest fell behind to a Des Walker own-goal, but Nigel Clough swept in an equaliser with four minutes remaining. A Sheringham hat-trick carried Forest to a 4–2 win in the replay. After the game, Roworth invited Clough up to the boardroom to get warm and meet the Palace directors. Clough, showing his contempt for the board, brought six apprentices with him and told them to 'get stuck in [to the soup] before these buggers have it all'.

At least, it sounds contemptuous, and it's easy to see why various directors felt aggrieved, but Clough had a habit of introducing youth players into unfamiliar environments as though to test them, perhaps to show them the rewards football could offer, or to demystify for them those running the club. Lee Glover, for instance, remembered an incident when he was one of the apprentices selected to travel to an away game with the first team. 'We played Watford away,' he said, 'and after the game, I was doing the kit and the gaffer says, "There's someone I'd like you to meet." And the gaffer brings in Elton John. He says, "Elton, do you know young Glover, from Corby, Northants?" And he says to me, "Glover, have you ever met Elton John?" That was surreal, but it was a sign of the esteem that Brian Clough was held in by people like Elton John.'

Whatever his motivation, that win over Palace and its aftermath suggested that whatever else was leaving Clough, his obstreperousness wasn't. The victory set up a semi-final against Tottenham. Forest had two goals wrongly ruled out in drawing the home leg, but after a bomb scare had delayed the second, a Roy Keane goal in injury-time saw them through to the final against Manchester United. Reaching the final earned Clough the Manager of the Month award for February, his twenty-fifth such title.

Before the final, Forest met United in the league. Clough had previously resisted calls all season to drop Crossley who, for all his ability, was error-prone, but he did finally drop him after an incident in Barnsley town centre that left him facing possible charges of criminal damage. 'I was thrown in too young and you make mistakes,' Crossley admitted. 'I had a few erratic performances as a youngster. He stuck by me and never mentioned leaving me out. There were times when I wanted to be left out – the crowd were on my back, I got in trouble with the law – but I think he liked me. We came from a similar background, I was from a mining family. When I became a professional footballer, it never changed me as a person. I was still game for a laugh, but I knew I was lucky to be paid to play football. If he ever asked me to do anything, like clean his shoes, or make his tea, I did it. It was quite amusing.'

Crossley's obvious replacement, Steve Sutton, had by unfortunate co-incidence been sold to Derby for £300,000 a fortnight earlier, so Clough turned to the 21-year-old Andy Marriott. 'I had got into a bit of trouble with some friends,' Crossley said. 'It was in the newspapers – "Crossley's clanger in the slammer" – and his punishment was to leave me out. He didn't tell me, he just read out the team and I wasn't in it. It was the best punishment he could have given me. Hitting footballers in the pocket doesn't work as well.'

Marriott kept a clean sheet as Forest beat United 1–0, and retained his place for the ZDS Cup final. Forest had got there with wins over Leeds, Aston Villa and Tranmere, and a two-legged victory over Leicester in the northern-area final, and looked on course for the trophy as Gemmill and Black gave them a 2–0 lead. Southampton battled back to take the game in to extra-time, but another goal from Gemmill gave Clough his last piece of silverware.

Three days later, Roworth quit as chairman after being arrested by police investigating his accountancy firm on suspicion of fraud; given Dryden's conviction for defrauding the post office, and the various charges later made about Clough, it's hard to avoid the thought that there was a culture of financial opportunism about Forest in those days. NatWest had written to Roworth advising him to make money available to meet his £250,000 overdraft and a creditor issued a writ for £100,000, which was paid off by what the *Evening Post* termed 'an associate'. It later turned out that the associate was Clough, who had loaned him £108,000 to, as he thought, get him over a short-term financial shortfall; precisely the same sort of loyalty he had shown to Dryden. Clough never got his money back as further writs were issued: one for £250,000 from the Forest director Chris Wootton and one for £350,000 from a Brian Smith of Scarborough, a long-time associate of Roworth. Bailiffs moved in to Roworth's accountancy firm, White and Co., that May and he filed for bankruptcy with debts of over £1million the following month. He ended up being jailed for two years after being convicted on eight counts of deception; he had had no professional qualification, and had been paying his clients' money into his own account while claiming he was investing it in the Isle of Man.

That was hardly the ideal preparation for the League Cup final, for which Marriott retained his place. Forest fell behind to a fourteenth-minute Brian McClair goal after which, as Lacey put it in the *Guardian*, 'they seldom looked like surrendering the initiative against Nottingham Forest, who could not sustain any sort of attacking pressure until the closing minutes of a skilful, imaginative but largely passionless match.' Paul Ince and Mike Phelan – preferred to Neil Webb, seemingly to combat Keane – broke up Forest's passing and Black and Crosby were left isolated on the flanks. Clough's final chance of glory passed with a whimper.

Clough's treatment of Sutton seemed symptomatic of a wider malaise. It was never entirely clear why he had lost his position to the error-prone Crossley. Martin O'Neill later suggested that Clough's sensitivity to criticism got in the way; that he persisted with Crossley precisely because his critics said he shouldn't. In his greater days, he would have been more ruthless, as he had been with Les Green. In his greater days, of course, he'd had Taylor offering another pair of eyes and another opinion that might have overcome his stubbornness.

Sutton thought the side that won the League Cup in 1990 had great potential, but then Webb, Parker and Carr were allowed to leave and Forest became increasingly predictable. Apart from Pearce, they very rarely scored from outside the box, while he felt they lacked fitness, largely because training was often either cut short or consisted of nothing other than a six-a-side. Sutton suggested the board was slow to act, and perhaps should have been tougher, but then Forest continued to prosper in the cups and, for all the concerns that became apparent in hindsight, there is a sense that Clough was still overachieving considering his budget. Besides, two European Cups and a league title didn't change the fact that this was still Forest, a club happy enough to go about doing things in the right way.

Clough was always distrustful of those he felt over-complicated the game, and in his later years would insist that a footballer had to entertain, comparing good play to the Mona Lisa, Marilyn Monroe or Frank Sinatra. 'Get the ball,' he said. 'Give it to your mate or try to go past someone. Score a goal. Make the people watching feel as if there's been some skill, some flair in what you've done.' Until the very end, his sides refused to hoof the ball – 'Give me time,' he said, 'and I could train a monkey to do that. What pleasure does anybody get from football like that?' – and they were almost uniquely respectful to referees, but the idea that Clough's conception of playing football 'the right way' extended to putting on a show is fanciful: his sides, certainly when he worked in tandem with Taylor, had always been built on a solid defence. His Derby won promotion with a string of 1–0 wins and, in Europe especially, Forest could be crushingly dull in seeking a clean sheet.

Maybe he did insist more upon attractive football as he got older, perhaps realising that with the resources available, playing well was a more achievable goal than winning trophies. 'It was something he stressed,' said Hodge. 'Winning was everything, and he was always delighted with a clean sheet, but he wanted to do it with the right style of play and with discipline. He was aiming for Utopia. But maybe in the eighties the emphasis changed.'

Rather than playing one winger tucked in, in the role Martin O'Neill had once occupied, Clough began to use two out-and-out wide men, extra cover in midfield being provided by Nigel Clough, who always played deep off a centre-forward. In his willingness always to offer an outlet, he carried on the lineage of O'Hare, Francis and Birtles. 'He was a brave, clever player, who was always prepared to receive the ball with his back to the goal and a hulking centre-half breathing down his neck,' Sheringham said in his autobiography. 'He used to get whacked so many times, but Nigel wouldn't flinch. He would receive that ball and, sure enough, he would be mugged again.'

Clough always referred to Nigel as 'the Number Nine' and did his best to play down the familial connection, but it did rankle with certain players. 'The one thing to which I could never quite get attuned,' Sheringham said, 'was Clough Senior's habit of basing everything around his son . . . I think that rankled a bit with a lot of the players, because we all felt we could play the game.' Yet when Nigel – neat, uncomplicated and effective – so clearly embodied his father's vision of how the game should be played, his centrality seems only natural.

In those later years, his insistence that football should be played in the right way became almost a monomania: concerned about feigning injury, for instance, he briefly banned his players from receiving treatment on the pitch, which led to a string of absurdities, such as Steve Hodge playing on even as blood oozed from a head wound. To an extent, playing neat football with a side of polite young men with short hair who didn't answer back to referees suited the club's traditions more than a raft of trophies would have done. The Corinthianism and sense of decorum that Clough had mocked when he'd arrived, and that he'd flouted repeatedly, became the thing that insulated him.

The Final Curtain

The final season was a long, painful drift towards relegation. Clough was rarely at the training ground and regularly seemed to lose track of what he was saying. 'Forest should not have been subjected to such humiliation,' Clough admitted in his first autobiography. 'But the club became a victim of my personal stubbornness, my supreme but misplaced optimism.' His inner torment was played out on his face. The familiar redness became blotchiness and then, as the pressure increased, his skin was ravaged by spots.

In retrospect, hints of the collapse to come were there, but who at the time could seriously have challenged Clough? And who, perhaps more pertinently, would have wanted to? 'I don't know when it first occurred to me we might actually go down,' said Dan Lawson, who saw every home game that season. 'The bad results were stacking up, and there was a feeling we were drifting, but I think we all thought Clough would get us out of the mess. I suppose we were in denial. You could see on his face that something was badly wrong, but we still believed in him. Even by the March I thought we'd somehow be OK.'

Clough was still a charismatic, provocative, larger-than-life character who had for over a decade defied financial pressures to deliver a side that challenged for silverware and whose position in the top half of the league table had come almost to be taken for granted. In June 1992, for instance, Forest signed the 21-year-old midfielder Ray McKinnon from Dundee United for £750,000. 'Forest were obliged to buy him to strengthen a squad depleted by the loss of Des Walker and Darren Wassall,' wrote Hamilton, the effect being – whether deliberately or not – to highlight the oddity of buying a midfielder to replace two defenders.

When the fixture list was released in early July, there seems to have been no sense of foreboding about the offices of the *Evening Post*. 'Brian Clough has been handed a tough start in his bid to land the inaugural Premier League title,' ran the intro on the brief news piece alongside the fixtures, which showed Forest set to start the first season of football's brave new world against Liverpool. That was also the first game shown live on Sky, a Sunday-afternoon fixture that began the game's television revolution.

There was perhaps a little disquiet at the lack of signings, but then that was hardly unusual at Forest. 'Just because the gaffer hasn't thrown money about this summer doesn't mean we're going to have a bad season ...' Pearce said after pre-season defeats to Sampdoria and Stuttgart. 'It's too early for me to say what we can do. We've got a good squad and plenty of talent. If we get a good start, who knows, but we are going to need some luck. Realistically our best chance of winning something probably lies in one of the cups.'

Forest actually began the season positively, Sheringham, who had been linked with a move to either Chelsea or Tottenham, getting the only goal in that game against Liverpool, as Forest followed Fenton's tactical advice and looked to expose their opponents' three-man defence with rapid cross-field passing. 'For several weeks there have been dark murmurings of doom and despondency circulating the city,' Ian Edwards wrote in the *Evening Post*. 'Apparently, Forest do not have the strength to mount a serious challenge to the kind of team they at times humbled yesterday. Humble is not too strong a word. For the opening forty-five minutes, Forest looked more like a team capable of lifting the championship.' It was the only time that season they would do, and talk of winning the championship was soon replaced by worries at the other end of the table.

Forest lost 2–0 at Sheffield Wednesday and 5–3 at Oldham, where the thirty-two-year-old Gary Bannister, picked up on a free transfer by Clough after being released by West Brom, scored twice on his debut. There had been serious doubts among fans and journalists about the wisdom of signing him – doubts that would in time be justified – but it seemed then that Clough's judgement, his willingness to go against the grain, once again, would be vindicated. Manchester United won 2–0 at the City Ground, and when Forest then went down 3–1 at Norwich, it meant they had fewer points after five games than they had ever had before under Clough. A 4–1 defeat at Blackburn left them bottom. 'For the second time in less than a week Forest conceded an early goal, fought their way back to take control of the match and then, in the space of ten crazy second-half minutes, committed defensive suicide,' Edwards wrote.

Crossley was guilty of another error, scoring the first own-goal in the Premiership. 'The rule was that if you wanted to go home for the weekend, you had to get it confirmed by the Thursday afternoon,' he said. 'I went to see Clough and he said "no problem", but then we got beaten 4–1 and I scored an own-goal. On the team coach we had a curtain to divide the players from the staff so they couldn't see what we were doing and we couldn't see what they were doing. We were approaching junction 36 on the M1, which was my stop and I was on tenterhooks. I went to see him and said, "Is it ok if I get dropped off?" and he turned round and said, "I'll see you on Friday." So he told me to have four days off.'

At least as much of a concern as Crossley's form was the central defensive pairing of Steven Chettle and Carl Tiler, but Clough was typically bullish. 'I've never been in this position before,' he said. 'It's a new experience for me. And it's not going to last very long. We're going to regroup, close ranks and keep doing the things we know best. We'll keep passing the ball on the grass the way it's meant to be and hopefully, sooner or later, we'll get a break.'

There were other disruptions, most of them related to money. Whatever the other factors in Wassall's departure, it can't have helped that he was on only £250 a week when he left. Pearce, meanwhile, who was on £4,000 a week, sought a significant rise. According to Clough, Pearce was offered an additional £100,000 a year for the remaining three years of his contract, but rejected it. Clough felt he was being greedy and would offer no more. 'Stuart Pearce's heart never seemed to be in the club after he failed to get his way with his contract,' Clough said, although there was little he could have done anyway after surgery on his groin restricted him to just one game between January and May.

Then Sheringham left for Spurs, largely because his son, Charlie, was living in London and the constant travel was exhausting him. His departure, plus that of Wassall and Walker, brought in £5million, so there was money available, but Clough struggled to reinvest it. He said he felt that fees were inflated and perhaps, in the aftermath of the new television deal, they were; but it may equally have been that he no longer had the wherewithal to assess a player and arrange the transfer. Sheringham, oddly, had been told he couldn't leave until a replacement had been brought in, only to be allowed to go anyway after three matches, once Spurs upped their offer to £2.1million. Clough said he had believed Lee Glover – 'a brave young man who had overcome serious injuries' – was just as good. He was wrong about that, and the Sheringham deal would lead to other problems further down the line.

In October 1993, Rick Parry, then the Premier League's chief executive, set up an independent inquiry into bungs that also included on its investigative panel Robert Reid QC and Steve Coppell, who was about to become the chief executive of the League Managers' Association. The case against Clough collapsed for lack of evidence, but Ron Fenton was banned from working with an English club again. In the end any action fizzled out because of Clough's deteriorating health.

Six years later, the inquiry long since completed, Parry spoke of grave doubts about Clough's probity. 'By the time the inquiry started,' Parry said, 'he was no longer in football and we could not compel him to appear. But he did come, on his own, to the offices of lawyers. He was lucid, treated our inquiry with respect, but it was not particularly productive. On the balance of evidence, we felt he was guilty of taking bungs.'

The signing of Lee Chapman from Niort had been complicated by the French club's financial problems, but inconsistencies still emerged. In Forest's internal accounts, the transfer price was recorded as £378,000 plus £135,000 for the agent Dennis Roach. More detailed accounts compiled by the auditors Price Waterhouse, though, listed the payment to Roach at £65,000, the other £70,000 unaccounted for. Similarly, in August 1989, Clough signed two youth players from Leicester City for £15,000: the official contract showed a fee of £40,875. Alf-Inge Håland, signed midway through the 1992–93 season, could have been bought for £150,000; Clough paid £350,000, the other £200,0000 unaccounted for. Håland's agent was Rune Hauge, who, of course, was found to have delivered 'an unsolicited gift' to the Arsenal manager George Graham after negotiating the transfer of Pål Lydersen to Arsenal. Hauge had also been involved in Todi Orlygsson's move to Forest; Parry's inquiry heard he had delivered £45,000 in cash to Fenton via a Norwegian trawler that landed in Hull. And the deal to sign Stan Collymore, Tom Bower claimed in *Broken Dreams*, broke down because the Southend chairman Vic Jobson refused to pay a bung of £350,000 on a £1.75million deal.

Clough's relationship with right and wrong, particularly where money was concerned, was complex, and he certainly would have had no qualms about taking what he believed was his right, even if it wasn't strictly legal. Pat Murphy quotes him admitting to operating in some grey areas – while denying the overt allegations that he took bungs – in an interview given six months before his death, 'I've given players money that I've fiddled out of the club,' he said, 'either to move them on or to seal a transfer or to tide them over when they were having domestic problems. But I've never taken a bung or made extra money for myself as a manager. I earned enough money. I was satisfied.'

It was the sale of Sheringham that came under the most scrutiny thanks to the former Tottenham chairman Alan Sugar's revelations in the High Court about the deal. Sugar said that when he asked his then-manager Terry Venables to explain an additional £50,000 payment, he received the answer, 'Cloughie likes a bung.' Venables denied this, as did Clough, but it was that comment that led to the inquiry into the Sheringham transfer, and that was the main subject of Clough's excruciating appearance on ITV's *Sport in Question* programme in 1995.

It was horrific television. Peter Taylor said Clough had become a cardboard cut-out by 1982; thirteen years on, he had descended to the very depths of caricature. He looked far better than he had in that last season as a manager, his skin less blotchy, the eyes perhaps regaining a flicker of the old spark, but this was a sickeningly diminished Clough. The charisma was still there as he held court, despite the presence on the panel of the former West Indies cricket captain Clive Lloyd and the then-*Times* football correspondent Rob Hughes, neither of them exactly shrinking violets, and there were glimmers of the old wit and comic timing, but he looked at least a decade older than he actually was, his face sagging and his hair brittle. More worryingly, he was, fairly obviously, drunk.

'Now I was accused by a guy called Sugar, who's a spiv from London,' he began, his eyes flicking from the presenters, Jimmy Greaves and Ian St John, as though to gauge the reaction of the studio audience. They responded with a ripple of knowing giggles, while St John, shifting awkwardly in his chair, ran a nervous tongue behind his upper lip. 'I hope you keep that in,' Clough went on, aware of how provocative he was being. The audience laughed, Clough laughed and Greaves, scribbling something on a pad, made a weak joke about it not being them who would get sued.

'And he accused me of taking money over the Sheringham deal in the High Court,' Clough said. 'And, like parliament, you can't touch them when they say it in High Court.' Thus far, the complaint was rational enough. But Clough continued, his voice rising in that familiar crescendo of fury. 'Now the second he's big enough, brave enough and gets a bloody shave, and doesn't walk like a spiv, I'll sue him if he repeats it.'

He paused. 'There you are,' he concluded with a flourish of the finger, a horribly ambiguous conclusion. He almost certainly meant, 'There you are, I've given my reaction to this allegation,' but he could equally well have meant, 'There you are, I've said something ludicrous and controversial; I've earned my appearance money.'

'Maybe Mr Sugar's watching tonight, Brian,' St John said, leaning back as though relieved that the worst was over. 'If he isn't,' Clough said, 'he'll watch it tomorrow.' The line was sharp and self-aware, and drew both laughter and applause. It was poignant, though, for unlike everything else he said that night, the delivery was pitch perfect, a reminder of what he had been.

A little later, he took up the theme again. 'Sugar got rid of.. . .' he began, at which St John tried vainly to head him off. 'Hang on. I haven't finished,' he said, wagging a finger at the audience. 'Sugar got rid of his manager, right? He then took on board – the chairman of Tottenham football club –

then took on board to oversee all transfer deals. He dropped such a clanger with the German, he's pissed off.' There was more laughter, although by then it was surely awkward, driven partly by memories of past Clough grandstanding, but surely mainly by embarrassment.

Lloyd turned and said something to Greaves – wondering how Clough could be stopped, perhaps – but Greaves decided to draw Clough out. 'Who has?' he asked. 'The German,' Clough replied, by which he meant Jürgen Klinsmann, who had left Tottenham for Bayern Munich after a single season in which he'd been named the Football Writers' Player of the Year. There was more laughter and an ugly, knowing smile appeared on Clough's face. 'And he,' he shouted, turning to the audience, 'did his contract. That's how clever he is.'

More chuckles encouraged him, although by then he was becoming increasingly incoherent, losing the clipped Teesside accent he had at his best – mocking, aware of his own superiority – to a generic northernness that made him sound less like himself than like a bad impersonation of himself. 'Hey,' he continued, seemingly desperate to ensure he remained the centre of attention, 'and lost a fortune as well on him ... So I don't know what these chairman goes [sic]. What I would like to say is – and I've said it over many times, and James [i.e. Jimmy Greaves] will forgive me if I'm talking too much ... I have been of the opinion for many years that if the chairman sacks the manager who he initially appoints, he should go as well.' The argument, of course, makes no sense on any level, but it was an opinion, and it had been expressed by Clough, and so the audience applauded.

It got worse. 'You're a journalist, aren't you?' he snapped when the broadcaster Darren Fletcher, sitting in the audience, raised his hand to ask a question. Fletcher nodded. 'And not a very good one,' Clough carried on. It wasn't funny or justified; it was a rude and unprovoked attack, designed only to belittle the target. Fletcher, fortunately, rose above it and asked his question calmly.

Clough was then asked how he'd have handled Eric Cantona. 'I'd have kicked him in the bollocks,' Clough replied to enthusiastic applause, for nothing was so popular as Clough being Clough. But here the sense was that he was being not himself but 'Clough', playing up to the stereotype, aware that that was the easiest way to win the approval he so craved.

Worst of all was the answer to a question about whether, by paying £1million for Trevor Francis, he felt responsible for inflating the transfer market. He could have answered the question straight, by pointing out that markets set their own values, or even by outlining, as he had before, what Francis had done for Nottingham Forest. Instead his mind drifted to the player he had bought two seasons later, Justin Fashanu. Perhaps it was only natural that Fashanu should haunt him, for he was the first big mistake he'd made in the transfer market, the player whose signing symbolised the breakdown of his relationship with Peter Taylor and the break-up of the European Cup-winning team.

That, though, wasn't what Clough focused on. 'I feel responsible for Justin Fashanu,' he said, with a nod and a knowing glance at the audience. 'It took me about three months to twig him, but I twigged him.' The tone and the context made his meaning obvious. Duncan Hamilton has suggested that, in private, Clough expressed sympathy for the troubled forward, but it was not evident here: this was base homophobia, playing to the gallery, further evidence of the bullying streak in Clough's personality. The term 'responsible' was probably accidental, picked up from the question – Fashanu hadn't been mentioned at all – but you wonder what Clough felt a year later when Fashanu committed suicide.

He certainly expressed little responsibility over Sheringham. 'Sheringham came to me after a year at Forest, saying he had to return to London to be with his young son,' Clough explained to Murphy. 'We agreed a fee of £1million and Sheringham asked me for some extra money for himself. I said he wasn't going to get an extra penny. If I'd decided to sell him, he would have been legally entitled to £25,000 from Forest, but he was the one agitating for the move. I was sure Terry Venables had tapped him up [something Venables denies and for which there is no evidence], so there was nowt from my end for Sheringham.

'Sugar never repeated the claim outside the court, which was good advice because I would have sued the arse off him. Terry later confirmed that I never got anything out of the Sheringham transfer, and I suspect he was covering himself by telling Sugar that everyone takes bungs in football because I'd told Sheringham that if he wanted anything extra he'd have to go to Tottenham for it. The deal became slightly more expensive to them than they'd envisaged because I wouldn't be a soft touch. So I suspect that

Terry had to spin a line to Sugar and it was convenient to drag me into it.' According to Tom Bower – although he admitted his 'veracity was questionable' – Fenton later corroborated allegations Venables had made that Clough was known to like receiving his cut in a bag or an envelope at service stations.

The explanation Clough gave in his autobiography is a little different. Sheringham was due a fee of £100,000 for each year he stayed at Forest under the terms of the three-year contract he'd signed after joining from Millwall. That was entirely standard. Sheringham had cost £2million so, resigned to losing him, Clough sought £2.1million to cover the initial fee plus that £100,000 payment. 'As far as I was concerned, when Teddy Sheringham signed for Tottenham, we received our money back. He was paid his £100,000 and all was legitimate and legal.' Yet, in Tottenham's books, the sum they recorded paying for Sheringham was £2.15million. Only months later, after the falling-out between Venables and Sugar and the case in the High Court, Clough claimed, did he find out anything about an additional £58,750 Tottenham revealed it had paid in cash on the day of the deal. They claimed they believed it to be a payment of £50,000 plus VAT to the former Arsenal player-turned-agent Frank McLintock for negotiating the deal between Clough and Venables.

'It has since been accepted,' Clough wrote, 'that the notorious £50,000 ... was paid to Frank McLintock and [his business partner] Graham Smith for their professional services as agents working on behalf of Tottenham Hotspur. It is said that the money was paid in cash, I don't know. What I do know is that it was not paid to me – not in fivers, not in a plastic carrier bag, not in a lay-by or a motorway service station.'

McLintock and Smith told Parry's inquiry that they split the money between them and spent it. Smith produced a builder's invoices to support this, even though these appeared to pre-date McLintock's own invoice to Tottenham. An alternative account was that the money was given to Fenton in the Posthouse Hotel in Luton, although what happened after that remains unclear. Parry and his inquiry were given various explanations, one of which, from Alan Hill, suggested Clough 'liked to play Robin Hood' with fees he received from various deals; between 1987 and 1993, the enquiry found, Clough was involved in fifty-eight transfers, with a total value of £19.5million, from which he received personal payments of around

£1million. 'Alan Hill told us there would be unsolicited gifts to staff and players,' Parry said, 'but even these were illegal and broke the rules of the FA.'

Forest mysteriously returned £8,750 to Tottenham, insisting no VAT was due. If it had been a payment to an agent, it would have been. In June the following year, McLintock sent a new invoice to Spurs for £50,000 + VAT, while his company, First Wave, made a voluntary disclosure to Customs and Excise of its failure to pay VAT on the £50,000 fee. Little wonder the Labour MP Kate Hoey felt moved to use parliamentary privilege to name Clough among a list of managers she believed to have 'siphoned off [millions of pounds] from the game in back-handers, bungs and fixes'.

But that was later. Even that autumn, there was an increasing sense that the end was nigh for Clough, something intensified that September when it was announced that he was to be given the freedom of the city. 'We had heard a rumour that Brian would not be in charge at Forest that much longer,' said Betty Higgins, the leader of Nottingham City Council. 'It was just something that someone said. I don't know whether it's true or not, but we wanted to do it while he is still in charge.'

Forest lost at home to Sheffield Wednesday, at which Clough at last moved to try to add a centre-back. A £2.5million bid to sign Craig Short from Notts County was rebuffed, and he ended up at Derby; then an attempt to bring Colin Foster back from West Ham broke down over personal terms.

As the rumours about Clough continued, Fred Reacher, the chairman, felt compelled to defend him. 'People keep saying that the manager has shot it,' he said. 'Nothing could be further from the truth. Now is the time for him to keep a cool head and not to panic. And he's the perfect man for the job in hand.' His reward for his loyalty was a row that led to Clough threatening to boycott a Monday night game against Coventry in protest at the damage he saw being inflicted on an already muddy pitch by the 150 dancers Sky wanted to perform as part of their pre-match entertainment. Perhaps it was widely perceived as Clough being Clough, stubbornly sticking up for tradition against the glitzy new world of Sky, but it also emphasised what an anachronism he seemed in the Premiership. He did turn up though, and after a 1–1 draw was in defiant mood. 'I'll outsee the lot of you,' he insisted. 'All this speculation about my job is ridiculous, just plain stupid. I've got a good bunch of lads – and they've got a good manager.'

His search for a centre-back led him to pursue Laurent Blanc, as Forest continued to look frail at the back, winning only 3–2 in the away leg of their League Cup tie at Stockport. Bannister suggested the problem might be the backpass law, which had been introduced the previous summer. 'Where we've suffered,' he said, 'is when we've had the ball, played it back to Mark [Crossley] and he has cleared it. On most occasions the ball has come straight back at us, putting us under even more pressure. Mark having to hump the ball up the field has not helped us at all. Last season a backpass would have kept us possession and Stuart Pearce, Brian Laws or Gary Charles would just have picked the ball up from the keeper to start us off again.'

The problem wasn't just that the rule change necessitated an alteration in Forest's style of play, but that with the ball in active play for more of the game, a greater premium was placed on fitness, something that had never really been a concern for Clough before. 'The backpass rule meant you had to be fit,' said Laws. 'To play ninety minutes you can't slow the game down by going back to the keeper. The game got quicker. Cloughie ignored it until we were already in trouble. Then he brought in fitness coaches and he hated fitness coaches; he thought they knew nothing about the game. He threw them out twice in the first few weeks.'

A goalless draw at Chelsea gave Forest their first away point of the season, but they were still three points adrift at the bottom. With Terry Wilson injured, Keane ended up being drafted into the back four for a 2–2 draw against Manchester City, and after Forest had completed their progress to the third round of the League Cup with a 2–1 home win over Stockport, Hamilton was scathing, describing their performance as 'ragged and flat': 'The overwhelming impression,' he went on, 'was of a side transparently lacking form and carrying only a sliver of self-belief.'

The Bridgford Road Stand, constructed at a cost of £4million to comply with the Taylor Report and blamed by Reacher for Forest's lack of spending on players, opened for a 1–0 defeat to Arsenal, whose manager George Graham joined a lengthening list of personalities insisting Forest were too good to go down, a view with which most fans seem to have concurred. A deflected shot gave Forest a 1–0 home win over Middlesbrough, but they remained bottom, two points from safety.

There was a draw at Sheffield United and a 1–0 League Cup win at Crewe, but after a 1–0 defeat at home to Ipswich, the patience of fans ran out and there was booing at the final whistle. Clough responded by flicking a V-sign at them. His attempts to bring in new players gathered pace. A bid for the centre-back Colin Cooper failed and there was talk of an attempt to sign the centre-forward Andy Cole from Bristol City. Alf-Inge Håland was signed from Bryne after Clough had been impressed by him while watching England play Norway on television; the contrast with the old days, when Taylor had Kenny Burns trailed to Perry Bar dogs to assess his personality, could hardly have been more marked. Perhaps the £45,000 delivered in cash by a Norwegian trawler, uncovered by the Parry inquiry, helped persuade Clough further investigation was unnecessary. As it turned out, complications over his registration meant Håland didn't arrive till the following summer, and by then it was too late.

Faith in Clough was waning fast, with even Nigel admitting to a growing terror of relegation. 'For the first time in my professional career I'm scared,' he admitted in his *Evening Post* column at the beginning of November. 'I've had eight years in the game and I've never tasted such a chilling fear. I've been trying to hide it and pretend it would go away. But the prospect of relegation makes me sick to the pit of my stomach . . . The darker moments are getting longer after every match and I can't see the light at the end of the tunnel.' Even with over six months of the season to go, there was a dreadful sense of inevitability about Forest's demise, rarely ever a sense that Clough had the energy or the brilliance any more to turn things around.

The players, Laws said, were aware of what was happening, but did nothing about it, either too scared to act or unable to believe that Clough was fallible. 'Everybody recognised it, but never mentioned it openly,' he said. 'The alcoholism was starting to show. Decisions were a bit strange, team selections were a bit strange, his whole mannerism was a bit strange. Many times it concerned us, but we weren't brave enough to stop him. He wouldn't acknowledge we had to change our training schedule. It was very relaxed, very easy. But we couldn't slow the game down any more, and in the last fifteen minutes of games we were knackered and very average teams were starting to put us under pressure. Our fitness caught up with us.'

*

A 1–0 defeat at home to Everton, who had been only two places above Forest before the game, intensified the gloom and led Reacher to issue another vote of confidence, this time adding that he believed Clough would see out his contract and that he had a verbal agreement with him to carry on for another year. Sure enough, later that week, Clough signed a one-year contract extension.

'I promised I'd get him [Reacher] to the top of the Premier League,' Clough said. 'Honest. That's how much the new contract means to me and it's no idle threat even though I'm bottom of the league. The chairman has proved his commitment to me and I'm going to prove to everyone I'm as good a manager as I've ever been. I'm as determined as ever to win things, especially the championship. On my passport it says I'm a Football League manager and managers get paid for winning the league.' It sounded fine, but none of it was true: the notion of Forest winning the league *was* an idle threat and there was little evidence Clough had anything like the requisite fight left in him.

Earlier that month, he had described his team as 'crap' and admitted he was 'in the shit'. In retrospect, the damage his alcoholism was doing to himself and the club was obvious, but this was Brian Clough. He was bigger than that, and it had reached the stage where Forest had a dependency upon him.

That was disastrous, for Clough had lost touch tactically and in terms of conditioning. As the rest of English football began to take preparation more seriously, Forest went backwards; being 'fresh', that magical quality that had sustained Clough from his playing career to his greatest successes as a manager, and which legitimised a less-than-industrious approach to training, was no longer enough. By the end, Clough was only showing up on a Friday morning and a Saturday afternoon; a concern for freshness, perhaps, was his excuse for his long absences from the training ground.

His tactical stubbornness had been seen the previous March, in a league game against Crystal Palace. Forest had experimented with Wassall as a sweeper, with Pearce and Charles pushing forward from full-back. For ten minutes, Alan Hill said, Forest dominated, but then Clough demanded a return to a back four and they ended up drawing 0–0. According to Fenton, the insistence on playing 4–4–2 with a winger meant that the central midfield pairing, even with a player as tenacious as Keane, often got swamped, especially if the other team advanced its full-backs. Clough seemed unwilling even to contemplate the possibility of change; perhaps by then he was incapable. Hamilton described how fatigued he seemed that season, tired in himself and wearied by the changes brought about by the advent of the Premiership, the increasing autonomy of players and demands of television.

Yet for all the problems, that season Forest dominated a lot of games. They lacked a cutting edge to take advantage, though, and their problems in central defence meant they were always vulnerable defensively, particularly from set-plays. That Keane and Nigel Clough both had spells that season playing in the centre of defence told its own story. 'One of the reasons Forest were relegated,' Clough wrote in his autobiography, 'was because I had nobody at the back who could head a ball.' And yet the player he signed when he had the chance was not a defender but Neil Webb, bought back from Manchester United for £750,000.

An Ian Woan equaliser seven minutes from time earned Forest a point at Palace, but Tim Flowers then saved a last-minute penalty from Pearce as Forest lost 2–1 at home to Southampton. As so often, the League Cup provided solace, Keane scoring his first goal in nine months as Forest beat Tottenham 2–0, and the momentum of that result was carried on in a 4–1 win at Leeds in Webb's first game back. Forest remained bottom because Palace beat Sheffield United, but ending the champions' thirty-one-game unbeaten home record at last kindled a spark of hope. They promptly lost at Villa, were denied a win over Wimbledon by a Crossley error, and then went down 2–1 at Tottenham to end the year bottom of the table. Nigel Clough suggested thirty points would be necessary from their remaining twenty-one games to keep Forest up.

Briefly, that January, it seemed possible. Forest lost to Arsenal in the quarter-final of the League Cup, and again in the fifth round of the FA Cup, but their league form improved radically. Woan's second-half goal gave them a 1–0 win at Coventry, then they thrashed Chelsea 3–0. They lost 2–0 at Manchester United, but beat Oldham 2–0 and managed a 0–0 draw at Anfield. Yet, just as everything seemed to be improving, just as it looked as if Clough might somehow, improbably, get away with it, might inspire the sort of great escape that would allow him to walk away, if not in glory, then at least with the satisfaction of having averted relegation, just at that moment, the men in grey suits struck as a group of rebel shareholders called for an Emergency General Meeting to investigate the administration of the club.

Steve Stone headed the winner on his debut away at Middlesbrough, and then Gary Crosby, back after injury, got the only goal as Forest beat QPR to climb out of the bottom three on goal difference. Crosby's return, though, could not cover the hole left when Webb suffered an Achilles injury that required surgery and kept him out for the season. With Pearce struggling with groin problems, there was a real dearth of experience.

In the last game before the EGM, Forest lost 2–0 at home to Manchester City, a performance bad enough that, even after the run of thirteen points from their previous six games, Edwards was moved to dismiss it as 'inept'. The rebels called for a four-man committee to investigate the running of the club, and made clear their concerns were not limited to its administration. 'There have been rumours and allegations as to the reasons for Clough's failure to move into the transfer market and replace players like Des Walker, Teddy Sheringham and Darren Wassall,' they said in a statement. 'His decisions and manner during Forest's alarming slump have been met with increasing disbelief and angry rebels are furious that no one at board level has dared challenge his authority.'

The board ended up beating the action by 121 votes to 41, which was portrayed as a humiliating defeat for the rebels. That is debatable, but what the vote exposed was that a quarter of Forest's members were seriously troubled by Clough's handling of the crisis, and that can only have been a destabilising factor.

The same day, Clough signed Robert Rosario from Coventry, which was widely perceived as further evidence of his failing judgement. Rosario was 'game but limited' as Clough later put it, and no great bargain at £400,000. Dean Saunders had been available from Liverpool, but Clough wanted nothing to do with him because he'd turned Forest down the previous season. 'We'd heard there was a big signing on the way,' said Dan Lawson. 'That we were about to sign a forward we desperately needed. Stan Collymore was suggested, Saunders as well, and then it ends up being Robert Rosario. Everybody was just sort of, "is that it?" I think that was when I realised we were going down.'

The slide accelerated with a home game against Palace, who began the day a place above Forest. Keane cancelled out a Gareth Southgate strike to earn Forest a draw, but they dominated the game, winning sixteen corners to Palace's one, and should have won comfortably. Clough, alarmingly, stayed sitting in the dug-out at half-time. In the past it might have been seen as some grand motivational gesture, but here it simply reinforced the suggestion that he was not merely losing his grip on his team but on reality.

In a 3–0 defeat at Everton, as Forest were forced to play a sweeper to keep the score down, chants of 'Sack the board' were heard for the first time. Reacher addressed the press after the game, insisting Forest would stay up; Clough remained strangely absent. This, surely, was a time for his belligerence, for him to attempt to yank Forest's season from the brink by force of will, but instead it was his chairman issuing the rallying cry.

They lost 3–0 at home to Norwich, after which Keane went to see Clough to ask for a couple of days off. He found Graham Taylor sitting in the corridor outside an unlit office. Assuming Clough was in the boardroom, Keane went in and sat down to wait for him, only to discover Clough in the corner, hiding from Taylor. The England manager was there to discuss Nigel and his place in the national side, but after another home defeat Clough couldn't face speaking to anybody.

On 21 March, Clough's fifty-eighth birthday and the twentieth anniversary of his mother's death, Forest faced Leeds at home. A Nigel Clough penalty earned a point that lifted Forest off the bottom, but it was a day of further controversy. The Trent End had welcomed Clough by singing Happy Birthday, but when they jeered his son for hitting a long ball, Clough flicked a V-sign in their direction. He claimed, unconvincingly, to have been issuing an instruction to Charles, who was wearing number two, but more pertinent was that Nigel should have been playing a long ball at all; that simply wasn't the Forest way and it suggested the lengths to which they had been forced. As David Lacey put it in the *Guardian*, under the new approach, Nigel Clough 'might have felt a little like Von Karajan conducting *Roll Over Beethoven*'.

Two days later, Clough was made a Freeman of the City of Nottingham, a moving occasion, but one that had a clear valedictory feel. At last he came out fighting, but even his words of defiance looked to the past. 'I've been through the lot,' he said. 'Highs and lows at places like Hartlepools and

Derby . . . That's why I don't feel under pressure or fear. Why should I? At my age – fifty-eight going on 107 – what have I got to be afraid of any more? I had no money at Hartlepools, struggled initially at Derby, got hammered by a non-League team at Brighton and got the sack at Leeds, bless 'em. Blow me, I think my skin is thick enough by now.'

That, though, was only one of two interviews he gave Hamilton that afternoon. In the other, intended for posterity and the book he knew Hamilton would write, he was far more candid, speaking of his exhaustion and his regrets. Hamilton was reminded of Joseph Heller, cursed by having produced his greatest work first and struggling always thereafter to live up to it.

A 2–1 win at Southampton raised hopes again, but later that week, as Gaynor was offloaded on a free to Millwall, Clough pulled out of a £1.75million deal to sign Stan Collymore from Southend, apparently persuaded by victory at the Dell that he would be all right with what he had – or perhaps because he refused to pay a bung. Clough's explanation to Hamilton for his hesitation on the day he received the freedom of the city was more poignant. 'I don't know if he's right for us,' he said. 'And yet the thing is I used to know. I'm just knackered.' In those final days, Clough came to resemble the ailing Simón Bolívar as rendered by Gabriel García Márquez in *The General in his Labyrinth*, his greatness behind him, mentally and physically shattered, futilely engaged in a final struggle he cannot win.

Clough was knackered a lot that season. In his autobiography he admitted he should have gone two years earlier. 'During that final, awful season,' he wrote, 'each time I looked in the shaving-mirror, I said, "You should have gone old pal. You missed the right time to call it a day."' Once Frank Clark had taken over from Clough, Collymore joined for £2.25million.

A Paul McGrath goal gave Aston Villa a 1–0 win at Forest, leaving them second bottom and two points from safety. The bad news continued. Pearce, who had barely played since January, was ruled out for the rest of the season after it was found that a muscle in his groin had become detached from the bone. A 3–1 home defeat to Blackburn followed, which left Forest bottom of the table. 'It was a dreadfully flat first half during which Forest did not produce one shot on target; it was impossible to believe you were watching a team fighting relegation,' wrote Edwards, as the *Evening Post* began to speak openly of 'the end of an era'.

541

Forest twice had the lead at QPR, but lost 4–3 as Les Ferdinand scored a hat-trick and even a home win over Tottenham on Easter Monday, in which Rosario scored his only goal for the club, left them two points from safety. That was a season when good news was soon followed by bad. That week Gary Charles was fined £1,600 for failing to provide a breath specimen after bumping into a neighbour's Ford Fiesta. That, allied to comments he'd made in a Sunday newspaper claiming Forest fans were trying to force him out, led Clough to tell him he'd played his final game for the club. Later that week, Roworth was convicted of fraud and detained in prison, a reminder of how far Forest had fallen, not merely in terms of league position, but from their Corinthian ideal.

A flat 1–0 defeat at Wimbledon left Edwards noting that, 'Brian Clough's decision to sell Teddy Sheringham will be the epitaph on his Premier League tomb.' It was a truer statement than he could have known. A last-minute Keane goal earned a draw at Arsenal, but it would be the last point Clough won. As the dictator's grip on power loosened, so the atmosphere around the club had disintegrated; when it became most important for players and backroom staff to pull together, so everything fell apart. Clough again, perhaps, could consider himself let down by the game. 'It was like the last days of an empire with characters desperate to settle old scores before everything changed for ever,' said Archie Gemmill. 'They were out to impress our chairman Fred Reacher and safeguard their jobs. Life was anything but harmonious. People were jockeying for position and the shit flew around left, right and centre.'

Finally, on 25 April, the conspirators who would end Clough's reign made their move, or at least that was how the *People* described it in a story outlining what their headline described as the 'amazing plot to oust Clough'. Whether there was a plot, though, seems debatable. The *People* reported that Chris Wootton, a director, had revealed that Clough had twice almost died because of his alcoholism, and had a tape in which Clough slurred his words as he tried to record his lines for a Shredded Wheat commercial, culminating in his admission 'I'm fucking sozzled'.

Wootton was in no doubt that Clough's ability to pilot the club had become severely compromised, but that did not make it a plot. Wootton, at first, defended Clough before loaning the tape, by then ten months old, to a local journalist, who sold it to the *People* in a deal done in a Happy Eater. He claimed he was naive and had tried to protect Clough. If he weren't looking to force Clough out, though, it's hard to understand why Wootton would have handed over the tape; perhaps he was merely looking to alert the public to what was going on behind the scenes, to spark a reaction. If so, he got one. The following day, Clough's face, the skin red and blotchy, knobbled with spots, stared out from the *Sun*. 'I don't have a drink problem,' he claimed, insisting he only had the occasional sherry or glass of white wine.

In the past, Clough had been able to manipulate events through his deployment of the media and by force of will. His will, though, had grown weak, and far from controlling the media, he was being mocked by it. His medals couldn't protect him any longer. That morning Clough had rung Fenton and got him to arrange a meeting with Fred Reacher at Fenton's house. Clough told him he wanted Wootton dismissed and said that he was planning to retire at the end of the season. Reacher called a press conference.

Journalists gathered at the City Ground, many of them still expecting to hear that Clough had been given a vote of confidence and that a rogue director, like so many before him, had been forced to resign. Sure enough, Reacher began by condemning Wootton and said that, as he had refused to resign, he had been suspended pending an emergency board meeting. And then came the bombshell as he let slip that Clough would be retiring at the end of the season. The media knew before the players. Alan Hill, the chief scout, found out only because he happened to be watching television when the news was announced. An hour earlier, he'd spoken to Clough to arrange meeting for lunch, and nothing had been said about an impending announcement; he, O'Kane, Gemmill and Fenton had known that Clough was leaving, but the timing of the announcement stunned him.

Clough's career ended where so much of it had been fought, in a boardroom. He had battled the blazers for three-and-a-half decades and finally, helped in no small measure by his self-destructiveness, the blazers did for him. Reacher later admitted the announcement had been tactless, but insisted the decision to go public had been Clough's. Given the timing, it was hard to avoid the conclusion that his retirement was linked to the drinking, and that Forest were keen to announce his decision before he went back on it. In the days that followed, it was reported that Clough had recently been found asleep in a ditch near his home. 'So what?' he asked when challenged about the claim. 'I often walk between my home and Nigel's. It's six or seven miles and hard work when you get to my age. On the day in question I had a kip in a field because I was tired. Why else do you have a kip?' Drunkenness, presumably, was not the answer he was looking for.

Barbara Clough and the three children issued a statement condemning the board. 'Brian has had no part whatsoever in this statement,' it said. 'Several months ago, the family dismissed the possibility of Brian retiring and some weeks ago we made a definite decision that he would do so at the end of the season. It goes without saying that he intended to do this properly so that the first people to be told would be his working colleagues at the ground and, of course, the players. He has such a tremendous respect and affection for them all that anything else would be unthinkable.

'We were, therefore, surprised and hurt when we heard on the one o'clock news of his impending retirement. We believe the timing could hardly have been worse. The implication is, of course, that his decision was forced on him and Mr Reacher, whose support and loyalty have been unswerving following the campaign to oust him. Indeed, the word used most often in the press this week is "resignation" rather than retirement. After forty years we feel disappointed that words like "hounded out" should accompany his retirement.'

Clough gave one final defiant interview to the *Evening Post*, which produced a farewell supplement of sufficient depth to suggest they had been preparing for Clough's departure for some time. 'I am not a boozer,' he insisted. 'My chairman told me yesterday he was prepared to say any-where that he has never seen me the worse for booze. Yes, I have a drink in the privacy of my own home – a drop of sherry. I have been known to take a glass of champagne when I've won a league title. I have been known to have a couple of glasses of champagne when I've won the European Cup. Twice. I have been known to have one before getting on an aeroplane because I'm a wee bit frightened of flying. Still am, at the age of fifty-eight. I have the occasional glass of wine with the chairman and my colleagues at the club over lunch. That's it.'

By that stage, the same old defence had begun to sound tired and it didn't take a logician to see how tenuous it was; just because a man had won the European Cup thirteen years earlier didn't mean he couldn't be an alcoholic now. Past successes were no defence against the problems of the present. Clough rebuffed any suggestion that alcohol was behind his departure. 'Booze?' he said. 'I'll give you booze. My decision to retire from the game I've lived in for a lifetime is based simply on the fact that Old Big 'Ead has just had enough. That's all.'

He did, though, accept that, 'I might have stayed in management a shade too long.'

In a moving piece in the *Post*'s supplement detailing his memories of working with Clough, Hamilton admitted he had found him an impossible puzzle. 'If you knew him personally as well as professionally, you found a contradictory character,' he wrote. 'A Chinese box of a man. There was the public persona determined to keep his home life private. The extrovert, with a sense of theatre bordering on pure ham, who basically disliked performing for a crowd.

'He could be an awkward cuss, curmudgeonly, unforgiving, bombastic, choleric and unnecessarily abrasive. Or he could be compassionate, emollient, charming, over-generous and go out of his way to be no bother to anyone . . . On occasions he could be all of these within the same hour.'

Forest faced Sheffield United in Clough's final home game, knowing that defeat would almost certainly relegate them. That was his farewell. Forest lost at Ipswich the following week, but by then relegation had been confirmed. The years that followed would be awkward and uneasy, marked by erratic television appearances and ill health bad enough that allegations that he had taken bungs would not be pursued. He cut his ties with football almost completely, rejecting the opportunity to become a life president or director at Forest because he didn't want to interfere with his successor whom he feared 'would feel like a husband who'd got his mother-in-law living in the spare bedroom'.

As his health worsened, Clough had a liver transplant in January 2003 that seemingly gave him a new lease of life, but he died on 20 September 2004, aged sixty-nine. The array of clubs represented by the flags left in tribute at the gates of the City Ground testified to Clough's appeal far beyond the east Midlands. 'I am often asked what was the magic, the secret, the quintessence of the man,' Martin O'Neill said after a memorial service

545

at the City Ground. 'Many who knew him little said that it was fear, but [his players] said they could hardly have achieved so much with fear being the motivating factor. Personally, he scared the life out of me. I was asked in an interview to sum up Brian in three words. I think he would have been insulted to be summed up in three volumes.'

Clough hadn't shown up to training on the Friday before the Sheffield United game, and by two o'clock on the Saturday he still hadn't turned up at the stadium. The players went out to warm-up and, as Keane put it, 'the sense of tension round the stadium was obvious'. By twenty to three, even Stuart Pearce was getting edgy. 'Where the fuck's the gaffer?' he asked. As they left the dressing-room, though, Clough appeared at the end of the tunnel, wearing a pair of wellington boots and a sheepskin coat, carrying a shovel and whistling. 'I think the point he wished to make was that this was just another game,' Keane explained. '"Don't worry lads. I'm not worried." Bizarre. Pure Clough.'

Forest lost 2–0, confirming their relegation, but that had long been anticipated. 'I've long told the players the ball is their friend,' said a spent Clough afterwards, 'but today we couldn't get hold of it.' They were, according to Patrick Barclay's report in the *Observer*, 'anxious, unduly hurried and soon breached by a ruthless demonstration of composure,' Glynn Hodges turning onto a Paul Rogers pass and curling a finish beyond Marriott. Roy Keane headed an Ian Woan cross wide of an empty net early in the second half, and with that whatever chance Forest had had was gone. Sheffield United's second, Barclay wrote, was 'a depressing summary of the flimsiness with which Forest have protected their net all season. A corner slipped through Marriott's hands, producing another. This went short to [Charlie] Hartfield, whose outswinging cross was met with the meaty thump of the head by the captain, [Brian] Gayle.'

This, more than anything, was an opportunity for the world of football to hail Clough, which fans of both sides did, long and loud, with the chant 'Brian Clough's a football genius'. 'When you look back,' said Laws, 'he was very quiet and subdued. He looked the worst I'd ever seen him, his whole body, his demeanour. You could see it was the right thing to go. It was very emotional for him, he was in tears saying his farewells.'

'If nothing becomes a man like his leaving,' Duncan Hamilton wrote in the *Evening Post*, 'Clough can comfort himself in the knowledge that he went with as much dignity as it's possible to muster while being mobbed. What Clough received was worship from the prayer mat, and those who witnessed it will not easily forget the outpouring of warmth to one man. Compassion for him swept through and across the City Ground like voltage from an electric charge.' For once, football did say thank you, but it had waited until one of its greatest figures was at his absolute lowest.

To some, his popularity remained mystifying, but although he could be selfish and unthinking, Clough could also be immensely generous. People who used to live in Derby tell of how his car would regular be seen on double-yellow lines or blocking driveways, and speak of a tacit assumption that the police and traffic wardens knew his registration and were under instruction never to take action. But if he saw an old couple waiting at a bus stop, he would give them a lift into town to do their shopping and would often pay if he saw an impoverished pensioner in front of him in a shop.

Aside from the obvious point that human nature is immensely complex and that it is unrealistic to expect uniformity or consistency, it's hard to know what to make of the contradictory examples: were the acts of charity in some way compensatory for Clough's frequent unpleasantness in other areas? Did he enjoy dispensing fury or favour as he felt like it, like some arbitrary and whimsical god? Or was it just that Clough in private was very different from Clough the public figure? 'There's a fallacy,' Clough said in 2000, 'that you take your boots off one day, become a manager the next. You've got to be hard-faced, do horrible things. You've got to tell people things that'll break their hearts and it breaks your heart as well, but you haven't got to let them find out.' So you wear the disguise, cover that tenderness and empathy with brashness; wear the mask for long enough though, and it can become hard to know which the true face is. 'There were a lot of people left Forest in an unsatisfactory way,' said Hodge, who had himself left with a sense of bitterness and relief. 'In terms of the relationship with Clough it didn't end in a nice way, once he wanted to move you on. Maybe he couldn't deal with it.'

'Brian never changed fundamentally,' Doug Weatherall said. 'Football changed him in that it made him hard, while retaining all the great qualities. He'd encountered so many people who cheated, it made him more cynical than he would otherwise have been.' And it wasn't just people who cheated, of course, it was life itself. Jimmy Greaves would almost certainly have become a regular for England anyway, but it was Clough's bout of flu that let him in. Then there was the injury, 'the great injustice', as Clough termed it. He was bitter that his career was truncated, and bitter too at the callous way Sunderland off-loaded him to ensure they got their insurance money. If football could treat somebody like that, could cast them adrift, then why not take what you could out of it when the opportunity was there? The world, he discovered, wasn't just. It wasn't only that there were fools who didn't recognise his talent, or team-mates who didn't try their all, or directors in it for their own self-aggrandisement; the world fundamentally wasn't fair and there was nothing you could do about it.

On the pitch, though, he tried. Relatively speaking, his teams didn't cheat, didn't dive, didn't argue with referees. They sought a purity of play, and in that quest Clough became an almost messianic figure. These days, any manager who leads his team to a series of good results is likely to be hailed as a Messiah, but Clough, with his charisma and his idealism, effectively became the leader of a cult that stretched far beyond Nottingham. There may have been a touch of sanctimony, hypocrisy even, about his insistence on playing 'the right way', but he was essentially, as he had termed himself in that interview with Don Revie, 'a utopian'.

'When you think about things,' said Lee Glover, trying to encapsulate Clough's legacy, 'the joy he brought to the Forest fans, the way he wanted the game played, the great players he brought through – I'm not talking about myself – but he picked a lot of younger players . . .' It was that that made people forgive Clough; his sense of style, his faith in youth, the impression he gave of, whatever else was going on behind the scenes, at least on the pitch trying to do things the right way. So popular has he remained that there are four statues to Clough in England: one in Middlesbrough, one in Derby and two in Nottingham. When he died, tributes piled up at the City Ground, not just from the fans of those clubs he had played for or managed, but from all over the country, all over the world. Whatever else he was, Clough's principles, his belief in how football could be played, touched people and there was a genuine public grief at his passing. It was not just Clough the man who was mourned, but what he stood for, an era of football that, for all its faults, was at least not wholly dominated by capital. Clough was the revolutionary hero who, without huge resources, stood up to the grandees, and did so with style. By the time he retired, though, the grandees were too great to be challenged; what he had done with Derby and Forest was almost impossible; to have done it after the sharing of gate receipts was abolished was impossible, and became ever more so with the advent of the Premiership and the Champions League.

'Clough's resilience as a popular hero,' wrote Barclay after that final game, 'was due partly to a combination of charisma and iconoclasm, but for football lovers he also came to represent a protest against the march of athleticism. However, portrayal of his whole career as a crusade is a half-truth. Early teams at the City Ground were based on "clean sheets and good habits" to use [Peter] Taylor's phrase and indeed had as much to do with blanket defence as swift counter-attack ... only later, after the split with Taylor, did he become the patron saint of passing. This, indeed, has been a truly noble period, bringing Forest a modest haul of trophies for their consistently pure football.'

The pressure of maintaining that, though, of retaining self-imposed standards that others ignored, of remaining apparently indifferent as your heart was broken by breaking the hearts of others, took a terrible toll. It led Clough to erratic outbursts, and it led him to seek solace in booze, and the bottle made the outbursts even more erratic, and the pressure of making up for that led him even more surely to alcohol, and so the familiar spiral turned ever faster. And in an ungrateful, unjust world, there was always – even after the settlement with Leeds – insecurity, something that could only have been heightened by his awareness of his own volatility and self-destructiveness, and by football's obsession with cash.

But perhaps that is too hard; perhaps it is rather that, as Harry Storer told Clough when his career was in its infancy, football is an ungrateful sport, an environment in which the wolves are always waiting to pounce on any weakness; it is a hard game, and for a time Clough played it harder than anyone. Perhaps it is simply that in a ruthless world in which hearts are constantly broken, there is an acceptance that you have to take what you can get when you can. That might not excuse Clough's worst excesses, but it does in some way explain them. In that sense, perhaps, he never changed, but remained always the cocky kid with a chip on his shoulder, stealing apples from those who had more than he did.

The Robin Hood image stuck, and was appropriate on multiple levels: he was a showman who challenged the usual rules of society and, while some saw him as a thief, others saw him fighting honourably for the underdog; and, of course, there is no reason for the two interpretations not to co-exist. 'Travellers at the end of the twentieth century can be sure that wherever they roam across the globe, mention of the city's name will bring a response which suggests an association with a mythical medieval renegade by the name of Robin Hood . . .' John Becket and Colin Griffin wrote in the conclusion to their history of Nottingham. 'Nottingham has rather more to its past than a folk hero, a castle and a wicked sheriff: although perhaps the same tradition was being kept alive when Brian Clough's Nottingham Forest twice robbed the rich clubs of Europe to bring the European Cup to what at the end of the 1970s was a rather humble City Ground.' Thanks to Clough, by 1996 that humble ground was one of eight venues chosen to host matches at the European Championship, a clear enough indication of how he raised the stature both of Forest and Nottingham.

In his final game at the City Ground, Clough remained standing by the dug-out throughout, seemingly determined that, whatever else had happened that season, at the last he should resemble Alan Brown's straight-backed ideal. As Hamilton put it, he seemed 'like a captain determined to be on the bridge when the ship went down'. As Ahab, perhaps, would have wanted to go. After the final whistle, a girl gave him a flower; he took it sadly and said, 'Hey, beauty, no more tears today, please.' This was the gentler, mellower Clough, touched by the affection in which he was held, but nonetheless broken by football, by the world. The reception demonstrated the gratitude of Forest fans for all the good times, but perhaps also something more general, an acknowledgement that there should be no recriminations, that age, life, gets us all in the end, even Brian Howard Clough.

There was still time, though, for one last quip before retirement, for one last assertion of his authority.

'Brian,' asked a television reporter, approaching him outside the ground. 'Can I have a word?'

'Of course,' he replied. 'Goodbye.'

Bibliography

Books

Anderson, Stan, *Captain of the North* (SportsBooks, 2010)

Ashurst, Len, *Left Back in Time* (Know the Score, 2009)

Bale, Bernard, *Bremner! The Legend of Billy Bremner* (Andre Deutsch, 1998)

Beckett, John (ed.) *A Centenary History of Nottingham* (Manchester University Press, 1997)

Beckett, John and Colin Griffin, 'Nottingham Today' in *A Centenary History of Nottingham* (Manchester University Press, 1997)

Bowles, Stan, *The Autobiography* (Orion, 2004)

Clavane, Anthony, *Promised Land: The Reinvention of Leeds United* (Yellow Jersey, 2010)

Clough, Brian, *Clough: The Autobiography* (Corgi, 1994)

—*Cloughie: Walking on Water: My Life* (Headline, 2002)

Cockayne, Michael, *Derby County: The Clough Years* (Parrs Wood Press, 2003)

Conn, David, *The Beautiful Game: Searching for the Soul of Football* (Yellow Jersey, 2004)

Craven, Maxwell, *An Illustrated History of Derby* (Breedon, 2007)

Crick, Michael, *The Boss: The Many Sides of Alex Ferguson* (Simon & Schuster, 2002)

Croker, Ted, *The First Voice You Will Hear Is . . .* (Collins Willow, 1987)

Dickinson, Wendy and Stafford Hildred, *For Pete's Sake: The Peter Taylor Story. Volume 1: The Backstreets to the Baseball Ground* (Matador, 2010)

Docherty, Tommy, *The Doc: Hallowed be thy Game* (Headline, 2006)

Edwards, George, *Right Place, Right Time: The Inside Story of Clough's Derby Days* (Stadia, 2007)

Edwards, Maurice, *Brian and Peter: A Right Pair: 20 Years with Clough and Taylor* (Derby Books, 2010)

Francis, Tony, *Clough: A Biography* (Stanley Paul, 1987, revised edn, 1993)

Francis, Trevor, with David Miller, *The World to Play For* (Granada, 1983)

Gemmill, Archie, *Both Sides of the Border* (Hodder & Stoughton, 2005)

Gray, Eddie, *Marching on Together: My Life with Leeds United* (Coronet, 2001)

Greenwood, Ron, *Yours Sincerely* (Willow, 1984)

Griffin, Colin, 'The identity of a twentieth-century city' in John Beckett (ed.), *A Centenary History of Nottingham* (Manchester University Press, 1997)

Hamilton, Duncan, *Provided You Don't Kiss Me: 20 Years with Brian Clough* (HarperPerennial, 2008)

Hardwick, George, *Gentleman George* (Juniper, 1998)

Hardy, Lance, *Sunderland, Stokoe and 73: The Story of the Greatest FA Cup Shock of All Time* (Orion, 2009)

Hermiston, Roger, *Clough & Revie: The Rivals who Changed the Face of English Football* (Mainstream, 2011)

Hodge, Steve, *The Man with Maradona's Shirt* (Orion, 2010)

Hopcraft, Arthur, *The Football Man: People and Passions in Soccer* (Aurum, 2006, first published Collins, 1968)

Howey, Martin and David Bond, *Meet Me in the Roker End: A Revealing Look at Sunderland's Footballing History* (Vertical, 2005)

Hunter, Norman, *Biting Talk* (Hodder and Stoughton, 2004)

Keane, Roy, *Keane: The Autobiography* (Penguin, 2003, first published Michael Joseph, 2002)

Kuper, Simon and Stefan Szymanski, *Why England Lose: and Other Curious Phenomena Explained* (HarperCollins, 2009)

Lawson, John, *Forest 1865–1978* (Wensum, 1978)

Lloyd, Larry, *Hard Man, Hard Game* (John Blake, 2009)

Luscombe, William (ed.), *The Park Drive Book of Football* (Pelham, 1970)

Mackay, Dave and Martin Knight, *The Real Mackay: the Dave Mackay Story* (Mainstream, 2004)

McKenzie, Duncan, *The Last Fancy Dan* (Vertical, 2009)

McLintock, Frank, *True Grit* (Headline, 2005)

Mellor, Keith, *The Garibaldi Reds: The Pictorial History of Nottingham Forest Football Club* (Sporting and Leisure Press, 1984)

Metcalf, Mark, *Charlie Hurley: The Greatest Centre-Half the World has Ever Seen* (SportsBooks, 2008)

Mourant, Andrew, *Don Revie: Portrait of a Footballing Enigma* (Mainstream, 1990)

Murphy, Patrick, *His Way: The Brian Clough Story* (Portico, 2004)

Pearce, Stuart, *Psycho* (Headline, 2000)

Pearson, Harry, *The Far Corner* (Little, Brown 1994)

Priestley, J.B., *English Journey* (Penguin, 1977, first published William Heinemann, 1934)

Rostron, Phil, *We are the Damned United: The Real Story of Brian Clough at Leeds United* (Mainstream, 2009)

Sandbrook, Dominic, *State of Emergency: The Way We Were: Britain 1970–74* (Allen Lane, 2010)

Sheringham, Teddy, *My Autobiography* (Little, Bown, 1998)

Shipley, John, *1977–78 Champions: Nottingham Forest* (Tempus, 2004)

Taylor, Daniel, *Deep into the Forest* (Breedon, 2009)

Taylor, Peter, *With Clough by Taylor* (Sidgwick and Jackson, 1980)

Todd, Colin, *Toddy: The Colin Todd Story* (Breedon, 2008)

Newspapers
Brighton Evening Argus
Daily Mail
Daily Mirror
Daily Telegraph
Derby Evening Telegraph
Express
Guardian
Hartlepool Mail
Middlesbrough Evening Gazette
News of the World
Northern Echo
Nottingham Evening Post
Observer
People
Sun
Sunday Express
Sunday Mirror
Sunday Times
Sunderland Echo
The Times

Websites
playerhistory.com
rsssf.com
soccerbase.com
statto.com

Index